Chelonian Library

Hermann's Tortoise, Boettger's and Dalmatian Tortoises

Testudo boettgeri, hercegovinensis and hermanni

HOLGER VETTER

Chelonian Library

Hermann's Tortoise, Boettger's and Dalmatian Tortoises

Testudo boettgeri, hercegovinensis and hermanni

Holger Vetter

Edition Chimaira

Holger Vetter
Hermann's Tortoise,
Boettger's and Dalmatian Tortoises
Chelonian Library
Edition Chimaira
Frankfurt am Main 2006
Germany
ISBN 3-89973-602-8

1. Edition, 2006

© 2006 Chimaira Buchhandelsgesellschaft
mbH
Andreas S. Brahm, Publisher
Heddernheimer Landstraße 20
60439 Frankfurt am Main
Germany
Telephone: +49 (0) 69 – 49 72 23
Telefax: +49 (0) 69 – 49 78 26
E-Mail: frogbook@aol.de
www.chimaira.de

ERPENT'S TALE
NATURAL HISTORY BOOK DISTRIBUTORS

in the US available from:
Zoo Book Sales
Serpent's Tale
PO Box 405
Lanesboro MN 55949 – 0405
Phone: (507)-4678733
e-mail: zoobooks@acegroup.cc
www.zoobooksales.com

Layout/Typesetting: Mirella Sciortino,
LINEARTE
Scans: Gerold Schipper
Editing: Gerold Schipper
Translation: www.herprint.com
Print: DCM, Meckenheim
Binding: Freitag, Kassel

TABLE OF CONTENTS

▶ **Preface** (ANDREAS NÖLLERT) ——————————— **8**

▶ **Acknowledgments** ————————————— **9**

▶ **Systematics** ———————————————— **10**

Genus *Testudo* LINNAEUS, 1758 – Palearctic tortoises ——————— 10
The *Testudo hermanni* species group ————————————— 11
Species *Testudo boettgeri* MOJSISOVICS, 1889 – Boettger's tortoise ——— 13
Species *Testudo hercegovinensis* WERNER, 1899 – Dalmatian tortoise —— 15
Species *Testudo hermanni* GMELIN, 1789 – Italian tortoise —————— 16

▶ **Description** ———————————————— **19**

Testudo hermanni species group ——————————————— 19
Morphology and coloration ————————————————— 19
Carapace ———————————————————————— 19
Plastron ————————————————————————— 20
Head and limbs ————————————————————— 21
Juvenile coloration ———————————————————— 21
Variability ————————————————————————— 24
Karyotype ———————————————————————— 25
Size and weight ————————————————————— 25
Sexual dimorphism ———————————————————— 26
Hearing ————————————————————————— 29

Boettger's tortoise ————————————————————— 29
Morphology and coloration ————————————————— 29
Carapace ———————————————————————— 29
Plastron ————————————————————————— 29
Head and limbs ————————————————————— 30
Variability ————————————————————————— 31
Size and weight ————————————————————— 32
Sexual dimorphism ———————————————————— 32

Dalmatian tortoise ————————————————————— 33
Morphology and coloration ————————————————— 33
Carapace ———————————————————————— 33
Plastron ————————————————————————— 33
Head and limbs ————————————————————— 34
Size and weight ————————————————————— 34

TABLE OF CONTENTS

Italian tortoise _____ 36
Morphology and coloration _____ 36
Carapace _____ 36
Plastron _____ 36
Head and limbs _____ 36
Variability _____ 37
Size and weight _____ 40

Distribution _____ 42

Testudo hermanni species group _____ 42
Boettger's tortoise _____ 42
Dalmatian tortoise _____ 45
Italian tortoise _____ 49

Fossil records _____ 58

Natural habitat _____ 60

Vegetation _____ 60
Vertical distribution _____ 63
Climate _____ 64
Population densities _____ 66
Age structure _____ 67
Sex ratios _____ 70
Home range _____ 71
Defensive behavior _____ 75

Diel and annual cycles _____ 76

Diel cycle _____ 76
Annual cycle _____ 79

Thermoregulation _____ 81

Diet and feeding _____ 84

Reproduction _____ 92

Growth and Life expectancy _____ 108

Growth _____ 108
Life expectancy _____ 110

▶ **Diseases and parasites** _____ 112

▶ **Husbandry** _____ 116

General _____ 116
Keeping in outdoor enclosures _____ 119
Keeping in an indoor terrarium _____ 129
Legal requirements _____ 132
Feeding _____ 133
Hibernation _____ 138
Breeding _____ 146
Rearing _____ 155
Health concerns _____ 162

▶ **Tortoise and man** _____ 168

Boettger's tortoise _____ 168
Italian tortoise _____ 174

▶ **Threats** _____ 176

Testudo hermanni species group _____ 176
Boettger's tortoise _____ 182
Dalmatian tortoise _____ 190
Italian tortoise _____ 191

▶ **Conservation** _____ 201

Testudo hermanni species group _____ 201
Boettger's tortoise _____ 206
Italian tortoise _____ 209

▶ **Addresses** _____ 227

▶ **Climate Tables** _____ 229

▶ **References** _____ 242

▶ **Internet Addresses** _____ 324

▶ **Photo Credits** _____ 325

Tortoises are a true miracle of evolution! Developing an armor in the form of a shell to protect the encased body from above as well as from below must certainly be viewed as one of nature's most ingenious protective strategies of all times. Indeed, so successful is this design that it guaranteed its bearers almost 300 million years of survival – with hardly any alterations to their "anatomical architecture". The build of the body, the diverse expressions of their ways of life, and a longevity that is virtually proverbial, secured them important places in the cultural histories of many peoples.

Alas, all this did nothing to keep "modern" man from destroying their natural habitats on a massive scale, collecting millions of specimens, and in the end leave nearly half of the about three hundred species living today threatened with extinction. This depressing history also applies to the representatives of the *Testudo hermanni* species group. Between the 1960' and 1980' in particular, they were exported as cheap mass products by the ton from the countries of the Balkans, arriving first in our pet stores, and then, more often than not, on the garbage dump. All this makes me want to mention two persons who, joined by many others, did not tire to fight this development and stand out like beacons in the effort of conserving the tortoises of the Palearctic. The field studies conducted by Michael Roderick KIRKBY LAMBERT in the late 1960' on the tortoises of Morocco demonstrated with brutal clarity the horrifying extent of the exploitation of these creatures. He is certain to have created an important basis for the international laws governing the protected status of the tortoises of Europe and North Africa today.

Then there was WALTER KIRSCHE, who since the early 1960' has been keeping Palearctic tortoises in exemplifying outdoor enclosures and breeding them in astound-

ing numbers every year. Documenting all observations and results in a painstakingly precise manner, and making them available to others through publication, he no doubt contributed greatly to the fact that the tortoises living in captivity today are no longer specimens removed from the wild, but instead originate from planned captive breeding. The observant reader of this book by HOLGER VETTER will note just how many scientific results were obtained by WALTER KIRSCHE.

Besides carefully researched data on the distribution, biology and ecology of the *Testudo hermanni* species group, HOLGER VETTER also introduces us to the many projects that exist today in an effort to conserve these unique monuments of nature in Europe, urges us to respect these animals, and as a result makes an excellent contribution to the public relations work of nature and species conservation. This makes his monograph particularly valuable to me.

While reading his book, and in particularly while phrasing this preface, I came to recall my own encounters with the tortoises of Europe – in particular with *Testudo boettgeri*. As early as during my years as a student in Jena, my wife and I were drawn to the natural paradises of Bulgaria that are all but forgotten today, but were in fact the "Mecca" of all East German herpetologists and terrarium enthusiasts. This, I tend to think, was a result of the motivation bestowed upon us by our friend and idol, FRITZ JÜRGEN OBST of Dresden. Equipped with backpack, measuring tape, scale, notebook, photographic gear, and even more enthusiasm, we cruised the oak forests along the coast of the Black Sea, the forests of the landmark loam mountains at Melnik, and the lands surrounding Sandanski, always in search of tortoises. When we eventually found our first Boettger's tortoise in the wild near Arkutino, we felt as though we had been granted a miracle. Thereafter, life was never the same again.

I was therefore more than pleased when I was asked to write a preface for this excellent book by HOLGER VETTER. I wish him and his publishers, Edition Chimaira, many more publications of the same caliber in that they impress by paying homage to the wonders of evolution, afford them due respect, and hopefully instigate the same in the general public as well.

ANDREAS NÖLLERT,
Jena, January 2006

Acknowledgements

I would like to express my gratitude to all my friends and acquaintances who made available to me photographs and drawings for this book project: HARALD ARTNER, SILVIA BLAHAK, ROGER BOUR, BERNARD BOUSSAC, HENRIK BRINGSØE, JACO BRUEKERS, BERNARD DEVAUX, MARKO DJURAKIC, BALÁZS FARKAS, ERWIN GONSCHOR, EDLEF HEIMANN, FELIX HULBERT, GÉRARD JAKUBOWICZ, HELMUT KANTZ, JÉRÔME MARAN, ALBERT MARTÍNEZ, the DE MARCO family, MANFRED MÜLLER, ANA PAUNOVIC, ALEXANDER PIEH, HANS-DIETER PHILIPPEN, GEORGI POPGEORGIEV, NEMANJA RISTIC, HANS-HERMANN SCHLEICH, HANS-ULRICH SCHMIDT, WOLFGANG SCHMIDT, BRUNO SEEGER, SHINTARO SEKI, ALEKSANDAR SUKIC, STEFAN THIERFELDT, MERCÈ VIADER, WOLFGANG WEGEHAUPT, and FRITZ WÜTHRICH.

In particular I would like to say Thank-you to ANDREAS NÖLLERT, who not only supplied several photographs, but also contributed to the present volume with a preface.

Also, I would like to thank ALINE FAURE for her work with the layout, and ANDREAS S. BRAHM and GEROLD SCHIPPER for their concept of the "Chelonian Library" series and its professional realization.

My very special thanks go to my parents, IRIS ADLON-VETTER and GERHARD VETTER, who, by buying a juvenile Testudo boettgeri for me some twenty-five years ago, laid the foundation for my interest in chelonians and who did not tire to actively support me in the pursuit of my hobby.

Bad Kreuznach, April 2006

HOLGER VETTER

Systematics

Genus *Testudo* LINNAEUS, 1758 – Palearctic tortoises

Original description
LINNAEUS (1758): Systema naturae per regna tria naturae secundum classes, ordines, genera, species, cum characteribus, differentiis, synonymis, locis. – 10th Edition, Volume 1, Stockholm (Salvii): p. 197.

Type species
Not specified in the original description, but subsequently designated as *Testudo graeca* LINNAEUS, 1758 by BELL (1828).

Synonyms
– *Chersus* WAGLER, 1830 (type species by monotypy: *Testudo marginata* SCHOEPFF, 1793)
– *Peltastes* GRAY, 1869 (type species: *Testudo graeca* LINNAEUS, 1758 – designated by LINDHOLM [1929]; an unavailable name that is preoccupied by *Peltastes* ILLIGER, 1807, for a genus of hymenopteran insects, by *Peltastes* AGASSIZ, 1838, for a genus of echinoderms, and by *Peltastes* FISCHER-WALDHEIM, 1846, for a genus of orthopteran insects)

– *Chersinella* GRAY, 1870 (type species: *Testudo graeca* LINNAEUS, 1758 – designated by LINDHOLM [1929])
– *Peltonia* GRAY, 1872 (a replacement name for *Peltastes* GRAY, 1869)
– *Medaestia* WUSSOW, 1916 (type species: *Testudo graeca* LINNAEUS, 1758 designated by MERTENS [1949])

Etymology
Testudo = (Latin) tortoise

Vernacular names
English: Palearctic tortoises, Eurasian tortoises, European tortoises, Mediterranean tortoises, True tortoises; **French:** Tortues paléarctiques (= Palearctic tortoises), Tortues eurasiennes (= Eurasian tortoises), Tortues européennes (= European tortoises), Tortues méditerranées (= Mediterranean tortoises); **German:** Griechische Landschildkröten (= Greek tortoises), also Eurasische (= Eurasian) Landschildkröten, Europäische (= European) Landschildkröten, Mediterrane (= Mediterranean) Landschildkröten, Eigentliche (= True) Landschildkröten

The Testudo hermanni species group

The Testudo hermanni species group is marked by a wide-ranging and distinct geographical variability, which affects in particular body size, shape of the shell, as well as coloration and color pattern. Notwithstanding, science at present distinguishes only between three forms whose systematic status is treated variably in the existing literature.

The genetic study conducted by VAN DER KUYL et al. (2002) demonstrated that the morphologically easily differentiated western and eastern European members of the species group in fact represent separate branches of evolution. According to the results of this study, the differences are, however, smaller than those between forms of Testudo from Europe and North Africa that are without dispute accepted as species. SQUALLI-HOUSSAINI & BLANC (1990) even found that a high degree of similarity exists between the western European representatives of the Testudo hermanni species group and the forms of the Testudo graeca species group on the one, and the eastern forms of the Testudo hermanni species group and the Central Asian tortoises of the genus Agrionemys on the other hand. Following these authors the eastern and western members of the Testudo hermanni species group appear to be genetically more distant from each other than from the Testudo graeca species group and Agrionemys, respectively. These results have to be treated with care, though, in particular because they are in the case of Testudo boettgeri based on only one specimen, and Testudo hercegovinensis was not taken into consideration at all because its specific status had not yet been clarified by the time of this study.

Based on the currently available information systematists arrive at different conclusions regarding the systematic status of the members of the Testudo hermanni species group. While PERÄLÄ (2002a, b, c) accepts

Testudo hercegovinensis as a separate species that owing to its distinctive morphology is easily identified (it still remains to be investigated genetically, though), and presumes, like ARTNER (2000), BOUR (2004b) and others, that this is also the case in Testudo hermanni and Testudo boettgeri, most other authors consider these three forms to be subspecies of Testudo hermanni. As for the purpose of this book, I will follow the phylogenetic species concept of PERÄLÄ (2002a, b, c) and accept all three currently recognized forms as separate species. This notion is supported by the statement of PERÄLÄ (2002b) that Testudo boettgeri and hercegovinensis would occur in sympatry in places where their respective distribution ranges overlap without producing hybrids (which is something that has not yet been documented properly, though), and by the fact that captive crossbreeding of Testudo hermanni with either of the other two eastern relatives often produces offspring with a distinctly reduced degree of fertility. Thus, if in the following text "Testudo hermanni" is mentioned, it always refers to the tortoises native to western Europe.

Most experts are quite certain that more than these three forms will eventually emerge taxonomically. I will therefore be careful to distinguish between a western (France, Italy, Spain) and an eastern (Balkan Peninsula) population group. Presently, the former includes only Testudo hermanni whereas the latter comprises Testudo boettgeri and Testudo hercegovinensis. "The usual suspects" for ranking as separate forms would include within the western population group the tortoises native to Corsica and Sardinia as well as those from Sicily and mainland Italy (in the course of their genetic studies, FRITZ et al. [2005], for example, found differences between tortoises from Tuscany and Sardinia). The same applies to the eastern population group where even greater geographical variability exists in a region that is much smaller than that inhabited by the western counterpart. Several populations may qualify for such reevaluation (see chapter "Distribution"), with one example being the tortoises from the southern Peloponnesus that can be distinguished also genetically (VAN DER KUYL 2002) and will be defined as a new taxon in the near future (BOUR 2004a). Based on the results of their genetic studies, VAN DER KUYL et al. (2002) voiced their assumption that the genetically less variable western population group may have retreated to a single refuge area during the glacial period of the Pleistocene, possibly in the south of today's Italy (Sicily). One might argue, though, that the populations of the French mainland may just as well have retreated to another region. On the other hand, the more pronounced genetic variability of the eastern population group suggests that the tortoises used a number of different glacial retreats.

The cladistic position of the forms of the *Testudo hermanni* species group within the Palearctic tortoises is also still a subject of widespread discussions. The conclusions drawn by SQUALLI-HOUSSAINI & BLANC (1990) in this respect have already been mentioned. While OBST & AMBROSIUS (1971) believed there was a close relationship between the eastern European representatives of the *Testudo hermanni* and *Testudo graeca* species groups (tortoises of Asia minor, central Asia, North Africa, the Caucasus and southeastern Europe) and a range of distinct differences between this group and the marginated tortoise (*Testudo marginata* SCHOEPFF, 1793) and the Central Asian tortoises of the genus *Agrionemys* KHOZATSKY & MLYNARSKI, 1966, LYKAKIS (1974) presumed a closer relationship between the entire *Testudo hermanni* species group and *Testudo marginata*. Together with several related fossil forms, CHKHIKVADZE (1970) placed the *Testudo hermanni* species group in a separate genus, *Protestudo*, which he introduced in the same publication, and considered this group to be closely related to the genus *Agrionemys*. He republished this concept once more in 1989, and it found acceptance amongst various other herpetologists of the former Soviet Union. Although DE LAPPARENT DE BROIN (2001) arrived at a similar conclusion, i.e., that the *Testudo hermanni* species group would form a cladistic group that was separate from the rest of the species of *Testudo*, he also found that the fossil type species of *Protestudo*, *Protestudo bessarabica* (RIABININ, 1915) from the upper Miocene of the Republic of Moldavia and the Ukraine, were to be placed within *Agrionemys*. This summarily rendered *Protestudo* a junior synonym of *Agrionemys*.

Based on a cladistic analysis, GMIRA (1993A) even concluded that the *Testudo hermanni* species group would need to be clustered with the Central Asian tortoises and incorporated it into *Agrionemys*. However, as this author based her findings merely on traits such as size, proportions and coloration, her presumed cladistic relationships must be considered not sufficiently secured. GMIRA also used in her cladograms the trait of an allegedly rigid plastron for the *Testudo hermanni* species group, which is a trait of doubtful use considering that many females of these forms have a movable rear part of the plastron at least at times of oviposition. Studying 61 morphological traits, PERÄLÄ (2002a, c), on the other hand, concluded that the *Testudo hermanni* species group would represent the most primitive grouping within the genus *Testudo* (in a wider sense) that would consequently clearly warrant their separate generic status. The genetic studies conducted by FRITZ et al. (2005) likewise revealed that the *Testudo hermanni* species group was slightly separated from the rest of the species of *Testudo*, and that the Central Asian tortoises (i.e., the genus *Agrionemys*, according to the concept used here) would represent a sister group of all other Palearctic tortoises, i.e., the genus *Testudo* (sensu lato) as it is accepted at present.

PARHAM et al. (2006) concluded from their genetic studies that the *Testudo hermanni* species group would not form part of the genus *Testudo* s. str., but were as yet unable to provide further details on the exact phylogenetic position of this species group within the cladistic group as defined and named Testudona by them. This group would, according to these authors, include next to the *Testudo hermanni* species group the Central Asian tortoises of the genus *Agrionemys*, the African pancake tortoise *Malacochersus tornieri* (SIEBENROCK, 1903), the Asian tortoises of the genus *Indotestudo* LINDHOLM, 1929, and the species of the genus *Testudo* s. str.. *Testudo* s. str. would only comprise the members of the *Testudo graeca* species group plus, as they see it, the closely related taxa *Testudo marginata* SCHOEPFF, 1793, and *Testudo kleinmanni* LORTET 1883 (INCLUDING *Testudo werneri* PERÄLÄ, 2001). A close relationship with *Testudo marginata* and *Testudo kleinmanni* was also presumed by GMIRA (1993a, 1995) and VAN DER KUYL et al. (2002). For these two species, the generic or subgeneric name *Chersus* WAGLER, 1830 (type species: *Testudo marginata*) would be available.

Here, the *Testudo hermanni* species group is preliminarily left within the genus *Testudo*, which (still?) conforms with the vast majority of opinions voiced in contemporary literature. If the concept proves true that this species group is better accommodated in its own genus, no existing generic name would be available. DE LAPPARENT DE BROIN (pers. comm. to PARHAM et al. 2006) intends to formally introduce such a name in due course, though.

Species *Testudo boettgeri* MOJSISOVICS, 1889 – Boettger's tortoise

Original description
MOJSISOVICS (1889): Zoogeographische Notizen über Süd-Ungarn aus den Jahren 1886–1888 – Zugleich ein III. Nachtrag zur "Fauna von Béllye und Darda". – Mitteilungen des Naturwissenschaftlichen Vereins der Steiermark, Graz, 25: p. 242.

Original combination
Testudo graeca var. *boettgeri* MOJSISOVICS, 1889

Type material
Lectotype, No. 7836 in the collection of the Naturmuseum und Forschungsinstitut Senckenberg in Frankfurt am Main, Germany; a female of 16 cm in carapace length, designated as a lectotype by BOETTGER (1893). BOETTGER indicated this specimen merely as "type", but because MOJSISOVICS (1889) had explicitly referred in his original description to several specimens, BOETTGER's treatment of a single specimen must be seen as the designation of a lectotype (BOUR pers. comm.).

Type locality
Not indicated; later designated through lectotype designation as Orsova, Tal der Cerna, Banat (= valley of the Cerna at Orsova, Mehedinti District, Romania) by BOETTGER (1893).

Fig. 1: Lectotype of *Testudo boettgeri* (No. 7836 in the *Senckenberg Museum*, Frankfurt/Main, Germany); lateral view (R. BOUR)

Figs. 2&3: Lectotype of *Testudo boettgeri* (No. 7836 in the *Naturmuseum und Forschungsinstitut Senckenberg*, Frankfurt/Main); carapacial and plastral aspects (R. BOUR)

Synonyms

– *Testudo graeca* var. *boettgeri* MOJSISOVICS, 1889

Testudo enriquesi PARENZAN, 1932 (holotype: a female of 20.5 cm in length; unlocated; type locality: Conca di Elbassan, Skumbi, Albania (= plains of Elbasan, Elbasan Prefecture, Albania)

– *Testudo hermanni hermanni* – (WERMUTH 1952)

– *Protestudo hermanni hermanni* – (CHKHIK-VADZE 1970)

– *Testudo hermanni boettgeri* – (BOUR 1987)

– *Agrionemys hermanni boettgeri* – (GMIRA 1993a)

– *Testudo boettgeri* – (BOUR 2004b)

Etymology

boettgeri = named in honor of Oskar BOETT-GER (1844–1910), the founder and first director of the Naturmuseum und Forschungsinstitut Senckenberg in Frankfurt am Main, Germany.

Vernacular names

Albanian: Breshkë e zakonshme e tokës (= common tortoise), Breshkë (= tortoise), Breshkë toke (= tortoise), Breshkë e ugareve (= fallow land tortoise); **Bulgarian:** Schipoopaschata kostenurka, Schipoopaschata suchosjemna kostenurka, Grácka kostenurka (= Greek tortoise); **Czech:** Zelva recká (= Greek turtle), Zelva zelenavá; **Danish:** Græsk landskildpadde (= Greek tortoise); **Dutch:** Griekse landschildpad (= Greek tortoise); **English:** Boettger's tortoise, Eastern Hermann's tortoise, Balkans Hermann's tortoise, Greek tortoise, Spur-tailed tortoise, Spur-tailed Mediterranean land tortoise; **Estonian:** Lôunaeuroopa kilpkonn (= Southern European tortoise); **Finnish:** Kreikankilpikonna (= Greek tortoise); **French:** Tortue de Boettger (= Boettger's tortoise), Tortue d'Hermann des Balkans (= Balkans Hermann's tortoise), Tortue d'Hermann orientale (= eastern Hermann's tortoise), Tortue grecque (= Greek tortoise); **German:** Griechische Landschildkröte (= Greek tortoise), also Boettgers Landschildkröte, Griechische Testude, Östliche Griechische Landschildkröte (= eastern Greek tortoise), Eigentliche Griechische Landschildkröte (= actual Greek tortoise), formerly also Gemeine Landschildkröte (= common tortoise); **Greek:** Chelóna i mesogeiakí (= Mediterranean tortoise), Onychochelóna (= nailed tortoise; referring to the horny nail that forms the tip of the tail of this species; **Italian:** Testuggine di Boettger (= Boettger's tortoise), Tartaruga greca (= Greek tortoise); **Macedonian:** Rid-

ska schelka (= Greek tortoise), Hermaniewa schelka (= Hermann's tortoise); **Hungarian:** Görög teknõs (= Greek tortoise); **Polish:** Zólw grecki (= Greek tortoise); **Romanian:** Broascâ testoasâ din Dobrogea (= Dobrudjan tortoise), Broascâ testoasâ banateana (= Banat tortoise), Broascâ testoasâ de uscat; **Russian:** Balkanskaja tscherepacha (= Balkans tortoise); **Swedish:** Grekisk landsköldpadda (= Greek tortoise), Grekisk sköldpadda (= Greek turtle), Östlig grekisk landsköldpadda (= Eastern Greek tortoise); **Serbian:** Sumska kornjaca; **Slovak:** Korytnacka zelenkastá; **Turkish:** Trakya tosbagasi (= Thrace tortoise); **Ukrainian:** Balkanska tscherepacha (= Balkans tortoise)

Species *Testudo hercegovinensis* WERNER, 1899 – Dalmatian tortoise

Original description
WERNER (1899): Beiträge zur Kenntnis der Reptilien- und Batrachierfauna der Balkanhalbinsel. – Wissenschaftliche Mittheilungen aus Bosnien und der Herzegovina, 6: p. 818.

Original combination
Testudo graeca var. *hercegovinensis* WERNER, 1899

Type material
Two syntypes, Nos. 1222 (11.87 cm-long shell of an adult male), and 1899 (mounted skeleton) in the collection of the Naturhistorisches Museum in Vienna, Austria; BOUR (1987) selected No. 1222 as lectotype.

Type locality
near Trebinje (= surroundings of Trebinje, Serbian Republic, Bosnia and Herzegovina)

Synonyms
– *Testudo graeca* var. *hercegovinensis* WERNER, 1899
– *Testudo hermanni hercegovinensis* (BLANCK & ESSER 2004)
– *Testudo hercegovinensis* – (PERÄLÄ 2002b)

Etymology
hercegovinensis = named after Herzegovina, a region in the south of Bosnia and Herzegovina, in which the type locality of this species is situated.

Vernacular names
Croatian: Èancara; **English:** Dalmatian tortoise, Herzegovina tortoise; **French:** Tortue d'Herzégovine (Herzegovina tortoise); **German:** Dalmatinische Landschildkröte (= Dalmatian tortoise); **Italian:** Testuggine della Dalmazia (= Dalmatian tortoise); **Slovenian:** Grska kornjaca (= Greek turtle), Balkanska zelva (= Balkans tortoise)

Species *Testudo hermanni* GMELIN, 1789 – Italian tortoise

Original description

GMELIN (1789): Caroli a Linné ... Systema Naturae per regna tria naturae, secundum classes, ordines, genera, species; cum characteribus, differentiis, synonymis, locis. Editio decimo tertia, aucta, reformata. Tom I. Pars III.ñ Leipzig (Georg Emanuel Beer): p. 1041.

Although the species was first described by SCHNEIDER (1783) on the basis of a specimen in the collection of Johannes (or Jean) HERMANN, a zoologist, botanist, chemist and philosopher in Strasbourg, France,

Fig. 6: Lectotype of *Testudo hercegovinensis* (No. 1222 in the

that later became the holotype, SCHNEIDER failed to suggest a scientific name so that the first description of taxonomic relevance must be ascribed to GMELIN (1789).

Original combination

Testudo hermanni GMELIN, 1789

There has been a great deal of confusion in the past about the correct scientific name of this species. Until the early 20th century it was usually referred to as *Testudo graeca* LINNAEUS, 1758, whereas the entire *Testudo hermanni* species group was known as *Testudo ibera* PALLAS, 1814 (Moorish tortoise), and *Testudo hermanni* GMELIN, 1789, was considered to be a junior synonym of *Testudo graeca*.

SIEBENROCK (1913) then eventually noted that *Testudo graeca* and *Testudo hermanni* were two different species, but hesitated to suggest a respective name change in order to not upset the well-established use of the species' name. FLOWER (1926) eventually assigned the correct name *Testudo hermanni* to the Italian tortoise and reclassified *Testudo graeca* and *Testudo ibera* as subspecies of one species. According to PERÄLÄ (2002a, c), however, all forms of the *Testudo graeca* complex represent species in their own rights.

Type material

Holotype, No. 121 in the Musée de Zoologie of the Université de Strasbourg in Strasbourg, France; a 10.8 cm-long plastron of a male specimen.

The type specimen of *Testudo hermanni*, i.e., the specimen that served Johann Friedrich GMELIN for his introduction of this species into science in 1789, was unlocated for many years. This became a serious problem when it was noted that the western and eastern population groups of the *Testudo hermanni* species group were sufficiently different to distinguish them as subspecies, or, as they are treated here, represent distinct species. Based on the assumption that the type specimen originated from the Balkans, WERMUTH (1952) used a semiadult female to define a "new" subspecies, *Testudo hermanni robertmertensi* (No. 37468 in the Naturmuseum und Forschungsinstitut Senckenberg in Frankfurt am Main) from the mountains north of the town Artá on the Spanish Balearic island of Mallorca, i.e., from the western portion of distribution range. In 1987, the French herpetologist Roger BOUR eventually discovered the plastron of the type specimen in the Zoological Museum of the University of Strasbourg. It was clearly identified by its agreeing with the color plate published by SCHOEPFF (1793). BOUR now noted that the specimen did not, as was commonly sup-

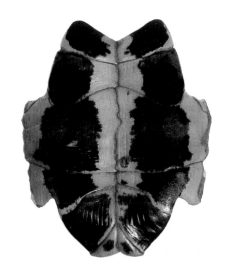

Fig. 7: Holotype of *Testudo hermanni* (No. 111 in the *Musée de Zoologie*)

Fig.8: Holotype of *Testudo hermanni* (No. 111 in the *Musée de Zoologie*)

posed, originate from the southeastern, but rather from the southwestern parts of Europe. Some time later, the 13 cm-long carapace with the extremities attached was also discovered in the same museum. All pieces were in an excellent state of preservation and substantiated what BOUR had concluded from his analysis of the plastron alone.

This led to the less than pleasing situation that the eastern tortoises, previously known as *Testudo hermanni hermanni*, had to be renamed with the next available name in line, i.e., *Testudo hermanni boettgeri* MOJSISO-VICS, 1889 (today *Testudo boettgeri*), while the western form, known as *Testudo hermanni robertmertensi* now had to be referred to as *Testudo hermanni hermanni* (today *Testudo hermanni*). This rearranging of names had a rather ironic effect, too. While it dissociated the famous German herpetologist and director of many years of the Frankfurt Naturmuseum und Forschungsinstitut Senckenberg, Robert MERTENS (1894–1975), whose name used to be linked to the western form, the founder

Fig. 9: Holotype of *Testudo hermanni* (No. 111 in the *Musée de Zoologie*)

and first director of the very same institution, Oskar BOETTGER (1844–1910), was now honored with another "officially" accepted form. In praxis the new arrangement means that literature dealing with "*Testudo hermanni hermanni*" published before 1987 actually refers to the animal today known as *Testudo boettgeri* (and/or in many cases probably to the recently revived taxon *Testudo hercegovinensis*). The data on "*Testudo hermanni robertmertensi*" published before 1987, on the other hand, refer to the tortoise today known as *Testudo hermanni*.

The situation becomes even more confusing by the fact that not all authors after

1987 applied the revised nomenclature so that it is in many cases unclear whether they refer to western or eastern representatives of the *Testudo hermanni* species group. Likewise, very old literature may be fairly puzzling, because this species group was regularly referred to as "*Testudo hermanni*" because, as was mentioned before, science did not for a long time distinguish between these two species complexes.

Type locality

Not indicated; designated as Collobrières, Massif des Maures, Var, France (= Collobrières in the Maure Mountains, Department of Var, Region Provence-Alpes-Côte d'Azur, France) by BOUR (1987).

Synonyms

– *Testudo graeca Bettai* LATASTE, 1881 (holotype: No. 1947.3.4.54 in the Natural History Museum in London, England; a 20.2 cm-long female; type locality: not indicated)

– *Testudo graeca* – (BOULENGER 1889)

– *Testudo (Testudo) hermanni* – (WILLIAMS 1952)

– *Testudo hermanni robertmertensi* WERMUTH, 1952 (holotype: No. 37 468 in the Naturmuseum und Forschungsinstitut Senckenberg in Frankfurt am Main, Germany; A 9.4 cm-long female; type locality: mountains north of Arta, Mallorca Island, Balearic Islands [= mountains north of Artà on Mallorca, Balearic Autonomous Region, Spain)

– *Protestudo hermanni robertmertensi* – (CHKHIKVADZE 1970)

– *Testudo hermanni hermanni* – (BOUR 1987)

– *Agrionemys hermanni hermanni* – (GMIRA 1993a)

– The name "*Testudo ermania*" used by ZAHND & PORTE (1961) is merely a lapsus calami.

Etymology

hermanni = named after Johannes (or Jean) HERMANN (1738–1800), whose extensive zoological collection also contained the type specimen of this species.

Vernacular names

Basque: Hermann dortoka (= Hermann's tortoise); **Catalan:** Tortuga mediterrània (= Mediterranean tortoise), Tortuga de garriga (= Garrigue tortoise); **Danish:** Hermanns landskildpadde (= Hermann's tortoise); **English:** Hermann's tortoise, Western Hermann's tortoise; **French:** Tortue d'Hermann (= Hermann's tortoise), Tortue d'Hermann occidentale (= western Hermann's tortoise), Tortue de Mertens (= Mertens' tortoise), Tortue française (= French tortoise); **Galician:** Tartaruga mediterránea (= Mediterranean tortoise); **German:** Italienische Landschildkröte (= Italian tortoise), also Robert-Mertens-Landschildkröte (= Robert Mertens' tortoise), Französische Landschildkröte (= French tortoise), Robert-Mertens-Schildkröte (= Robert Mertens' turtle), Mertens'sche Griechische Landschildkröte (= Mertens' Greek tortoise), Westliche Griechische Landschildkröte (= western Greek tortoise); **Italian:** Testuggine di Hermann (= Hermann's tortoise), Testuggine comune (= common tortoise); **Maltese:** Fekruna ta' l-art; **Sardinian:** Tostòinu (= tortoise), Tostòini (= tortoise); **Swedish:** Västlig grekisk landsköldpadda (= western Greek tortoise); **Spanish:** Tortuga mediterránea (= Mediterranean tortoise), Tortuga hermanni (= Hermanni tortoise), Tortuga de Hermann (= Hermann's tortoise), Galápago del Mediterráneo (= Mediterranean tortoise)

Description

Testudo hermanni species group
Morphology and coloration

Carapace

The dorsal shell (carapace) of the tortoises included in this species group is highly domed, oval to trapezoid when viewed from above, and has steep sides. Its highest point is situated behind the center. The nuchal region is slightly notched, while the posterior marginal scutes are curved downwards, feebly serrated, and may be distinctly elongated in very old specimens. The bony part of the carapace usually comprises an octagonal nuchal plate, eight vertebral plates (neurals; the three posterior ones are usually hexagonal in shape), a coccygeal plate (suprapygal), a caudal plate (pygal), eight pairs of rib plates (costals), and eleven pairs of marginal plates (peripherals). The posteriormost neural is often referred to as first suprapygal that is situated anterior to the second suprapygal, which in turn is then followed by the pygal. Anomalies and aberrations from this principal layout are not uncommon.

The bony shell is usually covered with a long, narrow nuchal scute (cervical), five narrow vertebral scutes (vertebrals), four pairs of rib scutes (pleurals), and eleven pairs of marginal scutes (marginals). Deviations are common here as well. The vertebrals are wider than long, the fifth of which is enlarged and distinctly wider than all other vertebrals, although the first vertebral may be nearly as wide in some individuals. The vertebrals 2–4 are distinctly narrower than the pleurals 1–3. The caudal scute (supracaudal) is usually divided (the split may only be present on the upper side, though), but may also be entire in more than half of the animals of certain populations. The areolae of the vertebrals and pleurals are often raised, although the surface of the carapace has only a weak relief. Exceptions due to disease are possible and include single, boxlike, separated, humped individual scutes; these are the results of inadequate husbandry conditions. Growth rings are visible in young to semiadult specimens, but become increasingly indistinct with age.

The ground color of the carapace can be lemon, gold, horn, straw or greenish yellow, yellowish orange, or dark brown and usually sports a conspicuous irregular, dark brown to black spotted pattern in the anterior and lateral parts of the vertebrals and pleurals and in the anterior and lower sections of the marginals. The areolae of the scutes are largely dark in color. In some instances, the carapace may be uniformly light in color, more rarely dark throughout.

According to WERMUTH (1952) *Testudo hermanni* has a higher domed carapace than the two other species. While STEMMLER (1959) refuted this statement especially as

Arrangement of carapacial scutes

C = cervical
M = marginals
V = vertebrals
P = pleurals
S = supracaudals

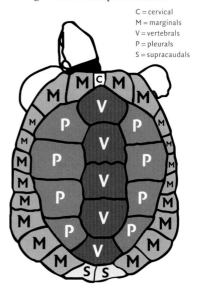

Arrangement of plastral scutes

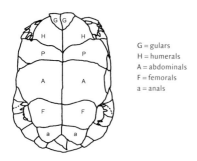

G = gulars
H = humerals
A = abdominals
F = femorals
a = anals

tapers to a point anteriorly, and is shorter and narrower than the posterior lobe. The bony part of the plastron consists of an entoplastron and two epi-, hyo-, hypo- and xiphiplastra each. Anomalies are commonly found here as well. Scutes comprise pairs of gulars, humerals, pectorals, abdominals, femorals, and anals. A distinct groove separates the anals. The gulars are thickened and regularly round, and do not protrude over the anterior margin of the carapace, or do so only slightly. The pectorals are relatively wide, as are the bridges, which each contain a small inguinal scute that is hardly visible from below and may also be entirely absent, and a small axillar scute. The length of the central suture separating the pectorals usually equals at least half the length of the central suture between the humerals.

far as Sardinian specimens were concerned, CHEYLAN (2001) confirmed that the carapaces of eastern European members of the *Testudo hermanni* species group were slightly compressed. GUYOT & DEVAUX (1997a, b) equally found differences in the proportions between carapace lengths and shell heights of female tortoises from the Albera Mountains and Corsica on the one, and their cousins from Greece on the other hand. According to the same authors, males would not exhibit these differences, though.

Plastron

The ventral shell (plastron) is well developed. Its anterior lobe is slightly, if at all, arched,

The ground color of the plastron and the bridges is lemon, gold or greenish yellow to yellowish orange, and is usually patterned with dark brown or black spots that are often clearly outlined and may be fused to form two wide longitudinal stripes.

The plastral formula for the three species dealt with here is: abdominals > humerals > anals > < gulars > femorals > < pectorals.

Head and limbs

The head of these tortoises is of moderate size, with the snout not projecting. The alveolar ridge is strongly pronounced, has sharp edges, and ends before the masticating surface of the upper jawbone. The hyoid ridge is strongly developed in its posterior section, sharply edged, and elongated and ending in a point before the weakly developed outer appendix of the sphenoid bone. It ends abruptly anteriorly and continues in a more or less arched maxillar rim. The cranial opening between orbit and nasal cavity is usually concealed by the marginal ledge of the masticating surface when viewed from below, while the cavities in the palatine are situated beside and behind the outer processus of the sphenoid. The quadrate bone envelops the stapes. The upper jaw sports a hooked beak.

The prefrontal and frontal scales are large. They may be split lengthwise or fragmented into several small scales. The rest of the head scales are small.

The head is dark or grayish brown in its anterior regions, lighter posteriorly. The upper side of the head is often slightly lighter in general. The lower jaw is usually dark, whereas the throat and neck are light. A sharply delimited, bright yellow spot is often present beneath the eye in the area of the massetericum (the temporal scale).

The anterior sides of the front legs are covered with small to moderately large scales that do not overlap, but there are also larger areas without scales. Just above the front feet there are numerous, very small, granular scales that show no distinct overlapping. The front feet usually have five, but sometimes only four visible claws. In the latter case the fifth claw is usually greatly reduced, or the respective toe is present in the skeleton, but not discernible on the outside. On Corsica, 44.2 % of male and 59.4 % of female specimens possess a fifth, often less well developed claw, but in 4.2 % of the males and 12.5 of the females this claw is very distinct and often as well developed as the fourth. This trait appears to vary with the sex, as these figures demonstrate that a distinct fifth claw is more commonly found in females. The rear feet are furnished with four claws each. The heels of the rear feet are covered with large scales, and the thighs lack spur-like horny scales. A longitudinally furrowed, horny nail forms the tip of the tail.

The upper arms and the rear sides of the lower arms are dark, while the anterior surfaces of the lower arms are light grayish brown. The hind legs and the tail are also light grayish brown with a more or less widespread darker tint on the outer surfaces.

Juvenile coloration

Hatchlings show on their carapaces much less contrasting colors than older conspecif-

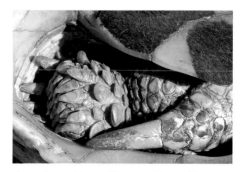

Fig. 10: A characteristic trait of the species of the *Testudo hermanni* species group is the horny nail on the tip of the tail. (W. WEGEHAUPT)

Boettger's tortoise,
Testudo boettgeri

Figs. 11&12: left: *Testudo boettgeri*, portrait (J. MARAN),
Testudo boettgeri, dorsal view (E. HEIMANN)

Dalmatian tortoise,
Testudo hercegovinensis

Figs. 15&16: left: *Testudo hercegovinensis*, portrait (J. MARAN),
Testudo hercegovinensis, dorsal view (A. SUKIC)

Italian tortoise,
Testudo hermanni

Figs. 19&20: left: *Testudo hermanni*, portrait (J. MARAN),
Testudo hermanni, dorsal view (J. MARAN)

Fig. 13: *Testudo boettgeri*, ventral view (G. POPGEORGIEV)

Fig. 14: *Testudo boettgeri*, carapacial aspect (A. PAUNOVIC)

Fig. 17: *Testudo hercegovinensis*, plastral aspect (J. MARAN)

Fig. 18: *Testudo hercegovinensis*, dorsal view (A. SUKIC)

Fig. 21: *Testudo hermanni*, ventral view (F. WÜTHRICH)

Fig. 22: *Testudo hermanni*, dorsal view (H.-U. SCHMIDT)

ics. It consists of a mix of shades of brown, black and yellow. Juveniles of a few weeks of age display a dark pigmentation on the anterior and central portions of the carapace scutes. Round to oval, dark spots are particularly common in the central sections of the vertebrals and pleurals. In the case of the pleurals these spots are often fused with the darkly pigmented anterior margins of the scutes. The plastron is marked with large black blotches, which are usually more extensive in specimens from the western parts of the distribution range than in those from the east. Newly hatched babies of *Testudo hermanni* exhibit a vivid yellow coloration on the head and neck as well as on the legs and soft parts, with black spots appearing on the sides of the head some time later. The light spots beneath the eyes that are typical for representatives from the west are whitish initially and turn yellow only later. The soft parts are yellowish, and the carapace is brownish in color. In contrast, the head, neck, limbs and soft parts of hatchlings of the eastern population group appear very dark, with small lighter patches being limited to the front and hind legs. It takes several months before the coloration lightens. The basis of the claws of the front feet is usually

distinctly darker in juveniles from the east than in those from the west, which applies in particular to specimens from the Italian mainland.

A less than perfect position inside the egg may cause some hatchlings to emerge with severely deformed shells, but these animals usually straighten themselves out within just a few weeks. The adult coloration appears with relative rapidness from the second year of life. The carapace maintains its oval outline up to the fifth or sixth year, at which age the shell of male specimens is still not widened at the level of the ninth and tenth marginals.

Variability

Specimens from coastal regions are usually much lighter in their colors than those from the inland or higher altitudes of mountainous areas. This may be explained by different climatic conditions affecting their natural habitats. Darker tortoises warm up more rapidly, and are thus better adapted to the often somewhat cooler climate in mountainous regions. JOST (1998a, b) noted in the southeast of Corsica that specimens from dryer environments were smaller and lighter in color than their cousins from moister

Figs. 23&24: Juvenile *Testudo hermanni* from Menorca (Spain); dorsal and ventral aspects (H.-U. SCHMIDT)

habitats. It is possible that the shape and surface structure of the shell is influenced by environmental factors at least to some extent. This is, for example, also suggested by the development of humped shells in animals kept in inadequate conditions in human care. However, free-ranging tortoises with boxlike carapace scutes similar in appearance to those raised in captivity were also found living in the closer vicinity of water bodies in the north of the Italian island of Sardinia and in Croatian Istria, whereas specimens from dryer habitats showed a much more regular growth.

As far as the traits that differentiate the three species dealt with here are concerned,

it must be said that these may be extremely variable. It is therefore quite impossible to provide a universal key to their identification. Instead, all traits separating them need to be evaluated together.

Karyotype

The body cells of the species of the *Testudo hermanni* species group each contain 52 chromosomes (20 metacentric or submetacentric, 10 subtelocentric and 22 acrocentric chromosomes).

Size and weight

The species of the *Testudo hermanni* species group may grow to reach a maximum carapace length of 35.7 cm, but are usually much smaller, i.e., they usually measure 20–24 cm only. The weight of adult specimens commonly ranges from 1 to 3 kg. The various species may substantially differ as to their body sizes, but the significance of these differences within the context of the entire distribution range is all but easy to rate. Available data are often incomplete and have not in all instances been gathered using the same standard methods. Some authors gave minimum adult sizes in a rather arbitrary manner, which severely limits their usefulness for comparisons.

Fig. 25–27: The small-sized form of *Testudo boettgeri* from the south of the Peloponnesus will soon be described as a separate taxon. Shown here is a female of this "dwarf form". (J. MARAN)

In the Balkans, a correlation is clearly discernible between the maximum size of adult specimens, climate (temperatures in particular), and the geographical range of a population. The largest specimens live in the coolest parts of the distribution range, which is in the north and at higher altitudes and in forests, whereas the smallest are found in the warmest areas, which is in the south and in the lowlands. There is obviously a link between the body sizes of the tortoises and their natural habitats – the dryer their environment, the smaller are the tortoises, or so it would appear.

Sexual dimorphism
Throughout their entire distribution range, male specimens of the *Testudo hermanni* species group are some 10–12 % smaller on average than their female counterparts. While males may grow to a maximum carapace length of 31.4 cm, this value is 35.7 cm for females. The weight of adult females may be up to 3 kg under normal circumstances, whereas males tip the scales at a maximum of only 1.5 kg. The only exception that seems to contradict these rules results from a study conducted in a population of *Testudo boettgeri* in the Iron Gate Nature Reserve in Romania where males were said to grow slightly larger than females. This statement is, however, not quite beyond doubts because only a relatively small number of animals were examined.

Another sex-dependent difference is found in the shape of the carapace. Males from the eastern reaches of the range in particular exhibit a shell that is widened at the level of the marginals 9 and 10 which lends it a distinctly pear-shaped outline and contrasts thus with the rather oval appearance of females. The following proportional ratios were recorded for 31 adult males and females of *Testudo hermanni* each from the

French Department of Var: carapace length/carapace width (measured between the sixth and seventh marginals): = 1,16–1,31 (on average 1,27 ± 0,03) in males, and 1,22–1,36 (on average 1,31 ± 0,03) in females; carapace length/maximum shell height = 1,74–2,08 (on average 1,90 ± 0,08) in males, and 1,72–2,06 (on average 1,92 ± 0,08) in females.

In males, the supracaudal is wider at its base and more arched than in females and thus appears pentagonal rather than trapezoid. The plastron of a male is slightly to distinctly concave in shape and shorter relative to the body length than that of a female. The posterior lobe of the plastron is always rigid in males, but becomes a little flexible in females at least during the oviposition period. Both sexes lack a truly hinged plastron, though. The groove between the anals is comparatively wider in male specimens, and the ratio of the length of the xiphiplastra to their width is 0.39 ± 0.04 on average in males, but 0.59 ± 0.05 in females. Male representatives of the *Testudo hermanni* species group are marked by a distinctly longer and sturdier tail than their female counterparts (about 26 % of the carapace length as compared to about 14.3 %). When walking, males usually carry the tail folded to one side, where it may almost reach the bend of the knee. Females often carry their tails sticking out straight, but when it is folded in as well, it does not extend beyond the margin of the supracaudal. The cloacal opening is situated closer to the tail tip in males, and the horny nail at the tip is distinctly more prominent and longer than the claws than in females where it is shorter than the claws.

AMIRANASHVILI (2000) noted that further differences between the sexes existed in their bony structures. Investigating Bulgarian *Testudo boettgeri*, the peripherals at the level of the bridges were found to be

Fig. 28: Sexual dimorphism in the Italian tortoise (female on the left, male on the right) (J. MARAN)

relatively narrower and higher in males than in females. The suture between the hyo- and hypoplastra was longer than the central suture between the hypoplastra by a factor of 3 to 3.5, whereas this factor was only 2.5 to 2.8 in females. In male specimens, the suture separating the humerals from the pectorals crosses over the entoplastron in male specimens, whereas in females it largely follows in its central section the suture between the hyo- and entoplastra. Males usually have quadrangular first and third neurals, an octagonal second, and the five posterior ones are hexagonal. This is less commonly so in females where the first, third and fifth neurals are more often quadrangular, the second and fourth octagonal, and the three posterior ones hexagonal. The jags of the suture between the hypo- and xiphiplastra are wider in females than in males.

The above-mentioned external differences become recognizable from reaching a carapace length of about 10 cm, which indicates an age of about four to seven years. However, with some experience and a sufficient number of specimens for direct comparisons, it is often possible to use the telltale shape of the tail nail make an educated guess about the sexual identity of a specimen as early as at about one year of age.

It is still insufficiently known at which age exactly sexual maturity sets in. Many authors link carapace sizes to the probable onset of sexual maturity rather than the functionality of the gonads. There is in fact only one study from Romania that refers to the size of the testicles. It indicates that some males in this country become sexually mature already at an age of seven years, which corresponds to a carapace length of about 13 cm. Most Romanian specimens are, however, able to reproduce only from an age of eight or nine years. The male *Testudo hercegovinensis* observed copulating by HERZ (2002) in Dalmatia (Croatia) did not exceed 10 cm in carapace length. Some populations in Greece are equally known to include specimens that begin to show mating behavior on attaining 10 cm in carapace length, but it is more commonly seen in specimens measuring 11–15 cm. A study of seventeen populations in this country revealed a close correlation between the age at the onset of sexual maturity and the size of adult specimens. Members of populations of small adult size matured in some instances much earlier than those of populations that consisted of large-growing specimens. For example, males of a small-growing population at Kalamáta in the south of the Peloponnesus became sexually mature already at an average age of just 6.4 years. This contrasted with the males of a large-growing population living in the vicinity of Deskáti in the central parts of Greece, which reached this point only at an average age of 14 years. The cross-country average lies at 10.3 years.

Being of an altogether smaller build, tortoises in France begin to show sexually motivated behaviors only on having grown to 12–13 cm in carapace length, which corresponds to an age of about 10–12 years. CASTANET & CHEYLAN (1979) even presumed for French specimens that sexual maturity would set in at an age of twelve years in males and fourteen years in females. Males on Corsica also become mature on having grown to 12–13 cm in carapace length, but it appears that they achieve this already by the time they are seven to eight years old. The tortoises living in the Ebro Delta of Spain mature at an age of 6–8 (males) and 8–10 years (females), respectively.

Females mature clearly later than their male counterparts. In Greece and the western parts of the distribution range, they measure about 2 cm more in carapace length when they become able to reproduce. Studies involving X-ray technology and examining the reproductive organs of female specimens were conducted in both Greece and Romania. In the latter country, females contained eggs from 15 cm in carapace length, while the smallest female with eggs was found living in the vicinity of Alíki, some 50 km southwest of Thessaloníki (Thessalonica) in Greece, and measured only 14.2 cm. The latter is, however, likely to represent an exception since all other females with carapace lengths of 14–15 cm from that area were not gravid. The typical minimum size of females with eggs therefore appears to be at least 15 cm in both Greece and Romania, which corresponds to an age of about eleven years. Like in the case of male specimens, it is apparent that, in females, the onset of sexual maturity is related to the body size of adult specimens in the respective population. Minimum and maximum values were once more found in the populations at Kalamáta (on average 7.2 years), and Deskáti (on average 16.6 years), respectively, with a cross-country average of twelve years. The smallest female observed laying eggs in nature in southern France measured 14.5 cm, which would indicate an age of about 12–14 years. Females raised and kept in outdoor enclosures began to produce fertile eggs at an age of about ten years, though. On Corsica, the carapace length of a female with eggs is at least 15 cm, which suggests an age of about eight to nine years. Two females of *Testudo hercegovinensis* in the care of HERZ (2005) deposited clutches of eggs for the first time at carapace lengths of 14 and 14.5 cm, and weights of 660 and 710 g, respectively.

Hearing

The importance of the sense of hearing in chelonians has hardly received any research effort as yet. Insofar as *Testudo boettgeri* is concerned, an interesting observation made in several specimens kept in an outdoor pen was documented by CHRISTIANSEN (1973). The animals were brought a bunch of fresh dandelion at a point of time when only one specimen was active outside their shelter. When this tortoise began to eat the crisp leaves, the other tortoises hurried to leave their shelter as well. Since they could not possibly have seen either the feeding specimen or the dandelion, it might have been the sounds of feeding that attracted them.

Boettger's tortoise
Morphology and coloration

Carapace

The dorsal aspect of the carapace is oval in females and about trapezoid and distinctly widened at the level of the ninth and tenth marginal in males. The highest point of the shell is situated posterior to the center. The lower sides of the seventh marginals are usually bent backwards and touch the inguinals. The division of the supracaudal is highly variable. For example, it is entire in more than 50% of the specimens living at Lakes Ohrid and Prespa, on the Greek island of Corfu, and in the northeast of the Greek mainland, whereas it is divided in 83.3% of the animals inhabiting former Yugoslavia, in 82% of those in Bulgaria, and in 72.2% of those in most parts of Greece.

The ground color of the shell is straw or dirty yellow to yellowish green, olive or light brown. The darker markings of the carapace usually have irregular outlines and commonly cover less than 50% of the surface. They often create little contrast with the basic coloration, but rather fade into it

via shades of brown or gray. Some specimens are uniformly light or almost entirely dark. The fifth vertebral lacks a keyhole-shaped marking.

Plastron

The bony pelvic supports of the plastron are not forked. The ratio of the length of the suture between the femorals to the length of the suture between the pectorals usually amounts to 0.83–1.17 in males whereas it is usually 0.68–0.72 in females. The ratio of the length of the suture separating the humerals to the length of the suture separating the femorals is 2.2–2.6 in males and 2.22–2.6 in females. PERÄLÄ (2002b), however, doubted the usefulness of the length ratios of the sutures between the individual plastral scutes as a tool to differentiate between the species of the *Testudo hermanni* complex, but conceded that this trait may be more reliable in females than in males. Although this feature would be fairly constant within each population, it would not be constant throughout any of the three species recognized at present. The suture between the humerals and pectorals usually runs in an almost straight line, in an outwards curved V-shape, or in a wavy line, but only in 20% of the specimens in an inward-curved V-shape. Inguinals are usually present.

The ground color of the plastron corresponds to that of the carapace. It usually sports two longitudinal rows of dark spots, of which at least those on the gulars and anals are isolated. The plastral pattern is highly variable, however, and ranges from a virtual absence of black pigment (e.g., in Bulgaria) to an almost entirely black appearance (especially on the Peloponnesus). A clinal change of plastron colors is notable in Greek specimens in particular, where the dark content increases steadily from northern to southern populations, with specimens native to the Peloponnesus having an almost completely black plastron. Earlier, it was presumed that this could be a result of temperature-dependent selective pressures, because there may be a connection between the dissipation of heat from the tortoise shell and the extent of the dark pattern. This theory was based on the assumption that light-colored tortoises from the cooler north would dissipate less heat than their light-colored cousins from the warmer south. This line of thinking was eventually disproved by the studies conducted by NUS-SEAR et al. (2000), which demonstrated that the coloration of the plastron had no influence on the thermoregulation of tortoises. The only explanation thus left for the differences in coloration is that they are determined genetically, which would also explain why specimens from the north have a light plastron, but not those from equally cool situations in the mountain regions of the south.

Head and limbs

The head of Boettger's tortoise is rather bulky and rounded. It usually lacks a yellow spot beneath the eye.

BOUR (2004a) noted that the members of the *Testudo hermanni* species group would also differ with regard to the scalation of the anterior surface of the lower arms. Specimens from Montenegro possess an about triangular patch around the wrist that consists of at least six (outer side) to twelve (inner side) irregular rows of 12–15 very small scales. These are followed by similarly small scales, which may in part protrude, before they connect with the small scales of the upper arm. Irregularly shaped, moderately large to large scales follow the line of the elbow, while the ulna itself is covered with

Fig. 29: A female Boettger's tortoise from Marathea, Peloponnesus (Greece) (A. NÖLLERT)

a row of large scales. These do, however, not extend as far as the wrist. Specimens from the south of the Peloponnesus exhibit a scalation of the anterior side of the lower arms that is rather similar to that of French *Testudo hermanni* (see below). The area around the wrist is covered with 5–6 rows of 10–12 scales each, while the patch above the wrist is relatively small and more or less rectangular in shape and is made up of slightly protruding scales.

It is of interest that HIGHFIELD (1988b) reported that nearly all of the "Bulgarian giants" he examined had only four claws on their front feet.

Variability

As has been mentioned before, the extent of geographical variability within the eastern population group is most obviously expressed in body sizes. However, differences in coloration are in part very evident, too. While, for example, some Greek populations show very light colors with almost no black content, those from other parts of the country may appear almost entirely black. In Albania, one in one-thousand specimens is said to be almost completely black with only a few yellow spots. These major differences may be based on age-related "lightening" or "darkening" in at least some instances, though.

Some aberrations in the color pattern are indeed specific to certain populations. Certain colonies on the Peloponnesus are, for example, relatively dark and have at the same time rather small adult sizes. Specimens living in the south of the peninsula are particularly reminiscent of their western cousins. For example, a population existing south of Kalamáta resembles in its plastral aspects very much animals from the western reaches of the range. SOFSKY (1982) almost exclusively found specimens with very dark,

almost black carapaces with a yellow spotted pattern behind the eyes in the vicinity of Édessa in northern Greece. ARTNER & ARTNER (1997) described a population of small (up to about 15.5 cm in carapace length) specimens from the arid areas of northeastern Greece near the coast that were notable for their extraordinarily light ground coloration; some specimens even had plain yellow shells. The tortoises living on the Greek island of Corfu are commonly grouped with the eastern population group. On the other hand, STUGREN & KAVVADIAS (1989) concluded from their study that the highly domed carapace, the contrasting yellow and black pattern of the shell, the light gray coloration of the soft parts, and the predominantly black plastron would indicate that the population on Corfu might possibly represent an intermediate form between the eastern and western population groups. It is furthermore interesting to note that these tortoises sometimes also sport the longitudinal blotches on the plastron and the yellow spot beneath the eye that are otherwise typical of *Testudo hermanni* from the western parts of the distribution range.

Size and weight

As far as its body size is concerned, this species displays an enormous extent of variability. In Greece alone, WILLEMSEN & HAILEY (1999a) found at least five different "size classes", each of which would occupy a relatively small geographic area. Besides very small and moderately large specimens there are also very large ones known. Moderately large animals have been found on Corfu (at maximum 15 cm for males, 19 cm for females), from Macedonia (19.6 cm for males, 21.4 cm for females), from the west coast of Greece (at maximum 17.8 cm for males, 20.6 cm for females), from central and northeastern Greece (at maximum 18.9–20.7 cm for males, 21.1–21.7 cm for females) and from the Peloponnesus (at maximum 17.1–19.0 cm for males, 18.0–19.5 cm for females). Average male specimens from the Peloponnesus measure 12.5 cm and females 14.7 cm. This peninsula is also home to a population, though, in which the maximum size of males does not exceed 10.5 cm and whose females grow to around 12 cm only. Populations of large specimens exist in the north and northeast of Greece (at maximum 21.2–23.8 cm for males, 24.8–25.8 cm for females), in Albania (largest specimen 26.4 cm, sex unknown), Bulgaria (at maximum 31.4 cm for males, 35.7 cm for females; this is the largest specimen known to date), and Romania (at maximum 24.2 cm for males, 23.3 cm for females).

Fig. 30: This female *Testudo boettgeri* exhibits the high-yellow coloration typical of Corfu specimens. (J. BRUEKERS)

The average carapace length in Greece is about 15.2 ± 1.08 cm for males, and 17.0 ± 1.26 cm for females. While adult female specimens usually weigh between 1.5 and 3.0 kg, males do not normally tip the scales at more than 1.5 kg (usually 0.8–1.2 kg). The largest male known as yet (31.4 cm in carapace length) was captured in 1915 by the teacher Vasil GEORGIEV north of the Bulgarian town of Kotel in a limestone area named Urushkite Steni at 1,050 m altitude and weighed 6.5 kg when alive. After its death, it was stuffed and is today preserved under the number 111-49/15 in the collection of the Natural History Museum in Sofia, Bulgaria. The largest known female (35.7 cm in carapace length) had been captured by BESHKOV (1997) on 05.07.1973 in the Malashevska Plains of Bulgaria as well, but had unfortunately never been weighed. It is thoroughly possible that *Testudo boettgeri* may even grow to carapace lengths around 37 cm in Bulgaria. A corresponding animal had been observed by SHKORPIL (1897) in the vicinity of the village of Goljam Dervent in the southwestern parts of the Burgas region near the border with Turkey. This author referred

Fig. 31: Some populations of Boettger's tortoise are notable for their aberrant color patterns, as is the case in these yellowish, small-sized animals from the northeast of Greece. (H. ARTNER)

to it as "*Testudo graeca*" (today *Testudo ibera*) as he, like most authors at that time, was under the impression that there was only one species of tortoise present in Bulgaria. BURESH & TSONKOV (1933a) later reidentified the animal as *Testudo boettgeri*, though. Because there is unfortunately neither an illustration nor a detailed description of this specimen, and both *Testudo boettgeri* and *Testudo ibera* occur in the surroundings of Goljam Dervent, its specific identity will probably remain a mystery forever. For this reason it cannot claim the size record for a member of the *Testudo hermanni* species group.

Sexual dimorphism

In addition to the sex-indicative morphological disparities listed above, WILLEMSEN

& HAILEY (1999b) discovered a sex-specific difference for Greek specimens that applies to the coloration of the plastron. Males show a higher content of black pigmentn in their plastral color pattern, and their black blotches are 1.3 times larger than those of their female counterparts.

Dalmatian tortoise
Morphology and coloration

Carapace

The carapace is oval in dorsal view in females, and rather trapezoid in males where it is distinctly widened at the level of the ninth and tenth marginals. The highest point of the shell is situated posterior to the center. The lower side of the seventh marginal is usually not bent backwards. The supracaudal is divided in most specimens (82–92 %).

The basic color of the shell is straw or dirty yellow to brownish yellow, yellowish green, yellowish olive or olive green. It ap-pears as though specimens from the north of the distribution range of this species are in general darker than those from the southern parts as well. The dark pattern of the carapace usually covers less than 50 % of the entire surface. The carapace pattern of juveniles is distinct and clearly defined, with the growth rings being clearly visible. This condition changes as the animal grows older, often starting as early as with the onset of sexual maturity. Older specimens eventually appear quite drab and show a more grayish ground color. The fifth vertebral often sports a yellow marking with black bordering that has the shape of a keyhole. Of the 33 specimens examined by WEGEHAUPT (2005) in Croatia, 65 % displayed this conspicuous marking.

Plastron

The bony pelvic supports of the plastron are usually distinctly forked. Inguinals are usually absent, and their place is com-

Fig. 32: Very light-colored specimen of *Testudo boettgeri* from Greece (H. BRINGSØE)

monly occupied by the laterally widened abdominals. WEGEHAUPT (2005) found that 61% of the 33 specimens he examined in Croatia had no inguinals, 14% possessed an inguinal on one side, and 25% on both sides. The ratio of the length of the suture between the femorals to the length of the suture between the pectorals is far too variable to be useful as a trait of differentiation, although it seems to tend toward a balanced state. The suture separating the humerals from the pectorals runs in an inward-curved V-shape.

The ground color of the plastron corresponds to that of the carapace. It is marked with two longitudinal rows of dark blotches of which at least those on the humerals and anals are isolated. The gulars are almost always, and the anals often, free of spots or marked on one side only.

Head and limbs

The head of this species is rather bulky and rounded. A yellow spot beneath the eye is often present. All specimens examined by WEGEHAUPT (2005) on the Adriatic coast of Croatia showed with no exception a yellowish olive occiput. BOUR (2004a) had no samples of *Testudo hercegovinensis* available for his studies of the scalation of the lower arm in species of the *Testudo hermanni* species group.

Size and weight

Testudo hercegovinensis is a small to moderately large species. So far, measurements

Fig. 33: Male *Testudo hercegovinensis* from Croatia (W. WEGEHAUPT)

Fig. 34: *Testudo hercegovinensis* (left) differs from *Testudo boettgeri* (right) by usually lacking inguinal scutes. (J. MARAN)

Fig. 35: Juvenile *Testudo hercegovinensis* from Croatia (J. MARAN)

have been published for specimens from Montenegro (at maximum 14–17 cm in carapace length for males, 17–19 cm for females) and Croatia (at maximum 14.5 cm for males, 16.4 cm for females), and from the Italian nature reserve of Bosco della Mesola (see below) (at maximum 16.2 cm for males, 18.4 cm for females). The average carapace length for males amounts to 12.6–13.5 cm, and for females 14.0–14.7 cm. However, a female specimen preserved in the Natural History Museum of Vienna, Austria (No. 19368) exceeds 20 cm in length, and EGER (2005) described a female in his care that measured 21.5 cm in carapace length. While female specimens may reach weights of about 500–1,820 g, males of this tortoise will not exceed 350–935 g.

Italian tortoise
Morphology and coloration

Carapace
The carapace is in both sexes rather oval in dorsal view (but distinctly trapezoid in some individual males) and only slightly widened at the level of marginals 9–10. The highest point of the shell is situated close to the center. The lower side of the seventh marginal is usually bent backwards and in contact with the inguinal. It appears that the supracaudal of French specimens is always, and that of Sardinian ones almost always (87.0–99.3 %), divided.

The ground color of the shell is bright lemon or golden yellow to yellowish ochre or orange. The dark markings of the carapace are arranged in a nearly symmetrical, highly contrasting pattern that often covers more than 50 % of the surface area. The fifth vertebral sports a black-bordered marking that is reminiscent of a keyhole. The basic coloration and pattern of the shell are fairly constant in specimens from Spain and the French mainland, but clearly more variable in those from Corsica, Sardinia, and the Italian mainland.

Plastron
The bony pelvic supports of the plastron are not forked. The ratio of the length of the suture between the femorals to the length of the suture between the pectorals is usually 1.57–2.00 in males, and usually 0.92–1.55 in females. The ratio of the length of the suture separating the humerals to the length of the suture separating the femorals is 1.23–1.93 in males, and 1.36–1.93 in females. The suture between the humerals and pectorals has an inward-curved V-shape. Inguinals are usually present.

The ground color of the plastron matches that of the carapace. Dark blotches are arranged in longitudinal rows paralleling the midline; they are fused to form wide continuous stripes. The gulars are free of any dark markings.

Head and limbs
The head of the Italian tortoise is rather elongated and shows regular contours. A sharply delimited, bright yellow spot is situated beneath the eye in the region of massetericum, which fades with the age of the animal.

In *Testudo hermanni*, the fold in the area of the wrist is separated from the lower arm by only 2–3 rows of very small, flattened scales numbering about ten. Approximately twenty scales make up the row of enlarged scales along the elbow, and the same number is counted in the area above the wrist. Those along the elbow are distinctly larger than those above the wrist, though. Furthermore, the area covered by these scales on the elbow is often much larger so that the anterior side of the lower arm is dominated by large, polygonal scales. Insofar as the size of the area covered by these "elbow scales" is concerned, BOUR (2004a) could not find that these would be indicative of the geographical origins of specimens or their sexes.

Variability

The specific identity of the Corsican and Sardinian populations has occasionally been discussed as these animals grow to substantially larger sizes than those living in the south of France or in Spain. Most authors, the present one included, currently treat them as *Testudo hermanni*, but some experts suspect the tortoises of these islands to represent a "hybrid" form between *Testudo hermanni* and animals from the Balkans. This is based on their high degree of

Fig. 36: Female *Testudo hermanni* from Ajaccio, Corsica (France) (J. MARAN)

morphological variability that distinguishes them from southern French and Spanish specimens. The more trapezoid shell of males from these islands is more reminiscent of the eastern population group, while

Fig. 37: Clearly visible in this female *Testudo hermanni* from the vicinity of Stintino, Sardinia (Italy) is the species-indicative yellow cheek spot. (J. MARAN)

Fig. 38: Head scalation of a female *Testudo hermanni* from Tuscany (F. WÜTHRICH)

the length ratios of the plastral sutures, on the other hand, are more typical of specimens from the French mainland and Spain. It must be conceded, though, that this may also represent an intermediate stage.

The coloration of the plastral and soft parts of Corsican and Sardinian specimens also corresponds better to the "type" found in *Testudo hermanni*, although Corsican ones exhibit a more fragmented striped pattern than is common in *Testudo hermanni*. They are furthermore notable for their less intense yellow coloration and sometimes smaller and less contrasting dark markings on a carapace that is relatively massive and lower than normal for the western population group. This condition again places these animals closer to specimens from the eastern parts of the range. The keyhole marking on the fifth vertebral that is characteristic of *Testudo hermanni* is not always clearly defined in Sardinian specimens. These furthermore appear altogether lighter than conspecifics from other parts of the range because the dark markings on the carapace are often "frayed" with the yellow color intruding from the margins and ap-

pearing as inclusions and dots in the black patches. Very dark specimens are occasionally found, though.

Sardinian specimens are fairly constant with regard to some other traits, too. This includes the altogether relatively light coloration of the soft parts, the number of claws on the front feet (usually four), and the yellow coloration of the claws. In summary it may be stated that although the populations living on Corsica and Sardinia differ from those in southern France and Spain, they still fairly agree with the "western basic type". Their allocation to *Testudo hermanni* therefore appears to be justified, at least for the time being, but further studies may arrive at the conclusion that the tortoises of these two islands may be more accurately placed taxonomically as representatives of yet another separate form.

Far from a final verdict is also the situation with regard to the animals living on Sicily and in the south of the Italian mainland. WERMUTH (1952) thought these populations should rather be included in *Testudo boettgeri*, but only two years later reported on a specimen from Calabria that was clearly assignable to *Testudo hermanni*. STEMMLER (1968a) presumed that the few tortoises examined by him from the Ital-

Fig. 39: Male *Testudo hermanni* from the Albera Mountains in Catalonia (Spain) (J. MARAN)

Fig. 40: Female Italian tortoise from Tuscany (Italy) (F. WÜTHRICH)

ian west coast would be closely related to their cousins on Corsica and Sardinia and should, like these, be regarded as intermediate between *Testudo hermanni* and specimens from the Balkans.

Another theory that was entertained for some time was to cluster the populations from Sicily and southern Italy with the eastern population group, while the remaining Italian populations were to be regarded as *Testudo hermanni*. Of the 137 specimens from all over Italy examined by BRUNO (1986), 32 % exhibited intermediate characteristics between the western and eastern forms, but the majority either resembled *Testudo hermanni* or could clearly be identified as this species. The tortoises living in the regions Apulia, Abruzzi and Marches in particular are said to display color patterns that would rather link them to the eastern populations. Following these research results, Italy could indeed be home to a transitory zone between the two population groups. However, other authors noted that Italian specimens from various regions (Apulia, Tuscany, Latium,

Molise) would conform with the western form – except of course the partly introduced populations of what is probably *Testudo hercegovinensis* in Emília-Romagna, Venetia and Friuli-Julish-Venetia. BRUNO (1986) voiced the opinion that the Italian specimens that would resemble those from the eastern parts of the distribution range in their external morphology could be the result of interbreeding with conspecifics from the Balkans that were introduced by man. This idea would find support in facts such as the incident of an Albanian car that was stopped in a roadblock and found to contain in the boot several specimens of the eastern European form of this tortoise. Since the police officer who had stopped that car did not quite know what to do with the animals, he released them in a nearby forest which he knew had been home to tortoises at least in the past. That the native population probably consisted of *Testudo hermanni* was beyond the comprehension of the policeman.

In summary it may be stated that influences from the eastern population group are only weakly expressed on the Italian mainland and may be, if at all, of importance only in the northeast. The main boundary between western and eastern population groups is surely situated in the plains of the Po River.

With regard to the Sicilian populations, BRUNO (1986) was unable to clearly identify as *Testudo hermanni* 14 out of 34 specimens originating from this island. A Sicilian specimen described by STEMMLER (1968a) had a relatively light ground color that was reminiscent of that of animals from the Balkans, but at the same time showed continuous stripes of black on the plastron and other traits that would group it with the western population group. BALLASINA (1995a) figured tortoises from Sicily that were hardly distinguishable from Italian, Sardinian or Corsican ones, but in comparison with southern French specimens showed a reduced, although still expansive black pattern. Their basic shell coloration resembled that of Corsican and Sardinian specimens, but the plastron bore the black stripes typical of the western population group.

Little information exists about the animals living in the Tuscan Archipelago and on the islands of Lampedusa, Linosa and Pantelleria that are presently generally referred to as *Testudo hermanni*.

The tortoises native to the Spanish northeast are marked by having a content of black on their carapaces that is greater than, e.g., that found in specimens from southern France or even those from the Balearic Islands. Their basic carapace coloration is dominated by yellowish ochre, whereas those from southern France show a greater influx of orange. Balearic animals exhibit a carapace that is more saddle-shaped, i.e., raised in the anterior portion, and rather dull yellowish green in color as compared with conspecifics from the Spanish mainland.

Size and weight

Testudo hermanni is a small to moderately large species whose females grow to 25 cm in carapace length whereas males do not exceed the 19.6 cm-mark. Fully-grown females of *Testudo hermanni* usually reach weights of up to 1.5 kg at maximum. Moderately large specimens are known from the islands of Corsica (at maximum 18.0 cm for males [on average 14.9 ± 0.87 cm], and 24.5 cm [on average 17.9 ± 1.0 cm] for females) and Sardinia (at maximum 19.6 cm [usually 13–16 cm, weight around 400–700 g] for males, 20 cm [usually 15–19 cm, weight around 580–1,200 g] for females). As far as Sardinia is concerned, BASSU et al. (2003) noted that the local tortoises were distinctly smaller and lighter than their cousins on the small island of Asinara off the northwestern coast of the main island. The populations on the Baleares have not yet been studied in detail with regard to their body sizes, and this is precisely the reason why highly contradictory information persists about just how large the tortoises on these islands grow. SCHMIDT (2000a), for one, reported about an about 25 cm-long female which he had found in a public garden on Menorca. Following other authors, Balearic specimens are said to resemble those from the Spanish mainland (at maximum 14–15 cm for males, 16–18 cm for females) and southern France (at maximum 16.6 cm [on average 13.8 ± 0.59 cm] for males, 19.1 cm [on average 15.9 ± 0.86 cm] for females; weights 350–450 and 550–1,000 g, respectively), which depicts them as rather smallish. According to MASCORT (1997b), specimens from the Balearic Islands reach even slightly smaller maximum sizes than those from the Spanish mainland, and MERCHÁN FORNELINO

& MARTÍNEZ SILVESTRE (1999) indicate for specimens from Mallorca an average carapace length of 11.0 cm for females and 10.6 cm for males, with maximum lengths of 20.0 and 18.1 cm, respectively.

It is at present equally difficult to rate the situation in Italy. According to BALLASINA & WILLEMSEN (1990), Tuscany is home to relatively large specimens, but this contradicts the values obtained by CARBONE (1988) (at maximum 15.8 cm [on average 13 cm] for males, 17.3 cm [on average 14.7 cm] for females). WEGEHAUPT (2003) mentioned a central Italian population in which individuals reached maximum sizes of just under 17 cm (weight ca. 1 kg) in the cases of females and about 12.5 cm (weight ca. 500 g) in males. Of a comparatively small growth appear to be the populations in the Italian south, in the regions of Calabria and Apulia. It is as yet uncertain how large Sicilian representatives of this species may grow.

Fig. 41: A pair of Italian tortoises on Menorca (Spain); the female on the left, the male on the right (H.-U. SCHMIDT)

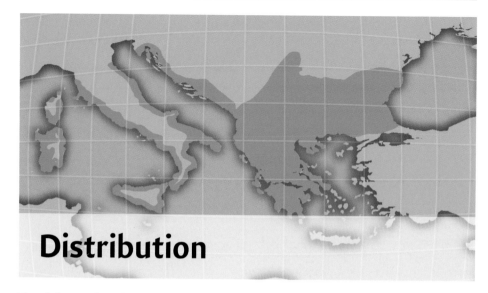

Distribution

Testudo hermanni species group

Besides the marginated tortoise (*Testudo marginata* SCHOEPFF, 1793), the members of the *Testudo hermanni* species group are the only species of tortoises that are exclusively distributed on the European continent. Until the end of the Pliocene (some 1.8 million years ago), the *Testudo hermanni* species group (or an ancestral form for that matter) were distributed north to the southern parts of today's Poland. They subsequently retreated to the more southern portions of Europe and have for the past 10,000 years been limited to the Mediterranean regions of Europe.

Today, the species grouped in the *Testudo hermanni* complex are found from the northeast of Spain (Catalonia) and southern France in the west, through Italy, (probably) Slovenia, Croatia, Bosnia and Herzegovina, Serbia and Montenegro, Albania, Macedonia, and Greece, to Bulgaria, Romania and the European part of Turkey in the east. Included in the distribution range are numerous islands in the Mediterranean Sea, including Mallorca, Menorca, Corsica, Sardinia and Sicily, with some of the populations being a result

of human introduction. With the exception of certain regions in the Balkans, the common distribution range of these species falls into the bioclimatic zone of the Mediterranean.

Boettger's tortoise

The distribution range of Boettger's tortoise stretches from Montenegro, Albania, the east of Serbia and Macedonia in the west to Bulgaria, Romania and European Turkey in the east. Records from Cyprus are based on specimens introduced by man, and no natural populations exist on this island. The occurrence of this species in Croatia that was still presumed by PERÄLÄ (2002b) is probably based on *Testudo hercegovinensis* as was suggested by SCHWEIGER (2005) and WEGEHAUPT (2005).

Albania: The species is present virtually throughout this country, probably including the islands of Sazan in the Vlorë Bay and Sverneci in the bay of Nartës, although records from these islands have as yet remained unconfirmed. Following HAXHIU (1995b), the largest populations exist in the Shëngjini Mountains at Lezhë, in the Div-

Fig. 42: Distribution range of *Testudo boettgeri*

Fig. 43: *Testudo boettgeri* is still relatively widely distributed in Bulgaria (shown here is a habitat at Melnik). (A. NÖLLERT)

Fig. 44: Natural habitat of *Testudo beottgeri* in the vicinity of Lake

Fig. 45: In Greece (here a natural habitat on the Peloponnesus), *Testudo boettgeri* is by far the most common species of tortoise. (J. MARAN)

jaka Nature Reserve near the coast west of Lushnjë, in the hilly country of Taraboshi at Shkodër, and in the surroundings of Libohovë in the rocky hills on the southeastern side of the Dropulli Valley in the southwest of the country.

Bulgaria: The species can be found throughout the country.

Greece: Boettger's tortoise is the most wide-ranging species of tortoise in this country. It is present in most parts of the mainland including the Peloponnesus Peninsula, and on several smaller and larger islands, including Corfu, Lefkas, Cephallenia, Provati, Zakynthos and Euboea. The species is only rare or even wanting in the extremely arid parts of the Peloponnesus in the provinces of Argolís and Lakonia, on the Maina Peninsula, and in the surroundings of Corinth. Population densities generally decrease with the farther one travels to the east from Thessaloníki. It

is also absent from all Aegean islands except Euboea. Although BADER & RIEGLER (2004) observed a Boettger's tortoise in an off-limits military installation near Pefka on Rhodos Island, their find was most certainly based on a released "pet" specimen. This island actually lies far outside the natural distribution range of this species and is not home to free-ranging *Testudo boettgeri*.

Macedonia: *Testudo boettgeri* is widespread in this country.

Romania: Records of this species exist from about forty localities from the surroundings of the Iron Gate in the districts of Caras-Severin, Gorj and Mehedinti in the southwest. The individual populations are almost completely divided here by the spurs of the South Carpathian Mountains into a smaller western and a larger eastern range. Older reports about populations in the Dobrudja and in the delta of the Danube on the

Black Sea coast (districts of Constanta and Tulcea) were in general based on misidentified Eurasian tortoises (*Testudo ibera*) that live in this area, but are in part also founded on the fact that the border between Romania and neighboring Bulgaria used to be situated farther to the south during earlier times.

IFTIME (2002) happened, though, upon three free-ranging *Testudo boettgeri* in the Dobrudja between July 2001 and July 2002 – a fully grown female and an adult male at Bâneasa (15 km north of the Bulgarian border), and a juvenile female of maybe three or four years at Adamclisi. This author therefore presumed that at least this part of the Dobrudja was home to a small population of Boettger's tortoises that also reproduce successfully. These three finds should be viewed in relation to the about fifty *Testudo ibera* IFTIME found in total within the same region over a period of five years.

Serbia and Montenegro: From the south of the Serbian Republic, the valleys of the rivers Vardar, Juzna Morava and Timok provide the species with a northern dispersal route into the eastern parts of Serbia up to the Danube. It can also be encountered in the extreme south of Montenegro at Ulcinj.

Turkey: The species is limited to the European part of this country. Despite the statement by ATATÜR (1995), who refuted its occurrence in the eastern sectors of this region, it is in fact distributed east to the province of Istanbul.

Dalmatian tortoise

The distribution range of the Dalmatian tortoise extends along the eastern coast of the Adriatic Sea from (probably) Slovenia, Croatia, Bosnia and Herzegovina to Montenegro. The presence of this species in the Italian northeast and its origin are not compre-

Fig. 46: A Boettger's tortoise in Bulgaria (G. POPGEORGIEV)

Fig. 47: Distribution range of *Testudo hercegovinensis* (? = questionable natural populations)

hensively explained as yet (see below). EISELT (1961) reported about attempts to reintroduce *"Testudo hermanni"* to the surroundings of Vienna, and at Ferlach and Ponfeld near Klagenfurth in the Austrian state of Corinthia. It remains unclear from his paper which of the three possible species exactly was involved, but it may be supposed that climatic conditions had been taken into consideration and animals from the northernmost parts of the range of the species group were used. These would have been *Testudo hercegovinensis*. Nothing further was ever published about the "success" of this project, but it appears to be safe to suppose that there are no free-ranging tortoise populations in Austria today. The same applies to the reintroduction project of tortoises near Lohr am Main in Hessian, Germany, that dates back to 1911 (MERTENS 1947).

Bosnia and Herzegovina: *Testudo hercegovinensis* can be found in Bosnia and Herzegovina in the Eumediterranean climatic zone near the coast and in the valley of the river Neretva. It ranges in the hinterland to the surroundings of Mostar, Trebinje and Bileca.

Italy: It is still uncertain whether the tortoise populations limited to the Po Delta (Bosco della Mesola Nature Reserve and Santa Giustina) in the province of Ferrara (Emília-Romagna region) are of natural origins. Chelonians have been released into the about 1,000 ha-large nature reserve on various occasions, but BALLASINA (1995a) suggested that it was possible that natural populations may exist, or may have existed, in the dunes of the regions Venetia and Friuli-Julish-Venetia as well. Records from the surroundings of Trieste are commonly regarded as based on released "pet" specimens, but considering the proximity of this city to the populations in Croatia, it cannot be safely supposed that the coastal areas were not once home to natural populations that subsequently interbred with introduced conspecifics.

The populations in the northeast of Italy have traditionally been assigned to *Testudo boettgeri*, but zoogeographic aspects suggest

Fig. 48: A Dalmatian tortoise in Croatia (W. Wegehaupt)

Fig. 49: Most populations of *Testudo hercegovinensis* live in Croatia. (J. MARAN)

Fig. 50: A typical natural habitat of the Dalmatian tortoise in Croatia (W. WEGEHAUPT)

that they may in fact be referable to *Testudo hercegovinensis* (see below). This question requires further studies. If it turned out that the tortoises in the northeast are in fact *Testudo boettgeri*, it would provide another indication that the species owes its existence here to the activities of man.

Records of tortoises representing the eastern population group in various other parts of Italy have been quite rightly explained as "escaped pets" by BALLASINA (1995a).

Croatia: The species is limited here to a coastal strip of between 5 and 15 km in width along the Adriatic coast that offers a Mediterranean climate. Besides populations on the mainland, there also insular ones, at least on the islands of Hvar and Korcula off the Dalmatian coast. Although PERÄLÄ (2002b) presumed that the species was again replaced by *Testudo boettgeri* to the north of Zadar, this was actually disproved by more recent studies. For example, the specimens examined by SCHWEIGER (2005) from farther north, i.e., from the islands of Pag and Krk in the Kvarn Bay, had in no case inguinals, and these plastral scutes were also absent in 61 % of the tortoises from the northern Adriatic coast examined by WEGEHAUPT (2005). This would indicate that the populations living on the two mentioned islands, those on the neighboring islands of Cres, Plavnik and Rab, and on the mainland north of Zadar (in Istria north to at least Rovinj) must be assigned to *Testudo hercegovinensis*.

Serbia and Montenegro: The species is present in this state union only along the coast of the Republic of Montenegro, ranging south to about Budva.

Slovenia: The question of whether or not *Testudo hercegovinensis* occurs in this country is still not comprehensively answered. FREYER (1842) for one supposed that the species could be found in Crain, whereas SIEBENROCK (1916) stated tortoises had never existed in Slovenia. His opinion was followed by most subsequent authors so that the occurrence of free-ranging populations in this country has been negated in general. TOME (1996) presumed that finds of specimens of this species in the wild, in particular those near towns along the Istrian coast, were based on released "pet" tortoises, some of which were believed to successfully reproduce in the wild. Taking into consideration that *Testudo hercegovinensis* is found on the Istrian west coast of Croatia though, it does not appear beyond reason to suppose its natural occurrence on the nearby Slovenian coast as well. The records marked in the distribution map published by BRUNO (1986) for the vicinity of the capital Ljubljana are most likely in error for fossil records from the Pleistocene (see below).

Italian tortoise

The distribution range of this species is highly fragmented today, which applies in particular to Spain and the south of France where only isolated relict populations persist. Much larger and continuous areas are still occupied on Corsica, Sardinia, Sicily and the Italian mainland. Records from Malta are based on introduced specimens, and no natural populations of tortoises exist on this island today. These finds of *Testudo hermanni* furthermore date back to the 1910' and have not since been confirmed.

Various authors presumed that man also introduced *Testudo hermanni* to Sardinia and Corsica and support this notion with the absence of fossil finds. In the case of Corsica, *Testudo hermanni* has also not been mentioned before the 19th century. Although a lack of fossil evidence alone may be less than a convincing argument for concluding that the populations of tortoises there are entirely based on human activity, the results of the genetic studies by VAN DER KUYL et al. (2002)

Fig. 51: Distribution range of *Testudo hermanni* (? = questionable natural populations; * = recently [re-]populated areas)

also point into this direction. The populations on Sardinia and Corsica fit, on the other hand, well into the zoogeography of the western Mediterranean region. The Italian tortoise is furthermore not limited to small distribution patches on both these islands as could be expected for artificially established populations and as is indeed the case with the introduced *Testudo marginata* on Sardinia. Another argument for an indigenousness of the Sardinian and Corsican populations is the fact that individuals are well distinguishable externally from other populations native to the western Mediterranean region. As has been mentioned before, FRITZ et al. (2005) even found some genetic differences between Sardinian specimens and those from Tuscany. Fossil records from Corsica made in the last few years furthermore showed that the populations there have been in existence for at least 157,000 years.

France: *Testudo hermanni* used to be distributed along the entire Mediterranean coast of France in earlier times. In 300 through 500

A.D., populations of tortoises still existed near Montpellier, in the mountain chains of the Alpilles, at Arles, and in the area of today's Marseille, as became evident from excavations made in the old harbor. As recently as in the mid-19th century the species used to occur in the south of France in a continuous population from the Albères Mountains (Department Pyrénées-Orientales, region Languedoc-Roussillon) on the Spanish border, to the western reaches of the mountainous country of Corbières. The species was still common in the Albères Mountains even during the early 20th century, but had all but disappeared there in the 1960' and 70'. After a disastrous bush fire ravaged the area on either side of the border and devastated several thousands of hectares of natural habitat in 1986, it must unfortunately be supposed that *Testudo hermanni* has now entirely disappeared from the French portion of the Albères Mountains.

The population in the Maure and Estérel massifs in the department Var (re-

Fig. 52: A specimen of *Testudo hermanni* from Italy (A. PIEH)

gion Provence-Alpes-Côte d'Azur) has been known at least since the beginning of the 20th century. It ranges from about Hyères in the west to Agay in the east, which corresponds to an area of about 750 km². This territory is home to about ten populations that are more or less isolated from each other and inhabit an area of some 160 km². To the north, the species occurs to an approximate line Carces-Draguignan-Fayence (from west to east). Most populations are, however, concentrated in the region around Collobrières, La Garde Freinet, Gonfaron and Gogolin. Whether or not the population living to the northwest of Mt. Aurélien in the department of Var is of natural origin, cannot be said at present. It is, however, certain, that juveniles have been encountered there. A population that had been reported from the surroundings of the village of Lamanon (department Bouches-du-Rhône) during the early 1930' was not since confirmed.

The species became extinct on the Hyères Islands in the early 19th century, being the result of unsustainable collecting by the local human populace. An attempt to reestablish it in the national park on the island of Port-Cros in 1975 failed due to keeping the animals safe from animal collectors. Captive propagation projects in outdoor enclosures on Port-Cros and the neighboring island of Poquerolles were equally unsuccessful, as park rangers did not monitor the pens closely enough to keep poachers out. It was only more recently that the French chelonian conservation organization SOPTOM managed to establish a population on the neighboring island of Levant whose about

Fig. 53: *Testudo hermanni* has been reduced to a few small populations on the Spanish mainland that persist, for example, in the Albera Mountains of Catalonia. (J. MARAN)

Fig. 54: The distribution range of the Italian tortoise has also been shrunk to small patches in France; shown here is a habitat at Roquebrune sur Argens in the department of Var (B. DEVAUX)

1,000 hectares are for 95 % controlled by the defense force.

FRETEY (1975) and STREET (1979) reported about an artificially established population of *Testudo hermanni* in the department Calvados in Normandy. According to FRETEY (1975), the animals had been released there before 1939. Nothing is known about the status of these tortoises today.

On Corsica, the tortoises are today found along the south and east coasts, from about the Golo River in the northeast to the capital of the island, Ajaccio, in the west. A few isolated populations also exist in the north, for example at Cape Corse as well as at Calvi and L'Île-Rousse. The individual specimens that have occasionally been found in the interior of the island are, possibly with the exception of those from the surroundings of Corte and the Tavignano Valley, most certainly tortoises that managed to escape from private gardens or were released into the wild.

Italy: This is the country with the largest of the remaining populations of this species. All told, *Testudo hermanni* is known from 114 localities. It is found both on the mainland and the large islands of Sardinia and Sicily as well as on some smaller islets. The two most significant centers of distribution today lie in Tuscany and Latium on the one, and Apulia on the other hand. Extinct are the natural populations that once roamed the Liguria region, with the few individuals that were observed there until the early 1990' having been released "pets". Today, efforts are being made to reestablish specimens from southern France there (see below). While the populations in northern Tuscany have been all but disappeared (there is still a relict group in the regional park of San Rossore), important populations still thrive south of Livorno, in particular in the Maremma National Park and in the WWF Reserve around Lake Burano.

Largely uncertain is the situation in Umbria. RAGNI et al. (2004) were the only ones to mention populations of this species in that region, but failed to provide further details. In Latium, several, locally rather dense populations are found along the coast, for example in the mountains at Tolfa, in the Circeo Nature Park, on the property of the estate Castel Porziano, and in the WWF Reserve Palo e Macchiagrande. Populations also persist in the province of Rome, for example in the relatively undisturbed nature reserve Decima Malafede and in the more remote regional parks Canale Monterano and Monti Lipini. Tortoises have even been observed in protected areas situated within the city limits of Rome itself, i.e., in the nature reserves Tenuta dei Massimi (with its high percentage of agriculturally used areas and remains of oak forest), Monte Mario (a hilly area with forests), and Insugherato (a catchment area of the river Acqua Traversa with narrow valleys and forests). The animals living there are, however, scarce and must be considered endangered. This is in spite of evidence that at least those in the Insugherato Reserve are able to reproduce with success.

Testudo hermanni has all but disappeared from the region Campania. A relict population may possibly still hold out in the vicinity of Caserta north of Naples, but BALLASINA (1995a) actually doubted the natural origin of this population and presumed them to be hybrids between various representatives of the Testudo hermanni species group.

A few populations persist in the Calabria region on the Gulf of Táranto, but at the Tyrrhenian side of the region they have become almost extinct. The situation in the region Basilikata is hardly known, and it appears as though the species would be limited to coastal areas. Important colonies still exist in the region Apulia, but even these have dramatically decreased in size over the past years. Here, the strongest populations live in the Murge Mountains, in the Gargano Na-

tional Park, and again on the Gulf of Táranto. Uncertainty dominates the distribution of Testudo hermanni in the region Molise, but it appears as though there is a natural population in the valleys of Biferno and Cigno. Records from the Abruzzi region are sparse and very localized. Some older reports exist from regions near the coast in the southeast. It appears that the species has managed to survive only in a small oak forest on the coast at Torino di Sangro Marina and in the nature reserve surrounding Lake Serranella. The population at La Pineta di Santa Filomena between Montesilvano Marina and Pescara is now extinct.

Recent investigations from the Marches region are limited to those published by FI-ACCHINI (2004) and FIACCHINI et al. (2004). The former surveyed the herpetofauna of the province of Ancon and found populations of this species on about 35 % of the surface area of this province. Together with his colleagues he reported in the same publication on a population living in the nature park Gola della Rossa e di Frasassi. In the region Emília-Romagna, notes on populations exist from the coasts of the province of Ravenna, but these could not be confirmed after 1979. With the exception of southern Italy, the distribution range rarely extends farther inland than 50 km from the coast.

Testudo hermanni has by now possibly become extinct on the island of Elba, where it used to be a very common sight still during the 19th century. A single free-ranging individual was, however, spotted in 1999 and has since been kindling the hope that a small relict population might still be surviving. During a stay on Elba in the spring of 2003, PAWLOWSKI et al. (2004) failed to discover tracks of this tortoise, and staff of the Hydra Institute in Fetovaia, who had been conducting various surveys for several years, were unaware of tortoises on their island. Several authors reported on *Testudo hermanni* from the neighboring islands of Capráia, Monte Argentário and Pianosa, but the present status of these possible populations is unknown. The species was introduced to the small island of Montecristo around 1960, but this attempt at repopulation eventually failed.

On the island of Sicily, the largest populations are concentrated in the coastal areas in the north and southeast. Although BALLASINA (1995a) suggested that only a few relict populations were surviving mainly to the northeast in the Nébrodi Nature Park and around Mount Etna, as well as in the northwest in the provinces of Palermo and Trápani, there are actually also numerous records from the Sicilian southeast, i.e., from the provinces of Ragusa and Siracusa. BALLASINA (1995a) stated that the population on Mount Etna would now be extinct, and tortoises could only be found in private gardens.

Contradictory information exists about an occurrence of *Testudo hermanni* on the Liparian Islands (islands of Lípari and Salina), and their status there is unclear at present. Populations of this species have also been recorded for the islands of Lampedusa, Linosa and Pantelleria, but their status has remained poorly documented. With Lampedu-sa being situated on the African shelf and its never having had a land connection with the European mainland or Sicily for that matter, it may be quite safe to suppose that the animals found on these islands owe their existence to human introduction.

The distribution of this species on the island of Sardinia is altogether inadequately researched. Most records are centered in the northwestern parts of the island, and the populations living there appear to be rather substantial. This does, however, not necessarily mean that these animals are really more scarce or even absent in other parts. It could well be that this picture is skewed by a lack of records. BRUNO (1986), for example, stated with confidence that the Italian tortoise would be present virtually throughout the entire island. Its occurrence in the northeast of the island has been refuted by some authors, though, as this would be an area where man has introduced *Testudo marginata*. Still, there is a possibility that both species exclude each other only by territory, as is the case in large parts of Greece, but still occur in the same regions. Populations of *Testudo hermanni* have also been mentioned for some of the small islets off the Sardinian coast, including Asinara, Piana di Asinara, Molara,

Fig. 55: The densest French populations of *Testudo hermanni* in France are today found on Corsica; this female was observed near Ajaccio. (J. MARAN)

Fig. 56: *Testudo hermanni* has probably been introduced to Mallorca during the late Stone Age. (A. PIEH)

Tavolara, La Maddalena, Caprera, Santo Stefano and Santa Maria, with those for Asinara having been confirmed even more recently (BORRI et al. 1988, BASSU et al. 2003). The record of *Testudo hermanni* from Mal di Ventre (MOCCI DEMARTIS 1987) is based on a misidentification as is obvious from the photograph in the respective article that clearly shows a tortoise that is assignable to the *Testudo graeca* complex. The island has furthermore been known to be home to tortoises of this species group that were released there by humans. It remains unclear, though, whether the populations existing on the small islands are of natural origin or have developed from specimens introduced by man.

Spain: Some 900,000 years ago, the distribution range of *Testudo hermanni* on the Iberian Peninsula used to be much more extensive than today and included the region around Coimbra on the Atlantic coast of Portugal, the Betica Mountains in the Spanish southeast and much of the northern parts of the peninsula. During the upper Stone Age (some 7,000 to 3,500 years ago), the spe-

cies still inhabited a continuous area along the Mediterranean coast from the Spanish region of Catalonia via southern France to Italy. It was only during subsequent times that connections were broken up and rendered today's populations isolated from each other. Natural populations are today limited to a small area on the northeastern Mediterranean coast of Spain. As recently as during the mid-1800', the species used to range over a large portion of the Catalonia coast, from about the Ebro River in the south to the French border in the north, covering a coastal strip of about 300 km in length. Although numerous records still exist from this region today, including some from the Galera Plains, the surroundings of Montsià, and other parts of Catalonia, most of these no longer represent natural populations, but are rather based on reintroduced animals. The same applies to individual records of tortoises from the surroundings of València (region Comunidad Valènciana) and the occasional finds of individuals in other regions (e.g., in Galician). Whether the population in the Catalonian province of Tarragona at the lower course and estuary of the Ebro River as well as at Montsià is of natural origin, is controversially discussed because specimens of *Testudo hermanni* were released there (or rather on some islets in the nature park Delta de L'Ebre) over the past few years by nature conservationists. The same is true for the Garraf Mountains south of Barcelona (see chapter "Conservation"). The only evidently natural population today exists in the Catalonian province of Girona at Alt Empordà in the extreme east of the Pyrenean Mountains. It is spread over an area of some 350 km² and comprises two centers: the region surrounding the Balmeta Mountain Chain and the valley of San Quirze in the eastern portion of the Albera Mountains. Population densities here are very low, though, and the specimens found are usually very old. Juveniles are scarce, and all this indicates that reproduction rates are very low.

Populations on the Balearic Islands of Mallorca and Menorca have been known in the literature since the 19th and 18th centuries, respectively. The animals on Menorca appear to have first been discovered by the British governor of the island of the time, ARMSTRONG, in 1752. Since the oldest finds of *Testudo hermanni* on these islands are not older than about 3,000 years, it is commonly presumed that the species has been introduced there by humans during the course of the upper Stone Age. BALLASINA et al. (2002) also concluded from their finding of genetic parallels between Spanish and Italian tortoises that the populations on the Spanish mainland were not of natural origin either.

On Mallorca, *Testudo hermanni* is found living in two more substantial populations in the northeast in the area of the Artá Mountains between the Bay of Alcúdia and Puerto Colom (an area of about 250 km²) and in the south on either side of the Cape Blanc (about 180 km²). Besides these, a few isolated remnants of habitats in a natural state still exist in the east of the island on fincas (farms) that are used for agriculture in a way that leaves room for tortoises to coexist, and small numbers of animals have survived there. While the populations at Cape Blanc, which range from near the coast to about 15 km inland, are distributed relatively irregularly (tortoises are, for example, entirely absent from some sections of the hilly country, but may occur in fairly dense populations in other regions), this is not the case as far as the other, larger population in the northeast of Mallorca is concerned. ROGNER (2005) found the largest population southeast of Son Baulo, ranging from the dunes behind the hotel of the same name to the Punta de sa Barraca and in more open situations of the pine forest that lie adjacent to the dunes. He also discovered another substantial population between Son Serra de Marina and Manacor (Cifre Nou and in the surroundings of the Barranco de Son Cifre).

Low-density populations of *Testudo hermanni* exist on Menorca along the southern coast between Santa Galdana and Es Canutells, as well as on the north coast on some forested hills at Alayarens. ESTEBAN et al. (1994) found tortoises in 31 of the 48 grid quadrants (each measuring 5 km²), which they used to subdivide the island of Menorca.

Whether *Testudo hermanni* also occurred in larger numbers on the smaller Balearic Islands of Ibiza and Formentera at one stage, has not been demonstrated beyond doubt as yet. At least, MALUQUER (1918) reported that it was still present on Ibiza during the 19th century. The individuals that are occasionally encountered today are most certainly escaped or released "pet tortoises". These are also found every now and then on Mallorca and Menorca.

Fossil records

The oldest fossil finds that can be assigned to the *Testudo hermanni* species group originate from the transitory period between Pliocene and Pleistocene (some 1.8 million years ago) of Poland, southern France, central Italy, and northeast and southeast Spain, possibly also of northern central Spain. AUFFENBERG (1974) grouped *Testudo canstadiensis* PLIENINGER, 1847, from the Pleistocene travertine of Baden-Württemberg with the *Testudo hermanni* species group. *Testudo szalai* MLYNARSKI, 1955, was described from the upper Pliocene of Poland, and *Testudo globosa* PORTIS, 1890, from the upper Pliocene and lower Pleistocene of Valdarno (Tuscany, Italy). *Testudo lunellensis* ALMERA & BOFILL, 1903, was defined from the lower Pleistocene of the small town Lunel-Viel in southern France and the cave Gracia in the nature park Guell near the Spanish city of Barcelona. Also dating back to the lower Pleistocene are remains of tortoises that were discovered in France in the grotto of Sartanette at Boucoiran in the department of Gard; these were preliminarily assigned to *Testudo hermanni* by CHEYLAN (1973b). Like *Testudo lunellensis*, these finds hardly differ from specimens of extant *Testudo hermanni*, other than maybe in that the shell bones are slightly thicker. This is, however, of little taxonomic value.

Numerous remains of members of the *Testudo hermanni* species group have become known from the mid and upper Pleistocene (some 900,000 to 25,000 years ago) from prehistoric human settlements who used these tortoises as a food resource. Mid-Pleistocene finds exist from southern France (including Corsica [grotto of Castiglione in Oletta]), Croatia, Slovenia, Italy (including Sicily), Portugal and Spain (in Catalonia for example from Barcelona, Llers, Crespià and Montjuic, Cau del Duc at Torroella de Montgrí as well as from the Garraf Mountains). From France, fossils from these times were recorded from the Rhône Valley upstream to Aven d'Orgnac on the Ardèche, but also from areas west of the central massif, including the grotto of Fontéchevade on the Charente, and from Abîmes de la Fage in Corrèze. In Montenegro, Italy (including the islands of Elba and Lípari), France (at least ten localities from the Wurm ice age near the Mediterranean coast and in the Rhône Valley from Abri Moula on

Figs. 57&58: Fossil shell remains of *Testudo antiqua* BRONN, 1831, from the Miocene of Germany. This extinct form was probably closely related to the the *Tetsudo hermanni* species group. (H.-H. SCHLEICH)

the Ardèche), and Portugal (Figueira-Brava grotto south of the capital Lisbon and the Columbeira cave in the Estremadura, both some 30,000 and 29,000–26,000 years ago) localities for remains of tortoises exist from the upper Pleistocene. It is likely that the western European finds of fossil tortoise remains and those from the Devil's Tower in Gibraltar and the Horá Cave in Granada (Spain) are ascribable to the *Testudo hermanni* of today's time, whereas the eastern European ones refer to *Testudo boettgeri* and *Testudo hercegovinensis*, respectively.

A gap in the records exists for the period between 25,000 and 10,000 before today. This may point to a decline in tortoise populations as a result of a final peak of cold conditions during the last ice age. Tortoises then became more common once more in deposits of the upper Stone Age. Subfossil records that are apparently referable to the *Testudo hermanni* species group also exist from Malta (including Gozo). The oldest records from the Bal-

earic Islands likewise date back to the upper Stone Age (Talayot culture) and are, as has been mentioned before, just some 3,000 years old.

Natural habitat

Vegetation

The species of the *Testudo hermanni* species complex inhabit a rather wide range of arid to submesic Mediterranean habitats. These include sandy heathlands, vegetated dunes, open wooded country, the margins of forests, rocky slopes, and scrublands such as maquis or garrigue. They also occasionally advance into the marginal areas of agriculturally used areas, and are found on garbage dumps and in fruit orchards. A distinct preference is notable for sun-exposed, dry habitats. It can be assumed that these species originally were inhabitants of the evergreen oak forests that once dominated the Mediterranean region, but were logged and cleared thousands of years ago and gave way to the replacement scrub vegetation that is typical for it today.

In the western Mediterranean region, *Testudo hermanni* is mainly found in rocky plains, heathlands, dune areas near the coasts, and in cultivated pastures and meadows. A preference exists for more or less forested regions in the coastal hinterland. Usually, these habitats are densely vegetated with trees and shrubs, with dominating tree species being, depending on soil compositions, holm (*Quercus ilex*) or cork oak (*Quercus suber*), but partly also chestnut (*Castanea sativa*). In some regions, such as the southern French Maure Mountains and the Italian Maremma National Park, open chestnut, fir and pine forests (*Pinus pinaster*, *Pinus pinea*) offer suitable habitats.

On the Balearic island of Menorca, the animals are mainly found in limestone ravines and hilly country. While the canyons are vegetated with partly rather tall trees, a discontinuous blanket of maquis that includes individual Aleppo pines (*Pinus halepensis*) dominates the hilly country, but is mainly vegetated with diss (*Ampelodesma mauritanica*), a sharply edged species of sweet grass with a high content of silica acid that is typical of the western Mediterranean region. Vegetation cover is comparatively dense in the habitats of these tortoises on Mallorca. Characteristic plants include Aleppo pines and high maquis that is composed mainly of olives (*Olea europaea*), kermes oaks (*Quercus coccifera*), mastic trees (*Pistacia* lentiscus) and linden trees of the genus Phillyrea, with a low undergrowth of shrubs and herbs that include rosemary (Rosmarinus officinalis), Montpellier and white-leaved rockroses (Cistus monspeliensis and Cistus albidus), daisies (genus Bellis), and diss. In the Albera Mountains, plants such as the rockroses already mentioned (plus the sage-leaved rockrose, Cistus salviifolius), heather (Erica spp.), aulaga (Ulex parviflora), Spanish broom (Spartium junceum), mastic tree and thorny broom (Calicotome spinosa) make up the characteristic plants of habitats for the Italian tortoise. The more shaded small forests of this region are frequented only at the peak of summer when the shrub vegetation has withered completely and the tortoises seek to escape the scorching heat. The islets in the Ebro Delta consist of sand dunes that are reinforced by sand-loving and salt-tolerant plants. In some parts, there are small forests of Aleppo pines present that likewise aid in the reinforcement of the loose soil and keep moisture.

On Corsica, the French mainland, and in the Pyrenean Mountains, Testudo hermanni prefers cork oak forests that are interspersed with clearings. HIGHFIELD (1987a) listed the following species of plants that he identified in the natural habits of these tortoises in southern France: prickly pear (Opuntia ficus-barbarica), Jenny's stonecrop (Sedum reflexum), white stonecrop (Sedum album), lavender (Lavandula stoechas), immortelle curry plant (Helichrysum stoechas), Mediterranean spurge (Euphorbia characias), scorpion gorse (Genista scorpius), Montpellier rockrose (Cistus monspeliensis), prickly juniper (Juniperus oxycedrus), willow trees (Salix spp.), and blackberry (genus Rubus). On Corsica, the animals are furthermore often encountered in traditionally cultivated areas that are marked by a side-by-side of many small fields (e.g., fallow land, olive groves, meadows), often with

separators in the form of hedges and small groups of trees. Hedges and shrubs offer the tortoises adequate shelters in these situations. This agriculturally used land is often intensely used for cattle and sheep farming. Testudo hermanni is absent in those parts of the island where the maquis (also often referred to as macchia although not on this island) and from vineyards and kiwi and lemon plantations, which do not offer enough shade and little food.

TREPTE (1993) observed these animals in Tuscany in a dry vegetation of maquis that consisted of common gorse (Ulex europaeus), rosemary (Rosmarinus officinalis), tree heath (Erica arborea), myrtle (Myrtus communis), and brean down (Helianthemum apenninum). In the Sardinian northwest, Testudo hermanni shows a preference for open garrigue country, which denominates a society of dwarf shrubs that includes aromatic herbs such as thyme and prickly ball shrubs. It is often possible to infer the presence of tortoises from the "tortoise trails" that have been "trampled" into the garrigue through continuous use. On this island, tortoises are equally present in the sandy dunes at the coast, in plains near the sea and adjacent chains of hills, in the valleys of rivers, on used cultivated lands, and in ravines and plateaus stretching into the inland.

Shrub-covered lands in the vicinity of watercourses and dunes near the beaches with a cover of salt-tolerant plants form preferred habitats of tortoises on Sicily. On this island, Testudo hermanni even advances onto the bare, rocky, elevated areas of the Nébrodi Mountains where only insular patches of ferns exist.

The natural habitats of the eastern forms are more diverse than those occupied by their western cousins. In contrast to the western Mediterranean regions you will have a hard time finding stands of cork oak here. The tortoises living on the east coast of the Adriatic Sea show themselves as particularly flexible. Here, they inhabit scrub lands (garrigue or phyrgana) interspersed with holm oaks, as well as hilly country with solitary cocklebur (*Agrimonia eupatoria*), fig trees (*Ficus carica*), olive trees (*Olea europaea*), Jerusalem thorn (*Paliurus spina-christi*), ivy (*Hedera helix*), and downy oaks (*Quercus pubescens*), or occur in areas densely overgrown with Italian cypress (*Cupressus sempervirens*), and in cultivated areas such as olive groves. In the surroundings of Lake Scutari, they even persist in a semidesert-like landscape that offers only a sparse vegetation of trees (fig trees [*Ficus carica*], mulberry [*Morus* spp.], locusts [genus *Robinia*], pear trees [genus *Pyrus*] and Mediterranean hackberry [*Celtis australis*]) and thorn bush (blackberries of the genus *Rubus* and greenbrier of the genus *Smilax*).

WERNER (1899) found *Testudo hercegovinensis* living in Bosnia and Herzegovina in the oak forests surrounding Trebinje and in the bushlands at the base of the mountain Golo-Brdo. In Albania, *Testudo boettgeri* can be encountered in pine forests (*Pinus halepensis*, *Pinus maritima*, *Pinus pinea*), near the coast, in rocky, hilly country with scrub vegetation (pomegranate [*Punica granatum*] and Mediterranean blackberry [*Rubus ulmifolius*]), but also at lower elevations in the mountains where Oriental hornbeam (*Carpinus orientalis*), Cornelian cherry dogwood (*Cornus mas*), Jerusalem thorn (*Paliurus spina-christi*), downy oak (*Quercus pubescens*) and Spanish broom (*Spartium junceum*) grow.

In Greece, the range of suitable habitats extends from sparsely vegetated riverbeds and sandy stretches, dunes, fields and their margins, via olive groves and mountain slopes, to partly very open holm oak forests, deciduous oak forests, pine forests with little, no, or plentiful undergrowth, and even the forests of water meadows that are in part marked by very dense vegetation. As has been mentioned before, oak forests were likely to have been the original natural habitat of *Testudo boettgeri* and *Testudo hercegovinensis*. After these had been cleared with great care, the animals were forced to adapt to new habitats if they were to survive. In central Greece, this led to their inhabiting fallow vineyards, meadows bordered with hedges and oak forests with little to rather dense underbrush today. In contrast, the animals largely avoid areas used for agriculture in the northeast of the country and prefer instead dry heathlands near the coast in hilly country, meadows surrounding lagoons, heavily grazed scrub heaths, pine woods, dense maquis with thornbrush, and olive groves. In the surroundings of the city of Thessaloníki, *Testudo boettgeri* is rather common in areas with sandy soils and near the coast where the salt-tolerant vegetation includes purslane (*Halimione* spp.) and glasswort (*Salicornia* spp.). Besides these, the species occurs in meadows with rush (*Juncus* spp.), in dry heathlands interspersed with plants of the lily family, silver king (genus *Artemisia*), butcher's broom (*Ruscus aculeatus*), thorn apple (genus *Crataegus*), sticky willy (genus *Galium*) and species of blackberry (genus *Rubus*), as well as in dunes overgrown with European beachgrass (*Ammophila arenaria*), sea holly (*Eryngium maritimum*), cottonweed (*Otanthus maritimus*), fourwing saltbush (*Atriplex* spp.), and tamarisks (*Tamarix* spp.). Other suitable habitats for this species in this region include bowl-shaped ravines that are nearly inaccessible to man due to their impenetrable maquis vegetation that consists predominantly of oak trees. In central and western Makedonia the animals live mainly at lower altitudes in landscapes dominated by oak trees. At higher elevations they are limited to south-facing situations.

On the Peloponnesus, the tortoises are commonly found on the coast where the vegetation consists of a patchwork of garrigue, meadows, fallow lemon plantations, terraced olive orchards, and garden-like landscapes of olives, natural hedges, cypress and small pine forests, but also in the immediate vicinity of human activity in pastures for sheep and around ruins. Grecian fir woods (*Abies cephalonica*) and mountain meadows are the dominant forms of vegetation upwards of altitudes of about 1,000 m, and although this may be an extreme habitat for *Testudo boettgeri*, the species has managed to persist also here. Near the border with Macedonia, the animals have been recorded from altitudes of about 1,000 m from juicy meadows with insular patches of beech (*Fagus sylvatica*) and oak trees (genus *Quercus*).

In Bulgaria, *Testudo boettgeri* often occurs in clearings, aisles, and meadows in rocky mixed oak forests (e.g., at Sveti Vlas, Slantshev Brjag, Kamtshija, Arkutino) and in partly rather dense black locust forests (*Robinia pseudo-acacia*) without any scrub or herbaceous undergrowth. Elm, ash, and hornbeam also form part of the habitats used by this species. Boettger's tortoise is also found in Bulgaria in larger public gardens (e.g., in the gardens of Evksinograd Castle), but more rarely on open, dry slopes with a loose cover of scrub, or on beaches (e.g., at Slantshev Brjag, Nesebâr, Burgas, Krajmorie, Sozopol and Kavarna). On the southern fringes of the Dobrudja, *Testudo boettgeri* occurs on coastal slopes that are free of scree, and on the margins of marshes (e.g., at Kavarna and Mihailbei).

Around the Iron Gate in Romania, the tortoises live in the open country around acacia and mulberry forests of the hilly country, but more rarely inside these forests. The transitory areas between grassland and forest are commonly used to retreat into

and escape the hottest time of the day. The animals prefer habitats that are not entirely plain, but rather sloped situations with a decline of at least 5E since these also offer suitable nesting sites.

Vertical distribution

The members of the *Testudo hermanni* species group are in general inhabitants of the coastal plains. However, on the French mainland most specimens live in relatively inaccessible situations in mountainous country at altitudes of 400–700 m. On Corsica, the majority of tortoises can be found between sea level and 200 m above, and it is only rarely that a specimen will be encountered at 600–900 m. On the Italian mainland, *Testudo hermanni* ascends to elevations of 400–500 m, in the south even up to 800 m. The animals are found in the center of Sardinia up to altitudes of 700–800 m, and in the Nébrodi Mountains of Sicily they are said to occur up to 1,550 m above sea level. In the Spanish region of Catalonia, *Testudo hermanni* is distributed at elevations of up to about 600 m.

In Albania, the distribution range of *Testudo boettgeri* extends from the coast of the Mediterranean Sea to about 1,200 m above sea level (surroundings of Kisait in the Drin-i-Bardië Valley between Kukës and the mountain Pastrik). In Bosnia and Herzegovina, populations of tortoises are limited to altitudes not exceeding 500 m, which results in a complete separation of populations living in valley basins. In Bulgaria, the highest altitude record is from about 1,400 m on the northern face of the Belasica Mountains, but most populations live below 1,300 m. The tortoises are found up to about 1,300 m elevation on the southwest-facing mountain slopes near the village of Vlahi in the Sofia region, but range only up to about 1,050 m on the northwest-facing side of the

Slavyanka Mountains. In the Greek region of western Makedonia, Boettger's tortoise can still be found at 1,400 m altitude at Néa Kotili, whereas it does not appear to ascend above 700 m at maximum in the region around the Iron Gate in Romania. According to information published by BARAN & ATATÜR (1998), Testudo boettgeri has a vertical distribution range of up to 1,500 m in Turkey, but this simply cannot be true for the highest point there only reaches 1,030 m (Yildiz Mountains). Testudo hercegovinensis is found in Bosnia and Herzegovina at altitudes below 500 m.

Climate

With the exception of certain parts of Bulgaria, Greece, Macedonia, Serbia, Montenegro and Romania, the members of the Testudo hermanni species group are almost exclusive to areas offering a typically Mediterranean climate. It is marked by mild winters, hot and dry summers, and a low amount of precipitation. An exception is found, for example, in the Bosco della Mesola Reserve in the Italian northeast where hot, rainy summers, and dry, cold winters prevail. In the west of the distribution range and on the eastern coast of the Adriatic Sea, average tempera-

Fig. 59: Tortoises are often found in a patchwork landscape of garrigue, meadows and other plant societies that line the coast of the Peloponnesus (Greece). (J. MARAN)

tures do not decrease to below 5 °C in January, and range between 22.5 and 25 °C in July. In contrast, temperature lows of at least -2.5 °C are reached in January on the central Balkans, around the Iron Gate in Romania, in Macedonia, in the Bulgarian north and Serbia, while the thermometer climbs to 20–27.5 °C in July. This is also the month when less than 50 mm of precipitation is recorded throughout the distribution range of these species. The western parts of the Mediterranean region and Bulgaria, Macedonia and Romania receive less than 800 mm of rain per annum, while precipitation amounts to a maximum of 1,200–1,400 mm per annum on the Dalmatian coast. The annual number of hours of sunshine averages 2,000–2,500 in these regions.

Testudo boettgeri is notably less common than *Testudo marginata* in the warmer regions, while the situation is reversed in relatively cool areas. This is illustrated, for example, on Mt. Olympus at 600 m altitude where numerous Boettger's tortoises have to share their habitat with only relatively few marginated tortoises. In general it may be stated though, that where *Testudo boettgeri* occur in sympatry with *Testudo marginata*,

Fig. 60: In the Garraf Mountains (Spain), plants such as rockroses, heather, aulaga and Spanish broom are character species of the natural habitats of *Testudo hermanni* (REPTILIA EDICIONES ARCHIVES)

the former is mainly found at the bases of slopes in more mesic situations and the latter at higher elevations. In Bulgaria, Boettger's tortoise occurs in sympatry with *Testudo ibera* in places, and while the former dominates in oak forests, the latter is more common in beach biotopes. A similar situation can be observed in the northeast of Greece, where *Testudo boettgeri* obviously prefers wooded biotopes in the lowlands, and *Testudo ibera* is more common on steeper, more open ground. There are, however, also habitats on the Chalkidiki Peninsula, where it appears to be just the other way round: near the coast, *Testudo ibera* is more common than *Testudo boettgeri* in hotter, dryer biotopes, which results in the former having a distinctly raised body temperature. While the Eurasian tortoise resides in the heathlands near the coast all year round, *Testudo boettgeri* puts in an appearance there only in summer.

Population densities

Research results on the densities of free-ranging populations of the *Testudo hermanni* species group are available for various parts of the distribution range. Considerable densities are often noted in open forests. These habitats are usually far removed from human settlements and in some cases even enjoy some form of legal protection. One of the best-studied populations of *Testudo boettgeri* lives, or used to live, in an about 75 ha heathland near the coast at Alíki in the Greek region of central Makedonia. In the early 1980', an average of 13.7–47.0 specimens per hectare were counted here, reaching peaks of more than 150 in particularly suitable sections with sandy soil and an overgrowth of lichens and herbs. This represents an extremely high value rarely recorded for any species of tortoise. The average biomass of specimens older than ten years amounted

to 26.27 kg per hectare, reaching as much as 73 kg per hectare in the areas with the highest densities. For Epanomí and Lágos, situated likewise in the Greek northeast, HAILEY et al. (1988) worked out a population density of ten tortoises with carapace lengths of 10 cm or more per hectare. Over all, the population densities are unnaturally high in some places in Greece, which HAILEY & WILLEMSEN (2000) suggests to be a result of an absence of natural predators.

In the Bosco della Mesola Nature Reserve in the Po Delta, which is home to a total of about 1,000 tortoises, an average of twelve tortoises was found to share one hectare. Average values of 80.9, 39.2–44.8 and 44.5 tortoises per hectare were calculated for populations in Croatia, Montenegro and Romania, respectively. Following an estimate by CRUCE (1978), the biomass could be 58.29 kg per hectare in Romania, but his calculations took into consideration only specimens that weighed at least 1.31 kg. For Croatia and Montenegro, biomasses of 55.2 and 39.9 kg per hectare, respectively, were calculated.

Most of the populations of *Testudo hermanni* investigated to this effect come not even close to these figures, with the extremely high value of up to 80 tortoises per hectare on the property of the private nature reserve Son Cifre des Baix on Mallorca being an outstanding exception. An average of 0.2–6.11 *Testudo hermanni* per hectare was counted in the Maremma National Park in Tuscany. In the nature park around the Garraf Mountains where tortoises live in an area totaling 160.25 hectares, a population density of ten specimens per hectare was calculated for an area of 23.75 hectares, whereas there were just two animals per hectare in the remaining land. In the Balmeta Mountain chain in the Spanish northeast, population densities have been on a continual decrease ever since the devastating fire in 1986, reducing the figure of 10.95 to now 2.4 tortoises per hectare. FRANCH et al. (2002a) investigated the surroundings of the Catalonian town of Garriguella after another raging bush fire. Including the finds of dead specimens, they worked out an average population density of a measly 0.21 tortoises per hectare. The latter result is likely to have been influenced by the fact that this was a population living on the fringes of the species' distribution range in Spain. These results show, however, that forest and bush fires represent an enormous danger to the continued existence of *Testudo hermanni* in this region, particularly because it is a species with a long life cycle and slow generation succession.

In an area in the south of Menorca, a comparatively high value of 9.4 specimens per hectare was found. For Corsica, calculations are available for traditionally farmed fields situated in the eastern plains (on average 3.2–11.7 [range 2.1–13.8] tortoises per hectare), and for cork oak and olive forests in the south of the island (on average 4.0–13.5 specimens per hectare). In the Maure Mountains on the French mainland, average values of 0.19–23.2 tortoises per hectare were determined, with the highest value being 42.7 (on average two tortoises per hectare; biomass 0.04–14.8 kg per hectare), but these figures cannot be applied to the entire region. There, the populations are distributed in a spotty fashion within large areas that are too heavily forested to allow an exact gathering of data. It may be safe to assume that population densities in southern France are in fact less that one tortoise per hectare, as was also noted, for example, by CHEYLAN (1981b) in the aftermath of a widespread forest fire. Research in southern France demonstrated that larger areas were home to populations that were smaller in size than those in optimum habitats. This suggests that the

partly very high densities on the Balkans are either exceptional concentrations of individuals that are facilitated by particularly favorable environmental circumstances, or simply flawed estimates that did not properly take into consideration migrating specimens. On the other hand, the figures produced for the surroundings of Alíki are likely to be reliable because they have been determined from a closed area of large size. In spite of the mentioned uncertainties and possible sources of error the impression remains that population densities on the Balkans are indeed much higher than those in the western parts of the distribution range.

Age structure

The content of juveniles within a population is often underestimated. The reason for this being so is that the probability of finding a two year-old specimen is about one-sixth of that of finding an adult conspecific (0.13 as compared to 0.81), simply because the former has shorter diel and annual phases of activity. Populations may, however, indeed differ substantially regarding their content of juveniles. Their figures are particularly low in the declining populations of the southern French Maure Mountains (12–18 %) and the Italian Maremma National Park (13 %). Juveniles are believed to be more common in the Maure Plains, where 21 % of the animals have carapace lengths of less than 11.5 cm, i.e., are less than nine years old. Even higher is the number of juveniles in the Albera Mountains of Spain. According to a study conducted by FÉLIX et al. (1989), 30 % of specimens living here measured less than 10 cm in carapace length, before the population was exposed to a forest fire. Thereafter, the portion of juveniles was found to have risen to 66 %. Following another fire, FRANCH et al. (2002) determined an average juvenile (specimens of less than

10 cm in carapace length) content of only 12 % in the surroundings of Garriguella in Catalonia. On Corsica, the portion of sexually immature specimens in a population appears to be particularly high. A survey conducted in the south of the island revealed that 42.6 % of the tortoises living there were five years of age or less, and 21.6 % were between six and nine years of age (HENRY et al. 1998). More than half of the tortoises investigated by WALLACE (1995) on Menorca were juvenile as well.

Partly contradictory data come from the eastern parts of the distribution range, in particular from Greece. Only a few or even no juveniles at all were found in some populations, as was the case in an old oak forest at Deskáti where no tortoises of less than twenty years of age have been observed since the 1930'. HAILEY & WILLEMSEN (2000) determined for another Greek population a juvenile content of 1 %, and in Bulgaria there are only 0.19 juveniles per one adult female. On the Croatian island of Pag, SCHWEIGER (2005) found subadult and juvenile specimens only every now and then, and in the population in the Bosco della Mesola Nature Reserve in the Italian northeast that owes its existence for a large part to artificial reintroduction, most specimens are older than

Fig. 61: Open garrigue country is the preferred natural habitat of *Testudo hermanni* in the Sardinian (Italy) northwest. (J. MARAN)

twenty years, and the juvenile content only amounts to 7,84 %.

At other localities, however, juveniles are rather numerous, and in many cases even more common than adult specimens. Nine populations in areas that were more or less strongly affected by agricultural use, comprised a total of 7,261 tortoises of which about 20 % were juveniles. This contrasted with a survey in a relatively pristine, largely wooded area where 1,276 specimens were marked, and a mere 3 % of these belonged to the juvenile age group.

A survey of seventeen populations from nearly all parts of Greece clearly suggested a correlation between the content of juveniles and the average size of adult females. Populations with relatively small females contained large portions of juveniles with carapace lengths of 10 cm or less, whereas in populations with large females only a few or even no juveniles could be found. Why this may be so is entirely enigmatic at present. STUBBS et al. (1985) furthermore noted in the population at Alíki in Greece that there were distinct differences between individual parts of that population. In a landscape dominated by heath, for example, 20.4 % of the tortoises were five years of age or less, and another 39.6 % were aged six to ten years. In

Fig. 62: Natural habitat of the Italian tortoise at Stintino, Sardinia (Italy) (F. WÜTHRICH)

another, larger heath area, these age groups made up only 4 and 18.7 %, respectively, and following a widespread fire, the content of sexually immature specimens even climbed to 25.9 %. Juveniles were, on the other hand, numerous in a Romanian population. Here, 47 % of the tortoises examined were sexually immature, which means females of not more than nine years of age and males of less than eight years. 31 % of the specimens were even younger than five years.

The mentioned differences in the juvenile content of individual populations have so far evaded plausible interpretation. It can be said, though, that predatory pressures on clutches and juveniles definitely have an impact. This is, for example, also underlined by the fact that the portion of juveniles of less than 12 cm in carapace length is about the same in four sympatric populations of *Testudo boettgeri* and *Testudo ibera* in the northeast of Greece.

Sex ratios

With regard to sex ratios in the wild, distinct differences have been noted relative to season, natural habitat and age groups, but some of these may be results of different survey methods. In theory, the structure of a population could only be portrayed accurately if all specimens were caught and individually marked. A census of this type, or any survey meant to investigate population structures, is also influenced by seasonal differences in the activity levels of both sexes.

In southern France, most surveys arrived at the conclusion that sex ratios were balanced or, if anything, slightly in favor of females. Different results came only from isolated, heavily decimated populations where more female than male specimens were found (up to 1.7 females per male). In the Spanish Albera Mountains and on the Balearic Islands, however, females make up

a distinct majority (2.6 and 2.4 females per male on average). In Italy (Tuscany), sex ratios once more appear to be balanced, but the respective ratios are clearly in favor of male specimens in the nature reserve surrounding the Garraf Mountains near Barcelona, Spain, where the studied populations of the western population group showed there were 1.43 males per female. It is interesting in this conjunction that this is a population that has been reestablished by man.

In contrast to the conditions in the western parts of the distribution range described before, the eastern population group appears to be dominated by male specimens. For example, 1.33 males per female were found in Croatia, and in the southeastern parts of Greece, this figure even rose to 2.1–6.3 (3.1 on average) at four different localities. Similar results were obtained by HAILEY (1990) at Alíki in the Greek northeast where 3.45 males were faced with one female. CRUCE (1978) was one of the few researchers who encountered a nearly balanced sex ratio in a Romanian population where 0.91 males matched the find of one female, and WALLACE & WALLACE (1985a) also determined a sex ratio of nearly 1:1 in a population comprising sixty-five specimens. MEEK (1989) investigated another population in Montenegro and worked out a ratio of 1.05 males per female as well. A similar situation exists in the tortoises populating the Italian nature reserve of Bosco della Mesola (1.13 males per females).

Like the differences in age structures, the discrepancies in sex ratios between individual populations could as yet not be explained. An attempt to this effect was undertaken by WILLEMSEN & HAILEY (2001b) for the Greek population living in the surroundings of Alíki, but was later partially retracted by these authors (see chapter "Growth and Life expectancy"). Over the years the originally determined sex ratio changed slightly in favor of the females here. While 4.1 males matched one female in 1982, it was only 2.4 in 1988. It also showed at Alíki that the microhabitat had an influence on the sex ratio within a population. While the proportional distribution was about balanced in some areas, others were clearly dominated by male specimens (up to 8.5 males per female on several small, insular, sandy patches). Other factors influencing sex ratios include the development of a population before a survey, its age group structure, and differences in the survival ratios of male versus female tortoises. An increased probability of survival in adult males, for example, means that together with the earlier onset of sexual maturity in males, a larger portion of a population is likely to be of the male sex.

Home range

The members of the *Testudo hermanni* species group obviously have a high degree of home range fidelity. In Tuscany, for example, twenty-seven specimens of *Testudo hermanni* of both sexes were traced after a period of two years at distances averaging just 50 meters from where they had been observed before (males 59 m on average, females 40 m). Similar results were obtained in Greece, where a study of 246 *Testudo boettgeri* over two years identified only a very few specimens that had relocated for more than 300 m since they had been marked. Here, the diel traveling distance amounted to some 80 m on average in males, and 85 m in females. STUBBS et al. (1985) noted that those specimens of a marked population of *Testudo boettgeri* that had survived a devastating fire and were forced to temporarily evacuate their microhabitats, had returned to their original sites two years later.
A six-year study of 124 specimens on Corsica likewise revealed that most animals stayed in

one spot for several years. The usage of the various sectors of a tortoise's "territory" is irregular during the course of the seasons, though, with activity being concentrated around the best feeding sites. Four Corsican tortoises of just a few months of age were rediscovered at distances of 21, 30, 77 and 79 m, respectively, from their original spots of discovery. Older juveniles appear to roam a little wider, and two- and five-years studies on Corsica revealed for this age group relocating distances of 122–411 m (230 m on average), whereas these values were only 122–268 m (184 m on average) for adult conspecifics.

All these figures fall within the limits of the normal home range. There are, however, also observations that suggest individuals with a more strongly pronounced urge to relocate. An about twelve year-old female, for example, that had been marked in the French Maure Mountains in 1981, was rediscovered at a distance of more than 1.5 km six weeks later and had moved almost 3 km from the original spot by the subsequent spring. Although these "hikers" are certainly rare exceptions, they might play a critical role in maintaining a gene flow between neighboring, but geographically separated populations.

Home ranges vary with the exact area in which members of the *Testudo hermanni* species group live:

Hilly, wooded country in the southern French Maure Mountains: males 1.56 ± 0.70 hectares on average, females 2.41 ± 0.92 hectares;

Forested area in southern France: 0.3–2.2 hectares;

Maquis in coastal Tuscany: males 0.25–1.20 hectares (0.65 on average), females 0.7–2.4 hectares (1.49 on average);

Maremma National Park, Tuscany, Italy: males 1.7–3.3 hectares, females 0.9–4.2 hectares;

Maquis, forests and heathland on Corsica: males 0.14–1.85 hectares (0.84 on average), females 0.75–3.50 hectares (1.37 on average);

Delta of the Ebro in Spain: adult males 1.69 hectares on average (semiadults 0.47 hectares), adult females 0.74 hectares (semiadults 0.89 hectares);

Heathland near the coast and marshy areas at Alíki in the northeast of Greece: males 1.23 ± 0.39 hectares on average, females 2.41 ± 0.67 hectares.

Fig. 63: Italian tortoise from the surroundings of Gonfaron, southern France (B. Devaux)

LONGEPIERRE et al. (2001) noted that the home range of French tortoises during the peak of the reproductive season in June was considerably larger than that of their Greek cousins. This was, however, not based on the French specimens traveling larger distances, but rather on the fact that French specimens make use of a wider variety of habitat types than do those in Greece. For the conservation of this tortoise in France this means that it takes the legal protection of a variety of neighboring habitat types, which obviously renders its implementation more difficult.

In the Italian Bosco della Mesola Nature Reserve, male specimens have activity ranges of 4.4–8.0 hectares (4.6 on average), while females roam on 1.6–10.8 hectares (7.4 on average). These comparatively high values are probably a result of this being a dense oak forest with a reduced availability of food that is limited to insular clearings with herbaceous cover and a relatively low population density. With the exception of the data from Spain and the Bosco della Mesola (it is rather interesting to note that both involve possibly reintroduced populations), these study results suggest that the home ranges of males may on average be smaller than those of the females. This is even true in cases, like in Tuscany and at Alíki, when there is no need for the females to walk larger distances to find suitable oviposition sites. It is likely that the females mate with several males within their expanded territories, resulting in an increased gene exchange.

In Greece (Alíki), *Testudo boettgeri* has a daily traveling range of 1–450 m (males 80, females 85 m on average), which means that males travel a total of approximately 11.7 and females 12.1 km per annum. Male specimens are less inclined to walk about in May, June and October, whereas this is the case in September and October in females.

Fig. 64: This juvenile *Testudo hermanni* shows the defense behavior typical of most tortoises. (H.-U. SCHMIDT)

For specimens in Tuscany, an average daily relocation of 14.7 m (females) and 29.2 m (males) was determined, with a maximum of about 100 m per day. A radio telemetry study in Tuscany conducted by CALZOLAI & CHELAZZI (1991) produced slightly different results: females traveled 7.3 ± 2.1 m per day on average, and males 10.5 ± 1.5 m. Here, males were more mobile than females in spring and fall (a daily average of 8.2 m as opposed to 1.8 m), whereas in summer the situation was reversed (males 22 m, females 44.7 m). These figures appear rather low when compared with those from Greece, but this is in fact easily explained by the measuring methods used. The Italian study did not consider the actual distances traveled, but rather measured the distances between the previous and the actual position of the animal every 24 hours. Measuring actual traveling distances is fairly easily done by means of a so-called "Ariadne thread". This tread runs off a reel when the tortoise moves forward and leaves a trail that can then be measured. Using this thread method in Tuscany revealed average diel traveling distances of about 80 m per day for a male in April and May, and 15.2 and 18 m, respectively, for two females monitored from late July through August. The average daily traveling distances of French specimens amounted to 150 m, with a maximum value of 500 m.

In spite of the site fidelity of the members of the *Testudo hermanni* species group, there is no "genuine" territorial behavior, and aggressive behavior does not aim at chasing off other specimens for good. Following information published by CHEYLAN (1981b), for example, a male *Testudo hermanni* on Corsica shares his habitat with an average of 24 females and 18.5 other males.

Seasonally induced migrations are likewise of nearly no importance for representatives of the *Testudo hermanni* species group.

Females that happen to live in wooded habitats, however, sometimes have to travel larger distances in order to find suitable oviposition sites. This means journeys of usually 200 to 300 meters, but in some extreme cases it may take much more than that as well. In southern France, for example, females had to and did travel up to 3 km.

Tortoises were also observed to travel to certain sources of food that was available only at specific times of the year (fruit). In Romania, for example, most specimens are found in hilly country in spring which is where mating takes place and eggs are laid. From mid-June, adult specimens are then seen traveling along valleys for up to 1.5 km to reach agricultural areas, while the juveniles remain in the hills and walk not more than 250–300 m. Toward the end of July, the adult tortoises return to their homeland, just in time to feast on the mulberries that have meanwhile become ripe. Conspecifics living in the heathlands in the surroundings of Aliki in the Greek northeast, on the other hand, display little inclination to hike over large distances in order to access seasonal food sources. In Tuscany, the tortoises always maintain their core territories, but rather expand their radius of activity in summer. On Corsica, females use certain areas for oviposition, but like their male counterparts they show a preference for cool and moist situations during the summer months. Amounting only to 200–300 m, these relocations do, however, not exceed the normal extent of their home ranges. On the island of Mallorca, the tortoises spend the moist winter mostly in hilly country, simply because their summer habitats at lower elevations are often flooded. Once the weather becomes warmer and dryer, they return to the lower elevations to make use of the lush vegetation and larger food resources. Although natural catastrophic events, such as forest fires, may trigger the animals to travel large distances to reach less dangerous sites, they will soon return to their "homelands".

A threat to the success of many re-introduction programs has been that large numbers of the released animals initially traveled large distances. In the process they often left the protected areas within which they were supposed to make a new home, and if they happened to come close to human settlements they often fell victim to the traffic or were collected by people. This motivated LIVOREIL et al. (2002) to investigate the reasons for this "nomadic lifestyle" and possibly contribute to solving the problem. Using the premises of the French chelonian conservation organization SOPTOM at Gonfaron, they experimentally placed some of the specimens earmarked for release in larger pens (20 m²) with a near-natural setup and afforded them a prolonged time of acclimatization. When these were eventually "released" into even larger pens (47 m²), it was found that they traveled much shorter distances and also spent less time walking about than control specimens released in the unlimited expanse of the wild. Although not even the largest outdoor pen will of course be a perfect replication of the conditions in nature, the results of this research suggest it would be of advantage to permit the tortoises to first adjust to their new surroundings within a controlled and spatially limited environment.

The members of the *Testudo hermanni* species group possess an excellent homing sense in which the sense of smell appears to play a leading role. The animals keep on returning to their shelters with impressive single-mindedness. In Tuscany, for example, 30 % of the hiding places beneath brush and 55 % of those in rabbit dens were used more than once during the course of a year, and 10 % of these were used more than three times. It is not uncommon to find two or three tortoises occupying the same shelter. The high degree of fidelity of females to certain oviposition sites and the purposeful return to their home territories also indicates the presence of a well-developed sense of orientation. Experiments demonstrated that displaced specimens soon found back to their actual home turf. Of the twenty-eight specimens in Italy that were displaced at distances ranging from 135 to 418 m from the spot at which they were found, all managed to make it back within just a few days – most notably on the most direct route possible.

Defensive behavior

The species of the *Testudo hermanni* species group respond to movement within a radius of about 15–20 meters. If a specimen is startled, it will usually quickly retract its head and limbs while emitting a loud hissing sound. As a result the shell will hit the ground with an audible clatter. More rarely will a startled tortoise try to run away. If an animal is lifted from the ground, it will usually move about its head and front legs frantically and empty its bladder.

Diel and annual cycles

Diel cycle

The period of daily activity of the species dealt with here varies over the course of a year. The most important determining factor is the length of the photoperiod. One to two hours usually pass between sunrise and the onset of activity, and the same applies in reverse to the ceasing of activity at sunset. As soon as the first rays of the morning sun reach the ground the tortoises will leave their night quarters and choose a spot for basking. They actively optimize the acquisition of warmth by aligning their shells toward the southeast in order to present as large a body surface as possible to the sun. Once an adequate temperature has been reached, the animals will then move off to forage. In the evening, the tortoises usually retreat into a shelter when the rays of the descending sun do not provide light on the ground anymore, which is the case, as was said before, some one to two hours before the astronomical sunset. Very warm weather, mainly during the time from July through September, may cause them to continue to be active until actual nightfall, though.

Daily activity during the cooler months (for example, from March through mid-May and in October and November in southern France) is generally limited to the hours around noon. If it is very hot, though, which is mostly the case from July through September, the tortoises are active in the morning and afternoon hours (in particular in the morning) and spend noon resting in a shady spot. This clear partition of activity periods is often obscured in certain types of natural habitats, specifically within forests, since the canopy formed by the trees has a moderating effect on light intensities and temperatures and creates a basis for more continuous activity.

CHEYLAN (1981b) divided the annual activity of southern French *Testudo hermanni* into five phases: awaking from hibernation (March/April), springtime (May/June), summer (July/August), fall (September through November), and hibernation (December through February). He also distinguished between the hours of a day that potentially facilitated activity for the tortoises and their actual time spent active. The latter is independent of the period of daylight hours. It is distinctly longer during the mating and nesting season from April through June than during the summer months of July and August, and then slightly rises once more in October when the animals attempt to compensate for lower temperatures with more extensive basking. The annual cycle of *Testudo hermanni* portrayed by CHEYLAN for the south of France is recognizable in other parts of the distribution range as well, although certain seasonal deviations must be expected.

Awaking from hibernation: In March and April the weather in southern France is still rather changeable and does not permit regular activity. It is usually not before the latter half of March that some 60–75 % of the tortoises will appear outside more regularly. This is usually the case only during the warmer hours of the day, i.e., between about 07.00 and 15.00 h. About 70 % of this period outside their shelters is then spent basking. This is preferably done by standing up against rocks or shrubs with the head and limbs extended from the shell, which obviously increases the exposed body surface and thus optimizes the collection of solar radiation. April eventually sees the end of hibernation for all tortoises. They begin to mate, and at an ambient temperature of 18 °C, the animals are active between about 9 and 14.00 h. Periods of bad weather, including late snows, are still common at this point of time. The number of hours of daylight per day gradually increases from 11.15 to 13.0 hours, of which the tortoises use eleven for activity. However, actual activity is limited to only 1.8 ± 0.6 hours during this period, and some

47.6 % of the day passes without any activity. Ambient temperatures now average 11 ± 7.3 °C. It is not uncommon for some tortoises to ignore food for the first eight to ten days after hibernation. It is only thereafter, and when their metabolism has been accelerated by the warming sun, that they begin to become more active and start foraging for food.

Spring: Facilitated by a more stable climate and longer days, the tortoises are active on a regular basis. Springtime sees an abundance of food with a great variety of feeder plants to choose from. Accordingly, most specimens spent a major part of the day foraging. In May, rising temperatures cause a shift of the peak of activity to 08.00 or 09.00 h. The tortoises spend a lot of time searching for food, roaming and mating, but still need to invest nearly 70 % of the daylight hours into basking. May then is the month with longest

Fig. 65: *Testudo boettgeri* in Greece (H. BRINGSØE)

activity periods. With the number of daylight hours rising from 13.0 to 15.18, the animals make use of thirteen of these for activity; the average period of actual activity amounts to 4.8 ± 1.2 hours now. Only 5.3 % of the days pass by without any activity. Ambient temperatures average 20.1 ± 8.2 °C. Males are particularly active since they are now very aware of the females. From the last week of May, the females begin to look for suitable nesting spots although most of them will not lay their eggs before some time in June. In June, peak activity is observed around 09.00 h, decreasing at round about 12.00 h, and only a few specimens remain active until late afternoon. Basking is now largely limited to the first two hours of activity and notably less extensive or frequent than before. The last specimens retreat into their shelters around 17.00 h, right after the ground is no longer directly illuminated and warmed by the sun. In Montenegro, the tortoises spend the morning hours basking in an attempt to raise their body temperatures to about 34 °C, and the rest of the day is then used for foraging, mating and roaming.

Summer: Rising ambient temperatures and the end of the nesting season cause a distinct drop in activity. A day now contains 13.13 to 15.18 hours of light, thirteen of which are used by the animals for activity, but the time spent on actual activity has now dropped to a mere 2.4 ± 0.6 hours. At this stage, two peaks of daily activity can be identified, one from 07.00 – 10.00 h (beginning of the daily rise in temperatures, about 20–25 °C) and another between 15.00 and 17.00 h. Sofsky (1982) even observed tortoises in the north of Greece that remained active until as late as about 20.00 h. By the end of July, only 10–25 % of the specimens in southern France stay outside their shelters. The winter quarters are exchanged for more simple shelters in or beneath vegetation or sometimes even in a rock fissure. Basking is much reduced, and the tortoises spend a lot of time "dozing" in the shade of plants. Approximately 6.3 % of the days pass without any activity at all, but in contrast to earlier phases these are now the times of greatest heat. Ambient temperatures now average 26.4 ± 8.6 °C.

Fall: In September, the first autumnal rains cause temperatures to drop. The tortoises respond with a gradual reduction of their activity. At first they feed less, then they stop altogether. Although the number of specimens that are still active is about the same as in summer, the number of days with unfavorable weather that forces the animals into inactivity increases. About 20.6 % (November: 72.6 %) of the days pass without any activity. Ambient temperatures average 16.1 ± 6.7 (November: 9.1 ± 4.9) °C. A day now contains 13.13 to 10.18 hours of light (November: 10.18–9.12), of which eleven (September) to eight (October, November) are used for activity by the animals, with the average period of activity amounting to 2.5 ± 0.6 hours (November 0.4 ± 0.6). In early September, the tortoises may be found outside their shelters between 07.00 and 17.00 h, but they will usually be active only during the warm morning hours between 08.00 and 12.00 h. 50–100 % of the specimens spend the first 2–3 hours basking, then have a brief period of activity, and by 12.00 h, almost all of them will have retreated into their shelters. October sees the tortoises spending most of their time basking, and in spite of frequent warm interludes, their activity levels decrease drastically. Only 20–25 % of the specimens will still be active at the same time. Short cold spells may temporarily bring all activity to a stop. The nights are once more spent in subterranean winter quarters, which, in November, are only exited on warm days, almost exclusively for the purpose of basking. Most tortoises will be active around 11.00 h at temperatures of about 13 °C in November.

During the course of a day, juveniles are less active than adults. Like their shorter annual period of activity, this may presumably be explained by their smaller body mass being more affected by temperature extremes (cold as well as heat) than their adult counterparts.

The continued decline of vegetation in many parts of Greece results in shelters for the local tortoises becoming increasingly scarce. The animals thus find themselves forced to use what "caves" are still left. Larger, deep cavities therefore often contain not only several *Testudo boettgeri*, but occasionally house Boettger's side by side with marginated tortoises. This is no natural behavior, however, and does not indicate the existence of interspecific social behavior.

Annual cycle

In the south of France, *Testudo hermanni* usually leave their winter quarters in mid-March (earliest date recorded 21.01., latest 15.04.). These consist of shelters beneath bushes, heaps of leaf litter, under fallen logs, larger rocks, or caves in the ground that have often been excavated by the tortoises themselves. Toward the end of October or during the course of November (earliest date recorded 01.10., latest 01.12.), the tortoises return there, after having been active for an average of seven and a half months.

Specimens living on the Spanish mainland observe a wintry period of dormancy from November through February. On Menorca, an about five month-long period of hibernation begins in late October. In the Corsican south, the animals usually reappear between March 15 and 20, more rarely as early as in late January. Here, hibernation usually commences in the second half of December (earliest date recorded 25.11., latest 25.12.), with the average period of annual activity amounting to some nine months here. In Tuscany, hibernation usually ends in February or March,

but at the very latest in early April, after having started in mid-November, and the average period of annual activity is eight to nine months. Here, TREPTE (1993) found animals that had obviously hibernated in the mud on the banks of a tributary of the river Ombrone. On Sardinia, local residents stated that hibernation periods would be rather brief with interruptions being not uncommon.

In Albania, where hibernation lasts from about the end of November to the end of March, *Testudo boettgeri* is active for approximately eight to nine months every year. The same period of dormancy extends to March, sometimes even to late April, in Bulgaria. A decrease in activity levels is notable here from early September, and the last tortoises finally retreat into their winter shelters around the end of October or beginning of November when night temperatures may already be as low as 1–2 °C. An average of 210 days of activity per year was determined for the tortoises living in the surroundings of Alíki in northeastern Greece. Here, hibernation commences around the beginning of November and ends in late March. 95 % of the local population are active from April through June, but only 49 % still are between July and October. Romanian specimens are active from March through October, with peaks of activity from April through June and from September through October. Specimens from the region around Sisesti usually enter their winter quarters in early October (earliest date recorded 12.09., latest 05.11.), and leave them not before the end of March or early April (earliest date recorded 24.03., latest 10.04.); they are active for 6.0–6.5 months of the year. Their peak of activity is observed during the first two week of May.

These observations suggest, amongst others, that the very mild climate on the southern coast of Corsica provides the local tortoises with conditions that enable them to be active for a period that is about two months longer than that available to their cousins in Romania. Interestingly enough, this has hardly any influence on their nesting and hatching seasons (see chapter "Reproduction"), which may be a result of the more continental climate on the Balkans.

Following information provided by BLANCK & ESSER (2004), hibernation usually occurs from early November through mid-February in *Testudo hercegovinensis*.

Tortoises cannot be found active throughout the entire periods of activity mentioned above. For example, the specimens living in the surroundings of Alíki were estimated by HAILEY (1989) to be active only on 140 (about 67%) of the 210 days per annum that would actually permit activity. Similar results were obtained in southern France where specimens were active on 52.4% of the days during March and April, rising to 93.7–94.7% between May and August, and decreasing once more to 79.4% in September and October. In Spain, activity peaks in spring, i.e., during the month of April, decreases during summer, and picks up again in September. The specimens existing in the sandy, dry coastal strip of Sardinia are exposed to comparatively high temperatures, and may, according to WEGE-HAUPT (2004), respond to hot spells with periods of literal estivation. The population introduced to the Italian nature reserve Bosco della Mesola are, in contrast, active throughout the period between the end of February and the end of October, which accounts for the comparatively mild summer temperatures at the northernmost fringes of the distribution range of this species group.

There do not appear to be sex-dependent differences in the total duration of annual activity according to CHEYLAN (1989). He considered statements to the contrary to be based on incidental observations of no general value or doubtful for various other reasons.

Juveniles become active at a much later point of time in the year than adults (in Romania, for example, only at the end of April as compared to end of March), and retreat into their winter quarters earlier in fall. An exceptional situation may, however, exist in Romania where more juveniles were observed toward the end of the period of annual activity. The shorter period of activity can probably be explained by their smaller body mass being more affected by temperature extremes (cold as well as heat) than their adult counterparts.

STUBBS & SWINGLAND (1985) noted in hibernating French specimens that some animals lost up to 7% of their body mass during this period, but most actually gained a little weight. These authors interpreted this phenomenon as being a result of intermittent activity on sunny winter days in the same fashion as had been observed before in Mallorcan animals.

Fig. 66: Italian tortoise on the island of Sardinia (W. WEGEHAUPT)

Thermoregulation

Members of the *Testudo hermanni* species group begin to be active on reaching body temperatures of at least 12–14 °C, but more commonly only at 15–16 °C. On attaining an "operational temperature" of 29–30 °C they begin to move about and forage. VELENSKY (pers. comm.), however, recorded that tortoises were feeding at body temperatures ranging from 20.0 to 34.5 °C on Corfu. Oviposition usually takes place at a minimum body temperature of 32 °C, although individual cases have been observed where this value was only 26 °C. The preferred body temperature is 25–30 °C, and tolerated maximum values in nature are 34–36 °C, with individual extremes being as high as 39.9 °C. On reaching the upper limits of their preferred body temperature, the animals retreat into shelters in order to avoid potentially lethal overheating. Temperature extremes they can just withstand, at least for brief periods of time, are −2 at the bottom and +44 °C at the top ends of the scale. The heartbeat of specimens hibernating at body temperatures of about 5 °C is reduced to a mere four beats per minute.

As far as body temperatures are concerned, MEEK (1984b) determined for Montenegro specimens values ranging from 20.0 to 34.2 °C (29.3 °C on average), whereas VELENSKY (pers. comm.) measured 17.9–37.2 °C in specimens on Corfu in May, and PULFORD et al. (1984) worked out a mean value of 28.5 °C for the French Maure Mountains. Juveniles show distinctly lower average values than adults. Body temperatures during courtship and mating are obviously variable

Fig. 67: Boettger's tortoises basking (B. SEEGER)

and extend throughout the entire range of preferred body temperatures. It should be noted, though, that the instances of mating at the lower limits of preferred body temperatures were observed in captive situations. The lowest body temperatures measured inside the cloaca were −0.4 and +1.6 °C, the latter of which was taken at an ambient temperature of −9 °C. In places where *Testudo boettgeri* occurs next to *Testudo ibera*, the former usually becomes active earlier than the latter species, with the difference amounting to 1.2 °C in July and August. Contradictory information exists for comparisons of this type with *Testudo marginata*, where WILLEMSEN (1991) determined for *Testudo boettgeri* on the Peloponnesus distinctly lower body temperatures than for the marginated tortoise (e.g., in May, a maximum of 34–35 versus 36–37 °C), whereas PANAGIOTA & VALAKOS (1992) noted slightly higher values in *Testudo boettgeri* in an outdoor enclosure situated in the Greek region of Attica. There are some indications that adult males may in nature operate at a body temperature that is about 2 °C above that of their female counterparts. This difference appears to be more pronounced in late summer and fall, which may have to do with their being more sexually motivated at this time of the year.

The individual representatives of the *Testudo hermanni* species group spend up to 60 % of their annual period of activity thermoregulating. This figure may even rise to 80 % during the cooler seasons. Morning basking sees the body temperature to rise faster than the ambient temperature. This is mostly a result of the animals thermoregulating actively in an attempt to heat up with as much efficiency as possible. Further factors include physiological processes involving glands with internal secretion, and the pineal organ that contributes the messenger substances melatonin and serotonin.

Like with other reptiles, the body temperatures of tortoises are closely linked to ambient temperatures, but the former generally range above the latter throughout the year. This suggests the animals to be able to regulate their body temperatures through physiological processes at least to a certain extent. Compared with air temperatures, the difference may be about 5 °C, but less when compared with ground temperatures. Body temperatures remain almost stable during hibernation and are maintained above freezing even at times of frost, further hinting at internal regulation mechanisms. This enabled, for example, specimens in the French Provence that had buried themselves at least 10 cm deep for hibernation, to survive a particularly cold spell with temperatures dropping to −18 °C in January of 1985. Similarly, a few specimens withstood the winter of 1956 hibernating in an outdoor enclosure in Munich, Germany, despite the fact that temperatures of −23 °C caused the ground to freeze rather deeply. Active specimens not only manage to raise their body temperatures to 4–8 °C above the maximum ambient values, but also to keep them at these levels. This is obviously of great advantage during the cooler times of the year (April-June and September-October) in particular. The difference is smaller (−4.6 to +2.6 °C) in summer, or even nonexistent, but again becomes more pronounced in fall (+2 to +3.6 °C). With this phenomenon being most apparent in spring, there is likely to be a connection with seasonal mitochondrial activity, which reaches its peak in May and June and thus coincides with the peak of metabolic production of heat. In contrast, mitochondrial activity is distinctly reduced when the tortoises hibernate.

Usually, body temperatures are also above ambient temperatures during the course of the day. A pattern of four distinct phases has been identified in southern

French specimens, during their main period of activity from May through mid-September. It comprises a nightly phase with minor fluctuations (body temperature 7.8–31.3 °C, on average 20.8–21.5 °C, between 01.00 and 07.00 h), morning where temperatures rise rapidly by 1.4 °C per hour between 07.00 and 10.00 h, a noon phase that varies in length according to month and weather (body temperature around 30 °C on average, but usually below the ambient temperature), and finally evening from 17.00 to 01.00 h, during which body temperatures decrease by 0.7 °C/hour to the nightly values. A much more complex situation is found in the month of November. The morning phase of warming up is much extended, the steady noon phase is reached later and very short, and the subsequent cooling-down sets in suddenly. While hibernating, body temperatures usually remain constant throughout the day for the animals remain motionless and make no attempts at active thermoregulation through selecting certain locations or body postures. Immediately on exiting their winter quarters, CHEYLAN (1989) noted that body temperatures followed an about bell-shaped graph during the course of a day. The morning phase of warming up was marked by rapidly rising body temperatures (4.5 °C/hour), noon lasted only for four to five hours, and the subsequent decrease in temperature was distinct and continuous until about 23.00 h. Body temperatures exceeded the ambient values mainly during the noon phase, but came near the air temperatures during the heating-up and cooling-down phases. Studies conducted in Tuscany (CHELAZZI & CALZOLAI 1986) furthermore revealed that a detailed knowledge of the environment had a major impact on how efficiently body temperatures could be regulated. Tortoises that had been placed in an unfamiliar environment needed up to three hours (two on average) more to reach their preferred body temperatures than conspecifics that called the same area their home. This fact could be of importance for reintroduction projects. It would be of particular interest to learn how long it effectively takes introduced animals to adjust to their new surroundings.

VELENSKY (pers. comm.) recorded nightly air temperatures of 13–20 °C on Corfu. The body temperatures of tortoises emerging from their night shelters ranged from 18.0–21.1 °C, and were 24.3–34.3 °C when they returned there. The highest body temperature noted was 37.2 °C; it was recorded while the air temperature was only 24 °C. This would indicate that substrate temperatures were well above that of the air, and the highest substrate temperature recorded from under an active tortoise was 43.5 °C. VELENSKY (pers. comm.) noted that juveniles made up the majority of active tortoises when substrate temperatures were very high, whereas older specimens preferred to retreat into their shelters then. The Czech zoologist concluded that substrate and body temperatures influenced the behavior of Testudo boettgeri more than ambient air temperatures.

MAYER (1996b) described another form of thermoregulatory behavior from a captive setting. He observed that if a specimen would happen to fall on its back while exposed to the sun, it would wet its head, neck and front legs with saliva and the hind parts of the body with a fluid from the cloaca. The resultant thin layer of fluid had a cooling effect through evaporation and prevented the tortoise from overheating. The same behavior has also become known from other tortoises that live in arid areas and are exposed to life-threatening heat.

When active, that is outside their period of hibernation, the members of the Testudo hermanni species group take four to six breaths per minute.

Diet and feeding

The digestive tract of the species dealt with here is both by its anatomy and its functionality adapted to the processing of relatively low-protein food that is rich in raw fibers. Digestion is facilitated mainly through fermenting processes initiated and regulated by the intestinal flora in the appendix and large intestine. To do so the microorganisms living there require raw fibers that are abundantly present in nature in the form of plant fibers. The tortoises are therefore for the largest part vegetarians that feed mainly on wild herbs, but occasionally also consume the green parts of woody plants growing in their natural habitats. The "quality" of their feeder plants varies with the seasons. While the tortoises are faced with a wealth of juicy plants in spring, the lack of rain and high temperatures in summer cause the diverse ground vegetation to wither and leave the animals with no choice but to feed on rather dry plant matter. This causes their food not only to contain less moisture and less protein, but also renders it increasingly difficult to digest. At this stage, it resembles hay in both composi-

tion and nutritional value, and its lingering time in the digestive tract often exceeds two weeks substantially. It is not before the rains in fall that the tortoises will once more have green feeder plants available.

So far, at least 132 species of vascular plants representing 46 families have been identified as food sources (CHEYLAN 2001). A clear preference exists, however, for species of the daisy family (Asteraceae), bean and acacia family (Fabaceae), and plantain family (Plantaginaceae), but comprises to a smaller extent also sweet grasses (Poaceae), the crowfoot and buttercup family (Ranunculaceae), and grasses (Graminaceae). Most of these plants are native to open country including steppes, meadows and pastures. Climbing plants and species with hard or thorny leaves are consumed only to a lesser extent and usually only at certain times of the year. These include wood asparagus (*Asparagus acutifolius*), wild madder (*Rubia peregrina*), butcher's broom (*Ruscus aculeatus*), Eurasian greenbrier or prickly ivy (*Smilax aspera*), and ivy (*Hedera helix*) and European blackberry (*Rubus fruticosus*). Leaves of trees and shrubs that contain large amounts of resin, or are notable for their intense resinous scent, such as prickly juniper (*Juniperus oxycedrus*), Phoenician juniper (*Juniperus phoenicea*), Aleppo pine (*Pinus halepensis*), and mastic tree are hardly consumed, and the same is true for some intensely aromatic shrubs like myrtle (*Myrtus communis*). The leaves of hard-leafed plants, e.g., olive (*Olea europaea*), narrow-leaved mock privet (*Phillyrea angustifolia*), large-leaved mock privet (*Phillyrea media*), holm oak (*Quercus ilex*), cork oak (*Quercus suber*) and Mediterranean buckthorn (*Rhamnus alaternus*), are eaten only if an acute shortage of better foods dictates. Like almost all other herbivores, the tortoises stay clear of probably all species of the family Euphorbiaceae (spurge; these plants produce a toxic, milk-like juice), rockroses (genus *Cistus*), heather (genera *Calluna* and *Erica*), aromatic and/or scenting, often very hairy and waxy species of the mint family (Lamiaceae; e.g., lavender of the genus *Lavandula*, rosemary [*Rosmarinus officinalis*], winter savory [*Satureja montana*] and thyme [*Thymus vulgaris*]), as well as some plants of the daisy family (Asteraceae; e.g., curry plants of the genus *Helichrysum* and false yellowhead [*Inula viscosa*]). On the other hand, the tortoises consume some rather dangerously poisonous plants without suffering negative effects. These include, for example, black bryony (*Tamus communis*) and most species of arum lily (genus *Arum*). It has been suggested that the tortoises would seek out and eat some of them as a remedy against intestinal parasites, such as threadworm. In certain situations, cultivated plants also form part of the food spectrum of these animals. This applies to the eastern population group in particular whose members are commonly spotted in areas used for agriculture. The tortoises also feed on mushrooms, including even hot and inedible species, in fall, for which they seem to have a reputation in the Maure Mountains in southern France. Lichen and moss are occasionally consumed, too, but it is possible that these are taken in rather accidentally.

As far as which parts of plants are consumed, these include leaves and stalks as well as flowers and fruit. Respective studies on Corsica and in Tuscany revealed the following ratios: 70 % leaves, 18.6 % flowers, 8.2 % fruit, and 3 % stalks. This result does, however, not portray actual dietary preferences, because certain parts of the plants are clearly more easily accessible than others. If only the most commonly ingested plant species are taken into consideration, the flower content rises to 34.4 %, which is a figure about twice as high as the one given before and an indicator of just how popular they are. The low fruit content is probably due to the fact that fruits are difficult to access for the tortoises. On Corsica, for example, the only fruits within reach are those of the Tyrrhenian arum lily (*Arum pictum*) and some species of vetch (genus *Vicia*). Most others become available to them only once they have dropped to the ground, as is the case with juniper (genus *Juniperus*), pear and blackberry, for example.

VINKE & VINKE (2004c) suggested that unsaturated fatty acids in seeds and young sprouts of plants might play a particular role in the diet of tortoises. To this effect, WILLIG (2005) also noted that her Boettger's tortoises would go to great lengths to obtain the seeds of grasses, field pennycress, shepherd's purse, vetch and even thistle. This subject would therefore be deserving of more detailed studies.

Some regional differences exist in the choice of feeder plants. On Corsica, about half of the plants growing in an area of 17 ha (open forest with cork oak and olive trees as well as dry grassland with rockroses) are eaten by the tortoises living there, totaling 61 species in all. With the exception of very aromatic and hard-leafed species, these comprise almost all plants within the reach of the tortoises. Preferred species are those of the families of the daisies (Asteraceae), beans and acacias (Fabaceae), buttercups (Ranunculaceae), arum lilies (Araceae), bellflowers (Campanulaceae), morning glories (Convolvulaceae), and madders, goosegrasses and bedstraws (Rubiaceae), in this order. However, only nine plant species were involved in 62 % of the instances of feeding, which suggests them to be the major food source for *Testudo hermanni* at least in this part of the distribution range. These were tuberous hawkbit *(Leontodon tuberosum)* and Mediterranean daisy *(Urospermum dalechampii)* of the family Asteraceae, bird vetch *(Vicia cracca)* of the family Fabaceae, fragrant virgin's bower *(Clematis flammula)* of the family Ranunculaceae, Tyrrhenian arum lily and cuckoo-pintle *(Arum vulgare)* of the family Araceae, sheep's bit *(Jasione montana)* of the family Campanulaceae, pink convolvulus *(Convolvulus cantabrica)* of the family Convolvulaceae, and wild madder *(Rubia peregrina)* representing the family Rubiaceae. With regard to cultivated plants, figs and grapes are amongst those consumed on Corsica. Madders, goosegrasses and bedstraws (Rubiaceae) accounted for about 25, beans and acacias (Fabaceae) for 20, daisies (Asteraceae) for 10, and buttercups (Ranunculaceae) for 8 % of their diet in southern France.

As compared to Corsica, the diversity of feeder plant species available to tortoises is much reduced in a 60 ha sandy stretch of coast in Tuscany that is overgrown with maquis. Direct observations and analyses of fecal samples revealed a mere twenty-seven plant species. This is probably a result of a more homogenous natural habitat. What showed, though, was that the pre-ferred feeder plants were representatives of the plant families Asteraceae, Fabaceae and Ranunculaceae in Tuscany as well. Like on Corsica, the tortoises appear to actively search for fragrant virgin's bower, although it is comparatively rare in Tuscany.

A similar situation exists in Albania where direct observations and analyses of stomach contents revealed the consumption of species of fabacean plants in twenty-four, cucurbitacean (pumpkin) in nineteen, vetch-like in three, and rubiacean plants in two cases. Here, it is claimed that *Testudo boettgeri* would cause substantial damage in melon fields in that they would feed on fruit and leaves. The food spectrum of the tortoises also includes the leaves and fruit of beans, peas and cucumbers. Furthermore, the animals revel in fallen fruit such as pear, fig, mulberry, blackberry and the fruit of Cornelian cherry dogwood.

In Spain, LÓPEZ-JURADO et al. (1979) noted that the tortoises living there would also include in their diet prickly pears of cacti of the genus *Opuntia*, bulbs of daffodil *(Asphodelus aestivus)*, lesser sea daisies *(Asteriscus aquaticus)*, and Montpellier rockroses *(Cistus monspeliensis)*. The feeder plants of Mallorcan specimens were identified as to comprise for a major part (30 %) species of plantain (genus *Plantago*), asteraceans (26 %), and rubiaceans (10 %), creating an average calcium : phosphorus intake ratio of 3.5 : 1, and a protein content of 2.75 %. Here, African grass (genus *Hyparrhenia*), daisies, and the fruit of the mastic tree and the strawberry tree *(Arbutus unedo)* were also consumed.

Studies conducted in Croatia and Montenegro came to similar conclusions and underlined the importance of fabacean plants for the dietary spectrum of *Testudo boettgeri* and *Testudo hercegovinensis*. In Montenegro, for example, fabaceans such as bur clover (*Medicago polymorpha*), star sedge (*Carex echinata*), garden vetch (*Vicia sativa*), bush vetch (*Vicia sepium*), field clover (*Trifolium campestre*), and various species of plantain (genus *Plantago*) made up the majority of plants consumed, complemented by ranunculaceans such as fragrant virgin's bower, showy buttercup (*Ranunculus acris*), arum lilies (genus *Arum*), grasses of the family Graminaceae, and ivy (*Hedera helix*), goosefoot (genus *Chenopodium*), and pipe vines (genus *Aristolochium*). The local tortoise population would also often enjoy a meal of cultivated plants such as collards. In Croatia, the animal's summer food included for a major part bur and field clover, vetches, plantains, and oxtongue (genus *Picris*), and fallen fruit such as plums, whereas during fall their diet mainly consisted of thyme, horse mushrooms (*Agaricus arvensis*), and apples.

On the north coast of Greece, the tortoises' spring food consisted mainly of the fabacean plants that were abundant in the lush meadows during this season, and sweet grasses such as trefoil (*Lotus peregrinus*) and the Mediterranean plantain (*Plantago maritima*), but also the sea squill (*Urginea maritima*), which is poisonous to mammalian consumers. Summer then sees the animals shift their diet mainly toward skeleton weed (*Chondrilla juncea*), but the flowers of several species of poppy (genus *Papaver*) and various species of chamomile (genus *Anthemis*) are consumed as well.

In Romania, it was noted that Boettger's tortoises would migrate for some distance in late June in order to reach gardens in which ripe beans and yellow plums could be found.

Besides a staple diet of plant matter, invertebrates are regularly consumed as well although these make up only a minor portion. Most commonly, slugs and snails

as well as earthworms and caterpillars are eaten, and this applies to both natural and captive settings. The shells of snails have repeatedly been discovered in the feces of tortoises living in Tuscany, and analyses of stomach contents in Albania came to a similar conclusion. HAXHIU (1995a), for example, found as many as twenty-three snails in the stomach of a single tortoise in Albania. Reports of beetles and millipedes having been consumed came from Tuscany, Croatia, Bulgaria and southern France. The feces of Bulgarian tortoises, for example, included wing sheaths of running beetles of the genus *Carabus*, and the analysis of the stomach contents of a *Testudo hercegovinensis* from the Croatian coast revealed, besides plant remains, three millipedes of the genus *Glomeris* (pill millipedes) and an unidentified arthropod.

Members of the *Testudo hermanni* species group are by no means above feeding on carrion, and the feces of other animals (e.g., dogs, rabbits, sheep and cattle) also appear to be quite attractive. Human excrement appears to be a particular "delicacy" around camping sites, and garbage dumps in the surroundings of human settlements

Fig. 68: Excrement of *Testudo hermanni* (J. MARAN)

Fig. 69: Prickly pear cacti with ripe fruit on Menorca (Spain); a delicacy for tortoises (H.-U. SCHMIDT)

Fig. 70: Some habitats on Menorca are peppered with empty snail shells that are a major source of calcium for tortoises. (H.-U SCHMIDT)

Fig. 71: A Bulgarian *Testudo boettgeri* surrounded by its natural feeder plants (G. POPGEORGIEV)

are regularly scoured for edible remains. Aided by their sense of smell, the tortoises are able to detect the mentioned smelly "tidbits" from a large distance. Stomach contents also included eggshells, bones, feathers, and small pebbles. The consumption of pebbles possibly serves an improved gastric crushing of ingested food, as is the case in crocodilians and birds.

Very little is as yet known about possible seasonal shifts in the feeding behavior of the species dealt with here. In former Yugoslavia and on Sardinia, the tortoises are particularly common in the surroundings of blackberry hedges in late summer. The animals are known to have a particular taste for these berries and are at this point of time often found with their faces stained blue. NOUGARÈDE (1998) reported that on Corsica about 30–35 species of annual plants that formed part of the herbaceous layer would be consumed when they flowered in May, whereas in July and August this number was reduced to 3–12. This figure would eventually rise to about 15 in late September when the rains of late summer triggered the flowering of other plant species. Overall, the dietary spectrum of Corsican tortoises would be widest in midsummer and around each beginning and ending of a vegetation cycle. The animals could "afford" to be more choosy in spring when food was plentiful and of a high quality, than during summer when feeder plants

Fig. 72: A Boettger's tortoise in a juicy meadow (M. Müller)

Fig. 73: Boettger's tortoise from Bulgaria (G. POPGEORGIEV)

were becoming less abundant. As far as the plant species were concerned that were eaten during the various seasons of a year, these comprised in spring mainly annual flowering plants that appeared only during this particular season such as the Mediterranean daisy (Urospermum dalechampii), sheep's bit (Jasione montana), and vetches of the genus Vicia. In summer, sufficiently moist spots still offer a limited number of favorite feeder plants, including once again the Mediterranean daisy, but also common sheep sorrel (Rumex acetosella) and tuberous hawkbit (Leontodon tuberosum), while fragrant virgin's bower can be found in dry meadows. Feeder plants within the forests are now limited to the green shoots of wild madder (Rubia peregrina). Autumn sees the availability of meadow plants to rise once more, now including species such as the Tyrrhenian arum lily and tuberous hawkbit, but also fruit such as strawberry, peach and pear.

Food is clearly found and identified with the sense of sight dominating, and the tortoises are particularly attracted to red, orange and yellow flowers and fruits. The sense of smell is likely to also play an important role, as is demonstrated by an observation made by RUDLOFF (1990) who found several specimens feeding on carrion in a rock fissure that was difficult to access. BRINGSØE (1986) even reported about a Testudo boettgeri that dug up from the soil strongly scented truffles of the genus Arcangeliella.

Besides of drinking directly from puddles or streams, which is mainly observed in the case of juveniles, the water requirement is covered mainly through the consumption of fresh, juicy feeder plants. During heavy rain showers, the tortoises can often be seen as they raise their rear parts and press the snout into the ground in order to drink from the small depression in the ground created thus. It is common for them to urinate at the same time.

Reproduction

At the beginning of the mating season, the epididymes of the males will distinctly enlarge, with the production of sperm reaching its peak in July or August. The production of sperm depends mainly on the ambient temperatures and only to a lesser extent on the hours of sunshine. It starts only once temperatures exceed about 26 °C and stops completely at values at or below the 21 °C-mark. A study of male specimens representing the *Testudo hermanni* species group kept in human care in central Europe showed that sperm production as well as androgen level fluctuation patterns were distinctly different from what was happening in males living in the wild, even if the captive specimens were kept in outdoor enclosures.

Male specimens can often be seen engaging in territorial arguments, which are particularly common after copulation took place. These fights include biting and shell-ramming and sometimes lead to one opponent ending up on his back. Most fights are, however, resolved by one of the antagonists running away. The explosive sounds of shell-ramming carry over a distance of about 50 meters.

Mating can be observed throughout the entire period of activity, but are particularly frequent between March and May and during August/September. While some authors feel that mating activity would be more pronounced in late summer, others failed to detect any differences between spring and late summer mating activities. It appears as though late summer mating is of critical importance for the fertilization rates of clutches laid in the spring of the subsequent year.

Courtship usually commences with the male sniffing the female, with particular attention being given to her head and front legs. This activity is usually interspersed with head bobbing. The male then takes to circling the female and sniffing her with the head and neck more or less extended. Eventually the male begins to ram the rear parts of the shell of his female partner in rhythmical forward and backward movements, but this activity is less strongly pronounced in the species dealt with here than it is in other species of the genus *Testudo*. If the female endures this phase with her head and legs retracted into her shell, the male intensifies his courtship, repeats his shell-ramming, and places bites into the female's head, front and hind legs. These bites may sometimes be so forceful that they draw blood. Eventually the male mounts the female, pushes his tail beneath that of the female, and feels with his tail tip for the cloaca of the female. Guiding the penis into the cloaca of the female is apparently aided by the strong horny nail that covers the tip of the male's tail.

If the female was stopped by the bites and shell-ramming, but is not actually ready to mate, she will now take to flight with quick, jerky steps or press the rear margin of her shell firmly onto the ground and thus effectively prevent copulation. If the female runs off, the mounted male cannot do much more than attempt to follow for a few steps in his upright position with some hopping movements before he finally slides off. He will then pursue the female and try to stop her with more bites and shell-ramming, but these attempts at copulation are in the most instances entirely futile.

In the case of a female that is ready to mate, she will raise herself on her hind legs, retract her head and front legs, stick out the tail and so facilitate copulation. In his attempt to initiate intercourse, the mounted male will open his mouth wide and produce high-pitched, piping, squeaking or grunting sounds in the rhythm of his body movements. These sounds are audible over large distances, although they are not the product of a true voice, but rather a byproduct of air pressed abruptly from the lungs. Because this production of sounds and the mounting would represent an increased energy expenditure for the males, it has been speculated on numerous occasions that the sounds may serve as a quality criterion by which females could select mating partners. GALEOTTI et al. (2005) therefore experimentally studied a group of tortoises kept in a nature-like setting in order to determine whether the mating sounds of Testudo hermanni

could possibly provide a relevant stimulus for both sexes. At the same time they analyzed the sound characteristics in order to find out whether and which sounds may play a role in partner selection or serve to deter rivals. It showed that while females responded to playback sounds, males appeared to ignore these entirely. Females were particularly attracted to short, high-pitched sounds that were emitted at high repetition rates, but also responded to short, continuous sounds. It was revealed that the males with the best vocal qualities were those that also had raised hematocrit levels (erythrocytes or red blood cells) suggesting that the call would indeed give an indication of the fitness of the respective male. This could thus enable females to choose the most promising mating partners for their offspring. This is the first study that managed to associate a function of attraction to the sounds produced by tortoises.

In a study in Greece, HAILEY (1990) found that courting males would execute between five and thirteen (eight on average) shell-rams per minute. A male that was observed for 20 minutes executed 133 shell-rams in a continuous sequence, before the female eventually managed to escape beneath a bush.

A common observation is that of males that appear to "rest" on a female's back. These

Fig. 74: Courtship in Testudo hermanni is often a rough affair with the male ramming and biting his potential partner. (W. SCHMIDT)

males would then be in an almost trance-like state and stroke with their front legs the carapace of their partners in a near compulsive fashion without showing the slightest inclination to actually copulate.

The courtship of biting, ramming and numerous unsuccessful attempts to mount that precedes mating usually persists for several hours or even days. Copulation then takes between 2 and 15 minutes, in rare instances up to one hour. According to observations made by MORETTO (quoted in CHEYLAN 2001), an ejaculation may take up to five minutes (!). Evidence of successful copulation remains in the form of slimy residue on the cloacae of both specimens involved.

It is entirely normal for a male to copulate with several females during the course of a year and vice versa. Observations made in captivity showed that males preferred to mate with the largest females available, whereas females did not seem to be likewise predisposed.

Female specimens are able to store the sperm of one successful copulation for at least ten months, but probably even for a number of years. This has been demonstrated on several occasions by females that were kept in captivity without a mating partner for respective periods of time, but still continued to produce fertilized eggs. Since, however, sperm vitality and quality decrease over time, fertilization rates of clutches decrease with the length of such periods.

Four to six weeks pass between copulation and the laying of eggs. In southern France, the oviposition season extends from late April to early July with a distinct peak in June. In some instances, eggs were laid as late as September. On Corsica, the nesting season falls into the months of May and June with a peak around June 10, but a case of particularly early oviposition was observed under captive conditions on this island on April 13 already.

SWINGLAND & STUBBS (1985) reported about an oviposition from Greece on April 30. Here, June is also the month of peak nesting activity, and the latest recorded date appears to be June 16. In València, that is a little south of the natural distribution range of *Testudo hermanni*, a captive female laid eggs in the first half of May, but even there most nesting activities were noted between the end of May and the end of June. These two months are also those during which egg-laying takes place in Albania and Croatia, and in Romania, 75 % of the eggs are laid in early June, with the earliest date recorded being May 21, and the latest June 20. In Bulgaria, instances of oviposition have to date been recorded for June and July.

Eggs may be laid at any time of the day, but are mostly deposited in the late afternoon and evening hours. SWINGLAND & STUBBS (1985) recorded in the French Maure Mountains twenty-one instances of oviposition before 12.00 h, eleven between 12.00 and 16.00 h., and thirty-three after 16.00 h. While many females finalized their nesting shortly before sundown, some continued until long after nightfall, and a few even until well after midnight. In the tortoise center CARAPAX in the Italian Massa Marittima (Tuscany), instances of morning oviposition were noted in June from about 09.30 h, in July from 08.50 h, and afternoon nesting from about 15.30 h in June, and from 18.00 h in July. Here, no differences were found between the frequency of morning and afternoon nesting in May and June, whereas in July the number of morning ovipositions is about twice as high as that for the afternoon. In Bulgaria, most of the observed instances of egg-laying were recorded from between 17.00 and 20.00 h, and one female was still busy with her nest at 23.00 h. In Romania, observations made by CRUCE & RÂDUCAN (1976) suggest that most clutches are laid between 17.00 and 19.00 h, and these two authors presume that this serves to prevent the plundering of nests by magpies (*Pica pica*) and common crows (*Corvus frugilegus*). It may be argued, though, that ambient temperatures would rather determine the time of day when eggs are best laid because the nesting season is usually marked by high temperatures around noon. A female building a nest in an open, fully sun-exposed area would certainly run a risk of succumbing to the excessive heat. This is outlined by the fact that every year dead, usually older females that obviously died of overheating can be found at their nests in the vicinity of the Meteóra monasteries (Greece). Oviposition is therefore often triggered by warm summer rains. BONIN et al. (1996) presumed that a shift toward longer days in the photoperiod might also have an influence on the point of time at which eggs are laid.

Females that are ready to lay their eggs are notable for their appearing very active and full of energy. They usually select a sunny spot in open land, commonly situated on the south-facing side of a hill, on a clearing in a forest, but also in cultivated fields. An important determinant of what makes a good spot is the condition of the substrate. It needs to be loose enough to be diggable. Therefore, sandy or loose earth is favored, and the substrate is normally slightly moist. Vineyards and olive groves with irrigated soils that have been ploughed recently therefore often exert an irresistible attraction on gravid females. Nests are also often dug between the roots of low shrubs where the moisture content appears to be particularly favorable.

Sun-exposure, soil composition and vegetation appear to determine the spatial distribution of nest pits. While there seems to be no "system" in the spacing of nests in flat, open and sandy situations, clutches are found in high concentrations at a few select sites in hilly or densely wooded areas, often reaching densities of two or three clutches per square meter. In the forested Maure Mountains of southern France, for example, gravid females literally converge on a few oviposition sites and spend between several hours and a few days there. This requires them to walk distances of up to 3 km. It is common in these situations that females show a high degree of fidelity to "their" nesting sites and return to them again and again for many years. Others often seem to choose nesting sites at random and even select different spots within one nesting season. Data gathered in the CARAPAX center indicate that the minimum ground temperature of a potential nesting site needs to be at least 20 °C (range 20.0–36.2 °C).

On reaching a potential nesting site, the female will first walk about nervously and thoroughly test with her nose temperatures and moisture levels of possible spots for her pit. She will also often be seen extending her head toward the sun. Once a particular spot has been picked, it is first cleared of obstructions with the aid of the front legs and the plastron. Then, the female uses her hind legs to excavate an about pear-shaped pit measuring approximately 6.0–7.5 H 7–10 cm in diameter by 5–15 cm deep. The size of the nest pit is determined by the number of eggs to be laid and the size of the female. The respective earthworks will only be finished when the female cannot reach to the ground of the pit with the claws of her hind feet anymore. The distance between the surface of the topmost eggs and the surface of the ground is about 7 cm on average.

Many females will excavate up to ten "test holes" before they eventually dig out the one which is to take their eggs. Observations in captive specimens revealed an average of four "dry runs" per successfully deposited clutch. The reason for why a certain pit is eventually aborted is not always recognizable, but in many cases disturbances by external sources or natural obstacles in the ground (e.g., roots or rocks) could be identified. EVANS (1982) reported about a female in captive care that discontinued oviposition for about two hours to let a heavy thunderstorm pass before she resumed her laying of eggs; she produced two eggs before the interruption and six thereafter. VINKE & VINKE (2004a) also observed that nest pits that had been excavated during the previous day were revisited on the next to be completed and take the eggs. This was a more common occurrence with females that had started the excavation of a pit only late during the previous afternoon. The older and more experienced a female is, the more straight forward the process of nesting will be, it would appear, but some specimens maintain their habit of digging "test nests" for many seasons.

A moistening of the soil with urine or the contents of the anal bladder, which is a common observation in other species of tortoises, is not, or at least only very rarely, seen in representatives of the Testudo hermanni spe-

cies group. In natural circumstances, up to thirty-six hours may pass from the first excavation attempt to the eventual laying of the eggs. Thirty to 385 minutes (with an average of 134 minutes) pass from the beginning of digging activities "in earnest" and the laying of the first egg.

Once the excavation works are finalized, the female will calmly sit above the pit and wait for labor contractions to set in. The actual laying of the eggs is usually a short affair. Mostly, not more than 60 to 90 seconds lay between the appearing of the individual eggs, although breaks of up to five minutes may occur. The female aids the expulsion of eggs through first extending the head and limbs and then retracting them in support of a labor contraction. This sequence of movements is often repeated until the first egg appears from the cloaca. HEIM (quoted in MAYER 1996b) described a rather interesting

Fig. 75: In Testudo boettgeri, mating can be observed throughout their activity period, but mainly during March through May and again in August/September. (G. POPGEORGIEV)

Fig. 76: Male *Testudo hermanni* emit high-pitched, squeaking or grunting, hoarse sounds with the mouth widely agape during copulation.
(J. MARAN)

observation and interpretation in this connection: "At the moment an egg is expelled, the tail assumes the features of a "face". The tip of the tail with its horny nail turns into a nose, and two dark scales on the tail become eyes. The shell now appears to have a head with a briefly opened mouth at the other end. This illusion may act to deter or confuse potential egg predators." Although this hypothesis sounds quite plausible, no evidence has as yet been presented that would confirm it must be taken seriously.

Each egg is guided down to the bottom of the pit with the tail and carefully adjusted in its position with the hind legs. Following observations made by SWINGLAND & STUBBS (1985) this may take more than thirty minutes in some cases, but I have never recorded periods of such length in my specimens. Right after their expulsion the eggs are covered in a viscose slime that protects them against cracking when they arrive at the bottom of the pit.

Once all the eggs are laid, the female commences to refill the nest pit with her hind legs and solidifies the soil with her hind legs and the plastron in a display of seemingly infinite tenacity. Finally, she will often turn around and around in order to spread leaf litter, blades of grass, small stones, twigs, etc., over the refilled nest, which may take another fifteen minutes or so. Having thus erased almost all traces of activity, she leaves a nest that is usually very difficult to spot.

Finally, the female moves off from the nesting spot on stiff hind legs in a jerky and visibly exhausted gait. Most specimens will resume feeding right after having laid their eggs and then take to extensive basking. According to various authors, the entire process of nesting from excavating a pit to its complete closure may take between one and a half and six hours in total, depending on the composition of the ground.

A clutch of a member of the Testudo hermanni species group may comprise between one and eighteen eggs, but usually consists of four to six. The following average numbers of eggs have been reported from various parts of the distribution range: Spanish mainland, 2.9 ± 1.1 (older females) and 2.5 ± 0.9 (younger females), respectively, Mallorca, 3–4, southern France, 2.93 ± 0.84 (1–8, usually 2–3 with an average of 2.8), Corsica, 3.97 (1–8, usually 3–5), Greece, 4.3 ± 1.13 (1–7), Bulgaria, 4.0 (with a maximum of 7), and Romania, 6.4 (3–11). In Albania, 4–9 eggs per clutch have been counted, while on Sardinia, these numbered 4–7. Fifteen clutches of female Testudo hermanni kept in human care in València consisted of 4.2 eggs on average (1–6 eggs). VINKE & VINKE (2004b) reported that their female Testudo hercegovinensis would produce clutches of usually three eggs with a maximum of five. Following BLANCK & ESSER (2004), the first clutch of a year would usually contain 2–3, rarely 4–6 eggs, and the (rare) second or even third clutch merely one or two. A female of this species on one occasion developed not less than eight eggs to a stage where they could have been laid, but then was unable to expel them unaided. When they were eventually forced out through an injection with Oxytocin, they showed distinct dents that indicated there had been too little space in the uterus for such a large number of eggs. Testudo boettgeri kept in enclosures in Germany produced an average of 5.5 ± 1.34 (3–8) eggs per clutch, and for the Netherlands, EENDEBAK (2002) worked out an average of six eggs (2–15, and 2–4 in first clutches). Eleven to fourteen year-old females in the care of KIRSCHE (1967) produced three or four eggs in their first clutches after reaching sexual maturity, older ones five to eight, and the average amounted to 7.6 eggs per clutch.

In some individual cases, not all the eggs of a clutch were laid at once, but rather spread over two nests. This would also offer an explanation for most of the finds of *Testudo boettgeri* nests that contained only one or two eggs.

The hard-shelled, white, and almost perfectly ball-shaped to slightly elongated eggs of the species discussed here are slightly compressed, which is likely to smoothen their passage through the pelvis during their expulsion. Within a clutch, the eggs are very homogenous regarding their shapes and sizes, but it is thoroughly possible that they differ between individual clutches of the same female. The larger a female is, the wider are the eggs produced by this female. In contrast, there appears to be no correlation between the size of a female and the weight of her eggs. What seems to be a paradox, though, is easily explained by the variability of the egg shape: small females with a small pelvic diameter produce eggs that are more elongated in shape, but still are of about

the same weight as the more spherical eggs of larger conspecifics. More correlations exist between the number of eggs in a clutch, the total weight of a clutch, and the size of the mother specimen. A large female *Testudo boettgeri* with a weight of 3.5 kg (which is a weight practically exclusive to captive conditions) may, according to data provided by EENDEBAK (2002), produce about twice as many eggs per year as one that weighs only 2 kg. It also appears that the volumes of individual eggs are slightly larger in clutches that comprise fewer eggs.

The following average egg sizes have been recorded for representatives of the *Testudo hermanni* species group from different parts of the distribution range:

Southern France: Length 31.5 ± 0.59 mm (28–42 mm), width 24.6 ± 0.57 mm (22–27 mm), weight 15.7 ± 2.7 g (12.1–18.8 g), carapace lengths of mother specimens 16.0 ± 1.4 cm;

Corsica: Length 34.7 mm (28.0–41.3 mm), width 27.8 mm (23.6–32.1 mm), weight 15.1 g (8–22 g), carapace length of mother specimens 17.9 ± 1.4 cm;

Northeastern Spain: Length 34.5 mm (26.4–38.0 mm), width 25.2 mm (24–26 mm);

Croatia: Length 30.3 mm (26–35 mm), width 23.3 mm (23–24 mm);

Greece: Length 37.6 ± 2.5 mm, width 27.97 ± 1.4 mm, weight 17.1 ± 2.3 g (10.5–23.5 g), carapace lengths of mother specimens 19.1 ± 0.9 cm;

Romania: Length 35.1–38.1 mm, width 28.6–28.8 mm, weight 18.1–18.3 g, carapace lengths of mother specimens 19.1 ± 2 cm.

Eggs obtained from female *Testudo hermanni* kept in human care in València averaged 32.8 ± 9.3 mm (29.4–44.8 mm) in length, 28.3 ± 1.7 mm (25.0–33.9 mm) in width, and weighed 15.3 ± 3.0 g. In Germany, female *Testudo boettgeri* of 17–19 cm in length that were kept in captive enclosures produced eggs that measured 32.9 ± 1.3 mm (28–37 mm) in length

Fig. 77: In the south of France, the oviposition season of *Testudo hermanni* extends from late April to early July. (J. MARAN)

Figs. 78–81: A clutch of southern French *Testudo hermanni* usually comprises only 2-3 eggs. (J. MARAN)

and 26.5 ± 1.7 mm (23–30 mm) in width, and weighed 13.7 ± 2.26 g (10–18 g) on average.

The weight of a clutch matches on average 4 to 7 % of the weight of the mother specimen. The following average values have been recorded from various parts of the distribution range:

Southern France: 46.13 g, Corsica: 58.12 ± 22.40 g (38–79 g),

Greece: 73.38 ± 18.33 g. The volume of an egg ranges around 35 ml. Eggs consist for 76.8 % of water, 6.6 % are lipids, and 16.7 % are dry matter. The energy content of an egg averages about 5.3 kj/g. The shell accounts for 14.1 % of the entire weight of an egg, and the shells of six eggs obtained from captive-bred specimens examined by COOPER (1983) weighed 2.65 g (0.93–4.27 g) on average and were 0.4 mm (0.29–0.55 mm) thick. A weight loss of some 30–40 % is experienced during the incubation period of the eggs.

Two subsequent instances of oviposition are spaced by between 10 and 31 days in southern France (15–18 on average), an average of 16 on Corsica, 15–19 in Italy, and an average of least 10 in Greece.

With the captive female *Testudo boettgeri* kept by EENDEBAK (2002) this interval ranged around twenty days, which is a figure I am able to confirm for my Boettger's tortoises. Reports about nesting intervals of about 40 days appear to be misleading and are probably based on incomplete observations.

The total number of clutches produced by a female in nature is largely unknown because free-ranging specimens have rarely been followed continuously in nature. HAILEY & LOUMBOURDIS (1988) concluded from a count of follicles and luteins in dissected specimens of a Greek population that two or three clutches per year were possible; the average values for three populations were 1.9, 2.4 and 2.4 clutches per annum. Up to three clutches per year have also been reported from Corsica and the Balearic Islands. Only two (very rarely three) clutches per annum at intervals of 19-31 days each have so far become known from the south of France, and in the Italian CARAPAX center, most female *Testudo hermanni* would produce only one clutch in a year. This appears to be the case also in *Testudo boettgeri* living in Bulgaria. *Testudo hercegovinensis* usually produce one clutch per annum, rarely two, and very rarely even three. On the Spanish mainland, an average of 1.1 clutches per female and year was determined. When pondering these data, it needs to be taken into consideration that distinct annual and individual variations exist. The larger average sizes of Corsican, Greek and even Romanian specimens and the average numbers (see above) of eggs per clutch in these populations, but also the fact that females in the northeastern parts of Greece and in Romania regularly produce a third clutch, suggest them to be more fertile than their cousins living in the south of France. According to BERTOLERO & CHEYLAN (2004), female *Testudo hermanni* would produce an average of 6–9

eggs per year, but some females would not reproduce every year.

In the Greek northeast (and presumably throughout the entire distribution range of the *Testudo hermanni* species group), the number of eggs per female and year is strictly correlated to the size of the respective mother animal. Specimens with carapace lengths around 17 cm produce the largest numbers of eggs, i.e., nine or ten per annum, whereas smaller and younger specimens with carapace lengths of 15 to 16 cm average lay only four or five. The latter also applies to very old, large females with carapace lengths of more than 18 cm. Such a decline in fertility was also noted in other parts of the distribution range, e.g., on the island of Corsica. The total number of eggs produced per female ranges from three to twenty-two in females living in northeastern Greece, but the average values vary with the population and the year. At Alíki, a female lays 7 ± 2.3 eggs per annum on average, in Deskáti 14 ± 4.5, in Litóhoro 10 ± 3.3. In Litóhoro, for example, each female produced 11.9 eggs in 1985, but the next

Fig. 82: Females of the *Testudo hermanni* species group excavate a nest pit of up to 15 cm deep. (W. WEGEHAUPT)

year saw this average decline to a "mere" 8.7. In Romania, a female *Testudo boettgeri* has an average annual output of 10.8–12.2 eggs, with the lower value having been determined on the basis of ovarian scars in July and August and the higher one in March and April on the basis of follicles measuring more than 17 mm in diameter. KIRSCHE (1967) recorded for captive female representatives of the eastern population group an average of 13.1 eggs per year. On Corsica, a study of twelve sexually mature females demonstrated an annual average production of 7.6 eggs, which is surprisingly low considering the body size of Corsican specimens. In the Maure Mountains of southern France, a female would produce 6–8 eggs on average per annum, with exceptional cases of up to ten eggs having become known. From the perspective of energy, a female invests about 15 % of her total energy household into her clutch.

During the course of incubation, fertilized eggs will change their shade of color from rather pale to bright white. This usually happens within the first fortnight following deposition. The first blood vessels can be seen as early as after six to eight days.

One successful mating enables the female to produce fertilized eggs in several subsequent clutches, which is a phenomenon called amphigonia retardata. For this purpose the females have tubular, protein-producing glands in the reproductive tract in which sperm is kept alive. EENDEBAK (2002) conducted a study to this effect using four *Testudo boettgeri* kept in human care. After having been separated from their male partners after laying their first clutches of the year, these specimens produced between seven and seventeen additional eggs, usually in the form of one more clutch, but in the case of the seventeen eggs these were spread over two. In two cases, fertilization rates remained at 100 %, but in the two others it was reduced to 70 and 86 %, respectively. Only two of the females continued to lay eggs also in the following year, numbering eight and nine, respectively. These were still all fertilized. Thereafter, no more eggs were produced until the females were once more placed in the company of males. This may indicate that the ability of producing fertilized eggs without renewed mating is limited to one to two years in the species of the *Testudo hermanni* species complex.

Incubation periods largely depend on incubation temperatures. Respective data from nature are so far available only from France and Romania. On Corsica, juveniles emerged from two clutches after 98 and 115 days, respectively, and the hatchlings of another four clutches deposited in an outdoor enclosure appeared after an average of 94 days. This largely corresponds to the data gathered on the French mainland where an average of three months (73–104 days) was determined. Extreme values of 110 and 124 days have been reported from Romania. At the Italian CARAPAX center, juveniles hatched after 69–103 days. In Albania, hatchlings with soft carapaces were encountered in October.

The long-term minimum temperature necessary for the development of the embryos is 23–24 °C, and the maximum long-term temperature that is still tolerated lies at 35 °C. These extreme values are, however, hardly ever reached inside a nest pit in nature, or at least not for longer periods of time. DEVAUX (1996b) monitored temperatures inside about 8 cm-deep nest pits for a period of three months. This revealed an absolute minimum of 8 °C and an absolute maximum of 42 °C, but the average temperatures ranged quite precisely around 20 °C, often increasing by about 10 °C in the early afternoon, and decreasing by about 10 °C in the early hours of the morning. According to EENDEBAK (2002), the temperature inside a nest pit may be up to 15 °C above the ambient temperature at night.

With regard to the reproductive success, a hatching ratio of 93 % was determined under the semi-natural conditions of an outdoor pen on Corsica. In this case, however, it needs to be taken into consideration that no predators had access to clutches of eggs, which would obviously be the case in a truly natural setting.

Rains during the early and middle stages of incubation have a delaying effect on embryonic development, but an accelerating one if they occur toward the end of the incubation period. Hatching is timed to coincide with the times of the first rains at the end of summer, when an increased moisture level of the ground makes it easier for the baby tortoises to exit their nest pits. This leads to hatchlings from clutches with different deposition dates to often emerge at about the same point of time. Although this may be as early as toward the end of July (around the 27th) in areas like Montenegro and the south of France, it usually takes until September. For example, hatchlings were found at Saint-Raphaël in the French department of Var on September 1, 16, 19, and 26 and on October 1, with the earliest hatching date in Var having been recorded as August 1. August also appears to be the earliest month of hatching in the northeastern parts of Greece. On Corsica, most hatchlings appear between September 15, and October 10, more rarely as early as from the end of August. In the Italian CARAPAX center, hatching of babies occurs between August and October. In Croatia, MEEK (1985) found freshly hatched juveniles in late September. In Romania, the time at which baby tortoises appear ranges from September 20, to the first week of October, but is most common between September 24 and 30. Various authors have pointed out that the babies of the species dealt with here may leave their nest pits only in the subsequent spring if a particularly dry year is experienced.

The embryos are positioned within their eggs across the longitudinal axis. Their shells are folded across the ventral shell from bridge to bridge, but begin to unfold already while they are busy emerging. Various authors recorded timespans ranging from two hours to several days to pass between the point of time at which the eggshell was first scratched with the egg tooth and created barely visible fissures, and the eventual emergence of a baby tortoise. This time is used by the hatchling to resorb almost all of the amniotic fluid that surrounds it and what has remained of its yolk sac.

Moving its head and front legs the baby eventually manages to break out a small piece of the shell, and then continues to widen the opening by biting and breaking off more pieces. The next step is to move the front legs and turn around inside the shell in order to crack it open. It usually takes the hatchling a number of strenuous attempts to achieve this. The hatching process may thus take up to three days during which period of time the hatchling inserts several phases of rest that may take between one and three hours each.

According to HIGHFIELD (1996a), up to twelve days may lie between the hatching of first and the last baby of a clutch. The tremors associated with the liberation attempts of the first hatchling serve as a trigger for its siblings to also try and leave their eggs. Uniting their physical powers, it becomes easier for all hatchlings to exit their common nest pit. Notwithstanding their concerted effort, their leaving the nest pit may still take several days, depending on weather conditions.

Upon emerging from the ground, the babies immediately take to the cover of shrubs and bushes. The originally almost circular shell extends to an elongated shape during the first two to four days, and the "belly button" in the plastron closes. Since the small tortoises are highly susceptible to heat and dryness, they spend most of their time in the cover of bushes (in Croatia, for example, beneath Spanish broom [Spartium junceum], in Montenegro, beneath slender false broom [Genus Brachypodium]) or rocks in relatively moist situations at the base of slopes where water collects after rain showers. Their color pattern makes the small tortoises blend in with their environment and renders them very difficult to spot. It will only be on their reaching about 10–11 cm in carapace length that juveniles can be encountered in the same microhabitats as the adults.

Southern French hatchlings emerge with carapace lengths of 3.0–3.37 cm (3.17 ± 0.035 cm on average), and Corsican ones with 2.6–4.2 cm (3.65 ± 0.022 cm on average). Spanish ones measure 3.3–3.9 cm (3.7 cm on average) on emergence, Italian ones 3.2–3.8 cm (3.4 cm on average), those from Croatia 3.1–4.5 cm (3.85 cm on average), Bulgarian ones 2.9–3.6 cm, Romanian ones 3.18–3.85 cm, and Greek hatchlings are 2.2–4.4 cm (3.81 ± 0.52 cm on average) in carapace length at this point of time. KIRSCHE (1967) determined for fourteen Testudo boettgeri that had hatched in human care carapace lengths of 2.8–3.3 cm (3.02 ± 0.037 cm on average). Hatchling Testudo hermanni are 2.2–3.7 cm in width and 1.5–2.2 cm in height when they leave their eggs, and conspecifics representing the eastern population group are 3.4–3.7 cm wide. Corsican hatchlings weigh between 5 and 20 g (12.7 ± 2.27 g on average), Spanish ones 9.1–12.7 g (11.5 g on average), Italian ones 7.0–14.0 g (8.8 g on average), Croatian ones 10–19 g (15 g on average), Greek ones average 9.6 ± 1.4 g, and captive-bred babies of the eastern population group weigh between 6 and 30 g (7.6 ± 0.18 g on average). Hatchling Testudo hercegovinensis produced in human care weighed 6–7 g (HERZ 2005), but

Fig. 83: In southern France, most juveniles hatch during the month of September. (J. MARAN)

according to BLANCK & ESSER (2004), the weight at hatching is about 12 g on average in this species. In all three species, the weight of the hatchlings accounts for 61.2% of the egg weight on average.

Like with most other chelonian species, incubation temperatures determine the sexes of the hatchlings. Here, it is the middle third of the incubation period that determines the sexes of the offspring. The vertex, i.e., the value at which specimens of both sexes hatch at a balanced ratio, appears to be 31.5 °C. This was the result of experiments conducted by EENDEBAK (1995) with 515 eggs of *Testudo boettgeri*. Lower temperatures produce more males, higher ones more females. In the study by EENDEBAK, eggs incubated at 25–30 °C produced exclusively males, and from those stored at 31 °C 79% were of the male sex. This ratio was reduced at 32 °C when only 26% of the hatchlings were males, and eggs incubated at 33–34 °C eventually produced exclusively

females. This author also noted that "female temperatures" had to be maintained for a period of at least five to seven days, while the production of males required a much longer period. Using constant temperatures of 30–31 °C, FRITZ & PFAU (2002) obtained almost exclusively males from *Testudo boettgeri* clutches, whereas most or even all of the offspring hatched were female when the temperature was kept at 32.5–34.0 °C for the first 40 days of the incubation period, then reduced to 29.0–30.0 °C, and the substrate moisture increased from about day 45. EENDEBAK (1995) noted that the sex of tortoises hatching from eggs that had been continuously exposed during their incubation period to temperatures of 30–33 °C could be identified only at a relative late stage, in part only in their eighth to tenth year of life. WEGEHAUPT (2003) provided the following vertex temperatures for *Testudo hermanni* and *Testudo boettgeri*: *Testudo hermanni* 32.5 °C, *Testudo boettgeri* 31.5 °C in the

Fig. 84: A joint effort makes it easier for all hatchlings of a clutch to emerge from a nest pit. (B. DEVAUX)

case of populations from cooler regions in the interior country or from higher altitudes, and 32.5 °C for specimens from warmer regions. The vertex for *Testudo hercegovinensis* appears to be distinctly lower than that of *Testudo boettgeri*. For example, VINKE & VINKE (2004b) over several years incubated Dalmatian tortoise eggs at 31.5 °C, and amongst those specimens raised to sexual maturity they only ever obtained two males.

Malformations are occasionally found in hatchling tortoises. They are more common in captive-bred specimens, which suggests these alterations to be a result of inadequate conditions during the incubation period and/or inadequate husbandry and/or noncompliance with the dietary requirements of the adult specimens. Affected parts of the anatomy most often include the skeleton (e.g., jaws of different lengths, supernumerary toes, or stunted limbs) and the number and arrangement of horny scutes. The latter phenomenon appears to be correlated to the incubation temperature during the early stages of embryonic development; it is also rather common in specimens living in the wild. This is demonstrated by 2.4 % of the members of a population in Montenegro, and 11.1 % of the animals in the French department of Var (vertebrals 5 %, pleurals 3 %, marginals 2.5 %, plastral scutes 0.6 %), and 10.9 % of the animals on Corsica (vertebrals 6.8 %, pleurals 1 %, marginals 2.6 %, plastral scutes 0.5 %) showed shell scutellation traits that differed from the norm. These include supernumerary and fused scutes, but also rearranged and usually asymmetrical scutellation patterns that are atypical for the respective species.

It is interesting to note in this connection that a female with a duplicated cervical kept by KIRSCHE (1967) produced exclusively offspring (five) with exactly the same anomaly. This female had been paired repeatedly with a male that also had a duplicated cervi-

cal scute. The same author reported about another female whose eleven babies from three subsequent years all displayed malformations of the same type, i.e., anomalies of the carapace scutes and a reduced number of toes. The cause of this phenomenon remained unclear as it was impossible to identify which of the seven males present had fathered these clutches. Furthermore, the possibility exists that these clutches had been fertilized from stored sperm, and the occurrence of an unvarying type of malformation throughout three years does therefore not necessarily prove it to be hereditary.

The formation of anomalies is obviously independent of the sex, and the exact mechanisms driving it are still unknown. Various authors have been speculating that this might be a result of inadequately high and constant temperatures during incubation, excessive handling of the eggs for candling, and/or inadequate husbandry conditions and/or deficient food supply to the parental specimens. REISS (2004) once more interpreted the scutellation anomalies of his hatchlings (all with a missing 5th vertebral) as a genetically fixed fault introduced by the mother tortoise. Every year, this animal would produce offspring amongst which about 30 % had only four or a much reduced 5th vertebral scute. Since there were several males available for fertilizing the eggs, the mother was "held responsible" for the scutellation anomalies of the offspring, in spite of the fact that she herself possessed five normally formed vertebrals. REISS (2004) also noted that mortality rates of juveniles affected by scutellation anomalies were higher than those of normally formed siblings. He therefore presumed that other, externally invisible genetic defects were being passed on as well. About 20 % of the hatchlings thus affected did not survive their first year of life.

An instance of extreme polydactyly was reported from a specimen kept in captivity in

Catalonia (Spain). It had eight toes on the left front foot, nine on the right, and six toes on each of the hind feet.

EENDEBAK (2002) found out that the number of claws appears to be hereditary at least to certain extent. His studies showed that female Testudo boettgeri with five claws on each of their front feet would produce substantially more juveniles with the same number of claws than those mothers with only four claws. Mothers with four claws, on the other hand, would produce four times more babies with the same number of claws than those with five claws. Similar results were obtained by this author also with regard to the heredity of an entire versus a divided supracaudal scute of the mother specimen.

Abnormal color patterns in members of the Testudo hermanni species group have been observed on several occasions. WERMUTH (1971a) for one described an albinistic specimen with bright red eyes that showed a pale olive brown coloration throughout. It had been an animal collected in Bosnia and Herzegovina that had made its way into the German pet trade. It fed normally, but tried to avoid bright light and spend more time than usual hiding beneath a piece of cork bark. After years of living in the company of about twenty tortoises in the garden of the WERMUTH family, it mysteriously disappeared without a trace one day. That albinistic tortoises are highly "desirable" is also demonstrated by the disappearance of another such specimen, i.e., a juvenile of 6 cm in length, from the collection of a keeper in Dortmund (Germany) in June 2003 (ANONYMOUS 2003f). Three albinistic baby Boettger's tortoises could be seen at the tortoise exhibition held at the Botanical Gardens of Basle (Switzerland) in August 2000. MARTÍNEZ-SILVESTRE & SOLER MASSANA (2001) reported about an amelanistic male with a very light-colored shell and light brown eyes.

The hatching of identical twins has been observed in nature as well as in captivity. These twins are substantially smaller than "normal" siblings. Siamese twins amongst members of the Testudo hermanni species group are not unheard of either. REISS (2004), for example, described a bicephalic (two-headed) hatchling Testudo boettgeri, which was additionally affected by fused gulars and a carapace that was slightly malformed in the regions of the anterior and posterior vertebrals. This hatchling was also substantially smaller than its normal siblings. It was closely studied as to its motoric functions, which revealed that the right head controlled the right pair of legs and the left head the limbs on the left, respectively. On its first day, the animal only managed uncoordinated movements and was unable to maintain any direction because the left and right pairs of legs were not moved in the typical alternating fashion. On the second day, however, the hatchling had already adapted to its handicap and moved about in some kind of "seizing" motion. This consisted of placing both front legs forward simultaneously and following up with both hind legs. On day three, the conjoined hatchlings began to feed with both heads. Most of the time both heads would feed at the same time, but there were also situations when one head showed no interest in food.

Various authors, including B. PETERS (1967) and KIRSCHE (1984b), supposed that Testudo boettgeri and Testudo ibera would occasionally hybridize in areas where their distribution ranges overlapped. BASOGLU & BARAN (1977) and AMIRANASHVILI (2000) assumed the same based on finds of individual specimens in Turkey and Bulgaria, respectively, that displayed characteristics of both species. Reports like these may possibly be based on specimens of Testudo ibera with divided, or those of Testudo boettgeri with entire supracaudals, however.

Growth and Life expectancy

Growth

In hatchlings, the shell is still very weakly ossified. The ossification process then begins to spread from a "vertebral center" at the neurals and radiates to the anteriorly, posteriorly and laterally adjacent areas. This results in the initially free arches of the ribs to be gradually fused from the top to the bottom ends. The gaps between the bones (fontanelles) between costals and neurals, and between suprapygals and peripherals, respectively, thus become increasingly narrow. Simultaneously, the initially more widely spaced peripherals gradually fuse with each other and with the nuchal and pygal. As far as the plastron is concerned, the ossification radiates from an anterior and a posterior bony clasp that are initially widely separated. The anterior clasp consists of the epi- and hyoplastra, the posterior one of the hypo- and xiphiplastra. From there, the ossification process spreads toward the center of the plastron causing the about T-shaped gap in the bone plates to become smaller and smaller. It takes about three to four years until carapace and plastron are ossified throughout with only small gaps remaining. There is a large amount of individual variation, though, and the last gaps will usually have disappeared only in the fifth or sixth year of life.

Juveniles grow relatively rapidly. This slows down clearly on reaching sexual maturity, and adult specimens eventually almost cease to grow altogether. Representatives of the species discussed here reach their final sizes at an age of about fifteen to twenty years, but since they continue to grow, even if ever so slightly, they are basically never "fully grown" in the strict sense of the term. This very minor growth then often adds hardly visible growth rings, or only faint incomplete indications of these, around the areolae of the shell scutes. At this stage, weight gains are limited to just a few grams as well.

Growth rates depend highly on hatching weights, the month of hatching, and the maximum size of the respective species and/or population. Although a lower hatching weight or the smaller size of hatchlings from a later clutch of the same year are slowly made up during the course of subsequent years, these animals will always be smaller. As a rule of thumb it may be expected that a baby tortoise will have about doubled its hatching weight by the time it retreats into hibernation for the first time and add some 50% per year over the following five years. The proportional growth is drastically reduced from the sixth year on and continues until the animal reaches its relative maximum size.

Female representatives of the *Testudo hermanni* species group grow faster than their male counterparts, and eastern European specimens grow faster than western European ones. The main reasons for the size differences between individual populations of the eastern population group are obviously neither hatching sizes nor the speed at which they grow, but rather the duration of substantial growth. Members of populations of smaller size cease to grow earlier and mature earlier than their cousins in large-growing populations. This is, however, not true for the western population group. The tortoises native to the Maure Mountains, for example, reach sexual maturity comparatively late, but still remain relatively small, whereas their Corsican cousins mature early, but still continue to notably grow thereafter.

Studies conducted on Corsica arrived at the conclusion that growth rates are influenced by the availability of food even if the climatic conditions are about identical. Juveniles that were monitored over a period of four years and examined at regular intervals showed very distinct differences in growth rates (1.17–1.85 mm per year), depending on whether they had access to green fodder in summer or not.

In their studies, ANDREU & LÓPEZ-JURADO (1998) came to the conclusion that Spanish specimens measured 4.2 cm in carapace length on average at an age of one year, 4.7 cm after two years, 6.7 cm after three, 7.2 cm after four, 9.4 cm after five, 9.9 cm after six, 11.0 cm after seven, and 12.3 cm after eight years in males and 11.5 cm in females. From a general point of

	Weight	Carapace length
on hatching	6–12 g	3.2–4.0 cm
before 1st hibernation	12–24 g	4.0–4.8 cm
before 2nd hibernation	20–36 g	4.6–5.4 cm
before 3rd hibernation	32–56 g	5.2–6.4 cm
before 4th hibernation	52–86 g	6.0–7.4 cm
before 5th hibernation	82–135 g	7.2–8.6 cm
before 6th hibernation	135–225 g	8.6–9.8 cm

WEGEHAUPT (2003) also provided growth data for the juveniles of a relatively small-growing population living in central Italy

Age in years	1	2	3	4
Carapace length in cm	4.6–5.8	5.2–7.4	7.0–8.9	9.8–9.9
Average carapace lengths in cm	5.2	6.4	8.0	9.9
Weight in g	19–40	27–77	72–130	170–173
Average weights in g	38	54.5	103	171.5
Numbers of juveniles examined	12	7	4	2

COUTARD (2005) is the source of information on the growth of Corsican juveniles from the Corsican chelonian center A Cupulatta

view, juvenile *Testudo hermanni* would grow during their first six years by an average of 1.05 cm in southern France, by 1.23 cm on Corsica, and by 1.0 cm per annum in Greece, so that as six year-olds they would measure 9.5, 11, and 10.2 cm on average, respectively. Sardinian yearlings are about 4.5 to 5.0 cm in length and weigh 20 to 25 g according to data published by WEGEHAUPT (2004). In a natural environment, juveniles weigh about 50 g at an age of three years, and ca. 150 g five years later.

A counting of growth rings on the shell scutes will provide fairly reliable information on the age of tortoises during the first few years of life. This applies up to an age of about seven years in the case of specimens living in the Ebro Delta (i.e., only to young and subadult animals), but in southern French ones it can be used up to an age of about ten to twelve years in males and twelve to fourteen years in females, and even up to eighteen or nineteen years in specimens of certain populations living in the Balkans. Thereafter the determination of a specimen's age on this basis becomes very difficult because the growth rings are then situated very closely together and can hardly be distinguished. Furthermore, the shells of older specimens are usually so worn that they are virtually smooth.

Another way of age determination is the examination of crosscuts from pipe bones that reveal clearly defined growth rings as well. This process is called skeletochronology, but for obvious reasons it is rather unsuited for the keeper of live tortoises. This method allows a determination of ages up to an age of about twenty years. Thereafter, problems of a similar nature as those associated with the counting of growth rings on the shell scutes are encountered.

The weight of a tortoise is not constant throughout the year, and there is usu-

ally no constant gain. The highest weight is reached at the height of summer, and by fall adult specimens in particular will once more have lost a lot of weight.

Life expectancy

Like other species of tortoises, the members of the *Testudo hermanni* species group are not particularly fertile and reach sexual maturity at a comparatively late stage in their lives. All this is compensated for by a high life expectancy. The succession of age classes is slow, and the balance of losses and additions in a population is ensured mainly through the long longevity of the animals. Mortality rates are in general highest amongst juveniles, and the annual reproductive output of a population depends almost exclusively on its number of adult females. These experience a distinct reduction of their fertility only toward the end of life (see chapter "Reproduction").

With regard to juvenile survival rates, PUCHADES LLORIS (1996) found that 90.7 % of the hatchlings kept in the semi-natural setting of an outdoor enclosure situated in the vicinity of València survived to the start of their first hibernation, and no losses occurred during this period of dormancy. Although predatory mammals were kept from accessing the babies with a fence, birds and rodents would have been able to catch them. For specimens living in the Corsican wild, a 29–75 % chance (52 % on average) of survival was determined for the first two years of life. Their three to nine year-old cousins living in the same area in the south of the island had an even higher survival rate of 79–93 % (88 % on average). STUBBS & SWINGLAND (1985) gave an estimated survival rate of 60 % for tortoises with carapace lengths of less than 10 cm inhabiting the Maure Mountains in the south of France, but this is actually a minimum

Fig. 85: Hatchling *Testudo hercegovinensis* usually measure about 39 mm in length on average. (A. SUKIC)

These could result in infections and consequently in the deaths of females. This theory by WILLEMSEN & HAILEY (2001b) was later retracted, though (HAILEY & WILLEMSEN 2003), when it was shown that the determined changes in population structure were not linked to the previously identified population density. WILLEMSEN & HAILEY (2001b) had determined an annual survival rate of adult specimens of 80–100 % (88.6 % on average) for eight Greek populations.

Amounting to 96 and 95 %, respectively, the rates of survival in southern French (Collobrières) and Corsican (Porto-Vecchio) specimens representing both sexes suggest that these animals are longer lived and reproduce for longer periods of time than their eastern relatives. Here, both males and females live for another 13.5 years on average after having reached sexual maturity. By comparison, this figure is 11.6 years on average in males and 8.1 years in females in the population at Alíki in Greece. It means that the tortoises here spend about 56 and 42 %, respectively, of their lives after reaching sexual maturity. Relatively high rates of survival of 95 % on average in males, and 96.6 % in females, were also established in the Maure Mountains.

BONIN et al. (1996) supposed for specimens representing the *Testudo hermanni* species group in nature a potential life expectancy of about eighty years, but presumed that fifty or sixty year-old specimens would already be a very rare occurrence. Most specimens may be presumed to live only to a maximum age of twenty to thirty years, according to BOURDEAU & TRONCO (1992).

value as neither a range was determined nor was the probability of incidental recaptures taken into consideration.

The average life expectancy of males of the population at Alíki (Greece) is 20.6, that of females 19.1 years. This suggests that a succession of generations takes about twenty years, corresponding to twice the age at which maturity is reached and three times the age at which secondary sexual traits are developed. It is estimated that 1 % of the tortoises of one such population live to an age of fifty years. However, this applies only to those populations that have a high content of juveniles and no balanced proportion of the sexes, as is commonplace in *Testudo boettgeri*. The annual survival rate in the Alíki population is an estimated 91 % in males, and 88 % in females. The higher mortality in females has in part been attributed to infections that were the result of injuries sustained during courtship. It was argued that in very dense populations, males and females would encounter each other frequently and the continued attempts of the males to mate could cause injuries to the sensitive skin of the female's tail region, particularly through the horny tail at the end of the male's tail.

Diseases and parasites

Like most of the viruses found in tortoises, those identified in members of the *Testudo hermanni* species group are herpes viruses of the family Herpesviridae. Specimens kept in captivity have become known to be hosts of viruses representing the genera *Herpesvirus, Iridovirus, Paramyxovirus* and *Sendaivirus*. It appears that these tortoises are particularly susceptible to infections with *Herpesvirus*.

Not very much is as yet known about the course of an infection and its consequences and thus about the risk for populations in the wild from the introduction or release of specimens that were kept in human care before. A study conducted by the German veterinary physician Karina MATHES of ninety *Testudo hermanni* in the "tortoise village" at Gonfaron in France and ninety-three free-ranging specimens in the Maure Mountains fortunately did not reveal any indications of infections with herpes viruses (MATHES 1997). The fact that 7 % of the tortoises cared for in Gonfaron and 12 % of their wild cousins in the Maure Mountains at the same time tested positive for mycoplasmae shows that these are also

not uncommon in nature and need not necessarily affect the health of tortoises unless aggravated by additional factors, and stress in particular. The US veterinarian Bobby COLLINS had come to the same conclusions a few years earlier.

Insofar as internal parasites of the species dealt with here are concerned, threadworms clearly play a dominant role, and amongst these, pinworms of the family Oxyuridae feature most prominently. A tortoise in good general health is host to an average of between 5,000 and 200,000 of these parasites. By now the following species of threadworms have been identified from *Testudo hermanni*: *Aleuris numidica, Atractis dactyluris dactyluris, Medhiella microstoma, Medhiella stylosa, Medhiella uncinata, Tachygonetria bainae, Tachygonetria conica conica, Tachygonetria conica nicollei, Tachygonetria dentata dentata, Tachygonetria longicollis longicollis, Tachygonetria longicollis pusilla, Tachygonetria longicollis setosa, Tachygonetria macrolaimus palearcticus, Tachygonetria numidica, Tachygonetria robusta robusta* and *Thaparia thapari thapari*. In six specimens from the

Fig. 86: Semiadult *Testudo hercegovinensis* from Croatia suffering from a shell disease (J. MARAN)

Fig. 87: Soft, mushy food paves the way for the development of a so-called "parrot's beak". (A. NÖLLERT)

surroundings of Gonfaron, the most common species were *Atractis dactyluris dactyluris*
(more than 37 %), *Tachygonetria longicollis
longicollis* (about 22 %), *Tachygonetria conica
conica* (15 %), and *Tachygonetria macrolaimus
palearcticus* (14 %). In the course of their investigations, LONGEPIERRE & GRENOT
(1999) noted that specimens with parasite
infections would specifically seek out and
eat poisonous feeder plants that would effectively reduce the extent of the infection.
The only study to this effect on *Testudo boettgeri* was conducted in Albania where only
the threadworms *Tachygonetria conica* and
Tachygonetria longicollis were identified. As
yet, nothing more is known about possible
geographical differences in the infestation
with endoparasites.

Ticks are common in tortoises representing the eastern population group, but
rarely found in their western relatives. The
extent of a tick infestation varies with the
locality, but it is obvious that *Testudo boettgeri* and *Testudo hercegovinensis* are distinctly
less severely affected than *Testudo ibera* and
Testudo marginata.

Fig. 87a: Even large-scale shell trauma often heals perfectly with the appropriate medical care.

In Greece, a *Testudo boettgeri* is host to
0.6–2.0 ticks on average, but it would appear that this is the case almost exclusively
during the summer months. Adult tortoises
are more frequently affected than juveniles
and subadults (40–60 % as compared to 5–
20 % each), and males more so than females
(60 % as compared to 40 %). All developmental stages of the parasites can be found

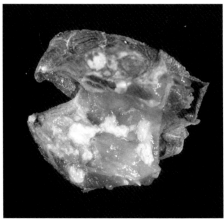

Figs. 88&89: These two tortoises exhibit the firmly attached deposits on the tongue and pharyngeal lining typical of an infection with herpes virus. (S. BLAHAK)

on infested tortoises. In Bulgaria, the tick species *Haemaphysalis taurica*, *Hyalomma aegyptium*, *Hyalomma excavatum*, and *Hyalomma plumbeum* were identified, whereas in Greece only *Hyalomma aegyptium* was found. Furthermore, attacks by the tick species *Hyalomma anatolicum* and *Hyalomma marginatum* have been reported from representatives of the *Testudo hermanni* species group.

Bloodsucking mites (e.g., species of the genus *Dermanyssus*) can also be found on the soft parts of these tortoises. Wounds are often infested with maggots of flies of the genus *Lucilia*, and in some Greek populations the tortoises are massively infested with these parasites.

Fig. 90: Tick infestation in a tortoise (W. SCHMIDT)

Fig. 91: Bulgarian *Testudo boettgeri* with a severe malformation of the posterior part of the plastron (G. POPGEORGIEV)

Husbandry

General

The members of the *Testudo hermanni* species group are certainly the species of tortoises most commonly kept in human care. Amongst these, the representatives of the eastern population group are those most widely kept and bred. Tortoises that were brought from Italy were kept in the gardens of monasteries as early as during the Dark Ages. Later, they were represented in just about every traveling menagerie. The first display specimens in a zoo appeared in the Viennese animal park at Schönbrunn (Austria) in 1816, and the "Greek tortoise" was first mentioned in a zoo guide to the Frankfurt Zoo (Germany) in 1860. The Basle zoo (Switzerland) obtained their first representative of the *Testudo hermanni* species group in 1903.

The species of tortoises discussed here become fairly tame after some time of keeping and begin to feed out of the hands of their keepers, or come to them when they expect food. MEYER (1998), however, noted that his *Testudo hermanni* were distinctly shyer than their relatives from the eastern parts of the distribution range. Be that as it may, you

should refrain from lifting the animals up often (no matter which species), as this is something only their predators in the wild would do. Losing contact with the ground therefore causes unnecessary stress to them.

Provided with good care and always respecting their natural requirements renders them excellently suited for being kept and bred in captivity. The species in this group are propagated on a regular basis and in large numbers. It is therefore entirely unnecessary to collect additional specimens from the wild. The captive breeding statistics released by the German Chelonia Group of the "Deutsche Gesellschaft für Herpetologie und Terrarienkunde e.V." (German Society for Herpetology and Terrariology) noted for the period 2001 through 2004 alone a total of 5,969 *Testudo boettgeri*, 921 *Testudo hermanni*, and 49 *Testudo hercegovinensis* that had all been hatched in human care, plus five specimens that were not identified to species level, but represented this species group nevertheless (SCHILDE 2003, 2004A, B, 2005). It is quite certain that many breeding records listed under *Testudo boettgeri* actually referred to *Testudo hercegovinensis* as this species was revalidated only recently. It must also be taken into consideration that it is still only a small number of members and associates of the Workgroup who regularly report their breeding figures, and that there are large numbers of unaffiliated breeders. It therefore appears reasonable to assume that in Germany alone a minimum of 10,000 babies of *Testudo boettgeri*, *Testudo hermanni* and *Testudo hercegovinensis* were produced during the given period.

It is a lamentable fact that by far most of the thousands of tortoises that were imported over the last decades ended up in the hands of animal-loving people who were well-meaning, but basically clueless, and succumbed to the appeal of animals that were weakened from lengthy transports and inadequate "storage" and offered for a few Deutschmarks in pet-shops. Fed with a "diet" of lettuce, minced meat, pasta and kitchen leftovers, they were then sentenced to a short life as "children's toys" in a garden or on the floor of an apartment, until they were mercifully released by death. About 83 % of the tortoises "cared for" in this manner did not live through their first winter in captivity. Most keepers did not really see a tragedy in that, because a new animal was certain to be available for a few Marks in spring. The import ban instituted by the European Union has meanwhile resulted in a greatly reduced availability of these species in the commercial pet trade. If you happen to find tortoises in general pet shops these days, they are captive-bred. The drastically higher prices they demand prevent purchases "on the spur of the moment".

Notwithstanding this, far too many mistakes are still made in the keeping and feeding of tortoises that turn their lives in captivity into an ordeal from which their only way out is a premature death.

Keeping these three species together or in the company of other tortoises is not rec-

ommendable. MAYER (1992a, b) described the hybridization of *Testudo hermanni* and *Testudo boettgeri*, but also pointed out that the animals would preferably mate with a partner of their own species if such was available. He presumed that there were certain key stimulants (presumably of an olfactory nature) that would under normal circumstances prevent "erroneous" mating. MAYER's hybrids between both population groups were dominated by the dark pigmentation of the (western) mother specimen, although the black was not particularly deep and rather tended toward brownish. The proportionate content of yellow was relatively high, with the boundaries between the light and dark elements being slightly blurred. Limbs and soft parts appeared light yellow as is common in the western population group, whereas the yellow spot beneath the eye that is typical for these, was absent with only one or two paler scales indicating its position. The dark wide stripes on the plastron were more pronounced than is common in representatives of the eastern population group, but appeared not quite as wide and less deeply black than in western ones. They were also partly interrupted. The shade of yellow of the plastron corresponded to that of the mother specimen. These juveniles grew faster than purebred "conspecifics" of the same age. There even was one case of hybrid twins hatching.

VEIDT & FRITZ (2001) also reported on hybrids between *Testudo hermanni* and *Testudo boettgeri*. Like the specimens produced by MAYER (1992a, b), the crossbreeds of these two authors more resembled *Testudo hermanni* than *boettgeri*. The sutures between pectorals and femorals were of about the same length in these animals. VEIDT & FRITZ (2001) noted, like MAYER (1992a, b) had before, their rapid growth, and in addition found them particularly robust and well-suited for captive situations. Quite rightly they pointed out that an indiscriminate dissemination of hybrid specimens could embody a grave danger to "purebred" collections in human care, if the information of their hybrid origin was lost at some point or other. This would create a terrarium tortoise that was no longer genetically identical to its cousins in the wild.

If only for this reason it would be sensible to withhold trading permits for hybrids in general. Crossbreeding experiments may serve a purpose in verifying the specific or subspecific status of a form, but can produce indicative results and are justifiable only in a strictly scientific setting. Other than that it has been shown that hybrid clutches are often less fertile and produce weak hatchlings.

Just how important it is to compose breeding groups of specimens that are really compatible is demonstrated by a variety of examples. The existence of a species now known as Testudo hercegovinensis was unknown to both scientists and terrarium enthusiasts. Being by no means rare in the collections, the respective animals were usually regarded as small specimens of Testudo boettgeri or light-colored Testudo hermanni. It was therefore common to keep them in the company of either (e.g., EGER 2005). One keeper of Testudo boettgeri then reported to VINKE & VINKE (2004a) of a female that would continuously produce unfertilized eggs. This tortoise differed substantially in its appearance from what was supposed to be its conspecifics. It was much smaller than these and displayed a much more contrasting color pattern. Eventually it was reidentified as a Dalmatian tortoise. The males in this group had never been seen attempting to mate with this female.

A group of very small Testudo hercegovinensis also included a very large female of unknown provenance (Testudo boettgeri?), which was so attractive to the males that they did not mate with the smaller females or did only

insufficiently so. All clutches produced by this group were infertile.

EGER (2005) once noted a male tortoise that would often hide in his outdoor enclosure, sleep beneath a shrub there, and hardly dare to enter a hotbed – all in order to avoid being attacked by other males. The other males, in contrast, seemed to get along quite well with each other. It was only later that this secretive animal was found to be the only Testudo hercegovinensis male in a group that otherwise comprised Testudo boettgeri. The moment this specimen was separated from the other males and in the company of females of its own species, it returned to showing an entirely normal behavior.

What can be learned from these stories is that one had better try and keep the local forms of the species group separated, even if they do not carry different scientific species names (as yet).

The joint captive housing of several species has also been demonstrated to lead to hybrids between Testudo hermanni and tortoises of the Testudo graeca species group, as well as between Testudo boettgeri and Testudo ibera and Testudo marginata, respectively, and even between Testudo boettgeri and species of the genus Agrionemys. From a clutch of four eggs laid in the collection of KIRSCHE (1984b), two viable hatchlings emerged after an incubation period of 70 and 74 days, respectively, from the union of a male Testudo boettgeri and a female Central Asian tortoise. Their unusual appearance immediately suggested them to be hybrids. The remaining two eggs were opened on day 80 and contained two perished embryos of 1 and 1.5 cm in length that appeared to be normally formed. The live hatchlings agreed in their carapace colorations with "genuine" baby Testudo boettgeri, but showed the yellowish brown skin typical of the Central Asian tortoise and had only four claws on all feet. The larger of the two hybrids exhibited the more rounded shell shape of the Central Asian tortoise, whereas its smaller sibling had the narrow shell of *Testudo boettgeri*. The latter also had a distinctly developed horny nail at the tip of its tail. The smaller specimen grew at a very slow pace, while the larger animal grew even faster than the juveniles of *Testudo boettgeri*. Its weight after seven months was 170 g as compared to an average of 135 g in "purebred" Boettger's tortoises. The smaller specimen eventually perished at an age of seven months without showing obvious symptoms, and the larger one about one year later following its outdoor hibernation. This is an indication of what was said before, i.e., that hybrids often tend to have a reduced vitality as compared with "purebred" specimens.

Hybrids between members of the *Testudo hermanni* species group and Central Asian tortoises have also been described by other keepers in Germany and France. ZIRNGIBL (2000), for one, also obtained a clutch of four eggs from a female *Agrionemys* as a result of a mating with a male *Testudo boettgeri*. In three of these the embryos perished at a fully developed stage, and from the fourth a hatchling emerged that was notable for its very small eyes that were kept closed for most of the time. It died after about one year. All these hybrids more resembled a Boettger's tortoise in their appearance than they did the Central Asian tortoise.

STEINLE had already reported on a supposed hybrid clutch between these two cladistic groups in 1977. He had found a clutch of eight eggs in an outdoor pen of which five contained perished embryos. This enclosure had been housing a male *Testudo boettgeri* and a female Central Asian tortoise for a period of eight years. The Central Asian tortoise had been about the size of a fist when it was purchased. As it is in any case unlikely that it would have been able to store sperm for eight

years, it must be presumed that these embryos were of hybrid parentage.

MERTENS (1968a) mentioned hybrids between *Testudo boettgeri* and *Testudo ibera* based on a case of a clutch of seven eggs from which only one hatchling emerged. It had a horny nail for a tail tip, but an undivided supracaudal scute. It must be borne in mind, though, that the latter trait is relatively common also in "purebred" *Testudo boettgeri*.

HEIMANN (1990) kept members of the eastern population group together with some *Testudo ibera* in an outdoor enclosure for a period of four years. As far as the eggs laid by the *Testudo ibera* were concerned, only 48 % developed embryos, and in the members of the *Testudo hermanni* species group the percentage was even lower at 37 %. When the two groups were eventually separated, the percentages immediately rose to 93 and 92 %, respectively. This made HEIMANN presume that the reasons for the low fertilization rates during the joint keeping lay in interspecific mating that produced embryos, which were perishing at very early stages of their development. The large numbers of infertile eggs may therefore be misleading because very early stages of embryonic development are easily overlooked when eggs are examined only macroscopically.

A hybrid from the union of a female *Testudo boettgeri* and a male *Testudo marginata* is stored in the Staatliches Museum für Tierkunde in Dresden (Germany) under the number 41567. This animal had hatched amidst four siblings from a clutch deposited in June 1996 in the collection of Michael REIMANN. Like its siblings it resembled a baby marginated tortoise closely in its appearance.

Keeping in outdoor enclosures

The members of the *Testudo hermanni* species group are probably the species of tortoises that are suited best for keeping in an outdoor enclosure in central Europe. As a general rule they should be able to enjoy unfiltered sunlight as often and as long as possible. Given these circumstances they do well and reproduce readily. Keeping them in an indoor terrarium offers no advantages whatsoever and must therefore be considered not in compliance with their biological requirements.

Keeping them outdoors is usually possible during the period from spring through late summer, though. Only if there are extended periods of bad weather with temperatures constantly below 12–15 °C is it recommendable to temporarily house them in a terrarium indoors. In order to avoid unnecessary transfers, they should be placed outside only around mid-May when the temperatures have become a little more stable. If you

have therefore decided for yourself that these tortoises are right for you, you need to have available both a suitable outdoor pen and an indoor terrarium that are both set up properly (see below).

A much better solution is, however, to append a greenhouse or a high-quality hotbed to the outdoor enclosure. These offer freely accessible climatic refuges into which the tortoises can retreat at night or during periods of cool weather. They should be fitted with UV-permeable polycarbonate sheeting and thus assist with making the most of the relatively weak solar radiation at these latitudes.

The soil beneath the greenhouse or hotbed needs to be removed to a depth of at least 80 cm if the tortoises are to hibernate outdoors and replaced with a mix of garden

Fig. 92: An example of an exemplary, well-structured outdoor enclosure for Mediterranean tortoises (B. SEEGER)

humus free of chemical fertilizers (no, it does not mold), river sand, and beech leaf litter (which rots rather slowly). The sheeting creates a desirable greenhouse effect that pushes temperatures to useful levels, which are, however, still not high enough to allow the animals to reach their preferred daily body temperatures of 35 °C. Therefore, a basking spot has to be set up in the greenhouse or hotbed, in whose center temperatures of 40–50 °C are created. This will enable the tortoises to find themselves a suitable spot that allows them to heat up relatively quickly. Halogen spotlights of 150 and 300 Watts have proved well-suited for this purpose. They can easily be controlled via a thermostat. Heating of the entire greenhouse or hotbed is necessary only during extended periods of moist/cool weather, however. Many keepers found it very useful to

raise the boxlike hotbed on a foundation of bricks as this does not only increase the air volume inside and thus its thermal stability, but also made it easier to install the basking spot. The same obviously also applies to a greenhouse that sits on a base of brickwork.

An interesting aid for °Conomically heating a small hotbed was suggested by BIDMON (in THIERFELDT 2004). It consists of a partially buried, closed water container that is equipped with an aquarium heater. If the weather is cool, the water is heated up and so releases warmth gradually but continually into the immediate surroundings. During warm weather, the sunlight heats up the water instead and creates a heat sink.

Finally, it should be noted that the greenhouse or hotbed should by all means be equipped with automated vents. This is a

Fig. 93: Male Testudo boettgeri in a lush "pasture" (F. WÜTHRICH)

safety measure to protect the tortoises from possible overheating on sunny days. For an absolute minimum a hotbed should be placed in a spot where it is partially shaded.

Another safety measure is the installation of a lightless heat spot that prevents nightly temperatures from dropping below 12 °C especially in spring and fall. It should also be automatically controlled with a thermostat. The latter is set up to switch the lightless heating device on if ambient temperatures decrease below 12 °C and off on reaching 15 °C. The greenhouse or hotbed should furthermore be secured and locked to protect the tortoises from possible nocturnal predators.

Since the tortoises prefer dark and tight shelters, the greenhouse or hotbed should offer a respective structure, maybe in the form of a small "house" or some other construction that is dark inside. A simple wooden box, with a hinged lid, will already do. It should also have the above-mentioned mix of garden soil without fertilizers added, river sand and beech litter. It has the advantage of not mildewing, whereas a bedding of hay develops mold quickly and straw dries out rapidly.

This type of outdoor husbandry management also eliminates the need for transporting the tortoises back and forth between their outdoor and indoor enclosures, and has proved the ideal setup for *Testudo boettgeri*, *Testudo hercegovinensis* and *Testudo hermanni*. New additions will usually soon accept the shelter, but if not, they will have to be collected in the evenings and during cold spells and placed in the greenhouse or hotbed until they have begun to "see the benefits".

The outdoor enclosure should be set up in the garden where it is warmest, most sun-exposed, and best protected from wind. A south-facing (in the northern hemisphere), sloped situation is ideal. Taking into consideration that the tortoises need to heat up in the morning, an exposure to morning sun is of particular importance. The pen should not include trees or high shrubs, as these would cast large shadows. The necessary shaded areas should be kept small. It is obvious that an outdoor pen should not be set up right next to a busy main road or other noisy places with a high degree of air pollution. The site should also be investigated as to the possibility of rising groundwater levels as a result of persistent rains that may flood the enclosure.

As far as its dimensions are concerned, the outdoor pen should not be made too large. A pair or a group of several juveniles can be adequately housed in an area of 2–5 m², and a small breeding colony may need just 10 m², if the pen is structured with thought. Right from the beginning the possible necessity of subdividing a pen or the need for a separate enclosure must be included in the planning. If the animals are to largely fend for themselves by feeding on wild herbs, a pair needs to be housed in an enclosure of at least 30 m², though.

You would need to find out for yourself whether the setting up of an outdoor enclosure of this kind requires a building permit, which is a distinct possibility if it is to be a

Fig. 94: Aspect of the entrance area of a hotbed (F. WÜTHRICH)

Fig. 95: A hotbed needs to be aired during summer. (B. SEEGER)

large and/or permanent structure. The respective regulations vary greatly not only
from country to country, but also from one
county or municipality to the next. There
may also be other laws and/or bylaws and/or
directives etc. that need to be complied with
regarding the outdoor keeping of animals
on non-farming, residential properties. It is
therefore highly recommendable to contact
the respective offices before and find out what
exactly is required.

Quite a few useful tips on how to set
up and decorate outdoor enclosures can be
found in the existing literature in most major languages. These include books, such as
ZIRNGIBL (2000), WEGEHAUPT (2003) and
MINCH (2006), but also numerous articles in
magazines, e.g., HOLFERT & HOLFERT (1999)
and SIMON (2000).

First and foremost the enclosure needs
to be fenced-in in a manner that makes it impossible for the tortoises to escape. They are
surprisingly skilled climbing artists, and the
risk is greater in a small enclosure than in a
large, well-structured one. SCHLÜTER (2005),
for example, found in the Bulgarian wild a
specimen that was busy scaling a wiremesh
fence and had reached about 1 m above the
ground already. The height of the surrounding barrier should be at least 45 cm. It is preferable to make it lean inwards, and the upper
edge may be bent over and in as well. This
is particularly important in corners that are
open invitations for "making a break", especially as it is here where the animals often climb on top of each other. The corners
should therefore also be rounded rather than
angular and covered on top with planks,
plastic sheets or concrete slabs. In order to
preclude a digging through under the fence,
it should be buried at least 30 deep. Suitable
fencing materials include slabs, semi-pipes
or angular casts of concrete, walls built from
natural rock, wooden beams or palisade fenc-

ing, and corrugated plastic or asbestos sheeting. Owing to their heat-storing properties, rock or concrete walls are probably the best choices to be made. If the fencing is not perfectly straight but runs in an irregular line as a result of your incorporating natural rocks in the ground, roots, low hills and depressions, it is often not regarded by the tortoises as a "prison wall", but rather as part of their environment. In my opinion, glass is just as unsuited as wiremesh fencing since it causes the animals to continuously walk along these borders in an attempt to get to the visible other side. They will also manage to overcome wiremesh fences of more than one meter in height, and many a tortoise has strangled itself in the mesh in the past. Although quite popular for this purpose, railway sleepers have been impregnated with tar oil that is often present in large quantities even after decades. The same applies to a number of scarcely volatile polycyclic aromatic carbohydrates that enter the body through contact with the skin and are known to cause cancer. As these substances increase their concentration when exposed to higher temperatures, railway sleepers are simply not fit to serve as fencing material for a tortoise pen.

It is of advantage to outfit the pen with an entrance large enough to allow, for example, a wheelbarrow through.

Of great importance are shaded spots where the tortoises can escape the midday heat. Dense bushes of moderate height are ideal for this purpose, but hollow logs also make shelters that are very popular amongst the tortoises as they offer a comfortable microclimate within. Small specimens also like to shelter under ridging tiles because these conserve heat very well.

Choosing the right composition of vegetation for the enclosure is not quite easy as many plants are either consumed by the tortoises or severely damaged. Grass, on the other hand, has the tendency to keep moisture near the surface for a long time. This moisture then evaporates slowly and creates a cooling effect right where the tortoises spend all their time. The pen must therefore not mainly be planted with grasses, especially because the grass is not normally eaten. In contrast, the animals can often be seen regurgitating grass that has accidentally been eaten together with other greens, or trying to pull it out of the mouth with the front feet.

An ideal vegetation cover consists of hard, herbaceous plants and low bushes, shrubs and trees. These may include creeping juniper, mountain pine, lilac, hibiscus, dog rose, grapevines, gooseberry, currant, blackberry, midland thorn, fig trees, honeysuckle, mulberry trees, knotweed, sugar loaf fir tree and other small conifers, cinquefoil, thicket-forming ornamental grasses, lav-

Fig. 96: Weather-protected outdoor setup for juveniles (B. SEEGER)

Fig. 97: A well-structured outdoor enclosure is a minimum requirement for keeping tortoises properly. (F. WÜTHRICH)

Fig. 98: Boettger's tortoises spare no effort to access their favorite feeder plants. (M. MÜLLER)

ender, lungwort, orach, rock roses, heath-er, rosemary, sage, thyme, mallow, Scotch heather, St. John's wort, yellow loosestrife, yucca, cabbage palm, immortelle, Cooper's hardy ice plant, prickly pear cacti, agaves, Yuccas, and Spanish broom. Not to be used are toxic plants such as yew tree, spurge lau-rel, and oleander. No vegetation should be present right along the fence where it might serve the animals as climbing aids. The rest of the pen should sport a dry slope that offers as large as possible a variety of feeder plants. These may include speedwell, lucern, white clover, red clover, rabbitfoot clover, hop tre-foil, strand medic, birdfoot deervetch, Berg-er's clouded yellow, common kidney vetch, yarrow, shepherd's purse, dead nettle, bush vetch, garden vetch, tufted vetch, spring vetch, winter vetch, spring pea, watercress, violet, wild strawberry, woodruff, dog vio-let, wild mallow, geranium, bull thistle, field sowthistle, daisy, wild pansy, forget me not, rose bush, mint, frostweed, showy butter-cup, common dandelion, lesser hawkweed, wild carrot, burnet saxifrage, sainfoin, lamb succory, wild chicory, groundsel, cat sear, bedstraw, fireweed, ribwort, comfrey, white mullein, common sheep sorrel, chickweed, lesser stitchwort, hen and chicken, house-leek, beach morning glory, bindweed, blad-der campion, charlock mustard, and colts-foot. Succulent plants such as stonecrop and white stonecrop are appreciated by the tortoises as delicious tidbits. The tortoises are thus enabled to pick and choose from a natural food source that emulates the plant society of a dry herbaceous grassland. Ad-ditional food needs to be supplied at regular intervals in spring and fall, though, as the natural vegetation within the pen will not be

Fig. 99: An outdoor pen for semiadult tortoises (B. SEEGER)

sufficient due to climatic conditions and/or the number of animals looking for food. If the size of the enclosure permits, particularly heavily grazed areas should be fenced off from time to time to allow the vegetation to recover and regrow with an increased raw fiber content.

The soil of the outdoor enclosure should be loose and well aerated as such a substrate warms up much better than a firmly compacted one. This means that an outdoor pen with a loose sandy ground will be warmer by several degrees Celsius during the day than one with a moist loamy soil, for example. If you are forced to set up a pen in an area with a heavy soil, you will have to remove at least some 20–40 cm of the top layer and replace it with a sand/gravel mix to which is added a generous amount of dolomite calcrete available from nurseries. This creates a substrate rich in lime, which raises the calcium content in the feeder plants growing on it as well. The excavated soil may be used to sculpture the pen with one or more low hills and walkways, its size permitting of course.

The sand/gravel/lime layer may be covered once more with a few centimeters of topsoil. Its color should preferably be dark since dark soils reflect less light and as a result warm up quicker than light-colored ones. Suitable additives, such as crushed lavalite (a dark, porous volcanic rock material) are available at various granulations from building supply stores. The individual layers of soil mix over time, forming a water-permeable, rapidly drying, loose substrate. Using fertilizers is of course a no-no. To the contrary, the soil should be managed as though to emulate the nutrient-deficient soils in the homelands of these tortoises. This ensures that the feeder plants growing in it will not turn into juicy calorie bombs, but remain the valuable, protein-deficient and raw fiber-rich food they are meant to be.

Hills, large rocks and roots make fabulous elements of decoration and should be used to create visual barriers. Patches with a rough surface ensure that the claws are constantly worn down to a healthy length. The enclosure should be structured as diversely as possible. Areas with no or little vegetation, where the sun can reach the ground unobstructed, are important as basking sites and dry spots and should therefore be situated in the immediate surroundings of the sleeping quarters. More of these patches should alternate with densely vegetated areas. To prevent them from overgrowing quickly, they can be dug over in fall or early spring when the tortoises are not active in the pen anymore or not yet. Doing the same at some vegetated spots brings dormant seeds to the surface that initially create a fairly loose and diverse plant society. Some flakes of rock can serve as heat sinks at the basking spots. In order to prevent the keeper from accidentally stepping on animals hidden in the vegetation when he enters their domain, some larger rocks can be used to create walkways made of stepping-stones.

A low hill of a few square meters in size and a height of maybe 30 to 50 cm should not be missing in a pen that houses females. A spot like this is often readily chosen for laying the eggs. Although females of the species in the *Testudo hermanni* complex do not necessarily need such a hill for their eggs and will just as readily excavate their nest pits next to large boulders or bushes, making a hill available is a simple way of "directing" their respective activities to a predetermined site that can be controlled much more easily. Contradicting other authors, MEYER (1998) reported that the female *Testudo hermanni* in his care preferred the flat parts of their enclosure for burying their eggs. They simply ignored the nesting hill so popular amongst females of the eastern population group.

A sun-exposed section of the hill (sloped by maybe 30–45E) is furnished with loose garden soil, or bark compost or humus mixed with sand at a ratio of about 1:1. Such a substrate remains easily diggable. VINKE & VINKE (2004a) recommended shaping the hill like a banana of which the outer, longer outline should point south. This would enable the females to choose between a southeast-, south- or southwest-facing spot for their individual nest pits. The dark color of the hill's soil facilitates a good warming rate, which makes it particularly attractive to nesting females. If you keep a layer of light soil beneath the dark top substrate, nest pits that have been dug without the keeper watching become more obvious. BIDMON (in THIERFELDT 2004) recommended framing the nesting hill with basalt rocks, as these would provide very good heat sinks. The hill should furthermore be planted with low-growing shrubs so that small, sunny, wind-protected spots would be created all over the hill. The areas to be used by the females for their nest pits must be kept free of vegetation and not measure more than maybe 30 H 30 cm. These predetermined nesting spots need to be watered every day during the nesting season and compacted. In order to prevent that subsequently excavated pits in these small spaces lead to the destruction of previously laid clutches, all spots require regular checking.

The tortoises will routinely use "the hill" also for basking, and males often climb it to survey their "territory". Its significance as an optical barrier must not be underestimated either. Lower-ranking specimens on the run from conspecifics of the same sex, or females trying to escape males obsessed with mating, can move out of sight around the hill at least for a period of time and so enjoy peace for a while. Large rocks, logs or roots create obstacles that have to be bypassed or climbed-over and thus add to the diversity of terrain. Besides, they make it possible for the individuals to avoid each other.

Females will accept a nesting site only if it offers the right amount of moisture and temperature range. This may become a problem during cool, rainy summers. It is therefore recommendable to either set up the hill at a spot that enjoys some protection from the elements, or to offer an "alterative hill" in the greenhouse or hotbed where temperatures and moisture levels are more easily controlled. A sudden deterioration of the weather can often be compensated for, as was described by HOLFERT & HOLFERT (1999), by the ad hoc installation of a hot spot and, in the worst case scenario, by an umbrella above the nesting female. If the nesting site is situated in the greenhouse or hotbed, it is in any case advisable to set up a 200-Watt halogen spot some 40 cm above the desired nesting spot. This is a quite failsafe way to make females deposit their clutches in the immediate surroundings of this source of warmth.

Setting up a fixed feeding site inside the outdoor enclosure is not a good idea. It actually deprives the tortoises of the motivation to go and look for food. There is no need for them to even move, and they convert all their energy into growth and not into motion as they would in the wild. It is therefore a much healthier approach to instead use portable food bowls that are placed in different locations every time. Also, these are much more convenient to clean. Still clean leftovers can be left inside the pen where they slowly turn into hay. As a matter of fact, they are often much more eagerly consumed than when they are fresh and green.

Fresh water needs to be available at all times and must be replaced every day. These tortoises like to drink while they take a bath, which enables them to take in additional water via their skin and cloaca. Since they, however, also rid themselves of liquid and solid wastes at the same time, their source of water has to be cleaned every day. The bowl must also not be too deep or steep-walled in order to preclude drowning accidents. Best suited are, for example, large, shallow earthenware undertrays for flowerpots.

There are some rather astounding reports about the successful resuscitation of drowned specimens that had been submerged for longer periods of time. WICHELHAUS (2002), for example, found an about two month-old juvenile *Testudo boettgeri* drifting lifelessly on the surface of a garden pond after she had accidentally dropped and lost it there two weeks earlier. Much to her surprise the little tortoise was then found walking around a few hours later after it had minimally warmed in the sun, and the next day it resumed feeding. RAU (1981) reported about a female that had fallen into a pond of about 80 cm in depth where it remained on the bottom in the 5 °C water for days. When eventually recovered the animal looked clearly drowned, but after grass had been removed from its mouth and water had been shaken out of it with the head held down, it began to slowly return to life. Originally it was handicapped by its milky and murky eyes and had difficulty finding food and detecting obstacles, but a few weeks later it had a clean bill of health and the eyes were clear and bright once more. ROGNER (2005) presumed that the respiratory tract of tortoises might be closed off completely in an accident of this type, and the low temperatures common to the described instances might have reduced the metabolism of the involved specimens to the absolute minimum enabling them to survive these periods without a supply of oxygen.

Keeping in an indoor terrarium

As has been said before, it is best to make available to the tortoises a greenhouse or hotbed that is directly connected to the outdoor pen and that the animals can make use of in spring and fall. If this is impossible to realize, a dry, heated, and spacious indoor setup is required. However, the yearly transfer of the animals from their outdoor enclosure into the indoor terrarium in fall is often a rather unpleasant experience for both the keeper and the tortoises. The animals suddenly feel trapped and will attempt to climb over the terrarium walls. This phase may continue for weeks on end.

As far as what is an appropriate size for the indoor terrarium, the formulae legally prescribed in Germany give an indication of what is reasonable and should therefore be adopted by responsible keepers as a minimum requirement the world over. The respective ordinance states that a terrarium for one or two specimens should at least be eight times the carapace length of the largest specimen in length and half this figure in width. Ten percent have to be added to these dimensions for a third and a fourth specimen each, and twenty percent for each additional specimen after that. BRABENETZ et al. (1996) called for a minimum ground space of 1.2 m² for one or two specimens of the western population group and 2 m² in the case of the eastern population group. For every additional specimen another 0.3 and 0.5 m² should be added, respectively. The detailed minimum requirements prescribed by the respective Austrian ordinance for the keeping of animals are dedicated a separate chapter below, and although they may not apply to your location, they are certainly worth a closer look.

ZIRNGIBL (2000) considered a ground space of at least 2 m² to be adequate for one pair, and an area of 0.5 m² for a group of three to five juveniles of up to 150 g in weight.

These figures indicate that keeping a breeding colony consisting of one or two adult males and three or four females neces-

Fig. 100: An example of keeping young *Testudo boettgeri* indoors (B. SEEGER)

sitates a terrarium that easily fills an entire room.

The walls of the terrarium should be at least three times as high as the height of the largest tortoise. Preparing for the distinct possibility that all tortoises gather in one corner and climb on top of each other, there is still a good chance that one specimen manages to climb over the wall and falls down on the other side. This needs to be prevented by mounting a barrier ledge on the inside at the top or by increasing the height of the walls.

With regard to the placement of the terrarium it needs to be said that it should be well lit, but not exposed to direct sunlight. If the sun shines directly into it, there is a distinct risk of overheating. A room with normal room temperature is ideal, but it is important that night temperatures there do not constantly lie above 20 °C. The terrarium also must be protected from drafts, for which reason the relative position of windows etc. must be given particular attention.

Regarding the design of an indoor set-up, MÄHN & WILMS (2001) provided many very useful hints. The terrarium must only contain materials that do not rot or mold readily. Since these tortoises love to dig in the ground, part of their enclosure should provide an opportunity to do so. This is easily realized by filling a section with sand or a sand/soil mix. This area should also be covered from light and prying eyes by an optical barrier, or better even, an artificial "cave" in the form of a box made from planed wood that is just a little higher than the highest specimen living in the terrarium. The substrate is to be moistened every now and then so that it never becomes wet, but does not dry out completely either.

The remaining bottom surface is best covered with modeling clay from which you can easily create surface structures that make the setup appealing to the eye. The clay is distributed and sculpted when moist. Once you are happy with your "landscaping", it is covered with a thin layer of sand or a sand/soil mix as a final touch. After it has dried it will form a hard and wear-resistant surface. A particularly natural appearance is achieved if the ground rises toward the back of the indoor pen. Sloping "steps" are ideal for this purpose. The raised rear part then also contains the predetermined oviposition spot.

In order to raise the level of humidity somewhat for the night and to prevent the bottom substrate from drying out completely and producing a lot of dust, the ground should be misted lightly in the evenings. The recommended clay ground makes cleaning easy, absorbs water readily and thus counteracts the accumulation of stagnant moisture. By releasing the absorbed water slowly during the drying out process, it contributes to a healthy level of humidity. The substrate used in the sand pit is largely contained there and can be easily replaced when the need arises.

Many keepers have made positive experiences with a substrate of sand or thoroughly rinsed, round-grained gravel, but in both cases there is a need for daily cleaning measures, and the bedding needs to be replaced completely at regular intervals. Tortoises have a surprising metabolic turnover, and keeping them in sanitary conditions requires an investment into work and time, which the prospect keeper must not underestimate.

Although often used for a substrate, bark mulch or beech wood shavings must be advised against. Both carry a distinct risk for the tortoises to accidentally swallow it with food and then cause injuries in the digestive tract that may end fatally!

It is of utmost importance that the females have a spot of diggable substrate available that is deep enough for them to excavate nest pits. This may become a critical factor when they encounter a cold spell during spring that necessitates a temporary retransfer to their indoor terrarium. A depth of one and a half times the carapace length of the largest female should be safe, although there may of course be individual deviations from this rule. If such a spot is not available, the eggs may simply be dropped anywhere on the hard ground where most of them will break on impact. The respective box or trough is filled with a substrate mixed from simple garden or forest soil or bark humus and river sand at a ratio of two to one. A suitably powerful halogen spotlight is mounted above this site at a distance of about 50 cm in order to provide the necessary bright light and warmth. The females will then choose a spot that appeals most to their instincts. The substrate must not be too dry, because bark humus in particular will then keep on falling back into the pit. Eventually the female may just give up trying to excavate a proper nest pit. It is therefore necessary to mist this spot on a regular basis and keep it slightly moist. Care must be taken to not make it wet, because the females will then reject it as a nesting site. If you cover the nesting site with a thin layer of wood shavings, you will easily notice when digging activities have taken place.

Some large rocks and roots can be used for decoration. The former need to be positioned in a manner that makes it impossible for the tortoises to topple them and become buried under them in the process. These items invite the tortoises to climb and thus further their behavioral enrichment. With some skill the terrarium is structured into various sectors. The rocks and roots furthermore serve as obstacles, between which the animals will establish paths that are used with varying frequency. When setting up these obstacles, you need to ensure that they can pass by them easily; tightness should be exclusive to the shelters because it is only there that the tortoises like to be in touch with walls and ceilings.

A small waterbowl, which is to be cleaned and refilled with fresh water every day, completes the furnishing.

Plants in the terrarium are not only unnecessary, but also impractical because many of them are just seen as a welcome addition to the tortoises' menu. If desired for esthetical aspects, a few potted greens can be positioned where the animals cannot reach them. Suitable plants for this purpose include cacti, euphorbias, cherry laurel (*Laurus nobilis*), green lilies (genus *Chlorophytum*), aloe (genus *Aloe*), sansevieras (genus *Sansevieria*), dragon trees (genus *Dracaena*), spiderwort (genus *Tradeskantia*) and species of the genera *Echeveria*, *Kalanchoe* and *Sedum*. Toxic plants have to be avoided, of course, but because little is as yet known about the tolerance of tortoises toward vegetal substances, there is always a risk involved if you try out a new plant. A list of definitely unwholesome plants can be found in DENNERT (2001).

As far as the illumination of the winter enclosure is concerned, you need to create a brightly lit environment.

HIGHFIELD (1996a) recommended that an array of 40 watt full-spectrum fluorescent tubes (True-Lite® and Sun-Glo®) be used. These would not only come closest to natural sunlight, but more important, also range into the ultraviolet part of the spectrum. The latter is also true for metal vapor (HQI) and mercury high-pressure lamps (HQL). These can be used for both general lighting and localized light and hot spots. Size and placement of the terrarium dictate how many spotlights may be required.

Day temperatures should range between 20 and 35 °C and reach peaks of 35–50 °C right under the hotspots. These values are usually ensured if the lamps are hung about 20 cm above the ground. At night, temperatures should decrease to 15–22 °C. An indoor terrarium necessitates an additional supply with UV-radiation, for which purpose lamps such as Osram's Ultra Vita Lux® 300, Philips TL 05, TL 09, TL 12 are suitable choices. Ultraviolet light is required for the synthesis of vitamin D3, which in turn is needed to metabolize calcium. The effects of such treatment become visible in increased levels of activity and improved food intake. The lamp should be installed at a distance of about 70–75 cm above the surface of the terrarium bottom and used up to three times per week for periods of initially five minutes. The duration of the radiation sessions should then be gradually increased to fifteen minutes. Some parts of the terrarium should be kept altogether more shaded and cooler. Large planting containers are often enough to provide these cool retreats.

Legal husbandry requirements in Austria

In Austria, the ordinance governing the keeping of animals, effective as of 17.12.2004, prescribes in detail what is required for the keeping of these tortoises. Although this is legally binding only for keepers living in that country, it may be of general interest and provide an idea of what officials think provides these tortoises with conditions that take care of their natural requirements. Also, it is a handy summary of many points discussed in more detail above.

Minimum size of the enclosure:

1–2 specimens of up to 6 cm in carapace length = 0,5 m² (for each additional specimen add 0.2 m²); 6–12 cm = 1,0 m² (+ 0,4 m²); larger than 12 cm = 2,0 m² (+ 0,5 m²).

Indoor terrarium:

Furnishings: must be structured with plants, rocks and branches; shelters; water bowl; HQI- and heating spotlights.

Substrate: loamy soil, sand, must permit digging, scree in places. Temperatures: 25–30 °C during the day; localized hotspots with heating spotlights that provide temperatures of 35–45 °C; nightly decreases by ca. 10 °C [the necessary presence of both warm and cool zones is mentioned only for *Testudo hermanni*, but in practical terms is applicable also to the other two species].

Photoperiod: 6–14 hours of daylight depending on the season; HQI-flooders for high light intensity; UV-radiation on a daily basis.

Humidity: 40–60 %; 60–80 % for juveniles; misting daily.

Outdoor enclosure:

Site: sunny, protected from wind.

Furnishing: dry shelter hut furnished with substrate for burying; opening of shelter hut east- to southeast-facing if possible; sunny spots where the substrate dries up quickly; hill for oviposition; shaded spots and hiding places beneath small bushes, shrubs, rocks, roots etc.; waterhole; for juveniles, metal mesh cover as protection from birds and predatory animals.

Substrate: flowering meadow, loamy soil, sand, scree in places.

Temperatures: at least 15 °C during the day; at least 10 °C at night.

Particular notes: Hibernation for 3–5 months at 4–6 °C

Feeding

Food for these tortoises should be based on plant matter that is rich in calcium (ca. 2 %) and raw fibers (at least 12 %, better 20–30 %). It should not contain easily digested, ballast-deficient constituents (such as tender lettuce leaves and herbs, sweet fruit) and starch, or foods rich in carbohydrates (such as muesli, bread, pastry, pasta or rice). There should

Fig. 101: Offering a variety of wild herbs for food is just as important in the indoor terrarium. (W. SCHMIDT)

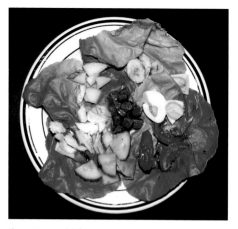

Figs. 102&103: Bad (left) and good examples of feeding Mediterranean tortoises (F. HULBERT)

also be little fat (10% at maximum) and not more than maybe 20% in proteins (25% in the case of juveniles). All percentages quoted here refer to dry mass. The food should have a calcium : phosphorus ratio of 1.5–2 : 1.

If the food is too nutritious, the animals tend to build up fat, initially in the liver, and later also beneath the peritoneum between the muscles and under the skin. While this condition is not particularly conducive to their health per se, it may be aggravated by an improperly conducted overwintering, which results in the fats not being metabolized properly and literally poisoning and killing the affected animal. Vegetables are often too rich in carbohydrates. Food that is deficient in raw fibers is metabolized far too quickly in the fermentation chamber that is the intestine. The pH existing there is altered and the result is the formation of alcohol and gases. This may in turn have devastating effects on the metabolic bacterial fauna in the intestine, which is then often replaced by much less beneficial bacteria such as E. coli and/or Salmonella. The lingering period is sometimes reduced to less than twenty-four hours, which is insufficient for a complete digestive process. The results are often a rapid onset of digestive problems and diarrhea, which appear to render the affected animals susceptible to infestations with flagellates and parasitic worms that the soft feces are no longer able to mechanically flush out. Most tortoises will instinctively try and remedy the diarrhea by consuming soil, which in turn may lead to most severe cases of constipation.

A diet of soft or even mushy foods furthermore paves the way for a development of the so-called "parrot beak" that is consequence of a lack of wear on the horny ledges of the upper jaws. Their excessive growth will eventually seriously impede the intake of food.

Having said all this, the question arises of what to feed these animals. Experience has shown that most indigenous wild herbs and a number of cultivated plants are compatible with the needs of these tortoises. In general, the flowers of dandelion make a particularly popular food, but preferences are very much a matter of individual likes and dislikes here as well. A suitable healthy diet may therefore be composed of, e.g., the leaves and flowers of dandelion, rose and hibiscus, lucern, vine leaves, pansy, kohlrabi and radish leaves, thistle, coltsfoot, prickly and wall lettuce, red

Fig. 104: Hay cobs make a good supplementary food that is rich in fiber and low in protein. (F. HULBERT)

purse, corn poppy, rape, yellow mustard, feeder lupine, stonecrop, white stonecrop, mullein, common evening primrose, chickweed, ribwort, garden vetch, spring pea, goose grass, vervain mallow, yellow goat's beard, mallow, balm mint, horse radish, wild chicory, yarrow, coneflower/echinacea, geranium, various types of vetch, garlic mustard, woodruff, chamomile, goatsfoot, absinth, water cress, nasturtium, garden cress, parsley, carrot green, melon leaves, and the young leaves of mulberry and birch trees.

This summery staple diet is obviously quite impossible to substitute completely at certain latitudes during the cold parts of the year. An alternative basis needs to be established then for which straw, leafy vegetables and lettuces have to be used. Suitable plants include green cabbage, marrowstem kale, Italian dandelion, radicchio, chicory, ru-

and white clover, cat sear, groundsel, hawkweed, sage, daisies, comfrey, lady's mantle, field penny cress, houseleek, stinging and dead nettle, nipplewort, marigold, shepherd's

Fig. 105: A Boettger's tortoise with a good appetite (B. SEEGER)

cola, silver beet, portulaca, fennel, sprouts, spinach, and Roman, common, iceberg, and field lettuce and endives. Note though, that spinach and the mentioned types of collard should not be offered at large quantities.

The animals will obviously eat just about anything green that is offered, but the fiber content in the mentioned vegetables and lettuces is too low and therefore needs to be raised. There are various means available for just that and at the same time reducing the moisture content. For one, you can leave the food to wither somewhat before offering it. Then you can mix it with hay cobs that are naturally rich in raw fibers and poor in fats and proteins; AGROBS® and Reptosan H® are just two appropriate products for this purpose (see below).

Fruit and vegetables should not account for more than 5–10 and 5–15 % of the food, respectively. They should also not be offered more frequently than maybe once a week. Of all the types of fruit, DENNERT (2001) regarded blackberry, currant, pineapple, banana, kiwi, fig, prickly pear, mangosteen, papaw and orange to be suitable additions to the main food. For vegetables she recommended radish, beans, zucchini, kohlrabi and carrot. Fruit and vegetables mainly serve to provide sufficient amounts of moisture. An oversupply of these carries, however, the risk of metabolic disorders that manifest themselves in diarrhea, colics, and infestations with flagellates and parasitic gut worms.

As has been mentioned in the chapter "Diet", carrion and invertebrates are occasionally consumed in the wild, and this also applies to an outdoor enclosure. This does by no means suggest an extent that would justify the feeding of these tortoises with cat or dog food, though. The results of a diet that contains large amounts of protein include an overly rapid growth (manifest in the formation of "humps" in the carapace), kidney damage, gout, and – very often – premature death.

As far as commercial foods are concerned, only the purely vegetal so-called hay cobs with their high content of raw fibers and low content of fats and proteins are suitable as supplements. Safe to use are products such as AGROBS® and Reptosan H® that are specifically made for the use with tortoises. Their beneficial effects from the viewpoints of veterinary medicine and dietary science were discussed by DENNERT (2000a, b). Most of the other commercial types of "dry food for tortoises" are simply unsuited for tortoises owing to their high protein content. The worst that can be fed to them are dog and cat foods.

Many keepers reported that their animals would initially not accept the mentioned hay cobs. VINKE & VINKE (2004b) solved this common problem by initially soaking the cobs in water, adding a generous dash of a multivitamin juice, and mixed about 5 kg of the cobs with three large handfuls of dry food without meat but with vegetables for dogs. Their tortoises were soon used to this new food that its "pepping" could first be reduced and then became entirely unnecessary. Other keepers obtained the same results with similar "recipes". Another advantage of the soaked hay cobs is that this food leaves smudges on the mouths of the tortoises, which is a clear indicator of whether all tortoises have resumed feeding after hibernation in spring.

Because these animals can also be literally "fattened" with vegetal proteins, foods like dandelion and clover should only be fed with moderation – no matter how much the tortoises love them. The seasonal changes in the availability of food in nature also need to be emulated in human care. Besides the natural deficiency in proteins, these changes are the main reason why tortoises in the wild produce rather regular growth rings and no shells deformed by humps. As summers in central Europe, and in many other parts of the world where these tortoises are kept, are rainy and comparatively cool though, there is an almost uninterrupted supply of fresh greens while regular cold spells hamper an optimized digestion. It is therefore often a matter of lucky circumstances whether or not the tortoises grow at a regular pace. As has been described above in the Chapter "Diet", the animals find food during the southern European summer mainly in the form of dry herbs and grasses only. This suggests that the tortoises in captivity should also only be able to graze on young, protein-rich shoots in spring, but then be forced to make do with fully grown, ballast-rich and at the same time protein-deficient plants and wilted, dried-up or artificially dried greens such as hay during the summer months. In fall, when the rains return in the wild, they should once more have access to fresh and new herbs. Particularly suitable for this purpose are perennial herbs as these grow and sprout also in fall. Plants of this type include, for example, dandelion, plantain, various types of clover, garlic mustard, nipplewort, and dead nettle (WILLIG 2005).

Feeding should take place in the morning and in the late afternoon, but no large portions should be offered on either occasion. Days of lent as a result of bad weather are entirely normal and in fact contribute to a regular and healthy growth of the animals. Withholding food during favorable weather,

Fig. 106: Lettuce should only be given every now and then as a "substitute" (F. HULBERT)

Fig. 107: *Testudo boettgeri* feeding on dandelion (W. SCHMIDT)

Fig. 108: Fresh drinking water must always be available to tortoises. (*Chimaira* Archives)

on the other hand, is unnatural for vegetarians such as these.

If you stick to these recommendations on feeding, the food supplies protein, raw fiber and trace elements at optimum ratios, even in the cases of gravid females and juveniles. Cuttlefish bone, calcium for puppies, mussel grit, whetstones for birds, and crushed egg shells (which need to be heated to counteract the risk of salmonella) all provide sources of additional calcium. Another alternative exists in the form of bones of wild animals that have been boiled and then buried for some time in a compost heap or in the garden until they have turned brittle. Owing to the risk of medication deposits, the bones of fattened livestock animals should not be used. The tortoises should be able to help themselves freely to calcium. Contrary to many recommendations in the literature it is not advisable to add calcium preparations of whatever kind to their regular food. This "forces" the calcium upon them, and nobody is really certain (yet?) about what might be a proper dosage. It could therefore be that in the end you cause more damage than good. The same actually applies to the routine addition of vitamin preparations.

Although not all representatives of the species portrayed here will drink on a regular basis, fresh water should be available to them at all times.

This chapter is destined to end with a little anecdote on a member of the *Testudo hermanni* species group that became the subject of a court battle. Some years ago, a Boettger's tortoise lived in an outdoor enclosure near the city of Mainz in Germany. One day the animal managed to escape and dared to enter the property of a neighbor where it nibbled a few holes into the juicy heads of lettuce growing there. Their raging grower claimed compensation for damage of property amounting to about US$ 25, which the owner of the tortoise found exaggerated. The dispute was taken to court with the central question being, "how much in monetary value did the tortoise eat?" The court requested an expert's opinion for which none other than Professor Bernhard GRZIMEK was contracted. Upon detailed research his assessment was that a tortoise of the given size would be able to eat lettuce to the value of about $ 1.50 during the given period of time. The magnitude of court, expert's, and lawyers' fees remained undisclosed.

Hibernation

A cool hibernation period is crucial if these tortoises are to stay healthy and reproduce.

This applies, of course, only to healthy and strong specimens. Failing to observe such a period of rest has negative effects on the overall health of the tortoises and causes a desynchronization of the sexual cycles, resulting in low fertilization ratios up to the loss of entire generations.

At some point in mid-September, the animals should therefore be contained in their greenhouse or hotbed. This prevents them from burying themselves somewhere in their outdoor pen. It also softens the drop in temperatures and thus enables the tortoises to reach their preferred daily body temperatures for an additional period of time that extends far into fall. This is also the time when all specimens should once more be subjected to a thorough external health check so that possible injuries or diseases are discovered before the animals begin to hibernate. Convalescent specimens should then only go through a truncated overwintering, whereas sick and/or emaciated or even newly acquired ones may be best housed warm in an indoor terrarium and spared the stress of hibernation altogether. Female tortoises also need to be checked for possible late gravidity. If they carry eggs again, they obviously need to be given the opportunity to lay them before they are sent into hibernation.

Because the weather in September is often already rather cold in some regions, central Europe included, an unheated greenhouse or hotbed may not provide the desired temperatures. If this is the case, artificial heating (for maybe four to six hours daily) may be required that will enable the tortoises to remain active until November. Artificial lighting may also be needed, and both should be timed as to emulate gradual decreases in intensity. With the shortening of the hours of daylight and night temperatures that at this time of the year may occasionally drop to 3–7 °C, the animals will reduce their food intake

and eventually stop feeding altogether. Activity and thermoregulatory and social behaviors are still continued for a while. The tortoises will regularly seek the hot spot beneath the heating lamps and produce feces; it is just that they do not feed anymore. Once the digestive tract has been emptied, they remain in their shelters for increasingly long periods of time and eventually bury themselves up to 20 cm deep for hibernation. Females usually begin to do so much earlier than males, which often continue to congregate under the heating lamps until these are eventually switched off.

Various keepers have noted that some specimens would not bury themselves. In these cases it was mostly futile if the keepers buried them instead, and they would usually reappear above the ground some time later. A better solution to keep them from harm would then be to overwinter them in the house.

In the existing literature it is often stated that the animals should be made to empty their bowels completely for which purpose they should be bathed in warm water. Most experts today agree, however, that this is entirely unnecessary. In fact, it is today believed that some of the commonly experienced problems, such as the refusal of food after hibernation and the resultant health issues due to enfeeblement, may be ascribed to the intensity of defecation induced by these warm baths before hibernation. This procedure also reactivates the animals' metabolic functions and causes substantial stress to their cardiocirculatory system. One should remember that no warm baths are available to these animals in nature either, and still, there appear to be no problems of this type after hibernation.

If the tortoises happen to be severely infested with parasites before hibernation, this is a genuine problem that needs to be addressed. Parasitic worms will maintain their metabolism throughout winter, even though the tortoises cease to feed. Their metabolic waste products may eventually overcome the intestinal barriers and cause a sepsis that is potentially lethal. Another result may be a post-hibernation ileus (intestinal obstruction), if the worms have formed a dense skein in the appendix that now effectively blocks the intestine. Deworming right before hibernation would, however, be irresponsible since there is a distinct chance that the dead worms and/or unicellular organisms are not excreted anymore, but mainly because it is quite certain that the agents of the medication will be not metabolized to an extent that is safe. Possible results include liver damage and blood poisoning, both of which are life-threatening conditions. Cases of blood poisoning often manifest themselves externally by the formation of large, dark red patches (hemorrhages) right under the horny scutes of the shell that do not fade even under pressure. Ideal points of time for the administration of parasiticides are therefore in spring and early summer, but not later than six to eight weeks before the commencement of hibernation.

The common practice of oiling the shell before hibernation or in general is entirely unnecessary.

Once all specimens have eventually disappeared and temperatures are constantly low, the tortoises may be dug up with great care and transferred to a cold place in the house where they are safe from extreme temperatures. In order to not expose them to substantial temperature fluctuation in the process, this should preferably be done in the evening hours.

A more natural type of overwintering is, however, to leave them in their greenhouse or hotbed (see below) because they have buried themselves in a familiar environment and will awake there as well. The only general exception concerns juveniles of less than 200 g in weight; these should always be overwintered in the house where they can be monitored closely.

If the tortoises are kept in an indoor terrarium during the transitional period of the year, preparations for their hibernation need to begin about eight weeks prior to their scheduled overwintering. Firstly, lighting in-

Fig. 109: Many keepers overwinter their tortoises successfully in a hotbed. (F. WÜTHRICH)

tensity and duration are gradually reduced to zero, and temperatures are lowered to 10–12 °C on a step-by-step basis as well. About two weeks before they commence with their hibernation, all food supply is stopped, and the keeper must not yield to the tortoises' begging that is likely to ensue. Eventually the animals will bury themselves in the substrate of the terrarium.

Places in cold, dark rooms, such as garages, storerooms and unheated cellars, have been proved suitable for hibernation many times over. However, overwintering the tortoises in a greenhouse or hotbed, where temperatures may rise to 20 °C on warm and sunny days, as they would in nature, was considered a more "natural" way of hibernation by some authors (e.g., WILMS & LÖHR 2000) as opposed to the rather constantly low values in those rooms. According to FRIESLEBER (2005), the foundations of the greenhouse or hotbed should in this case reach at least 50 cm deep into the soil, though, and be additionally insulated on the inside for this purpose. If the animals are to be overwintered in their hotbed, the soil should be dug over and thoroughly moistened in September already. It is then furnished with a good layer of beech leaf litter. Adverse effects of the increased moisture level are not to be expected because it is only a brief period of time, and by mid-October, when the tortoises begin to bury themselves in the substrate, an adequate level of moisture should have restored itself. Now the soil should be neither wet nor dry so that no additional moistening should become necessary during the actual hibernation period.

Once all tortoises have disappeared into the ground, it is additionally covered with a layer of straw and another of leaf litter, and the entire construction is protected from rain and snow with a translucent tarmac. Such a hotbed should at least have a ground space of

1 by 1 m since larger volumes provide greater safety margins against freezing through.

If the tortoises are to hibernate in a greenhouse, it is usually sufficient to fill their shelter hut with beech leaf litter.

The advantages of overwintering them in a greenhouse or hotbed are not only a fairly low workload for the keeper, but also and foremost that the tortoises are enabled to determine their own pace and rhythm. The smaller space inside a hotbed reduces their options considerably, though.

An important aspect of overwintering tortoises in such an outdoor building is to protect them from mice and rats or other potential predators that might be particular to your area of residence. A reasonably fine-meshed fence that is sunk into the ground should keep undesirables out. A concrete floor, on the other hand is not recommendable as it prevents the exchange of moisture with the surrounding ground.

This type of overwintering ensures that temperatures beneath the layer of leaf litter do not decrease below 0 °C even if the outside temperatures sink to values of -15 to -20 °C. At a depth of 20 cm, temperatures usually still range between 2 and 4 °C on these occasions.

Overwintering in cold rooms is best effected by using individual boxes that are placed standing freely at elevated spots. The latter prevents frost from reaching the containers via the walls or floor. Since the tortoises will obviously continue to breathe air, their boxes must not be airtight. Suitable materials include untreated wood, but also various types of durable plastic (e.g., hods from a hardware store). In order to protect the tortoises from vermin and from falling out of the box when they begin to resume their activity, its top should be covered with wiremesh. The box itself should be about three times as high as the carapace length of its content, and about four times the plastron surface area in ground space. It is first furnished with a layer of blowing clay that has been soaked in water before. This layer serves to raise humidity levels inside the hibernation quarters. It is then followed by a mix of slightly moist beech leaf litter, garden soil and river sand. Other materials may do the job as well, but you should in general avoid dusty substrates such as peat, for example. The height of the substrate should be equal to about twice the carapace length.

With these preparations completed, the tortoise can now be placed on the substrate and covered with a layer of beech leaf litter. If a specimen remains animated in spite of low temperatures and moves about in its winter quarters for longer than a few days, it may be an indication of a disease. The respective animal then needs to be monitored closely and possibly examined by a veterinarian.

Fig. 110: Hibernation in a refrigerator is a good and practicable method. (S. THIERFELDT)

The winter boxes should be checked every three to four weeks. This is to see whether the animals are still buried and to ensure the moisture level of the substrate is still appropriate. The substrate should be moist and crumbly and must not smell stale. If it is too dry, it will desiccate the animals, which causes them excessive weight loss and possibly leads to respiratory infections. Wet nose syndrome and gummed-up sunken eyes in spring are then often the result. Misting the substrate lightly if and when necessary preempts those undesirable problems. This requires some good instinct, however, since a soaked substrate molds and rots easily and causes a different set of health hazards in the form of skin and shell rot.

To say it with the words of ZIRNGIBL (2000), "Now all there is left for you to do is to hope that you did everything right." The advantages of overwintering your tortoises in the house are an improved level of control and conditions that are sure to be without extremes. The great disadvantage is that it often involves temperatures that are simply too high. If you therefore settle for an air vent to a cellar instead, you need to ensure that it is really safe from rain and thaw and cannot be reached by severe frost. Sometimes the latter only takes leaving the respective cellar window open.

Overwintering tortoises in old and vibration-free refrigerators has been proved particularly well-suited for members of the *Testudo hermanni* species group. This necessitates the tortoises to be accommodated in small, airy boxes of at least three times the size of the respective animal. These are filled with a slightly moist mix of sand, soil and beech leaf litter. Every box is covered with a lid that has been perforated and so makes provision for an exchange of air. A water-filled tray is placed on the bottom of the fridge as to ensure that an appropriate level of humidity is maintained. Another way of achieving the same goal is to place wet towels between the individual boxes. The boxes are then stacked inside the fridge. The substrate in each box needs to be checked for its moisture every six to eight weeks and remoistened if necessary. Opening the fridge door for brief periods every three to four days, ensures proper ventilation.

The advantages of "fridge hibernation" are a setup that is easily monitored, constant conditions, and full control over temperatures and duration of the overwintering. Two major disadvantages are that the animals can be conditioned for hibernation only with difficulty in a fridge, and that you are bound to run out of space quickly if you have to overwinter a larger collection.

If you decide that "fridge-hibernation" is right for you and your tortoises, you need to take into consideration that many refrigerators, and older models in particular, offer substantially different temperatures at various spots inside. Near the rear wall of the appliance it may be particularly cold so that the hibernation boxes must not be in contact with it. The difference between the lowest and the highest level may be as much as 2 °C. All this makes it necessary that you check and map the exact temperatures throughout the entire appliance.

The substrate is not the only thing that needs be checked at regular intervals; the animals themselves must also be monitored.

Fig. 111: Overwintering tortoises in a refrigerator ensures constant conditions and makes monitoring easy. (B. SEEGER)

This involves taking a look at their nostrils, the mouth, eyes and eyelids, the cloaca, and checking the shell for possible hemorrhages beneath the scutes. The eyelids are good indicators for the state of hydration of a specimen. The lower lid must not form a deep furrow, be gummed-up with its upper counterparts, or sunken in. Weighing the tortoises every few weeks enables you to realize whether they are losing weight rapidly.

Specimens that turn out to be medically unfit for hibernation only right before they are supposed to commence their wintry period of dormancy, are often rather resistant to warm overwintering as a result of their hormonal programming. In these cases the photoperiod has to be lengthened once more to 12–14 hours of daylight using high-output lamps. Localized basking spots offering temperatures of 40–45 °C must be set up next to cool retreats to enable the animal to thermoregulate at optimum levels. If all this does nothing to "prevent" the affected tortoise from hibernating, BAUR & HOFF-

Fig. 112: Juvenile *Testudo boettgeri* shortly after emerging from their winter quarters (B. SEEGER)

MANN (2004) recommend complying with its hormonal "inner clock", but restricting the period of rest at low temperatures to just a few weeks. Thereafter the temperatures are raised once more, fooling the tortoise's organism into assuming it was spring again. Keeping an animal "awake" by force results in a rapid loss of weight because fat reserves are used up while no feeding takes place that could replenish them at this stage. Consulting with an experienced veterinarian is advisable as it will be he who must take care of the sick tortoise afterwards.

Hibernation should take place at temperatures of 2–8 °C, with a range of 3–7 °C being preferable. Although a short-term (!) drop to +0.5–1 °C has, according to observations made by various keepers, no negative effects, extreme values like these ought to be avoided. Temperatures above the 8 °C-mark keep the metabolism of the liver going, which is often the cause of so-called "posthibernal anorexia" (a consumption syndrome following hibernation) (see below). It is best to monitor temperatures with a digital thermometer whose probe is placed in the substrate right next to the tortoise.

Briefly rising temperatures during the transitional periods, but even warm spells during winter, are no problem for specimens that have enjoyed a healthy diet during their preceding active period. However, if temperatures rise above 12 °C for longer periods of time, the animals may wake up and reappear on the surface.

As far as the duration of their hibernation is concerned, *Testudo hermanni*, *Testudo hercegovinensis* and specimens of *Testudo boettgeri* originating from warmer parts of their distribution ranges should be overwintered for about three months. Four to five months are appropriate for representatives of *Testudo boettgeri* from the cooler regions of southeastern Europe.

When temperatures rise to values around the 12–15 °C mark in spring, the tortoises soon begin to move about inside their winter quarters. If they were hibernating in a hotbed outside, and provided there is no chance of renewed frost, the thick outer layer of leaf litter can now be removed so that the first warm days may wake the tortoises up. Then the straw and most of the inner layer of leaf litter can also be removed so that only a thin blanket of leaf litter remains for the time being. It is best heaped up in a place or two as to provide shelters for as long as the animals are not yet fully active. One corner is fully cleared though to make space for a freshly filled water dish and some herbal hay.

If they were overwintered in a greenhouse, the tortoises usually also wake up without assistance by the increasing intensity of the spring sun that drives temperatures up. Those hibernating in a cellar or fridge can now be placed back into their hotbed, greenhouse or terrarium. In the case of a hotbed, the animals should be covered with beech leaf litter, and if they are moved to a greenhouse, they are placed inside their shelter huts. Again, the transfer should take place at night in order to spare them sudden radical changes in temperatures.

The hotbed or greenhouse can and should be opened on sunny days without frost, first, so that the animals can once more enjoy unfiltered sunlight, and second, to prevent the hotbed or greenhouse from becoming unseasonably warm. Once the night temperatures reach about 15 °C with the aid of a heating lamp and the days are additionally warmed with halogen spotlights, the first tortoise will soon appear outside its shelter in order to bask. This is the right time to now also remove the last of the leaf litter. Sunny and warm weather draws the animals outside where they can bask in the sun. The doors of their shelter house must be kept closed on days with bad weather, though, as to prevent the tortoises from leaving it, burying themselves unnoticed somewhere in the outdoor enclosure, and being exposed to the moist and cold conditions that are likely to prevail there.

When the animals have resumed their activity, they should be bathed in lukewarm water. This enables them to replenish body fluids lost during hibernation, and flush metabolic waste products from the kidneys. It altogether favors their readjustment to an active life. The tortoises are exposed to brief but heavy showers also in nature at this time of the season, and they seek out deep puddles to bathe in and drink extensively. Spring rains in central Europe are too long-lasting by comparison and are usually accompanied by substantially dropping temperatures so that the tortoises are unable to make use of them. They much rather have to shelter from them in the protection of their retreats. Various keepers have made the best experiences with using chamomile tea of about 30 °C for their "bath water".

If the animals are moved from their winter quarters to a terrarium first, its lighting is switched on and the heating raised gradually only a few days later. The photoperiod is likewise slowly prolonged from initially eight to later twelve hours according to the photoperiod outside.

The tortoises will usually soon resume feeding. If a specimen remains without appetite after hibernation, a drop in blood sugar levels is the result. The ensuing low glycogen content in the liver requires the attention of a veterinarian. As a general rule, all animals should now be subjected to a detailed health check in order to identify possible injuries and diseases that may need to be treated before they become really serious. Again, the nostrils, mouth, eyes and eyelids, and the cloaca and shell, require particular checking.

Also, you may want to check each specimen's weight and compare it with the figure taken before hibernation. The weight loss during hibernation should not exceed 5%. If it is more than 5%, it indicates that hibernation conditions were too dry; a weight loss of more than 15% is a distinct health hazard.

In a study conducted in the 1970', the British veterinarian Dr. Oliphant JACKSON compared weights and sizes of healthy versus sick members of the *Testudo hermanni* and *graeca* species groups. He concluded that there was an optimum body weight that could be used for evaluating the state of health of a specimen, but also indicated the quality of its hibernation (e.g., JACKSON 1978a, b). Based on his data he developed a graphic that was meant to enable every owner of a tortoise representing these species groups to determine whether a specimen was too light, too heavy, or had a "perfect" weight for its size. This diagram became known as the "Jackson index" or "Jackson curve", and many inexperienced tortoise keepers and veterinarians soon thought it to be the ultimate tool that allowed a reliable determination of the state of health of a tortoise without the need of complicated and time-consuming tests in laboratories. However, it must be borne in mind that this method focuses on just one criterion, i.e., the weight, which is a variable that can be influenced by a range of factors in tortoises in particular. For example, it is not at all unusual that an adult *Testudo boettgeri* disposes of 50 ml urine at once, which means a sudden change in weight of nearly 50 g as well. A gravid female whose body cavity is filled with eggs almost to the brim can eat only very little, but still appears to be rather heavy. Even a human with the ideal weight for his size cannot by default be considered entirely healthy.

It is therefore indispensable to also take into consideration other factors besides the weight when attempting to evaluate the state

of health in a tortoise. These range from the appearance of the eyes and nostrils, via that of feces and urine, to the overall behavior. What JACKSON achieved, though, is that many tortoise keepers (at least in the UK) now weigh their animals on a regular basis and in the process are able to note drastic changes at a reasonably early stage if there is a health problem.

A study similar to that of JACKSON's was the one conducted by MÜLLER & SCHWEIGER (2002). It also included *Testudo marginata*, *Testudo kleinmanni*, *Testudo werneri*, and the Central Asian tortoises of the genus *Agrionemys* and led to comparable conclusions. These two authors were quite aware of the possible pitfalls of the "Jackson curve", but were most certainly right in stating that an index value much below the minimum of their and JACKSON's graphs would be reason enough to subject a specimen to further health tests. In such a case, the husbandry conditions need to be checked by and large. If no shortcomings can be detected in this area, a disease may be suspected. MÜLLER & SCHWEIGER (2002) developed from their data a table of minimum hibernation weights, that is the weight a tortoise should at least have to be sent into cold hibernation with a good conscience. Because this table is easier understood than the indices calculated by MÜLLER, SCHWEIGER and JACKSON and is very useful in practical terms, it is reproduced on page 147. Note that only specimens measuring between 10 and 27.9 cm in carapace length have been taken into consideration since the numbers of both smaller and larger specimens were too low to produce conclusive values.

Breeding

As has been mentioned before in a byline, the species dealt with here are meanwhile bred by many keepers, in large numbers, and in many instances over several generations. It can be

Size class (mm)	Minimum hibernation weight (g)
100–109	187
110–119	250
120–129	336
130–139	395
140–149	540
150–159	625
160–169	790
170–179	884
180–189	998
190–199	1.000
200–209	1.160
210–219	1.360
220–229	1.480
230–239	1.545
240–249	1.625
250–259	2.050
260–269	2.300
270–279	2.430

ten sets in earlier in central Europe than in southern Europe, and summer sometimes resembles premature fall, this temperature-dependent mating season may coincide with times when conditions are less than favorable, last too long, or are too intense.

A fairly firm pecking order exists amongst the males at least during the mating season. It is initially established through biting and ramming fights. This is the reason why territorial disputes are limited to rare and brief squabbles between males even on muggy warm days. Otherwise, the animals coexist side by side and can therefore be kept together in their outdoor enclosure throughout the year.

Quite brutal fights may ensue, though, when a new male is introduced to an existing group. This suggests that the tortoises are quite able to recognize individuals. ZIRNGIBL (2000) described specimens from the western parts of the distribution range as far more tolerant in this respect than their eastern European cousins.

Males often become literally obsessed with mating and will ram and bite anything that even remotely resembles a female tortoise. This necessitates composing breeding groups in which there are distinctly more females than males. As a rule of thumb, there should be three to five females per male. Otherwise the females are unable to find respite from the continuous attentions of the males, which results in an extremely stressful situation for both sexes, but for the females in particular. Indicators that this may be the case include that the females are hardly seen at the basking spots because they would be subjected to copulation attempts there. They are also kept from feeding, become susceptible to diseases, and may eventually die if the situation is not remedied.

Optical barriers and a large number of retreats are therefore crucial for the wellbeing

said that if the natural requirements of these species are met, it just happens. The numbers of captive-bred *Testudo boettgeri* have by now become larger than what can be accommodated by responsible keepers. The fact that the majority of captive-bred specimens are of the male sex simply results from the fact that most of the commonly used literature gives incubation temperature ranges that are too low to produce females (see chapter "Reproduction").

Courtship and mating activities can be observed throughout the entire period of annual activity, but peaks are clearly discernible shortly after hibernation and again in late summer. The animals have a second mating season also in the wild. But because fall of-

Fig. 113: Many private keepers breed *Testudo boettgeri* on a regular basis. (J. MARAN)

of the females in a group. You may therefore want to fit your outdoor pen with a number of "female safe houses". These can easily be constructed from a piece of concrete slab that is securely placed on some bricks. Retreats of this type must only slightly higher than the shells of the pursued animals so that they are effectively protected from above from the males. Furthermore, there should be separate pens in which females can be kept at least before and a while after laying their eggs during the second half of summer. In general it is recommendable to keep the sexes of these species (as in most others) separated and only place them together for brief periods of time after hibernation in spring and again in late summer for the purpose of their mating.

After the females have once more been returned to their familiar "ladies club", they will show increased levels of activity, feed better, and abandon their predominantly secretive lifestyle. A few days in the company of the males are all that is needed for a successful fertilization of their eggs. The male specimens hardly consume any food during this time and copulate with the females several times each day. It appears that even the females are more ready to mate when not in the constant company of males, and you will note that the ratio of fertilized eggs rises under such a husbandry regime.

At the very least should the males be separated from the females shortly before or at the latest during the egg-laying period because they become particularly persistent then. This results in females being kept from nesting, and as a consequence they may develop egg binding or just drop their eggs somewhere. Even a brief delay of oviposition may terminate the development of embryos. Health risks for the female must also be feared if they are exposed to copulation attempts while they are nearing the full term of their gravidity. Eggshells may be cracked in the process and finally burst when the eggs are eventually laid resulting in severe injuries to the female's oviduct. The females are also often pestered while they are busy excavating their nest pits, and some instances have been documented where males attempted to mate while the female was busy laying her eggs. Disturbances of this nature may lead to a disruption of the oviposition process, subsequent egg binding, or at least the loss of the clutch. Even otherwise rather timid males are apparently unable to resist a female that is busy laying eggs. CASARES (1995) presumed this might have to do with the fact that the depositing of eggs is followed immediately by another ovulation.

The second mating season in late summer is indicated under the conditions of captivity by the females mounting each other several times a day; they may even open the mouth wide as is typical of mating males. This is the right time to once more place the males into the pen of the females. As soon as enough males are present, the described homosexual behavior ceases, and the females participate in courtship only passively. Courtship at this time of the year is much shorter than in spring, and the females appear much more willing to mate. This period of time equally lasts for about three weeks after which the males lose interest rapidly. They can now be left with the females until it becomes time for all of them to hibernate, unless you have opted for keeping the sexes separated as a principle.

Fig. 114: Good oviposition sites are hotly contested in an outdoor pen. (J. MARAN)

A particular difficulty presents itself if a specimen that has been living alone for a long time, is to be integrated into a breeding colony. Following an account by VINKE & VINKE (2004a), for example, the tortoise expert Gerhard WAGNER noted that formerly single males are very commonly hyperactive and aggressive and therefore hardly suitable for breeding purposes. Single females, on the other hand, often become lethargic when added to a group and may even cease to feed. According to this keeper, juveniles may respond to a few years of solitary husbandry conditions with stunted growth, feeding disorders (e.g., the formation of food preferences to the point where all other food is ignored), and no or an abnormal sexual imprint. The highly experienced tortoise keeper Hans-Jürgen BIDMON, on the other hand, noted that juveniles would always grow faster if they were kept one by one for their first six to seven years of life than conspecifics of the same ages that were kept in groups. It appears as though there is still some research to be done on this particular subject.

In human care, oviposition takes place some five to seven weeks after hibernation. This usually coincides with the time from May through June, although isolated instances have been observed as early as around mid-April or as late as August as well. More than one clutch per year is a distinct possibility. MITCHELL (2004), for one, recorded not less than six clutches with thirty-five eggs in total (6/7/6/5/6/5) from one of his female Testudo boettgeri in a single year. Clutches were produced at intervals ranging from twenty-two days to four months.

Gravid females begin to restlessly cruise their pen in search of a good nesting site already days before the eggs are due. They investigate potential spots thoroughly by sniffing the soil, sometimes even tasting it, and scratching the ground with their front and hind feet. If they cannot find a spot to their liking, their nervousness increases visibly, and they often attempt to escape from their enclosure. Older and experienced females often return to the nesting spot of previous years, whereas younger and recently acquired specimens tend to dig a number of "test pits".

While some females cease to feed a few days before the great event, others continue to accept food until shortly before they lay their eggs. Some females also behave like males during this period, and will bite and ram any other tortoise that happens to cross her path. They may even mount the other animal and in the process produce the copulation sounds typical of a male.

Females that are kept in an outdoor pen and whose behavior indicates that oviposition is imminent should be monitored closely. This may possibly enable you to recover her eggs right away. In such a setting, two days on average pass between the first digging attempts and oviposition, but it may also be as many as eight. Adverse factors such as the absence of suitable oviposition sites, bad weather, or obnoxious males may lead to egg binding that has to be diagnosed (e.g., by means of an X-ray examination) and treated by a veterinarian. Particularly nosy specimens can be kept away from the nesting female by simply covering the latter with a wiremesh basket.

Oviposition normally takes place on a particularly warm day with a raised level of humidity as is the case, for example, after a spring or summer thunderstorm. Eggs that have not been buried, "lost" somewhere in the open, or laid inside the shelter hut usually turn out to be infertile.

The interval between two clutches in captivity largely corresponds to observations made in the wild and amounts, according to a number of authors, to 14–30 days.

Fig. 115: Abnormally large (53 x 31 mm), infertile egg of a *Testudo hermanni* from the surroundings of Ajaccio, Corsica (J. MARAN)

Although incubation outdoors is possible in principle if the clutch has been deposited in a hotbed or greenhouse (see below), the relatively low incubation temperatures will produce exclusively male offspring. It is therefore best to carefully dig up the nestpit with a spoon, uncover the eggs with a paintbrush, mark their tops with a soft pencil, and then remove and transfer the eggs to an incubator. Turning the eggs shortly after they have been laid does not normally cause problems.

Simple incubation containers can be made from standard plastic cricket containers commonly used in petshops. They are filled to half or two-thirds of their height with an incubation substrate such as sand, vermiculite, perlite, fine gravel, or a mix of garden soil and sand at a ratio of 2:1. The eggs are then placed in depressions in the slightly moist substrate (water potential according to KÖHLER [2004] -400 to -600 Kilopascal). They must not be buried in fine substrate for more than one third of their diameter as otherwise the exchange of gases through the eggshell would be impeded. A lack of oxygen and raised concentrations of carbon dioxide can cause premature hatching, the perishing of embryos shortly before hatching, or malformations. The incubator itself should obviously not be exposed to vibrations or harmful influences such as tobacco smoke.

Fig. 116: This infertile clutch of eggs was removed from a female that died of egg-binding (vicinity of Ajaccio, Corsica, France). (J. MARAN)

Clutches left in the outdoor enclosure do not normally hatch under the climatic conditions of central Europe, although a few isolated instances from particularly favored areas have become known. For example, a single baby Testudo boettgeri hatched from a clutch laid in a garden in Nonsbach in the lower Inn Valley in Upper Austria on 20.09.1992. ZAPLETAL (2002) reported on the hatching of three offspring of the same species from a clutch that had been overlooked in the ground of a hotbed in September 2001. Interestingly, these hatchlings differed from siblings hatched from other clutches in having almost entirely black limbs and a highly contrasting carapace. ZAPLETAL reasoned that this might be a result of the substantial temperature fluctuations the eggs had been exposed to during their incubation. It is a regular phenomenon in many species of reptiles with large distribution ranges that dark color varieties occur in the cooler parts of the

range, and this is also the case with Testudo boettgeri (see chapter "Description"). ZAPLETAL (2002) presumed that this clutch had been deposited some time during the first half of June 2001 when the family had been on holidays. It would correspond to an incubation period of about 105 days, which about matches the incubation period under natural conditions (see chapter "Reproduction"). These "hotbed hatchlings" were noteworthy for their surprising agility.

The "summer of the century" experienced during the year 2003 brought about a number of additional records of "natural broods" from central Europe. These included Switzerland from where forty-one instances of natural breeding of Testudo boettgeri were reported, exclusive of the regions Western Switzerland and Ticino, from where no reports were logged. In Austria and Germany the situation was similar (e.g., ANONYMOUS 2003a, BAUER 2003, KUNDERT 2003b, BRAUN 2004, NEUMANN & WENNING 2004, WICHELHAUS 2004, WÜTHRICH 2004), and various keepers even reported that their animals responded to the excessive heat and drought with inserting several weeks of "estivation". A tortoise keeper from the canton of Aargau in Switzerland described that eggs that had been placed in a letter case of her daughter's for decoration during the summer of 2003 hatched to everybody's surprise (ANONYMOUS 2003a). The first hatchlings from clutches left outdoors emerged toward the end of July, but most appeared only in August and September. Several reports pointed out that the babies hatched after one of the rare downpours had softened the dry and hard soil. Some of the hatchlings were even not found before the spring of 2004, which means they hibernated outside without suffering ill effects.

The maximum number of hatchlings found alive was twenty-one, to which must be added an unknown number of those that fell victim to crows and magpies in an outdoor enclosure set up in Berne, Switzerland. About one-quarter of the records from Switzerland indicated losses. Some babies were lost to predatory animals such as crows, magpies and marten, and others were run over when they managed to venture out on an adjoining parking lot. One specimen was "retrieved" alive by the neighbor's cat and suffered only a minor bite wound. If the numbers of hatchlings found is compared with average clutch sizes, it becomes apparent that many more losses than were reported would have to be lamented.

In Switzerland, most reports of natural breeding originated from places that were situated at less than 600 m above sea level, and there was in fact only one observed in the canton of Wallis above that altitude, i.e., at 670 m a.s.l..

It appears that all instances of natural breeding involved specimens of *Testudo boettgeri* with the possible inclusion of some *Testudo hercegovinensis*, which have remained unidentified in many collections of supposed "Boettger's tortoises" until today. In general it can be said that although instances of natural breeding had been known from climatically favored spots in central Europe before, there has never been such a large number in a particular year that would compare with 2003.

Whether or not embryonic development takes place inside an egg, can be determined through candling after only a few weeks. In fact, it is common for a dull white spot to appear in the middle of the egg after just a few days. This spot subsequently spreads to form a "belt" all around the egg. It indicates the position of the blastodisc, below which lies the white portion of the yolk. About two weeks later, candling will reveal a dark spot of several millimeters in size that is the embryo floating on the yolk, and the inside of the

Fig. 117: Eggs are recovered after they have been laid and transferred into an incubator. (W. WEGEHAUPT)

shell is crisscrossed with a road map-like pattern of blood vessels. The embryo will continue to grow, and another four weeks down the line, you will be able to make out the outlines of a tiny tortoise already. Attempts at candling will then usually fail after about seven weeks as the embryo now fills the egg almost entirely. Soon thereafter small air pockets form inside the egg in the upper areas or on the sides.

As the egg becomes heavier during the course of its development, its progress is easily monitored through regular weighing on a preheated scale. Like with the eggs of all other species of tortoises those of the species dealt with here must never be turned or exposed to excessive heat because this would inevitably kill the embryos inside. Right after oviposition the heavier yolk sinks to the bottom of the egg where it will have accumulated after about one week. As the developing embryo rests on the yolk, turning the egg would cause it to be smothered by it. Candling should not be attempted with the aid of a light bulb of more than 25 Watts; a penlight is by all means preferable.

It needs to be emphasized that eggs should not be handled excessively; many of the commonly observed anomalies in hatchlings might be a result of just that!

Fig. 118: When unearthing eggs, their tops should be marked to prevent an accidental shift of their original positions. (W. Schmidt)

Accidentally damaged eggs can usually be incubated without problems if the damage to the shell is limited to a crack or a small indentation that leave both the inner and outer membranes intact. If the damaged spot is dirty, it needs to be cleaned of all larger particles and then dabbed with a moist piece of kitchen or toilet paper. If you want, you may disinfect the site with an antiseptic

(such as Spitacid or Sterilium), which must, however, not find entry into the egg. The crack or dent is then patched up with melted paraffin jelly that must for obvious reasons have cooled down to 30–32 °C. This prevents an excessive loss of fluids and infections with bacteria and/or fungi. You must ensure that only a maximum of one-third of the egg's surface is covered thus, as otherwise the paraffin sealant would impede the exchange of gases through the eggshell. Very small cracks can often be sealed simply with a small patch of sticky tape. A detailed description of how to patch-up cracked eggs can be found in ROGNER (2005).

If it so happens that the hatchling attempts to emerge from the egg right at this spot, the keeper should for once assist with the opening up of the shell. The "paraffin method" may of course also be used if the egg has been opened "on purpose" because you

thought it would be spoilt, but found a live, still underdeveloped embryo instead.

Provided with a relative humidity of 65–90 % (mainly 70–80 %) and an incubation temperature of 25–34 °C, development takes between 40 and 140 days. This is on average a much shorter period than in nature (comp. chapter "Reproduction"). The discrepancy is explained by clutches in human care being usually exposed to a far more constant temperature regime than in the wild. Although many breeders swear by decreased night temperatures, these are unnecessary and in fact render it quite impossible to influence the sex ratio amongst the offspring (see below). Even in nature, the temperatures inside the nest pit are fairly constant with the surrounding soil acting as a buffer that allows ambient temperature changes to reach the eggs only with substantial delay or not at all.

Incubation temperatures of between 25 and 26 °C prolong the incubation period (usually to more than 80 days), those between 28 and 34 °C shorten it (usually 50–80 days). Since the keeper hardly ever knows which region exactly his animals, or rather their predecessors, originated from, the incubation of females in particular should make use of an incubation temperature above 32.5 °C, which is likely to produce females (see chapter "Reproduction").

The hatchlings of a clutch of eggs usually emerge within a period of about three days between the first and the last baby. Longer periods of up to nine days have been observed, though. VINKE & VINKE (2004a) even reported that one of their hatchlings appeared only with a delay of sixteen days from a clutch that hatched "on time" after 59–60 days of incubation. This was, however, a unique exception. EENDEBAK (1995) demonstrated that there is no linear correlation between a constant incubation period and the incubation temperature. Instead, the resultant graph shows a distinct kink at about 27.5 °C. Keepers are therefore often tempted to "help" their babies hatching once the "normal" incubation period has expired, or ponder "unraveling" one that has been sitting for days in an egg that is already open. This is a very bad idea, though. Hatchlings usually need this additional period of time to complete their embryonic development and await favorable conditions. Disturbed, they may leave the protection of their eggs too early, exposing the yolk sac to mechanical damage or dirt. Injuries to the yolk sac can be as lethal as substrate that is accidentally resorbed into the body cavity with the yolk sac.

If a hatchling has genuine problems with leaving the egg, it is usually an indication of a pathological problem of some kind or other. Such a tortoise would perish in nature, and even in human care it is very likely to not keep pace with its siblings and die after a few months at the latest anyway. Problems with hatching always suggest improper husbandry conditions and feeding regimes for the mother specimen and should always be more than enough reason to reexamine all relevant parameters.

As far as fertilization rates are concerned, 515 of the altogether 741 eggs obtained from ten *Testudo boettgeri* females and examined by EENDEBAK (1995) were fertile. Of these, 312 eventually hatched, resulting in a fertilization rate of 69.5 % and a hatching success of 42.1%. HAILEY & LOUMBOURDIS (1988) investigated the same species under the conditions of a terrarium and worked out a fertilization rate of 89.2 % and a hatching rate of 79.4%, HEIMANN (1986) calculated for his Boettger's tortoises that 46.7–66.6 % were fertile with 2.5 % of the fertilized eggs containing embryos that perished during the course of development or grew into non-viable malformed hatchlings. KIRSCHE (1997) observed six of his females representing the

eastern population group over a period of six years and counted during this period a total of 58 clutches comprising 424 eggs. Babies emerged from 326 of these, which equals a hatching success of 76.9 %. COUTARD (2005) calculated a fertilization rate of 83 % for the clutches laid by the female *Testudo hermanni* at the Corsican tortoise center of A Cupulatta.

The first clutches of young females are often 100 % infertile, but this need not be the case in each and every instance. If their eggs are fertile, they often yield only very small non-viable hatchlings or those that develop very slowly if they survive. MEYER (1998) reported on a clutch of three eggs that had been laid by an older female *Testudo hermanni*, from which hatched two normally sized babies and a "midge" of only 27 mm in carapace length and a weight of 6 g. The egg containing this abnormally small tortoise was indistinguishable from its sibling eggs as to its size and appearance. The minute baby was very lively and fed continuously, but had only grown to a mere 29 mm in length and 7 g in weight after six months.

There appears to be a positive correlation between the mortality rate of embryos and the incubation temperature. The lowest mortality rate (20–30 %) was found to exist

Fig. 119: Newly hatched baby in the incubator (W. SCHMIDT)

Fig. 120: Depending on incubation conditions, the babies emerge after about 40–140 days. (W. SCHMIDT)

in eggs incubated at between 26 and 32 °C. At temperatures of 25, 33 and 34 °C, respectively, it was around 50%, and at 24 and 35 °C it reached 100%. Juveniles emerging from eggs incubated at constant values at the lowest possible temperature range were in general small, weakly, and hardly able to make it out of the shell unaided. Another paper by EENDEBAK (2002) provides further insights into the effects of incubation temperatures. With regard to *Testudo hercegovinensis*, the incubation temperatures must not be too high, according to the experiences made by several keepers. To this effect, EGER (2005) noted that a high percentage of hatchlings would emerge with scutellation anomalies already at incubation temperatures of 31.5 °C. Out of a total of ninety-three hatchlings thirty-two (34.5%) showed more or less obvious anomalies of this type, and the hatching success was reduced to 54%. At 24%, the content of prematurely perished embryos of was again very high. Clutches of *Testudo boettgeri* and *Testudo hermanni* incubated by EGER (2005) under the very same conditions yielded a hatching success of more than 70 and 80%, respectively,

and the loss of embryos was reduced to 14 and 8%.

Rearing

Raising baby tortoises is not a particular problem if only a varying diet is made available. Hatchlings should be kept as "sterile"

Fig. 121: Freshly hatched juveniles first drink their fill. (B. SEEGER)

Fig. 122: Hatchling *Testudo boettgeri* with a freshly closed navel (G. POPGEORGIEV)

Fig. 123: Juvenile *Testudo hercegovinensis* (W. SCHMIDT)

as possible on moist paper or kitchen towels until the possibly still present yolk sac has been used up and the plastron has closed. If the yolk sac is still very large, the hatchling can be affixed with sticky tape to a ring cut from a cardboard tube with a suitable diameter so that the yolk sac hangs freely in its center. Once the belly buttons have eventually closed, the hatchlings are placed in a tub filled with a few millimeters of warm (ca. 30–32 °C) water. The low depth guarantees that the babies can keep their heads above the water without having to struggle. Here, the hatchlings will usually drink their first fill. Thereafter they can be transferred to their raising tanks.

Releasing juveniles into the outdoor enclosure is only possible after about four years. This is due to the fact that smaller juveniles would simply be "lost" in a normally structured outdoor pen as a result of their naturally very secretive way of life. They leave their shelters only for brief periods during the morning and afternoon hours, bask, feed, and will soon dig themselves in once more or retreat into the protection of thickets of vegetation. Owing to the fact that juveniles overheat and/or desiccate rather quickly

and predators are a major factor, they refrain from basking extensively at this stage.

If the weather permits, hatchlings should be kept outdoors, though, for which a clearly organized small pen, e.g., a hotbed, is a suitable place. They may remain there from May through September provided climatic conditions are appropriate. As hotbeds are typically fitted with two lids that swing open to the sides, one of these can be removed and replaced with a frame covered with chicken wire. This enables the babies to benefit from unfiltered sunlight while potential predators such as marten, rats, mice, crows, magpies, blackbirds, dogs and cats are kept out. Beginners often underestimate the dangers posed by their own pets, and while most cats will indeed ignore the baby tortoises most of the time, dogs very often will not. Veterinarians are used to the sight of juvenile and subadult tortoises with bite marks from encounters with dogs, which they have to treat – if at all possible.

Another risk, which has unfortunately been on a steady increase over the past years, exists in the form of human "predators". These are contemporaries who illegally enter the properties of tortoise keepers and "help

Fig. 124: A semiadult Boettger's tortoise (S. Seki)

themselves" to a tortoise or two or even the complete collection. Besides suffering the unsettling feeling of having become a victim of crime and having lost a substantial asset, the despairing owner will also be extremely worried about the wellbeing of his animals. In this scenario it will help to have a set of photographs by which the tortoises can be identified individually (see chapter "Conservation"). They are proof of rightful ownership, and the investigating authorities will know precisely what they have to look out for. In order to keep all this from happening in the first place, standard measures of home security such as proper fencing all around, and locks at greenhouses and hotbeds should exist, and if necessary be tightened by motion detectors coupled with flood lights, alarm systems, CCTV etc.

Like for the adult specimens, the enclosure for juveniles needs to be fitted with a heating lamp that protects the animals from adverse weather conditions during early spring and late fall or summery cold spells. To prevent the baby tortoises from escaping, the frame of their hotbed may either be sunk some 10 cm into the surrounding ground or filled with soil to the same depth. A larger rock or two of a dark color will absorb heat during the day and slowly release it when it becomes cooler and thus act as a natural heat sink. A piece of meadow, easily cut out with a spade, is just as easily replaced after it has been grazed. You may alternatively want to sow white clover or other feeder plants. The ground needs to be kept slightly moist at all times and must never be allowed to dry out completely. Keeping the juveniles in conditions that are too dry results in a malformed growth of the shell even if they are properly supplied with vitamins and minerals. In order to keep the ground from becoming soaked, but rather make it draw moisture as is needed from below, it is best to drill some

Fig. 125: Juvenile *Testudo boettgeri* from Rujan, Serbia and Montenegro (N. RISTIC)

Fig. 126: Juvenile *Testudo hermanni*, Albera Mountains, Catalonia (Spain) (J. MARAN)

holes into it at various places of the hotbed, which are then used for "watering". You may furthermore want to emulate a rain shower by spraying the hotbed with warm water, which is something the small tortoises will quite visibly enjoy.

Various keepers swear by covering at least the largest part of the ground of the hotbed with a layer of straw a few centimeters thick. This emulates quite effectively the herbaceous layer in the wild in which the juveniles prefer to hide. The baby tortoises accept this substitution readily and will soon have established a maze of tunnels in it. The straw also maintains a relatively humid microclimate that is highly beneficial to their health. You need to check it for signs of mold on a regular basis, though, and replace it when necessary. The babies will also feel safe from predators beneath the straw and have something to help them right themselves if they happen to fall on their backs.

Other natural shelters and protection from the sun include *Erica* plants or small species of shrubs. Additional retreats must be available in the form of, e.g., pieces of cork bark or halved flowerpots. An ideal solution may be to provide them, like the adults, with a small shelter hut with a lid that can be flipped open.

A small water bowl, preferably again an earthenware undertray for flowerpots with a diameter of about 10 cm, must not be missing. It should not be placed near one of the walls of the hotbed, though, as the baby tortoises tend to wander along these in particular and would thus walk through it all the time, tipping it over or at least carrying dirt into it. During their first year of life it is important to cover the bottom of the undertray with large pebbles so that the animals can easily exit it and, what is even more important, can right themselves if they somehow end up in it upside down.

The baby tortoises should furthermore be bathed at regular intervals. This takes care of their increased need for moisture. Because sudden cloudbursts are common throughout the Mediterranean summer (comp. the reports by SCHMIDT [2000a, b, 2004a, b] on the tortoises of Menorca), this emulates quite well the conditions in the wild. Obviously, it should not be overdone, and WEGEHAUPT (2003) suggested a regime of six times per month during spring up to and including June, twice per month in July and August, and four times per month from September.

If circumstances dictate that the juveniles are kept in an indoor terrarium during the transitional periods in spring and fall, their environment must obviously offer about the same conditions as described above. Garden soil can be used as a substrate, and should be moistened with warm water every other day. Again, you need to be careful not to soak the soil, but only use so much water that the soil can dry up within the course of a day.

Juveniles feed exclusively on the green parts of plants during their first year and will usually refuse flowers as well as fruit. Other than that they have the same dietary requirements as have the adults. It is important to prevent them from growing too fast, which takes care of no humps disfiguring their carapaces.

Hatchling tortoises often ingest grains of sand right after they have left their eggs. These probably help them to digest their food properly. They usually begin to consume "genuine" food only one to three days later.

Although many keepers do not overwinter their baby tortoises during the first year, you should take into consideration that nobody spares them this period in the wild. It therefore makes sense to let them hibernate as well, and a shortened period of hibernation of maybe four to six weeks is still better than no hibernation at all.

A result of "pampering" babies too much can be an unnaturally rapid growth and an increased susceptibility to diseases. FRITZ & PFAU (2002) pointed out that specimens that were allowed to hibernate did not only develop nice and smooth shells, but also

Fig. 127: Juvenile *Testudo hermanni* from Ajaccio, Corsica (France) (J. MARAN)

showed much prettier colors than conspecifics of the same age that had been kept warm in winter. They may hibernate in their terrarium, which is to be fitted for this purpose with fresh and well-moistened substrate. The tank must be placed where it is safe from drafts, but must of course not be made airtight. Overwintering them in a fridge is preferable to keeping them in a cellar or similar room. This is simply because the inevitable changes in temperatures in a room may wake the tortoises temporarily, which poses a great risk to them due to their reserves being smaller than those of adult tortoises. A fridge, on the other hand, ensures a constantly low temperature and thus reduces the risk of losses.

In spite of all precautions it may occasionally happen that the one or other juveniles does not survive its first hibernation. You should take this as a form of natural selection because runts or weak animals would usually also perish earlier or later even if they had not been sent into hibernation.

One month after their hibernation, the babies should show clear signs of growth. Their slow growth should be facilitated also in human care by means of feeding them sparingly as this is the only way to ensure their healthy development. Although the shell of "powered" juveniles may often be highly domed and smooth as well, the bony structure under the horny scutes will usually be rather porous and permanently damaged. The shell of a rapidly growing specimen is in most cases not typically shaped, though. It may be too low, humped or unshapely. Humps are not only an esthetical problem, but they correspond to damage to the inner

	Spec. 1	Spec. 2	Spec. 3	Spec. 4	Spec. 5
Age: 1 day					
Weight in g	7,0	7,5	8,0	8,0	6,0
Carapace length in mm	31,0	32,0	33,0	31,0	30,0
Carapace width in mm	28,0	27,0	29,0	27,0	25,0
Shell height in mm	18,0	18,0	19,0	18,0	19,0
Age: 12 months					
Weight in g	38,0	25,0	70,0	43,0	66,0
Carapace length in mm	52,0	48,0	65,5	55,0	63,0
Carapace width in mm	48,5	41,7	58,0	49,0	56,0
Shell height in mm	31,5	26,8	37,5	33,8	39,3
Age: 24 months					
Weight in g	68,0	48,0	210,0	96,0	225,0
Carapace length in mm	61,4	56,0	98,0	72,0	97,0
Carapace width in mm	55,5	49,0	83,0	65,0	84,5
Shell height in mm	38,0	33,8	49,0	40,8	54,3

organs of the tortoise as well. Because the lungs are situated right beneath the carapace, the lung volume is affected by such a formation of humps. Furthermore, the vertebral column is usually more or less deformed in tortoises affected thus.

Specimens that grow notably faster than others should be separated and kept on a "spartan" diet of fiber-rich foods. In summer, all young can be exposed to a "dry period" by offering them nothing but hay. To make consumption easier for them, the hay may be cut up before with a pair of scissors.

KIRSCHE (1967) published two tables showing the growth of juveniles representing the eastern population group. The one depicts the growth of five specimens during raising, and the other shows the relationships between body weight and age for ten

specimens. These data demonstrate once more that most juveniles in human care grow way too fast.

It should be noted for the table below that weights (in g) were always taken on May 1. The letter "a" signifies the first attempt at mating, "b" indicates the first clutch, and "c" refers to the excavation of a nest pit without subsequent oviposition by the respective specimen.

SCHIPPAN (2004) took measurements of her captive-bred Testudo boettgeri over a period of several years and recorded the following weights: hatchlings 15–30 g, one year-olds 30–60 g, two-year-olds 40–100 g, three year-olds 80–200 g, and four year-olds 150–300 g.

The weights of ten year-old captive specimens of Testudo boettgeri range around 850 g, and the animals measure about 15 cm in car-

Age	Spec. 1 (C)	Spec. 2 (C)	Spec. 3 (C)	Spec. 4 (C)	Spec. 5 (C)	Spec. 6 (C)	Spec. 7 (C)	Spec. 8 (C)	Spec. 9 (X)	Spec. 10 (X)
1 day	?	?	7,5	8,0	6,0	7,5	6,5	7,0	8,0	8,0
8 months	?	?	24	45	44	26	14	21	22	19
2 years	?	?	40	166	169	41	40	28	58	46
3 years	95	55	49	231	255	79	58	40	88	78
4 years	180	120	66	305	320	116	75	65	134	120
5 years	246	160	95	380	375	183	78	104	158 a	148 a
6 years	340	240	122	550	485	200	136	120	275	285
7 years	430	300	126	640	565	355	158	165	255	290
8 years	510	380	200	885	790	365	185	200	345	410
9 years	605	445	228	855	715	500	230	250	420	500
10 years	718	515	255	1.090	950	640	–	–	440	560
11 years	820	620	315	1.285 b	1.010	710	–	–	470	590
12 years	770	630	335	1.290	1.050	800	–	–	–	–
13 years	870 c	620	–	–	–	–	–	–	–	–
14 years	920 b	650	–	–	–	–	–	–	–	–

apace length then. Another ten years later, they tip the scales at approximately 1.6 kg and have grown to 20 cm.

In human care, male tortoises reach sexual maturity at an age between four and eight years, whereas females need eight to fourteen years. Expressions of sexual dimorphism can often be discerned already in specimens as young as three years. Instances of "test mating" that may often be observed at this age as well are, however, no reliable indicators of the sexes of the specimens engaging in them. It appears that females train the mounting of conspecifics just as much at this age as do males. Even specimens of just a few months of age have been known to mount each other. What triggers this behavior and its purpose are still unknown.

A captive-bred female in the collection of HEIMANN (1992) grew from 3.4 cm in carapace length and 12 g in weight in 1984 to 18 cm in carapace length and 1,250 g in 1990. It turned out to be sexually mature at an age only 6.5 years as it produced at this point of time a clutch of seven eggs from which six babies eventually hatched. This early onset of sexual maturity was attributable in the present case to the offspring not hibernating, but having been made to spend the winters in a warm indoor terrarium. This is in contrast with a female of a second-generation litter in the collection of KIRSCHE (1984a, see table above) that matured only at the age of fourteen years – his tortoises were kept in an outdoor pen in Berlin (Germany) all year round.

Health concerns
Generally speaking the species dealt with here are fairly robust animals that can withstand cooler temperatures during summer without necessarily developing severe health problems. In this respect they are in general less sensitive than, let's say, representatives of the *Testudo graeca* species group from North

Africa. Notwithstanding this, you should keep a close eye on your specimens and weigh them on a regular basis. Changes in their behavior and appearance, and/or continued weight loss, may well be early warning signs of a developing health problem.

Healthy tortoises of the *Testudo hermanni* species group are rather lively during their active periods. They are very inquisitive and always busy foraging. The shell of a healthy adult specimen is hard and dry. Shedding takes place by losing only small pieces of old skin (particularly in the case of juveniles). The nostrils are dry and free of any discharge, and the same applies to the cloaca. Healthy specimens produce feces that are elongate in shape, compact and interspersed with fibers, and show a dark green to black coloration. Soft, greasy feces point to gastrointestinal problems.

As soon as a tortoise shows notable changes to this effect, you should consult with a veterinarian experienced in the medical treatment of tortoises. What you should not do is experiment with medication yourself. Chances are that inappropriate types, dosages and applications cause more damage than good.

Addresses of veterinarians specializing in this field can usually be obtained from organizations such as those listed in the Appendix "Addresses" below. In general it is recommendable to have all specimens checked out routinely by a vet once a year during their activity period.

Juveniles often suffer from a softening of the shell. The disease is often progressive and in many cases cannot be stopped in spite of different treatments. Microscopic post mortem examinations then usually reveal an insufficient ossification. In a study of six young tortoises that had perished thus, ZWART (2002) diagnosed an inflammation of the large intestine as a result of endoparasitic infections with cryptosporids, balantids and flagellates. This inflammation inhibited the absorption of calcium from the ingested food, which in turn prevented the formation of solid bone matter; the result was a shell that remained or turned soft. It coincided in four of the six cases with kidney disorders, with two specimens having hatched with cystic kidneys and the other two having acquired inflammations of the kidneys. One specimen had even suffered from severe articular gout. Kidney disorders also afflict the calcium metabolism. According to ZWART (2002), the mentioned parasites had probably been acquired even before hatching. He managed to experimentally prove that the risk for problems of this type could be reduced by about half if an incubation substrate was used that had been sterilized before in a common microwave oven.

Diseases as a consequence of colds are rare and usually take a less severe course. Serious cases of nasal catarrh or pneumonia are practically limited to grossly inappropriate husbandry conditions. These would include a housing on a drafty balcony or allowing them to roam the house or apartment freely.

More common are purulent infections of the skin that are likely to be a result of too much moisture in the immediate environment. Their treatment with, e.g., antibiotic ointments, will obviously only be effective if the cause is eliminated as well.

Endoparasites are present in virtually all tortoises and are usually no threat to their health. They will only escalate into a problem if they proliferate, which is in most cases facilitated by an inappropriate diet or the keeping of large numbers of tortoises in a small space. Common round worms (ascarids), threadworms and even hexamites may then turn into serious threats to the infected animals. Afflicted specimens do not normally show outward signs of parasitoses, but very

heavily infested ones lose weight rapidly, become lethargic, and eventually perish if left untreated. Once a veterinarian has determined a parasitic infestation on the basis of a cloacal smear or fresh fecal sample, the administration of deworming medication via a stomach tube or by injection may be required. Fresh fecal samples are obtained naturally and usually right during the course of the drive to the annual health check.

These tortoises must probably be considered to be amongst the species that are most susceptible to infections with herpes. An infection often destroys entire collections, with only one example being the outbreak in the Aachen Zoo (Germany) in 2003, which appeared to have been triggered by the addition of a new specimen. Signs may often appear within a few weeks after infection, and many animals perish within the next six weeks. This does, however, by no means suggest that specimens with no symptoms are by default free of herpes! The herpes virus reproduces even inside eggs and usually causes the contained embryos to perish. It appears that very many cases of infections with *Herpesvirus* result from a joint keeping of members of the *Testudo hermanni* and *Testudo graeca* species groups, and *Testudo ibera* in particular. During the course of her studies in the "tortoise village" at Gonfaron, in the Maure Mountains, and in Morocco, MATHES (1997) noted that tortoises of the *graeca* complex were to a large extent carriers of the herpes virus whereas none of the examined *Testudo hermanni* tested positive. If nothing else is, this is one major argument for the strictly separate housing of these species.

A study of thirty-five different strains of the virus, which had been extracted from six species of tortoises including members of the *Testudo hermanni* species group, showed that these could be clustered in two groups. The tortoises dealt with here were found to be carriers of the so-called "testudo type", which appears to be the more dangerous one of the two (BLAHAK 2004a). It is presumed that the "testudo type" entered Europe from Turkey since members of the *Testudo graeca* species group usually survive an infection with this virus. This would mean that the immune system of these species has over time adapted to this pathogen. In contrast, the members of the *Testudo hermanni* species group usually die of such an infection, which suggests that their immune system is not "familiar" with this strain and cannot fight or contain it successfully.

Telltale signs of an infection are a thick white deposit on the mucous membranes of the mouth and tongue with a resultant severe difficulty of swallowing. Afflicted specimens lose control of the movement of their limbs, often walk backwards, and suffer fainting spells. This already indicates brain damage, and nothing will save them

Figs. 128&129: A hatchling *Testudo boettgeri* with an atypical color pattern (J. MARAN)

Fig. 130: Albinistic and normally pigmented juveniles of *Testudo boettgeri* (H.-D. PHILIPPEN)

at this stage. Some specimens are known to have just dropped dead from one moment to the next without their having displayed any signs of an infection before. It is exactly this what makes this disease so perilous – infected specimens may appear entirely normal and healthy for a long time, until their immune system is weakened and the virus begins to wreak havoc. Such a breakdown may be caused by another disease or simply by stress. Also, it is only at this stage that the pathogen will be detectable, e.g., through a smear from the pharyngeal mucous membranes. In the meantime, the carrier tortoise may have spread the virus to others. Symptom-free carriers of the virus can only be identified by the presence of antibodies in their blood. However, because the formation of these antibodies may take several months, newly acquired specimens should be kept in quarantine for at least one year and checked on a regular basis during this period. Only then will it be reasonably safe to place them with others.

Herpes in tortoises is at present not curable, and treatment must be limited to treating the symptoms. But even if this is successful, the afflicted tortoise will remain a carrier of the virus as long as it continues to live, and symptoms may flare up again at any time. It also means this specimen must be kept in isolation for the rest of its life, or, as some keepers are practicing already, in "herpes colonies". Breeding with such a colony is, however, not a good idea because an infection of the babies in their eggs is not only possible – it is quite likely. Humans and other pets are not at risk of contracting an infection with "tortoise herpes", but a keeper may well spread the disease from infected to "clean" specimens if his regime of minimum hygiene is not up to scratch. It should therefore go without saying that you first care for the healthy animals, then disinfect

your hands, and only then look after sick or possibly sick specimens.

Inappropriately housed tortoises often also suffer from mouthrot and/or diseases of the liver that are also caused by viral infections.

A common problem under the circumstances of captivity is bite wounds that rivaling males or those obsessed with mating inflict on conspecifics. Injuries resulting from copulation attempts also fall into this category and often lead to the formation of abscesses deep beneath the skin in the tail and cloacal region of females. These are mostly caused by the horny nail at the tip of the male's tail. Males may also suffer from wounds in the cloacal area. All specimens should therefore be checked for injuries on a regular basis. Open wounds that are left unattended often tend to weep and thus attract flies to lay their eggs in them. These eggs hatch after one to two days, and the maggots anchor themselves in the surrounding tissue and begin to eat themselves to deeper layers. In such a case all maggots need to be removed and the wound treated with a disinfectant. If the inflammation has already spread over a larger area, it may be necessary to have a veterinarian treat it with antibiotics.

Some specimens remain lethargic following their hibernation, do not resume feeding, and show a rapid loss of weight, dry skin, sunken, tearing or gluey eyes, and occasionally a runny nose and a reddening of the mucous membranes lining the oral cavity. Many specimens will at this stage also show a reddened plastron. These changes were interpreted by WIECHERT (2000) as indicators of an imbalanced metabolism. Possible causes for this syndrome appear to include hibernation conditions that were too warm or too dry, but may also be referable to a disease that remained undetected before hibernation. This period then stressed the organism trough metabolic products (metabolic stress) that weakened the overall immune system and thus manifested itself fully. Light cases of this so-called "posthibernal anorexia" (referred to as PHA) can be remedied by rehydration (administering up to 40 ml in total per kilogram body mass in several sessions per day) with a 5 % glucose solution, but even mineral water may already do the trick. It is furthermore recommendable to bathe afflicted specimens in warm water every day to monitor the discharge or urine and feces, exposure to unfiltered sunlight and/or particularly bright artificial light. Temperatures should be kept constant at 28–30 °C. This therapy may be supported by a veterinarian administering a range of anabolitic products. In light cases, the tortoises will resume feeding after just a few days. Eyes that are gummed shut can be opened and kept open through long baths and the application of a vitamin A eye ointment. If the eyes are overlain with a cheesy substance, a veterinarian may need to remove it through flushing or with a special tool. This may then need a follow-up course of several days with an antibiotic ointment. Obviously you will have to have blood tests done to determine the exact cause of the problem.

Kept in compliance with their natural requirements, the members of the *Testudo hermanni* species group may live in human care to an age of between 80 and 120 years. Although one instance of 115 years has been documented for a *Testudo boettgeri*, this is certainly an exception. On the other hand, reports on specimens of more than 50 years of age are rather common. At least in the past, most specimens were not given a chance to live to such an age, though. Disease due to bad diet usually reduced the average life expectancy of a tortoise of the *Testudo hermanni*

species group hatched in human care to a mere 1.75 years in Great Britain during the 1980'.

Baytril

Although Baytril® is undoubtedly an excellent antibiotic for the elimination of bacteria in warm-blooded animals, it should not be used for tortoises. At body temperatures of less than 37 °C, which is a value rarely reached by tortoises, Baytril® may have a nephrotoxic effect. It has been proven to cause the formation of condensation nuclei of uric acid within the glomeruli and proximal tubuli of the kidneys. This may eventually be aggravated by the deposition of calcium phosphate that blocks the tubuli. Specimens that have been treated with Baytril® die painfully of gout in the kidneys only years later. Because by then no connection is usually made to the treatment with this antibiotic, it mostly appears enigmatic (JENNEMANN pers. comm.).

Recent years saw the publication of several books in a variety of languages on the topic of tortoise and/or reptile diseases in general that can be recommended to the keeper (and his veterinarian!). These include, for example, ACKERMAN (2000a, b), KÖHLER (1996), EGGENSCHWILER (2000b), and SASSENBURG (2000, 2006).

Tortoise and man

Boettger's tortoise

The representatives of the *Testudo hermanni* species group played a role in the history of mankind already during the times of antiquity. For example, they served as a motif on trade weights in ancient Greece. DUMOULIN (1994) described finds of shells and shell fragments that could be assigned to *Testudo boettgeri* from archeological excavation sites in Greece. Oftentimes only the bony constituents have remained, but the shells of some finds show traces of alteration such as drilled-in holes. In most cases it is obvious that these shells once served as sounding bodies of so-called "chelyes" (= "tortoises"), which were antique string instruments. There are, however, also some tortoise shell objects that defy explanation as musical instruments for reasons of timeline or technical peculiarities.

Tortoises or certain parts of these were furthermore attributed medicinal properties that were supposed to be effective against a range of ailments. Their meat and bile were thought to be an antidote against snakebite and scorpion sting as well as against epi-

leptic fits. Tortoise blood was administered in the case of various eye diseases including cataracts, and was supposed to prevent toothaches if only one used it to rinse the mouth three times a year. Blood was also dripped into aching ears and massaged into the scalp in cases of thinning hair. It was believed to help against headaches and tumors if, as relayed by PLINIUS and NIKANDROS, it was collected in a new earthenware bowl from the head of a tortoise cut off with a copper knife (SÜSS & MALTER 1991). The list of exotic remedies (which are certainly highly detrimental to tortoise populations) goes on and on, and many "recipes" are linked to ancient folk beliefs. For example, the ancient Greeks believed that "danger" in the form of hailstorms and vermin could be avoided if a tortoise was buried alive while lying on its back.

Ancient Greek literature contains a variety of tales and myths whose animal lead roles were probably played by *Testudo boettgeri*. The Greek philosopher ZENO, for example, once engaged in a theoretical experiment that required the fast runner Achill to

Fig. 131: Banner of the "District of the Tortoise" in Siena, Italy
(*Chimaira* Archives)

Fig. 132: Wine label from the province of Grosseto, Italy
(*Chimaira* Archives)

Fig. 133: A music instrument manufactured from the shell of a Mediterranean tortoise (B. DEVAUX)

compete against a particularly slow contestant for which he chose the tortoise. "Imagine the fast runner Achill is pitted against the tortoise. Because he is a friendly man, he allows the slow animal a good headstart, thinking, ‚I'll soon catch up with you.' But this is in fact an impossible task." ZENO calculated that Achill would start off, but when he reached the spot at which the tortoise had been when he started, the tortoise would have moved forward too, not by much, but still by some distance. Achill would now be required to catch up more, which would result in the tortoise having moved a little farther. This would continue on and on, with the tortoise staying ahead by ever decreasing margins, but because it would continue to move, the fast Achill would, according to ZENO's thought game, never actually catch it.

Another Greek fable is that of AESOP. It relays a race in which tortoise and hare compete (SÜSS & MALTER 1991). The hare sneered at the tortoise because he considered him lazy and lame. "Listen, you fast runner," the tortoise answered, "I shall defeat you in the race." "Idle words," responded the hare, "If you dare to start the race, you will be surprised." The fox was entrusted with marking the racetrack. The tortoise knew how unwieldy he was, but did not hesitate and started right away. The hare, full of confidence of his superior speed, took his time, got bored and fell asleep on his way. The tortoise continued to walk slowly but steadily and eventually passed the sleeping hare and arrived at the finish line first. A sluggish tortoise had thus defeated an otherwise invincible adversary simply by perseverance. Later this fable made use of a pair of hedgehogs that caused a dull-witted hare to run himself to death by exhaustion between the two spiky smartheads that positioned themselves at either end of the racetrack.

Besides the perseverance of the tortoise obvious from this tale, the old Greeks also admired its composure. This is still obvious in the popular saying, "to be as unperturbed as a tortoise by mosquitoes".

ROSCHER's (1884) Lexicon of Myths contains the following story. Dryope, the only daughter of the king, tended her father's herds at the river Oita. The nymphs of this area were very fond of her and took her in their midst as a playmate. They also taught her to sing and dance. When Apollo saw her dance on one occasion, he instantly fell in love with her, and transformed his appearance into that of a tortoise so that he could approach her. The girl was curious and drawn to the animal and placed it on her lap. Here, Apollo quickly transformed into a snake, which sent the nymphs scattering. Apollo had reached his goal, and the result of this union was a son, which Dryope named Amphissos. In the eyes of the ancient Greeks, the tortoise was a particularly ugly animal and thus the exact opposite of Apollo, the God of Beauty, Master of the Muses, and Regent of Heavenly Spheres. This tale may actually have been the foundation of the failsafe recipe of storytellers and playwrights along the lines of "The Beauty and the Beast". Insofar, the second transformation comes as a surprise: the tortoise makes the advances, establishes the initial contact, but the snake

is then left to "do the job" (SÜSS & MALTER 1991).

Many cultural circles in ancient Greece regarded the tortoise as a symbol of fertility, but it eventually mutated into an embodiment for chastity and domesticity. The temple at Elis contained two statues, with one depicting Venus Urania (= the heavenly) that stood with one foot on a tortoise, while the other, Venus Pandemos, was seated on a ram. The writer PLUTARCH of old stated that Venus Urania was meant to embody the guardian of marriage, and remind one of the female virtue of domesticity. The tortoise had obviously by then been demoted to a symbol of "tamed femininity" or "house wife". A custom in ancient Greece was to pin a tortoise to the door of the wedding bedchamber as to remind those inside of the virtue of domesticity. Following SÜSS & MALTER (1991), the two types of Venus could be described in modern words as Venus Urania symbolizing the woman as a possession, and Venus Pandemos the woman as an independent partner.

The tortoise also played a role in a popular saying in ancient Greece for a situation that was highly improbable, "rather a tortoise will fly". A "flying" tortoise, however, made a fatal impact on the Greek poet Aischylos when it fell on his head and killed him in Gela on the island of Sicily in the year 456 B.C.. The poet had even been prophesied that he would be killed by an object falling from above on a particular day. When this day arrived, Aischylos thought he was clever enough to cheat destiny and sat down under a cloudless blue sky where he considered himself safe. But it was exactly there that his fate caught up with him. A bearded vulture had carried a tortoise into the sky and dropped it in the fashion several birds of prey do habitually to crack the shell and make the meat accessible (see chapter "Threats"). These birds usually choose a boulder for this purpose, but the "vulture of death" had apparently confused the bald head of old Aischylos that gleamed in the bright sun with such a boulder. "Nobody can escape destiny," is the message conveyed by this chiding tale that was commonly retold in 18th century books on morale. Bald-headed people may furthermore learn from this story that it might be of benefit to wear something solid on the head during excursions out in the open (not only) in the Mediterranean region.

The art collection of the Musée d'Orsay (France) includes a beautiful painting by Gustave MOREAU (1826–1898). It depicts a young woman at the base of a boulder that holds a lyre on which rests the head of Orpheus; on the right side of the painting are two *Testudo boettgeri*.

Testudo boettgeri has also been playing a role as a motif in the realm of philately. Albania, for example, issued a series of postage stamps with reptile motifs on 10.08.1966, of which the 10 Qindarka-stamp (Michel No. 1083, Scott No. 957) is supposed, according to the caption, to depict a "*Testudo graeca*" (i.e., probably a *Testudo ibera*), but following a personal communication received from BOUR actually shows a *Testudo boettgeri*. This would also make more sense as *Testudo ibera* does not occur in Albania. Azerbaidzhan issued on 12.06.1995 a five-piece series of postage stamps with tortoise motifs, of which

S.O.P.T.O.M.
LE VILLAGE DES TORTUES
BP 24
83590 GONFARON - FRANCE

the 300 Manat-value (Michel No. 227, Scott No. 524) (Fig. 140) shows a *Testudo boettgeri*, even though this species does not occur in this country. On 12.09.1996, Romania published a series on indigenous animals including a 150 Leu-stamp (Michel No. 5209, Scott No. 4122) (Fig. 141) that carried a Boettger's tortoise for a motif. It is uncertain when exactly a series of "postage stamps" with tortoise motifs from the West African country of Guinea appeared on the market. Showing "Postes 1998" as a publication date this is a set of eighteen pieces that were printed in two continuous sheets. All pieces have nominal values of 150 Guinea-Francs, and one depicts a beautiful *Testudo boettgeri* (Fig. 144). These "postage stamps" are, however, so-called vignettes, which are postage stamp-like printed matters without any real post-age value that are produced by unsound agencies to the detriment of collectors. This is also the reason why they are not listed with numbers in stamp collectors' catalogs. Bulgaria published on 08.10.1999 a four-piece set of stamps with tortoise motifs of which the 30 Lew-stamp (Michel No. 4427, Scott No. 4095) is supposed to depict a *Testudo boettgeri*, but it appears as though the caption has been mixed up with that of the 10 Lew-piece (Michel No. 4425, Scott No. 4093) that carries the caption "*Testudo graeca*" (which, judging from the geographical position of this country, is again likely to be a *Testudo ibera*). On 24.11.1999, a "block issue" ap-

Fig. 136: Bulgarian telephone card with *Testudo boettgeri* for a motif

Fig. 137: Spanish telephone card with a picture of *Testudo hermanni* (1997)

peared in Angola that united three chelonian "postage stamps" with "nominal values" of 3,500,000 Kwanza each. One of these depicts a *Testudo boettgeri*. However, the entire issue is in fact just a vignette (see above). The same motifs also appeared on two vignettes of the Russian Federation republic of Karachai-Tcherkessia in 2000; this republic is not a member of the World Post Association. Hungary issued on 09.05.2001 a series dedicated to the animals of Europe, which contained a 70 Forint-postage stamp (Michel No. 4671, Scott No. 3759) (Fig. 143) showing a *Testudo boettgeri*.

MONACO (WWF)

1.25
TORTUE D' HERMANN TESTUDO HERMANNI
W OLIVER

MONACO (WWF)

1.25
TORTUE D' HERMANN TESTUDO HERMANNI
W OLIVER

MONACO (WWF)

1.25
TORTUE D' HERMANN TESTUDO HERMANNI
W OLIVER

MONACO (WWF)

1.25
TORTUE D' HERMANN TESTUDO HERMANNI
W OLIVER

Fig. 139: French 3-Franc postage stamp with first issue postmark, 1991

Fig. 138: Set of postage stamps from Monaco, 1991

POÇTU 1995

300m AZƏRBAYCAN

Fig. 140: 300-Manat postage stamp from Azerbaidzhan, 1995

ROMÂNIA 150L

Testoasa de uscat

Fig. 141: 150-Leu postage stamp from Romania, 1996

TESTUDO GRAECA ESPAÑA

TORTUGA TERRESTRE

CORREOS 1 PTA

Fig. 142: 1-Peseta postage stamp from

70ft

Görög teknös – Testudo hermann MAGYARORSZÁG

Fig. 143: 70-Forint postage stamp from Hungary, 2001

150GNF
Postes 1998

République de Guinée

Fig. 144: 150-Guinea-Franc vignette from

REPOBLIKAN'I MADAGASIKARA

1500FMG
300ARIARY

Fig. 145: 1,500-Madagascar-Franc vignette, 2001

Testudo boettgeri also served as a motif on telephone cards in Bulgaria and the People's Republic of China.

Italian tortoise

The Louvre in Paris holds two splendid silver salt castors from the period of King Louis XIV in the shape of tortoises, presumably *Testudo hermanni*. A large silver bowl in the same museum, crafted by the Nuremberg artist Wenzel Jamnitzer between 1550 and 1560 for the collection of the Sun King, is embellished with various animal motifs, amongst which are three juvenile tortoises. These are likely to depict the Italian tortoise as well. Staying with the Louvre, you can find the painting "Paradise on Earth" by the Dutch painter Jan Bruegel (1568–1625). If you look more closely, you will find a tortoise that is likely to be a *Testudo hermanni*. It is situated near the right front leg of the cow. Another painting in the Louvre collection with a *Testudo hermanni* is the "Still-life with Musical Instruments" by Pieter Claesz (1597–1660) painted in 1623. Besides a variety of foodstuffs and string instruments in the foreground it also contains a finely detailed tortoise. Most interesting, however, was the find of a sketch of the great Leonardo da Vinci in the vaults of the Louvre. Titled "The Woman and the Tortoise" it shows a woman with a *Testudo hermanni* in her hands. In a later version of this draft the artist removed the tortoise, changed the position of the arms, and it became – the "Mona Lisa". A depiction of the Italian tortoise can also be found on a pillar of the convent of Saint Genis des Fontaines in France.

DUPRÉ (1998) took the readers of her article on a tour through Florence, pointing out the various artful expressions of *Testudo hermanni* throughout the capital city of Tuscany. These include frescos, sculptures (e.g., the obelisks on the Piazza Santa Maria Novella or the "tortoise well" in the Gardens of Boboli), mosaic windows, and even salt and pepper castors. In the equally Tuscan city of Siena, *Testudo hermanni* has been given a place of honor as the symbol of one of the twenty-two historical districts. Beginning in the early 14th century, the people of Siena were focused on the social, cultural and religious life that played out in their particular district, and they were loyal only to it. Today, only seventeen districts remain, and their individual importance has greatly diminished. Still, there are symbols marking the roads to inform the observant traveler in which district he presently finds himself. The seventeen remaining districts are each assigned to one of three groups. The "tortoise quarter", Tartuca, is situated in the southwest of the city, bordering the districts of the Eagle, Snail, Wave, Panther and Forest with their respective symbols. Tartuca sports a blue and yellow banner with a tortoise (Fig. 131.) and enjoys the patronage of Saint Antonius of Padova. The latter was a Franciscan monk who lived in the early 13th century and to whose honor the inhabitants of this district build a church in the 16th century. Since the Dark Ages, the districts compete against each other in a festival named Palio, which is basically a horse race that is often decided more by the tricks employed by the riders than by the speed of their horses. On this occasion the banners of all the districts and the colorful robes of the participants of the tournament dominate the sights throughout the city.

In recent years, *Testudo hermanni* has also attracted the attention of postage stamp designers. On a 300 CFA-Franc-stamp from Tchad (Michel No. 579 [Block 50], Scott No. 292 F) issued on 01.04.1973 as part of a block dedicated to music, the above-mentioned painting, "Still-life with Musical Instruments", is reproduced (the caption erroneously states the year of birth of the artist as 1590, though). A year later, on 03.07.1974,

Spain published a set of postage stamps with reptile motifs, of which the 1 Peseta-piece (Michel No. 2087, Scott No. 1819) (Fig. 142) is supposed to depict a "*Testudo graeca*" according to its caption, but which much rather shows a *Testudo hermanni* (BOUR pers. comm.). A French set dedicated to protected wildlife was issued on 14.09.1991, and its 3 Franc-value (Michel No. 2854, Scott No. 2262) (Fig. 139) had an Italian tortoise for a motif. Above and to the right of the depicted tortoise is a line drawing that points out the usually divided supracaudal scute of *Testudo hermanni*. Under the patronage of the WWF, Monaco issued on 07.11.1991 a set of stamps dedicated to the worldwide conservation of nature that comprises four pieces (Michel Nos. 2046–2049, Scott Nos. 1778–1781) (Fig. 138), which were printed as a continuous strip or block and all showed *Testudo hermanni* from four different angles. The drawings are of excellent quality and highly naturalistic. One of the most recent "postage stamps" with a *Testudo hermanni* for a motif comes from Madagascar and is dated 2001 (Fig. 145). Twelve pieces were printed as two continuous small sheets, both in a perforated and smooth-margined version. The Italian tortoise is shown on one of the "stamps" with a nominal "value" of 1,500 Madagascar-Franc. In spite of this series being actually quite attractive, it is merely a set of vignettes.

In 1993, the municipal administration of Gonfaron (Fig. 134) in France introduced a postmark that had been sponsored by SOP-TOM. It points out the tales, the wines, and the tortoises this town is famous for. One year later, SOPTOM was granted their own postmark, which contains the logo of the station, its name and postal address (Fig. 135). This postmark received a general optical "overhaul" in 2005.

The Spanish telephone service provider CabiTel issued a set of telephone cards titled "Fauna Ibérica" in March 1997 of which the 2,000 Pesetas-card depicts on both sides various aspects of *Testudo hermanni* (Fig. 137); a brief text on the rear side of the card provides information on the geographical distribution and natural habitats of this species in Spain.

Testudo hermanni has also been immortalized on the labels of wines. One example is that of the light, fruity "Vin de Pays des Maures", introduced by the vintagers cooperative of Gonfaron in 1992. It depicts as drawings three tortoises in the vineyards as well as a flying donkey, which is the town's coat-of-arms. This wine was followed up by the rather spicy and strong "Tortues Passion" in 2000, which is a "Château de Campuget" of the "Costières de Nîmes". Its label shows the photograph of a beautiful Italian tortoise and contains a note on the "l'Association de Protection et de Sauvegarde des Tortues". A red wine of the "Motta" vineyards from the province of Grosseto (Tuscany, Italy) shows on its label a stylized tortoise in the center of a laurel wreath (Fig. 132). The producing vineyard is named "La Tartaruga" and provides several red wines and a white Chardonnay under the "Tartaruga" label. The same label is also used for the olive oil and honey produced on this estate.

Threats

Testudo hermanni species group

The species of the Testudo hermanni species group are listed under the collective name Testudo hermanni in the Red Data Book of the IUCN (International Union for the Conservation of Nature) in the subcategory "Near Threatened" of the category "Lower Risk" (2004; www.redlist.org). This means that the survival of these species is as yet not dependent on conservation measures, but that they are close to being classified as endangered. Even though populations are still large in wide parts of the distribution range, drastic declines have been observed in some regions over the past few years rendering local populations threatened in their continued existence. The chelonian specialist group of the IUCN has included these species in Appendix X of their action plan because they are already subjects of conservation measures. The European council has rated these species as "Rare".

The period during which the life of a tortoise is most at risk is when it is still inside its egg. Numerous are the predators that just wait for an opportunity to ravage the clutches of these animals. Most studies to this effect have come to the conclusion that more than half of the clutches are lost to predators. No such losses were recorded in the surroundings of Alíki in Greece, though, and only 10–20 % of artificially created nests were plundered there despite the presence of badger and red fox. The numbers of nests that were destroyed by predators in the more forested parts of Greece were substantially higher, however, and came close to the figures determined in southern France and in the Italian Maremma National Park. In the Maure Plains, it was estimated that between 6.9 and 33.3 % of the eggs fell victim to predators. A study conducted in the French Provence showed that nine of a total of twenty-three clutches were lost to badger and beech marten in the first night following oviposition. This figure rose to fifteen within five nights, and was twenty-two after thirty-seven nights. A similar result was obtained for forty-five artificially created nests: twenty-two had been destroyed during the first night, thirty-three after four nights, and thirty-seven by day 37. Another study in the Provence revealed losses of between 34.4 and 98 % after thirteen nights in places with a high density of nest pits, but only 47.0 to 66.6 % where clutches were more widely spread. About 86 % of clutches are lost to predators in the Italian Maremma National Park, and on Corsica, 83 % of the artificially created nests in the surroundings of Porto-Vecchio had been destroyed after seventeen nights.

Losses are also very high during the first few years of life, but they decrease as the tortoises grow and their shells ossify. Animals that are known to prey on clutches and/or juveniles include the cinereous vulture (*Aegypius monachus*), golden eagle (*Aquila chrysaetos*), lesser spotted eagle (*Aquila pomarina*), bearded vulture (*Gypaetus barbatus*), white-tailed eagle (*Haliaeetus albicilla*), Egyptian vulture (*Neophron percnopterus*), common raven (*Corvus corax*), hooded crow (*Corvus cornix*), carrion crow (*Corvus corone*), rook (*Corvus frugilegus*), Eurasian jay (*Garrulus glandarius*), magpie (*Pica pica*), Caspian gull (*Larus cachinnans*), crested porcupine (*Hystrix cristata*), western and eastern hedgehogs (*Erinaceus europaeus* and *Erinaceus concolor*), brown rat (*Rattus norvegicus*), black rat (*Rattus rattus*), wood mouse (*Apodemus sylvaticus*), beech marten (*Martes foina*), European badger (*Meles meles*), least weasel (*Mustela nivalis*), ferret (*Mustela putorius*), golden jackal (*Canis aureus*), domesticated dog (*Canis familiaris*), red fox (*Vulpes vulpes*), brown bear (*Ursus arctos*), and wild boar (*Sus scrofa*). Even some colubrid snakes have been observed feeding on baby *Testudo hermanni*. Hatchlings with their soft shells are commonly consumed whole so that no evidence in the form of remains can be found. Only some birds will hack a hole into the shell to access the meat of the tortoises.

Hedgehogs have so far only been recorded as nest raiders, but badger, fox, beech marten, ferret, golden jackal, rats, and wild boar also regularly plunder the clutches of the tortoise species dealt with here. In France, the beech marten is the major threat, whereas on Corsica, western hedgehog, least weasel and red fox cause most losses.

Only a few of the above-mentioned species remain a threat once the tortoises have managed to survive into semiadulthood or even adulthood. These are mainly the domestic dog, wild boar, porcupine, bear, and large birds of prey. The latter play a role in the Balkans in particular where both the tortoises and these birds are comparatively common. In contrast, only a single such incident has become known from the western parts of the Mediterranean where *Testudo hermanni* made up 50–90 % of the diet of a pair of golden eagles on Corsica (CHEYLAN 2001). The taste of Balkan birds of prey for tortoises can sometimes reach surprising proportions. For example, ANDRINOS (1987) reported from Greece that a pair of eagles would bring about 90–100 tortoises back to their nest to raise one or more chicks. Some birds of prey, such as the Egyptian and the white-tailed eagles, but also raven and gull, appear to predominantly prey on juveniles and specimens found dead. Bearded vulture and golden eagle have developed a unique method for cracking the shells even of large adults: they carry their prey high into the air and eventually drop them onto a boulder or rocky ground where the shell bursts or at least cracks on impact.

Domestic dogs have become a problem in certain parts of the southern French Maure Mountains in particular. Many tortoises found here show the distinctive bite mark scars or fresh bite wounds of stray dogs, ranging from gnawed or chewed-up shells to mutilated limbs. SCHWEIGER (1992a) and TREPTE (1993) found in Tuscany a relatively large number of tortoises with missing limbs, and both authors attributed these injuries to porcupines that are numerous in this region. Like most rodents, the omnipresent rats take advantage mainly on sleeping or hibernating tortoises. As they mainly go for the terminal parts of the limbs and margins of the carapace, the type of injury usually makes identification of the culprit easy. While some tortoises survive these injuries, others are eventually eaten out of their shells, which is then the only evidence that remains of the drama.

Today, the largest threat by far to the natural populations of the members of the *Testudo hermanni* species group is the destruction of their habitats. Beginning during the middle late Stone Age, some 4,000 years B.C., man started to reshape the natural landscapes of the Mediterranean region. Most valleys were cultivated, and hills were fire-cleared on a regular basis to provide and maintain grazing for his livestock. During the course of the 18th century, the explosive proliferation of people and modernized agricultural methods resulted in a rapid expansion of the areas used by man. Only some mountain chains were spared for a long time, examples for which include the Albères/Albera Mountains in the eastern Pyrenean Mountains, the massifs of Maure and Estérel in the southern French department of Var, and a few limestone mountains in the French regions of Languedoc-Roussillon and Provence-Alpes-Côte d'Azur (e.g., the mountains of Clape, Gardiole, Sainte-Victoire, and Sainte Baume). The very high annual survival rate of specimens in the wild (comp. chapter "Growth and Life expectancy") is to an increasing extent negatively influenced by man's activities. The most devastating of these are without a doubt the forest and bush fires that break out with predictable regularity all over the Mediterranean region as a result of negligence or intentional arson. The effect of a fire on the local

tortoise population varies from case to case and depends on a number of factors. The latter include, for example, the local vegetation density, wind speed and direction, lay of the land, time of day, and season. Although the members of the *Testudo hermanni* species group appear to be in general less affected by these fires than, for example, *Testudo ibera* or *Testudo marginata*, because they are preferably found in areas where fires are less common, there are exceptions. In general, fire is a brief event, but it very often has lasting effects on the vegetation in the habitat of a tortoise population. For example, a single firestorm ravaging the open country of Albera in Spain was estimated to have claimed about 30% of the local tortoise population, and one that set the heathland near the coast at Alíki in the Greek northeast ablaze destroyed some 40% of the original population of about 3,000 heads. Fires can be even more devastating in the more wooded parts on Corsica and in the south of France. Here it is estimated that 69.5 and 80%, respectively, of the local tortoise populations were lost to fires. The number of fatalities appears to be correlated to vegetation densities and the extent of the fire. In Spain, it is believed that juveniles and adult female specimens are particularly at risk of dying in fires. Although the latter could not be confirmed for the animals living at Alíki in Greece, it was the juveniles that had to pay the highest price here as well. Large specimens often manage to survive a fire by pressing themselves into a depression in the ground so that the fire actually sweeps over them. Often, this still leaves them with severe burn wounds, at least to the posterior parts of the carapace. In some instances the entire horny and epidermal layers may be burned off so that the bony understructure becomes visible. Surprisingly, many specimens recover from these injuries.

The booming tourism industry of the Mediterranean region has a distinctly negative impact on the tortoises, too. While the construction of holiday resorts accounts only for a relatively small percentage of lost habitats over all, its qualitative impact on important habitats along the coasts is by far greater.

More recent studies concluded that the use of herbicides also has negative repercussions on tortoise populations. While the effects of Grammoxone and Atrazine on tortoises have not yet been investigated, it is known that 2.4 D and 2.4.5 T at least are lethal for these animals. This was outlined by the fact that after these herbicides were used in the surroundings of Olympia on the Peloponnesus (Greece) from 1980, mortality rates for tortoises with carapace length of more than 10 cm increased to up to 34 %, which is about three times the natural mortality rate. Condemned specimens appeared almost normal, were not even underweight, but in most cases showed swollen eyes and severely congested upper respiratory tracts, and hardly moved from their spot. None of these specimens was ever found again so that it remains uncertain when exactly and how they actually died. The number of specimens with less than 10 cm in carapace length also decreased by about half during this period. WILLEMSEN & HAILEY (2001a) interpreted this to be a direct result of poisonings with the mentioned herbicides and feared that their continued use would eventually spell doom for many a tortoise population. In fact, the monitored population had been all but eradicated by 1984, which these authors attributed to the high mortality rates rather than emigration, especially in the light of the fact that during this period more specimens had immigrated than had left the area. Mortality rates in the study area were altogether reminiscent of those following a severe bush fire. However, the use of herbicides is potentially much more dangerous as respective events are much more frequent. Other reports speculated that the use of herbicides and related chemicals had a negative impact on the fertility of the tortoises and would reduce the chances of survival for the embryos, but this could as yet not be proved.

On the island of Corfu, the numbers of sightings of Boettger's tortoises declined in the wake of an increased farming of olives and the increased use of pesticides and fungicides that came with it; between 1980 and 1984 the respective figures diminished from 284 to 159. HILL (2003), on the other hand, stated the species could (once more?) be encountered in partly high population densities and a wide range of habitats throughout the island

The consumption of these animals by the local human population does not generally pose a severe threat to the continued existence of the involved species, but very much does so to individual populations. In some countries of the Balkans, roasting of tortoises over a campfire is still a common practice amongst shepherds. The pitiable animals are mostly impaled alive on a stick, broiled in the glowing embers, and then cracked open so that the muscle meat can be eaten.

In the Greek town of Lárissa, tortoises were still collected for a local turtle soup factory until about 1970, although *Testudo marginata* were preferred over *Testudo boettgeri* due to their greater size. The wild populations of the Balkan Peninsula also had to suffer through a succession of wars that took place throughout the 20th century, beginning with WW I and ending with the Kosovo War. Troops and a starving civilian populace helped themselves freely to this easily acquired source of valuable protein.

There are reports that during WW I, French soldiers stationed in Greece would regularly entertain themselves with "tortoise races" prior to slaughtering the animals, with the first prize being that the winner would temporarily be spared the cooking pot. In Spain and Italy, where the poorer classes of the human population used to regularly enhance their scant diet with the meat of tortoises, this practice has now largely ceased. The fall of the "iron curtain", however, also made some "speciality restaurants" in the Czech Republic and other eastern European countries rediscover tortoises for their menus and now import these animals by the truckloads. For example, a shipment of 473 tortoises from Greece was confiscated and two smugglers were arrested on the Slovakian/Czech border on 16.05.1997; all these animals were intended for restaurants. One large suitcase was found to contain not less than 150 specimens, with the remaining ones being spread between another suitcase and two plastic bags. Sixteen of these animals were already dead. The surviving ones were temporarily accommodated in the zoo of the Slovakian capital Bratislava. Here, they were cared for in an exemplifying manner by staff so that "only" another thirty-four specimens perished. Unfortunately Greek authorities were unwilling to carry the costs of return transportation of the tortoises so that it took four months before a concerted effort of the department of forestry at Thessaloníki, various hunting associations, and the Slovakian Ministry of the Environment brought the tortoises back to Greece. They were released in the forested surroundings of Thessaloníki where they now enjoy freedom once more.

For decades, thousands and thousands of tortoises of the species dealt with here were collected for the international pet trade. Even minor collecting may, however, have a severe impact on less dense popu-

Fig. 146: Victims of a fire in southern France (B. DEVAUX)

lations. Considering the scandalous and opaque practices that persisted until only a few years ago (see below) it is not really surprising that, for example, the German Central Association of Petshops R.A. has "no statistic material on the trade in tortoises available" for the second half of the 20th century. Exporting countries, on the other hand, kept track of the lamentable forex-generating trade, and it is there where figures can found. Thus, during the course of 1971, the former Yugoslavia alone exported 400,727 specimens of *Testudo boettgeri* and *Testudo hercegovinensis*, largely stacked by the dozen in wooden crates. About 10,000 animals were processed into banjos. Major importing countries in 1971 were Germany (124,236 tortoises), Belgium (90,060), the Netherlands (60,945), Italy (50,691), France (36,201), Great Britain (22,737), Switzerland (9.942), Austria (5,373), and Denmark (870). The total number of imports by the mentioned countries was, however, much higher than that as they were augmented by imports from countries such as Bulgaria and Greece. Great Britain, for example, imported about

Fig. 147: Tortoises are regular victims of bushfires also on Corsica. (J. MARAN)

347,000 specimens of the species dealt with here between 1965 and 1977, some 10,000 from Turkey and another 70,500 from former Yugoslavia in 1978, 5,003 in 1979, and another 22,500 heads during the period from 1980 to 1983. France was the destination of about 60,000 *Testudo boettgeri* and *Testudo hercegovinensis* from the Balkans in 1967, and in total imported ca. 165,000 representatives of the *Testudo hermanni* species group over a period of four years. From July 1975 through December 1980, Switzerland imported a total of 16,365 tortoises representing these species. Beginning in the 1960', the US joined the ranks of regular importers of these three species, accounting for 5,354 specimens between 1989 and 1997. From 1977 to 1999 the international trade in tortoises of the *Testudo hermanni* species group involved an official total of 227,971 specimens.

After trading legally in wild-caught tortoises was made nearly impossible by new legislation, their collection assumed a less prominent role as a threat to their survival. This is despite the fact that as a tourist one is still offered on a regular basis specimens of *Testudo boettgeri* and *Testudo hercegovinensis* (usually babies) in the various states that once made up Yugoslavia. Although such trade is illegal, it usually plays out without any effort being made on concealing it. It is unfortunate that many holidaymakers then cannot resist the temptation and return home with a tortoise or two in their baggage. Most of them will be aware of their breaking laws, which shows in many a new owner of a tortoise changing their minds on the journey back home. It used to be rather common on homeward bound trains from Bulgaria to the former GDR to see tortoises being thrown out the windows of the rolling train. If these animals were not smashed into pieces on impact on the ballast of the railway track, they found themselves in a strange environment. Often they managed to survive there for a few years until a severe winter eventually got the better of them.

For the past few years, "farmed" animals from Slovenia have been appearing in pet shops. Their actual origins are dubious, though, and nobody seems to know where exactly the respective farms are supposed to be.

In the past, the tortoises were usually treated so badly during collecting already that their chances of survival were practically reduced to zero. In many parts of Greece, for example, farmers used to have a large box somewhere on their fields into which every tortoise was thrown that was found while they were working their fields. When the box was full, it was taken to a central collection point and emptied out. The animals were then shoveled with pitchforks into even larger crates that were then shipped either by land or sea to northern and central Europe. The life-preserving moisture during these many days of transportation came in the form of feces from the tortoises lying above. When such a shipment arrived at the importer's, the lower third layer of tortoises had degraded into a bloody, stinking mass. The animals in the middle third were dead as well, and what still moved in the top third was sold to unsuspecting animal lovers. Prices were very moderate at this point of time, demanding investments of just $ 3-7 for a tortoise, so that 99% of them ended up as "toys for the kids" in the hands of people who had no idea what the keeping of these animals entailed. Within a year, 80% of the imported animals were dead as a result of poor care, and, according to a study conducted by BLATT & MÜLLER (1974), only 1.8% of them were tough enough to hang on to life for five years. Often their owners eventually lost interest and abandoned them in the wild or made them "presents" to the nearest zoo. Zurich zoo (Switzerland), alone received 221 of these unwanted tortoises in 1974 and another 228 in 1975. Even long before the European Union banned the imports, OBST (1980), for one, demanded that mass imports be stopped. At the same time he promoted that strictly controlled small numbers of carefully collected and transported animals be exempted and made available for keeping and breeding to serious keepers.

The import ban imposed by the European Union unfortunately also has some negative side effects. Since selling the tortoises is longer possible – other than illegally to tourists – their value to the populace in many Balkan countries has diminished greatly. Being now practically worthless in monetary terms, they are often killed with deliberation and great cruelty. Cases have become known of pits being dug, filled with tortoises, soaked with petrol, and set alight.

In some instances tortoises were used as "live constituents" in the construction of new roads. In Greece, tortoises make good secondary targets for "sport shooters" that were less lucky shooting down more agile targets, rare birds for example. Officials look at such barbaric activities with consternation and helplessness, but maybe the problem could be overcome with large-scale information campaigns, and the enforcement through drastic fines of the existing species protection laws.

Boettger's tortoise

In Albania, *Testudo boettgeri* is still widely distributed and common in all size classes in areas not affected by man. The situation of the populations has been worsening since the 1970', though. HAXHIU (1995b) reported that the animals were deliberately killed in the central parts of the country in particular, mainly by shepherds who considered tortoises as competitors for food to their livestock herds. They are rarely consumed by the native people. Although HAXHIU had stated in 1985 that Albanians would regularly use these tortoises as food, he admitted ten years later that this statement had been made on a specific request by the then-communist regime that wanted to see information published on the economic value of the animals (HAXHIU 1995a). Like in the other countries, the major threat to its continued existence in Albania stems from the ongoing destruction of natural habitats. Originally vegetated mainly with maquis and forests, thousands of hectares have been cleared in this mountainous country since the 1960' to make space for fields, vineyards and fruit plantations. Since deforestation measures were usually taken in winter, large numbers of tortoises were killed by the heavy machinery used to flatten the forests. Some survived their severe injuries so that today tortoises with healed injuries to their shells can be found in many places. In some areas specimens disfigured thus were found to account for up to 16% of the populations. The socioeconomic changes that followed in the wake of the fall of the iron curtain also in Albania are particularly obvious on the free trade markets. As the country moves away from being an almost exclusive farming nation, the vegetation has begun to regain ground in many deforested areas. A threat to the tortoises that has remained, though, is the frequent forest and bush fires. The number of fires has in fact distinctly increased since the early 1990'. Most of these are started deliberately, for example by shepherds, in an attempt to "rejuvenate" the vegetation and thus create better grazing for their livestock herds. Many natural habitats are also lost to the increased construction of roads and settlements, and road kills of tortoises have as a consequence become more common. The tortoises used to be collected, partly on a large scale, and processed into chicken and pig feed until the early 1990'.

Like all reptiles, tortoises have a bad reputation in Albania and are considered symbols of evil in many folk tales. People therefore treat these animals accordingly. After the collapse of the old regime, smuggling of these animals ensued on a very small scale in the form of refugees taking them along in the hope of being able to sell them later (HAXHIU 1995b). Using hopelessly overcrowded ships and boats, an exodus of people tried to reach Italy. Earlier or later the Italian coastguard spotted these boat people, and what may have happened in more than one instance is illustrated by the following account: a boat with refugees from Albania was stopped within Italian territorial waters. Besides drugs and weapons a traveling bag containing several *Testudo boettgeri* was found. The Italian authori-

ties denied the owner of this bag permission to bring the animals into the country due to their protected status and the absence of valid import documents. The Albanian solved the problem instantly by ridding himself of the bag and its contents by dumping it overboard.

An increase in smuggling activity from Albania was notable during the following years. For example, about 400 Boettger's tortoises were illegally imported into Italy in 1995. They were discovered, confiscated and sent back to Albania. Tortoises of Albanian origin have also been appearing in the US pet trade on various occasions where they demand very high prices.

In Bulgaria, *Testudo boettgeri* used to be widely distributed and a rather common sight in areas such as the lowlands between the Stara Planina and the Sredna Gora Mountains. Today, the species is on the retreat everywhere as a result of man's activities. In some regions, particularly the more densely populated coastal areas and plains and valleys used intensely for agriculture, it has already been eradicated. Populations that exist at higher elevations on forested mountain slopes are less severely affected, but various smaller populations that used to live in some parts of the highlands in the Bulgarian west have now disappeared. The exact reasons for this phenomenon have not been identified, but it is quite certain that it is a result of anthropogenic influences as well. *Testudo boettgeri* has by now become very rare along the southern fringes of the Dobrudja and may in fact be already extinct there. It is likely that the highest population densities are now limited to the southern slopes of the Emine Balkans.

Bulgaria ranks amongst the poorer European nations, and the consumption of tortoises by the local populace is a factor that is still often underestimated. While this practice was largely limited to the city of Plovdiv and surroundings until the First World War, it became more widespread during the early 1940' when large numbers were not only exported to Germany, but also supplied to Bulgarian restaurants. Starting in the early 1960', rural Bulgarians began to believe that the consumption of tortoise blood, meat, eggs and other body parts could heal cancer, and leukemia in particular. Relatives of sufferers or "physicians" in some cases collected dozens or even hundreds of tortoises for this purpose. A former mayor of Chukarevo in the Burgas region estimated that 90% of the tortoises that used to live in the surroundings of his village were collected between 1941 and 1944. His fellow mayor of the neighboring village Drama reported that traders from Plovdiv caught tortoises there in so large numbers between 1942 and 1943 that populations were reduced by about 90% as well. Large specimens were usually affected the most since they were the easiest to find. In regions heavily sampled by tortoise collectors most remaining specimens were therefore small and not sexually mature or barely so. It is likely that the age structures of these populations have not fully recovered even until today.

During the mid-20th century, the consumption of tortoises was particularly popular in the eastern buttresses of the Stara Planina Mountains, in the eastern Rhodopes, in Svilengrad and Strandzha. These are areas where the animals are still more common today. Specimens were, however, also supplied to consumers and restaurants in towns such as Pazardzik, Sofia, Burgas, Varna, Stara Zagora and Plovdiv. Plovdiv and neighboring towns like, for example, Rakovski, were the unrivaled centers of tortoise consumption, though. Here, tortoise meat was a regular item on the menu of up to 98% of the populace until the late 1970'. In

Fig. 148: This Corsican *Testudo hermanni* survived a fire by hiding in a hare's burrow. (J. MARAN)

a poll involving several hundred randomly interviewed dwellers of Bulgarian towns at this time, some 35–40% admitted to having eaten tortoise meat at least once. Males were particularly familiar with this dish as most had encountered it during their military service.

For a long time, the majority of tortoises were collected in the eastern parts of Bulgaria. After these populations had been drastically reduced by the 1960', collectors focused more on the regions in the southwest and northwest of the country. Most of the animals that appeared on the markets during the 1970' therefore originated from the regions of Sofia and Montana where intact populations still existed. Tortoises are rarely consumed in the region of Sofia itself, and most people living there even despise the idea of eating these animals. In the plains of Petric, and in the foothills of the Malashevska, Ograzden, Pirin and Belasica Mountains, the intense collecting of tortoises during the 1970' eventually resulted in specimens of more than 20 cm in carapace length being limited to localities at altitudes between 900 and 1,400 m. Here, the population densities were too low to make commercial collecting profitable.

Even today the consumption of tortoises is still, respectively again, no exception in Bulgaria. It is particularly common amongst poor people and mainly entertained by members of the catholic minority. Again, the region around Plovdiv is the center of this practice. IONEV (1999), for one, often found remains of tortoise shells in camp-fires of gypsies. Restaurants now also offer *Testudo boettgeri* on a more regular basis than during the previous decades, particularly in towns such as Haskovo, Blagoevgrad and Harmanli.

Their use for "medicinal" purposes has not been relinquished in some parts of the country either. With local tortoise populations being on a constant decline, instances of hundreds of these tortoises being smuggled over the Romanian border have become known. It is not an uncommon practice to "stock" animals for months for the next family feast. The market price for a tortoise in Bulgaria is equivalent to between $ 3 and 6.

Another problem in Bulgaria is the meanwhile large number of wild boars that harass mainly the juvenile tortoises in the regions of Burgas, Montana, Plovdiv and Haskovo, as well as in the eastern reaches of the Stara Planina Mountains. In some parts of the country, e.g., in the vicinity of the villages of Rabisha (Montana region) and Daskotna (Burgas region) tortoise popula-tions have apparently become all but extinct by now.

The expansion of human settlements, industrial plants and the development of tourism obviously bear no good for the tor-toises either. The main reasons for their de-clining numbers, however, are certainly to be found in the destruction of natural habi-tats through the clearing of natural vegeta-tion, burning of stubble fields, use of heavy agricultural machinery, and the subsequent establishment of monocultures, though. The

Fig. 149: This young female *Testudo hermanni* on Corsica did not bury herself deep enough to escape a fire unscathed. (J. MARAN)

collection of semiadult tortoises for sale to local and international tourists contributes to their disappearance in coastal regions and certain areas in the center of the country. This practice could as yet not be stopped completely. Tortoises are also still used for crafting "tasteful" objects such as lampshades and ashtrays in some villages, e.g., in the Ran Haskovo region.

The largest Bulgarian populations of *Testudo boettgeri* today still exist in the Struma Plains, in the surroundings of Strandzha, in the eastern Rhodopes, and in the Bulgarian part of Thrace. This is in part a result of the environmental conditions in these regions and the more traditional methods of agriculture employed there, but mainly of Ordinance # 1578 of the Forest Administration. Issued in 1970 and valid until at least a few years ago, this bylaw prohibited the collection of tortoises throughout the Haskovo region. The remaining populations there are small and isolated from one another so that they have to be regarded as highly endangered. Right now, however, it is exactly this area that is the target of organized gangs of animal collectors that catch the tortoises for the international pet trade and the Bulgarian food market. Collected specimens are usually smuggled across the border into Greece or Turkey and shipped from there.

In Greece, the species is still widely distributed, and although a general decline in numbers is noted here as well, healthy populations still exist particularly in the northeast of the country. Future prospects for *Testudo boettgeri* are not all that bright here either, though. The heathlands near the coast are highly susceptible to fires that are usually started by people both accidentally and deliberately for fire clearing. These fires sometimes have devastating effects on local tortoise populations. A study conducted by WILLEMSEN & HAILEY (1989) showed that

the plant society rising from the ashes of a forest or bush fire does not provide a basis of life for *Testudo boettgeri* initially. This often prevents the tortoises to recolonize such an area for several years after it has been ravaged by fire.

The population at Alíki, which is one of the largest and densest populations of *Testudo boettgeri*, comprised some 5,000 specimens in the early 1980'. In spite of assurances by the officials that neither tourism installations nor pastures would be expanded, the spread of both was eventually tolerated. As had been predicted, they caused a substantial population decline. This involved, for example, the overnight destruction of some 150 ha of pristine nature in the surroundings of Alíki through means such as fire clearing and heavy earthmoving equipment on 19.07.1980, following an environmental impact study that had led to the rejection of an application to erect holiday bungalows there. The developers of the settlement thus created a different environmental scenario, and were now applying for otherwise worthless ground, with the price to be paid by some 1,400 tortoises and a multitude of other animals that lost their lives. It was therefore even more laudable that this did not lead to the issuing of development permits. Aided by the University of Thessaloníki, the area was eventually placed under police guard.

In spite of all these protection efforts, the population kept on declining slowly but steadily until about 1990. Reasons for this development were likely to be based on an increasing salinity of the soils that caused the heathlands to become drier and so reduced the tortoises' feeder plants. At the same time, the number of badgers rose drastically, which saw the loss of clutches and juveniles rise as well. At this time, a mere 1% of the monitored animals were representing the juvenile age group. The population has been recovering slowly since the 1990', though, and now lives within a fully fenced-in nature reserve (for waterfowl) that can only be entered with an official permit.

Wheat is the most widely farmed grain in the plains of northern Greece. Farmers unfortunately still continue to burn their fields after harvest here, and the widely ranging fires often spread into what has remained of the natural vegetation between the individual wheat fields. As a consequence the tortoises that used to persist there have by now all but disappeared completely. Even the rocky hills in this region with their natural garrigue vegetation are often not spared by these fires. A hill in the vicinity of Kilkís, for example, used to be home to a large population of Testudo boettgeri and a smaller one of Testudo ibera. A bush fire then ravaged parts of this hill in the 1980', leaving behind the remains of numerous tortoises that could not escape the catastrophe and could still be found years later. If the resident farmers cannot be convinced to stop the burning of their harvested fields, this could pose a serious threat to the continued existence of Boettger's tortoise in the wheat belt of Greece.

The common practice of dumping garbage and setting it alight at some stage represents a death trap for tortoises that forage or seek shelter amongst the garbage.

Greek farmers occasionally stone tortoises to death in the widespread belief they would cause damage to crops in general, and to the tasty young shoots of melon plants in particular.

The presence of Testudo boettgeri in agriculturally used areas in the south of Greece proves that more traditional methods of farming pose no threat to the species. In contrast, it appears that these even favor the survival of tortoises. The changeover to modern agrarian deserts, on the other hand, has had devastating effects on tortoise populations just like it did in other countries. It is therefore doubtful that Boettger's tortoises still live in areas that have been altered thus.

A population of Testudo boettgeri living in the vicinity of Olympia on the Peloponnesus was more closely investigated between 1975 and 1984. The investigation involved the capture, marking and re-release of 879 specimens in total during this period of time. It showed clearly that numbers dwindled when farmers began to burn down separator hedges from 1980, which spelt death to many hiding beneath them.

Large stretches of natural habitat were lost in the surroundings of Kalamáta when houses were built and tourism was developed. In this area, there is little hope for a future for the tortoise populations. A single population of Boettger's tortoise was discovered near Sparta that has been living within an old fruit orchard. It is a small but dense population that is likely to disappear from one day to the next when this plantation will eventually be recultivated if it is not placed under protection by law. It would mean the loss of the probably largest population in the Sparta Plains.

Sometimes even relatively minor changes to a natural habitat have disastrous consequences for a local tortoise population. One such example was a study area near the monasteries of Meteóra. For a long time, this area had been accessible only by means of a donkey ride, but in 1984 a network of roads was built to open it up for cars and tractors. The construction of the new roads claimed many hedges, which had a direct lethal impact on those tortoises resting beneath them even though their clearing affected only a relatively small portion of the entire area. Since then the increased traf-

Fig. 150: The cause of death is not always identifiable, as is the case with this *Testudo boettgeri* from Loutra Kilini, Greece (F. WÜTHRICH)

fic has been claiming the lives of (not only) tortoises on a regular basis, and some local residents freely admit to running them over deliberately whenever they feel like it.

The use of modern agricultural machinery such as harvesters and ploughs also has a negative impact on tortoises. This has been demonstrated again in the surroundings of Arfai, Antirrion and Préveza where populations declined drastically after respective machinery was introduced there.

Another problem that is particularly common in the surroundings of human settlements is the bad habit of people to just dump their garbage somewhere in nature. Garbage usually attracts rats that practically reduce to zero the chances of survival for young tortoises and often even cause fatal injuries to adults. Since *Testudo boettgeri* mainly occurs in cultivated lands and near human settlements in the southern parts of Greece, the proliferation of rats has become a major threat to them here. For example, in the surroundings of Olympia, an increased number of rat attacks on tortoises were noted from 1978. From 1982, hardly any juvenile *Testudo hermanni* could be found, and

since 1984, large numbers of rats can be "admired" there at any time of the day every day.

In contrast to other Mediterranean countries, there never was a large-scale trade in tortoises in Greece. However, inhabitants of a small village in the remote parts of the Greek central mountains reported in 1984 that a migrant trader had asked for tortoises and made an offer for 50 Drachms (about 20 US Cent) per head. This "top price" was too insignificant though to motivate people to now go out and look for tortoises. The implementation of European Union legislation has effectively stopped all legal trading in tortoises in Greece. Illegal trading has obviously been continued, but appears to be only a minor factor here.

RICHARDS & RICHARDS (1990), on the other hand, reported that many an inhabitant of the island of Corfu had a few tortoises "in store" for sale mainly to German and Italian tourists still in 1989. Dried tortoises and marine turtles were also offered as souvenirs.

An Austrian citizen was arrested in Vienna in November 1996, after he had tried to illegally import 450 *Testudo boettgeri*. These animals originated from the surroundings of the Greek mountain Kíssavos, and the smuggler thought he could sell them for prices of about $ 300–1,000 (!) per head. Forty-eight of these tortoises had already perished in transit, and the remaining survivors were temporarily accommodated in the Viennese animal park of Schönbrunn. Three-hundred and seventy-seven tortoises were then flown back in the company of a versed zoo keeper to Thessaloníki on 19.06.1997, with another 25 being retained in Vienna due to their still fragile states of health. The returned specimens were eventually released into the wild at Ambelákia and Spiliá on the foot of the mountain Kíssavos a short time later.

The former Yugoslavian republic of Macedonia used to be another hotspot for tortoise collectors. Exact information of the population status is not available at present.

In Romania, at least the populations in the border region with Serbia used to be safe from collectors for decades. Since Romanian citizens often tried to escape their communist regime via the "green border" into former Yugoslavia, police maintained permanent roadblocks, and access to the

border region was limited to a small number of villagers living there and people in possession of official permits. Since the demise of communism also in this country in 1990, the situation has drastically changed. The border region is now freely accessible. Its local inhabitants are usually reluctant to even touch a tortoise because they believe them to be carriers of the most dreadful diseases. If a farmer happens upon a tortoise in his fields, however, he will usually turn it on its back and "leave it to God's mercy". Notwithstanding that, specimens are also illegally caught and kept as pets. Meanwhile, a drastic decline of the wild populations existing in Romania has been noted. This development is due to factors including the damming up of artificial lakes and the resulting flooding of some regions, but also to other forms of habitat destruction.

There are only a few studies dealing with the Romanian populations of this species, and a lot of the information that has been published has meanwhile turned out to be either wrong or imprecise (ROZYLOWICZ et al. 2003). There are hardly any data pertaining to the geographical distribution of *Testudo boettgeri* in this country, and information on its biology is even scarcer. This is the main reason why scarcely any measures have been taken to protect and conserve Romanian populations.

The populations of Serbia and Montenegro have in the past been prime targets of animal collectors. In Serbia, villagers often already awaited the tortoises when they left their hibernation quarters. They were collected, transported to a collection point, and payment equal to about 60 US Cents per head was received. The Belgrade-based export agency GRUDA then arranged for the export of the animals to destinations in central and northern Europe. Their records indicate that in 1978 alone, about 100,000 tor-

Fig. 151: Road traffic regularly claims the lives of tortoises, as happened to this specimen on the Peloponnesus, Greece (J. MARAN)

toises were exported to Germany and Great Britain each. A single shipment of tortoises that were stacked in piles of wooden crates and transported north on trucks on journeys of several days could easily comprise some 12,000 specimens.

Stable populations still exist in some parts of Montenegro. Here, a census in an area of 2 km² conducted in the early 1980' revealed the presence of 125 individuals. However, an ongoing loss of habitats has been fragmenting once-continuous populations. Furthermore, many tourists from Belgrade had in the past the disturbing habit of taking back home from their holidays at the coast of Montenegro "live souvenirs" in the form of tortoises; many were also used for stuffing. That the illegal collecting of tortoises can still pose a serious threat to a population today is illustrated by the arrest of a smuggler by Croatian customs officials in May of 2005. The man had attempted to cross the border from Serbia into Croatia at night when he was checked by the customs officer on duty. His baggage was then found to contain not less than 504 Boettger's tortoises, which the man claimed to be taking along as a present to his German friends for them to use as garden ornaments. He claimed to have collected the animals over the past two months in Serbian forests. The smuggler was subsequently sentenced to a term in jail and has to expect an additional fine. The tortoises were temporarily accommodated in a rescue station and later handed back to Serbian officials.

In Turkey, the species appears to have never been particularly common. The existing populations are on the decline as a result of intensified agriculture.

Dalmatian tortoise
Owing to its relatively small geographical distribution range, *Testudo hercegovinensis* is probably the most threatened of the three species portrayed here. During the international "pet rush" of the 1960' and 70', entire regions were depleted of their natural tortoise populations.

The populations native to Bosnia and Herzegovina have for decades suffered from the activity of animal collectors that kept on supplying the international pet trade and in the process bled the natural population substantially.

Like in some other countries, thousands of tortoises used to be collected in Croatia and sold for a little money to tourists or professional animal dealers. The centers of this trade were the port town of Zadar and the region around the villages of Murvica and Policnik to the northeast of it. An estimated 60,000 live specimens from this region were traded between the early 1960' and the early 1980', which obviously reduced the natural populations to a substantial extent. *Testudo hercegovinensis* must equally be considered severely threatened on the Croatian islands, such as Cres, as a result of previously intense collecting, but also due to the heavy fragmentation of their habitats by means of a multitude of demarcation walls between low-grade farmed pastures. Since an import ban was imposed by the European Union, but in particular since the bloody secessionist war from the former Yugoslavian Federation, clear signs of recovery are notable in many Croatian populations, though. This is particularly true for border regions that are still densely dotted with landmines and therefore had a chance to see natural vegetation return. WEGEHAUPT (2005), for example, noted that numerous tortoises of all age groups were particularly common in the marginal areas of minefields. But the day will come when these minefields have also been cleared, which will then of course have the usual negative effects on nature. Due to the rocky structure of many of the mined areas, mine disposal vehicles are often of little use. Many farmers therefore resort to burning these areas and trigger the mines through the ensuing heat. This obviously kills most the tortoises, and the few that survive with usually severe injuries are still beaten to death by the farmers who regard them as vermin and competitors for food to their herds of sheep and goats. With the assistance of his son, WEGEHAUPT (2005) investigated twenty potential tortoise habitats on the Croatian Adriatic Coast in May 2005, but found the animals only in nine of these. This showed that tortoises are already absent from many agriculturally used areas today. SCHWEIGER (2005) encountered numerous tortoises on the island of Pag where they were particularly common in the northern parts. He concluded that the demarcation walls that crisscross the entire island might pose a problem to the regular finding of mating partners. Many of the parcels created thus can only be entered or left by climbing over the walls so that a tortoise living there is effectively "imprisoned". In spite of an intense search, SCHWEIGER often found only one tortoise living in a particular parcel. Reproductive groups were limited to some individual instances.

What has been said above with regard to the situation of *Testudo boettgeri* in Serbia and Montenegro also applies to this species.

Italian tortoise

As recently as during the late Stone Age, the Italian tortoise used to be distributed along the entire Mediterranean coast of France and also ranged much farther to the north than it is the case today. Ever since then, populations were on the back foot, be it for climatic changes or influences exerted by man. Today, *Testudo hermanni* must be regarded as seriously endangered in France. Although it appears that its distribution range has not shrunk substantially during the past few decades, the densities of the remaining populations have decreased continually. As a result of the devastating forest fires the Estérel Mountains experienced during the past decades, *Testudo hermanni* has become all but extinct here. There are hardly any suitable habitats left for the species to recolonize. The population has therefore become limited to small relicts in the less severely affected western parts of the mountain chain in the surroundings of Saint-Raphaël. Passably stable populations only still exist in the Maure Mountains, particularly at higher elevations, and on the island of Corsica. The Maure Mountains somehow escaped centuries of obsessive cultivation by the local people. This was certainly helped by the presence of Arabian pirates who used it as a base and were dispelled only in the 11th century A.D.. Loggers and shepherds then pillaged the mountains for a longer period during the 19th century before it was largely "forgotten" again after the First World War. The local fauna and flora obviously benefited from this anonymity until the expansion of towns and a booming tourism industry extended their tentacles from the Mediterranean coast to the Maure Mountains around 1950. The first residential buildings appeared right in the center of the mountain chain, and roads were built even to the remotest parts of this region. Originally intended as access roads for firefighters in the case of forest fires, the sheer presence of roads led to an increased presence of people that in turn caused an increase in those forest fires. It also raised the extent of illegal tortoise collecting.

The original estimate by CHEYLAN (1981a), based on a rather small study area in the Maure Plains, of only about 10,000 specimens of *Testudo hermanni* in the Maure

Mountains was fortunately proved too low just four years later when STUBBS & SWINGLAND (1985) reinvestigated the matter. These authors demonstrated that the average number of individuals at altitudes below 300 m was higher than presumed by CHEYLAN (1981a). Nevertheless, they also considered their situation as worrying. A census conducted between 1991 and 1994 then produced the following estimates: 85,000 tortoises inhabit an area of about 200 km² at a population density of 0.4 tortoises/ha. This is insufficient to guarantee continuous reproduction. 20,000–30,000 tortoises live in a "core area" of about 30 km² in size, which corresponds to an average population density of 0.7–1.1 specimens per hectare. However, because some sections of this core area are thinly or not at all populated while the tortoises concentrate in others, such an average value is of little practical use. An additional area of 70 km² is home to an another estimated 25,000–50,000 tortoises. Lastly, an area of ca. 60 km² on the fringes of the southern French distribution range contains another 5,000–10,000 specimens. Although these more recent estimates of the total number of southern French tortoises are distinctly higher than what was calculated by CHEYLAN (1981a), they are still relatively low if you take into consideration that the entire range covers some 200 km². Even more worrying is that more than one-third of the total population lives in only 20 % of the range. This seems to suggest that the numbers are on the decrease within the larger part of the range. If no protective measures are taken to reverse this trend, it must be feared that the distribution range will eventually shrink to the extent of the core area. This situation is further aggravated by the fact that the content of old specimens in this population is very high and that juveniles are rarely recorded from outside the larger concentrations. It is entirely possible that there are more specimens in human care in France than in nature. Another census that was started in 2001 and ended in 2005 will allow comparisons that may then paint a clearer picture of the status of this species. The results, scheduled for publication early in 2006, were unfortunately not yet available when this book went to print. First results, however, indicated that the habitat of the tortoises has shrunk even further, with some large populations now living in privately owned grounds.

To understand the situation of *Testudo hermanni* in southern France, one needs to recall that most of the habitats suitable for this species simply do not exist anymore today. It is likely that these tortoises were once widely distributed at low altitudes. The largest part of the southern French coastal plains is today fragmented through settlements and cultivated areas and virtually cut up by roads, railway tracks, canals and the like. The fact that the tortoises today are more common in the Maure Mountains than in the Maure Plains is therefore probably attributable to man's preference for the lowlands as an area for settlement. While the plains became less and less hospitable to tortoises, the mountains and their foothills were largely left alone or were used in a manner that left room for tortoises as well. Herds of goat and sheep kept the vegetation low and thus facilitated the growth of wild herbs in the open cork oak forests. This in turn reduced the risk of forest fires, which became less frequent in these foothills as a consequence. It also made the control of predators such as badger, marten and fox easier, from which the tortoises benefited. Olive groves and clearings in the forests now provided them with ideal places for their nests as the risk of losing them to predatory animals was greatly reduced.

The situation for the tortoises has been deteriorating since recently, though. A reduction in livestock farming and the return to more traditional forms of agriculture in many places now favors potential nest raiders once more. Beech marten, badger and wild boar populations recover, and some of them have literally specialized in locating and plundering tortoise nests that become more and more concentrated in fewer and fewer suitable spots. In some areas, the losses of clutches thus destroyed now amount to up to 90%. This is a direct result of reduced grazing through livestock herds that allows brush to grow taller, produce dry underbrush and therefore an increased fire hazard. It at the same time hampers the growth of the wild herbs that serve the tortoises as food. The reasons for this change are mainly found in the social and economic changes that developed in the wake of World War I. In general, there are much fewer people living in rural regions now, and this means less livestock farming.

The management of forests is a responsibility of the Office national de Forêt, the National Forest Office. Their main focus is on setting up firebreaks, but they do not seem ambitious enough to improve the living conditions for the native fauna.

The fires that ravage the south of France on an almost regular basis are a major problem. Often started by profiteering land developers, they devastate entire regions and kill everything alive that cannot flee fast enough - and that obviously includes tortoises. These fires are therefore a major threat to the remaining populations of Testudo hermanni. At earlier times, when widespread fires swept through a region only every thirty to fifty years, they were no problem for the local flora and fauna. Just the opposite was true: fires eliminated larger trees and dense scrub, and left a fertile soil behind that facilitated the growth of new and low vegetation. This rejuvenation of the flora provided excellent food resources for the recovering tortoise populations. Small summery fires were a regular occurrence between the major firestorms since times immemorial. Even the ancient Greek seafarers who some 3,000 year ago cruised off the coast at the foot of the Maure Mountains between the cities of Toulon and Fréjus

Fig. 152: Ill-fated encounters like this can unfortunately still be seen on roads in the south of France. (B. DEVAUX)

of today noted that fires turned huge forests into charcoal. It is an interesting byline that it was these Greeks who first introduced the term "maurun" for the mountain massif and its surroundings – it means "dark" or "black".

The mountain range was thus swept by fires again and again for thousands of years. Fires have therefore become a vital aspect of life for this type of habitat. They are the basis for regeneration and rejuvenation in that they facilitate the aeration of the soils and a renewed growth of vegetation. Some plants, such as the cork oak that is so characteristic of the Mediterranean coast, are well adapted to and even need an occasional fire to thrive. Fires thus are even of an advantage for the tortoises and their ecosystem – if they break out at larger intervals. During the 1970' though, not less than 103,450 hectares of maquis and pine forest were destroyed in the Département Var, of which some 7,000 hectares of forest burned down and killed some 20% of all the tortoises living on the French mainland in one catastrophic fire in August of 1979 alone. Since 1956, the loss of area to fires averages about 38,000 hectares per year. In 1990, even about every third tortoise of the Maure Mountains succumbed in this gruesome manner, with some 25,000 carcasses littering the landscape afterwards. This particular firestorm devastated about 15,000 hectares of forest and bushland. The forest fires that broke out in the surroundings of the small town of Vidauban during the "summer of the century" in 2003 did not only claim the lives of six people, but also those of between 3,500 and 5,000 tortoises. Started by arsonists in mid-July and late August, and favored by an extreme drought and strong winds, the fires spread rapidly and consumed another 20,000 hectares or so of forest and brush, including some 5,000 hectares of tortoise habitat.

Including Corsica in the calculations, it can be stated that an average of 4% of the natural habitat of *Testudo hermanni* in France is lost to fires every year. According to CHEYLAN (1984), about 90% of all forest fires spring from human activity, with some 25% being attributable to the carelessness of tourists.

There were, fortunately, no fires in areas with tortoise populations between the two major events of 1990 and 2003 so that the survivors were able to reproduce, increase the numbers of sexually mature specimens, and thus ensure the survival of the populations for the time being.

In areas devastated by fires, such as the Maure Plains, it had been noted at earlier times that it took the tortoises three to four years to recolonize the burnt-down sections from neighboring regions. This meant that recolonization was slow, but took place steadily. In all it took about ten years before such an area one more contained the largest part of its natural fauna and flora.

Now that large fires are an almost annual occurrence, nature is hardly left with a chance to recover. These catastrophic events become particularly threatening to tortoise populations when they are exacerbated by other factors such as settlements and roads, which fragment the natural habitats, and various others that reduce the numbers of these animals. The combination of fires and increasingly isolated insular habitats as a result of building activities has a particularly destructive effect on tortoise populations. Southern France has over the course of the past fifty years or so been literally flooded with holiday resorts, golf courses, but mainly with industrial installations and highways. All these shredded the natural habitats of the tortoises and left them only with insular patches to live in. Being suitable relict habitats these patches are then not rarely inhabited by thousands of tortoises. If such an island is devastated by fire – as happened at Vidauban in 2003 – there is no chance of recolonization because the nearest "island" is still too far away.

Since *Testudo hermanni* is rarely distributed at altitudes of more than 400 m a.s.l., mountains are an effective barrier for the dispersal of these tortoises. This leaves the areas along the foothills of these mountains and the plains as the only contact zones between populations. But these potential contact zones are exactly where man has erected his own barriers. In the end this spells extinction for the affected populations. Their natural habitats shrink more and more, and one day the tortoises are gone.

Tourism and environmental pollution are further threats to the continued existence of tortoises in France. Considerable numbers of them lose their lives on southern French roads. In the Provence, the animals are still being collected by tourists, hunters and mushroom collectors, with DEVAUX (2004a) estimating that some 2,000 tortoises disappear in the suitcases of tourists every year. Even occasional instances of theft from the zoological gardens in the region or the "Tortoise Village" (see below) have become known.

Collection for the commercial pet trade that used to be big business in the past in France as well is no longer a major problem today. After the very strict conservation laws of the European Union have come into effect, only a few professional animal collectors continue to operate illegally. *Testudo hermanni* used to be, and still is, a popular "garden ornament" in France itself. It is a "custom" imported from the French colonies in Africa, and in the beginning had less to do with a fondness for the animals than with the erroneous belief that a tortoise in the garden would keep snails and slugs

at bay. As early as at the beginning of the 19th century, thousands of tortoises from Corsica and Sardinia were unloaded in the Marseille harbor every year and sold on the market of Beaucaire to animal dealers from all over France and neighboring countries. It is therefore little surprising that the first escaped or released specimens were documented from otherwise tortoise-free regions already back then.

The consumption of tortoises by the local populace used to be commonplace during previous centuries. It persisted until the early 20th century in the form of the Friday meatless meals in Christian monasteries and experienced a revival during both World Wars when other foodstuffs were scarce. Today, the practice has been discontinued. Participants of the wars reported that tortoises were barbecued in their shells in an open fire, and the liver and the little meat on the limbs were consumed in particular. Later, the animals were in part marketed via fish shops, but this was soon halted for health concerns. A German army deserter who had fled into the wilderness of the Maure Mountains during the second World War built himself a contraption in the style of a "laying battery" for tortoise eggs, from which he then made omelets in early summer.

According to DEVAUX (1997a), the tortoise populations of the islands of Port-Cros and Poquerolles had already been all but completely consumed by the soldiers of Napoléon by 1811. A few surviving specimens were still seen around 1850, but the populations had eventually ceased to exist by the beginning of the 20th century.

A problem of more recent times is the possible interbreeding of native *Testudo hermanni* with tortoises of other species that have been released into the wild by people. This is illustrated by the find of several *Testudo boettgeri* within a population of *Testudo*

hermanni in the surroundings of Les Mayons. Here, GUYOT & PRITCHARD (1999) found between May and October of 1995 a total of thirty-five *Testudo hermanni* living in an area of some 35-40 hectares, but also seven specimens that were either "pure" representatives of the eastern population group or hybrids between western and eastern animals. PERÄLÄ (2002b), on the other hand, argued that based on the range of variability in the proportional length of the suture between femorals and abdominals identified by him for French specimens and the fact that said authors used this trait for their identifications, it may simply be a case of misidentification. GUYOT & PRITCHARD (1999) contemplated several possibilities to eliminate the prospective problem:
– do nothing,
– destroy the animals,
– resettle them in areas where previous populations have become extinct,
– leave them to the care of people where they cannot reproduce.

No interference would only be successful if *Testudo hermanni* were better adapted than the eastern form to a life in the south of France and would therefore eventually dominate in a competitive situation. This is unlikely, however, because the eastern animals are altogether substantially larger than their western cousins, and by laying more eggs have a larger reproductive potential. Although the collection of free-ranging tortoises is generally prohibited in France, scientists should be permitted to remove alien or bastard specimens if and when they encounter them during the courses of their studies. Destroying these tortoises is unacceptable due to reasons of ethics and animal protection. Resettling the problem animals in regions where tortoise populations have become extinct sounds tempting, but in reality meets with difficulties. A precondition

would be to eliminate the causes that led to the extinction of the native tortoises in the first place. Most practical therefore appears to be to accommodate the animals in the care of trustworthy private enthusiasts.

That the situation of the populations on Corsica can be considered quite good, was referred (CHEYLAN 1995) to the fact that the pressure on the tortoises and their habitats exerted by local people was minimal. A major factor for this being so was the more traditional ways of farming that was more in harmony with nature. Corsica is furthermore free of many of the common predators, such as magpie, badger and marten, which have a distinct taste for tortoise eggs and juveniles. Predatory risks exist, however, in the form of stray domestic pigs that have interbred with the local wild boar population and do not hesitate to eat eggs and juveniles.

Fires are a matter of concern on Corsica as well, particularly in the regions surrounding Porto-Vecchio, Saint Trinité and Sotta. Expanding human settlements, the illegal collection of tortoises for and by tourists (mainly in the surroundings of Porto-Vecchio and Casinca), the construction of new roads, and an increase in tourism aggravate the problems. Furthermore, the traditional ways of farming are more and more abandoned in favor of modern agricultural methods. Many a farmer and farmhand still views a tortoise as a competitor for the food for his livestock, and the finds of specimens that were beaten to death with a pickaxe or shovel suggest that *Testudo hermanni* are occasionally killed on purpose. First amongst the alterations nature has had to endure over the past years are by all means the erection of industrial installations in the surroundings of Bastia, and the expansion of human settlements in the regions around Casinca, Porto-Vecchio, Bonifacio and along the Gulf of Valinco. Even on Corsica, only those populations of *Testudo hermanni* appear to be quite safe, which happen to live in areas that are largely spared the influx of tourists, where fires are rare, and that are thinly populated by people. This is the case, for example, in the surroundings of Aléria, in the plains of Stabiacciu, in Figari region, and on the estuary of the river Rizzanese.

In Italy, *Testudo hermanni* has been largely reduced to small, scattered populations. The species has disappeared from large parts of the coastal strips, and healthy populations are limited mainly to national parks and private lands. Some populations with large numbers of individuals still exist in Latium, for example, but there are also regions that have been severely exploited by animal collectors in the past and that are presently being investigated for possible reinforcement release programs.

The main reason for the general decline in populations is the ongoing conversion of valuable coastal country into developed land. On Sardinia, the densest populations exist in the valleys and hills immediately adjacent to the coastal strip. Owing to their sandy and rocky, often even boulder-strewn and shallow soils with a predominantly garrigue-type vegetation, these wide expanses are largely unsuited for agricultural or pastoral purposes. Tourism, on the other hand, has so far been limited to some bays that have been made accessible via roads or tracks. Over the past few years mainland Italians in particular have discovered the northeast of the island to be a worthwhile holiday destination, but besides some luxury installations of the Aga Khan on the Costa Smeralda, there are as yet relatively few hotels with the required infrastructure that have detrimental effects on the local tortoise population. In places where the animals find relatively undisturbed living conditions, their populations still appear to be quite stable.

Fig. 153: Tortoises often recover even from massive trauma to their shells, as is the case with this Bulgarian *Testudo boettgeri* (G. POPGEORGIEV)

In centuries past, the consumption of tortoises by the local populace used to be a factor contributing to the decline of populations. Tortoises used to be regular trade items on food markets still during the 19th century, and in some cases they were literally bred for slaughtering. Like in the south of France, they made an acceptable Friday meal in monasteries even during the early 20th century. Until a few decades ago, it is said that tortoises were processed by the tons into meaty broths and soups on Sardinia.

According to BRUNO (1971b), an estimated 54,200 tortoises and freshwater turtles were collected on the Italian mainland for the pet trade between 1968 and 1970. These figures were augmented during the same period by about 7,500 specimens from Sicily, and another 5,230 from Sardinia. Today, both consumption by humans and the pet trade have come to play negligible roles as threats to the continued existence of *Testudo hermanni* as compared to the destruction of natural habitats. Obviously there is still the one or other tortoise that is illegally removed from the wild to end up in the enclosure or garden of an "animal lover"; on average, five or six people are caught illegally collecting or trying to export tortoises every year. It appears that the work of the conservation center CARAPAX (see chapter "Conservation") may have unintentionally provided motivation for people to do this. Obviously they did not only attract the attention of nature lovers to the plight of the native tortoise populations, but also that of terrarium keepers who are not too worried about laws. Like with the French equivalent organization SOPTOM, cases of theft and attempted theft of tortoises from this conservation center have been reported on various occasions.

The continued spread of the wild boar in Italy, including the islands, has resulted in the lamentable situation that in some areas all tortoise clutches are lost these days. Predators (besides wild boar these are mainly fox and marten) find the eggs of *Testudo hermanni* an easy target as they are often deposited in a rather concentrated manner in certain spots. On Sardinia, the pigs plough over entire areas in search of eggs, and eat the clutches, juveniles and even adults including their shells. On Sardinia, stray dogs are a serious problem for the tortoises as well. The fauna and flora in the northeast of this island are furthermore under threat to an increasing extent from the development of the tourism industry. An expanding agriculture also consumes many a small paradise as well (a saddening example for this was given by VINKE & VINKE 2002b). Expansive agricultural areas are presently created in the valleys of rivers and on the plains in the interior of this island. This once more results in a severe fragmentation of habitats, and animals die under heavy machinery, are beaten to death because they are regarded as vermin, poisoned through herbicides or fertilizers, and their nesting spots are eliminated or made unusable through ploughing. A local resident freely told WEGEHAUPT (2004) that the easiest way of killing a tortoise was to turn it on its back and then beat on its extended head with a stick.

The practice of fire clearing of areas for pastures and cornfields is also on the increase and results in large numbers of fires that spring from negligence or arson. These obviously kill many tortoises every year on Sardinia as well.

A general decrease in precipitation and the resultant summery aridity in the coastal areas of the Sardinian northwest has become a serious problem over the past few years. In the affected areas, finds of Italian tortoises that have died of thirst are becoming increasingly common. WEGEHAUPT

(2004), for example, found fifteen dried-up adult specimens outside their shelters in the immediate vicinity of the sea in fall of 2003 alone.

The presumed extinction of *Testudo hermanni* on the island of Elba is thought to be a result, at least for a major part, of the presence of the large numbers of rats living there.

Many an Italian population has escaped extinction for now only due to the natural longevity of these tortoises. Conservation measures are therefore urgently required, particularly in view of the fact that some 90% of all free-ranging specimens of *Testudo hermanni* occur in Italy. BALLASINA (1995a) presumed that numerous representatives of the eastern population group that reached Italy via the pet trade were eventually released into the wild by their owners, interbred with indigenous animals and thus rendered many Italian populations genetically impure. This would be particularly true for the populations in Tuscany, Latium and Campania. Bastards of this kind would be virtually impossible to identify as their color patterns would usually resemble that of *Testudo hermanni*. The greater body size of members of the eastern population group would be the only distinctive trait, but it was rather difficult to use due to the fact that rather large-growing populations also existed on the Italian mainland. BALLASINA (1995a) therefore thought it crucial to conduct genetic studies in order to determine the genotypes of Italian *Testudo hermanni* and then establish a number of "biogenetic reserves" where certified pure tortoises could live and reproduce.

Six populations comprising an estimated 5,000 tortoises still exist in the northeast of Spain. The populations have shrunk substantially in comparison with past decades and usually show only low densities. The species has entirely disappeared from many regions. More recent studies, however, also revealed hotspots where adult specimens still lived at fairly high densities, and where juvenile to semiadult ones were rather numerous.

A primary reason for the species' decline in Spain is once more the increased frequency of firestorms. These dry out the soils and favor the growth of some particularly resistant plant species, which in turn completely alters the habitats of the tortoises. Effects of agriculture and the collecting of specimens for the pet trade in the past have been and are equally detrimental to the local populations. During the 1970' alone, 10,000 to 15,000 tortoises were collected in Spain every year. Tortoises also used to be kept as "pets" by local people in the past, but this practice has become more rare in recent times. Notwithstanding, specimens are still offered for sale on black markets in the larger cities and by migrant dealers in the Spanish northeast.

FÉLIX et al. (1989) estimated the density of a population in a valley at 10.95 specimens per hectare. This was before a forest fire claimed some 25,000 hectares of forest and almost the entire natural habitat of this population in 1986. About 3,000 tortoises, equal to ca. 30% of the population, mainly on the southern slope of the mountain massif, lost their lives as a result. On the morning of 06. August 2000, a huge bush fire broke out in the surroundings of the Catalonian village of Garriguella, which is the home of the conservation organization "Centre de Reproducció de la Tortuga de L'Albera" (CRT) (see chapter "Conservation"). The fire flared for more than 30 hours and left 5,800 hectares of devastated land behind, mainly cork oak forest and Mediterranean brush. Although this region had only a relatively thin population of tortoises, a subsequently conducted ten-day survey showed that the fire had destroyed about 80% of the animals living there. Considering these figures it may be feared that the recurrence of wide-ranging fires alone is enough to drastically reduce the numbers of Spanish tortoises or even eradicate them completely.

Testudo hermanni used to be a common sight in large parts of eastern Mallorca only a few decades back. Numbers of this species on this island were estimated to exceed 20,000 still in the early 1980. Like with the neighboring island of Menorca, the collection of tortoises for the pet trade played a major role, with about 300–400 specimens being exported from Mallorca annually and mainly for the pet trade on the Spanish mainland during the early 1980'. To a much lesser extent tortoises were collected for stuffing and sale as souvenirs.

Since wild boar, fox and badger do not occur on the Balearic Islands, the tortoises are not under pressure from this side. However, bush and forest fires are a regular occurrence here as well, and the insatiable mass tourism has been consuming one pristine piece of land after the other on Mallorca as it did and does on Ibiza. The resultant "entertainment deserts" obviously leave no room for tortoises. During the course of the summer of 1981 alone, 300 hectares of habitat in the east of Mallorca fell victim to intentionally started fires, and the annual loss of habitats destroyed in this manner amounted to an estimated 500 hectares during the early 1980'. More and more old fincas were bought up and surrounded with solid walls by their new owners, which often made it impossible for the tortoises living in the lands to migrate to their traditional nesting and seasonal grazing spots; small gaps in the walls at ground level to let the animals pass through would already make a big difference for them. With the newly occupied

fincas came guard dogs that turned out to be a lethal menace for the tortoises. Meanwhile the Balearic Islands were plagued by a proliferation of rats that also represented a major risk of predation for young tortoises in particular.

All things considered it can be stated that the remaining Mallorcan populations are still stable, but their distribution range has become heavily fragmented by now.

On Menorca, population densities have substantially diminished over the past few years. The island had long been spared the effects of mass tourism, but eventually entered the line of sight of travel organizers as well. Tortoises have since completely disappeared from the surroundings of many settlements. Between 1965 and 1976, a single dealer exported ca. 5,000 tortoises annually from this island. It is therefore particularly delightful to learn that the numbers of individuals in the more remote parts of Menorca are experiencing a distinct increase now as it suggests that populations are recovering from the intense collecting of animal dealers.

Conservation

Testudo hermanni species group
The species discussed here are listed under the name of *Testudo hermanni* in CITES Appendix II and Appendix A of Ordinance No. 338/97 of the European Union. They are furthermore protected through EU Ordinance No. 1808/2001, and a variety of laws and ordinances in the individual EU member countries, usually in a category equal to "strictly protected". To illustrate the consequences of this legislation, we will take a closer look at what it means for the private enthusiast in Europe.

Ownership, purchase, display, or the commercial trading in *Testudo boettgeri*, *Testudo hercegovinensis* and *Testudo hermanni* are in general prohibited. Exemptions are granted only in certain circumstances and mainly for captive-bred specimens from within EU countries or legal imports from countries without. This requires the potential keeper to apply for an exemption from the ownership and marketing prohibition (EU permit No. 224), which may be issued by the regional office overseeing this type of administration in the respective country and/or prov-

ince. For specimens that have been in the possession of a person already before the EU species protection ordinance came into effect, the owner needs to be able to produce on request a certificate of their legal acquisition or legal import. If a specimen that was acquired through a once off lifting of the marketing prohibition is to be sold again, another application for such an exemption must be made.

In order to be recognized as captive-bred specimens, the subject tortoises need to have hatched in a controlled environment. This means that both the parental specimens and hatchlings must not have been able to exit this territory, nor must alien specimens have been able to enter it. Only then is a breeding group of certified legally procured tortoises considered a group that can legally produce marketable hatchlings. Feeding these animals and protecting them from predators and diseases are legally prescribed.

The export or re-export of species listed in Appendices A and B of the EU ordinance, or those protected by local laws if applicable, requires that an official export or re-export permit be issued by the relevant authorities.

Specimens representing any of the species dealt with here can only be imported if the relevant office of the Nature Conservation authority has issued import permits up front. Wild-caught specimens may in general not be imported for commercial or private purposes. The import of captive-bred ones is possible in certain cases. Import permits are directly linked to the export permits issued by the exporting country (CITES documents) and will only be issued if the export/import of these animals and the trade volume in the respective species are not considered harmful to the natural populations. Also, their import must be shown to serve the conservation of this species or further it by serving a purpose in either scientific research or education. The import permits and the documents issued by the country of origin must be presented to customs when the respective shipment is processed.

In Germany at least, a scientific authority decides whether an applicant is sufficiently qualified to house the animals in conditions that are in agreement with their natural biological requirements, from which they cannot escape, and that conform with the requirements for animal protection in general. The tortoises furthermore have to be registered in writing with the relevant authorities of the respective federal state. Changes in the extent of the collection, such as the hatching of babies, deaths, permitted sales etc., need to be logged at these offices without delay. These notifications need to contain information on the number of specimens involved, species, age, sex, origin, whereabouts, and individual traits. If the animals are moved to a different location due to their owner relocating or because they have been built a new enclosure somewhere else, the relevant authorities have to be notified as well. If such relocation involves wild-caught specimens for which a certain locality of keeping was fixed, a relocation permit has to be obtained before they can be moved. Exempted from these regulations are visits to a veterinarian if the animals are to be brought back right thereafter.

The overseeing office may demand that the rightful acquisition of the animals in question be proved. This procedure is subject to the law of free evidence, for which reason all documents relating to an acquisition should be kept safe. Import documentation, confirmation of presentation, official confirmation of registration, and CITES documents may therefore all become very important at one stage or another. Like additional paperwork, such as cash slips, deeds of gift and deeds of exchange, they should contain as many details as possible. These should preferably include the vernacular and scientific names, date of hatching, sex of the animal (as far as can be identified), name and address of the breeder, cross references to documents in the possession of the breeder ("stud book"), information on parental animals, and in the case of imported specimens also details of the import permit such as number of permit, date of arrival and country of origin. The buyer should never accept documents that merely attest to the purchase of "a tortoise", or appear otherwise deficient in detailed information. On the other hand, if officials pose unreasonable demands as to providing evidence about the rightful ownership, an objection may be raised. After all it is just not possible to have every piece of paper validated by a conveyancer.

Some national ordinances may furthermore demand, as is the case in Germany, that reptile species of the Appendix A of the EU ordinance be marked. As far as the tortoise species dealt with here are concerned, the implantation of microchips (transponders) is prescribed. Alternatively, (photographic) documentation is to be compiled that provides clear evidence of the identity of individual specimens. In most countries, it is left to the owner how this is complied with. Such documentation has to depict the traits identifying an individual either by a respective drawing or photographs. In the case of the species dealt with here these are usually the contours of the carapace scutes and the crosslines of the plastral scutes. This depiction is furthermore to be complemented by a description of the animal including at least data on its dimensions, weight, sex and age, and possible unique particulars. This documentation needs to be updated at intervals that permit to chronologically follow the possible change of certain traits. The original documentation has to accompany the original registering of an animal with the relevant office, and subsequent ones must be produced upon request.

Photographs to this effect have to be clear, full format, and well lit. The carapace must be photographed from above without an angle to the side so that both the cervical and 5th vertebral are clearly visible. The plastron also needs to be photographed at a zero angle. These photographs should preferably be taken with a background of paper with a 1 cm grid (a master copy can be found in ROGNER 2005).

Individuals of the three present species may be identified on the basis of eleven variable traits (BENDER 2001a). These include on the carapace the shape of the lateral sutures between the cervical and adjacent marginals (altogether nine different states) and the suture to the first vertebral (sixteen different states) as well as the contours of the sutures between the fifth vertebral and the two pleurals and the fourth vertebral (also sixteen states). The individual points of reference are to be numbered and entered into a proto-

col of characteristics ("reptile pass") so that there cannot be any doubts as to the identity of a particular specimen. The plastron contains another five traits that are usable for the identification of individuals. These are the shapes of the "crossings" that form the meeting points of the individual plastral scutes at the midline of the plastron. Here, a total of ten different states can be found.

The illustrated documentation needs to be redone after five years for tortoises with weights of more than 500 g, and every year for those weighing less than that. This accounts for the fact that it is as yet unknown which and how many of these traits there are in juveniles and how fast these can possibly change. An individual characterization should therefore, for the time being at least, be based on the traits listed above for adults.

In order to find out whether these traits are present already at hatching and whether and if so how rapidly they may change until a specimen reaches adulthood, a detailed study was commissioned. It involved the recording of traits in hatchlings and re-recording these again and again at regular intervals over a period of four to five years. It was of utmost importance in this quest to use for this procedure a statistically sufficient number of samples (= tortoises) to comply with scientific demands. The absence of such data had led to the dissatisfactory situation that neither keepers nor officials knew what to do when to comply with what laws in Germany have been demanding since 01.01.2001 and be legally on the safe side. This was the reason why the German Chelonia Group of the Deutsche Gesellschaft für Herpetologie und Terrarienkunde (DGHT, German Society for Herpetology and Terrariology) formed in March of 2001 a task team "Photographic Documentation of Juveniles". This team was to take care of all aspects involved, including organization, coordination, recruiting of participants, dissemination of information, and portrayal of the activities of the task team in magazines and other media. The mission of this team was to take photographs of as many baby tortoises as possible (at least 200–300) during their first two to three years of life at regular intervals of six to eight weeks. This was to determine when it was sensible to take the first photograph and the intervals at which new photographs needed to be taken. All participants had access to a mailing list on the Internet where relevant dates were published on a notice board, and participants made good use of a forum discussing all aspects of raising juveniles in captivity. As of 15.08.2002, this project was then financed jointly by the DGHT and the Federal Ministry for the Environment, Nature Conservation and Reactor Safety and accompanied by the Federal Office for Nature Conservation (F+E-Project "Individual Identification of Juvenile Tortoises", FKZ 802 86 070). This research project has meanwhile been concluded, and the results will be published shortly.

Marketing of captive-bred tortoises within the European Union requires that the relevant authorities issue a permit. This will only be granted if the babies hatched in a controlled environment from a closed breeding group of legally acquired parental animals. The applicant should apply for a breeder's certificate right away as it enables him to legally market his offspring of Appendix A-species throughout the European Union without having to apply for further permits. For captive-bred offspring of Appendix A-species this is the most important document to prove the legal acquisition and ownership of the animals.

Export from the European Union requires customs to be presented with an export or re-export permit issued by the relevant authorities. The shipment must furthermore comply with the regulations in place for a humane shipment of live animals.

Authorities are compelled by EU execution ordinances to decide on the issuing of documents and permits within fixed timeframes. In the present case these decisions need to be made within four weeks from receipt of a complete application. It is therefore in the applicant's best interest to always submit a complete set of documents and to ensure that all questions in questionnaires have been answered. Delays must be expected and accepted if another country has to be contacted in the approval process, or if the office has to consult with scientific advisors. The documents thus issued have a limited period of validity; for example, import and export permits for the EU expire after a maximum of six months. If no use has been made of them, they have to be returned to issuing authority.

Testudo boettgeri, *Testudo hercegovinensis* and *Testudo hermanni* are furthermore listed (once more under the collective name of "*Testudo hermanni*") in Appendix II of the Berne Convention of 1979. This compels all signatory states to take adequate legal and administrative measures to strictly protect these species and their natural habitats. It prohibits the collecting, killing and other utilization of the animals, disturbing them

Figs. 154&155: An example of taking ID photographs of a tortoise on scaled paper (B. SEEGER)

intentionally, and affecting their protected habitats. Signatory states meanwhile include almost all European and many African countries.

The European Union has also included the species dealt with here (again under the collective name "Testudo hermanni") as species of "common interest" in the Appendices II and IV of their Fauna-Flora-Habitat directive (92/43/EWG) of 1992. This translates the demands imposed by the Berne convention into European law. The EU member countries are therefore obligated to take appropriate measures to establish a strict protection system for the species concerned. Again, this outlaws the collection and deliberate killing of animals in the wild, disturbing them willfully during their mating and hibernation seasons in particular, the deliberate destruction or collection of their eggs, as well as causing damage of any kind to or destroying their breeding or resting places. Prohibited are also the ownership, transport, trade, exchange, as well as the offering for sale or exchange of specimens collected from nature. Specimens that were legally collected before this directive took effect are exempt from it. Member states are to introduce a system that allows a continuous monitoring of incidental collection or killing of specimens of these species. Based on the information gathered

thus, the member states are to initiate research and/or conservation measures that are required to ensure that such incidental collecting and/or killing has no significant negative effects on the continued existence of these species. The Network Natura 2000 is to assist with the realization of this directive by coordinating the placement under legal protection of particularly important habitats, their conservation and rehabilitation.

These species are also protected through national laws in their native countries. Unfortunately though, their enforcement leaves much to be desired in most of them. Considering the vast range of variability in Testudo hermanni and Testudo boettgeri (see chapter "Description") and that species protection includes the conservation of the entire genetic diversity of a species, one will soon arrive at the conclusion that protective measures must preferably be effected throughout the distribution range of the Testudo hermanni species group and not limited to a few large "model populations". Required protective measures must include, for example, curbing the illegal collecting of tortoises and the establishment of more protected areas. It will obviously be quite impossible to fully stop the collection of individual tortoises by tourists, for which reason it is imperative to bar the general public from accessing the core habitats of the individual populations. Prime sites for additional protected areas for these tortoises would be the remaining habitats on Mallorca and Menorca. Research as to the suitability of envisaged areas would need to be done with great care and consideration, though, in order to prevent from recurring acts of terror in the style of Alíki in Greece (see chapter "Threats") where local interest groups tried by means of arson to create new facts and thus prevent the establishment of a new nature reserve.

Several organizations dedicated to the conservation of tortoises (CARAPAX, SOP-TOM, C.R.A.R.C., CRT, and Son Cifre de Baix; for further details on the individual organizations see below), together with the Cyprus Ministry of Fisheries and the University of Pisa in 1992 founded an umbrella organization (TORMED), mainly with the purpose of coordinating repopulation programs. It was also meant, for example, to facilitate the exchange of specimens in cases where members of a certain population group could be accommodated and looked after better in one center than in another. Since 1999, TORMED has been fully equipped with organizational structures such as a mission statement and a board of directors (its first president was THIJS KRAMER of Son Cifre de Baix) with official headquarters in Brussels, Belgium. Aims of this organization include the awarding of "seals of approval" for tortoise conservation centers, to inform the European public about their work, lobby for support in Brussels and other European capitals, develop nature and species conservation strategies, and further repopulation projects. TORMED has thus been responsible for several international operations in Italy, France, Greece, Morocco, Tunisia and Albania. A total of about 6,000 tortoises have since been rehomed in protected areas in their countries of origin. In many cases, repopulation takes place in regions that have previously been devastated by fires that also destroyed the local tortoise population. This is done to prevent a destabilization of existing population structures by the introduction of additional specimens. One such example was the rehoming of 250 tortoises (200 *Testudo boettgeri* and 50 *Testudo ibera*) from France (SOPTOM and Chizé Zoo), Italy (CARAPAX), Belgium (R.A.N.A.), and The Netherlands (Iguana Reptile Zoo at Vlissingen) early in

October of 1997. Originating from confiscations from private owners, the animals were subjected to thorough health checks and then flown to Greece with the support of British-based Virgin Airlines, where they were released into the wilderness of a region north of Thessaloníki. Here a raging forest fire had stripped the land of tortoises a few years before. While the *Testudo ibera* were set free in the dry hilly country, the Boettger's were released in the moister valleys. In spite of all the goodwill demonstrated through actions like this one it cannot be emphasized enough just how problematic the release into the wild of animals of uncertain origin may eventually turn out to be.

Boettger's tortoise

In their report on the threatened amphibians and reptiles of Eastern Europe, the Societas Europaea Herpetologica (1994) categorized this species as relatively wide-ranged. Although the report suggested a number of protective measures to be taken, it soon showed that hardly any fundamental knowledge on nature and species conservation existed in the countries of the former Eastern Block. The result was that the putting into effect of those measures has been leaving a lot to be desired until today. Some of the SEH's suggestions included:

Signing into effect of respective legislation in these countries to protect and conserve natural habitats and outlaw the direct persecution of tortoises;

Education of the local human population;

Setting up of various protected areas, e.g., within the Bulgarian forested regions in the Rhodopes near the border with Greece and for the population living in the drainage region of the Evros;

Field studies and ecological research with the aim to identify particularly large populations in order to be able to take conservation measures at an early stage.

For Albania, HAXHIU & ORUÇI (2002) pointed out the urgent necessity to soften the negative attitude of the human population toward reptiles in general and tortoises in particular. The mentioned authors therefore have been organizing throughout the past few years open forums mainly for children and students. The Natural History Museum in the Albanian capital Tirana dedicated an entire room to the portrayal of the tortoises of this country; it also has on display tortoise clutches and specimens senselessly killed by people. Children and adolescents from all over Albania have meanwhile visited the exhibition. A TV documentary outlining the importance of tortoises, the threats they face, and what can be done to protect them from forest fires, traffic on roads, and their deliberate killing has also been filmed. These measures are of course by far not sufficient, and the few existing Albanian nature activists depend heavily on sponsorships for their various projects. It would be of great importance that officials enforce the existing protective legislation.

In Bulgaria, *Testudo boettgeri* is protected by law. Collection, ownership and transport of these animals are prohibited, and contravention of these laws carries a maximum penalty of an equivalent of US$ 6,000, a jail term of up to three years, and the forfeiture of the vehicle used while committing the offence. In 2004, this law was indeed applied for fining a poacher who with the aid of an accomplice had on 15.05.2003 illegally collected fourteen tortoises in the vicinity of the village of Ovcharovo in the Harmanli District. While the accomplice had managed to escape over the border into Greece, the arrested poacher eventually agreed to pleading guilty and accepting a fine equivalent to $ 600 as suggested by the prosecutor's office.

The tortoises were released in a remote region of the eastern Rhodopes.

Enforcement of conservation laws still needs to be improved, though. This would also include the more thorough checking of tourists' baggage on exiting the country, as this is the most common manner in which tortoises are smuggled to destinations in western and central Europe. A wide-ranging campaign to educate the human population about tortoise products being entirely unsuited to curing diseases would also be of great importance. In regions plagued by wild boar to an extent that threatens the continued existence of tortoises, appropriate measures should be decided on including, e.g., an increased hunting of these wild pigs. Because suitable natural habitats have all but disappeared in the plains in particular, repopulation programs for tortoises in these regions cannot possibly be contemplated at the present point of time.

A small research center was established in Banya in 2002 that is aimed at the study and conservation of the tortoises of this region (*Testudo boettgeri* and *Testudo ibera*) and their natural habitats. The study area covers about 80 km² and borders the coast of the Black Sea in the south, the highway between Burgas and Varna in the west, and the river Ghin in the north. Here, fifty-seven Boettger's tortoises and one *Testudo ibera* were monitored during the course of an entire year. An outdoor enclosure of 2000 m² in size houses ten *Testudo boettgeri* whose clutches are recovered and incubated artificially. The resultant hatchlings are then kept in a smaller enclosure and monitored in the framework of a long-term study in order to learn more about the habits of Bulgarian *Testudo boettgeri*. The initiator of this center, Ivo Evstiatev IVANCHEV, recommended that more of these small, specialized centers be established and select populations be augmented through the release of tortoises bred in captivity for exactly this purpose. Another goal of the conservation efforts is to convince the local populace that nature and species conservation are necessary.

Legal protection for Boettger's tortoise also exists in Greece. Although *Testudo boettgeri* could almost be termed a synanthropous species by comparison with the other tortoise species in this country, many a population will not survive the alterations to their habitat effected by man. The best way of conserving the species in the long run would therefore again be to conserve their natural environments. This would necessitate the establishment of numerous, relatively small protected areas in the south of Greece in particular. Even Recommendation No. 26 of the Permanent Committee of the Berne Convention from 1991 suggested to the Greek government that the habitat of the population of *Testudo boettgeri* at Alíki be placed under legal protection in order to prevent further deterioration of the local environment. The country subsequently specified numerous conservation-worthy habitats in the framework of Natura 2000, which also included those with populations of Boettger's tortoise. These were, for example, a wetland of some 1,400 hectares around Alíki, which includes a narrow strip of dunes and expansive heathland.

In areas where the numbers of juvenile *Testudo boettgeri* are very low, an obvious approach would be to consider reducing the numbers of predators, but such measures are impossible to introduce because animals like marten and badger rank amongst the endangered animals in Greece as well. A more practicable option would be the recommendation expressed by WILLEMSEN (1995), i.e., to create clearings in forested areas that would provide the tortoises with adequate nesting spots. A rather unrealistic idea is to make farmers return to more traditional forms of agriculture, although it would be of vital importance to regulate, or better even completely stop, the practice of fire clearing. The use of the herbicides 2.4 D and 2.4.5 T should be declared illegal, as these are not only lethal for the tortoises but also harmful to the health of the local human population. Furthermore does the elimination of vegetation favor soil erosion in many areas. The often entirely senseless destruction of vegetation, and the removal of hedges in farming areas in particular, should also be stopped. Conserving these hedges is pivotal to the survival of tortoise populations in cultivated regions.

Conservation breeding programs like those existing in France are presently not considered necessary in Greece or any other country that is home to members of the eastern population group for that matter. Actively involved in safeguarding tortoises are, amongst others, the German/Greek animal and environment activist association O AETOS. Under the presidency of Bernd PITZER, a German living in Greece, the association strives to educate school children in the region around the head office of the association at the foot of Mt. Olympus, but also managed to convince several large-scale farmers to rather collect tortoises from their fields in troughs than beat them to death on sight. The animals collected thus are then taken and released in a large, fully fenced-in olive grove, or in the nearby mountains. The members of O AETOS also collect tortoises in areas heavily affected by tourism. Here, it was noted that mainly tourists from Eastern Europe illegally removed many specimens. The collected tortoises are then transported to safer areas and released there.

Néa Póri, for example, is a tourist village that has risen from virtually nothing, but the extensive construction measures that make its rise possible are rapidly encroaching on

Figs. 156&157: Signboards along the highway at Gonfaron, southern France (B. Devaux)

a nearby marsh area with salt meadows and river country, pinning the local tortoises in a dead end from which there is no escape. In the east there is the sea, a river cuts off the south and west by running parallel to the beach at a distance of about 1 km from the shoreline before it eventually drains into the Aegean Sea, and from the north come building machines on a wide front. Here, PITZER and his team managed to collect some 170 Boettger's tortoises in 2001 and 2002 alone that were then released at a distance of ca. 800 m on the other side of the river. Animals that sustain injuries during the construction of roads are cared for until they are fit enough to be set free once more. The work of this association is financially supported through donations and income generated by the organization through guided tours for eco-tourists in the region around Mt. Olympus, as well as the income from a gliding and paragliding camp the German runs together with a lady friend. On 15. September 2004, O AETOS was sanctioned by the state-owned Hellenic Wildlife Hospital to act as the official rescue station for tortoises and other reptiles in northern Greece. The Hellenic Wildlife Hospital itself has taken on the responsibility of caring for injured or sick wild animals and rehabilitates them for a release into the wild. The organization maintains a

network of staff in various places throughout Greece who arrange for the transport of such animals to where they can be looked after properly. Until recently, the main focus of the hospital was the medical treatment of birds. It is most unfortunate that the Greek government did only order that this organization care for injured and sick wild animals, but did not make available the required funding.

Testudo boettgeri is also strictly protected in Romania, but here the enforcement of the existing legislation is rather lenient as well. The region around the Iron Gate, in which populations exist, is a nature reserve covering an area of 128,160 hectares.

Italian tortoise

The IUCN has been recommending for the conservation of this species that plans be made to control the further expansion of tourism, and the land and forest use in the countries where it occurs. Furthermore, it has been suggesting that nesting facilities be monitored and expanded, and that the predatory pressures (e.g., by excessive numbers of wild boars) be reduced. Of particular importance are considered the prevention of further fragmentation of habitats through the indiscriminate construction of roads and railway lines, and the curbing of further loss of vegetation (maquis, garrigue) through forest and bush fires, intensified and expansion of farming, clearing of forests, settlement dispersal, tourism (e.g., through the construction of holiday bungalows and resorts), and the construction of sport and entertainment installations such as golf courses.

The use of heavy earthmoving machinery during summer should by all means be avoided in the most important habitats at least. These machines often kill or injure tortoises and destroy their nests of eggs. The use of pesticides and similar chemicals in all habitats of the animals and neighboring buffer zones should be discontinued. The illegal collection of, and trade in, tortoises need to be subjected to more stringent controls. On the other hand, the release of specimens from other populations into the wild, i.e., animals from other countries or even from captive keeping, must be stopped. Exceptions to this demand are obviously projects through which areas in which tortoise populations have become extinct are to be recolonized with animals from neighboring populations. This would obviously necessitate the release, for example, of animals from the Spanish Albera Mountains in the French Albères Mountains, or tortoises from the south of France in the Italian region of Liguria.

France granted Testudo hermanni legal protection as far back as in 1970. Any trade with these animals, their killing, release into the wild, as well as the destruction of their eggs, and any action to the detriment of their natural habitats are strictly prohibited. Tortoises may only be transported under a special permit issued by the relevant veterinary authority and only if this is for other than commercial purposes.

Recommendation No. 26 of the Permanent Committee of the Berne Convention of 1991 contained the appeal to the French government that a nature reserve for the Italian tortoise be established within the natural distribution range in the Maure Mountains and the Maure Plains in order to curb the persisting dangers to the continued existence to this species' last populations on the French mainland. It also called for the establishment of a state-supported breeding and recolonization program and improved conservation measures for the natural habitats of the major populations on Corsica. The IUCN also recommended to the French government that important habitats for Testudo hermanni in the Maure Mountains, Maure Plains and on Corsica be placed under particular protection within the framework of Natura 2000. Regions that had previously formed part of its distribution range in the Maure and Albères Mountains should be renaturalized and prepared for recolonization. The French government has meanwhile responded to these appeals by declaring as nature reserves six areas with populations of Testudo hermanni on the mainland and fifteen on Corsica. Three of these are of vital importance for the survival of this species (for example, a large reserve now exists in the surroundings of Porto-Vecchio on Corsica).

The IUCN recommends that repopulation programs be continued for as long as is necessary, particularly in the Maure Mountains and on the island of Levant.

In response to the worrying results of studies investigating the population status of Testudo hermanni on the French mainland, a private initiative had founded the chelonian research center

"La Station d'Observation et de Protection des Tortues des Maures" (SOPTOM) in fall of 1985. This organization then published their species conservation program in September 1986, which amongst others included the construction of a specialized research center on a plot of about one hectare in size on the outskirts of the small village of Gonfaron in the Département Var in the Maure Plains. It resulted in a large-scale drive for financial support. Assisted by the work of hoards of volunteers, numerous generous donations (e.g., by Ford Motors and the Office for Agriculture of the Department of Var to the tune of about $ 4,200 each), and the expedient sale of souvenirs, the project soon took shape. Its main source of income was an "adoption program" that has been continuing until today with many people adopting individual tortoises. On 28.05.1988, the center with the name "Village des Tortues" (= "village of the tortoises") was ceremoniously opened to the public in the presence of the British naturalist and writer Gerald Durrell and the mayor of Gonfaron. The construction of the "village" had by then cost the equivalent of only about $ 30,000. These astoundingly low costs had been made possible by the mentioned help of many unpaid volunteers from France and other countries. Already during their first summer of operation, staff of SOPTOM welcomed about 25,000 interested visitors including many groups of school children. This instant success was certainly a result of an excellent exercise in public relations work that attracted a huge response particularly by the French public. The year of 1993 saw the numbers of visitors rise to 65,000, which generated an income for SOPTOM of an equivalent of about $ 300,000. This enabled the project to financially sustain itself without the need of any government funding.

From amongst the numerous donors that keep on making money available willingly for SOPTOM's goals must be mentioned the British Chelonia Group in particular. A single donation of about $ 2,200 by this group facilitated, for example, the construction of an entire rearing pen.

During the course of 1996, the center expanded its grounds to now cover two hectares, and the numbers of visitors have been rising to figures of between 100,000 and more than 150,000 every year.

The "tortoise village" is equipped with a multimedia lecture auditorium seating sixty people, sports a diorama of the region, offers accommodation for the winter months, has a "fossil trail" (with life-sized illustrations of fossil chelonian species), an incubation and rearing station, as well as numerous outdoor enclosures. A gift shop can be found in the reception building. Visitors can stroll through the "village" on slightly raised walkways, which afford a clear view of the tortoises without disturbing them. Information boards have been placed in strategic places informing visitors in French, English and German language about various aspects of "tortoisology" and the work of SOPTOM. A larger-than-life sized plastic cross section model of a female during oviposition depicts anatomical details of a tortoise's interior.

The almost natural outdoor pens are home to several hundred tortoises, most of which are of southern French origin. A majority of them were donated by private keepers and now serve to keep their species extant in the framework of a captive breeding program. Not a single tortoise was removed from the wild for being kept at the station. Sexually mature males and females join each other in the "reproduction area" for mating purposes. Once they have copulated, the females are transferred to their own pens where they are safe from further harassment by the males and where they can lay their eggs without disturbance. These pens are checked thoroughly for clutches several times a day. If one is located, it is carefully dug up and incubated artificially. Juveniles hatched at the station or donated by private keepers are raised to an age of five years by which time they are large enough to be safe from most predators. In the station itself a variety of predator safeguards are used, ranging from netting and trellises to tiger feces (!), the latter of which are supplied by the Mont Faron zoo. Placed in strategic places throughout the village, they are meant to intimate to marten and fox that it may be safer for them to avoid the property of the village.

A separate enclosure is dedicated to juveniles that are due to be released into the wild. It sports an environment that is very similar to what the young animals will encounter in nature. Following an adjustment period of about six months in this pen, they are eventually set free in suitable habitats together with "supernumerary" adults. Since the late 1990', every specimen has been furnished with a microchip that is implanted into a skin fold on a hind leg. This enables researchers to re-identify individual specimens in the field.

The practice of releasing specimens into the wild is not without controversy, though, since it appears, for example, that animals have been released that were infected with the herpes virus. This may of course spell disaster for wild populations. In his study of repopulation programs for the Italian tortoise, GAGNO (2001) arrived at the conclusion that no health risks would exist for free-ranging populations if tortoises that temporarily lived in human care were subjected to a quarantine period of at least one year in duration and a subsequent two-year period in a separate enclosure. This verdict has not been met with unanimous acceptance either, though.

In 1997, SOPTOM set up several pens in which captive-bred crossbreeds between the western and eastern population groups are housed. These animals can of course never be released into the wild, but at present there are no plans of what to do with them eventually.

The numbers of tortoises released by SOPTOM into the wild have risen continually over the years. In 1990 alone, it was 750 specimens that served to strengthen wild populations, and in 1998, the station was housing a total of 1,800 juveniles. By 2005, SOPTOM had released more than 10,000 tortoises into suitable habitats. These included, for example, the island of Levant in the Hyères Archipelago, where man had hunted the tortoises to extinction, but where a population now exists once more. A total of 1,100 tortoises were released there in an area of 950 hectares between 1990 and 1998. These were composed for one third of semiadults, with adults making up the other two thirds at a ratio of 45 % males to 55 % females. These animals are regularly checked, and a very low mortality rate of just 3 % has been recorded. Reproductive activity was noted for the first time already in 1992, which subsequently resulted in the find of newly hatched babies. It appears, though, that all, or at least most, juveniles are lost to predators, presumably rats. This follows from the fact that so far no semiadult specimens could be observed, which should roam the island in larger numbers by now (LIVOREIL 2003). Owing to its military installations, this island is off limits to the public, which curbs the risk of bush fires enormously.

SOPTOM furthermore serves as a base and starting point for field studies in the region that are undertaken to disclose details of the natural history of Testudo hermanni. In the framework of species conservation programs, threatened natural habitats have been and still are being identified and areas suitable for repopulation projects are earmarked. Nesting sites are created, existing populations monitored, and protection measures are designed and effected.

2001 saw the foundation of the "Centre de Recherche et de Conservation des Chéloniens" (CRCC) under the umbrella of SOP-TOM. This division is to coordinate and drive forward all conservation measures involving *Testudo hermanni*. At present, the CRCC is occupied mainly with genetic studies. A "tortoise clinic" has been in existence since 1989 and offers facilities for laboratory and veterinary research. Some 300 sick or injured tortoises are treated and nursed back to health here every year. Besides cases of bronchitis, burns, and broken bones, injuries to the shell from agricultural harvesters, fires, or encounters with road traffic make up the majority of cases. These injuries are often repaired with polyester resin and fiberglass, which leaves "patches" that are highly durable and watertight. They remain in place until the

shell has renewed itself over the course of a few years and then simply fall off. As soon as a sick or injured tortoise has recovered a little, it is transferred to the safety of a quarantine pen (which, according to LOEHR [2002], is in a less than good condition at present, though). If it then shows that everything is quite all right, the convalescents are eventually placed in a "normal" pen. Depending on the severity of the injuries, specimens may at a later stage be released into the wild, or will spend the rest of their lives in the safety of the "village". All tortoises living at the station are dewormed at semiannual intervals.

The "mayor" of the "tortoise village" at Gonfaron is the French environmentalist Bernard DEVAUX, who used to earn his keep as a designer of water features and TV sets, as a writer, moderator of radio broad-

Fig. 158: Outdoor pens for tortoises in the *Centro de Recuperación de Anfibios y Reptiles de Catalunya* in Masquefa, Spain (A. MARTÍNEZ)

casts, and lecturer. A turning point in his career came with his military service in Algeria from 1959 through 1961. He was so impressed with the Sahara Desert and its reptile fauna that he decided to become an animal filmographer. He then bought and restored an old farmhouse in the Provence, where he wanted to live and work. It was also where the first, rather incidental encounter with the British biologist David STUBBS took place, who at the time was busy investigating the remaining populations of Testudo hermanni in the Provence. Both became friends quickly, and from this friendship soon arose the idea of SOPTOM and the "tortoise village" that were both founded with the assistance of the French herpetologist Jean-Pierre POUVREAU.

The team of SOPTOM soon realized that effective nature conservation could only be achieved with the support of the general public and in cooperation with the authorities. For this reason, the organization has been doing intense public relations work both at national and international levels, making use of newspapers, radio and TV. Media campaigns thus inform the public that, for example, tortoises do not need to be protected in residential backyards, but rather in the Provence, next to the cork oak trees of the garrigue. Their program is not limited to guided tours through the village itself, but also includes the publication of books, videotapes and DVDs, posters and informational pamphlets, and giving lectures. The flagship is, however, their quarterly published journal, "La Tortue", which has by now achieved an international reputation of being an excellent journal.

With the station now being widely known, it has become a strong base for environmentalists, which can have a substantial influence on talks with local authorities about questions of nature conservation. For example, it helped to prevent the construction of a test track by the tire manufacturer Michelin that would have cut right through the natural habitat of the tortoises. Public pressure on the company became intolerably high, and the nature conservation organization "Le Conservation du Littoral" eventually bought the area in which the test track was planned to be built. Less successful was the attempt to stop the construction of Highway 57 between Le Cannet and Toulon in the years 1989/1990, though, which severely affected the natural habitat of one of the four largest remaining tortoise populations. However, the still young organization managed at least to enforce protective measures for the affected population. It entailed the removal of about 300 tortoises between May 1989 and October 1990 from a 4 km long and 100 m–wide strip along the construction site that were then housed for a year in a 1,500 m² seminatural enclosure at the station of SOPTOM. After construction had been completed in 1990, 284 specimens (100 males, 169 females, 15 semiadults) were released once more. This took place after a 4 km-section of the highway had been secured with a fence whose erection had been supported by the regional highway company ESCOTA and two tunnels had been built that now enabled the tortoises to safely cross from one side to the other. The divide between the lanes of the highway is open at the crossing points of the tunnels so that light (but unfortunately also a lot of garbage) can enter and the tortoises are not deterred from using the tunnels due to their being in deep darkness. SOPTOM takes care of maintaining the tunnels and cleans them out on a regular basis. Field studies conducted in this region from 1993 to 1995 showed that the population remained for the largest part in its traditional place, that only a few specimens had moved off, and that only five tortoises lost their lives on the highway. The

Fig. 159: The "tortoise hospital" of the tortoise village in Gonfaron, France (B. DEVAUX)

roadhouse at Sigues is by all means worth a stop — it is entirely dedicated to the tortoises of the Maure Mountains, sporting a large mural painting, an entertainment area for children with toys in the shape of tortoises, and information boards on the biology of the animals and the "tortoise village". Along the highway itself, three huge, sequential signboards point to SOPTOM: the first shows an egg, the second a hatching tortoise (which is, by the way, the logo for SOPTOM designed by Marc CHEYLAN), and finally a tortoise with the caption "Tortue des Maures".

Visitors to the station are given the feeling of being part of the protection program. During the guided tours through the premises they learn a lot about the threats facing tortoises in the wild and the work of SOPTOM. The organization has thus acquired an excellent international reputation – aside from its controversial release policies – and enjoys worldwide support. Theirs was the first project of this kind in Europe that received official recognition by the IUCN. The French government and the authorities of the European Union became aware of the problems caused by the trade in tortoises only through the activities of SOPTOM. In 1995, SOPTOM played host to an international congress on the subject of tortoise conservation.

It was attended by 230 experts from thirty-six countries, and followed up with a symposium organized by SOPTOM in Senegal in June of 2003.

SOPTOM has meanwhile greatly expanded its activities both nationally (construction of a "tortoise village" on Corsica; see below; funding of the marine turtle reserve at Les Hattes in French Guyana) and internationally (construction of a "tortoise village" each for the breeding of the African spurred tortoise [*Centrochelys sulcata*] in Senegal and for the radiated tortoise [*Astrochelys radiata*] and the spider tortoise [*Pyxis arachnoides*] on Madagascar).

The station is today situated in the middle of the largest and most important French nature reserve that is dedicated to the conservation of the Italian tortoise. The reserve covers an area of altogether 33,485 hectares and comprises, besides the largest population of tortoises of this country, also large portions of open forest and maquis. Furthermore, the French government announced in June 2005 that three additional "forest reserves" would be at a planning stage, one of which was to be situated in the Maure Mountains.

In a quest to conserve the natural habitats of *Testudo hermanni*, SOPTOM cooperates closely with the "Conservatoire et Étude des Ecosystèmes de Provence" (CEEP). This is an organization that has been striving since the 1970' to conserve and manage what has remained of nature in this region. This is done, for example, by buying up large tracts of land that are then placed under protection, and by entering into agreements to this effect with landowners and authorities. The organization meanwhile owns eleven properties with a total size of 460 hectares in this region. By purchasing "Green Shares" at a price of about $ 40 each, everybody can participate in the nature conservation efforts of the CEEP. Since 2005, SOPTOM has furthermore been enjoying the support of another nature conservation organization, Noé-Conservation, which supports a variety of research projects both through funding and with personnel.

SOPTOM has also become active over the last years in the Albères Mountains on the border with Spain. Although the local tortoise populations vanished from here at the latest during the catastrophic fires of 1986, some members of these populations still exist in human care. SOPTOM now hopes to resurrect these populations on the basis of these specimens. This quest found the support of the municipality of Argelès-sur-Mer, which undertook in 1995 to inform the inhabitants of the town about these plans and to gather information on the tortoises living in human care. Keepers were asked to consider "donating" their tortoises for this purpose or at least let SOPTOM have their eggs. Genetic examinations done at the Muséum nationale d'Histoire naturelle in Paris were to ensure that only those tortoises were used for this project that evidently originated from this very region. Plans are to investigate in a feasibility study the establishment of a breeding station in the parklands surrounding Valmy Castle, which would then be managed in a joint effort by SOPTOM and the municipality of Argelès-sur-Mer and headed by an expert person. A section of this station will be open to the public, but limited to enclosures housing tortoises that cannot be incorporated into the breeding project due to their origins or other reasons.

A permanent exhibit to this effect was opened already in May of 1998. Here, interested people can find information on the biology of local tortoises, the reasons for their being threatened with extinction or why they have disappeared already, and what plans have been made to conserve them. Information events are held in schools and for the local and national press at a regular

basis. Offspring arising from these efforts are scheduled for release after a few years in suitable areas, and a task team is presently busy with the identification of potential sites. Hopes are that these areas will then be declared official nature reserves.

Plans of repopulating the Estérel Mountains are also being made. At present, feasibility studies are to identify suitable areas in which released tortoises will have a good chance of survival. The mountain range is already a region monitored by the national Office of Forestry, ONF. Like all repopulation projects this undertaking has to be sanctioned by the Ministry of Environmental Affairs and accompanied by scientific research projects.

SOPTOM will in future shift its focus more on the conservation of the tortoises' natural habitats. A species simply cannot be saved if its natural habitats within a natural environment are not conserved at the same time. The absolute necessity of approaching the problem in this manner is illustrated by the fact that despite all repopulation efforts the population in the surroundings of Les Mayons has shrunk as a result of human activities from about 800 tortoises in 1981 to a mere 65 in 1999. Conservation measures in some regions include, for example, the thinning out of forests on a regular basis, which not only reduces the risk of wild fires and makes access easier for firefighters, but also favors the growth of grasses and herbs. These, in turn, create improved feeding grounds for the tortoises.

The ultimate aim must be to reliably conserve the natural landscape of the Maure Mountains and the surrounding lowlands. This requires that authorities at departmental and municipal level and the office of forestry be actively involved, and that SOPTOM continues to be supported by other nature activist groups. There are no guarantees,

Fig. 160: STÉPHANE GAGNO treating a patient with massive shell trauma in the "tortoise hospital" in Gonfaron, France (B. DEVAUX)

though, that the purchase of land, the declaration of more nature reserves, and restrictions on land consumption for the expansion of human settlements will breed the desired effects. Although they will be crucial to the long-term conservation of *Testudo hermanni*, they will likely be met with fierce opposition.

SOPTOM personnel obviously have a lot of stories to tell, and some are really rather weird. One such story unfolded on 14.05.1998: the station received a telephone call from a man in Avignon, who confessed to having recently collected three tortoises in the Maure Mountains. He now wanted to return them and would arrive in about an hour's time. Considering the distance and nature of the call, it was put aside the next moment, but a short while later staff began to hear engine noises from above. A helicopter appeared in the sky and landed on the open field next to the tortoise village. The pilot jumped out, imposed on the dumbstruck

Fig. 161: The initiators of the *Centro de Recuperación de Anfibios y Reptiles de Catalunya* in the Spanish Masquefa, J. SOLER and A. MARTÍNEZ (A. MARTÍNEZ)

SOPTOM people three tortoises and the equivalent of about $ 210, jumped back into his chopper, and disappeared as quickly as he had appeared.

As has been mentioned before, fifteen protected areas exist within the network Natura 2000 on the island of Corsica. These are also home to large populations of *Testudo her-*

manni. They are situated at Terrenzana, Pinia, and on Lake Urbino on the east coast, at Lavu Santu, Santa Giulia, Bruzzi, Saint-Jean, Roccapina, and on Lake Chevanu in the southeast, and in the region of Belvédère-Campomoro and on Cape Senetosa in the southwest. The reserve "Mucchiatana", for example, is a narrow strip of coastal land of only 170 hectares in size, but it comprises valuable natural land in the form of juniper thickets, bush and grasslands, and maquis. The existing nature reserves should be investigated which exact requirements could be met to improve the protection of the tortoises living there, be it through reducing the risk of fires by thinning out the vegetation or moderate grazing by livestock, restricting the access for both locals and tourists, and in some cases maybe even augmenting the wild populations with captive-bred stocks. Interlinking several protected areas to a network could play an important role in this respect as well. The large reserve Agriates in the northwest of the island contains no tortoises at present, but may prove to be an area in which tortoises can be reestablished at a later stage. A "tortoise village" modeled after the one in Gonfaron was set up in Moltifao in the center of the island in June of 1997. It was funded by the national parks board, the regional government of Corsica, but mainly by SOPTOM. It is today managed and maintained by the national parks board. The "founder population" consisted of 120 specimens, and the development of a breeding program and the planning of conservation measures will earlier or later be linked to the success of the "head office" in Gonfaron.

In Italy, several populations exist in protected areas, as is the case in the Maremma National Park on the Tuscan coast and the nature reserve surrounding Lake Serranella in the region Abruzzi. Recommendation No. 26 of the Permanent Committee of the Berne Convention of 1991 contained an appeal to the Italian government to further extend legal protection to the natural habitats of major populations of Testudo hermanni. The IUCN also recommended to the country that particular protection be granted within the network Natura 2000 to habitats of Testudo hermanni on the mainland, in the Sardinian northeast, on Elba, and a number of other islands. Areas previously inhabited by this species should be renaturalized and prepared for repopulation programs. Several of the protected areas have meanwhile been established, for example, a narrow strip of coastal duneland to the north of Marina di Grosseto in Tuscany with a vegetation of pine and juniper, and others are sure to follow.

Since 1985, the Belgium-based nature conservation foundation R.A.N.A (Reptiles and Amphibians in Nature) has been working with the WWF on the development of a breeding and repopulation program for the Italian tortoise. Three years down the line, R.A.N.A founded the species conservation project CARAPAX (which is not without controversy today). A concerted effort by R.A.N.A., the European Union, and the regional government of Tuscany, with the support of the Italian Ministry for the Environment, then led to the opening of the CARAPAX tortoise center near the small town of Massa Marittima in Tuscany in July of 1989. This center is about 15 hectares in size and lies near a nature reserve of 35 hectares that is entirely dedicated to the conservation of Testudo hermanni. The station strives to conserve all Italian species of tortoises and their natural habitats, as well as making the public aware of the needs of and threats to this animal group. The main focus of CARAPAX is directed at Testudo hermanni. A total of thirteen wild populations of this species have been investigated scientifically since 1990, the two largest ones of which even on a continuous basis.

The center is run by eight people in the employ of R.A.N.A. plus about one hundred volunteers that find their way to Massa Marittima every year from all over the world. For a small contribution they can make use of a mess and accommodation, and it is their work in the center and in the habitats of the tortoises that everything necessary gets done. As far as funding is concerned, the center requires the equivalent of about $ 400,000 per year.

In the quest of keeping wild populations genetically "pure" within the center, the animals are housed according to their regions of origin as defined by borders in the form of natural barriers such as rivers etc.. In the mid-1990', the center thus sported twelve quarantine pens for *Testudo hermanni*, in which the animals were accommodated according to their sex. Nineteen enclosures housed breeding colonies from various geographical regions, thirteen pens were reserved for gravid females, twenty-four for hatchlings, six for raising juveniles up to two years of age, and eighteen for three to six-year olds.

Besides attending to its breeding and repopulation programs, CARAPAX strives to increase the understanding for these animals in the public through newspaper articles, TV documentaries and lectures for the about 25,000 visitors to the center, of which some 35 % are school children.

Since the species has been eradicated in Liguria, CARAPAX has been trying since 1994 to reestablish it there in more isolated situations such as islands. This is done using founder stock from southern France that has been made available by SOPTOM. The choice in favor of French specimens was based on the presumption that the original Ligurian tortoises were more closely genetically re-lated to these as a result of closer geographical distances than to conspecifics from other parts of Italy.

The populations of northern Tuscany (regional park of San Rossore) are scientifically monitored with the support of the park's management and the Natural History Museum of the University of Pisa. One breeding colony at the CARAPAX center every year produces some 35–50 juveniles that are all transferred eventually to San Rossore. However, doubts have emerged as to whether the tortoises in this park are really of natural origin. San Rossore used to be part of the lands owned by the Italian kings who established a variety of animal species here, including, for example, camels, but also tortoises representing the *Testudo graeca* species group and *Testudo marginata*.

The populations in the center and south of Tuscany are considered to still be genetically pure. Every year, the station produces about 300 babies from this region, which are raised for six years and then released into the wild. This routine began in 1994 (with about 200 offspring) and serves to keep losses through the omnipresent wild boar in check and give the young tortoises a chance of survival. The necessity of this was shown by WILLEMSEN (1995) who failed to find any tortoises of the age group 0–8 years in this area. Within the central and southern Tuscany population group, CARAPAX furthermore keeps specimens from isolated areas, such as the Parco di Montioni, from the surroundings of Siena and (probably) the island of Elba, separated, and the same applies to tortoises from the surroundings of Florence as this population is quite far removed from the other populations on the Italian west coast. Chances are, though, that man has established the species there. The breeding success with these isolated populations amounts to about 100 offspring per year in total. Another breeding and repopulation program exists for the tortoises from south of the river Ombrone (Maremma National Park), which is coupled with a program to reduce the number of wild boars.

The region of Latium has long been suffering from the influx of unauthorized releases of "pet" tortoises of unknown origin. As a consequence, the populations existing here cannot be considered genetically pure anymore. CARAPAX produces approximately seventy babies from/for this region annually.

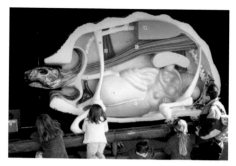

Fig. 162: Visitors to the tortoise village in Gonfaron can learn about the biology of *Testudo hermanni* from models. (B. DEVAUX)

The situation in the region Campania is particularly complicated. For centuries the port of Naples has seen the import of tortoises from other parts of the distribution range that were eventually released into the wild by their buyers. BALLASINA (1995a) therefore supposed that no genetically "pure" populations would exist in this region at all anymore. CARAPAX has been producing approximately thirty to forty babies of this population per year, which are also released into the wild in compliance with demands posed by the regional administration and a number of nature conservation agencies. They are intended to augment the wild populations in various areas such as the Mt. Vesuvius National Park.

CARAPAX also keeps strictly separated tortoises from the western and eastern parts of the Calabria region after BALLASINA (1995a) had found them to be clearly distinct. About 50–60 babies are produced annually of the western form, which in nature suffers badly from habitat fragmentation due to expanding settlements. The eastern form is under siege mainly from wild boars and is bred to the tune of several dozen every year. CARAPAX and the University of Calabria have been cooperating in planning a repopulation project for the Pollino National Park.

The annual production of baby tortoises from the Gargano National Park in the Apulia region amounts to approximately 75. CARAPAX is also busy establishing a breeding group for the Murge Mountains in the same region. According to BALLASINA (1995a), this population has been plundered by animal collectors in general and German enthusiasts in particular. In the long run, the CARAPAX management is hopeful to strengthen the Murge population through the release of captive-bred specimens and thus create one of the "biogenetic reserves" mentioned in the chapter "Threats".

As far as the eastern parts of the island of Sicily are concerned, WWF staff have been collecting tortoises from habitats that were to be built over. A breeding group of this origin has been accommodated in the CARAPAX center where it produces about forty babies every year. The other specimens from these collections were placed in a breeding program on the island itself. CARAPAX has been trying to improve the coordination of activities to this effect by WWF, Associazione Erpetológica Sizilienna, and Ente Fauna Sizilienna on Sicily. The populations in the west and south of the island have not received much attention. A few babies are hatched every year at the CARAPAX center, and some specimens are in the care of a variety of persons commissioned to do so by the WWF.

Sardinian tortoises are kept and bred at the station only in very small numbers, producing about fifty juveniles per year. The reason for this being so is that the situation of the species on this island is still considered to be reasonably safe.

For a number of years, CARAPAX has also been accepting members of tortoise species that do not naturally occur in Italy. Housing these specimens has meanwhile become a major problem of space for the station, though, and has forced the organization to engage in release programs also outside of Italy. Unfortunately, CARAPAX has not shown the same strict discrimination in this respect as it has for repopulation programs within its own country. The result is that in other states surrounding the Mediterranean tortoises are often "dumped" rather than "released" irrespective of their usually unknown origins.

Fig. 163: The continued successful breeding in Gonfaron creates hope for the future of the southern French tortoise populations. (B. DEVAUX)

This included, amongst others, the release of 289, 364, 296 and 133 Testudo boettgeri from (mainly Belgian) terrarium animals in the years 1991, 1994, 1995 and 2001, respectively, in Greece. These principally thoughtless actions may be well meant, but are entirely irresponsible. Besides of the distinct risks of "genetic pollution", there is also a high risk of introducing pathogens into wild populations, which may be extremely hazardous to local tortoise populations. The former is particularly bewildering considering that CARA-PAX must also be aware of the "rediscovery" of Testudo hercegovinensis and presents itself as extremely discriminate as far as the geographic variability of Testudo hermanni is concerned. The idea of releasing animals whose exact origins are unknown must therefore be categorically rejected. This was also stated in a resolution agreed upon at the AGM of the German Chelonia Group of the DGHT in March of 2001 that centered around the Testudo graeca species group.

Its repopulation policy is one of the reasons for the reputation of the CARAPAX center being surrounded by a lot of controversy amongst expert chelonologists today. On some occasions, stories have surfaced about the mass dying of tortoises at the station that in some instances is said to have caused an intolerable stench. Management of the center decided some years ago to expand their attention to storks and donkeys, which unfortunately drew the focus away from the tortoises. Although this offers variety to visitors, it also appears that staff (of mainly volunteers from various countries) are unable to cope with the workload.

This appears to be the right place to discuss a few fundamentals pertaining to the subject of repopulation of tortoises. Any form of repopulation program merely eases the symptoms, but does very little to nothing to correct the causes for the declining popu-

lations of the relevant species. Many experts share the opinion that attempts at repopulation for species that are not acutely threatened with extinction – as is the case with Testudo hermanni – are no adequate means to their conservation. Exceptions may be experimental projects, of course. If the destruction of the natural habitats of Testudo boettgeri, Testudo hercegovinensis and Testudo hermanni continues at the pace of the past years and decades, there will come the day when there are more tortoises than habitats to release them in. In the past, the IUCN used to support repopulation projects for various tortoise species. Many of these have meanwhile been halted at least temporarily for the medical reasons and genetic concerns mentioned before. Today, the organization recommends that in cases of not acutely endangered tortoise species the highest priority be granted to the protection of wild populations.

In Spain, legal prescriptions for the conservation of Testudo hermanni have been in place since 1973. Their original aim was to bring down the trade in these animals, which was threatening the survival of populations in the wild. The laws did, however, little to this effect. Rather, dealers gradually shifted their focus toward members of the eastern population group and other species and genera (e.g., Central Asian tortoises of the genus Agrionemys or box turtles of the genus Terrapene), which were now assuming the role of the indigenous tortoises. Testudo hermanni has since been upgraded to a "species of particular interest" in 1990, which means, for example, that the private possession of an Italian tortoise, even if captive-bred, is principally illegal in Catalonia. Recommendation No. 26 of the Permanent Committee of the Berne Convention of 1991 furthermore suggested to the Spanish Government that the natural habitats of this species in the dunelands of Serra Nova and in the surroundings of Artá on Mallorca be placed under protection. The IUCN also recommended to this country that particular protection be extended to important habitats of the Italian tortoise within the network of Natura 2000 in parts of Mallorca, Menorca, and in the Albera Mountains. Areas previously inhabited by this species in the Albera Mountains should be renaturalized for repopulation projects. This resulted in the establishment of six new protected areas. As far as repopulation programs were concerned, the IUCN recommends that these be continued for as long as was necessary, in particular in the Albera Mountains.

The regional government of the Balearic Islands has been maintaining a small study project on Mallorca that is to gather data on the biology of these tortoises. It is also planned to establish a rescue and breeding station there. Other than this, there is the privately owned tortoise reserve Son Cifre de Baix, situated some 10 km outside of Manacor in the center of the island, that has been open since 28. September 1978. This center of 25 hectares in size is dedicated exclusively to Testudo hermanni. As of September 1990, it was home to more than 1,260 specimens of this species representing all age groups. The estate sports, amongst others, a large (ca. 5.000 m²) and several smaller enclosures where tortoises can be housed under supervision if and when necessary. The need for this arises regularly in the course of scientific studies or for accommodating specimens confiscated by customs etc. that are to be released into their natural environment. This reserve lies within the private property of the Dutch couple Mr. and Mrs. Kramer who take care of the conservation of this tortoise population with exemplifying commitment. Although a little makeshift in places, it is completely surrounded by a wall (or wiremesh fence in some places) that keeps out stray pigs, sheep and goats. While the former

have a distinct taste for tidbits in the form of baby tortoises, the latter are attracted by the lush green of the reserve, which creates a stark contrast to the withered vegetation on the other side of the wall during the dry season. Large numbers of damaged spots in the wall attest to attempts, mainly by goats, to somehow overcome the "obstacle". Within the reserve, firebreaks of about 1,200 meters in length are cleared and maintained to curb the spread of potentially devastating wildfires. These breaks are cleared from vegetation either by hand or with carefully controlled light machinery at regular intervals and are particularly popular as egg-laying sites amongst the tortoises. A small, restored finca serves visiting biologists as a base camp for their studies.

Son Cifre de Baix is not open to the public. Lacking the means of constant monitoring, it had been decided already in 1983 to remove the reserve from the national and international eye and thus reduce the temptations for dubious "tortoise lovers".

The island is also the home of the organization "Amics de les tortugues/Amigos de las tortugas" (A.D.L.T), that aims at informing the public and authorities about the threats and needs of the tortoises, helping to improve the conservation of their natural habitats, investigating the husbandry conditions with private keepers, and quite generally promoting the conservation of chelonians worldwide. The organization demands, amongst others, that every tortoise sold in petshops be accompanied by an information pamphlet that describes in detail how the animal must be kept. Persons known to keep tortoises are visited and given advice about how to care for them properly and even offered active assistance if and when necessary. Education for the authorities includes convincing them not to simply release confiscated tortoises in nature reserves in arid areas that have never been part of the natural distribution range of *Testudo hermanni* because some 70% of these animals do not survive this. Owners of properties with a population of tortoises are made aware of the problems associated with walls (see chapter "Threats"). Watering places are established on these fincas in order to improve the living conditions for the local tortoises.

Like with the rest of Spain, collecting tortoises is strictly prohibited on the neighboring island of Menorca. SCHMIDT (1999) reported about the case of a tourist who tried to smuggle a juvenile specimen through customs by hiding it in the pocket of his trousers. He was caught, though, and fined the approximate equivalent of $ 200.

Almost the entire distribution range of *Testudo hermanni* on the Spanish mainland was declared a protected area in 1986. This did not stop the collection of tortoises, though, and although the numbers of illegally removed animals decreased initially, they later increased once more as a result of increasing numbers in tourists visiting this region. Conservation projects for *Testudo hermanni* also exist in Catalonia under the management of the Ministry of the Environment. One of these was founded by the Catalonian regional government in October of 1984. It centers around Mas Pòlit, which is situated in the Albera Nature Park where two years later the Albera Project was launched under the name of "Centre de Reproducció de la Tortuga de L'Albera — CRT". It focuses on the conservation and breeding of the last populations of natural origin from the northeast of Spain. However, management was unable to stop the ongoing large-scale theft of tortoises from this site, and the station was eventually moved to Garriguella in the extreme south of the Spanish distribution range in 1992. Here, the project had been donated a hermitage including the surrounding

land in a relatively undisturbed area by the Catholic Church.

The project is managed by the "Amics de la Tortuga de L'Albera", an organization founded in November of 1992, in cooperation with the Faculty of Biology of the University of Barcelona and the Sociedad Herpetológica de Catalunya. This organization aims, amongst others, at an improvement of the legal protection status of the tortoises and their natural habitats and assists nature conservation authorities with the enforcement of the existing laws. By the mid-1990', the station was home to about eighty adult tortoises of which not a single one had been removed from nature. This breeding group meanwhile produces some 150–200 babies per year from eggs that are incubated artificially. It must be said, though, that not all clutches are actually found within the expansive main enclosure.

In 1997, some 200 three year-old juveniles were released into protected areas by the Catalonian regional government. This was followed up with other repopulation attempts. Juveniles produced by a separate breeding group of adults dumped at the station by private persons or from confiscations by the authorities and therefore without information about their exact origin, are used to repopulate a reserve near Barcelona where tortoises have become extinct.

The project also takes care of lectures in schools and at public gatherings to heighten the awareness of local people of the threats and needs of their native tortoises. This is also the reason why the station has been open to the public since March of 1994. It even sports a "class room" in which visiting school classes and other groups can obtain information on the work done at the station. Besides large numbers of pupils, about 10,000 people visit the station every year.

Several specimens have also been released on an experimental basis in the nature park at Cape de Creus in Catalonia. The original tortoise populations that used to live here had become extinct as a result of forest fires that were rampant in this area throughout the last decades. These animals are fitted with radio transmitters that provide information as to their adjustment to the new environment and thus about the suitability of this nature park for a repopulation project. Captive-bred juveniles from the CRT station have also been released into the wild since 2002.

The second Spanish center, the "Centro de Recuperación de Anfibios y Reptiles de Catalunya" (C.R.A.R.C.), is situated at Masquefa. It is run by the Commissió Medi Ambient Ajuntament de Masquefa (or short COMAM) in cooperation with various Catalonian authorities and the Liga para la Defensa del Patrimonio Natural (DEPANA). It is dedicated to the research and conservation of the entire indigenous fauna.

Since 1993, tortoises have been released into the wilderness of the nature park surrounding the Garraf Mountains and in the mountain landscapes of L'Avellana and Mossons south of Barcelona. The animals now living in the Mossons Mountains form a research population that is kept within a fenced-in area of 2–3 hectares in size. It is studied to find out more about the habits and abilities of released specimens to adjust to new surroundings.

In May of 1997, C.R.A.R.C. opened their new and expanded facilities, which now also include a "tortoise hospital", a small museum, and quarantine holdings.

The Garraf Mountains form part of a mountain chain that stretches along the Catalonian coast some 20 km from Barcelona. It used to be an area within the distribution range of *Testudo hermanni* and appears to

have been one of the last regions from which the species vanished. The aim is here, like in other places, to reestablish the species in a part of its original distribution range. This is done with tortoises that used to be kept as "pets" in gardens in and around Barcelona, in some instances for decades, before they were donated to the project or confiscated. They originate in most cases either from the area or from the Balearic Islands. Animals earmarked for release are first kept at the center in quarantine for three months during which time they receive veterinarian care. Housed in large outdoor pens they have an opportunity to adjust to a life in the wild. The first twenty-nine tortoises arrived at the center in June of 1992, and the first six specimens were released in September of 1993. They had been fitted with radio transmitters so that their whereabouts could be monitored. A forest fire then destroyed some 4,800 hectares of the nature park in April of 1994. Four of the released tortoises perished in the fire, and the other two sustained serious injuries and later died at the station to which they been taken for treatment.

Another seventeen tortoises, nine of which had been fitted with radio transmitters, were released in July of 1995 in an area of the nature park that had not been affected by the fire. In a study on the prospects of the project that was based on parameters such as weight and reproductive activity, it was demonstrated that 80% of the released animals had survived their first year in the wild during which period they had moved off from their point of release by a maximum distance of 550 m. In 1996, another fifty-three tortoises were set free, and by 2005 the total number of released specimens had risen to 598.

Meanwhile, juveniles have been spotted in the repopulated area (seventy-six in total by 2005), which are left to their own devices so that they can perfectly adapt to their environment. A census conducted in 2005 revealed a total population of 701 tortoises in this region, and the mortality rate was estimated to amount to 25.1 %. As it also revealed a shift in the sex ratio clearly in favor of males (see chapter "Natural habitat") future releases will mainly involve females.

Other repopulation efforts are scheduled for the Catalonian Montserrat and Cadiretes Mountains.

A total of ninety adult specimens of *Testudo hermanni* were released on the islets within the nature reserve Punta de la Banya that forms part of the nature park Delta de L'Ebre between 1987 and 2001. This was a repopulation project run by the "Estación Biológica Parc Natural del Delta de l'Ebre". Forty-four animals were set free in 1987 and 1988 in a "patchwork" of islets that were more or less linked to each other and thus covered a total of 5.8 hectares of land. In order to speed up reproduction, females made up the clear majority of specimens. A second population was established on an island of 2.8 hectares (nine specimens in 1990, and another five in 1993). These releases involved specimens caught in the region around Montsià, but also some of unknown provenance, which the station had received for this purpose from confiscations by the Catalonian authorities and excess stock and captive-bred ones from the Barcelona zoo. Other than these, the center has been receiving "gifts" from private owners who were no longer interested in their "pets".

All this led to the nature park surrounding the Ebro estuary being once more populated with a few tortoises that have been under constant surveillance since 1991. Studies conducted there showed that 94 % of the released females and 95 % of the males have managed to survive in the wild. By 1995, 222 juveniles have been recorded from here. These definitely benefit from the fact that predators are largely absent from the area.

The population of the nature park is today considerably denser than others in the wild. It has been expanding its range on a continuous basis, and juveniles have also been spotted in newly colonized areas.

A prediction model indicated, however, that this population would probably be able to maintain its present size only for some fifty years, and this only if the release of captive-hatched juveniles is continued. In general, it was found that small populations of less than one hundred specimens cannot persist if one to two adult females die every year or are lost to the population for other reasons.

It is planned to relocate some specimens at a later stage to other places in Spain where the species used to be naturally present. This excludes the locality Alt Empordà, though, where a population exists that is thought to be still genetically pure. LOEHR (2002) quite rightly raised the question why the organizers would not wait with the foundation of "new" tortoise populations in various reserves until "supernumerary" offspring of Albera specimens became available and so maintained the "genetic purity" of Spanish mainland populations in general.

On the outskirts of València lies the Centro de Protección y Estudio del Medio Natural (CPEMN). It is run by the regional government of the Autonomous Region Comunidad Valènciana and another place where, amongst others, *Testudo hermanni* are bred in captivity. The resultant babies are earmarked for later release into a nature park in this region.

A tortoise population furthermore exists in the nature park "Desert de les Palmes" near Castellón-Benicássim in the same Autonomous Region. These animals live in the center "Mas de les Tortugues" in an enclosure covering 4,900 m² with semi-natural

Asociación de Naturalistas del Sudeste
C/Medieras
6. Entslo. Izqda.
30201 Cartagena (Murcia)
Spain
E-Mail: anse-cartagena@wanadoo.es
Internet: www.asociacionanse.org

CARAPAX Center
CP 34
58024 Massa Marittima
Italy
E-Mail: info@carapax.org
Internet: www.carapax.org

Centre de Reproducció de la Tortuga de L'Albera
s/n Santuari de la Mare de Déu del Camp
17780 Garriguella (Girona)
Spain
E-Mail: crt@wanadoo.es
Internet: www.tortugues.org

Centro de Protección y Estudio del Medio Natural
Conselleria de Medi Ambient
Avenida del Pinars, 106
46012 El Saler (València)
Spain

Centro de Recuperación de Anfibios y Reptiles de Catalunya
C/Santa Clara
s/n 08783 Masquefa (Barcelona)
Spain
E-Mail: Crarc_Comam@hotmail.com

dauvi-Verlag
Jenseitsstraße 79
50127 Bergheim
Germany
E-Mail: redaktion@dauvi.de
Internet: www.schildkroeten-im-fokus.de
Journal: Schildkröten im Fokus (published quarterly)

Deutsche Gesellschaft für Herpetologie und Terrarienkunde e. V.
Geschäftsstelle
Postfach 1421
53351 Rheinbach
Germany
E-Mail: gs@dght.de
Internet: www.dght.de
Journals: SALAMANDRA, Der Salamander, *elaphe* (all published quarterly), MERTENSIELLA (supplemental publication, published occasionally)

Deutsche Gesellschaft für Herpetologie und Terrarienkunde e. V. – German Chelonia Group
Druslachstraße 8
67360 Lingenfeld
Germany
E-Mail: ag-schildkroeten@dght.de

(English: radiata-ag@dght.de)
Internet: www.ag-schildkroeten.de
(English: www.radiata.de)
Journals: RADIATA, RADIATA English Edition, MINOR (all published quarterly)

The German Chelonia Group maintains, amongst others, a "*Task Team Mediterranean Tortoises*" with the following aims:
• exchange of information and knowledge between keepers of Mediterranean tortoises
• support for members and beginners
• optimizing of keeping, breeding and raising conditions in nature-like settings
• coverage of the demand by the pet trade through local production (avoiding of farming and ranching)
• detailed study of species (subspecies, local varieties)
• establishing stud books for animals whose exact origins are known
• conservation of the European tortoises in their native countries, not by means of unchecked releases of captive-bred specimens, but rather through the conservation of still functional biotopes in the quest to secure populations in their natural environment
• cooperation with authorities and animal protection organizations in the realization of legal and animal protection requirements
If you are interested in the work of this task team and want to support it, please contact its chief executive:
Christoph Fritz
Fax: Germany-1212-510216511
E-Mail: christophfritz@web.de
Internet: www.dght.de/ag/schildkroeten/akeuropland.htm

Estación Biológica Parc Natural del Delta de l'Ebre
Plaça 20 de Maig
s/n 43580 Deltebre (Tarragona)
Spain
Internet: www.ebre.com

European Studbook Foundation
The *European Studbook* Foundation has also set up a captive breeding program for the species portrayed here. Their aim is to register as many specimens kept in European collections as possible in a central database and thus ensure that a healthy captive population is maintained throughout Europe. Contact addresses are as follows:
Testudo hermanni
Laurens Woldring
De La Reijstraat 124
2987 XG Ridderkerk
The Netherlands
E-Mail: testudo-hermanni-hermanni@studbooks.org
Testudo boettgeri, Testudo hercegovinensis
Ruurd van Donkelaar
Laantje 1
4251 EL Werkendam
The Netherlands
E-Mail: testudo-hermanni-boettgeri@studbooks.org
Internet: www.studbooks.org

herpetofauna-Verlags-GmbH
Römerstraße 21
71384 Weinstadt
Germany
E-Mail: info@herpetofauna.de
Internet: www.herpetofauna.de
Journal: HERPETOFAUNA (published bimonthly)

Internationale Schildkröten Vereinigung
Kirchenplatz 6
3562 Stiefern
Austria
E-Mail: gerhard.schaffer@isv.cc
Internet: www.isv.cc
Journal: SACALIA (published quarterly)

Natur und Tier Verlag GmbH
An der Kleinmannbrücke 39/41
48157 Münster
Germany
E-Mail: verlag@ms-verlag.de
Internet: www.ms-verlag.de
Journals: REPTILIA (terrarium magazine, published bimonthly), DRACO (terrarium journal dedicated to individual subjects, published quarterly), MARGINATA (chelonian magazine, published quarterly)

Nederlandse Schildpadden Vereniging
Lumeystraat 11c
3039 ZM Rotterdam
The Netherlands
E-Mail: voorzitter@schildpaddenvereniging.org
Internet: www.trionyx.nl
Journal: TRIONYX (published bimonthly)

O AETOS
Artemidos 50
60065 Platamonas/Pieria
Greece
E-Mail: eagles-club@kat.forthnet.gr
Internet: www.oaetos.de

**Österreichische Gesellschaft für Herpetologie –
Workgroup Chelonians**
Robert-Stolz-Straße 28
2301 Neuoberhausen
Austria
E-Mail: egretzberger@netzundplan.at
Internet: www.nhm-wien.ac.at/nhm/herpet/
Journal: HERPETOZOA (published quarterly)

Schildkrötenfreunde Österreich
Maria Ponsee 32
3454 Sitzenberg-Reidling
Austria
E-Mail: h.artner@pgv.at
Internet: www.sfoe.at
Journal: EMYS (published bimonthly)

Schildkröten Interessen-Gemeinschaft Schweiz
Postfach
4416 Bubendorf
Switzerland
E-Mail: info@sigs.ch
Internet: www.sigs.ch
Journal: TESTUDO (SIGS) (published quarterly)

Terrariengemeinschaft Berlin e V
Planetenstraße 45
12057 Berlin
Germany
E-Mail: abo@sauria.de
Internet: www.sauria.de
Journal: SAURIA (published quarterly)

Verlag Eugen Ulmer GmbH & Co
Wollgrasweg 41
70599 Stuttgart
Germany
E-Mail: datz@ulmer.de
Internet: www.datz.de
JournaL: DATZ (published monthly)

Village des Tortues – SOPTOM
Centre d'études et de protection des tortues
B.P. 24
83590 Gonfaron
France
or
Route d'Asco lieu dit Tizzarella
20218 Moltifao
France
E-Mail: soptom@wanadoo.fr
Internet: www.villagetortues.com
Journal: LA TORTUE (published in 3–4 issues annually)

Weather stations in the distribution range of:

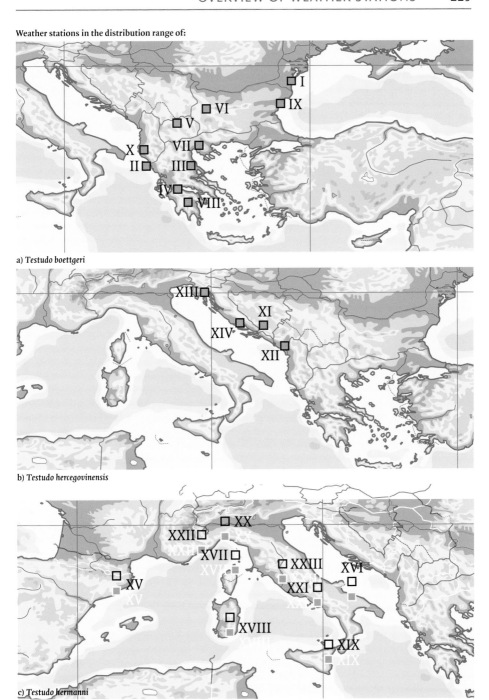

a) *Testudo boettgeri*

b) *Testudo hercegovinensis*

c) *Testudo hermanni*

The following is a selection of climatic data compiled from MÜLLER (1996, 5th Edition).

Weather stations were selected in an attempt to represent as many parts of the distribution ranges of the three species portrayed here as possible.

All temperatures are given in °C, amounts of precipitation in mm, relative humidity in %, and hours of sunshine in hours (h).

Boettger's tortoise

Weather station I
Constanta/Constanta/Romania
situated at: 44°10´N / 28°37´E, 52 m above sea level
Warm/temperate, suboceanic, permahumid rainy climate without distinct dry seasons, with moderately warm to warm and long summers and mild to moderately cold winters; vegetation period longer than 200 days; precipitation maximum in summer and fall; suboceanic deciduous and mixed forests

	J	F	M	A	M	J	J	A	S	O	N	D	Year
Mean temp.	0.8	0.5	3.8	9.1	14.9	19.5	22.2	22.0	17.8	12.8	7.2	2.1	10.9
Mean max. temp.	3.0	4.3	7.9	13.2	18.7	23.7	27.0	26.5	22.6	17.4	10.7	5.9	15.1
Mean min. temp.	-3.7	-2.5	0.6	5.7	11.1	15.6	17.6	17.3	13.8	9.2	4.3	-0.5	7.3
Absol. max. temp.	16.7	19.6	30.4	29.4	36.6	36.4	35.6	36.2	35.0	29.4	24.4	20.4	36.6
Absol. min. temp.	24.7	-20.2	-11.6	-4.5	1.0	3.8	7.6	7.0	1.0	-5.4	-12.8	-18.6	-24.7
Mean rel. humidity	88	86	83	80	81	77	74	74	78	82	86	88	80
Mean precipitation	30	26	24	32	37	49	35	32	27	40	44	37	413
Days with precipitation	10	9	8	7	9	8	6	4	4	6	9	10	90
Hours of sunshine	81	102	135	188	236	292	342	320	240	166	82	74	2,258

Weather station II
Corfu/Ionian Islands/Greece
situated at: 39°37′S / 19°55′E, 25 m above sea level
Warm/temperate, Mediterranean rainy climate with dry, hot summers and moist winters; usually more than five months with rain; subtropical hard-leafed and coniferous forests

	J	F	M	A	M	J	J	A	S	O	N	D	Year
Mean temp.	10.0	10.4	11.8	14.5	18.2	22.5	25.3	25.4	22.5	18.8	14.9	11.8	17.2
Mean max. temp.	14.0	14.6	16.0	19.1	23.3	28.2	31.4	31.5	27.8	23.4	19.1	15.9	22.0
Mean min. temp.	5.9	6.1	7.5	9.9	13.1	16.8	19.2	19.2	17.2	14.2	10.7	7.7	12.3
Absol. max. temp.	20.0	21.4	23.8	28.7	32.1	36.6	40.2	40.7	37.8	33.2	25.0	21.0	40.7
Absol. min. temp.	-4.4	-3.3	-2.8	-0.1	3.6	10.2	12.0	13.0	6.8	3.8	-2.5	-2.5	-4.4
Mean rel. humidity	74	73	73	74	71	65	62	62	71	71	74	76	70
Mean precipitation	196	132	100	70	41	14	4	20	95	184	237	259	1,352
Days with precipitation	15	14	12	10	6	3	1	2	6	11	15	17	112

Weather station III
Lárissa/Thessalia/Greece
situated at: 39°37′N / 22°15′E, 76 m above sea level
Warm/temperate, Mediterranean rainy climate with dry, hot summers and moist winters; usually more than five months with rain; subtropical hard-leafed and coniferous forests

	J	F	M	A	M	J	J	A	S	O	N	D	Year
Mean temp.	5.8	7.4	9.2	13.7	19.7	25.4	28.0	27.8	22.4	16.2	11.4	7.4	16.2
Mean max. temp.	10.0	12.9	15.1	20.4	25.7	31.3	34.4	34.0	29.1	23.1	16.3	12.1	22.0
Mean min. temp.	0.5	1.3	3.4	6.5	10.7	15.1	18.1	17.7	14.3	10.4	6.9	3.0	9.0
Absol. max. temp.	21.0	24.0	31.8	31.8	38.5	41.8	45.0	45.0	40.0	36.6	26.0	22.6	45.0
Absol. min. temp.	-11.8	-9.5	-7.0	-2.6	3.1	7.0	10.6	10.6	6.0	0.3	-6.0	-14.0	-14.0
Mean rel. humidity	81	74	74	71	65	52	47	45	58	73	82	82	67
Mean precipitation	51	40	49	35	45	30	15	13	31	88	64	61	522
Days with precipitation	10	8	8	7	9	6	3	2	4	9	10	10	86
Hours of sunshine	104	129	156	228	272	295	339	326	259	170	130	83	2,491

Weather station IV
Patras/Western Greece/Greece
situated at: 38°15′N / 21°45′E, 43 m above sea level
Warm/temperate, Mediterranean rainy climate with dry, hot summers and moist winters; usually more than five months with rain; subtropical hard-leafed and coniferous forests

	J	F	M	A	M	J	J	A	S	O	N	D	Year
Mean temp.	9.7	10.4	11.9	15.6	19.6	23.8	26.3	26.4	23.1	18.7	14.4	10.9	17.6
Mean max. temp.	14.3	15.2	16.5	19.8	23.4	27.5	30.6	31.1	28.2	24.2	19.8	16.2	22.2
Mean min. temp.	5.3	5.6	6.3	9.2	12.3	15.8	17.9	17.8	15.6	12.9	9.7	7.0	11.3
Absol. max. temp.	20.8	25.3	31.0	33.6	36.0	37.8	38.8	40.0	37.5	34.5	27.8	23.0	40.0
Absol. min. temp.	-4.1	-5.0	-1.3	1.0	5.8	9.5	11.5	10.5	8.0	3.0	-1.5	-3.8	-5.0
Mean rel. humidity	74	71	69	68	67	64	61	62	67	71	74	74	69
Mean precipitation	123	87	72	50	27	13	1	6	27	82	113	148	749
Days with precipitation	14	11	11	8	6	3	<1	1	4	8	12	14	92
Hours of sunshine	133	136	182	233	286	295	358	338	281	219	156	108	2,725

Weather station V
Skopje/Skopje City/Macedonia
situated at: 42°0′N/21°6′E, 245 m above sea level
Warm/temperate, suboceanic, permahumid rainy climate without clear dry seasons, with moderately hot warm to warm, long summers and mild to moderately cold winters; vegetation period longer than 200 days; precipitation maximum in summer and fall; suboceanic deciduous and mixed forests

	J	F	M	A	M	J	J	A	S	O	N	D	Year
Mean temp.	1.1	2.9	6.5	12.1	17.0	21.6	23.8	23.7	18.6	11.9	7.2	2.9	12.4
Mean max. temp.	4.7	8.3	11.9	19.3	23.3	28.0	30.8	31.1	26.0	18.5	11.7	7.4	18.4
Mean min. temp.	-2.9	-2.5	0.6	5.3	10.1	13.4	15.2	14.3	11.1	5.9	2.9	-1.1	6.0
Absol. max. temp.	19.0	18.1	25.0	30.2	33.5	37.0	41.2	40.5	38.5	34.2	24.8	19.4	41.2
Absol. min. temp.	-23.0	-23.9	-18.4	-4.5	-0.6	3.3	5.5	5.7	-3.2	-4.4	-9.7	-21.8	-23.9
Mean rel. humidity	85	79	73	66	69	63	58	57	67	80	85	87	72
Mean precipitation	46	41	38	34	52	49	35	37	42	58	71	43	546
Days with precipitation	7	6	8	8	11	8	4	5	4	8	6	11	86
Hours of sunshine	66	116	135	197	220	285	318	306	220	153	72	60	2,128

Weather station VI
Sofia/Sofia City/Bulgaria
situated at: 42°42´N/23°20´E, 550 m above sea level
Warm/temperate, suboceanic, permahumid rainy climate without clear dry seasons, with moderately hot warm to warm, long summers and mild to moderately cold winters; vegetation period longer than 200 days; precipitation maximum in summer and fall; suboceanic deciduous and mixed forests

	J	F	M	A	M	J	J	A	S	O	N	D	Year
Mean temp.	-1.7	0.6	4.6	10.6	15.5	19.0	21.3	20.7	17.0	11.1	5.5	0.7	10.4
Mean max. temp.	1.8	4.1	10.4	15.8	20.7	24.4	27.1	26.0	22.1	17.4	9.1	3.5	15.2
Mean min. temp.	-4.0	-2.9	0.8	5.3	10.2	13.5	15.6	14.9	11.3	7.9	2.5	-2.1	6.1
Absol. max. temp.	16.9	20.7	30.9	28.5	32.1	34.0	36.7	37.3	37.5	33.2	24.2	20.0	37.5
Absol. min. temp.	-27.5	-24.5	-14.9	-4.8	-1.5	2.5	6.9	6.1	-1.5	-3.3	-10.7	-20.3	-27.5
Mean rel. humidity	84	78	72	66	68	67	62	61	68	75	83	85	72
Mean precipitation	42	31	37	55	71	90	60	43	42	55	52	44	622
Days with precipitation	14	13	14	15	17	15	11	9	8	11	13	14	154
Hours of sunshine	55	91	138	187	221	261	314	304	233	155	75	49	2,083

Weather station VII
Thessaloníki/Central Makedonia/Greece
situated at: 40°39´N/23°7´E, 2 m above sea level
Warm/temperate, Mediterranean rainy climate with dry, hot summers and moist winters; usually more than five months with rain; subtropical hard-leafed and coniferous forests

	J	F	M	A	M	J	J	A	S	O	N	D	Year
Mean temp.	5.5	7.1	9.6	14.5	19.6	24.7	27.3	26.8	22.5	17.1	12.0	7.5	16.1
Mean max. temp.	9.4	11.7	14.4	19.7	24.8	29.4	32.4	32.1	27.7	21.7	15.9	11.4	20.9
Mean min. temp.	1.9	2.5	5.2	9.5	14.2	18.3	20.9	20.7	17.2	12.6	8.6	4.1	11.3
Absol. max. temp.	19.5	24.2	30.1	30.0	37.8	37.8	41.8	40.0	37.4	32.7	24.2	21.2	41.8
Absol. min. temp.	-10.3	-8.9	-4.7	-1.0	5.2	9.7	14.4	10.3	8.1	3.8	-2.8	-7.4	-10.3
Mean rel. humidity	78	71	69	67	66	56	51	52	60	69	76	78	66
Mean precipitation	44	34	35	36	40	33	20	14	28	55	56	54	449
Days with precipitation	6	6	7	7	6	6	4	3	4	6	7	8	70
Hours of sunshine	117	149	169	227	277	309	367	345	253	182	119	110	2,624

Weather station VIII
Trípoli/Peloponnesus/Greece
situated at: 37°31′N / 22°21′E, 661 m above sea level
Warm/temperate, Mediterranean rainy climate with dry, hot summers and moist winters; usually more than five months with rain; subtropical hard-leafed and coniferous forests

	J	F	M	A	M	J	J	A	S	O	N	D	Year
Mean temp.	5.3	6.1	7.7	11.5	15.4	20.1	23.1	22.9	19.3	15.5	10.5	7.1	13.7
Mean max. temp.	9.1	10.6	12.8	17.5	22.3	27.5	30.5	30.4	26.0	21.6	15.1	11.0	19.5
Mean min. temp.	1.5	1.6	2.5	5.5	8.5	12.7	15.6	15.4	12.6	9.3	5.8	3.1	7.8
Absol. max. temp.	18.0	21.0	29.6	29.0	33.2	37.6	39.8	40.2	36.4	33.4	26.0	19.0	40.2
Absol. min. temp.	-12.4	-16.4	-5.6	-1.0	1.0	5.5	9.0	9.0	4.0	0.6	-5.0	-10.2	-16.4
Mean rel. humidity	78	74	69	61	57	48	41	42	53	65	75	78	62
Mean precipitation	127	104	94	62	51	36	20	13	37	82	133	178	932
Days with precipitation	14	10	11	9	7	5	2	2	4	7	12	15	98

Weather station IX
Varna/Varna/Bulgaria
situated at: 43°12′N/27°55′E, 3 m above sea level
Warm/temperate, suboceanic, permahumid rainy climate without clear dry seasons, with moderately hot warm to warm, long summers and mild to moderately cold winters; vegetation period longer than 200 days; precipitation maximum in summer and fall; suboceanic deciduous and mixed forests

	J	F	M	A	M	J	J	A	S	O	N	D	Year
Mean temp.	1.2	2.4	5.0	10.0	15.5	20.2	22.9	22.6	18.9	14.0	8.6	4.1	12.1
Mean max. temp.	5.8	6.2	10.8	15.7	21.6	26.1	29.8	29.3	25.5	20.5	13.0	7.1	17.6
Mean min. temp.	-1.2	-1.1	2.3	6.8	11.9	15.9	18.5	17.9	14.4	10.9	5.9	1.0	8.6
Absol. max. temp.	20.4	21.4	27.5	29.5	34.7	35.4	38.7	39.4	35.4	32.4	24.2	21.0	39.4
Absol. min. temp.	-23.5	-15.8	-9.7	-2.3	2.4	7.2	10.1	9.8	0.0	-1.6	-8.2	-12.8	-23.5
Mean rel. humidity	85	81	78	76	76	73	68	70	73	78	80	84	77
Mean precipitation	36	31	26	35	40	56	39	38	25	43	49	56	474
Days with precipitation	10	9	8	9	10	9	6	4	4	7	10	10	96
Hours of sunshine	72	96	134	188	255	275	336	311	247	176	91	72	2,253

Weather station X
Vlorë/Vlorë/Albania
situated at: 40°29′N/19°30′E, 10 m above sea level
Warm/temperate, Mediterranean rainy climate with dry, hot summers and moist winters; usually more than five months with rain; subtropical hard-leafed and coniferous forests

	J	F	M	A	M	J	J	A	S	O	N	D	Year
Mean temp.	9.2	10.2	11.8	14.9	18.7	22.4	24.7	24.6	22.0	18.4	14.6	11.0	16,9
Mean max. temp.	13.1	13.5	15.7	19.1	23.1	27.1	29.6	30.4	27.1	23.1	18.9	15.0	21,3
Mean min. temp.	5.7	5.5	7.5	10.4	13.8	17.3	19.0	19.0	16.2	14.0	11.4	8.0	12,3
Absol. max. temp.	24.0	26.0	28.1	30.0	36.0	38.8	39.0	41.0	38.0	35.0	32.0	23.5	41,0
Absol. min. temp.	-7.2	-3.5	-3.0	3.0	5.0	10.8	12.5	12.8	4.0	1.0	-2.6	-4.5	-7,2
Mean rel. humidity	68	68	67	69	70	63	62	63	67	70	71	67	67
Mean precipitation	148	102	73	60	49	29	9	25	65	133	167	170	1,028
Days with precipitation	11	8	8	8	6	3	1	2	4	8	8	12	79
Hours of sunshine	132	143	173	226	274	317	369	344	279	211	117	100	2,685

Dalmatian tortoise

Weather station XI
Mostar/Federation Bosnia and Herzegovina/Bosnia and Herzegovina
situated at: 43°20′N/17°49′E, 99 m above sea level
Warm/temperate, Mediterranean rainy climate with dry, hot summers and moist winters; usually more than five months with rain; subtropical hard-leafed and coniferous forests

	J	F	M	A	M	J	J	A	S	O	N	D	Year
Mean temp.	5.4	6.5	9.7	13.8	18.3	22.4	25.4	25.5	21.4	15.8	10.7	7.8	15.2
Mean max. temp.	8.7	10.5	14.3	19.1	24.0	28.4	31.7	32.1	27.2	20.6	14.2	11.1	20.2
Mean min. temp.	2.1	2.5	5.1	8.5	12.6	16.3	19.0	18.8	15.5	10.9	7.1	4.5	10.2
Absol. max. temp.	18.8	22.2	25.8	29.6	34.8	40.0	43.0	40.2	38.2	30.3	22.9	19.2	43.0
Absol. min. temp.	-10.2	-6.9	6.0	1.2	3.3	8.4	11.0	9.6	7.1	4.0	-4.0	-4.3	-10.2
Mean rel. humidity	66	64	60	59	59	56	49	48	56	64	70	71	60
Mean precipitation	136	131	116	107	104	71	38	52	102	171	201	226	1,455
Days with precipitation	13	12	11	11	11	9	6	5	8	12	14	16	128
Hours of sunshine	109	119	177	192	226	272	340	315	232	160	106	90	2,338

Weather station XII
Podgorica/Montenegro/Serbia and Montenegro
situated at: 42°26′N/19°16′E, 40 m above sea level
Warm/temperate, Mediterranean rainy climate with dry, hot summers and moist winters; usually more than five months with rain; subtropical hard-leafed and coniferous forests

	J	F	M	A	M	J	J	A	S	O	N	D	Year
Mean temp.	5.6	6.2	9.5	14.0	18.6	23.5	26.4	26.3	21.6	15.3	10.6	6.7	15.4
Mean max. temp.	9.1	10.6	14.3	19.3	24.3	29.0	32.5	32.6	27.5	21.0	15.0	11.9	20.6
Mean min. temp.	2.3	2.5	5.4	9.3	13.6	17.8	20.8	20.6	17.0	11.7	7.5	4.4	11.1
Absol. max. temp.	18.0	20.4	26.2	31.0	33.1	37.6	40.6	41.2	39.0	30.0	23.0	19.4	41.2
Absol. min. temp.	-9.4	-9.7	-5.0	1.5	4.6	9.7	14.2	8.8	9.6	3.4	-5.4	-6.5	-9.7
Mean rel. humidity	73	74	66	63	63	56	48	48	58	68	77	75	64
Mean precipitation	179	195	135	98	105	60	40	63	113	202	213	229	1,632
Days with precipitation	10	9	12	11	12	8	3	5	7	14	12	14	117
Hours of sunshine	109	109	180	199	241	296	348	329	245	192	115	107	2,470

Weather station XIII
Rijeka/Primorje-Gorski kotar/Croatia
situated at: 45°20′N/14°28′E, 104 m above sea level
Warm/temperate, Mediterranean rainy climate with dry, hot summers and moist winters; usually more than five months with rain; subtropical hard-leafed and coniferous forests

	J	F	M	A	M	J	J	A	S	O	N	D	Year
Mean temp.	5.9	6.3	8.7	12.8	17.2	21.0	23.5	23.1	19.6	14.9	10.4	8.1	14.3
Mean max. temp.	8.8	9.3	12.0	16.2	21.1	24.9	28.0	27.5	23.9	18.3	13.3	10.7	17.8
Mean min. temp.	3.0	3.2	5.4	9.3	13.2	17.0	19.0	18.7	15.3	11.4	7.5	5.5	10.7
Absol. max. temp.	18.4	20.0	21.4	26.3	31.2	32.1	36.8	35.8	34.8	28.8	20.1	17.0	36.8
Absol. min. temp.	-8.3	-12.8	-3.6	0.8	3.0	9.3	12.0	12.0	8.4	2.8	-1.2	-2.5	-12.8
Mean rel. humidity	64	65	61	60	61	62	56	56	61	66	69	69	63
Mean precipitation	132	101	110	105	111	102	82	83	171	191	185	175	1,548
Days with precipitation	10	10	10	10	10	12	10	8	9	11	13	13	126
Hours of sunshine	108	107	139	175	222	249	297	263	206	165	86	91	2,108

Weather station XIV
Split/Split-Dalmatia/Croatia
situated at: 43°31′N/16°26′E, 128 m above sea level
Warm/temperate, Mediterranean rainy climate with dry, hot summers and moist winters; usually more than five months with rain; subtropical hard-leafed and coniferous forests

	J	F	M	A	M	J	J	A	S	O	N	D	Year
Mean temp.	7,8	8,1	10,3	14,0	18,6	22,9	25,6	25,4	21,6	16,8	12,3	10,1	16,1
Mean max. temp.	9,9	10,8	13,6	17,8	22,8	26,9	30,2	30,1	25,9	20,1	15,1	11,8	19,6
Mean min. temp.	4,9	5,0	7,4	11,1	15,5	18,9	21,8	21,8	18,7	14,0	10,1	7,2	13,0
Absol. max. temp.	17,7	19,5	21,2	26,8	33,2	36,3	37,8	37,1	34,9	30,8	22,0	17,9	37,8
Absol. min. temp.	-8,3	-8,1	-3,3	1,9	4,8	10,7	12,2	11,2	7,4	3,0	-4,5	-6,0	-8,3
Mean rel. humidity	62	63	63	60	60	57	52	50	58	63	66	67	60
Mean precipitation	76	74	53	62	60	53	40	32	55	71	110	130	816
Days with precipitation	13	9	11	11	14	9	5	5	8	11	13	13	122
Hours of sunshine	148	158	195	206	255	323	354	345	246	185	128	115	2.656

Italian tortoise

Weather station XV
Barcelona/Catalonia/Spain
situated at: 41°24′N/2°9′E, 95 m above sea level
Warm/temperate, Mediterranean rainy climate with dry, hot summers and moist winters; usually more than five months with rain; subtropical hard-leafed and coniferous forests

	J	F	M	A	M	J	J	A	S	O	N	D	Year
Mean temp.	9.4	9.9	12.3	14.6	17.7	21.6	24.4	24.2	21.7	17.5	13.5	10.2	16.4
Mean max. temp.	12.7	13.7	15.6	18.2	21.4	25.4	27.9	27.7	25.0	20.5	16.4	13.1	19.8
Mean min. temp.	6.3	7.1	8.9	11.0	14.0	18.1	20.7	20.8	18.7	14.5	10.5	7.5	13.2
Absol. max. temp.	20.8	21.1	24.3	27.8	32.2	34.5	35.4	36.1	32.6	27.5	24.5	20.0	36.1
Absol. min. temp.	-2.4	-6.7	0.8	3.9	4.8	11.0	14.3	13.2	10.4	5.0	2.8	-2.5	-6.7
Mean rel. humidity	68	65	68	66	66	64	65	69	73	71	70	67	68
Mean precipitation	33	42	46	47	52	43	29	48	77	80	49	47	593
Days with precipitation	5	5	8	8	8	6	4	6	8	9	5	6	79
Hours of sunshine	150	164	175	213	252	280	313	274	202	175	150	132	2,480

Weather station XVI

Bari/Apulia/Italy
situated at: 41°7′N/16°52′E, 12 m above sea level
Warm/temperate, Mediterranean rainy climate with dry, hot summers and moist winters; usually more than five months with rain; subtropical hard-leafed and coniferous forests

	J	F	M	A	M	J	J	A	S	O	N	D	Year
Mean temp.	8.7	9.5	11.1	14.2	18.1	22.2	24.9	24.5	21.3	17.8	14.1	10.8	16.5
Mean max. temp.	11.5	12.6	14.4	17.7	21.7	25.9	28.5	28.6	25.5	21.0	17.3	13.8	19.9
Mean min. temp.	5.8	6.4	7.8	10.6	14.5	18.4	21.2	21.2	18.3	14.5	10.9	7.8	13.1
Absol. max. temp.	20.0	21.9	25.7	28.2	35.7	37.9	41.0	41.9	38.8	29.7	26.2	22.0	41.9
Absol. min. temp.	-2.8	-2.0	-3.1	2.0	5.0	11.2	13.6	13.2	11.0	5.8	2.6	-2.8	-3.1
Mean rel. humidity	75	70	68	66	65	60	60	60	67	73	74	75	68
Mean precipitation	68	57	57	42	39	29	25	24	46	73	79	70	609
Days with precipitation	9	6	7	6	5	4	3	3	4	6	8	8	69
Hours of sunshine	120	145	195	235	310	325	355	320	265	210	140	105	2,725

Weather station XVII

Bastia/Corsica/France
situated at: 42°33′N/9°29′E, 10 m above sea level
Warm/temperate, Mediterranean rainy climate with dry, hot summers and moist winters; usually more than five months with rain; subtropical hard-leafed and coniferous forests

	J	F	M	A	M	J	J	A	S	O	N	D	Year
Mean temp.	7.9	8.6	10.3	12.7	16.2	20.2	23.0	23.0	20.4	16.0	11.9	9.1	14.9
Absol. max. temp.	23.6	22.0	23.8	24.2	29.7	32.6	35.8	36.0	34.0	27.6	23.8	24.0	36.0
Absol. min. temp.	-4.6	-5.0	-3.8	0.5	1.3	8.2	10.2	11.8	7.8	3.0	1.2	-1.8	-5.0
Mean precipitation	75	65	60	65	50	20	10	25	65	110	95	95	735
Days with precipitation	10	80	10	9	9	4	1	2	6	10	11	11	91
Hours of sunshine	137	132	188	223	258	306	364	313	249	197	128	110	2,603

Weather station XVIII
Cagliari/Sardinia/Italy
situated at: 39°13′N/9°6′E, 75 m above sea level
Warm/temperate, Mediterranean rainy climate with dry, hot summers and moist winters; usually more than five months with rain; subtropical hard-leafed and coniferous forests

	J	F	M	A	M	J	J	A	S	O	N	D	Year
Mean temp.	9.4	9.9	11.8	14.2	17.8	21.7	24.5	24.7	22.1	18.3	14.0	11.0	16.6
Mean max. temp.	14.2	14.6	16.5	19.1	23.4	27.1	30.3	29.9	27.2	23.3	18.8	15.6	21.7
Mean min. temp.	6.9	7.4	8.6	10.6	13.7	17.7	20.7	20.8	18.7	15.1	11.3	8.7	13.3
Absol. max. temp.	21.2	21.2	24.5	28.1	35.0	37.4	40.2	37.9	35.2	28.8	26.2	24.2	40.2
Absol. min. temp.	-2.0	-1.2	0.7	4.2	6.9	10.1	14.2	15.4	11.7	7.7	4.2	-1.0	-2.0
Mean rel. humidity	80	78	77	76	75	70	70	72	74	77	77	80	76
Mean precipitation	50	50	45	31	26	13	1	10	32	54	72	67	451
Days with precipitation	8	7	7	5	4	1	0	1	3	6	9	9	60
Hours of sunshine	128	122	187	206	269	274	327	304	229	193	122	105	2,466

Weather station XIX
Catania/Sicily/Italy
situated at: 37°30′N/15°6′E, 45 m above sea level
Warm/temperate, Mediterranean rainy climate with dry, hot summers and moist winters; usually more than five months with rain; subtropical hard-leafed and coniferous forests

	J	F	M	A	M	J	J	A	S	O	N	D	Jahr
Mean temp.	10.9	11.5	13.0	15.3	19.3	23.4	26.6	26.6	24.0	19.8	16.0	12.6	18.3
Mean max. temp.	14.1	15.1	16.6	19.0	23.3	27.5	30.8	30.7	27.7	23.2	19.2	15.7	21.9
Mean min. temp.	7.7	7.9	9.3	11.6	15.2	19.3	22.3	22.5	20.2	16.3	12.7	9.4	14.5
Absol. max. temp.	22.7	24.6	28.5	29.0	34.0	36.0	44.0	40.6	38.2	31.3	27.2	22.7	44.0
Absol. min. temp.	-0.8	0.6	1.2	4.4	8.2	13.5	18.2	17.0	14.1	9.8	4.4	2.4	-0.8
Mean rel. humidity	79	73	74	74	71	64	66	66	69	76	76	78	72
Mean precipitation	93	54	102	60	37	8	3	12	41	171	113	92	786
Days with precipitation	9	5	6	4	3	2	1	1	3	7	7	8	56
Hours of sunshine	123	128	172	199	241	287	319	291	247	186	170	39	2,493

Weather station XX

Genova/Liguria/Italy

situated at: 44°25′N/8°55′E, 54 m above sea level

Warm/temperate, suboceanic, permahumid rainy climate without clear dry seasons, with moderately hot warm to warm, long summers and mild to moderately cold winters; vegetation period longer than 200 days; precipitation maximum in summer and fall; suboceanic deciduous and mixed forests

	J	F	M	A	M	J	J	A	S	O	N	D	Year
Mean temp.	7.9	8.3	11.0	13.7	17.5	21.3	23.7	24.1	21.2	16.8	12.0	9.2	15.6
Mean max. temp.	10.5	11.2	13.9	17.1	20.8	23.9	26.7	26.5	24.2	20.3	14.8	12.1	18.5
Mean min. temp.	5.1	5.9	8.1	11.1	14.6	17.9	20.6	20.4	18.2	14.5	9.9	7.9	12.8
Absol. max. temp.	18.7	19.9	23.7	26.7	30.2	32.6	36.9	35.0	34.0	29.2	23.7	20.4	36.9
Absol. min. temp.	-5.2	-8.0	-1.0	3.1	7.3	11.0	14.3	11.9	11.0	3.3	-1.0	-2.8	-8.0
Mean rel. humidity	64	65	68	69	70	70	67	69	69	67	68	66	68
Mean precipitation	99	108	144	94	77	72	49	53	110	181	174	136	1,297
Max. Niederschlag	435	340	452	286	247	250	216	344	440	776	733	646	2,451
Min. Niederschlag	1	0	0	6	4	0	0	0	4	5	3	1	572
Days with precipitation	7	7	10	9	7	6	3	4	6	9	9	9	86
Hours of sunshine	127	126	167	189	236	252	298	270	264	171	105	112	2,217

Weather station XXI

Naples/Campania/Italy

situated at: 40°51′N/14°15′E, 25 m above sea level

Warm/temperate, Mediterranean rainy climate with dry, hot summers and moist winters; usually more than five months with rain; subtropical hard-leafed and coniferous forests

	J	F	M	A	M	J	J	A	S	O	N	D	Year
Mean temp.	9.0	9.6	12.0	14.6	18.7	22.2	24.8	25.0	22.1	18.3	13.9	10.9	16.8
Mean max. temp.	11.7	12.6	14.8	18.2	22.2	26.3	29.1	29.0	26.0	21.7	17.0	13.6	20.2
Mean min. temp.	4.3	4.8	6.4	8.9	12.3	16.0	18.1	18.1	15.9	12.4	9.0	6.4	11.1
Absol. max. temp.	18.3	21.5	24.7	27.5	32.2	35.2	37.9	36.6	33.8	29.6	24.9	20.8	37.9
Absol. min. temp.	-4.4	-4.0	-3.8	0.9	2.9	7.1	11.0	12.7	8.0	3.1	-1.8	-4.4	-4.4
Mean rel. humidity	73	73	71	72	71	67	65	66	69	71	75	76	71
Mean precipitation	93	82	75	67	45	46	16	19	71	130	114	137	895
Max. Niederschlag	190	197	201	99	198	99	73	115	202	211	276	267	1,188
Min. Niederschlag	9	7	3	4	11	0	0	0	4	10	26	43	520
Days with precipitation	10	11	10	9	7	5	2	3	9	10	11	13	98
Hours of sunshine	118	128	161	198	254	279	322	307	243	198	123	93	2,422

Weather station XXII

Nice/Provence-Alpes-Côte d'Azur/France
situated at: 43°40´ N/7°12´ E, 5 m above sea level
Warm/temperate, Mediterranean rainy climate with dry, hot summers and moist winters; usually more than five months with rain; subtropical hard-leafed and coniferous forests

	J	F	M	A	M	J	J	A	S	O	N	D	Year
Mean temp.	7.5	8.5	10.8	13.3	16.7	20.1	22.7	22.5	20.3	16.0	11.5	8.2	14.8
Mean max. temp.	12.5	13.3	14.8	17.1	20.4	23.9	26.5	26.6	24.8	20.7	16.5	13.2	19.2
Mean min. temp.	4.2	4.6	6.7	9.0	12.5	16.0	18.2	18.0	16.3	12.0	8.0	5.0	10.9
Absol. max. temp.	22.2	21.0	21.2	26.0	29.9	31.2	34.0	35.8	32.0	28.6	22.8	22.6	35.8
Absol. min. temp.	-1.6	-4.6	-1.5	3.2	5.1	10.6	12.8	11.4	10.0	4.2	1.2	-2.2	-4.6
Mean rel. humidity	68	68	73	75	75	75	72	74	73	72	70	69	72
Mean precipitation	68	61	73	73	68	35	20	27	77	124	129	107	862
Max. Niederschlag	200	208	195	160	157	150	160	95	211	279	317	270	1,211
Min. Niederschlag	0	0	0	0	3	1	0	0	2	10	7	5	503
Days with precipitation	9	7	8	9	8	5	2	4	7	9	9	9	86
Hours of sunshine	148	165	196	243	272	312	362	324	263	200	153	137	2,775

Weather station XXIII

Rome/Latium/Italy
situated at: 41°54´ N/12°29´ E, 46 m above sea level
Warm/temperate, Mediterranean rainy climate with dry, hot summers and moist winters; usually more than five months with rain; subtropical hard-leafed and coniferous forests

	J	F	M	A	M	J	J	A	S	O	N	D	Year
Mean temp.	6.9	7.7	10.8	13.9	18.1	22.1	24.7	24.5	21.1	16.4	11.7	8.5	15.6
Mean max. temp.	11.1	12.6	15.2	18.8	23.4	27.6	30.4	29.8	26.3	21.5	16.1	12.6	20.5
Mean min. temp.	4.5	5.4	7.2	9.8	13.3	17.2	19.6	19.4	16.9	12.8	9.3	6.4	11.8
Absol. max. temp.	18.1	20.7	25.3	29.8	32.8	34.9	40.1	39.2	34.2	28.2	24.6	19.3	40.1
Absol. min. temp.	-5.0	-5.4	-1.2	0.3	2.1	9.2	11.9	13.2	8.0	2.1	-2.4	-5.0	-5.4
Mean rel. humidity	77	73	71	70	67	62	58	59	66	72	77	79	69
Mean precipitation	76	88	77	72	63	48	14	22	70	128	116	106	874
Max. Niederschlag	179	189	157	144	130	86	55	66	138	425	254	246	1,056
Min. Niederschlag	12	1	0	10	5	0	0	0	0	19	21	12	369
Days with precipitation	6	6	8	8	6	4	2	2	5	6	8	8	70
Hours of sunshine	133	132	205	210	267	282	335	307	243	198	123	102	2,537

ACKERMAN (1997): The Biology, Husbandry and Health Care of Reptiles. – Neptune City (TFH Publications), 1068 pp.

ACKERMAN (2000): Atlas der Reptilienkrankheiten. – Ruhmannsfelden (bede-Verlag): 37, 57, 137, 141, 143, 210, 212-213, 238-239, 250-252, 254, 256, 457.

ACKLIN (2003): Schildkrötengeschichte. – Testudo (SIGS), Wimmis, 12 (3): 5.

ADAM (1993a): Überwinterung von europäischen Landschildkröten in einem Kühlschrank. – elaphe (N. F.), Rheinbach, 1 (4): 13-14.

ADAM (1993b): Überwinterung von europäischen Landschildkröten in einem Kühlschrank. – Journal der AG Schildkröten & Panzerechsen der DGHT, Bürstadt, 2 (3): 11-13.

ADAM (1996): Überwinterung von europäischen Landschildkröten in einem Kühlschrank. – DATZ, Stuttgart, 49 (9): 583-584.

ADAM (1997): Ein einfacher Inkubator für Schlangeneier – mit Bemerkungen zur Zeitigung von Schildkröteneiern. – elaphe, 5 (1): 20-23.

ADAMS (2001): Die Kennzeichnungsregelungen der Bundesartenschutzverordnung sind seit dem 1. Januar 2001 in Kraft. – BNA-aktuell, Hambrücken, 2: 17-23.

ADANSON (1845): Cours d'Histoire Naturelle fait en 1772. – 2, Paris.

D'ADDA (1990): Biologia ed ecologia della testuggine terrestre, Testudo hermanni hermanni GM., 1789 nel Parco Naturale della Maremma (GR). – Dissertation, Univ. di Milano, Milan.

ADLAM (1980): The trade in Mediterranean tortoises. – British Chelonia Group Newsletter, 19: 9-10.

ADRIAN (1983): Schildkröten. – Stuttgart (Franckh'sche Verlagshandlung): 7, 9, 18, 28, 30, 40-41.

ADRIAN (1986): Unsere Landschildkröte. – Stuttgart (Franckh'sche Verlagshandlung): 15-18, 37, 54-55.

AGUILAR (1990): La protecció de les tortugues terrestres i marines a les Balears. – Govern Balear, Direcció General d'Estructures Agràries i Medi Natural, Servei de Conservació de la Naturalesa, Documents Tècnics de Conservació, Palma de Mallorca, 6, 50 pp.

AGUILAR (1997): Situación actual de las poblaciones de Testudo graeca y Testudo hermanni en las Baleares. – Jornadas de conservación de la tortuga mediterránea, Consellería de Medio Ambiente, Generalitat Valenciana: 50-61.

AHNE (1992): Viruses of Chelonia. – In: SOPTOM (Eds.): Proceedings of the First International Congress of Chelonian Pathology, Gonfaron, France, 25-27 April 1992. – Gonfaron (SOPTOM): 58-78.

AHNE (1993): Viruses of Chelonia. – Journal of Veterinary Medicine, B, 40 (1): 35-45.

ALCOVER, MOYÁ-SOLÁ & PONS-MOYÁ (1981): Les Quimeres del Passat – Els Vertebrats fòssils del Plio-Quaternari de les Balears i Pitiüses. – Palma de Mallorca (Editorial Moll), 260 pp..

ALDERTON (1988): Turtles & Tortoises of the World. – New York & Oxford (Facts on File Publications): 26, 67, 102, 157, 159-160.

ALDERTON (1992): Griechische Landschildkröten schützen sich vor Überhitzung. – DATZ, Stuttgart, 45 (4): 244.

ALLARD (1998): Suivi de pontes et description de populations de tortues d'Hermann. – Situationsbericht an BTSA, Gestion et Protection de la Nature.

ALMERA & BOFILL (1903): Condideraciones sobre los restos fósiles cuaternarios de la caverna de Gracia (Barcelona). – Boletín de la Real Academia de Buenas Letras de Barcelona, Barcelona, 4 (33): 447-459.

ALONSO-ZARAZAGA (1998): Nomenclatura – lista de sinónimos y combinaciones. – In: SALVADOR, SÁNCHEZ, TERCEDOR, BELLÉS I ROS, GOSÁLBEZ I NOGUERA, GUERRA SIERRA, MACPHERSON MAYOL, MARTÍN PIERA, MARINO & GONZÁLEZ (Eds.): Fauna Ibérica, Vol. 10, Reptiles. – Madrid (Museo Nacional de Ciencias Naturales): 645-685.

ALVAREZ LÓPEZ (1934): Los caracteres geográficos de la herpetofauna ibérica (Contribución al estudio de la zoogeografía peninsular). – Boletín de la Real Sociedad Española de Historia Natural, Sección Biología, Madrid, 34: 327-373.

AMBROSINO, PASSADORE, GAMBARI, DELOGU & MAZZOTTI (1997): PCR-mediated amplification of genomic regions of Testudo hermanni GMELIN from Bosco Della Mesola (northern Italy). – Abstracts of the 3rd World Congress of Herpetology: 5.

AMIRANASHVILI (2000): Differences in shell morphology of Testudo graeca and Testudo hermanni, based on material from Bulgaria. – Amphibia-Reptilia, Leiden, 21 (1): 67-81.

AMIRANASHVILI (2001): Peculiarities of postembryonic development of the epiplastrons in recent terrestrial tortoises of the Palearctic. – In: ANANJEVA, DAREVSKY, DUNAYEV, IORDANSKY, KUZMIN und ORLOVA (Eds.): The Problems of Herpetology. – Moscow (Pushchino): 13-15.

AMORI, ANGELICI, FRUGIS, GANDOLFI, GROPPALI, LANZA, RELINI & VICINI (1993): Vertebrata. – In: MINELLI, RUFFO & LA POSTA (Eds.): Checklist delle specie della Fauna d'Italia. Vol. 110. – Bologna (Ed. Calderini & Ministero dell'Ambiente e Comitato Scientifico per la Fauna d'Italia), IV + 83 pp.

AMOS (1980): Knaurs Tierleben auf Inseln. – Gütersloh (Bertelsmann-Club): 171.

ANDERS (1994): Beiträge zur vergleichenden Anatomie des Verdauungstraktes bei Reptilien. – Thesis, Universität München, Munich.

ANDEWEG (2003): Verslag najaarslanddag. – Trionyx, Eindhoven, 1 (4): 110-113.

ANDRADA (1980): Guia de campo de los anfibios y reptiles de la Península Ibérica. – Barcelona (Ediciones Omega), 159 pp.

ANDRÉN & NILSON (1975): Observations on the Herpetofauna of Turkey in 1968-1973. – British Journal of Herpetology, London, 5: 575-584.

ANDREU & LÓPEZ-JURADO (1998): Testudo hermanni GMELIN, 1789. – In: SALVADOR, SÁNCHEZ, TERCEDOR, BELLÉS I ROS, GOSÁLBEZ I NOGUERA, GUERRA SIERRA, MACPHERSON MAYOL, MARTÍN PIERA, MARINO & GONZÁLEZ (Eds.): Fauna Ibérica, Vol. 10, Reptiles. – Madrid (Museo Nacional de Ciencias Naturales): 117-123.

ANDREU & PASCUAL (1978): Informe sobre los Reptiles catalogados de especies protegidas en el territoria español. – Bol. Est. Cen. Ecología, 7: 53-58.

ANDRINOS (1987): L'Aigle royal en Grèce. – In: L'Aigle royal en Europe. Premier Colloque international sur L'Aigle royal en Europe, 13-15 juin 1986, Arvieux. – Besançon (Maison de la Nature): 18-22.

ANGEL (1946): Faune de France. Vol. 45: Reptiles et Amphibiens. – Paris (Lechevalier), 204 pp.

ANON. (19??a): Merkblatt über die Pflege von Landschildkröten. – Berlin (DGHT-Landesverband Berlin), 6 pp.

ANON. (19??b): Deine Schildkröten. – Bremen (Kapust Verlag): 6, 8, 13, 16-17, 27, 31.

ANON. (19??c): Mediterranean Tortoises Testudo graeca & hermanni. – Care Sheet, British Chelonia Group, 8 pp.

ANON. (1907): Collections du Musée d'Histoire Naturelle de Son Altesse Royale Ferdinand I, Prince de Bulgarie (Amphibia et Reptilia). – Naturhistorisches Museum, Sofia: 251, 258.

ANON. (1969a): Tortoises of the World: Testudo hermanni. – International Turtle and Tortoise Society Journal, Los Angeles, 3 (1): 29.

ANON. (1969b): 1969 California Turtle and Tortoise Club Exibit. – International Turtle and Tortoise Society Journal, Los Angeles, 3 (4): 21-25, 37.

ANON. (1969c): Tortoises. – International Turtle and Tortoise Society Journal, Los Angeles, 3 (5): 37-38.

ANON. (1969d): Fewer tortoises in Britain. – Nature, London, 223: 1302-1303.

ANON. (1971): Courtship and Mating. – International Turtle and Tortoise Society Journal, Los Angeles, 5 (6): 36-37.

ANON. (1978a): Tortoises becoming extinct. – Bristol Chelonia Group Newsletter, Bristol, 8: 2-3.

ANON. (1978b): The Tortoise Trade. – British Chelonia Group Newsletter, 11: 1-2.

ANON. (1978c): The tortoise trade. – British Chelonia Group Newsletter, 12: 1-4.

ANON. (1979a): The tortoise trade. – Testudo, 1 (2): 5.

ANON. (1979b): The tortoise trade – A report on an investigation carried out by The Royal Society for the Prevention of Cruelty to Animals (RSPCA). – Horsham (The Royal Society for the Prevention of Cruelty to Animals), 15 pp.

ANON. (1979c): Schildkrötenimport = Schildkrötenmord? – Die Schildkröte, Haar, 1 (1): 26-33.

ANON. (1980): Schildkröten brauchen mehr als nur Salat. – Das Tier, Leinfelden-Echterdingen, 21 (4): 63.

ANON. (1983): A 'Wildtrack' Film (1978) on the Yugoslav Tortoise Trade. – Testudo, 2 (2): 22.

ANON. (1987a): Heinsberg: Student züchtet winzige Schildkröten. – BILD, 09.01.1987: 3.

ANON. (1987b): Wakey, wakey, rise and shine. – British Chelonia Group Newsletter, 56: 11-12.

ANON. (1987c): »Tiger haben wir bis jetzt noch nicht registriert«. – Mainzer Allgemeine Zeitung, 11./12.07.1987.

ANON. (1988a): Waking up hints. – British Chelonia Group Newsletter, 62: 4.

ANON. (1988b): Das Schildkrötendorf. – Das Tier, Leinfelden-Echterdingen, 29 (12): 39.

ANON. (1989): The B.C.G. 1989 Appeal: Conservation of the Tortoises and Terrapins of Europe. – British Chelonia Group Newsletter, 67: 10.

ANON. (1990a): Verheerende Waldbrände gefährden Frankreichs Schildkrötenbestand. – Westfalen-Blatt, Bielefeld, Oktober.

ANON. (1990b): Tortoise fingerprinting. – British Chelonia Group Newsletter, 74: 2-5.

ANON. (1990c): Das Jahr der Schildkröte. – Das Tier, Leinfelden-Echterdingen, 31 (6): 57.

ANON. (1990-1994a): How to Tell the Age of Your Tortoise. – In: HIGHFIELD (Ed.): Tortoise Trust Caresheet Collection, London (The Tortoise Trust): 3.

ANON. (1990-1994b): General Care of Mediterranean Tortoises. – In: HIGHFIELD (Ed.): Tortoise Trust Caresheet Collection, London (The Tortoise Trust): 8-10.

ANON. (1990-1994c): Rearing Healthy Hatchlings. – In: HIGHFIELD (Ed.): Tortoise Trust Caresheet Collection, London (The Tortoise Trust): 11-12.

ANON. (1990-1994d): Outdoor (Natural) Hibernation. – In: HIGHFIELD (Ed.): Tortoise Trust Caresheet Collection, London (The Tortoise Trust): 13.

ANON. (1990-1994e): Easy Vivarium Design for Small Tortoises. – In: HIGHFIELD (Ed.): Tortoise Trust Caresheet Collection, London (The Tortoise Trust): 17-18.

ANON. (1990-1994f): Post-Hibernation Problems in Mediterranean Tortoises. – In: HIGHFIELD (Ed.): Tortoise Trust Caresheet Collection, London (The Tortoise Trust): 23-24.

ANON. (1991a): From other sources. – British Chelonia Group Newsletter, 79: 8-9.

ANON. (1991b): Kontrollierter Schildkröten-Import. – Das Tier, Leinfelden-Echterdingen, 32 (10): 28-29.

ANON. (1991c): Aktuelle Adresse: S.O.P.TO.M., das Dorf der Schildkröten. – Das Tier, Leinfelden-Echterdingen, 32 (11): 32.

ANON. (1992a): Digest of the Turtles: 11, 85.

ANON. (1992b): Extract from a reptile survey undertaken by B. DEVAUX for SOPTOM magazine »La Tortue«. – British Chelonia Group Newsletter, 86: 6-10.

ANON. (1992c): News from France. – British Chelonia Group Newsletter, 92: 9.

ANON. (1992d): Mairies et SOPTOM – même combat. – La Tortue, Gonfaron, 19: 14-17.

ANON. (1992e): La plaine de Maures – Etat et lieux. – La Tortue, Gonfaron, 19: 20-21.

ANON. (1992f): Travaux d'hiver. – La Tortue, Gonfaron, 19: 21.

ANON. (1992g): Les nouveaux Permanents. – La Tortue, Gonfaron, 19: 22-23.

ANON. (1992h): Sponsor – 1. – La Tortue, Gonfaron, 19: 24-25.

ANON. (1992i): Sponsor – 2. – La Tortue, Gonfaron, 19: 25.

ANON. (1992j): Brice Lalonde. – La Tortue, Gonfaron, 19: 25.

ANON. (1992k): La TORMED est née. – La Tortue, Gonfaron, 20: 5-6.

ANON. (1992l): Comité scientifique. – La Tortue, Gonfaron, 20: 19.

ANON. (1992m): Assemblée Générale. – La Tortue, Gonfaron, 20: 20-21.

ANON. (1992n): Moltifao. – La Tortue, Gonfaron, 20: 21-22.

ANON. (1992o): Retour au pays. – La Tortue, Gonfaron, 20: 23-24.

ANON. (1992p): Nouveaux programmes de lâchers. – La Tortue, Gonfaron, 21: 15-17.

ANON. (1992q): À quoi servent les médias?. – La Tortue, Gonfaron, 21: 20.

ANON. (1992r): Incendies en Corse. – La Tortue, Gonfaron, 21: 20-21.

ANON. (1992s): Bilan de l'été. – La Tortue, Gonfaron, 21: 21.

ANON. (1992t): Sponsor. – La Tortue, Gonfaron, 21: 22.

ANON. (1992u): Plaine des Maures. – La Tortue, Gonfaron, 21: 22-23.

ANON. (1992v): Travaux en Corse. – La Tortue, Gonfaron, 21: 23.

ANON. (1992w): Étude sur les téguments. – La Tortue, Gonfaron, 21: 23-24.

ANON. (1992x): Île du Levant. – La Tortue, Gonfaron, 21: 24.

ANON. (1992y): Courrier. – La Tortue, Gonfaron, 21: 25-26.

ANON. (1992z): Leben mit Tieren – Terrarienbewohner. – Rastatt (Verlagsunion Erich Pabel-Arthur Moewig): 85-86.

ANON. (1992aa): Waking up! – Tortoise Trust Newsletter, London, 7 (1): 12-13.

ANON. (1992bb): Question Box. – Tortoise Trust Newsletter, London, 7 (1): 15.

ANON. (1992cc): Question Box. – Tortoise Trust Newsletter, London, 7 (2): 6.

ANON. (1992dd): Hermann's tortoise disease – the latest. – Tortoise Trust Newsletter, London, 7 (3): 1-2.

ANON. (1993a): Tortoises hibernation hints. – British Chelonia Group Newsletter, 95: 19.

ANON. (1993b): Tortues sans drontières. – La Tortue, Gonfaron, 23: 3.

ANON. (1993c): Le 15 Mai, la Corse..... – La Tortue, Gonfaron, 23: 29.

ANON. (1993d): Courrier. – La Tortue, Gonfaron, 23: 30.

ANON. (1993e): La »flamme« de Gonfaron. – La Tortue, Gonfaron, 23 b: 33.

ANON. (1993f): Examen des tortues-duc. – La Tortue, Gonfaron, 23 b: 34.

ANON. (1993g): Nourrissage. – La Tortue, Gonfaron, 24: 28.

ANON. (1993h): Corse. – La Tortue, Gonfaron, 24: 30-31.

ANON. (1993i): Plaine des Maures...suite. – La Tortue, Gonfaron, 24: 31-32.

ANON. (1993j): Bilan de l'été. – La Tortue, Gonfaron, 24: 33.

ANON. (1994a): Etudes et Recherches. – La Tortue, Gonfaron, 25: 27-30.

ANON. (1994b): ESCOTA nous aide. – La Tortue, Gonfaron, 25: 31.

ANON. (1994c): Les tortues de St. Tropez. – La Tortue, Gonfaron, 25: 33.

ANON. (1994d): Une aide du B.C.G.. – La Tortue, Gonfaron, 25: 33-34.

ANON. (1994E): Le Village des Tortues s'agrandit. – La Tortue, Gonfaron, 26: 24-26.

ANON. (1994f): Un centre en Espagne. – La Tortue, Gonfaron, 26: 29.

ANON. (1994g): Nouvelles de la Corse. – La Tortue, Gonfaron, 26: 29-30.

ANON. (1994h): Vétérinaire pour tortues; une spécialité rare. – La Tortue, Gonfaron, 27: 2-7.

ANON. (1994i): Retour en Ligurie. – La Tortue, Gonfaron, 27: 8.

ANON. (1994j): Plaine des Maures, suite. – La Tortue, Gonfaron, 27: 37.

ANON. (1994k): Does the common tortoise lay eggs? – British Chelonia Group Newsletter, 10: 7.

ANON. (1994l): Steckbriefe der europäischen Landschildkröten. – Schildkröten, Linden, 1 (2): 3-6.

ANON. (1994m): The Albera tortoise breeding centre. – Tortoise Trust Newsletter, London, 8 (6): 7.

ANON. (1994n): On the management of land tortoises in captivity. – British Chelonia Group Newsletter, 100: 6.

ANON. (1994o): Tortoise Fingerprinting. – Care Sheet, London (British Chelonia Group), 4 pp.

ANON. (1994p): Schildkröten – Winterschlaf muss nicht immer sein. – Ein Herz für Tiere, Ismaning, 11: 26.

ANON. (1995a): Pilzbefall. – Das Tier, Leinfelden-Echterdingen, 36 (2): 43.

ANON. (1995b): KARL LAPP – Schonzeit für Schildkröten. – Das Tier, Leinfelden-Echterdingen, 36 (5): 29-31.

ANON. (1995c): Winterschlaf. – Das Tier, Leinfelden-Echterdingen, 36 (10): 45.

ANON. (1995d): Schnabelpflege. – Das Tier, Leinfelden-Echterdingen, 36 (11): 44.

ANON. (1995e): Test your tortoise's health statistics – The Jackson Ratio. – Care Sheet, London (British Chelonia Group), 4 pp.

ANON. (1995f): Winter hints. – British Chelonia Group Newsletter, 103: 17.

ANON. (1995g): Jung und alt – Farnhams Schildkröten. – Das Tier, Leinfelden-Echterdingen, 36 (12): 70.

ANON. (1995h): Hibernating juvenile tortoises. – Tortoise Trust Newsletter, London, 10 (3): 8.

ANON. (1995i): Members' questions. – Tortoise Trust Newsletter, London, 10 (3): 10.

ANON. (1995j): Réintroduction de la tortue d'Hermann. – CITS bulletin, Bramois, 4: 2

ANON. (1995k): Rejoignez la S.H.F. – La Tortue, Gonfaron, 30: 34-35.

ANON. (1995l): Etude sur les »tortues-duc«. – La Tortue, Gonfaron, 30: 40.

ANON. (1995m): Une solution pour la Corse. – La Tortue, Gonfaron, 30: 40-41.

ANON. (1995n): La tortue »écorchée«. – La Tortue, Gonfaron, 31: 14-17.

ANON. (1995o): Effets pervers d'une loi. – La Tortue, Gonfaron, 31: 26.

ANON. (1995p): Tortues-ducs en question. – La Tortue, Gonfaron, 31: 28.

ANON. (1995q): Enfin! – La Tortue, Gonfaron, 31: 29.

ANON. (1995r): TORMED, un grand pas en avant. – La Tortue, Gonfaron, 31: 30.

ANON. (1995s): Pincés! – La Tortue, Gonfaron, 31: 30-31.

ANON. (1995t): Avec le CEEP. – La Tortue, Gonfaron, 31: 31.

ANON. (1995u): Methusalem trifft junge Hüpfer. – Ein Herz für Tiere, Ismaning, 7: 56.

ANON. (1995v); Madame Hermann. – La Hulotte, Boult-aux-Bois, 58: 18.

ANON. (1995w): EC Regulation 3626/82 – Sales Exemptions. – British Chelonia Group Newsletter, 106: 19.

ANON. (1996a): Digest of the Turtles III: 8, 79, 85.

ANON. (1996b): Der große Reibach mit geschützten Schildkröten. – Mainzer Allgemeine Zeitung, Mainz, 09.07.1996.

ANON. (1996c): Current law on tortoise sales within the UK. – Tortoise Trust Newsletter, London, 11 (1): 13.

ANON. (1996d): SOPTOM (Station d'Observation et de Protection des Tortues des Maures). – British Chelonia Group Newsletter, 112: 19-20.

ANON. (1996e): Le cas Heidmann. – La Tortue, Gonfaron, 32/33: 48-49.

ANON. (1996f): Bilan très positif pour 1995. – La Tortue, Gonfaron, 32/33: 49.

ANON. (1996g): Le pays des Maures et les tortues d'Hermann. – La Tortue, Gonfaron, 34: 4-11.

ANON. (1996h): Les débuts de la SOPTOM. – La Tortue, Gonfaron, 34: 34-39.

ANON. (1996i): Neige sur les tortues. – La Tortue, Gonfaron, 34: 43.

ANON. (1996j): Reprises des stages SOPTOM. – La Tortue, Gonfaron, 34: 44.

ANON. (1996k): Acquérir pour protéger. – La Tortue, Gonfaron, 35: 10-11.

ANON. (1996l): Etude pathologique. – La Tortue, Gonfaron, 35: 36.

ANON. (1996m): Réseau NATURA 2000. – La Tortue, Gonfaron, 35: 36-37.

ANON. (1996n): Trafic démantelé. – La Tortue, Gonfaron, 35: 37-38.

ANON. (1996o): Un bon été pour les tortues. – La Tortue, Gonfaron, 36: 45.

ANON. (1996p): Dans les Albères. – La Tortue, Gonfaron, 36: 45-46.

ANON. (1996q): A la découverte..... – La Tortue, Gonfaron, 36: 50.

ANON. (1996r): Sale of hatchlings and juvenile tortoises from pet shops and garden centres – how widespread is it? – British Chelonia Group Newsletter, 114: 18-19.

ANON. (1996s): Schildkröte gequält. – Odenwälder Zeitung, 05.09.1996.

ANON. (1996t): Nachzuchtprojekt 95 der SIGS. – SIGS-Info, Siblingen, 5 (1): 13-14.

ANON. (1996u): Die Griechische Landschildkröte (Testudo hermanni) – Merkblatt zur Haltung und Nachzucht. – Sankt Pölten (Schildkrötenfreunde Österreich), 2 pp.

ANON. (1996v): When a tortoise stops feeding in the autumn ... – Tortoise Trust Newsletter, London, 11 (3): 9.

ANON. (1996w): Dear Tortoise Trust ... – Tortoise Trust Newsletter, London, 11 (3): 10-11.

ANON. (1996x): A gentle reminder on dietary management for Mediterranean tortoises ... – Tortoise Trust Newsletter, London, 11 (4): 7.

ANON. (1996y): ROGER BOUR, des locomotives ... aux tortues! – La Tortue, Gonfaron, 34: 18-22.

ANON. (1997a): Schildkrötendiebstahl. – elaphe (N. F.), Rheinbach, 5 (1): 31.

ANON. (1997b): 38. Internationales Symposium über die Erkrankungen der Zoo- und Wildtiere. – SIGS-Info, Siblingen, 6 (2): 34-36.

ANON. (1997c): Der Winterschlaf – Schlüpflinge wollen auch schlafen. – SIGS-Info, Siblingen, 6 (3): 10-11.

ANON. (1997d): Overwintering tortoises. – Tortoise Trust Newsletter, London, 12 (3): 11.

ANON. (1997e): Tortoise hatchlings. – British Chelonia Group Newsletter, 115: 11.

ANON. (1997f): Deux pour le prix d'une! – CITS bulletin, Bramois, 8: 2.

ANON. (1997g): Un hiver bien rude. – La Tortue, Gonfaron, 37: 34.

ANON. (1997h): Enfin, Moltifao est ouvert. – La Tortue, Gonfaron, 39: 10-11.

ANON. (1997i): Le Congrès S.H.F. – La Tortue, Gonfaron, 39: 34.

ANON. (1997j): Inauguration en Espagne. – La Tortue, Gonfaron, 39: 37.

ANON. (1997k): La passion n'excuse pas tout. – La Tortue, Gonfaron, 39: 39.

ANON. (1997l): Retours au Sénégal et en Grèce. – La Tortue, Gonfaron, 40: 12-17.

ANON. (1997m): Séquence »irritation«. – La Tortue, Gonfaron, 40: 37.

ANON. (1997n): Importante découverte en Corse. – La Tortue, Gonfaron, 40: 38.

ANON. (1997o): Crottes de lion!. – La Tortue, Gonfaron, 40: 40.

ANON. (1997p): Amélioration au VILLAGE. – La Tortue, Gonfaron, 40: 40.

ANON. (1997q): Tortoise sales – new regulations. – Tortoise Trust Newsletter, London, 12 (1): 13.

ANON. (1997r): Restaurant-bound tortoises released into wild. – Tortoise Trust Newsletter, London, 12 (3): 9.

ANON. (1997s): Ich habe eine Schildkröte. – SIGS-Info, Siblingen, 6 (3): 2-6.

ANON. (1997t): Die Griechische Landschildkröte. – SIGS-Info, Siblingen, 6 (4): 13-14.

ANON. (1997u): Illegal import and sale of tortoises. – British Chelonia Group Newsletter, 115: 8.

ANON. (1997v): SOPTOM – Station d'Observation et de Protection des Tortues des Maures. – British Chelonia Group Newsletter, 117: 23.

ANON. (1998a): Le VILLAGE va avoir 10 ans. – La Tortue, Gonfaron, 41: 35.

ANON. (1998b): En Corse, réunion du Comité Scientifique. – La Tortue, Gonfaron, 41: 38.

ANON. (1998c): Vol à frontière. – La Tortue, Gonfaron, 42: 41-42.

ANON. (1998d): Dernier lâcher au Levant. – La Tortue, Gonfaron, 42: 45.

ANON. (1998e): Bon Anniversaire! – La Tortue, Gonfaron, 43: 40.

ANON. (1998f): Le VILLAGE poursuit sa croissance. – La Tortue, Gonfaron, 43: 40.

ANON. (1998g): Rien n'est trop beau pour les tortues!. – La Tortue, Gonfaron, 43: 41.

ANON. (1998h): Etrange animal. – La Tortue, Gonfaron, 43: 41.

ANON. (1998i): Entrée en fonction de la Responsable Scientifique de la SOPTOM. – La Tortue, Gonfaron, 43: 42.

ANON. (1998j): La TORMED à Majorque. – La Tortue, Gonfaron, 44: 28.

ANON. (1998k): Deux autres »monstres«. – La Tortue, Gonfaron, 44: 30.

ANON. (1998l): SOPTOM – Station d'Observation et de Protection des Tortues des Maures. – British Chelonia Group Newsletter, 121: 18.

ANON. (1998m): SOPTOM (Station d'Observation et de Protection de Tortues des Maures) – The Tortoise Village. – British Chelonia Group Newsletter, 122: 23.

ANON. (1998n): SOPTOM (Station d'Observation et de Protection de Tortues des Maures) – The Tortoise Village in France. – British Chelonia Group Newsletter, 123: 22-23.

ANON. (1980): SOPTOM (Station d'Observation et de Protection de Tortues des Maures). – British Chelonia Group Newsletter, 126: 21-22.

ANON. (1998p): Ostrasse und Westrasse der Griechischen Landschildkröte. – SIGS-Info, Siblingen, 7 (1): 26-27.

ANON. (1998q): For new members ... – Tortoise Trust Newsletter, London, 13 (1): 13.

ANON. (1998r): To ensure success, reliable temperature control is essential ... – Tortoise Trust Newsletter, London, 13 (2): 6, 11.

ANON. (1998s): Sie fragen, wir antworten. – Fachmagazin Schildkröte, Rothenfluh, 1 (6): 26-27.

ANON. (1998t): 18 essential »dos and dont's« to ensure that your tortoise has a safe hibernation. – Tortoise Trust Newsletter, London, 13 (3): 5.

ANON. (1998u): How to overwinter tortoises. – Tortoise Trust Newsletter, London, 13 (3): 12.

ANON. (1998v): Members write. – Tortoise Trust Newsletter, London, 13 (4): 10.

ANON. (1999a): Vom Mundraub einer Schildkröte. – Öffentlicher Anzeiger Bad Kreuznach, 10.08.1999: 11.

ANON. (1999b): Autumn feeding behaviour. – Tortoise Trust Newsletter, London, 14 (2): 4.

ANON. (1999c): The Jackson Ratio Graph – Inappropriate Use. – Tortoise Trust Newsletter, London, 14 (3): 4.

ANON. (1999d): What should I do immediately after hibernation? – Tortoise Trust Newsletter, London, 14 (3): 5.

ANON. (1999e): Hibernation Q & A. – Tortoise Trust Newsletter, London, 14 (3): 15.

ANON. (1999f): So your child wants... a tortoise! Do you realise the pitfalls? – British Chelonia Group Newsletter, 131: 16-17.

ANON. (1999g): CITES Identification Guide – Turtles & Tortoises. – Ottawa (Minister of Supply and Services Canada): Grün 19, Gelb 16, Grau A3, B24.

ANON. (1999h): TORMED – l'âge de raison!. – La Tortue, Gonfaron, 46/47: 18-19.

ANON. (1999i): Du nouveau à Gonfaron. – La Tortue, Gonfaron, 46/47: 40-41.

ANON. (1999j): Pas d'indencies cette année. – La Tortue, Gonfaron, 48: 5.

ANON. (1999k): Tortue sur pneus. – La Tortue, Gonfaron, 48: 53.

ANON. (1999/2000): Temperaturbedürfnisse von Schildkröten. – Fachmagazin Schildkröte, Rothenfluh, 2 (5): 18-21.

ANON. (2000a): Succès pour le gala TORMED. – La Tortue, Gonfaron, 49: 5.

ANON. (2000b): Congrès International sur le Genre Testudo. – La Tortue, Gonfaron, 49: 20-21.

ANON. (2000c): Braconniers en Bulgarie. – La Tortue, Gonfaron, 49: 51.

ANON. (2000d): Très bonne année au Levant. – La Tortue, Gonfaron, 50/51: 24.

ANON. (2000e): Notre équipe se renforce. – La Tortue, Gonfaron, 50/51: 62.

ANON. (2000f): Hibernation over. – British Chelonia Group Newsletter, 134: 16-17.

ANON. (2000g): Mediterranean tortoises – Vital steps for success. – Tortoise Trust Newsletter, London, 15 (1): 12-13.

ANON. (2000h): Managing juvenile growth – How much to feed? – Tortoise Trust Newsletter, London, 15 (3): 15.

ANON. (2000i): Landschildkröte sucht neue Freunde. – Öffentlicher Anzeiger Bad Kreuznach, 14.07.2000: 23.

ANON. (2000j): Winterschlaf – leicht gemacht. – SIGS-Info, Siblingen, 9 (3): 14.

ANON. (2001a): Natural Hibernation. – Tortoise Trust Newsletter, London, 16 (2): 13.

ANON. (2001b): Your Questions. – Tortoise Trust Newsletter, London, 16 (3): 10-11.

ANON. (2001c): Histoire d'une tortue d'Hermann. – Manouria, Mezzavia, 10: 6.

ANON. (2001d): Congrès International sur le Genre Testudo. – La Tortue, Gonfaron, 53: 10-11.

ANON. (2001e): Un Corse atypique. – La Tortue, Gonfaron, 53: 62

ANON. (2001f): Premier Congrès International sur le Genre Testudo. – La Tortue, Gonfaron, 54: 6-7.

ANON. (2001g): Etrange pouvoir de la calcification!. – La Tortue, Gonfaron, 55: 62.

ANON. (2001h): Sur le Net. – La Tortue, Gonfaron, 55: 65.

ANON. (2001i): La recensement de la tortue d'Hermann – 10 ans après. – La Tortue, Gonfaron, 56: 54-59.

ANON. (2001j): Autobus bulgare. – La Tortue, Gonfaron, 56: 67.

ANON. (2001k): Berichtigung zum Beitrag »Änderung der Bundesartenschutz-Verordnung in Aussicht gestellt«. – elaphe (N. F.), Rheinbach, 9 (2): 29.

ANON. (2001l): Trafficking in tortoises – the great »captive-bred« deception revealed. – Tortoise Trust Newsletter, London, 16 (2): 3-5.

ANON. (2001m): Identification guide – Testudo hermanni hermanni. – Tortoise Trust Newsletter, London, 16 (2): 18.

ANON. (2001n): The Conservation Appeal 2002 – CARA-PAX European Centre for Chelonia Conservation. – British Chelonia Group Newsletter, 144: 4-6.

ANON. (2001o): Réintroduction de tortues dans la nature. – Manouria, Mezzavia, 11: 3-4.

ANON. (2002a): The Conservation Appeal 2002 – »CARA-PAX« (European Centre for Chelonia Conservation). – British Chelonia Group Newsletter, 145: 3-5.

ANON. (2002b): Durée de vie – quatre ans. – La Tortue, Gonfaron, 57: 4.

ANON. (2002c): La tortue d'Hermann – Un programme »musclé« pour la sauvegarder. – La Tortue, Gonfaron, 58/59: 8-13.

ANON. (2002d): Zusammenfassung einiger Vorträge vom 2. Workshop der DGHT-AG Schildkröten in Norddeutschland. – Minor, Haan, 1 (1): 6-10.

ANON. (2002e): Repfile – Vol. 02. – Tokyo (PISCES Publishers): 12, 33, 41.

ANON. (2002f): Weicher Kern unter Schale. – Öffentlicher Anzeiger, Bad Kreuznach, 14.-15.12.2002: 9.

ANON. (2002g): Du nouveau sur l'Herpesvirus des Testudo hermanni. – Manouria, Mezzavia, 14: 3-4.

ANON. (2002h): Schildkröten nicht im Karton. – Öffentlicher Anzeiger Bad Kreuznach, 15./16.06.2002: 8.

ANON. (2002i): Appetit auf Salat muss da sein. – Öffentlicher Anzeiger Bad Kreuznach, 28.10.2002: 8.

ANON. (2002j): Weicher Kern unter Schale. – Öffentlicher Anzeiger Bad Kreuznach, 14./15.12.2002: 9.

ANON. (2003a): Sommer-Überraschung. – Testudo (SIGS), Wimmis, 12 (4): 43.

ANON. (2003b): Herpetologische Änderungen der CITES-Anhänge. – elaphe (N. F.), Rheinbach, 11 (1): 11.

ANON. (2003c): Das Schildkrötendorf Gonfaron in Frankreich. – Schildkröten, Linden, 10 (2): 13-14.

ANON. (2003d): News from CARAPAX. – British Chelonia Group Newsletter, 155: 4.

ANON. (2003e): Reptilia Responds. – Reptilia (GB), Barcelona, 29: 12-13.

ANON. (2003f): Reptilia Responde: »Mantengo una tortuga terrestre que encontré hace 30 años«– Reptilia (E), Barcelona, 42: 12-13.

ANON. (2003g): Verschwundene Schildkröte. – Reptilia (D), Münster, 44: 4.

ANON. (2003h): De pen van…ROB VERHOEKS. – Trionyx, Eindhoven, 1 (3): 77-79.

ANON. (2003i): Letters to the editor. – Tortoise Trust Newsletter, 18 (1): 8-10.

ANON. (2003j): Désastre pour la tortue d'Hermann. – La Tortue, Gonfaron, 63/64: 4.

ANON. (2003k): Une aide de la Fondation 30 Millions d'Amis. – La Tortue, Gonfaron, 63/64: 5.

ANON. (2003l): Un »Plan d'urgence pour la tortue d'Hermann«. – La Tortue, Gonfaron, 63/64: 5.

ANON. (2003m): Record chez les Hermann. – La Tortue, Gonfaron, 63/64: 81.

ANON. (2004a): 100 Jahre Reptilienhalle – Geschichte der Reptilienhaltung im Zoo Frankfurt. – Frankfurt (Zoo Frankfurt): 6.

ANON. (2004b): Les autres reptiles de la garrigue. – La Tortue, Gonfaron, 66: 52-59.

ANON. (2004c): Après les incendies. – La Tortue, Gonfaron, 66: 68-69.

ANON. (2004d): Golf de Vidauban; K.O. débout! – La Tortue, Gonfaron, 66: 70.

ANON. (2004e): Bravo les Forestiers-Sapeurs. – La Tortue, Gonfaron, 67: 5.

ANON. (2004f): Digestion et parasites. – La Tortue, Gonfaron, 67: 72-73.

ANON. (2004g): Réintroductions réussies en Espagne. – La Tortue, Gonfaron, 67: 78.

ANON. (2004h): Merci Maxime! – La Tortue, Gonfaron, 67: 80.

ANON. (2004i): Entr'aide pour les tortues d'Hermann. – La Tortue, Gonfaron, 67: 81.

ANON. (2004j): Retour de flammes. – La Tortue, Gonfaron, 67: 82.

ANON. (2004k): Les mystères de la natalité. – La Tortue, Gonfaron, 68: 81.

ANON. (2004l): La tortue de ZÉNON. – La Tortue, Gonfaron, 68: 82.

ANON. (2004m): Voleur démasqué. – La Tortue, Gonfaron, 68: 71.

ANON. (2004n): La Catalogne toujours dynamique. – La Tortue, Gonfaron, 68: 72.

ANON. (2004o): Testudo hermanni boettgeri – Eastern Hermann's Tortoise – MOJSISOVICS, 1889. – Reptilia (GB), 35: 39-42.

ANON. (2004p): Frau kidnappte Schildkröte. – Öffentlicher Anzeiger, Bad Kreuznach, 07.10.2004: 24.

ANON. (2004q): Schildkröte entführt. – Öffentlicher Anzeiger, Bad Kreuznach, 06./07.11.2004, Journal zum Wochenende: 7.

ANON. (2004r): Questions & Answers. – World Chelonian Trust Newsletter, Owatonna, 2 (3): 11-12.

ANON. (2004s): Questions & Answers. – World Chelonian Trust Newsletter, Owatonna, 2 (4): 11-12.

ANON. (2004t): Amphibien und Reptilien – Arten, Lebensräume, Verhalten. – Köln (VEMAG Verlags- und Medien Aktiengesellschaft): 70.

ANON. (2004u): Bei 30 Grad werden Schildkröten munter. – Öffentlicher Anzeiger, Bad Kreuznach, 05.08.2004: 11.

ANON. (2004v): Sachkundenachweis VDA & DGHT. 4. überarbeitete und erweiterte Auflage. – Bochum & Rheinbach (Verband Deutscher Vereine für Aquarienkunde e.V./Deutsche Gesellschaft für Herpetologie und Terrarienkunde e.V.).

ANON. (2005a): ANTOINE CATARD, du CEEP. – La Tortue, Gonfaron, 69/70: 68-73.

ANON. (2005b): Une initiative en Bulgarie. – La Tortue, Gonfaron, 69/70: 74-75.

ANON. (2005c): Une réserve dans les Maures? – La Tortue, Gonfaron, 71/72: 3.

ANON. (2005d): La tortue d'Hermann dans le Var – études et conservation. – La Tortue, Gonfaron, 71/72: 68-79.

ANON. (2005e): Le courrier des lecteurs. – La Tortue, Gonfaron, 71/72: 88-89.

ANON. (2005f): 7000 Tierarten weltweit in Gefahr. – Öffentlicher Anzeiger, Bad Kreuznach, 17.01.2005: 5.

ANON. (2006a): Eine interessante Initiative in Bulgarien. – Sacalia, Stiefern, 4 (10): 27-31.

ANON. (2006b): Une ferme qui nous inquiète. – La Tortue, Gonfaron, 73: 4.

ANON. (2006c): Pleine forme. – La Tortue, Gonfaron, 73: 5.

ANON. (2006d): Etrangetés. – La Tortue, Gonfaron, 73: 79.

ANON. (2006e): Nouvelles du TGV. – La Tortue, Gonfaron, 73: 80.

ANTENBRINK-VETTER & VETTER (1996): Der Panzer der Schildkröten. – Schildkröten, Linden, 3 (4): 3-24.

APELT (1993): Die Anwendung von Tiletamin-Zolazepam zur Injektionsanästhesie und Prämedikation einer Isofluranarkose bei der Schildkröte. – Dissertation, Tierärztliche Hochschule Hannover.

APPLEBY & SILLER (1960): Some cases of gout in reptiles. – Journal of Pathology and Bacteriology, Chichester, 80: 427-430.

APREA (1996): Testuggine comune, Testudo hermanni GMELIN, 1789. – In: SCILLITANI, RIZZI & GIOIOSA (Eds.): Atlante degli Anfibi e dei Rettili della Provincia di Foggia. – Monogr. Museo Prov. Stor. nat., Centr. Studi. Nat., Foggia: 68-69.

ARDIZZONI (1996): Bemerkungen zu den Eiern von mediterranen Landschildkröten. – Emys, Sankt Pölten, 3 (2): 20-22.

ARILLO (1968): Acido G amminobutirrico in encefalo di Testudo hermanni GMELIN sottposta ad anossia. – Bolletino Musei Istituti Biol. Univ., Genua, 36 (234-248).

ARILLO & CHERCHI (1971): Relazioni intercorrenti tra produzione di acido lattico, capacita di resistenza agli stress anossici ed ipertermici, e filiogenesi. – Bolletino Musei Istituti Biol. Univ., Genua, 39 (270): 39-54.

ARILLO & DeGUILI (1968): Aspartato, aparagini ed anossa; Bolletino Musei Istituti Biol. Univ., Genua, 36 (234-248): 53-58.

ARILLO & DeGUILI (1970a): Variazioni del ciclo di Krebs in anaerobiosi – I. Studi su Testudo hermanni GMELIN (Reptilia, Testudinidae). – Bolletino Musei Istituti Biol. Univ., Genua, 38 (261): 43-63.

ARILLO & DeGUILI (1970b): Variazioni del contenuto di GABA in Vertebrati sottoposti ad anossia. – Bollettino di Zoologia, Modena, 37.

ARILLO & DeGUILI (1972): Anaerobic synthesis of succinic acid in Testudo hermanni and Eisenia foetida. – Bollettino di Zoologia, Modena, 38 (4): 489-490.

ARILLO & NEVIANI (1968): Alanina ed anossia. – Bollettino Musei Istituti Biol. Univ., Genua, 36 (234-248): 47-51.

ARILLO, BALLETTO & CHERCHI (1972): The effect of anaerobiosis on free amino acid concentrations in tissues: first observation on the brain of Testudo hermanni (Reptilia, Testudinidae). – Boll. Musei Istituti Biol. Univ., Genua, 40: 5-13.

ARILLO, BALLETTO & CHERCHI (1974): Anoxia in the vertebrates: Preliminary studies on free aminoacids of the liver. – Bollettino die Zoologia, Modena, 41.

ARILLO, BALLETTO & CHERCHI (1975): Environmental adaptation of free amino acidsin the liver of anoxic vertebrates. – Bolletino Musei Istituti Biol. Univ., Genua, 43: 115-121.

ARILLO, BALLETTO & CHERCHI (1977): Quantitative variations of some compounds of the tricarboxylic acid cycle in specimens of Testudo hermanni GMELIN after exposure to hyperthermic conditions. – Journal of Thermal Biology, 2 (3): 131-134.

ARILLO, BALLETTO, CHERCHI, DeGUILI & MELODIA (1970): Glicerolo e a-Glicerofosfato in Alcune

Specie di Vertebrati ed Invertebrati Sottoposti ad Anossia. – Bolletino Musei Istituti Biol. Univ. Genua, **38** (263): 73-84.

ARNOLD & BURTON (1983): Pareys Reptilien- und Amphibienführer Europas. – Hamburg & Berlin (Verlag Paul Parey): 91-92, 96, plate 13, map 45.

ARNOLD & OVENDEN (2002): A field guide to the reptiles and amphibians of Britain and Europe. – London (Harper Collins Publishers), 288 pp.

ARNOLD, BURTON & OVENDEN (1978): Field guide to the reptiles and amphibians of Britain and Europe. – London (Collins), 272 pp.

ARNOULT (1958): Présence de *Testudo hermanni* F. G. GMELIN (Chélonien) en Normandie. – Bulletin de la Muséum National d'Histoire Naturelle, Paris, **2** (30): 123-124.

ARRAS (1996): Haltung von Landschildkröten, Terrarienbeheizung und -beleuchtung sowie Hygiene und Ernährung. – Schildkröten, Linden, **3** (2): 5-11.

ARTNER (1995): Die Überwinterung Europäischer Landschildkröten. – Emys, Sankt Pölten, **2** (5): 17-18.

ARTNER (1997): Rezension: GERHARD und KARIN POLASCHEK (1997): Die Griechische Landschildkröte. – Emys, Sankt Pölten, **4** (6): 36-37.

ARTNER (2000): Zur Frage des Unterartstatus der Ostrasse der Griechischen Landschildkröte *Testudo hermanni boettgeri* MOJSISOVICS, 1889. – Emys, Sitzenberg-Reidling, **7** (2): 4-8.

ARTNER (2003): Nomenklatur aktuell. Die rezenten Schildkrötenarten der Erde. – Emys, Sitzenberg-Reidling, **10** (6): IV-XXXVIII.

ARTNER & ARTNER (1997): Freilandbeobachtungen zum Vorkommen und zur Habitatwahl der drei Landschildkrötenarten *Testudo hermanni boettgeri*, *Testudo graeca ibera* und *Testudo marginata* in Griechenland. – Emys, Sankt Pölten, **4** (3): 5-15.

ARTNER, BUDISCHEK & FROSCHAUER (2000): Freilandbeobachtungen, Haltung und Nachzucht der Griechischen Landschildkröte *Testudo hermanni boettgeri* MOJSISOVICS, 1889. – Emys, Sitzenberg-Reidling, 7 (2): 9-27.

ARVY & FERTARD (2001): Pathologie des Tortues – Étude synthétique. – Bulletin de la Société Herpétologique de France, Paris, **100** (4): 7, 12, 19, 25, 29, 32-33, 37-38, 52-53, 58, 61, 63, 72, 74, 76, 80-82, 84, 93, 100, 125, 127-130, 132, 136, 138, 140-142, 144, 148-150.

ASIMAKOPOULOS (1990): On the legal status concerning the protection of amphibians and reptiles in Greece. – Herpetological Review, New Haven, **21**: 30-32.

ASTUDILLO & ARANO (1995): Europa y su herpetofauna: responsibilidades de cada país en lo referente a su conservación. – Boletín de la Asociación Herpetológica Española, Leganés, **6**: 14-45.

ATATÜR (1995): A preliminary report on the present status of Turkey's terrestrial and fresh-water turtles from the viewpoint of conservation. – In: BALLASINA (Ed.): Red Data Book on Mediterranean Chelonians. – Bologna (Edagricole): 183-190.

ATATÜR & YILMAZ (1986): A Comparison of the Amphibian Fauna of Turkish Thrace with that of Anatolia and Balkan States. – Amphibia-Reptilia, Leiden, **7**: 135-140.

AUER, REIMANN & TAPKAVAK (2004): Siamesische Zwillinge bei der Maurischen Landschildkröte *Testudo graeca ibera* PALLAS, 1814 und der Griechischen Landschildkröte *Testudo hermanni boettgeri* MOJSISOVICS, 1889. – elaphe (N. F.), Rheinbach, **12** (1): 63-66.

AUFFENBERG (1966): The carpus of land tortoises (Testudinidae). – Bulletin of the Florida State Museum, Gainesville, **10** (5): 159-191.

AUFFENBERG (1974): Checklist of Fossil Land Tortoises (Testudinidae). – Bulletin of the Florida State Museum, Biological Sciences Series, Gainesville, **18** (3): 196, 201, 203-204.

AURAHS (1996): Aus dem Schulgarten wurde eine Arche Noah. – Ein Herz für Tiere, Ismaning, **3**: 14-15.

AVANZI (2002): Les tortues terrestres. – Paris (Editions de Vecchi), 127 pp.

AVERY (1990): Parasites and the Biology of Chelonians. – Testudo, **3** (2): 3-8.

BACESCU (1934): Contributions à la faune des Reptiles de Dobrodgea. – Ann. Sci. Univ. Jassy, Jassy, **19**: 317-330.

BACHMANN (1994): Ferienbericht von Korfu und Kerkyra. – SIGS-Info, Siblingen, **3** (1): 21-22.

BACHMANN (1996): Was ich schon immer fragen wollte, aber nie zu fragen wagte. – Schildkröten, Linden, **3** (2): 28-29.

BÄCHTOLD-STÄUBLI (Ed.) (2000): Handwörterbuch des deutschen Aberglaubens. Band 7. – 3. Auflage, Berlin & New York (Walter de Gruyter).

BADER & RIEGLER (2004): Herpetologische Beobachtungen auf Rhodos (Griechenland). – ÖGH-Aktuell, Vienna, **13**: 6-9.

BAGNOLI (1985): Anfibi e Rettili della Provincia di Roma. – Rome (Assessorato Sanità e Ambiente WWF Lazio).

BAILLIEN (1961): Le pool intracellulaire des acides amines libres de l'Epithelium intestinal de la tortue grecque, *Testudo hermanni* J. F. GMELIN. – Annales de la Société Royale Zoologique de Belgique, Brussels, **92**: 187-190.

BAILLIEN & SCHOFFENIELS (1961): Origin of potential difference in the intestinal epithelium of the turtle. – Nature, London, **190**: 1107-1108.

BAILLIEN & SCHOFFENIELS (1963): Difference de potential, acides amines et calcium au niveau de l'intestin grêle de la tortue grecque. – Arch. int. Physiol. Biochim., **70**: 286-288.

BAILON, BOUR & RAGE (1988): Quand les espèces de l'Herpétofaune française sont-elles apparues? – Bulletin de la Société Herpétologique de France, Paris, **45**: 1-8.

BALL (1987): The chelonian trade. – Zoo Reptile News, **2**: 14-18.

BALLASINA (1982a): Le seul et dernier voyage des tortues terrestres ... – Nos Meilleurs Amis, **74** (1): 13-15.

BALLASINA (1982b): Stoffel de schildpad bedreigd! – De Wielewaal, Lier.

BALLASINA (1982c): L'herpétofaune européenne menacée – Les tortues terrestres. – L'Homme et l'Oiseau, Brussels.

BALLASINA (1983): Belgie en de handel in schildpadden ... – Mens en Vogel, Sint-Niklaas, **21**: 34-38.

BALLASINA (1990): The CARAPAX project: objectives, biological and socio economic aspects. – Résumés du IV Symposium Europaeum Chelonologicum, Massa Marittima.

BALLASINA (1992a): Report on the repatriation of tortoises to Greece by the Carapax Centre (Italy). – British Herpetological Society Bulletin, London, **40**: 2-4.

BALLASINA (1992b): Health care and management of terrestrial and fresh water chelonians based upon their ecological needs and techniques of stress reduction. – Proceedings of the 1st International Congress of Chelonian Pathology, Gonfaron (SOPTOM).

BALLASINA (1995a): Distribuzione e situazione delle tartarughe terrestri in Italia. – In: BALLASINA (Ed.): Red Data Book on Mediterranean Chelonians. – Bologna (Edagricole): 147-160.

BALLASINA (1995b): Salviamo le tartarughe! – Bologna (Edagricole), 216 pp.

BALLASINA (1996): Conservation and reproduction techniques at the Carapax Center, Italy. – In: SOPTOM (Eds.): International Congress of Chelonian Conservation – Proceedings. –Gonfaron (Editions SOPTOM): 210-213.

BALLASINA (2003): Report from CARAPAX 2002: this was the year that was. – British Chelonia Group Newsletter, 151: 6.

BALLASINA & WILLEMSEN (1990): Morphological aspects of Testudo hermanni hermanni in Tuscany, compared with individuals coming from southern Italy. – Abstracts of IV Symposium Europaeum Chelonologicum, Massa Marittima.

BALLASINA, VANDEPITTE, CAPECCHI & WILLEMSEN (1992): Testudo hermanni hermanni, dix ans de recherche, élevage et réintroduction au centre CARAPAX. – Chelonii, Gonfaron, 3: 315.

BALLASINA, VAN DER KUYL, DEKKER, MAAS, WILLEMSEN & GOUDSMIT (2002): Phylogenetic relationships among the species of the genus Testudo (Testudines: Testudinidae) inferred from mitochondrial 12S rRNA gene sequences. – Chelonii, Gonfaron, 3: 117-129.

BALLET, BERTOLERO, AGUIOLO GISBERT & CONESA GUILLES (2002): Haematological parameters in the Hermann's tortoise Testudo hermanni hermanni anf their application to conservation projects. – Chelonii, Gonfaron, 3: 346-348.

BALLETTO & CHERCHI (1970): Biosintesi di acidi grassi in Testudo hermanni GMELIN sottoposta ad anossia. – Bollettino di Zoologia, Modena, **37**.

BALLETTO, CHERCHI, ARILLO, DORIA-LAMBA, MELODIA & MENSI (1978): Gamma-amino-butyric acid synthesis in erythrocytes of Testudo hermanni. – Comparative Biochemistry and Physiology, C, Comparative Pharmacology, Vancouver, **61** (2): 281-282.

BALZEREIT (1979): Nachzucht der Griechischen Landschildkröte. – DATZ, Stuttgart, **32** (2): 64-65.

BANNIKOV & DROZDOV (1997): Family Testudinidae. – In: The Life of Animals, IV (2), Amphibians and Reptiles. –Moscow (Ed. Prosveshtenye), 486 pp.

BANTOCK (1994): Members' letters. – British Chelonia Group Newsletter, 97: 9-10.

BÄNZIGER (2005): Afrastering van het buitenverblijf. – Trionyx, Eindhoven, **3** (4): 110-111.

BARAN (1986): Biblio of the Amphibians and Reptiles of Turkey. – In: KASPAREK (Ed.): Zoological Biblio of Turkey. – Heidelberg: 79-118.

BARAN & ATATÜR (1998): Turkish Herpetofauna (Amphibians and Reptiles). – Ankara (Ministry of Environment), 214 pp.

BARBADILLO (1987): La Guía de Incafo de los Anfibios y Reptiles de la Península Ibérica, Isolas Baleares y Canarias. – Madrid (INCAFO), 694 pp.

BARBADILLO, LACOMBA, PÉREZ-MELLADO, SANCHO & LÓPEZ-JURADO (1987): Anfibios y Reptiles de la Península Ibérica, Isolas Baleares y Canarias. – Barcelona (Editorial Planeta).

BARBIERI, DORIA & SINDACO (1996): Atlante provvisorio degli Anfibi e dei Rettili Italiani. – Annali Mus. Civ. Storia Naturale »G. Doria«, Societas Herpetologica Italica, Genua, XCI: 95-178.

BARNAGAUD (1993): Prospections herpétologiques. Complément à l'Atlas national de 1989. – La Gazette de l'Eure et Loir, No. Spécial SI-93: 14-18.

BARNES (2004): Member's letters. – British Chelonia Group Newsletter, 160: 3, 17.

BARROWS (2001): Nutrition and nutritional disease in chelonians. – Testudo, **5** (3): 10-15.

BARTLETT (1995): Small Tortoises in the Home Collection. – Reptiles Magazine, Boulder, 4: 52-69.

BARTLETT (2003): Where Have All the Europeans Gone? – Reptiles Magazine, Boulder, 7: 30-38.

BARTLETT & BARTLETT (1996): Turtles and Tortoises. – Hauppauge (Barron's Educational Series): 97, 106.

BARUS & JOHNSON (1973): Notes on *Mehdiella microstoma* (new record) from *Testudo hermanni*. – Folia Parasitologica, Ceské Budejovice, 20 (2): 139-140.

BASILE (1989): Faszinierende Schildkröten – Landschildkröten. – Stuttgart (Verlag Stephanie Naglschmid): 16-21, 122-131, 140.

BASILE (2003): In jedem Sommer ... – turtles press international, Rodenbach, 1 (1): 20-21.

BASOGLU & BARAN (1977): Türkiye Sürüngenleri. Kisim I. Kaplumbaga ve kertenkeleler. – Ege Üniversitesi Fen Fakültesi Kitaplar Serisi, Bornova-Izmir, 76: 18, 32, 36, 194, 198, 230, plate 1.

BASSU, CORTI, FRESI, SATTA & ZUFFI (2003): Body size differences between insular populations in the Hermann's tortoise, *Testudo hermanni hermanni* from two Western Mediterranean islands. – In: SOCIETAS EUROPAEA HERPETOLOGICA (Eds.): Programme & Abstracts, 12th Ordinary General Meeting Societas Europaea Herpetologica (SEH). – Saint Petersburg (Zoological Institute of the Russian Academy of Sciences): 36-37.

BAUER (2003): Wie die Jungfrau zum Kind. – *Testudo* (SIGS), Wimmis, 12 (4): 44.

BAUMGÄRTNER (2000): Schildkröten-Ruhe. – Das Tier, Leinfelden-Echterdingen, 41 (2): 54.

BAUR (2000): Physiologie und Pathologie der Fortpflanzung bei Schildkröten. – In: ARTNER & MEIER (Eds.): Schildkröten. – Münster (Natur und Tier-Verlag): 165.

BAUR (2003): Untersuchungen zur vergleichenden Morphologie des Gastrointestinaltraktes der Schildkröten. – Frankfurt am Main (Edition Chimaira): 56, 64, 79, 96, 102, 109-110, 116, 120, 201, 226, 329, 333

BAUR & HOFFMANN (1999): HERPES – in aller Munde – oder längst verdrängt. – Radiata, Bennstedt, 8 (3): 3-10.

BAUR & HOFFMANN (2000): Europäische Landschildkröten – Haltung, Ernährung, Krankheiten. – BNA-aktuell, Hambrücken, 1: 67-71.

BAUR & HOFFMANN (2004): Winterruhe bei Europäischen Landschildkröten. Naturnahe, physiologische Vorbereitung und »Aufwachphase«. – Marginata, Münster, 1 (1): 48-54.

BAUR, HOFFMANN & SCHLECHT (2002): Mineralstoffwechselbedingte Erkrankungen und Deformationen des Panzers bei Schildkröten. – Schildkröten, Linden, 9 (2): 21-35.

BAUR, HOFFMANN, KÖLLE, BLAHAK & VON HEGEL (2001): Kennzeichnung von Reptilien des An-

hangs A mittels Transponder aus fachtierärztlicher Sicht. – Radiata, Haan, 10 (1): 15-19.

BECHTEL (1978): Terrarientiere II – Schildkröten, Krokodile, Echsen. – Hannover (Landbuch-Verlag): 9, 28-31.

BECK, RAPAPORT, STANLEY PRICE & WILSON (1994): Reintroduction of captive-born animals. In: OLNEY, MACE & FEISTNER (Eds.): Creative conservation – Interactive management of wild and captive populations. – London (Chapman & Hall): 265-286.

BECKER (1960): Lautäußerungen einer Schildkröte. – DATZ, Stuttgart, 13 (8): 254.

BEDRIAGA (1881/1882): Die Amphibien und Reptilien Griechenlands. – Bull. Soc. Imp. Nat. Mus., Moscow, 56 (2): 242-310, (3): 13-103, 278-344.

BEDRIAGA (1883a): Die Amphibien und Reptilien Griechenlands. Berichtigungen und Nachträge. – Zoologischer Anzeiger, 6: 216-220.

BEDRIAGA (1883b): Beiträge zur Kenntniss der Amphibien und Reptilien der Fauna von Korsika. – Archiv für Naturgeschichte, Berlin, 49 (1): 124-273.

BELCHEVA, BISSERKOV, ILIEVA & BESHKOV (1992): Karyological study on four species of turtles. – Ann. Univ. Sofia »Kliment Ohridski«, Fac. Biol., Sofia, 80: 212-219.

BELL (1828): Characters of the Order, Families, and Genera of the Testudinata. – Zoological Journal, London, 3 (12): 513-516.

BELLAIRS (1971): Die Reptilien. – Lausanne (Editions Rencontre): 469, 474, 608, 647, 651.

BELON (1553): Les observations de plusieurs singularitez et choses mémorables, trouvés en Grèce, Asie, Judée, Egypte, Arabie ... – Paris (G. Cauellar), XXII + 211 pp.

BENDER (2000): DGHT-Projekt »Individualerkennungsmethoden für Reptilien«. – Radiata, Bennstedt, 9 (1): 21-24.

BENDER (2001a): Fotodokumentation von geschützten Reptilien. – Rheinbach (Deutsche Gesellschaft für Herpetologie und Terrarienkunde): 6-9, 13.

BENDER (2001b): Weiterführung des Projekts »Fotodokumentation«. – Radiata, Haan, 10 (2): 18-19.

BENDER (2001c): Individualerkennung von Anhang A-Reptilien mittels Fotodokumentation. – BNA-aktuell, Hambrücken, 2: 29-33.

BENDER (2002): Teilnehmer gesucht – Fotodokumentation von jungen europäischen Landschildkröten (*Testudo graeca, T. marginata*). – elaphe (N. F.), Rheinbach, 10 (3): 22-23.

BENDER (2003a): Neuster Stand bei der Fotodokumentation junger europäischer Landschildkröten (*Testudo graeca, T. hermanni, T. marginata*). – Minor, Haan, 2 (1): 24-25.

BENDER (2003b): Aktuelle Informationen aus der Untersuchung zur Fotodokumentation junger europäischer Landschildkröten (*Testudo graeca*, T. *hermanni*, T. *marginata*). – Minor, Lingenfeld, **2** (3): 21-22.

BENDER (2004): Ein Streifzug durch den Schildkrötenpark »A Cupulatta« auf Korsika. – elaphe (N. F.), Rheinbach, **12** (3): 45-49.

BENDER (2005a): Identificatie van beschermde reptielen m.b.v. foto's. – Trionyx, Eindhoven, **3** (3): 66-72.

BENDER (2005b): Photodocumentation of Protected Reptiles. – Rheinbach (Deutsche Gesellschaft für Herpetologie und Terrarienkunde): 6-9, 13.

BENDER & DAUBNER (2001): Zwischenstand Jungtierprojekt – Suche weiterer Anhang-A Reptilien. – Radiata, Haan, **10** (3): 28.

BENDER & HENLE (2001a): Können Sie sich ausweisen? Forschungsvorhaben weist individuelle Identifizierbarkeit geschützter Reptilienarten nach. – Natur und Landschaft, **76** (4): 168-170.

BENDER & HENLE (2001b): Individuelle fotografische Identifizierung von Landschildkröten-Arten (Testudinidae) des Anhangs A der europäischen Artenschutzverordnung. – Salamandra, Rheinbach, **37** (4): 193-204.

BENNETT (1972): Turtles of Yugoslavia. – International Turtle and Tortoise Society Journal, Los Angeles, **6** (2): 15-34

BENNETT (1978): Turtles of Yugoslavia. – Testudo, **1** (1): 14-16.

BENYR, GEMEL & SCHWEIGER (2003): Weiterführende kritische Betrachtungen zur Veröffentlichung der Royal Society for the Prevention of Cruelty to Animals und Pro Wildlife über »Morbidity and mortality in private husbandry of reptiles« von S. ALTHERR und D. FREYER (2001). – ÖGH-Aktuell, Vienna, **11**: 11-14.

BERGER, COLLEAU, DUVAL, MANDIGOUT & TROTTEREAU (1985): Herpétologie, Batrachologie, Répartition. – Naturaliste Orléanais, Orléans, **4** (11): 1-50.

BERGIER & CHEYLAN (1980): Statut, succès de reproduction et alimentation du vautour percnoptère *Neophron percnopterus* en France méditerranéenne. – Alauda, Paris, **48**: 75-97.

BERGMANN (2003): »Schildkröten sterben niemals«. – Münster Westfälische Tageszeitung, 01.06.2003.

BERGMANS (1967): Gesjacher II. – Lacerta, Zoetermeer, **4**: 33.

BERGOUNIOUX (1935): Contribution à l'étude paléontologiques de Chéloniens – Chéloniens fossiles du Bassin d'Aquitaine. – Mémoires de la Société géologique de France (N. S.), Paris, **11** (25): 7-215.

BERGOUNIOUX (1958): Les Reptiles fossiles du Tertiaire de la Catalogue. – Estud. Geol., Madrid, **14** (39): 129-219.

BERGTHALER (1991): Landschildkröten naturgemäß gepflegt. – DATZ, Stuttgart, **56** (5): 337.

BERNER (1955): Amphibiens et reptiles des environs de Marseille. – Bulletin de la Société Linnéenne de Provence, Marseille, **20**: 45-46.

BERTOLERO (1991): La reintroducción de *Testudo hermanni* en el Parque Natural del Delta del Ebro. – Bulletin Parc Natural Delta de l'Ebre, **6**: 22-25.

BERTOLERO (2002a): What has happened with the Hermann's tortoise thirteen years after its introduction in the Ebro delta (NE Spain). – Chelonii, Gonfaron, **3**: 320.

BERTOLERO (2002b): Biología de la Tortuga mediterránea *Testudo hermanni* aplicada a su conservación. – Dissertation, Univ. Barcelona.

BERTOLERO (2003): Assessment of reintroduction projects: the case of the Hermann's tortoise. – Proceedings of the IUCN Turtle Survival Alliance 2003 Conference.

BERTOLERO (2006): La Tortue d'Hermann *Testudo hermanni* sur les îles de Majorque et de Minorque. – Chéloniens, Saint Auban, **1**: 12-19.

BERTOLERO & CHEYLAN (2004): *Testudo hermanni* GMELIN, 1798. – Manouria, Mezzavia, **22**: 21-22.

BERTOLERO & DONOYAN (2002): Le projet de conservation de la tortue d'Hermann dans le Parc Naturel du Delta de l'Ebre (Espagne). – Manouria, Mezzavia, **17**: 22-28.

BERTOLERO & MARÍN (2000): Detección de huevos en la tortuga Mediterránea mediante palpado inguinal. – Boletín de la Asociación Herpetológica Española, Leganés, **11** (2): 93-95.

BERTOLERO & MARÍN (2002): Paramètres reproducteurs de la Tortue d'Hermann *Testudo hermanni hermanni*. – Chelonii, Gonfaron, **3**: 134.

BERTOLERO & MARÍN (2005): Efficacy of inguinal palpation for detecting oviductal eggs in Hermann's tortoise, *Testudo hermanni*. – Amphibia-Reptilia, Leiden, **26** (4): 523-526.

BERTOLERO & MARTÍNEZ-VILALTA (1994): Presencia histórica de *Testudo hermanni* en las comarcas del Baix Ebre i Montsià (Sur de Catalunya). – Boletín de la Asociación Herpetológica Española, Leganés, **5**: 2-3.

BERTOLERO & MARTÍNEZ-VILALTA (1997): Diseño de proyectos de reintroducción. – Jornadas de conservación de la tortuga mediterránea.

BERTOLERO & PRETUS (2004): Caracteristiques de les poblacions de tortuga mediterrània a Menorca. – In: PONS (Ed.): IV. Jornades de Medi Ambient de les Illes Balears. Ponències i Resums. – Palma de Mallorca (Soc. Hist. Nat. Balears): 110.

BERTOLERO, CARRETERO & LLORENTE (2005): An assessment of the reliability of growth rings counts for age determination in the Hermann's Tortoise

Testudo hermanni. – Amphibia-Reptilia, Leiden, **26** (1): 17-23.

BERTOLERO, CARRETERO, LLORENTE & MARTÍNEZ-VILALTA (1996): Dominios vitales en una población de tortuga mediterránea (*Testudo hermanni*) en el Delta del Ebro. – IV Congreso Luso-Español de Herpetologia, Porto: 19.

BERTOLERO, CARRETERO, LLORENTE, MARTÍNEZ-VILALTA & MONTORI (1996): The importance of introduction in species conservation – the case of *Testudo hermanni* in the Ebro Delta Natural Park (NE Spain). – In: SOPTOM (Eds.): International Congress of Chelonian Conservation – Proceedings. – Gonfaron (Editions SOPTOM): 187-191.

BERTRAND (2006): Questions au vétérinaire. – Chéloniens, Saint Auban, 1: 47.

BESHKOV (1960): La tortue terrestre. – Turist, Sofia, V (XLVI), 3: 28.

BESHKOV (1961a): Beitrag zur zoogeographischen Untersuchung der Herpetofauna in Bulgarien. – Bull. Inst. Zool. Mus., Sofia, 10: 373-380.

BESHKOV (1961b): Über die Helminthenfauna einiger Lurche und Kriechtiere aus der Gegend von Burgas und dem Strandûagebirge. Vorläufige Mitteilung. – Natural Centres of disease in the Strandza area, Sofia: 141-145.

BESHKOV (1962): Über die Helminthenfauna einiger Lurche und Kriechtiere aus den Gebieten von Petric und Goce Delcev – Vorläufige Mitteilung. – Natural Centres of disease in the Petrich and Gotse Delchev areas, Sofia: 185-189.

BESHKOV (1984a): On the distribution, relative abundance and protection of tortoises in Bulgaria. – Ekologiya, Sofia, **14**: 14-34.

BESHKOV (1984b): Znacenieto na Stara planina za razprostranenieto na herpetofaunata v Balgarija. – Acta Zoologica Bulgarica, Sofia, **25**: 9-15.

BESHKOV (1985): Amphibians and reptiles. – In: Red Data Book of Bulgaria, Band 2, Animals. – Ed. Bulg. Acad. Sci., Sofia: 32-41.

BESHKOV (1993): On the distribution, relative abundance and protection of tortoises in Bulgaria. – Chelonian Conservation and Biology, Lunenburg, 1 (1): 53-62.

BESHKOV (1997): Record-sized tortoises *Testudo graeca ibera* and *Testudo hermanni boettgeri* from Bulgaria. – Chelonian Conservation and Biology, Lunenburg, 2 (4): 593-596.

BESHKOV & BERON (1964): Catalogue et Bibliographie des Amphibiens et Reptiles en Bulgarie. – Acad. Bulg. Sci., Sofia, 39 pp.

BESHKOV & NANEV (2002): Amphibians and reptiles in Bulgaria. – Sofia & Moscow (Pensoft), 120 pp.

BESHKOV, UNDSHIAN, SIMEONOV & DARAKCIEV (1967): Neue Angaben über die Verbreitung einiger Amphibien und Reptilien in Bulgarien. – Bull. Inst. Zool. Mus., Sofia, **25**: 5-10.

BESSON (1975): La réintroduction de la tortue d'Hermann *Testudo hermanni robertmertensi* (WERMUTH) à Port-Cros. – Trav. Sci. Parc national Port-Cros, 1: 37-40.

BETREMIEUX & SCHILLIGER (2006): Travaux préliminaires: Correlation entre hyperazotemie (urémie) et insuffisance rénale chez les Chéloniens. Et si l'urémie était bien un marqueur de l'insuffisance rénale chez les tortues? – Manouria, Mezzavia, **9** (30): 21–29.

DE BETTA (1868): I rettili ed anfibi del regno della Grecia con alcune notizie sulla deistribuzione geografica delle specie. – Atti del Reale Istituto Veneto di Scienze, Lettere ed Arti, Venedig, **13** (3): 1-91.

DE BETTA (1874): Fauna d'Italia. IV. Rettili ed Anfibi.

BEVAN (1986): Representations of Animals in Sanctuaries of Artemis and other Olympian Deities. – British Archaeological Reports, International Series, Oxford, **315**: 164.

BEVAN (1988): Ancient Deities and Tortoise-Representations in Sanctuaries. – **BSA**, 83: 1-6.

BIANCHI, REPETTO, GIORDANA & CAPRARO (1972): Serosal and mucosal permeability coefficients for acetamide and thio urea in turtle *Testudo hermanni* jejunum. – Comparative Biochemistry and Physiology, A, Comparative Physiology, Vancouver, **43** (2): 337-340.

BIBRON & BORY DE SAINT-VINCENT (1833): Reptiles. – In: GEOFFROY SAINT-HILAIRE, GEOFFROY SAINT-HILAIRE, DESHAYES, BIBRON & BORY DE SAINT-VINCENT (Eds.): Travaux de la Section des Sciences Physiques 3 (1) (Zoologie – 1e section. Animaux vertébrés, Mollusques et Polypes). – In: BORY DE SAINT-VINCENT, PEYTIER, PUILLON, BOBLAYE, SERVIER, BRULLÉ, VIRLET, GEOFFROY SAINT-HILAIRE, GEOFFROY SAINT-HILAIRE, BRONGNIART, BIBRON, DESHAYES, GUÉRIN, CHAUBARD & FAUCHÉ (Eds.): Expédition scientifique en Morée. – Paris & Strasbourg (F. G. Levrault): 57-76.

BIDMON (2001): Regulation der Ruhephasen bei Schildkröten: Was ist bekannt und welche Konsequenzen ergeben sich für die erfolgreiche Haltung? – Radiata, Haan, 10 (4): 3-19.

BIDMON (2004): Die Inkubation von beschädigten Eiern und die Versorgung bei Schlupfproblemen. – Schildkröten im Fokus, Bergheim, 1 (1): 12-19.

BIDMON (2006): Eine kostengünstige Methode zur Inkubation von Landschildkrötengelegen. – Schildkröten im Fokus, 3 (1): 25-31.

BIEDERMANN (1998): Knaurs Lexikon der Symbole. – Munich & Zürich (Droemer Knaur), 592 pp.

BIEGLER (1966): A survey of recent longevity records for reptiles and amphibians in zoos. – International Zoo Yearbook, London, 6: 487-493.

BIERMANN (1995): Isolierung und Charakterisierung von Herpesviren bei Landschildkröten. – Dissertation, Justus-Liebig-Universität, Gießen.

BIERMANN & BLAHAK (1993): First isolation of herpesvirus from tortoises with diphtheroid necrotising stomatitis. – Second World Congress of Herpetology, Adelaide: 27.

BIGOT DU CHAPELET (1960): Notes sur les Chéloniens français. – Bulletin Mayenne-Sciences, Rennes: 38-48.

BLACKWELL (1959): Seasonal weight of a European tortoise. – Naturalist, **870**: 92.

BLAHAK (1996): Repatriierung von Reptilien. – elaphe (N. F.), Rheinbach, **4** (4): 61-64.

BLAHAK (1998): Herpes! Wie geht es weiter? Oder: Der Stomatitis-Rhinitis-Komplex der Landschildkröten. – Fachmagazin Schildkröte, Rothenfluh, **1** (5): 60-61.

BLAHAK (1999): Stiftungsnachrichten. – SIGS-Info, Siblingen, **8** (1): 42-43.

BLAHAK (1999/2000): Herpes. – Fachmagazin Schildkröte, Rothenfluh, **2** (1): 64.

BLAHAK (2000): Virusinfektionen bei Reptilien. – Der praktische Tierarzt, Hannover, **81** (2): 92-112.

BLAHAK (2001): Erste Ergebnisse zum Vorkommen von *Mycoplasma agassizii* bei Landschildkröten. – SIGS-Info, Siblingen, **10** (3): 28.

BLAHAK (2004a): Vergleich von 35 Herpesvirus-Isolaten von 6 unterschiedlichen Landschildkrötenspecies. – Arbeitstagung AGARK Düsseldorf, 12.-13. Juni 2004.

BLAHAK (2004b): Herpesvirus im Schildkrötenbestand – was ist zu tun? Übertragungsprophylaxe und Desinfektion. – Schildkröten im Fokus, Bergheim, **1** (3): 17-20.

BLAHAK (2006): Infectious diseases in turtles and tortoises. – In: ARTNER, FARKAS & LOEHR (Eds.): Turtles. Proceedings: International Turtle & Tortoise Symposium Vienna 2002. – Frankfurt am Main (Edition Chimaira): 593-612.

BLAHAK & BIERMANN (1996): Herpesvirus infection in land tortoise as a problem of Chelonian conservation. – In: SOPTOM (Eds.): International Congress of Chelonian Conservation – Proceedings. – Gonfaron (Editions SOPTOM): 240-243.

BLAHAK & TORNEDE (2004): Comparison of 35 herpesvirus strains from 6 different species of tortoises. – Path. Med. Rep. Amph. 7th Int. Symp.

BLAKE, SHERRIFF & HAYWARD (1994): Husbandry of the Baltic Race of *Testudo hermanni boettgeri*. – NYTTS NewsNotes, New York, **5** (2): 9-11.

BLANC, SQUALLI-HOUSSAINI & BLANC (1989): Diversité génétique de la population de tortues du Massif des Maures (France) *Testudo hermanni hermanni* GMELIN, 1789. – Mésogée, Marseille, **48**: 7-11.

BLANCK (2006): Unterscheidungsmerkmale der drei Unterarten von *Testudo hermanni*. – Sacalia, Stiefern, **4** (10): 49-56.

BLANCK & ESSER (2004): Zur Kenntnis von *Testudo hermanni hercegovinensis* (WERNER, 1899) oder Neues Licht auf eine »alte« Art. – Sacalia, Stiefern, **2** (2): 17-31.

BLAS & COSTELLO (1978): Guía ecológica de Baleares. – Madrid (INCAFO), 205 pp.

BLATT & MÜLLER (1974): Die Mortalitätsrate importierter Schildkröten im Saarland. – Salamandra, Frankfurt am Main, **10** (3/4): 115-125.

BLUM (1971): Die Reptilien und Amphibien Europas. – Hallwag Taschenbuch 96 (Zoologie), Bern & Stuttgart (Hallwag Verlag): 24, 48-49.

BNA (Eds.) (2000): BNA-Artenschutzbuch – Teil I – Wirbeltiere. – Hambrücken (Bundesverband für fachgerechten Natur- und Artenschutz): 76, 287.

BOCK (1994): Voyage en Toscane et visite du centre CARAPAX. – CITS bulletin, Bramois, **3**: 13-14.

BODDINGTON (1994): Members' letters. – British Chelonia Group Newsletter, **99**: 7-8.

BODENHEIMER (1944): Introduction into the knowledge of the Amphibia and Reptilia of Turkey. – Rev. Fac. Sci. Univ. Istanbul, Ser. B Sci. Nat., Istanbul, **9**: 1-93.

BOESSNECK (1973): Die Tierknochenfunde aus dem Kabirenheiligtum bei Theben (Böotien). – Munich (Institut für Palaeoanatomie, Domestikationsforschung und Geschichte der Tiermedizin der Universität München): 26.

BOETTGER (1881): Beitrag zur Kenntnis der Reptilien und Amphibien Spaniens und der Balearen. – Abhandlungen der Senckenbergischen Naturforschenden Gesellschaft, Frankfurt am Main, **12**: 371-392.

BOETTGER (1888): Verzeichnis der von E. v. OERTZEN aus Griechenland und aus Kleinasien mitgebrachten Batrachier und Reptilien. – Sitzungsberichte der Preußischen Akademie der Wissenschaften, Berlin, **5**: 139-186.

BOETTGER (1889): Herpetologische Miscellen – I. Epirus – II. Corfu. – Berichte der Senckenbergischen Naturforschenden Gesellschaft, Frankfurt am Main, 1888-1889: 267-276.

BOETTGER (1893): Katalog der Reptilien-Sammlung im Museum der Senckenbergischen Naturforschenden Gesellschaft in Frankfurt am Main – I. Teil (Rhynchocephalen, Schildkröten, Krokodile, Echsen, Chamäleons). – Frankfurt (Knauer), X + 160 pp.

BOHNSTEDT (1956): Lautäußerung einer griechischen Landschildkröte. – DATZ, Stuttgart, **9** (10): 278.

BOLKAY (1919): Prinosi herpetologiji zapadnoga dijela Balkanskog poluostrva. – Glasnik zemaljsk. Muz. Bosn. Hercegov., Sarajevo, **31** (1), 38 pp., 5 plates.

BOLKAY (1924): Popis vodozemaza i gmizavaza, koje se nalaze u bos.-herc. zemaljskom muzeju u Sarajevu s morfoloskim, bioloskim i zoogeografskim biljeskama. – Spomenik Srp. Kralj. Akad., Belgrade, **61** (11), 39 pp., 7 plates.

BOLKAY (1928): Die zoogeographische Bedeutung des Neretva- (Narenta-) Tales. – Glasnik zemaljsk. Muz. Bosn. Hercegov., Sarajevo, **40** (1): 35-44.

BOLKAY (1929): Die Amphibien und Reptilien von Sarajewo und Umgebung. – Glasnik zemaljsk. Muz. Bosn. Hercegov., Sarajevo, **41**: 57-77.

BOLOGNA (Eds.) (1999): Studi propedeutici ai piani delle aree naturali protette gestite da Roma-Naura. – Technischer Bericht, Università degli Studi di Roma Tre, 11 Bände, 1243 pp.

BOLOGNA & LA POSTA (2004): The conservation status of threatened Amphibian and Reptile species of Italian fauna. – Italian Journal of Zoology, Modena, **71** (Suppl. 1), 183 pp.

BOLOGNA, CAPULA & CARPANETO (2000): Anfibi e rettili del Lazio. – Rome (Fratelli Palombi Editori), 159 pp.

BOLOGNA, CAPULA, CARPANETO, CIGNINI, MARANGONI, VENCHI & ZAPPAROLI (2003): Anfibi e rettili a Roma – atlante e guida delle spcie presenti in città. – Rome (Comune di Roma), 112 pp.

BOMMELI (1894): Die Thierwelt. – Stuttgart.

BONAPARTE (1835): Iconografia della fauna Italica per le quattro classi degli animali vertebrati – Tomo II – Amfibi. – Rome (Typografia Salviucci), 65 pp., 54 plates.

BOND (1998): Young Mediterranean tortoises. – British Chelonia Group Newsletter, 126: 11.

BONE (1992): Gastrointestinal system. – In: BEYNON, LAWTON & COOPER (Eds.): Manual of reptiles. – Cheltenham (BSAVA): 101-116.

BONFIGLIO & INSACCO (1992): Paleoenvironmental, paleontologic and stratigraphic significance of vertebrate remains in Pleistocene limnic and alluvial deposits from southeastern Sicily. – Palaeogeogr., Palaeoclimatol., Palaeoecol., **95**: 195-208.

BONFIGLIO & LATINO (1986): Primo rinvenimento di un vertebrato fossile (*Testudo* cfr. *hermanni*) nell'Isola di Lipari (Isole Eolie, Messina, Sicília). – Atti Soc. italiana Sci. Nat. Mus. Civ. Stor. Nat., Milan, **127** (3/4): 301-308.

BONIN (1991): Les Chéloniens – classification, caractères généraux, reproduction, pathologie et thérapeutique. – Dissertation, Univ. Lyon.

BONIN, DEVAUX & DUPRÉ (1996): Toutes les Tortues du Monde. – Lausanne & Paris (Delachaux et Niestlé): 108-110.

BONS, CHEYLAN & GUILLAUME (1984): Les reptiles méditerranéens. – Bulletin de la Société Herpétologique de France, Paris, **29**: 7-17.

BORRI, AGNELLI, CESARACCIO, CORTI, FINOTELLO, LANZA & TOSINI (1988): Preliminary notes on the herpetofauna of the satellite islands of Sardinia. – Boll. Soc. Sarda Sci. Nat., Sassari, **26**: 149-165.

BOSCÁ (1880): Catalogue des reptiles et amphibiens de la Peninsule Ibérique et des Iles Baléares. – Bulletin de la Société Zoologique de France, Paris, **5**: 240-287.

BOSCÁ (1881a): Catálogo de los Reptiles y Anfibios observados en España, Portugal y Islas Baleares. – Sociedad Española de Historia Natural, Madrid, **24**: 39-64.

BOSCÁ (1881b): Correciones y adiciones al catálogo de los Reptiles y Anfibios de España, Portugal y las Islas Baleares. – Anales de la Sociedad Española de Historia Natural, Madrid, **24**: 89-112.

BOSSCHERE & ROELS (2003a): *Tachygonetria bainae* in a Hermann's tortoise (*Testudo hermanni boettgeri*). – Tortoise Trust Newsletter, London, **18** (1): 3-5.

BOSSCHERE & ROELS (2003b): *Balantidium* sp. and *Nyctotherus* sp.: two common members of the digestive-tract flora in Mediterranean tortoises. – Tortoise Trust Newsletter, London, **18** (2): 9-11.

BOSSUTO, GIACOMA, ROLANDO & BALLETO (2000): Caratteristiche delle aree familiari in una poolazione di *Testudo hermanni* GMELIN del Parco Nazionale della Maremma (GR). – In: GIACOMA (Eds.): Atti I Congressa Societas Herpethologica Italica. – Turin (Museo Regionale Scienze Naturali): 543-551.

BOULENGER (1889): Catalogue of the Chelonians, Rhynchocephalians, and Crocodiles in the British Museum (Natural History). – London (Taylor and Francis): 177.

BOUNHIOL & LAHARGUE (1956): Nouvelle récolte à Bordeaux d'œufs fécondés de Tortue grecque. – P. V. Soc. Linn., Bordeaux, **96**: 25-26.

BOUR (1980): Essai sur la taxinomie des Testudinidae actuels (Reptilia, Chelonii). – Bulletin de la Muséum National d'Histoire Naturelle, Paris, 4, **2 A** (2): 541-546.

BOUR (1984): Les Tortues terrestres du Paléarctique. – In: DE BEAUFORT (Ed.): Espèces menacées et exploitées dans le Monde, Guide pratique pour leur connaissance et leur identification, 28. – Secrétariat de la Faune et de la Flore, Muséum National d'Histoire Naturelle, Inventaires de Faune et de Flore, Paris, **24**: 1-11.

BOUR (1987): L'identité des Tortues terrestres européennes: spécimens-types et localités-types. – Revue française d'Aquariologie, Nancy, **13** (4): 111-122.

BOUR (1989a): Caractères diagnostiques offerts par le crâne des tortues terrestres du genre *Testudo*. – Mésogée, Marseille, **48**: 13-19.

BOUR (1989b): *Testudo hermanni*. – In: CASTANET & GUYETANT (Eds.): Atlas de répartition des amphibiens et reptiles de France. – Paris (Société Herpétologique de France): 110-111.

BOUR (2002): Gravures et lithographies anciennes figurant des tortues terrestres du genre *Testudo*. – Chelonii, Gonfaron, 3: 12-27.

BOUR (2004a): A new character for the identification of populations of the Hermann's tortoise, *Testudo hermanni* GMELIN, 1789 (Chelonii, Testudinidae). – Salamandra, Rheinbach, 40 (1): 59-66.

BOUR (2004b): *Testudo boettgeri* MOJSISOVICS, 1889. – Manouria, Mezzavia, 22: 9-10.

BOUR, CADI, GUYOT, LOUCHART, MARAN, MAGNAN, MÉTRAILLER, MOSIMANN & SCHILLIGER (2002): Atlas de la terrariophilie – Volume 2 – Les tortues. – Campsegret (Animalia Éditions): 10, 14, 31, 33, 35, 45, 55, 76-78, 118, 144-145.

BOURDEAUX (1988): Pathologie des Tortues. – Maisons-Alfort (Editions du Point Vétérinaire), 20 (117): 761-775, 20 (118): 871-884, 21 (119): 45-62.

BOURDEAU & TRONCO (1992): Pathologie des tortues de compagnie: bilan des consultations à Maisons-Alfort. – Proceedings of the 1st International Congress of Chelonian Pathology, Gonfaron (SOPTOM): 136-154.

BOUSBOURAS & BOURDAKIS (1997): The amphibians and reptiles of some mountaineous areas of West Macedonia (Greece). – Biologia gallo-hellenica, 24 (1): 5-22.

BOUSBOURAS & IOANNIDES (1994): Amphibien und Reptilien des Prespa-Nationalparks und der Gebirgsregion um Florina (Mazedonien, Griechenland). – Salamandra, Rheinbach, 30 (3): 209-220.

BOUSSAC (1992): Herpétophilatélie. – La Tortue, Gonfaron, 19: 27.

BOUSSAC (1994): Herpétophilatélie. – La Tortue, Gonfaron, 26: 34-35.

BOUSSAC (1997): Herpétophilatélie. – La Tortue, Gonfaron, 40: 42-43.

BOUSSAC (2000): Herpétophilatélie. – La Tortue, Gonfaron, 50/51: 67-68.

BOUSSAC (2004): Consommer avec modération. – La Tortue, Gonfaron, 66: 76-79.

BOUVARD (1992): Contribution à l'étude des affections tégumentaires des tortues terrestres méditerranéennes. Observations personnelles dans le village des tortues de Gonfaron (Var-France). – Dissertation, Alfort.

BOYCOTT, TAYLOR & DOUGLAS (1953): Salmonella in tortoises. – Journal of Pathology and Bacteriology, Chichester, 65: 402-411.

BOYER (1965): Ecology of the basking habit in turtles. – Ecology, Ithaca, 46: 99-118.

BRABENETZ, LUTTENBERGER & SCHWAMMER (1996): Haltungsrichtlinien, Mindestansprüche für Schildkröten. – Vienna (Literas Universitätsverlag): 22, 38.

BRANDSTÄTTER (1990): Das »Village des Tortues« – Ein Projekt zur Erhaltung der letzten südfranzösischen Landschildkröten. – Vortragszusammenfassungen der DGHT-Jahrestagung, Bonn.

BRANDSTÄTTER (1993): The lost tortoise. – British Chelonia Group Newsletter, 94: 3-4.

BRANDSTÄTTER (1995): Behavioural und Environmental Enrichment bei Landschildkröten. – Journal der AG Schildkröten & Panzerechsen, Bürstadt, 4 (1): 22-25.

BRANDSTÄTTER (1996): Behavioural und Environmental Enrichment bei Landschildkröten. – Emys, Sankt Pölten, 3 (3): 20-23.

BRANDSTÄTTER & REDL (1994): Explanations of the scientific names of some common pet chelonia. – British Chelonia Group Newsletter, 102: 10-12.

BRANDSTETTER-HALBERSTADT (1994): Überwinterung von Landschildkröten im Kühlschrank. – Schildkröten, Linden, 1 (2): 31-33.

BRATISLAV (1988): The golden eagle (*Aquila chrysaetos chrysaetos*) in south-eastern Yugoslavia. – Larus, Zagreb, 38/39: 95-135.

BRATTSTROM (1965): Body temperature of reptiles. – American Midland Naturalist, Notre Dame, 73: 376-422.

BRATTSTROM & COLLINS (1972): Thermoregulation. – International Turtle and Tortoise Society Journal, Los Angeles, 6 (5): 15-19.

BRAUER (1980): Allgemeines über Landschildkröten. – Sauria, Berlin, 2 (1): 8-11.

BRAUN (1998a): Schildkrötendiebstahl. – Schildkröten, Linden, 5 (3): 11-15.

BRAUN (1998b): Schildkrötenüberwinterung im Kühlschrank. – Schildkröten, Linden, 5 (4): 29-33.

BRAUN (1999): Schildkröte und Hund – nicht immer ein gutes Gespann. – Schildkröten, Linden, 6 (1): 36-39.

BRAUN (2003): Große Ereignisse im Frühbeet. – Schildkröten, Linden, 10 (4): 38-44.

BRAUN (2004): »Naturbrut« von *Testudo hermanni boettgeri*. – Minor, Lingenfeld, 3 (2): 32-34.

BRAUNE, GEISS & THIEL (1989): Eine neue durch Herpesviren verursachte Erkrankung bei Landschildkröten. – Die Tierärztliche Praxis, Stuttgart, 17 (4): 416-419.

BRELIH & DZUKIC (1974): Catalogus Faunae Jugoslaviae. – Consil. Acad. Sci. Rei Publ. Soc. Foed. Jugosl., Acad. Sci. Art. Slovenica, Ljubljana, 33 pp.

BREHM (1927): Brehms Tierleben – Band I – Kriechtiere. Nach der zweiten Originalausgabe bearbeitet von OTTO EVERS. – Hamburg (Uhlenhorst-Verlag Curt Brenner): 43-46, plate 1.

BRELIH & DZUKIC (1974): Catalogus Faunae Jugoslaviae. Reptilia. – Acad. Sci. Art. Sŏov., Ljubljana, 4 (2): 1-33.

BRESSOUS (1993): Einzigartige Tierklinik – Letzte Zuflucht für Schildkröte Hermann. – Auf einen Blick, 16: 4-5.

BRIDLE (1984): The Bridle tortoise family. – British Chelonia Group Newsletter, 41: 1.

BRINGSØE (1986): A check-list of Peloponnesian amphibians and reptiles, including new records from Greece. – Annales Musei Goulandris, Kifissia, 7: 271-318.

BRÖDEMANN (1991): Futterneid. – Das Tier, Leinfelden-Echterdingen, 32 (10): 57.

BROGARD (2002): Les maladies des reptiles. 2. Auflage. – Maisons-Alfort (Editions du Point Vétérinaire), 320 pp.

BROGGI (1994): Feldherpetologische Beobachtungen und Bemerkungen zu schützenswerten Biotopen auf griechischen Inseln. – Herpetozoa, Vienna, 7 (1/2): 29-34.

BROGHAMMER (1998): Albinos – Farb- und Zeichnungsvarianten bei Schlangen und anderen Reptilien. – Frankfurt am Main (Edition Chimaira): 85.

DE BROIN (1977): Contribution à l'Étude des Chéloniens – Chéloniens Continentaux du Crétacé et du Tertiaire de France. – Mémoires du Muséum National d'Histoire Naturelle (Nouvelle Série) , Série C, Sciences de la Terre, Paris (Éditions du Muséum), 38, 366 pp., 38 plates.

BROSE (1925): Naturkundliche Streifzüge an den Ufern des Ochridsees. – Blätter für Aquarien- und Terrarienkunde, Stuttgart, 36 (16): 417-430, (17): 462.

BROUARD (1995): La tomodensimétrie – Application aux Chéloniens. Atlas tomodensimétrique et étude statistique comparative de 2 espèces de Chéloniens – une espèce aquatique, Chrysemys scripta elegans (GRAY, 1844) et une espèce terrestre, Testudo hermanni hermanni (GMELIN, 1789). – Dissertation, Univ. Nantes.

BRUEKERS (1986): Waarnemingen aan de Griekse landschildpad (Testudo hermanni robertmertensi) in Zuid-Frankrijk. – Lacerta, Zoetermeer, 44 (4): 63-65.

BRUEKERS (1995): De Landschildpadden van Mallorca, deel 1. – De Schildpad, Eindhoven, 21: 1.

BRUEKERS (1998a): Hardy exotic plants for outdoor vivariums in temperate zones. – Tortoise Trust Newsletter, London, 13 (1): 3-4.

BRUEKERS (1998b): Palmen und andere exotische Pflanzen für das Schildkröten-Freilandterrarium. – Reptilia (D), Münster, 14: 58-61.

BRUEKERS (2000): Palmen im Freilandterrarium für Landschildkröten – einige Anregungen für ein Experiment. – Radiata, Haan, 9 (3): 23-29.

BRUEKERS (2003a): Palms and other exotic plants for outdoor tortoise enclosures. – Reptilia (GB), Barcelona, 29: 35-38.

BRUEKERS (2003b): Palmeras y otras plantas exóticas para recintos al aire libre de tortugas terrestres. – Reptilia (E), Barcelona, 42: 39-42.

BRUEKERS (2004): Een Testudo hermanni hermanni met een snotneus. – Trionyx, Eindhoven, 2 (3): 70-72.

BRUEKERS (2005a): Griechische Landschildkröte (Testudo hermanni hermanni) im Habitat als Beute von Vögeln. – Schildkröten im Fokus, Bergheim, 2 (1): 33-34.

BRUEKERS (2005b): Rampen en schildpadden. – Trionyx, Eindhoven, 3 (2): 52-54.

BRUGAROLAS (1995): Centre de Reproducció de Tortugues de l'Albera in Spain. – Chelonian Conservation and Biology, Lunenburg, 1 (3): 249.

BRÜGGEMANN (2000): Zuchtbücher in den Niederlanden – ein Beitrag zur Arterhaltung. – Radiata, Haan, 9 (4): 17-20.

BRUINS (1999): Terrarien Enzyklopädie. – Erlangen (Karl Müller Verlag, Erlangen): 11, 258-262.

BRÜNNER (1950): Überwinterung subtropischer Landschildkröten. – DATZ, 3 (10): 157-158.

BRUNO (1968): Gli anfibi e i rettili dell'isola di Montecristo. – Atti della Società Toscana di Scienze Naturali, Ser. B, Pisa, 75: 31-71.

BRUNO (1970): Anfibi e Rettili di Sicília (Studi sulla Fauna Erpetologica Italiana IX). – Atti Accad. Gioenia Sci. Nat., Ser. Settima, Catania, 2 (7): 185-326.

BRUNO (1971a): Gli Anfibi e i Rettili dell'Appennino abruzzese con particolare riferimento alle specie del parco nazionale d'Abruzzo. – Lavori Soc. Italiana Biogeografia (N. S.), 5 (2): 697-783.

BRUNO (1971b): Red Book – Testudo hermanni GMELIN. – Notiz. Unione Erpetologica Italiana, 1 (2): 30.

BRUNO (1973): Problemi di conservazione nel campo dell' erpetologia. – Atti 3rd Simp. Naz. Conserv. Nat. Bari, 2: 117-226.

BRUNO (1975): Note riassuntive sull'erpetofauna dell'isola di Montecristo (Arcipelago Toscano, Mare Tireno). – Lavori Soc. Ital. Biogeogr. (N. S.), 5: 743-838.

BRUNO (1980): L'Erpetofauna delle isole di Cres, Trstnik, Plavnik e Krk (Kvarner, Jugoslavija). – Atti Mus. civ. Stor. nat., Triest, 31 (3): 249-282.

BRUNO (1981): Ricerche ecologiche, floristiche e faunistiche sulla fascia costiera mediotirrenica italiana. – Rome (Accademia Nazionale Lincei), 254: 31-76.

BRUNO (1986): Guida a Tartarughe e Sauri d'Italia. – Florence (Giunti-Martello), 256 pp.

BRUNO (1988a): L'Erpetofauna delle isole di Cres, Krk e Ada (Jugoslavia, Albania). – Bulletin d'Ecologie, Paris, 19 (2/3): 265-281.

BRUNO (1988b): Considerazioni sull'erpetofauna della Sicília. – Bulletin d'Ecologie, Paris, 19 (2/3): 283-303.

BRUNO (1989a): Introduzione a uno studio sull' erpetofauna del Monte Conero. – R.A.N.A., Italia: 23-44.

BRUNO (1989b): Introduction to a study of the herpetofauna of Albania. – British Herpetological Society Bulletin, London, **29**: 16-41.

BRUNO & GUACCI (1993): Appunti di erpetofauna Molisana. – Ann. Mus. civ. Rovereto, Sez. Arch., St., Sci. nat., **8**: 249-332.

BRUNO & MAUGERI (1976): Rettili d'Italia. I: Tartarughe e Sauri. – Florence (Giunti-Martello), 160 pp.

BRUNO & MAUGERI (1979): Rettili d'Italia. I: Tartarughe, Sauri, Serpenti. – Florence (Giunti Martello), 363 pp.

BRUNO, DOLCE, SAULI & VEBER (1973): Introduzione a un studio sugli Anfibi e Rettili del Carso Triestino. – Atti Mus. civ. Stor. nat. Trieste, Triest, **28** (2): 487-576.

BRUNS (1979): Behaucht von Jahrmillionen: Landschildkröten (Die Pflege von *Testudo hermanni* und *Testudo graeca*). – aquarien magazin, Stuttgart, **13** (2): 68-72.

BUCK (1897): Einiges über meine griechische Landschildkröte (*Testudo graeca*). – Der Zoologische Garten, Berlin, **38**: 293-294.

BUDISCHEK (2000): Schildkrötenpudding für europäische Landschildkröten. – Emys, Sitzenberg-Reidling, **7** (4): 26-28.

BUDISCHEK (2001): Keeping and breeding of *Testudo hermanni boettgeri*. – International Turtle & Tortoise Symposium, Vienna, Austria, January 17-20, 2002, Final Program with Abstracts: 54.

BUDISCHEK (2006): Haltung und Nachzucht der Griechischen Landschildkröte *Testudo hermanni boettgeri* MOJSISOVICS 1889. – Sacalia, Stiefern, **4** (10): 5-26.

BUDÓ & MASCORT (2001): El cangrejo de río americano (*Procambarus clarkii*), alimento ocasional de la tortuga mediterránea (*Testudo hermanni hermanni*). – Boletín de la Associación Herpetológica Española, Leganés, **12** (2):87-88.

BUDÓ, CAPELLERAS, FÉLIX & MASCORT (1996): The population status of *Testudo hermanni hermanni* in northeastern Spain and management by l'Albera Captive Breeding Centre (C.R.T. l'Albera). – In: SOPTOM (Eds.): International Congress of Chelonian Conservation – Proceedings. – Gonfaron (Editions SOPTOM): 196-197.

BUDÓ, CAPELLERAS, FÉLIX & MASCORT (2002): Western Hermann's tortoise (*Testudo hermanni hermanni*) in Catalonia, state of conservation and recovery projects. – Chelonii, Gonfaron, **3**: 321-322.

BULSING (2002a): Kweekresultaten. – De Schildpad, Eindhoven, **28** (1): 10-12.

BULSING (2002b): Waaschuwing bij het gebruik van graszoden. – De Schildpad, Eindhoven, **28** (3): 133.

BULSING (2002c): Schildpaddencommunicatie, daar durf je niet over te praten! – De Schildpad, Eindhoven, **28** (5): 219-222.

BULSING (2005): Microchiptransponders in schildpadden. – Trionyx, Eindhoven, **3** (2): 34-47.

BUNDESMINISTERIUM FÜR ERNÄHRUNG, LANDWIRTSCHAFT UND FORSTEN (Eds.) (1997): Gutachten über Mindestanforderungen an die Haltung von Reptilien. – Rheinbach (DGHT): 67.

BURCKHARDT (1960): Siena – The City of the Virgin. – Oxford: 117-121.

BURESH & TSONKOV (1933a): Untersuchungen über die Verbreitung der Reptilien und Amphibien in Bulgarien und auf der Balkanhalbinsel. 1. Teil: Schildkröten (Testudinata) und Eidechsen (Sauria). – Izv. Tsarsk. Prirodonausch. Inst., Sofia, **6**: 150-207.

BURESH & TSONKOV (1933b): Untersuchungen über die Verbreitung der Reptilien und Amphibien in Bulgarien und auf der Balkanhalbinsel. Teil II. Schlangen. – Izv. Tsarsk. Prirodonausch. Inst., Sofia, **7**: 106-188.

BÜRKI & REPOND (1998): Garriguella, Centre de reproduction des tortues de l'Albera (Espagne). – Manouria, Mezzavia, **2**: 8-9.

BURTON (1972): The role of the pet trade in the extinction of reptiles. – International Turtle and Tortoise Society Journal, Los Angeles, **6** (3): 29-31.

BURTON & LAMBERT (1977): Reptiles – tortoises come to Britain. – In: SITWELL (Ed.): The World of Wildlife. – London (Hamlyn).

BUSKIRK (1990): More on tortoises in Greece. – Tortoises & Turtles, **5**: 7-8.

BUSTARD (1999): Identifying individual tortoises. – British Herpetological Society Bulletin, London, **69**: 50-51.

BUSTARD (2002a): UK captive-breeding of European tortoises 1997-2000: background and potential problems. – Herpetological Bulletin, London, **79**: 2-4.

BUSTARD (2002b): UK captive-breeding of European tortoises 1997-2000: supply and demand. – Herpetological Bulletin, London, **79**: 4-6.

BUTTLE (1987): Observations on some of the herpetofauna of the Peloponnese. – British Herpetological Society Bulletin, London, **20**: 22-28.

BUTTLE (1988): Further notes on reptiles and amphibians of the Peloponnese. – British Herpetological Society Bulletin, London, **26**: 14-20.

BUTTLE (1989): Notes on reptiles and amphibians of northeastern Greece and the island of Samothraki. – British Herpetological Society Bulletin, London, **29**: 49-53.

BUTTLE (1995): An Introduction to Reptiles & Amphibians of the Greek Islands. – International Reptilian Magazine, **3** (7): 16-27.

BUXTON (1996): A tale of two dear friends. – British Chelonia Group Newsletter, 113: 7-9.

CAGLE (1944): Home range, homing behaviour and migration in turtles. – Miscellaneous Publications of the Museum of Zoology, University of Michigan, 6i: 1-34.

CALABRESI (1932): Anfibi e Rettili d'Albania. – Atti Accad. Sci. Ven.-trent.-istr., Padua, 23: 83-86.

CALCARA (1847): Descrizione dell'isola di Lampedusa. – Palermo (R. Pagano), 25 pp.

CALINESCU (1931): Contributuni sistematice si zoogeograficala studiul Amphibiilor si Reptilelor din România. – Acad. Rom. Mem. Sect. stiintifice, Ser. III, Bukarest, 7: 119-291.

CALMONTE (1968): Zwei bemerkenswerte Schildanomalien bei Testudo hermanni hermanni GMELIN 1789, der Griechischen Landschildkröte. – Aquarien Terrarien, Leipzig, Jena & Berlin, 5: 34-36.

CALOI & PALOMBO (1978): Anfibi, rettili e mammifera di Torre del Pagliaccetto (Torre in Pietra, Roma). – Quaternaria, 20: 315-428.

CALOI, KOTSAKIS & PALOMBO (1988): La faune a Vertebrati terrestri del Pleistocene delle isole del Mediterraneo. – Bull. Ecol., Paris, 19: 131-151.

CALOI, KOTSAKIS, PALOMBO & PETRONIO (1981): Il giacimento a vertebrati del Pleistocene superiore di San Giovanni in Sinis (Sardegna occidentale). – Rome (Accademia Nazionale Lincei), 8 (69): 185-197.

CALZOLAI & CHELAZZI (1991): Habitat use in a central Italy population of Testudo hermanni GMELIN (Reptilia Testudinidae). – Ethol. Ecol. Evol., 3 (2): 153-166.

CAMPANA (1917): Resti di »Testudo« del miocene superiore di Capudjar presso Salonica. – Bolletino della Società Geologica Italiana, Rome, 36: 69-78.

CAMPBELL (2002): Members' letters. – British Chelonia Group Newsletter, 145: 13.

CAMPI (1996): Wilma, eine griechische Landschildkröte (T. H. Boettgerie, Ostrasse) aus Albanien. – Schildkröten, Linden, 3 (4): 28-33.

CAMPI (1997a): Wie eine gute Absicht sich in ihr Gegenteil verkehren kann. – Schildkröten, Linden, 4 (3): 38-41.

CAMPI (1997b): Bavaria, eine deutsche Landschildkröte, fährt zur Kur nach Italien. – Schildkröten, Linden, 4 (4): 19-21.

CAMPI (1997c): Panzergrüße aus dem Süden. – Schildkröten, Linden, 4 (4): 24-29.

CAMPI (1998a): Plötzlicher Tod einer einjährigen Landschildkröte. – Schildkröten, Linden, 5 (1): 22-23.

CAMPI (1998b): Vom Eierlegen und von Sorgen mit Schlüpflingen. – Schildkröten, Linden, 5 (1): 32-33.

CAMPI (1998c): Weiche Panzer bei Nachzuchten. – Schildkröten, Linden, 5 (2): 21-26.

CAMPI (1998d): Lungenentzündung oder was sonst? – Schildkröten, Linden, 5 (4): 3-6.

CAMPI (1999a): Hallo, wir haben ausgeschlafen! – Schildkröten, Linden, 6 (2): 39-40.

CAMPI (1999b): Manchmal sollte man viel Geduld haben. – Schildkröten, Linden, 6 (3): 21-25.

CAMPI (1999c): Skandal – »Carapax-Zentrum«. – elaphe (N. F.), Rheinbach, 7 (2): 35-37.

CAMPI (2000a): Züchterglück oder reiner Zufall. – Schildkröten, Linden, 7 (1): 34-35.

CAMPI (2000b): Hurra – der Frühling ist da. – Schildkröten, Linden, 7 (2): 33-34.

CAMPI (2000c): Zoppi. – Schildkröten, Linden, 7 (4): 25-26.

CAMPI (2001): Schildkröten im Gehege und in der Natur sind uns immer ein Rätsel. – Schildkröten, Linden, 8 (1): 36-38.

CAMPI (2002a): Kinder und Schildkröten. – Schildkröten, Linden, 9 (2): 42-43.

CAMPI (2002b): Bastarde, Hybriden, Kreuzungen und die Folgen. – Schildkröten, Linden, 9 (3): 11-19.

CAMPI (2002c): Winterschlaf – ja oder nein? – Schildkröten, Linden, 9 (4): 26-29.

CAMPI & CAMPI (1997): Bemerkungen zu Freilandhaltung und Nachzuchten von Testudo hermanni boettgeri (Griechische Landschildkröte) in Italien. – elaphe (N. F.), Rheinbach, 5 (1): 7-10.

CAPECCHI (1994): 5 years of reproduction – more than 2.000 hatchlings! – R.A.N.A News, 1: 16-17.

CAPECCHI (1995): Analisi quantitativa e qualitativa sulla riproduzione della Testudo hermanni in Toscana. – Master's thesis, Universitá di Pisa, 129 pp.

CAPULA (1989): Anfibi e Rettili. – Milan (Ed. Arnoldo Mondadori), 255 pp.

CAPUTO (1989): Gli anfibi e i rettili del cratere degli Astroni (Campi Flegrei, Napoli). – Bol. R.A.N.A. Italia: 45-49.

CAPUTO & GUARINO (1992): L'erpetofauna del Cilento. – Atti Soc. italiana Sci. Nat. Mus. Civ. Stor. Nat., Milan, 132 (22): 273-292.

CAPUTO & GUARINO (1993): Primo contributo per la realizzazione dell'Atlante erpetologico della Campania. – Suppl. Ric. Biol. Selvaggina, Ozzano dell'Emilia, 21: 393-406.

CAPUTO, KALBO & DE FILIPPO (1985): Gli Anfibi e i Rettili del massicio degli Alburni (Appennino Campano-Lucano). – Natura, Milan, 76 (1-4): 94-104.

CARBONE (1988): Caratteristiche della popolazione di Testudo hermanni GMELIN del parco naturale della Maremma. – Dissertation, Università di Genova, 124 pp.

CARBONE & PAGLIONE (1991): Metodi di censimento e di studio delle popolazioni di Testudinidae. – In: FASOLA (Ed.): Atti II Seminario italiano Censimenti faunistici Vertebrati, Brescia 1989. – Suppl. Biol. Selvaggina, Ozzano dell'Emilia, 16: 149-156.

CARRETERO, BERTOLERO & LLORENTE (1995): Thermal ecology of a population of Testudo hermanni in the Ebro Delta (NE Spain). – In: LLORENTE, MONTORI, SANTOS & CARRETERO (Eds.): Scientia Herpetologica. – Barcelona (Societas Europaea Herpetologica/Asociación Herpetológica Española): 208-212.

CARTER (1993): Members letters. – British Chelonia Group Newsletter, 94: 5.

CASARES (1995): Untersuchungen zum Fortpflanzungsgeschehen bei Riesenschildkröten (Geochelone elephantopus und G. gigantea) und Landschildkröten (Testudo graeca und T. hermanni) anhand von Ultraschalldiagnostik und Steroidanalysen im Kot. – Der Zoologische Garten (N. F.), Jena, 65 (1): 50-76.

CASTA (1982): Les Agriates – Étude préalable à l'aménagement. – Ed. Ass. Amis Parc Nat. Régio. Corse et Conser. Esp. Litt. et Riv. Lac, 103 pp.

CASTANET & CHEYLAN (1979): Bone and scale growth marks as age indicators in Testudo hermanni and Testudo graeca (Reptilia, Chelonia, Testudinidae). – Canadian Journal of Zoology, Ottawa, 57 (8): 1649-1665.

CASTANET, MEUNIER & RICQLÈS (1977): L'enregistrement de la croissance cyclique par le tissu osseux chez les vertebrés poikilothermes – Données comparatives et essai de synthèse. – Bulletin Biologique de la France et de la Belgique, III (2): 183-202.

CEI (1943): Sopra una piccola raccolta erpetologica fatta dal Sig. L. CARDINI nei dintorni di Butrinto (Albania). – Soc. Trosc. Sci. Nat. Proc. Verb., Pisa, 52: 35-39.

CERNY (1959): Ein Beitrag zur Zeckenfauna Bulgariens. – Acta Acad. Sci. Cechoslov, Basis Brunensis, Brno, XXXI (7): 361-364.

CESARECCIO & LANZA (1984): Nuovi dati sull'erpetofauna dell'Arcipelago della Maddalena (Sardegna NE). – Boll. Soc. Sarda Sci. Nat., Sassari, 23: 137-143.

CHABANAUD (1920): Contribution à l'étude des Reptiles de France. – Bulletin de la Société Zoologique de France, Paris, 44: 287-289.

CHABANAUD (1925): La tortue grècque dans le Midi de la France. – Mém. 1er Congrès. Prot. Nat., Paris, 1923.

CHAPELLE & GILLES-BAILLIEN (1981): Variation in the lipids in the intestinal membranes of active and hibernating tortoises Testudo hermanni hermanni. – Biochemical Systematics and Ecology, 9 (2/3): 233-240.

CHAPMAN (1991): Excerpts from members' letters. – British Chelonia Group Newsletter, 80: 14.

CHAPMAN (1998): Hibernation temperature management in mild weather. – Tortoise Trust Newsletter, London, 13 (1): 13.

CHATELAIN-BURKHARDT (1989): Schildkröteneier auf dem Kühlschrank. – Das Tier, Leinfelden-Echterdingen, 30 (5): 55.

CHATFIELD (1987): Basic Nutrition and Feeding in Aquatic and Terrestrial Chelonia. – Testudo, 3 (1): 46-53.

CHATFIELD (1993): SOPTOM – the tortoise village. – British Chelonia Group Newsletter, 92: 3-4.

CHATFIELD (2000): Tortoises and the solar eclipse, 1999. – Testudo, 5 (2): 42-47.

CHELAZZI & CALZOLAI (1986): Thermal benefits from familiarity with the environment in a reptile. – Oecologia, 68 (4): 557-558.

CHELAZZI & CARLÀ (1986): Mechanisms allowing home range stability in Testudo hermanni GMELIN (Reptilia, Testudinidae). Field study and simulation. – Monitore Zoologico Italiano (N. S.), Florence, 20 (3): 349-370.

CHELAZZI & DELFINO (1986): A field test on the use of olfaction in homing by Testudo hermanni. – Journal of Herpetology, New Haven, 20 (3): 451-455.

CHELAZZI & FRANCISCI (1979): Movement patterns and homing behaviour of Testudo hermanni GMELIN (Reptilia, Testudinidae). – Monitore Zoologico Italiano (N. S.), Florence, 13 (2/3): 105-127.

CHELAZZI & FRANCISCI (1980): Homing in Testudo hermanni GMELIN. – Monitore Zoologico Italiano (N. S.), Florence, 14: 102.

CHELAZZI, CALFURNI, GRANDINETTI, CARLÀ, DELFINO & CALLONI (1981): Modification of homing behaviour in Testudo hermanni GMELIN (Reptilia, Testudinidae) after intranasal irrigation with zinc sulfate solution. – Monitore Zoologico Italiano (N. S.), Florence, 15: 306-307.

CHELIUS (1999): Aufgeschnappt – im wahrsten Sinne. – SIGS-Info, Siblingen, 8 (1): 29-30.

CHERCHI (1956): Termoregolazione in Testudo hermanni GMELIN. – Bolletino Musei Istituti Biol. Univ., Genua, 26: 5-46.

CHERCHI (1960a): Microvariazioni di temperatura in Testudo hermanni GMELIN. – Bolletino Musei Istituti Biol. Univ., Genua, 30: 15-50.

CHERCHI (1960b): Ulteriori ricerche sulla termoregolazione in Testudo hermanni GMELIN. – Bolletino Musei Istituti Biol. Univ., Genua, 30: 35-60.

CHERCHI & ARILLO (1964a): Resistenza di Testudo hermanni GMELIN a ipossia e suo comportamento cardiaco. – Bolletino Musei Istituti Biol. Univ., Genua: 95-107.

CHERCHI & ARILLO (1964b): Variazioni de quoziente respiratorio in Testudo hermanni GMELIN. – Bolletino Musei Istituti Biol. Univ., Genua: 127-148.

CHERCHI & ARILLO (1966): Considerazioni sulla capacita di resistenza de alcune specie di Testudinati all'ipossia. – Bolletino Musei Istituti Biol. Univ., Genua, **34** (209): 135-138

CHERCHI & ARILLO (1968): Effetti del monoiodoacetato dissodio su *Testudo hermanni* GMELIN trattata con una sostanza ipermetabolizzante. – Bolletino Zoologico, Rome, **35**: 445-446.

CHERCHI & BANDIERA (1961): Effetto delle variazioni di temperatura sull'elettrocardiogramma in *Testudo hermanni* GMELIN. – Bolletino Musei Istituti Biol. Univ., Genua, **31** (184):37-46.

CHERCHI, ARILLO & ACQUARONE (1966): Ipossia e variazioni del glicogeno in *Testudo hermanni* GMELIN (Nota 1 a). – Bolletino Musei Istituti Biol. Univ., Genua, **34**: 193-200.

CHERCHI, ARILLO & VALENTINI (1967): Note sul metabolismo anaerobio di *Testudo hermanni* GMELIN. – Bolletino Musei Istituti Biol. Univ., Genua, **35**: 101-104.

CHERCHI, BALLETTO & DEGUILI (1970): Biosintesi di acidi grassi in *Testudo hermanni* GMELIN sottoposta ad anossia (Nota II). – Bolletino Musei Istituti Biol. Univ., Genua, **38** (259): 19-25.

CHERCHI, BALLETTO & MELODIA (1972): Biosynthesis of L-levo-glycerol-1-phosphate in anoxic and high temperature stressed specimens of *Testudo hermanni*. – Bolletino Zoologico, Rome, **38** (4): 506.

CHERCHI, HOLZER, SCORTECCI & SERRATO (1958): Microvariazioni di temperatura in *Testudo hermanni* GMELIN. – Bolletino Musei Istituti Biol. Univ., Genua, **28**: 9-77.

CHERCHI, ARILLO, BALLETTO, MENSI & GAINO (1987): The seasonal cycle in tortoise mitochondria: evidence for a role in the control of circannual activity. – Bolletino Zoologico, Rome, **4**: 319-324.

CHEREPANOV (1985): Development of the horny shell in the Grecian tortoise. – Vestn. Leningr. Univ. Biol., Saint Petersburg, **1**: 22-28.

CHEYLAN (1973a): The genus *Testudo* in the Mediterranean basin. – Bulletin de la Société Zoologique de France, Paris, **98** (4): 594-595.

CHEYLAN (1973b): Les tortues préhistoriques de Boucoiran (Gard) preuve de l'indigénat de la tortue terrestre dans le sud de la France. – Bulletin de la Société des Études des Sciences Naturelles de Nîmes, Nîmes, **53**: 23-35.

CHEYLAN (1978): *Testudo hermanni*. – In: CASTANET (Ed.): Atlas Préliminaire des Reptiles et Amphibiens de France. – Montpellier (Société Herpétologique de France): 76.

CHEYLAN (1981a): Actual status and future of Hermann's Tortoise in western Europe. – 2nd European Chelonian Symposium, Oxford.

CHEYLAN (1981b): Biologie et écologie de la Tortue d'Hermann *Testudo hermanni* GMELIN, 1789 – Contribution de l'espèce à la connaissance des climats quaternaires de la France. – Mémoires et Travaux de l'Institut de Montpellier de l'Ecole Pratique des Hautes Etudes, Montpellier, **13**, 404 pp.

CHEYLAN (1983): Statut actuel des Reptiles et Amphibiens de l'archipel des îles d'Hyères (Var, S.E. de la France). – Trav. Sci. Parc Nation., Port-Cros, **9**: 35-51.

CHEYLAN (1984): The true status and future of Hermann's tortoise *Testudo hermanni robertmertensi* WERMUTH 1952 in Western Europe. – Amphibia-Reptilia, Leiden, **5** (1): 17-26.

CHEYLAN (1989): La Tortue. – In: CAMPS (Ed.): Terrina et le Terrinien, Recherches sur la chalcolithique de la Corse. – Rome (Ecole Fran₃aise de Rome, Palais Farnèse).

CHEYLAN (1992): La Tortue d'Hermann, *Testudo hermanni* GMELIN, 1789. – In: DELAUGERRE & CHEYLAN (Eds.): Atlas de répartition des batraciens et reptiles de Corse. – Pamplona & Paris (Parc Naturel Régional de Corse & École Pratique des Hautes Études): 43-46.

CHEYLAN (1995): Les tortues d'Hermann et cistude en Corse – Situation actuelle et mesures de sauvegarde. – In: BALLASINA (Ed.): Red Data Book on Mediterranean Chelonians. – Bologna (Edagricole): 69-93.

CHEYLAN (2001): *Testudo hermanni* GMELIN, 1789 – Griechische Landschildkröte. – In: FRITZ (Ed.): Handbuch der Reptilien und Amphibien Europas, Band 3/IIIA, Schildkröten (Testudines) I (Bataguridae, Testudinidae, Emydidae). – Wiebelsheim (Aula-Verlag): 179-289.

CHEYLAN, CONDAMINE, BOYER & MANIÈRE (1993): Plan d'action pour la protection des tortues d'Hermann et Cistude. – Aix en Provence (Espaces Naturels de Provence).

CHISZAR, TOMLINSON, SMITH, MURPHY & RADCLIFFE (1995): Behavioural consequences of husbandry manipulations: indicators of arousal, quiescence and environmental awareness. – In: WARWICK, FRYE & MURPHY (Eds.): Health and welfare of captive reptiles. – London (Chapman & Hall): 186-204.

CHKHIKVADZE (1970): O prois'chosdenii sowremennych suchoputnych cerepach paleoarktiki. – Soobsceniia Akademii Nauk Gruzinskoi SSR, Tiflis, **57** (1): 245-247.

CHKHIKVADZE (1973): Treticnye cerepachi Zajsanskoj kotlowiny. – Metzniereba, Tiflis, 100 pp.

CHKHIKVADZE (1983): Iskopajemyje cerepachi Kawkasa i Sewernogo Pricernomorja. – Metzniereba, Tiflis, 149 pp.

CHKHIKVADZE (1989): Neogenowyje cerepachi SSSR. – Metzniereba, Tiflis, 104 pp.

CHLEBICKI (1985): Some notes on the amphibians and reptiles in Sakar Mountains, Thrace, Greece. – Przegl. Zool., Warsaw, **29** (2): 193-198.

CHRISTEN (2005): Die posthibernale Anorexie – ein häufig gesehenes Problem in der Tierarztpraxis. – *Testudo* (SIGS), Wimmis, 14 (1): 5-8.

CHRISTIANSEN (1973): Iagttagelser og erfaringer med skildpadder i frilandsterrarium. – Nordisk Herpetologisk Forening, 16: 137-148.

CHRISTOPHEL (19??): Freude mit Terrarientieren. – Hamburg (Verlagsgesellschaft R. Glöss + Co.): 124-127.

CHRYSSOU (2000): From the Hellenic Wildlife Hospital. – Tortoise Trust Newsletter, London, 15 (2): 4.

CIHAR (1979): Taschenatlas der Terrarien. – Hanau (Verlag Werner Dausien): 100-101.

CIMATTI (2002a): Herpetofauna of Sardinia. – Reptilia (GB), Barcelona, 23: 60-64.

CIMATTI (2002b): Herpetofauna de Cerdeña – Reptilia (E), Barcelona, 36: 60-64.

CLARK (1967): Herpetofauna of the islands of the Argo-Saronic Gulf, Greece. – Proceedings of the California Academys of Sciences, San Francisco, 35 (2): 23-36.

CLARK (1970): A further contribution to the herpetological fauna of the islands of the Argo-Saronic Gulf, Greece. – British Journal of Herpetology, London, 4: 185-188.

CLARK (1972): New locality records for Greek reptiles. – British Journal of Herpetology, London, 4: 311-312.

CLARK (1989): A Check List of the Herpetofauna of the Argo-Saronic Gulf District, Greece. – British Herpetological Society Bulletin, London, 28: 8-24.

CLARK & CLARK (1973): Report on a collection of amphibians and reptiles from Turkey. – Occasional Papers of the California Academy of Sciences, San Francisco, 104: 1-62.

CLARO & BOURDEAU (1994): Tortues d'eau douce et tortues terrestres – élevage et soins. – Maisons-Alfort (Editions du Point Vétérinaire): 10, 14, 18-19, 29-30, 41, 44-45, 49-51, 53, 80, 89-95.

CLAUSEN (1981): Wurmbefall von Landschildkröten und Therapieversuche mit neueren Anthelminthika. – Dissertation, Univ. München, Munich.

VON CLAUSSEN & FORSTNER (1981): Untersuchungen über die Helminthen der Landschildkröten und Versuche zur medikamentellen Entwurmung. – Berliner und Münchener Tierärztliche Wochenschrift, Berlin & Munich, 94: 411-414.

COBB (1989): Tortues terrestres et aquatiques. – Lüttich (Humblet).

COBORN (1993): The Proper Care of Turtles. – Neptune City (T. F. H. Publications): 23, 218-219.

COBORN (1997): Turtles – Keeping & Breeding Them in Captivity. – Neptune City (T. F. H. Publications): 58-59.

COBORN (1998): Turtles yearBOOK. – Neptune City (yearBOOKS): 47-48.

COGALNICEANU & VENCZEL (1993): Considerations regarding the present status of amphibians and reptiles in Romania. – Ocrot. nat. med. înconj., Bukarest, 37 (2): 109-114.

COLBOURNE (1981): Hand feeding tortoises. – British Chelonia Group Newsletter, 24: 3.

COLEMAN (2000): Life in the cooler. – British Chelonia Group Newsletter, 138: 7-10.

COLLINS (1980a): The general husbandry of Mediterranean tortoises in captivity. – *Testudo*, 1 (3): 27-40.

COLLINS (1980b): The Captive Breeding of Mediterranean Tortoises in Britain. – In: TOWNSON, MILLICHAMP, LUCAS & MILLWOOD (Eds.): The Care and Breeding of Captive Reptiles. – London (British Herpetological Society); 21-36.

COLOM (1957): Biogeografia de las Baleares. – Palma de Mallorca, 568 pp.

COMPANYO (1863): Histoire naturelle du département des Pyrénées-orientales. – 3, Perpignan, 942 pp.

CONNOR (1993): Hermann's tortoise, *Testudo hermanni*. – the Tortuga Gazette, Van Nuys, 29 (8): 1-3.

CONNOR (1996): Hermann's tortoise *Testudo hermanni*. – Tortoise Trust Newsletter, London, 11 (2): 3-4.

COOPER (1983): Preliminary Studies on the Eggs of Three Species of Chelonians. – *Testudo*, 2 (2): 33-36.

COOPER (1994): Viral Diseases of Reptiles. – British Herpetological Society Bulletin, London, 47: 9-11.

COOPER (2000a): Tortoise news from other sources. – British Chelonia Group Newsletter, 134: 14-15.

COOPER (2000b): A happy ending for Homer. – British Chelonia Group Newsletter, 135: 10.

COOPER, GSCHMEISSNER & BONE (1988): Herpes-like virus particles in necrotic stomatitis of tortoises. – Journal of Comparative Pathology, 98: 117; The Veterinary Record, London, 123: 544.

COOPER, JACKSON & HARSHBARGER (1983): A neurilemmal sarcoma in a tortoise (*Testudo hermanni*). – Journal of Comparative Pathology, 93 (4): 541-546.

COOPER, LAWTON, JACOBSON & ZWART (1991): Deaths in tortoises. – The Veterinary Record, London, 128 (15): 364.

CORBETT (Ed.) (1989): Conservation of European reptiles and amphibians. – London (Christopher Helm), 274 pp.

CORBETT (1995): Protection of the herpetofauna. – Naturopa, Strasbourg, 79: 12-13.

CORBETTA & PETTENER (1976): Lineamenti vegetazionali del Bosco della Mesola. – Giornale Botanico Italiano, Florence, 110: 448-449.

CORSETTI & CAPULA (1992): The Amphibians and Reptiles of the Lepini Mountains (Latium, Central Italy): Checklist and provisional Atlas. – British Herpetological Society Bulletin, London, **39**: 8-16.

CORTI & ZUFFI (2003): Aspects of population ecology of *Testudo hermanni hermanni* from Asinara Island, NW Sardinia (Italy, western Mediterranean Sea) – preliminary data. – Amphibia-Reptilia, Leiden, **24** (4): 441-447.

CORTI, MASSETI & DELFINO (1997): The herpetofauna of anthropochorous origin of the Mediterranean islands. – In: ROCEK & HART (Eds.): Abstracts of the Third World Congress of Herpetology, Prague: 44.

CORTI, MASSETI, DELFINO & PEREZ-MELLADO (1999): Man and herpetofauna of the mediterranean islands. – Revista Española de Herpetología, Leganés, **13**: 83-100.

CORTI, NISTRI, POGGESI & VANNI (1991): Biogeographical analysis of the Tuscan herpetofauna (Central Italy). – Revista Española de Herpetología, Leganés, **5**: 51-75.

COSTA, NOUGARÈDE & CHEYLAN (2005): Les tortues de Porto-Vecchio. – Stantari, Ajaccio, **1** (1): 10-17.

COTTE (1909): Sur la ponte de *Testudo graeca*. – Bulletin de la Société Linnéenne de Provence, Marseille, **1**: 42.

COTTE (1912): Observations sur »*Testudo graeca*«. – Bulletin de la Société Linnéenne de Provence, Marseille, **1**: 58-59.

COTTE (1930): Indigénat de la tortue grecque en Provence. – Ann. Mus. Hist. Nat., Marseille, **22**: 83-93.

COUTARD (2005): Reproduction en captivité de la Tortue d'Hermann, *Testudo hermanni* GMELIN, 1789. – Manouria, Mezzavia, 27: 16-26.

COUTARD (2006): La sortie d'hibernation chez les tortues terrestres méditerranéennes. – Manouria, Mezzavia, 30: 2-3.

COUTARD (2006): L'accouplement chez les tortues terrestres méditerranéennes. – Manouria, Mezzavia, 30: 4-6.

COUTARD (2006): La ponte chez les tortues terrestres méditerranéennes. – Manouria, Mezzavia, 30: 7-9.

CRAMP & SIMMONS (1980): Handbook of the Birds of Europe, the Middle East and North Africa – Volume 2 – Hawks to Bustards. – Oxford (Oxford University Press), 695 pp.

CRNOBRNJA-ISAILOVIC & DZUKIC (1995): First report about conservation status of herpetofauna in the Lake Skadar region (Montenegro): Current situation and perspectives. – In: LLORENTE, MONTORI, SANTOS & CARRETERO (Eds.): Scientia Herpetologica. – Proceedings of the 7th Ordinary General Meeting of S.E.H. in Barcelona 1993. – Barcelona (Asociación Herpetológica): 373-380.

CROSS (1978): Unwanted tortoises discarded. – British Chelonia Group Newsletter, 11: 2.

CROSS (1979): The rearing of hatchling European tortoises – *Testudo hermanni* and *Testudo graeca*. – Testudo, **1** (2): 21-22.

CROUDACE (1989): The Husbandry, Management and Reproduction of the European Tortoises *Testudo graeca* and *T. hermanni*. – Testudo, **3** (1): 25-44.

CRUCE (1978): Structure et dynamique d'une population de *Testudo hermanni hermanni* GMEL. (Reptilia). – Trav. Mus. Hist. Nat. »Grigore Antipa«, Bucarest, **19**: 325-328.

CRUCE & NIEUWENHUYS (1974): The cell masses in the brain stem of the turtle *Testudo hermanni* – a topographical and topological analysis. – The Journal of Comparative Neurology, **156** (3): 277-306.

CRUCE & RADUCAN (1975): Activity cycle in the land tortoise (*Testudo hermanni hermanni* GMEL.). – Rev. Roum. Biol., Sér. Biol. Anim., Bucarest, **20** (4): 285-289.

CRUCE & RADUCAN (1976): Reproducerea la broasca testoasa de uscat (*Testudo hermanni hermanni* G.). – Stud. Cercet. Biol., Ser. Biol. Anim., Bucarest, **28** (2): 175-180.

CRUCE & SERBAN (1971): Contributii la studiul broastei testoase de uscat (*Testudo hermanni hermanni* G.). – Stud. si Cercet. Subcom. mon. nat. Dolj, Bukarest: 179-184.

CRUCITTI & TRINGALI (1986): The genus *Testudo* in Greece (Reptilia, Testudines, Testudinidae). – Istituto Lombardo Accademia di Scienze e Lettere, Rendiconti Chimiche e Fisiche, Geologiche, Biologiche e Mediche, B, **120**: 27-44.

CRUMLY & SÁNCHEZ-VILLAGRA (2004): Patterns of Variation in the Phalangeal Formulae of Land Tortoises (Testudinidae): Developmental Constraint, Size, and Phylogenetic History. – Journal of Experimental Zoology (Molecular and developmental evolution), **302B**: 134-146.

CSIKI (1923): Explanations zoologieae in Albanie peraetae. – Budapest.

CUNNINGHAM (2000): Emerging infectious diseases and amphibian declines. – Proceedings of the British Veterinary Zoological Society, London: 35-37.

CYRÉN (1909): Herpetologisches von einer Balkanreise. – Zoologischer Beobachter (Zoologischer Garten), Frankfurt am Main, **50**: 265-271, 295-300.

CYRÉN (1935): Herpetologisches vom Balkan. – Blätter für Aquarien- und Terrarienkunde, Stuttgart, **46**: 129-135.

CYRÉN (1941): Beitrag zur Herpetologie der Balkanhalbinsel. – Bull. Inst. R. Hist. Nat., Sofia, **14**: 36-125.

DÄMMRICH (1967): Pathomorphologische Befunde am Panzer der Schildkröten. – Verhandlungsbericht über Erkrankungen der Zootiere, **9**: 271-274.

DÄMMRICH (1985): Bewegungsorgane – Knochen, Gelenke und Skelett. – In: IPPEN, SCHRÖDER & ELZE

(Eds.): Handbuch der Zootierkrankheiten, Band 1, Reptilien. – Berlin (Akademie-Verlag): 215-240.

DANI (1970): Fauna e amfibëve në Myzeqe. – Bul. Shkenc. Nat, Tirana, 1: 39-43.

DANILOV (2005): Die fossilen Schildkröten Europas. – In: FRITZ (Ed.): Handbuch der Reptilien und Amphibien Europas, Band 3/IIIB, Schildkröten (Testudines) II (Cheloniidae, Dermochelyidae, Fossile Schildkröten Europas). – Wiebelsheim (Aula-Verlag): 329-419.

DASZAK & CAWTHRAW (1991): A Review of the Reptiles and Amphibians on Turkey, including a Literature Survey and Species Checklist. – British Herpetological Society Bulletin, London, 36: 14-26.

DATZBERGER (2005): Schildkröten in Athen. – Sacalia, Stiefern, 3 (8): 43-45.

DAUBNER (2001): Wissenschaftliche Untersuchung zur Fotodokumentation von Jungtieren in den ersten Lebensjahren. – Schildkröten, Linden, 8 (4): 25-29.

DAUM (1998): Europäische Landschildkröten. – Hannover (Landbuch-Verlag): 9, 16-22, 32, 42, 47-48, 50, 52, 55, 59-60.

DAUNER (1988): Tortues Terrestres et Aquatiques. – Paris (Editions de Vecchi S. A.): 113, 120.

DAVENPORT (1995): Regeneration of the Tail Spur in Testudo hermanni Part Two. – Testudo, 4 (2): 79-80.

DAVID (1976): Chirurgische Intervention bei einer Torsio oviducti sin. einer Griechischen Landschildkröte (Testudo hermanni); Kleintier-Praxis, 21: 57-59

DAVID (1994): Liste des reptiles actuels du monde – I – Chelonii. – Dumerilia, Paris, 1: 46.

DAVIS (1984): Feral tortoises – (again). – British Chelonia Group Newsletter, 42: 7.

DAVYDOVA & GONCHAROVA (1978): Comparative analysis of neuronal and synaptic organization of the mesencephalic visual center in the Grecian tortoise and Horsfield's terrapin. – Arkh. Anat. Gistol. Embriol., Moscow, 75 (12): 40-45

DECKERT, DECKERT, FREYTAG, GÜNTHER, PETERS & STERBA (1991): Urania Tierreich – Fische-Lurche-Kriechtiere. – Leipzig, Jena & Berlin (Urania-Verlag): 488-490.

DEFLEUR, BEZ, CRÉGUT-BONNOURE, DESCLAUX, ONORATINI, RADULESCU, THINON & VILETTE (1994): Le niveau moustérien de la grotte de l'Adaouste (Jouques, Bouches-le-Rhne) – Approche culturelle et paléoenvironnements. – Bulletin du musée d'Anthropologie préhistorique de Monaco, Monaco, 37: 11-48.

DELAUGERRE (1988): Les amphibiens et les reptiles de la montagne corse: le massif du Monte Cinto. – Travaux Scinetifiques du Parc Naturel Régional du Corse, Ajaccio, 14: 1-29.

DELAUGERE & CHEYLAN (1992): Atlas de répartition des Batraciens et Reptiles de Corse. – Ajaccio (Parc. Natur. Rég. Corse, Ecole Pratique des Hautes Etudes), 128 pp.

DELFINO (1997): Italian Palaeoherpetofauna Database: Neogene-Quaternary. – In: Abstracts of the 3rd World Congress of Herpetology, Prague: 51-52.

DELFINO, BIGAZZI & CHELAZZI (1986): Olfactory mucosa of Testudo hermanni GMELIN (Reptilia, Testudinidae) occurrence of paracrystalline inclusions in supporting cells. – Zeitschrift für Mikroskopisch-Anatomische Forschung, Leipzig, 100 (6): 867-880.

DELLBRÜGGER (2001): Überwinterung von Testudo hermanni boettgeri im Freiland. – Schildkrötenfreunde intern, Gelsenkirchen, 4 (1): 4-11.

DELLBRÜGGER (2002a): Nagerüberfall. – Vereinszeitschrift der Schildkrötenfreunde Horst, Gelsenkirchen, 1: 7-9.

DELLBRÜGGER (2002b): Illegale Jagd im Pinios-Delta oder ein klarer Fall von Amtsmissbrauch. – Vereinszeitschrift der Schildkrötenfreunde Horst, Gelsenkirchen, 1: 26-29.

DELLBRÜGGER (2003): Jahrestagung AG Schildkröten. – Turtle-News, 1: 5-12.

DELORME (1995): Les tortues de nos jardins et bassins. – Gerona (Jeanne Delorme).

DEMETROPULOS & HADJICHRISTOPHOROU (1982): Chelonians of Cyprus. – Biological Society of Cyprus, Bulletin No. 1, Nikosia.

DEMETROPULOS & HADJICHRISTOPHOROU (1995): Distribution of Chelonians. – In: BALLASINA (Ed.): Red Data Book on Mediterranean Chelonians. – Bologna (Edagricole): 21-23.

DENNERT (1997): Untersuchung zur Fütterung von Schuppenechsen und Schildkröten. – Dissertation, Tierärztliche Hochschule Hannover, 189 pp.

DENNERT (1999): Ernährung Europäischer Landschildkröten. – Reptilia (D), Münster, 17: 32-39, 18: 51-58.

DENNERT (2000a): Verwendung von Heucobs als Ergänzungsfutter für Landschildkröten. – elaphe (N. F.), Rheinbach, 8 (2): 23-24.

DENNERT (2000b): Verwendung von Heucobs als Ergänzungsfutter für Landschildkröten. – Draco, Münster, 2: 52-55.

DENNERT (2000c): Die Entwurmung der Landschildkröte vor dem Winterschlaf. – Radiata, Haan, 9 (3): 20-22.

DENNERT (2001): Ernährung von Landschildkröten. – Münster (Natur und Tier-Verlag): 9, 28-29, 33, 52, 64, 70-71, 93, 96-96, 98-99, 109, 115.

DENNERT (2004): Was Sie beim Kauf einer Landschildkröte beachten sollten. – Schildkröten im Fokus, Bergheim, 1 (2): 30-34.

DEPERET (1906): Los vertebrados del Oligoceno inferior de Torrega (Prov. de Lerida). – Memorias de la Real Academia de Ciencias y Artes de Barcelona, Barcelona, Ser. 3, 5 (21): 1-31.

DESPOTT (1918): Excavations conducted at Ghar Dalam (Malta) in the summer of 1917. – Journal of the Royal Anthropological Institute, London, 48: 214-221.

DEVAUX (1988): Le centre de repeuplement des tortues d'Hermann. – Courrier de la Nature, Paris, 115: 16-21.

DEVAUX (1990): Réintroduction de tortues d'Hermann (Testudo hermanni hermanni) dans le Massif des Maures. – Revue d'Ecologie (Terre et Vie), Supplément 5: 291-297.

DEVAUX (1992a): Tortues françaises et méditerranéennes. – Annales S.S.N.A.T.V., Toulon, 44: 275-277.

DEVAUX (1992b): L'Autoroute A57 – des engagements tenus. – La Tortue, Gonfaron, 19: 5-7.

DEVAUX (1992c): 7.000 Tortues sous la terre ... – La Tortue, Gonfaron, 19: 8-11.

DEVAUX (1992d): Du nouveaux chez les Testudo. – La Tortue, Gonfaron, 21: 3-4.

DEVAUX (1992e): Les mystères de »l'adaptologie«. – La Tortue, Gonfaron, 21: Essai, 7 pp.

DEVAUX (1993): Différenciation des Testudo. – La Tortue, Gonfaron, 24: 4-10.

DEVAUX (1994a): Des hauts et des bas. – La Tortue, Gonfaron, 25: 1.

DEVAUX (1994b): Monstres et curiosités. – La Tortue, Gonfaron, 26: 3-6.

DEVAUX (1995): Les Tortues. – Paris (Éditions Sang de la terre), 189 pp.

DEVAUX (1996a): Fin de règne?. – La Tortue, Gonfaron, 32/33: 2.

DEVAUX (1996b): La croissance. – La Tortue, Gonfaron, 36: 4-9.

DEVAUX (1997a): Ten years of conservation of Testudo hermanni in France – evaluation and results. – Abstracts of the 3rd World Congress of Herpetology: 52-53.

DEVAUX (1997b): BERNARD PALISSY au Louvre. – La Tortue, Gonfaron, 38: 8-11.

DEVAUX (1997c): A propos de réintroduction. – La Tortue, Gonfaron, 40: 4-11.

DEVAUX (1998a): La Tortue Martyre. – Gonfaron (Editions SOPTOM): 18-19, 46, 203, 210-213, 216, 220.

DEVAUX (1998b): La passion des tortues. – Paris (Éditions Sang de la terre), 214 pp.

DEVAUX (1999a): La tortue sauvage ou tortue d'Hermann. – Paris (Éditions Sang de la terre), 182 pp.

DEVAUX (1999b): Terrariophile ou terrariophobe?. – La Tortue, Gonfaron, 45: 7-12.

DEVAUX (1999c): Un concept neuf – le Village des Tortues. – La Tortue, Gonfaron, 45: 13-14.

DEVAUX (1999d): Risques et Conservation. – La Tortue, Gonfaron, 48: 44-47.

DEVAUX (2000a): Le Panda sort ses griffes. – La Tortue, Gonfaron, 49: 34-37.

DEVAUX (2000b): Entropie et conservation. – La Tortue, Gonfaron, 50/51: 2.

DEVAUX (2000c): Pour ou contre les N.A.C. – La Tortue, Gonfaron, 50/51: 50-55.

DEVAUX (2001a): L'Hibernation des Tortues. – Gonfaron (Editions SOPTOM): 1-3, 5-17, 19-28.

DEVAUX (2001b): L'arbre à palabres. – La Tortue, Gonfaron, 55: 46-49.

DEVAUX (2001c): David Stubbs – La fidélité. – La Tortue, Gonfaron, 56: 6-11.

DEVAUX (2001d): Aux Pays-Bas, un centre de soins exemplaire!. – La Tortue, Gonfaron, 56: 60-61.

DEVAUX (2002): Symbolisme et figuration des chéloniens, et plus particulièrement du genre Testudo. – Chelonii, Gonfaron, 3: 28-31.

DEVAUX (2003a): Incendies et Déraison. – La Tortue, Gonfaron, 63/64: 3.

DEVAUX (2003b): Brände und Schildkrötenschutz in der Provence. – Radiata, Lingenfeld, 13 (4): 23-29.

DEVAUX (2004a): Devoir de mémoire. – La Tortue, Gonfaron, 67: 3.

DEVAUX (2004b): La tortue du Péloponnèse. Une espèce très fragile. – La Tortue, Gonfaron, 67: 8-17.

DEVAUX (2004c): JEAN HERMANN. – La Tortue, Gonfaron, 67: 70-71.

DEVAUX (2005a) Bonne année pour la tortue d'Hermann. – La Tortue, 71/72: 3.

DEVAUX (2005b): SOPTOM – Station d'Observation et de Protection des Tortues des Maures. – Minor, Lingenfeld, 4 (3): 23-25.

DEVAUX & MADEC (1998): Plan de conservation pour les tortues des Albères. – La Tortue, Gonfaron, 42: 4-9.

DEVAUX & STUBBS (1997): Species Recovery Programme for Hermann's Tortoise in Southern France. – In: VAN ABBEMA (Ed.): Proceedings – Conservation, Restoration, and Management of Tortoises and Turtles – An International Conference. – New York (New York Turtle and Tortoise Society): 330-332.

DEVAUX, POUVREAU & STUBBS (1986): Programme de sauvegarde de la tortue d'Hermann dans le Massif des Maures (France). – La Station d'Observation et de Protection des Tortues des Maures, Gonfaron.

DE VILLENEUVE (1821): Statistique du département des Bouches-du-Rhne. – Marseille (Ricard, Marseille), 944 pp.

DIESENER & REICHHOLF (1995): Lurche und Kriechtiere. – Munich (Mosaik Verlag), 288 pp.

DIESSELHORST & FECHTER (1981): Knaurs Tierleben von A-Z. – Gütersloh (Bertelsmann-Club): 353

DIESSENBACH (1986): Testudo hermanni in Jugoslawien. – Die Schildkröte (N. F.), Heinsberg, 1 (1/2): 25-29.

DIETHELM (2002): Tagebuch einer Griechenlandreise. – Testudo (SIGS), Wimmis, 11 (1): 10-20.

DIETIKER & HERZOG (2000): Heiri oder Henriette? – SIGS-Info, Siblingen, 9 (4): 25-26.

DIETRICH (1996): Betr.»Winterkatastrophe bei Landschildkröten«. – DATZ, Stuttgart, 49 (10): 675.

VAN DIJK (2004): CITES Handelsregulierungen für Schildkröten – Hilfe oder Hindernis für den Artenschutz? – Schildkröten im Fokus, Bergheim, 1 (4): 19-28.

DIMOV (1965): Über die Dauer der fäkalen Salmonellenausscheidung bei den Landschildkröten der Gattung Testudo graeca und Testudo hermanni. – Zeitschrift für Hygiene und Infektionskrankheiten, medizinische Mikrobiologie, Immunologie und Virologie, Berlin, Göttingen & Heidelberg, 151: 326-330.

DIMOV (1966a): Versuche, Landschildkröten der Arten Testudo graeca und Testudo hermanni mit Salmonella-Bakterien zu infizieren. – Zentralblatt für Bakteriologie, I. Abteilung Originale, Stuttgart, 199: 181-184

DIMOV (1966b): Die Verbreitung der fäkalen Salmonella- und Arizona-Dauerausscheidung bei den freilebenden Schildkröten Testudo graeca und Testudo hermanni. – Zeitschrift für medizinische und mikrobiologische Immunologie, 152: 198-203.

DIMOV (1966c): Über den Charakter der fäkalen Arizona-Dauerausscheidung bei den Landschildkröten Testudo graeca und Testudo hermanni. – Zeitschrift für medizinische und mikrobiologische Immunologie, 152: 204-210.

DIMOV (1966d): Über den Charakter der fäkalen Salmonella-Dauerausscheidung bei den Landschildkröten Testudo graeca und Testudo hermanni. – Zentralblatt für Bakteriologie, I. Abteilung Originale, Stuttgart, 201: 201-206.

DIMOV (1968): Die epidemiologische Bedeutung der Ausscheidung von Salmonellabakterien bei Reptilien. – Zentralblatt für Bakteriologie, I. Abteilung Originale, Stuttgart, 214: 627-634.

DIMOV & ROHDE (1965): Die Verbreitung der Arizona-Bakterien unter den freilebenden Landschildkröten der Arten Testudo graeca und Testudo hermanni. – Zeitschrift für Hygiene und Infektionskrankheiten, medizinische Mikrobiologie, Immunologie und Virologie, Berlin, Göttingen & Heidelberg, 151: 107-110.

DIMOV, WESSELNIKOFF & ROHDE (1961): Salmonellenbefall von Landschildkröten (Testudo graeca) in Bulgarien I. – Zeitschrift für Hygiene und Infektionskrankheiten, medizinische Mikrobiologie, Immunologie und Virologie, Berlin, Göttingen & Heidelberg, 148: 135-141.

DIMOVSKI (1959): Prilog kon herpetofauna na Makedonija. I. – Fragmenta Balcanica, Skopje, 3 (1): 1-4.

DIMOVSKI (1963): Herpetofauna na Skopska kotlina. I. Zoogeografski i ekoloski pregled. – Godisen zbornik, Biologija, Skopje, 14 (12): 188-224.

DIMOVSKI (1964): Prilog kon herpetofauna na Makedonija. II. – Fragmenta Balcanica, Skopje, 5 (4): 19-22.

DINKEL (1979): Auf Schildkrötenjagd in Griechenland. – herpetofauna, Weinstadt, 3: 6-7.

DIVERS (1995): Gastro-Intestinal Nematode Parasites of Mediterranean Tortoises. – Reptilian Magazine, 4 (7): 47-50.

DIVERS (1996a): The structure and disease of the Chelonia Shell. – Reptiles Magazine, Boulder, 13: 51-56.

DIVERS (1996b): Certain Aspects of the Veterinary Care of Chelonia. – Testudo, 4 (3): 21-32.

DIVERS (1997): Thermoregulation in Chelonia. – British Chelonia Group Newsletter, 118: 13-15.

DIVERS (1998): Emergency care of the critically ill tortoise. – Testudo, 4 (5): 16-27.

DODSON (1980): My experience of reptiles and how I started to keep chelonians. – British Chelonia Group Newsletter, 19: 11-13.

DOLDER (1997): Tiere sehen dich an. – Bergisch Gladbach (HONOS Verlagsgesellschaft): 140-141.

DONHAUSER (1997): Blutreferenzwerte Europäischer Landschildkröten (Testudo hermanni, Testudo graeca, Testudo marginata, Agrionemys horsfieldi). – Dissertation, Ludwig-Maximilians-Univ., Munich.

DONOGHUE (1996): Nutrition of the tortoise. – Proceedings of the Association of Reptilian and Amphibian Veterinarians, Chester Heights: 21-30.

DORIA & SALVIDIO (Eds.) (1994): Atlante degli Anfibi e Rettili della Liguria. – Cataloghi dei beni naturali N°2, Mus. civ. Stor. Nat., Genua, 151 pp.

DOTTRENS (1963): Batraciens et Reptiles d'Europe. – Neuchâtel (Delachaux & Niestlé), 261 pp.

DOWLER & BICKHAM (1982): Chromosomal relationships of the tortoises (family Testudinidae). – Genetica, Dordrecht, 58: 189-197.

DRAAIJER & DRAAIJER (2002): Populaire pagina's. Zomaar een verhaaltje van een paar 'schildpaddengenieters'. – De Schildpad, Eindhoven, 28 (6): 280-283.

DRAAIJER & DRAAIJER (2004): De pen van ... GERARD en IRENE DRAAIJER. – Trionyx, Eindhoven, 2 (6): 180-183.

DRENSKI (1924): Nos et étrangers Reptiles au Musée Royal Priroda. – Sofia, XXV (3): 37-39.

DRENSKI (1934): La faune des régions de Lovec et de Trojan. – Lovec i Lovcansko, Sofia, VI: 107-125.

DRENSKI (1955): Artbestand und Verbreitung der Zecken (Ixodoidea) in Bulgarien (im Hinblick auf ihre medizinische und tierärztliche Bedeutung). – Bull. Inst. Zool., Sofia, IV/V: 109-168.

DREWES (2002): Faszination Terraristik. – Wachtberg-Berkum (Wachtberg Verlag): 136-139, 355, 394.

VON DEN DRIESCH & BOESSNECK (1990): Die Tierreste von der mykenischen Burg Tiryns bei Nauplion/Peloponnes. – In: JANTZEN (Ed.): Tiryns. Forschungen und Berichte. – Mainz, 11: 116.

DRIGGERS (2001): Causes and Prevention of URTD in Grazing Tortoises. – the Tortuga Gazette, Van Nuys, 37 (1): 4-5, 9.

DRURY (2000): Viruses, herpesviruses, and the detection of herpesvirus infections in tortoises. – Testudo, 5 (2): 4-12.

DRURY, GOUGH, McARTHUR & JESSOP (1998): Detection of herpevirus-like and papillomavirus-like particles associated with diseases of tortoises. – The Veterinary Record, London, 143: 639.

DUBBELDAM (1978): Geslaagde kweek van Griekse landschildpad, Testudo hermanni. – Lacerta, Zoetermeer, 36 (5): 68-71.

DUBBELDAM (1982): Testudo hermanni, de Griekse landschildpad. – Lacerta, Zoetermeer, 40 (10/11): 264-266.

DUCKWORTH (1984): Notes from Hereford. – British Chelonia Group Newsletter, 41: 6-7.

DUCOTTERD (1996): Maintenance des tortues terrestres européennes – les serres de jardins. – CITS bulletin, Bramois, 6: 15-18.

DUCOTTERD (1997): Protection et récupération des tortues de Chavornay (PRT) inaugure ses bassins d'acclimatation. – CITS bulletin, Bramois, 8: 12-14.

DUCOTTERD (1999a): Conseils sur l'hibernation. – Manouria, Mezzavia, 4: 10-13.

DUCOTTERD (1999b): Sortie d'hibernation – un moment difficile. – Manouria, Mezzavia, 5: 9-12.

DÜHR (1995): Legen Sie die Schildkröteneier in einen Brutkasten. – Ein Herz für Tiere, Ismaning, 6: 26-27.

DUMAS (2002): L'insertion écologique de l'autoroute. – Chelonii, Gonfaron, 3: 324.

DUMÉRIL & BIBRON (1835): Erpétologie générale ou Histoire naturelle complète des Reptiles. II. – Paris (Roret), 2, II + 680 pp.

DUMONT (1972): Les chéloniens de France – Leur avenir, leur protection. – Naturaliste Orléanais, Orléans, 3 (5): 10-12.

DUMONT (1974): Les chéloniens de France – Leur avenir, leur protection. – Courrier de la Nature, Paris, 33: 224-227.

DUMONT (1979): Halte aux importations des tortues. – Courrier de la Nature, Paris, 61: 20-22.

DUMOULIN (1992): Die Chelys – Ein altgriechisches Saiteninstrument. – Archiv für Musikwissenschaft, Berlin, 49, 2/3: 85, 225.

DUMOULIN (1994): Antike Schildkröten. – Würzburg (Verlag Königshausen & Neumann): 1, 3-6, 12-14, 16-19, 89, 155-158.

DUPRÉ (1995): Les tortues de Vienne. – La Tortue, Gonfaron, 30: 28-29.

DUPRÉ (1997): Les tortues au Louvre. – La Tortue, Gonfaron, 38: 4-7.

DUPRÉ (1998): »Qui va piano, va sano«. – La Tortue, Gonfaron, 41: 26-29.

DURHAM (1997): Albanian tortoises. – In: McNAMEE & URREA (Eds.): A World of Turtles. – Boulder (Johnson Books): 68-69.

DURRELL (1956): My Family and Other Animals. – Harmondsworth (Penguin books): 52-55.

DZUKIC (1972): Herpetoloska zbirka Prirodnajackog muzeja u Beogradu. – Glasnik Prir. muz., Belgrade, Ser. B, 27: 165-180.

DZUKIC (1974): Prilog herpetofauni Srbije. – Glasnik Prir. muz., Belgrade, Ser. B, 29: 105-110.

DZUKIC (1991): Fauna Durmitora, 4: Vodozemci i gmizavci. Gradja za faunu vodozemaca i gmizavaca Durmitora (Amphibia-Reptilia). – Crnog. Akad. Nauk. Umet. Pos. Izd., knj. 24, Odelj. prir. nauk., knj. 15, Podgorica: 9-78.

DZUKIC (1995): Diverzitet vodozemaca (Amphibia) i gmizavaca (Reptilia) Jugoslavije sa pregledom vrsta od medjunarodnog znacaja. – In: STEVANOVIC & VASIC (Eds.): Biodiverzitet Jugoslavije sa pregledon vrsta od medjunarodnog znacaja. – Bioloski fakultet i Ecolibri, Belgrade: 447-469.

DZUKIC & KALEZIC (2001): The Biodiversity of Amphibians and Reptiles in the Balkan Peninsula. – In: GRIFFITHS, KRYSTUFEK & GRIFFITHS (EDS.): Balkan Biodiversity, Papers from the ESF Exploratory Workshop on Balkan Biodiversity, Koper, September 2001. – Amsterdam (Kluwer).

DZUKIC, KALEZIC, PETKOVSKI & SIDOROVSKA (2001): General remarks on batracho- and herpetofauna of the Balkan Peninsula. – In: BOSKOVA (ED.): 75 years Maced. Mus. of Nat. Hist., Skopje (Prirodonaucen Muzei na Makedonija): 195-204.

EADE (1886): Tortoises. – Transactions of the Norfolk and Norwich Naturalists' Society, 4: 316-322.

EADY (1990a): Egg laying with a difference. – British Chelonia Group Newsletter, 74: 8.

EADY (1990b): A bumper year for tortoise eggs. – British Chelonia Group Newsletter, 76: 4-6.

EADY (1992): Some general suggestions for good tortoise husbandry. – British Chelonia Group Newsletter, 88: 2-3.

EADY (1993): Second generation. – British Chelonia Group Newsletter, 93: 7.

EADY (1997): Alternative method for hibernating Testudo graeca ibera, T. hermanni and T. marginata. – British Chelonia Group Newsletter, 115: 17-18.

EADY (1998a): Some observations on the durability of Mediterranean tortoise eggs. – British Chelonia Group Newsletter, 122: 9.

EADY (1998b): Members' letters. – British Chelonia Group Newsletter, 123: 18.

EADY (1999): Members' letters. – British Chelonia Group Newsletter, 127: 8-9.

EATWELL (2005): Seasonal and gender variation in serum levels of isolated calcium and 25-hydroxycholercaciferol in Testudo species. – Exotic DVM Veterinary Magazine, 7 (4): 17-22.

EBNER (1913): Beiträge zur Herpetologie von Griechenland. – Verhandlungen der zoologisch-botanischen Gesellschaft Wien, 63: 307-314.

EDEL (1997): Asyl für Exoten. – Leinfelden-Echterdingen, 38 (8): 38-39.

VAN DEN EECKHOUDT (1954): Quelques aspects de la faune provencale. – Naturalistes Belges, Rhode-Sainte-Genèse, 35 (4/5): 81-103.

EENDEBAK (1988): De Griekse landschildpad (Testudo hermanni) in het buitenterrarium. – Lacerta, Zoetermeer, 49: 87-90.

EENDEBAK (1995): Incubation period and sex ratio of Hermann's tortoise Testudo hermanni boettgeri. – Chelonian Conservation and Biology, Lunenburg, 1 (2): 227-231.

EENDEBAK (2001): Testudo hermanni boettgeri and Testudo marginata – A sustainable breeding program. – International Turtle & Tortoise Symposium, Vienna, Austria, January 17-20, 2002, Final Program with Abstracts: 53.

EENDEBAK (2002): Incubation period and sex ratio of Testudo hermanni boettgeri. – Chelonii, Gonfaron, 3: 257-267.

EENDEBAK (2006): Testudo hermanni boettgeri and Testudo marginata, a sustainable breeding program. – In: ARTNER, FARKAS & LOEHR (Eds.): Turtles. Proceedings: International Turtle & Tortoise Symposium Vienna 2002. – Frankfurt am Main (Edition Chimaira): 531-539.

EGER (2005): Gemeinsame Haltung von Testudo hermanni boettgeri und Testudo (hermanni) hercegovinensis – Erfahrungen eines Züchters über einen längeren Zeitraum und Auswertung der Nachzuchtdaten. – Schildkröten im Fokus, Bergheim, 2 (2): 25-30.

EGGENSCHWILER (1992): Die Ost- und Westrasse der Griechischen Landschildkröte. – SIGS-Info, Siblingen, 1 (3): 15-17.

EGGENSCHWILER (1993a): Eggi's Leserseite. – SIGS-Info, Siblingen, 2 (2): 12-13.

EGGENSCHWILER (1993b): Unterschiede zwischen Testudo graeca und Testudo hermanni. – SIGS-Info, Siblingen, 2 (2): 13-15.

EGGENSCHWILER (1994a): Der Tierschutz und die Schildkröte – Wo bleibt die Lobby?. – SIGS-Info, Siblingen, 3 (3): 22-25.

EGGENSCHWILER (1994b): Vergleich der Körpertemperaturen zwischen der Griechischen Landschildkröte (Testudo hermanni) und der Breitrandschildkröte (Testudo marginata) in ihrem natürlichen Biotop. – SIGS-Info, Siblingen, 3 (4): 5-7.

EGGENSCHWILER (1995): Die Ost- und Westrasse der Griechischen Landschildkröte. – Emys, Sankt Pölten, 2 (5): 12-14.

EGGENSCHWILER (1996a): Die Legenot der Schildkröte. – Emys, Sankt Pölten, 3 (3): 15-17.

EGGENSCHWILER (1996b): Die Landschildkröten in der tierärztlichen Praxis. – Siblingen (privately printed): 6, 21, 56.

EGGENSCHWILER (1996c): Die Vorbereitung und Durchführung des Winterschlafes. – SIGS-Info, Siblingen, 5 (3): 19-23.

EGGENSCHWILER (1997a): Über die Ernährung von pflanzenfressenden Landschildkröten – Der Einfluss auf Wachstum und Entwicklung. – SIGS-Info, Siblingen, 4 (2): 25-31.

EGGENSCHWILER (1997b): Über die Ernährung von pflanzenfressenden Landschildkröten. – Schildkröten, Linden, 4 (3): 20-27.

EGGENSCHWILER (1998a): Die Ernährung von Landschildkröten. – Merkblatt 6, SIGS, 4 pp.

EGGENSCHWILER (1998b): Winterschlaf Europäischer Landschildkröten. – Merkblatt 7, SIGS, 4 pp.

EGGENSCHWILER (1998c): Frühjahrserwachen europäischer Landschildkröten. – Fachmagazin Schildkröte, Rothenfluh, 1 (1): 52-54.

EGGENSCHWILER (1998d): Bebrütung von Eiern von mediterranen Landschildkröten. – SIGS-Info, Siblingen, 5 (2): 25-27.

EGGENSCHWILER (1998e): Todesfälle bei Schildkröten. – SIGS-Info, Siblingen, 5 (3): 3-10.

EGGENSCHWILER (1998f): Bissverletzung bei einer jungen Griechischen Landschildkröte. – SIGS-Info, Siblingen, 5 (3): 31-32.

EGGENSCHWILER (1999): Die verflixte Jackson Kurve. – SIGS-Info, Siblingen, 6 (1): 34-39.

EGGENSCHWILER (2000a): Wärme – wieviel, wie und warum. – SIGS-Info, Siblingen, 6 (2): 27.

EGGENSCHWILER (2000b): Die Schildkröte in der tierärztlichen Praxis. – Siblingen (Schöneck Verlag): 5-6, 15, 19, 21-22, 35-36, 47, 62, 76, 81, 83-84, 86, 91-92, 97, 101, 107-108, 115, 119, 122, 125.

EGGENSCHWILER (2001): Wie erkenne ich, ob meine Schildkröte gesund ist? – SIGS-Info, Siblingen, 7 (4): 4-11.

EGGENSCHWILER (2004a): Respiratory Diseases in Turtles – Recognition, treatment,and prevention. – Reptilia (GB), Barcelona, 34: 70-73.

EGGENSCHWILER (2004b): Patologías respiratorias en tortugas. Diagnóstico, tratamiento y profilaxis. – Reptilia (E), Barcelona, 47: 10-14.

EGGENSCHWILER & HERSCHE (1995): Aufzucht von europäischen und aus dem Mittelmeerraum stammenden Landschildkröten. – SIGS-Informationsblatt, 3, 2 pp.

EGGENSCHWILER & JOST (1998): Die Griechische Landschildkröte (Testudo hermanni). – Merkblatt 1, SIGS, 2 pp.

EGGENSCHWILER-LEU (1994): Auswertung der Jungtierausfälle. – SIGS-Info, Siblingen, 1 (4): 17-19.

EGGENSCHWILER-LEU (1999): Die ausbleibende Eiablage – Ursachen, Diagnose, Therapie, Konsequenz. – SIGS-Info, Siblingen, 6 (3): 33-40.

EGGERS (1985): Naturschutz – Artenschutz. – DATZ, Stuttgart, 38 (4): 267-269.

EGLIS (1962): Tortoise Behavior: a Taxonomic Adjunct. – Herpetologica, Emporia, 18: 1-8.

EGLIS (1967): Tortoise Behavior: a Taxonomic Adjunct. – International Turtle and Tortoise Society Journal, Los Angeles, 1 (2): 6-9, 33.

EGRETZBERGER (1995): Eindrücke aus Griechenland. – Emys, Sankt Pölten, 2 (4): 4-6.

EGRETZBERGER (1996): Vermessen von Schildkröten in Griechenland. – Informationsblatt der Fachgruppe Schildkröten der ÖGH, Vienna, 2 (3): 20-21.

EGRETZBERGER (1997a): Superlative. – Informationsblatt der Fachgruppe Schildkröten der ÖGH, Vienna, 3 (3): 9-18. – SIGS-Info, Siblingen, 4 (3): 18-25.

EGRETZBERGER (1997b): Buchbesprechung: Prof. Dr. WALTER KIRSCHE (1997): Die Landschildkröten Europas. – Informationsblatt der Fachgruppe Schildkröten der ÖGH, Vienna, 3 (3): 19-22.

EGRETZBERGER (1997c): Außergewöhnlich großes Gelege einer Griechischen Landschildkröte Testudo hermanni boettgeri. – Informationsblatt der Fachgruppe Schildkröten der ÖGH, Vienna, 3 (3): 23-24.

EGRETZBERGER (1998): Buchbesprechung: URSULA FÖHR-CAMPI (1997): Europäische Landschild-

kröten. – Informationsblatt der Fachgruppe Schildkröten der ÖGH, Vienna, 4 (2): 33-37.

EHLERS, BORCHERS, GRUND, FRÖHLICH, LUDWIG & BIHK (1999): Detection of New DNA Polymerase Genes of Known and Potentislly Novel Herpesviruses by PCR with Degenerate and Deoxyinosine Substituted Primers. – V. Gen., 18: 211-220.

EHRENGART (1971): Zur Pflege und Zucht der Griechischen Landschildkröte (Testudo h. hermanni). – Salamandra, Frankfurt am Main, 7 (2): 71-80.

EHRENGART (1976): Brutanlagen für Schildkröten-Eier. – Salamandra, 12 (1): 27-31.

EISELT (1961): Catalogus Faunae Austriae XXI ab: Amphibia, Reptilia. – Vienna (Springer-Verlag).

EISELT & SPITZENBERGER (1967): Ergebnisse zoologischer Sammelreisen in der Türkei: Testudines. – Annalen des Naturhistorischen Museums Wien, Ser. B, 70: 357-378.

EISENBERG (2004a): Prophylaxe statt Therapie. – Reptilia (D), Münster, 45: 16-25

EISENBERG (2004b): Avoiding Health Problems Associated with Captive Maintenance. Prevention Rather Than Treatment. – Reptilia (GB), Barcelona, 33: 12-20.

EISENBERG (2004c): Más vale prevenir que curar. Profilaxis de las patologías relacionadas con el cautiverio. – Reptilia (E), Barcelona, 46: 16-24.

ELIASSEN & REITE (1974): Metabolism of carbon-14 histamine in amphibians (Bufo bufo) and reptiles (Pseudemys scripta and Testudo hermanni). – Acta Physiologica Scandinavica, 90 (1): 52-56.

ENCKE (2001): Neues aus dem Allwetterzoo Münster. – Reptilia (D), Münster, 29: 13.

ENDANGERED SPECIES IMPORT AND EXPORT MANAGEMENT OFFICE (Eds.) (2002): Identification Manual For Common Turtles and Tortoises. – Beijing (China Forestry Publishing House): 128-129.

ENGELMANN (1846): Index Librorum Historiam Naturalem – Verzeichniss der Bücher über Naturgeschichte. Pars 1. – Leipzig (W. Engelmann), VIII + 786 pp.

ENGELMANN, FRITZSCHE, GÜNTHER & OBST (1993): Lurche und Kriechtiere Europas. – Radebeul (Neumann Verlag): 37, 49, 200-202.

ENGERT (1992): Besuch des CARAPAX-Zentrums in der Toskana. – Journal der AG Schildkröten & Panzerechsen der DGHT, Bürstadt, 1 (2): 8-9.

ERLER (2003): Saisonale Veränderungen hämatologischer und blutbiochemischer Werte bei europäischen Landschildkröten (Testudo graeca, Testudo hermanni, Testudo marginata). – Dissertation, Ludwig-Maximilians-Univ., Munich, 295 pp.

ERNST & BARBOUR (1989): Turtles of the World. – Washington & London (Smithsonian Institution Press): 265-268.

ERNST & NICHOLS (1974): Internal Ciliates of Tortoises. – British Journal of Herpetology, London, **5** (3): 450-451.

ERNST, ALTENBURG & BARBOUR (2000): Turtles of the World. – CD-ROM, Amsterdam (ETI).

ESTEBAN (1982): Estudio de la reproducción de *Testudo hermanni* (GMELIN) en cautividad. – Aquamar, Madrid, **27**: 12-20.

ESTEBAN & PÉREZ (1988): Contribución al conocimiento de los testudínidos españoles. – Dissertation, Univ. Complutense, Madrid.

ESTEBAN, FILELLA, GARCÍA PARÍS, MENORCA, MARTÍN, PÉREZ MELLADO & ZAPIRAIN (1994): Atlas provisional de la distribución geográfica de la herpetofauna de Menorca (Islas Baleares, Espaa). – Revista Española de Herpetología, Leganés, **8**: 19-28.

ESZTERLE (2001): Wer hat hier die Hosen an? – Schildkröten, Linden, **8** (2): 9-10.

EUROPEAN COUNCIL (Eds.) (1998): Seminar on implementation of Action Plans for Amphibians and Reptiles. – Strasbourg (European Council), T-PVS (98), 28, 69 pp.

EVANS (1979): Breeding Mediterranean tortoises in an English garden. – British Herpetological Society Newsletter, London, 20: 16.

EVANS (1980): *Testudo graeca* v *T. hermanni*. – British Chelonia Group Newsletter, 23: 3.

EVANS (1982): Egg-laying with a difference. – *Testudo*, **2** (1): 39.

EVANS (2004): Member's letters. – British Chelonia Group Newsletter, 160: 4.

EWALD (1983): Sue quelques Reptiles et Amphibiens du Péloponnèse oriental (Grèce). – Riviera Scient., Nizza, IX, **67** (III-IV): 2-14.

DI FABRIZIO (1992): Aree protette d'Abruzzo. – Penne (Cogecstre), 233 pp.

FASOLA, GALEOTTI, BALLASINA & PEDRAZZOLI (2002): »Le chant des tortues« – la fonction des vocalisations pendant le comportement reproducteur des *Testudo*. – Chelonii, Gonfaron, 3: 133.

FEHRINGER (1996a): Das Schildkrötenzentrum in Massa Marittima. – Informationsblatt der Fachgruppe Schildkröten der ÖGH, Vienna, **2** (2): 4-6.

FEHRINGER (1996b): Nach Griechenland der Schildkröten wegen. – Informationsblatt der Fachgruppe Schildkröten der ÖGH, Vienna, **2** (3): 7-13.

FEHRINGER (1997): Temperaturhaushalt eines Wintergartens und eines überdachten Freilandteiches. – Informa-

tionsblatt der Fachgruppe Schildkröten der ÖGH, Vienna, **3** (1): 12-20.

FEILER (2002): Ein Loch im Schildkrötenpanzer. Gedanken über die Gestaltung eines Freilandgeheges für mediterrane Landschildkröten. – *Testudo* (SIGS), Wimmis, **11** (4): 12-24.

DE FÉJERVÁRY (1923): Explorationes zoologicae ab E. CSIKI in Albania peractae. Pars I. Batrachians and Reptiles. – Mag. Tudom. Akad. Balkan-Kutat. Tudom. Eredm., Budapest, **1** (1): 7-65.

FÉLIX (1984): Les tortugues continentals del Empordá – Proposició d'estació zoològica a la serra de la Balmeta. – Figueras (IAEDEN), 40 pp.

FÉLIX (1985): Grave peligro de extinció de la tortuga mediterránea en la península Ibérica. – Quercus, **17**: 10-12.

FÉLIX, BUDÓ, CAPALLERES & FARRÉ (1990): Conseqüències dels incèndis forestals en una població de tortuga mediterrània (*Testudo hermanni hermanni* GMELIN, 1789) de l'Albera. – Annals de l'Institut d'Estudis Empordanesos, Institut d'Estudis Empordanesos, Ed. Figueres, **23**: 13-36.

FÉLIX, CAPALLERES, BUDÓ & FARRÉ (1989): Estructura de una población de tortuga mediterránea (*Testudo hermanni* robertmertensi, WERMUTH), antes y despues de un incendio forestal. – Treb. Soc. Catal. Ictiol. Herpetol., **2**: 210-223.

FENWICK (1982): Taking Care of Your Pet Tortoise. – Kingston (privately printed).

FENWICK (1984): Response to ROB HARPER's article in newsletter 40 »European tortoises – what now?«. – British Chelonia Group Newsletter, 42: 4-5.

FENWICK (1986): Breeding Tortoises in Captivity – Has Nature a Way of Protecting Its Own? – *Testudo*, **2** (4): 60-64.

FENWICK (1987): Landschildpadden kweken in gevangenschap – Bewchermt de natuur zichzelf? – De Schildpad, Eindhoven, **13** (4): 30-36.

FENWICK (1989): Feeding in Captivity. – *Testudo*, **3** (1): 58-74.

FENWICK (1990): Influences of the Food Choice of Hatchling Tortoises with Relation to Colour, Smell and Size of Food. – *Testudo*, **3** (2): 69-84.

FENWICK (1991): CARAPAX Review. – British Chelonia Group Newsletter, 83: 16.

FENWICK (1995): Taking Care of Tortoises, Their Eggs and Hatchlings. – Kingston (privately printed): 5, 9, 11, 15, 37, 56, 63, 73, 76-78, 88, 90.

FENWICK (1996a): Husbandry of Terrestrial Tortoises. – *Testudo*, **4** (3): 13-20.

FENWICK (1996b): Conservation – in a cold climate. – In: SOPTOM (Eds.): International Congress of Chelonian Conservation – Proceedings. – Gonfaron (Editions SOPTOM): 237-239.

FENWICK (2002a): Egg formation and development. – Chelonii, Gonfaron, 3: 240-241.

FENWICK (2002b): Hibernation of Mediterranean tortoises. – Testudo, 5 (4): 25-30.

FERGER & HOHL (1992): Die Zucht von Testudo hermanni hermanni (Westrasse der griechischen Landschildkröte) in Gefangenschaft. – SIGS-Info, Siblingen, 1 (2): 12.

FERRI (1993): Les tortues terrestres et aquatiques. – Paris (Editions De Vecchi SA), 156 pp.

FERRI (1994): Le grand livre des tortues terrestres et aquatiques. – Paris (Editions De Vecchi SA), 193 pp.

FERRI (1999): Tartarughe e testuggini. – Milan (Mondadori): 17, 19, 25, 30, 34, 38, 58, 68-71.

FERRI (2002): Turtles & Tortoises. – Willowdale & Buffalo (Firefly Books): 17, 19, 25, 30, 34, 38, 58, 68-71.

FERTARD (1989): La rétention d'œufs chez les reptiles (Chéloniens, ophidiens). – Maisons-Alfort (Editions du Point Vétérinaire), 21 (120): 153-168.

FERTARD (1992): Étude des caractéristiques radiographiques et chronologiques de la ponte chez Testudo hermanni en semi-liberté. – In: Proceedings of the First International Congress of Chelonian Pathology, Gonfaron, France, 25-27 April 1992. – Gonfaron (SOPTOM): 190-199.

FERTARD (1999a): Recherches en pathologie à Gonfaron. – La Tortue, Gonfaron, 48: 10-15.

FERTARD (1999b): Rétention d'oeufs chez une tortue. – Point Vétérinaire, N° spécial NAC, 30: 219-221.

FERTARD & DEVAUX (1997): Quelles recherches...et dans quels buts?. – La Tortue, Gonfaron, 38: 12-13

FIACCHINI (2004): Il progetto »Atlante degli Anfibi e dei Rettili della Provincia di Ancona«. – In: ZUFFI (Ed.): V° Congresso Nazionale della Societas Herpetologica Italica, 29 settembre - 3 ottobre 2004, Calci (Pisa). – Turin (Societas Herpetologica Italica): 20-21.

FIACCHINI, SCOTTI, ANGELINI, BURATTINI & FUSCO (2004): Aspetti naturalistici del Parco naturale regionale Gola della Rossa e di Frasassi (Marche), con particolare riferimento alla comunità erpetologica. – In: ZUFFI (Ed.): V° Congresso Nazionale della Societas Herpetologica Italica, 29 settembre - 3 ottobre 2004, Calci (Pisa). – Turin (Societas Herpetologica Italica): 28.

FILELLA-I-SUBIRA (1996a): Gaudí und die Herpetologie. – Reptilia (D), Münster, 1: 58-63.

FILELLA (1996b): Gaudí y la Herpetología. – Reptilia (E), Barcelona, 7: 58-64.

FILELLA (2001c): Gaudí and Herpetology – Reptilia (GB), Barcelona, 14: 70-75

FILELLA-I-SUBIRÀ (2002): On the morphometry of the Hermann's tortoise of the Empordà, Mallorca and Menorca (Catalan countries). – Chelonii, Gonfaron, 3: 368.

FILIP & KÜBBER-HEISS (2005): Ein Update zur Herpesvirose bei Schildkröten. – Marginata, Münster, 2 (3): 36-43.

FINLAYSON (1965): Spontaneous arterial disease in exotic animals. – Journal of Zoology, London, 147: 239-243.

FIRMIN (1996): La consultation des Tortues. – Maisons-Alfort (Editions du Point Vétérinaire), 28 (177): 223-232.

FIRMIN (1997): Cours de base du GENAC. – Prat. Med. Chir. An. Comp., Paris.

FISCHBACHER (1999): Erste Erfahrungen mit dem Brutapparat. – Schildkröten, Linden, 6 (3): 16-21.

FISCHBACHER (2002a): Schilderanomalien bei griechischen Landschildkröten. – Schildkröten, Linden, 9 (2): 9-11.

FISCHBACHER (2002b): Der Rollwagen. – Schildkröten, Linden, 9 (2): 38-39.

VON FISCHER (1884): Das Terrarium – seine Bepflanzung und Bevölkerung. – Verlag von Mahlau & Waldschmidt, Frankfurt am Main: 120-123.

FISCHER & HOMUTH (2006): Herpesvirusinfektion bei Landschildkröten – Erkrankung, Diagnose und Prophylaxemöglichkeiten. – Reptilia (D), Münster, 57: 56-63.

FITZGERALD (1989): International Wildlife Trade – Whose Business Is It? – Washington (World Wildlife Fund).

FITZINGER (1826): Neue Classification der Reptilien nach ihren natürlichen Verwandtschaften. – Vienna (Verlag J. G. Heubner): 44.

FITZINGER (1835): Entwurf einer systematischen Anordnung der Schildkröten nach den Grundsätzen der natürlichen Methode. – Annalen des Wiener Museums der Naturgeschichte, Vienna, 1 (1): 122.

FITZINGER (1843): Systema Reptilium. Fasciculis primus. Amblyglossae. – Wien (Braumüller und Seidel), 106 + VI pp.

FITZINGER (1853): Versuch einer Geschichte der Menagerien des Österreichisch-kaiserlichen Hofes mit besonderer Berücksichtigung der Menagerie zu Schönbrunn nebst einer Aufzählung der in denselben gehaltenen Thiere von der ältesten bis auf die neueste Zeit. – Vienna (W. Braumüller).

FITZINGER (1864): Bilder-Atlas zur wissenschaftlich-populären Naturgeschichte der Amphibien in ihren sämmtlichen Hauptformen. – Vienna (Hof- und Staatsdruckerei), 107 plates.

FLANK (1997): The Turtle – An Owner's Guide to a Happy Healthy Pet. – Foster City (Howell Book House): 115.

FLEISSIG & JAKOB (2002): Diebstahl von 58 wertvollen Landschildkröten bei Privat-Züchter! – Schildkröten, Linden, 9 (4): 35-36.

FLETCHER (1993): Cases from Veterinary Practice. – Testudo, 3 (5): 26-28.

FLOERICKE (1912): Kriechtiere und Lurche fremder Länder. – Stuttgart (Kosmos, Franckh'sche Verlagshandlung): 74-76.

FLOERICKE (1927): Der Terrarienfreund. – Stuttgart (Kosmos, Franckh'sche Verlagshandlung), 222 pp. + 16 plates.

FLOWER (1925): Contributions to our knowledge of the duration of life in vertebrate animals. III. Reptiles. – Proceedings of the Zoological Society of London, London: 931.

FLOWER (1926): Species of land tortoises of the genus Testudo found in the countries bordering the Mediterranean Sea. – Copeia, Lawrence, 150: 133.

FÖHR-CAMPI (1997): Europäische Landschildkröten. – Porto Mantovano (privately printed), 160 pp.#

FORLANI, CRESTANELLO, MANTOVANI, LIVOREIL, ZANE, BERTORELLE & CONGIU (2005): Identification and characterization of microsatellite markers in Hermann's tortoise (Testudo hermanni, Testudinidae). – Molecular Ecology Notes, 5: 228-230.

FORMAN & FORMAN (1981): Herpetologische Beobachtungen auf Korsika. – herpetofauna, Weinstadt, 10: 12-16.

FOX (1977): The urogenital system of reptiles. – In: GANS & PARSONS (Eds.): Biology of the Reptilia, Morphology E, Vol. 6. – New York (Academic Press): 1-157.

FOXWELL (1980a): Tortoise eggs laid early. – British Chelonia Group Newsletter, 20: 8.

FOXWELL (1980b): The tortoise trade. – British Chelonia Group Newsletter, 21: 11.

FRAIR (1967): Blood group studies with turtles. – International Turtle and Tortoise Society Journal, Los Angeles, 1 (2): 30-32.

FRANCH, BUDÓ, CAPALLERAS, CARBONELL, FELIX, MASCORT & LLORENTE (2002a): Consequences of the forest fire of the 6th of August 2000 on a population of Western Hermann's tortoise (Testudo hermanni) from Masif de l'Albera; Northern Iberian peninsula. – Chelonii, Gonfaron, 3: 226-229.

FRANCH, BUDÓ, CAPALLERAS, CARBONELL, FELIX, MASCORT & LLORENTE (2002b): Comparison of movements and growth rate of wild and captive bred juveniles of the Western Hermanns tortoise at Serra de l'Albera, northeastern Iberia. – Chelonii, Gonfaron, 3: 316-319.

FRANCK (1987): Schildkröten in Frankreich. – Die Schildkröte (N. F.), Heinsberg, 1 (3): 28-35.

FRANÇOIS-FRANCK (1906): Etudes de mécanique respiratoire comparée – III – Resumé des résultats fournis par les expériences antérieures sur le mécanisme de la respiration des Chéloniens (Testudo graeca); Comptes-Rendus de la Société de Biologie, Paris, 61: 127-129.

FRANÇOIS-FRANCK (1908): Etudes critiques et expérimentales sur la mécanique respiratoire comparée des reptiles – I Chéloniens (Tortue grecque). – Arch. Zool. Experi. et Gen., 4 (9): 31-187.

FRANK (1988): Amphibien und Reptilien als Hobbytiere. – Deutsche Tierärztliche Wochenschrift, Hannover, 95: 69-72.

FRANZE (2001): Die griechische Landschildkröte Testudo hermanni boettgeri als Streitgegenstand vor dem Amts- und Landgericht. – BNA-aktuell, Hambrücken, 1: 25-27.

DE FRESCHEVILLE (1965): Les Amphibiens et Reptiles corses. – Bull. Soc. Sci. Hist. Nat. Corse, 576: 50-69.

FRETEY (1975): Guide des Reptiles et Batraciens de France. – Paris (Hatier), 239 pp.

FRETEY (1986): Les reptiles de France – Tortues et lézards. – Paris (Hatier).

FRETEY (1987): Guide des Reptiles de France. – Paris (Hatier), 255 pp.

FRETEY (1996): État de santé des populations de chéloniens de l'Europe et du Moyen-Orient. – In: SOPTOM (Eds.): International Congress of Chelonian Conservation – Proceedings. – Gonfaron (Editions SOPTOM): 164-166.

FRETEY & NOUTET (1979): Commentaires à »Attention, tortues!«. – Bulletin de la Société Herpétologique de France, Paris, 10: 35-37.

FREYER (1842): Fauna der in Krain bekannten Säugetiere, Vögel, Reptilien und Fische. – Ljubljana.

FRIEDL (1984): Tierknochenfunde aus Kassope/Griechenland: (4.-1. Jh. v. Chr.): 189.

FRIEDMAN (1970): Orpheus in the Middle Ages. – Cambridge (Harvard University Press).

FRIEDMANN (1903): Spontane Lungentuberkulose bei Schildkröten und die Stellung des Tuberkelbazillus im System. – Zeitschrift für Tuberkulose, Leipzig, 4: 430-457.

FRIEMEL (1995): Oh, diese Schildkröten. – Schildkröten, Linden, 2 (4): 33-34.

FRIEMEL (1996a): Beobachtungen über das Verhalten meiner Schildkröten – drei Geschichten. – Schildkröten, Linden, 3 (1): 38-40.

FRIEMEL (1996b): Julchen, steinreich. – Schildkröten, Linden, 3 (3): 30-31.

FRIEMEL (1997): Zwei Episoden. – Schildkröten, Linden, 4 (3): 41-42.

FRIEMEL (1998): Fressgier. – Schildkröten, Linden, 5 (2): 36-37.

FRIEMEL (2000): Drei Begebenheiten mit unseren Schildkröten. – Schildkröten, Linden, 7 (4): 29-31.

FRIESLEBER (2005): Überwinterung von Europäischen Landschildkröten im Freigehege – ein Erfahrungsbericht. – Schildkröten im Fokus, Bergheim, 2 (4): 27-32.

FRINGS (1996): Das Simonsche Schildkrötenparadies. – elaphe (N. F.), Rheinbach, **4** (4): 67-73.

FRISENDA (1988): Situazione attuale delle testuggini terrestri e palustri in Italia con particolare riferimento alle regioni meridionali. – Bolletino dello Gruppo R.A.N.A. Italia, Bari: 13-18.

FRISENDA & BALLASINA (1988): Statut et protection des tortues en Italie. – Société Herpétologique de France, IIIme Symposium Europaeum Chelonologicum, Marseille.

FRISENDA & BALLASINA (1990): Le statut des Chéloniens terrestres et d'eau douce en Italie. – Bulletin de la Société Herpétologique de France, Paris, **53**: 18-23.

FRITZ (1995a): Schildkröten-Hybriden – 2. Halsberger-Schildkröten (Cryptodira). – herpetofauna, Weinstadt, **95**: 19-34.

FRITZ (1995b): Wie heißt die Griechische Landschildkröte denn nun wirklich? – DATZ, Stuttgart, **48** (12): 811-812.

FRITZ (1996): Nomen est Omen, auch bei Hermanns. – SIGS-Info, Siblingen, **5** (3): 31.

FRITZ (2001): Der Arbeitskreis Europäische Landschildkröten stellt sich vor. – Radiata, Haan, **10** (3): 33-34.

FRITZ (2002): Arbeitskreis Europäische Landschildkröten. – Minor, Haan, **1** (1): 28-29,

FRITZ & CHEYLAN (2001): Testudo LINNAEUS, 1758 – Eigentliche Landschildkröten. – In: FRITZ (Ed.): Handbuch der Reptilien und Amphibien Europas, Band 3/ IIIA, Schildkröten (Testudines) I (Bataguridae, Testudinidae, Emydidae). – Wiebelsheim (Aula-Verlag): 113-124.

FRITZ & PFAU (2002): Die Griechische Landschildkröte – ideal für das Freilandterrarium. – DATZ-Sonderheft Schildkröten, Stuttgart (Verlag Eugen Ulmer): 14-20.

FRITZ, PETTERS, MATZANKE & MATZANKE (1996): Zur Schildkrötenfauna Nordsardiniens. – herpetofauna, Weinstadt, **99**: 29-34, **100**: 14-20.

FRITZ, IROKY, KAMI & WINK (2005): Environmentally caused dwarfism or a valid species – Is Testudo weissingeri BOUR, 1996 a distinct evolutionary lineage? New evidence from mitochondrial and nuclear genomic markers. – Molecular Phylogenetics and Evolution, **37** (2): 389-401.

FRITZSCHE (1952): Über den Umgang mit Schildkröten. – DATZ, Stuttgart, **5** (3): 75-78.

FROLOV & ZWETKOVA (1997): Die Überwinterung von zentralasiatischen und Mittelmeerschildkröten in Gefangenschaft. – Schildkröten, Linden, **4** (3): 14-16.

FROMMHOLD (1957): Wie werde ich Terrarianer? – VII – Schildkröten und Echsen. – Aquarien Terrarien, Leipzig, Jena & Berlin, **4** (5): 11-13.

FROMMHOLD (1959a): Wir bestimmen Lurche und Kriechtiere Mitteleuropas. – Radebeul (Neumann Verlag), 219 pp.

FROMMHOLD (1959b): Als Tiergärtner und Herpetologe in Albanien. – Aquarien Terrarien, Leipzig, Jena & Berlin, **6**: 115-118, 144-147, 179-182, 214-217.

FROMMHOLD (1965): Sorgen um Landschildkröten. – Aquarien Terrarien, Leipzig, Jena & Berlin, **12**: 224-228.

FROST & SCHMIDT (1997): Serological evidence for susceptibility of various tortoise species to herpesvirus infection. – 38. Internationales Symposium über Erkrankungen der Zoo- und Wildtiere, 7.-11. Mai 1997, Zürich: 25-27.

FRÜHAUF (2005): Ach du dickes Ei ... Die Ablage eines »Rieseneis« durch ein Weibchen von Testudo hermanni boettgeri. – Marginata, Münster, **2** (3): 54.

FRYE (1981): Biomedical and surgical aspects of captive reptile husbandry. – Edwardsville (Veterinary Medicine Publishing Company), 456 pp.

FRYE (1991a): Biomedical and surgical aspects of captive reptile husbandry. 2. Auflage. – Malabar (Krieger Publishing Company), 712 pp.

FRYE (1991b): Reptile Care – An Atlas of Diseases and Treatments – Nutrition – A Practical Guide for Feeding Captive Reptiles – Volume 1. – Neptune City (T. F. H. Publications): 41-100.

FRYE (1993): A Practical Guide for Feeding Captive Reptiles. – Malabar (Krieger Publishing), 171pp.

FRYE (2003): Reptilien richtig füttern. – Stuttgart (Verlag Eugen Ulmer): 37.

FUHN (1956): Specie Mediterraneene de Broasce Testoase de Uscat in R. P. R. (Testudo graeca ibera PALLAS, Testudo hermanni hermanni GMELIN). – Ocrotirca Nat. Bukarest, **2**: 178-180.

FUHN (1969): Broaste, Serpi, Sopirle. – Bukarest (Natura si Omul Editura Stiintifica), 246 pp.

FUHN (1970): Aspects on the current situation of the fauna of the Hagieni Forest Nature Reserve, Constanza Department, Romania. – Ocrotirca Nat. Bukarest, **14** (1): 65-69.

FUHN (1981): Rare and endangered amphibians and reptiles in Romania, proposal for conservation. – Vienna (Societas Europaea Herpetologica).

FUHN & VANCEA (1961): Fauna Republicii Populare Romîne. Reptilia (Testoase, Sopirle, Serpi). – Bukarest (Editura Academiei Republicii Populare Romîne), **14** (2), 352 pp.

FUNKE (2005): Die LSA. – Minor, Lingenfeld, **4** (3): 30.

FURIERI (1965): Osservazioni ultrastrutturali suo spermio di Testudo hermanni GMELIN. – Boll. Soc. ital. Biol. sper., **41**: 144-145.

FURNWEGER (1970): The Dime Store Turtle. – International Turtle and Tortoise Society Journal, Los Angeles, **4** (2): 13.

FURRER (1972): Wiederbelebungsversuche an ertrunkenen Landschildkröten. – DATZ, Stuttgart, 25 (8): 287.

GABRISCH (1984): Die häufigsten Schildkrötenkrankheiten in der tierärztlichen Praxis. – Der Praktische Tierarzt, Hannover, 65: 483-489.

GABRISCH & ZWART (1995): Kapitel Schildkröten, Schlangen. – In: GABRISCH & ZWART (Eds.): Krankheiten der Heimtiere. – 3. Auflage, Hannover (Schlütersche Verlagsanstalt): 663-807.

GABRISCH & ZWART (2005): Krankheiten der Schildkröten. – In: FEHR, SASSENBURG & ZWART (Hrsg.): Krankheiten der Heimtiere. – 6. Auflage, Hannover (Schlütersche Verlagsanstalt): 681-682.

GAGNO (2001): Parasitologie intestinale chez les tortues d'élevage et les tortues sauvages. – La Tortue, Gonfaron, 55: 58-59.

GAGNO (2002): Préparation aux réintroductions de Testudo hermanni hermanni – contrle parasitologique intestinal – premiers résultats. – Chelonii, Gonfaron, 3: 157-160.

GALEOTTI, SACCHI, FASOLA & BALLASINA (2004): Vocalizzazioni dei maschi e scelta femminile in Testudo hermanni – un approccio sperimentale. – In: ZUFFI (Ed.): V° Congresso Nazionale della Societas Herpetologica Italica, 29 settembre - 3 ottobre 2004, Calci (Pisa). – Turin (Societas Herpetologica Italica): 33-34.

GALEOTTI, SACCHI, ROSA & FASOLA (2005a): Female preference for fast-rate, high-pitched calls in Hermann's tortoises Testudo hermanni. – Behavioral Ecology, 16: 301-308.

GALEOTTI, SACCHI, FASOLA, ROSA, MARCHESI & BALLASINA (2005b): Courtship displays and mounting calls are honest, condition-dependent signals that influence mounting success in Hermann's tortoises. – Canadian Journal of Zoology, Ottawa, 83: 1306-1313.

GANNON (1992a): Press Release MOT for Tortoises. – The Peoples Dispensary for Sick Animals, Head Office, Telford.

GANNON (1992b): Tortoises and Terrapins – PDSA advice leaflet to the public. – The Peoples Dispensary for Sick Animals, Head Office, Telford.

GANNON (1992c): Treatment of tortoises at PDSA centres – Internal memo of 152 animals treated over 12 months. – The Peoples Dispensary for Sick Animals, Head Office, Telford.

GARDINER (1978): Differentiation of Testudo graeca and Testudo hermanni. – British Herpetological Society Newsletter, London, 18: 15-16.

GARDINER (1980a): Testudo hermanni in France. – British Chelonia Group Newsletter, 22: 3-4.

GARDINER (1980b): The hibernation of young tortoises. – Testudo, 1 (3): 24-26.

GARDINER (1982): Is this a record?. – British Chelonia Group Newsletter, 32: 4.

GARDINER (1990): Successes and Failures in Rearing Captive-Bred Mediterranean Tortoises. – Testudo, 3 (2): 46-51.

GARDINER & GARDINER (1990): Further Notes on Testudo hermanni in Corfu. – Testudo, 3 (2): 42-45.

GARROD, BUXTON, SMITH & BATE (1928): Excavation of a Mousterian rock-shelter at Devil's Tower, Gibraltar. – Journal of the Royal Anthropological Institute of Great Britain and Ireland, London, 58: 34-113.

GASC, CABELA, CRNOBRNJA-ISAILOVIC, DOLMEN, GROSSENBACHER, HAFFNER, LESCURE, MARTENS, MARTÍNEZ-RICA, MAURIN, OLIVEIRA, SOFIANIDOU, VEITH & ZUIDERWIJK (Eds.) (2004): Atlas of Amphibians and Reptiles in Europe. – Second Edition, Paris (Muséum National d'Histoire Naturelle): 12, 177-179, 411, 500.

GAVANELLI, GEROSA & SCARAVELLI (1996a): Protection and care activities for chelonians in Romagna, Italy. – In: SOPTOM (Eds.): International Congress of Chelonian Conservation – Proceedings. – Gonfaron (Editions SOPTOM): 325-327.

GAVANELLI, GEROSA & SCARAVELLI (1996b): »The turtle and the man« – a research and teaching laboratory at Imola (Italy); In: SOPTOM (Eds.): International Congress of Chelonian Conservation – . – Gonfaron (Editions SOPTOM): 328.

GAYDA (1940): Su alcuni anfibi e rettili dell'Albania esistenti nel Museo Zoologico di Berlino. – Atti Soc. italiana Sci. Nat. Mus. Civ. Stor. Nat., Milan, 79: 263-272.

GEE (1991): Excerpts from members' letters. – British Chelonia Group Newsletter, 80: 12-13.

GEIER (2005): Fester Panzer – weiches Herz. – Biebertal (LSK-Verlag), 82 pp.

GEINECKER (1999): Über meine Erfahrungen mit fünf Landschildkröten. – Schildkröten, Linden, 6 (2): 36-39.

GEJVALL (1969): Lerna: The Fauna (Lerna I). – Athens (The American School of Classical Studies at Athens): 6, 49.

GENÉ (1838): Synopsis reptilium Sardinia indigenorum. – Mem. R. Accad. Sci. Torino, Turin, 1/2: 257-285.

GENIEZ & CHEYLAN (1987): Atlas de distribution des Reptiles et Amphibiens du Languedoc-Roussillon. – Montpellier (Laboratoire Biogéographie et Écologie des Vertébrés E.P.H.E./G.R.I.V.E.), 114 pp.

GERIQUE & ALBERT (1997): Manejo de quelonios en el Centro de Protección y Estudio del Medio Natural. – Proceedings Jornadas de Conservación de la Tortuga Mediterránea, Benicassim: 89-95.

GERLACH (1960): Salamandrische Welt. Amphibien und Reptilien. – Frankfurt am Main (Büchergilde Gutenberg): 76-79.

GERLACH (1973): Die Geheimnisse im Reich der Amphibien und Reptilien. – Munich (König Verlag): 84-87.

GÉROUDET (1965): Les Rapaces diurnes et nocturnes d'Europe. – Neuchâtel (Delachaux et Niestlé), 426 pp.

GERRITS & VOOGD (1973): The distribution of the purkinje cells in the cerebellum of Testudo hermanni turtle. – Acta Morphologica Neerlando-Scandinavica, 11 (4): 357.

GESSNER (1554): Conradi Gesneri Medici Tigurini – Historiae animalium liber II. de quadrupedibus oviparis – Adjunctae sunt etiam oviparorum quorundam appendiae. – Zürich (C. Froschoverus), VI + 110 pp.

GEYER (19??): Katechismus der Terrarienkunde. – Magdeburg (Creutz'sche Verlagsbuchhandlung): 92.

GHIRA & STUGREN (1988): Verteilung von Amphibien und Reptilien auf die Höhenzonen im Retezat-Gebirge. – Studia Univ. Babes Bolyai Biol., Cluj-Napoca, 33 (2): 69-75.

GIGLIOLI (1879): Beiträge zur Kenntniss der Wirbelthiere Italiens. – Archiv für Naturgeschichte, 45: 93-99.

GIL (1995): Conservación de la tortuga mora en Murcia; In: BALLASINA (Ed.): Red Data Book on Mediterranean Chelonians. – Bologna (Edagricole): 41-49.

GILBERTAS (1999): Das Schildkrötenkrankenhaus. – Das Tier, Leinfelden-Echterdingen, 40 (12): 34-35.

GILLES-BAILLIEN (1966): L'hibernation de la tortue grecque. – Arch. Int. Physiol. Biochim., 74: 328-329.

GILLES-BAILLIEN (1967): Action de la L-Bvasopressine sur certain caractères de permeabilité de la vessie isolée de la tortue grecque. – Annals of Endocrinology, 28: 716-719.

GILLES-BAILLIEN (1968): The extracellular space of the isolated intestinal epithelium of the Greek tortoise. – Arch. Int. Physiol. Biochim., 76: 731-739.

GILLES-BAILLIEN (1969a): Intracellular inorganic ions and amino-acid pool in the isolated intestinal mucosa of the tortoise Testudo hermanni hermanni GMELIN. – Arch. Int. Physiol. Biochim., 77: 305-313.

GILLES-BAILLIEN (1969b): Seasonal changes in the permeability of the isolated vesical epithelium of Testudo hermanni hermanni. – Biochimica et Biophysica Acta, 193 (1): 129-136.

GILLES-BAILLIEN (1969c): Seasonal variations in blood and urine constituents of the tortoise T. hermanni hermanni. – Arch. Intern. Physiol. Biochim., 77: 427-440.

GILLES-BAILLIEN (1970a): Permeability characteristics of the intestinal epithelium and hibernation in Testudo hermanni. – Arch. Int. Physiol. Biochem., 78: 327-338.

GILLES-BAILLIEN (1970b): Modifications of the intracellular inorganic ion content in the presence of L-alanine in the jejunum mucosa of Testudo hermanni hermanni. – Life Sciences Part 1, Physiology, Pharmacology, 9 (10): 585-590.

GILLES-BAILLIEN (1972): Inexchangeable fraction of the cationic content in the intestinal epithelium of the tortoise Testudo hermanni hermanni and its modification during hibernation. – Arch. Int. Physiol. Biochim., 80 (4): 789-797.

GILLES-BAILLIEN (1973): Seasonal variations in weight and hematological data of Testudo hermanni hermanni. – Arch. Int. Physiol. Biochim., 81 (4): 723-732.

GILLES-BAILLIEN (1976): Sodium ion compartmentation in the jejunal mucosa of the tortoise. – In: ROBINSON (Ed.): Intestinal ion transport. – Proceedings of the International Symposium, Titisee, Mai 1975, University Park Press, Baltimore, Vol. XIII: 75-77.

GILLES-BAILLIEN (1979): Sodium potassium atpase activity and hibernation in tortoise Testudo hermanni hermanni intestinal mucosa. – Annual Meeting of the American Society of Zoologists, Society of Systematic Zoology and the American Microscopical Society, Tampa, 27.-30.12.1979.

GILLES-BAILLIEN (1980): Trans-epithelial fluxes of amino-acids and metabolism in the tortoise Testudo hermanni hermanni intestinal mucosa. – Arch. Int. Physiol. Biochim., 88 (1): 15-24.

GILLES-BAILLIEN (1981a): Osmoregulation in reptiles. – Acta Zoologica et Pathologica Antverpiensia, Antwerp, 76: 29-33.

GILLES-BAILLIEN (1981b): Sodium cyclo-leucine and insulin compartments in tortoise Testudo hermanni hermanni intestinal mucus – possible role of the mucus in intestinal absorption processes. – Molecular Physiology, 1 (5): 265-272.

GILLES-BAILLIEN (1981c): Seasonal changes in the inorganic ion content of various tissues in the tortoise Testudo hermanni hermanni GMELIN. – Life Sciences, 2: 763-766.

GILLES-BAILLIEN & BOUQUEGNEAUX-TARTE (1972): Cationic distribution within the bladder mucosa of the tortoise Testudo hermanni and its modification during hibernation. – Arch. Int. Physiol. Biochim., 80 (3): 563-572.

GILLES-BAILLIEN & SCHOFFENIELS (1961): Origin of the potential difference in the intestinal epithelium of the turtle. – Nature, London, 190: 1107-1108.

GILLES-BAILLIEN & SCHOFFENIELS (1965a): Site of action of L-alanine and D-glucose on the potential difference across the intestine. – Arch. Int. Physiol. Biochim., 73: 355-357.

GILLES-BAILLIEN & SCHOFFENIELS (1965b): Variations saisonnières dans la composition du sang de la tortue grecque Testudo hermanni J. F. GMELIN. – Annales de la Société Royale Zoologique de Belgique, 95: 75-79.

GILLES-BAILLIEN & SCHOFFENIELS (1967a): Action of L-alanine on the fluxes of inorganic ions across the intestinal epithelium of Greek tortoise. – Life Sciences, 6: 1257-1262.

GILLES-BAILLIEN & SCHOFFENIELS (1967b): Bioelectric potentials in the intestinal epithelium of the Greek tortoise. – Comparative Biochemistry and Physiology, Vancouver, **23**: 95-104.

GILLES-BAILLIEN & SCHOFFENIELS (1967c): Fluxes of inorganic ions across the isolated intestinal epithelium of the Greek tortoise. – Arch. Int. Physiol. Biochim., **75**: 754-762.

GILLES-BAILLIEN & SCHOFFENIELS (1968): Amino acids and bioelectric potentials in the small intestine of the Greek tortoise. – Life Sciences, **7**: 53-63.

GILLES-BAILLIEN & SCHOFFENIELS (1970): Changes in the inorganic ion content of the jejunum mucosa in conditions causing modifications of the transfer of L-alanine (*Testudo hermanni hermanni*). – Life Sciences, Part I, Physiology, Pharmacology, **9** (10): 591-599.

GILLES-BAILLIEN & SCHOFFENIELS (1971): Bio-electric potential profiles in the bladder mucosa of the tortoise *Testudo hermanni hermanni*. – Life Sciences, Part I, Physiology, Pharmacology, **10** (6): 309-316.

GILLES-BAILLIEN & VERBERT (1978): Seasonal changes in the electrical parameters of the small intestine, colon, and bladder mucosa of land tortoises (*Testudo hermanni hermanni*). – Experientia, Bangor, **34** (9): 1174-1175.

GILLES-BAILLIEN, AGUILAR-PERIS & FERNANDEZ-TEJERO (1978): Analysis of a model of biological membrane transport intestinal – transport of cyclo-leucine. – Rev. Esp. Fisiol., **34** (1): 25-32.

GIRTANNER (1892): Die Griechische Landschildkröte im Garten. – Der Zoologische Garten, Berlin, **33**: 349-350.

GLAESSNER (1933): Die Tertiärschildkröten Niederösterreichs. – Neues Jahrbuch für Mineralogie, Geologie und Paläontologie, Abteilung 3, Stuttgart, **69**: 353-387.

GMELIN (1789): Caroli a Linné ... Systema Naturae per regna tria naturae, secundum classes, ordines, genera, species; cum characteribus, differentiis, synonymis, locis. Editio decimo tertia, aucta, reformata. Tom I. Pars III. – Leipzig (Georg Emanuel Beer): 1041.

GMIRA (1993a): Une nouvelle espèce de tortue Testudininei (*Testudo kenitrensis* n. sp.) de l'Inter Amirien-Tensiftien de Kénitra (Maroc). – Comptes Rendus de l'Académie des Sciences, Paris, Série II, **316**: 701-707.

GMIRA (1993b): Nouvelles données sur les espèces actuelles du *Testudo* (Chelonii, Testudinidae) – Bulletin de la Société Herpétologique de France, Paris, **65**: 49-56.

GMIRA (1995): Étude des Chéloniens Fossiles du Maroc – Anatomie, Systématique, Phylogénie. – Cahiers de Paléontologie, Paris (C.N.R.S Éditions), 140 pp.

GÖBEL (1986): Clinical use of fluoroquinolones in exotoc animals and small mammals. – Proceedings of second international veterinary symposium on Baytril®, Leverkusen, 18: 53-55.

GÖBEL & SPÖRLE (1991): Blood collecting technique and selected reference values for Herman's tortoise (*Testudo hermanni hermanni*). – Proceedings 4th International Colloquium on Pathology and Medicine of Reptiles and Amphibians, Bad Nauheim (Deutsche Tierärztliche Vereinigung): 129-134.

GÖBEL & SPÖRLE (1992): Blutentnahmetechnik und Serumnormalwerte wichtiger Parameter bei der griechischen Landschildkröte (*Testudo hermanni hermanni*). – Die Tierärztliche Praxis, Stuttgart, **20**: 231-234.

GÖBEL, SCHILDGER & SPÖRLE (1990): Propädeutik und diagnostische Verfahren bei Reptilien. – Der Praktische Tierarzt, Hannover, **71**: 14-25.

GOMILLE (1991): Jugoslawien – Der Ausverkauf der Schildkröten. – Das Tier, Leinfelden-Echterdingen, **32** (7): 69.

GOMIS (2004): Anatomie de la Tortue, ses applications à la pratique vétérinaire. – CD-ROM, Mulhouse (Parque zoologique).

GORSEMANN (1968): Het houden van Europese landschildpadden en huis. – Lacerta, Zoetermeer, **26** (1): 6.

GOTCH (1995): Latin names explained, a guide to the scientific classification of Reptiles, Birds and Mammals. – London (Blandford): 56.

GOTTSCHALK (1996): Ungewöhnliche Überwinterung einer *Testudo h. boettgeri*. – DATZ, Stuttgart, **49** (10): 675.

GRANIT (1940-1941): The »Red« Receptor of *Testudo*. – Acta Physiologica Scandinavica, Stockholm, **1**: 386-388.

GRANO & GRANO (2006a): Herpetofauna of the Capocotta sand dunes. – Reptilia (GB), Barcelona, **44**: 47-51.

GRANO & GRANO (2006b): Herpetofauna de las dunas de Capocotta. – Reptilia (E), Barcelona, **57**: 51-55.

GRANO & GRANO (2006c): L'erpetofauna delle dune di Capocotta. – Reptilia (It), Barcelona, **6**: 47-51.

GRAY (1869): Notes on the families and genera of tortoises (Testudinata), and on the characters afforded by the study of their skulls. – Proceedings of the Zoological Society of London, London: 165-225.

GRAY (1870): Supplement to the Catalogue of Shield Reptiles in the Collection of the British Museum. Part I. Testudinata (Tortoises). – London (Taylor and Francis): 8.

GRAY (1872): Appendix to the Catalogue of Shield Reptiles in the Collection of the British Museum. Part I. Testudinata (Tortoises). – London (Taylor and Francis): 4.

GRILLITSCH (1993): Freilandnachzucht der Griechischen Landschildkröte, *Testudo hermanni* GMELIN, 1789, unter den Klimabedingungen des unteren Inntales (Oberösterreich). – Herpetozoa, Vienna, **6** (3/4): 145.

GROLET (1996): Techniques et procédés de rapatriement – Bilan de six années d'expérience. – In: SOPTOM (Eds.): International Congress of Chelonian Conservation – Proceedings. – Gonfaron (Editions SOPTOM): 214-220

GROLET (1999): Opération »Apalone«. – La Tortue, Gonfaron, 48: 36-39.

GROLET (2002): Operation Apalone – Testudo part. – Chelonii, Gonfaron, 3: 277-287.

GROOMBRIDGE (1982): The IUCN Amphibia-Reptilia Red Data Book – Part 1 – Testudines, Crocodylia, Rhynchocephalia. – Gland (IUCN): 127-131.

GROOMBRIDGE (1988): Hermann's tortoise. – In: GROOMBRIDGE & BROODS (Eds.): Significant Trade in Wildlife – A Review of Selected Species in CITES Appendix II, Vol. 2. – Gland (IUCN): 23-29.

GROSS (1995): Landschildkröten – Die Pflege nach der Winterruhe. – DATZ, Stuttgart, 48 (7): 446-448.

GROSSI (2003): Autopsie d'une forêt meurtrie. – Manouria, Mezzavia, 21: 21-23.

GRUBAC (1987): L'Aigle royal en Macédoine. – In: L'Aigle royal en Europe, Premier Colloque international sur L'Aigle royal en Europe (13-15 juin 1986, Arvieux). – Briançon (Maison de la Nature): 37-39.

GRUBER (1982): Herpetofauna Griechenlands. – Karlsruhe (Hellenic Society for the Protection of Nature).

GRUBER (1999): Landschildkröten – Altersbestimmung möglich? – Ein Herz für Tiere, Ismaning, 2: 56.

GRUNDKE (1988): Reptilien auf Korfu. – DATZ, Stuttgart, 41 (5): 426-428.

GUERIN & WALLON (1975a): Effect of 2-4 dinitrophenol and ouabain on the ability of cesium ions to substitute for intracellular potassium ions in isolated and perfused turtle heart. – The Journal of Physiology, London, 70 (4): 467-477.

GUERIN & WALLON (1975b): Effets de la substitution du césium au potassium dans le milieu de perfusion du coeur isolé de tortue – 1 – Vitesse de pénétration du césium et de fuite du potassium. – C. R. Séanc. Soc. Biol., Paris, 163: 313-319.

GUERIN & WALLON (1979): The reversible replacement of internal potassium by cesium in isolated turtle (Testudo hermanni) heart. – The Journal of Physiology, London, 293: 525-538.

GULIA (1914): Uno sguardo alla zoologia delle »Isole Maltese«. – In: IX. Congrès intern. Zool., Monaco, 25-30 mars 1913, Monaco: 545-555.

GUMPENBERGER (1996a): Steroidhormongehalt in Kot von Griechischen und Maurischen Landschildkröten im Jahresgang und Kontrolle der Ovarien mit Ultraschalluntersuchungen. – Dissertation, Veterinärmedizinische Univ. Wien, Vienna.

GUMPENBERGER (1996b): Untersuchungen am Harntrakt und weiblichen Genitaltrakt von Schildkröten mit Hilfe bildgebender Diagnostik. – Dissertation, Veterinärmedizinische Univ. Wien, Vienna.

GUNDACKER (2006): Kühlschranküberwinterung europäischer Landschildkröten – ein Erfahrungsbericht. – Sacalia, Stiefern, 4 (10): 32-36.

GÜRTLER (1994): Landschildkrötenanlage im Ruhr-Zoo. – DATZ, Stuttgart, 47 (9): 552.

GUSSONE (1839): Notizie sulle isole Linosa, Lampione, et Lampedusa e descrizione di una nuova specie di Stapeliache che trovasi in questa ultima – lette nell'anno 1832. – Atti R. Accad. Sci., Sez. R. borbon., Sez. Bot., 4: 74-97.

GUYOT (1996a): Biologie de la conservation chez la tortue d'Hermann française. – Dissertation, Univ. Pierre et Marie Curie, Paris, 156 pp.

GUYOT (1996b): État d'une population de tortues d'Hermann après perturbation du site par la construction d'une autoroute. – In: SOPTOM (Eds.): International Congress of Chelonian Conservation – Proceedings. – Gonfaron (Editions SOPTOM): 184-185.

GUYOT (1996c): Biologie de la conservation chez la tortue d'Hermann française. – La Tortue, Gonfaron, 38: 14-17.

GUYOT (1997a): Étude d'impact sur la zone du centre d'élevage et d'information du Village des Tortues. –; SOPTOM Report, Gonfaron, 15 pp.

GUYOT (1997b): Conservation measures for a population of Hermann's tortoise Testudo hermanni in southern France bisected by a major highway. – Biological Conservation, 79 (2/3): 251-256.

GUYOT (1999a): Quelques aspects de la dynamique des populations chez Testudo hermanni hermanni dans le sud-est de la France – Conséquences pour sa conservation. – Bulletin de la Société Herpétologique de France, Paris, 89: 5-16.

GUYOT (1999b): La tortue face aux infrastructures routières – problèmes et aménagements expérimentés en France et à l'étranger. – In: Actes des troisièmes Rencontres »Routes et Faune Sauvage«, Ministère de l'Equipement, des Transports et du Logement und Ministère de l'Aménagement du Territoire et de l'Environnement, Strasbourg: 123-131.

GUYOT (2000): Un symposium consacré aux espèces de tortues vivant en Floride. – Manouria, Mezzavia, 6: 9-10.

GUYOT (2001a): La tortue d'Hermann française, étude écologique et perspectives. – Manouria, Mezzavia, 12: 10-22.

GUYOT (2001b): Du nouveau sur la tortue d'Hermann et les herbicides. – Manouria, Mezzavia, 13: 3-4.

GUYOT (2002): Some Biological Comments on Hermann's Tortoise, Testudo hermanni. – Reptile & Amphibian Journal, www.kingsnake.com, 3: 9-15.

GUYOT JACKSON (2004): Les cris de la Tortue d'Hermann, un moyen de sélection reproductive. – Manouria, Mezzavia, 25: 6.

GUYOT & CLOBERT (1997): Conservation measures for a population of Hermann's tortoise Testudo hermanni in southern France bisected by a major highway. – Biological Conservation, **79**: 251-256.

GUYOT & DEVAUX (1997a): Variation in shell morphology and color of Hermann's tortoise, *Testudo hermanni*, in southern Europe. – Chelonian Conservation and Biology, Lunenburg, **2** (3): 390-395.

GUYOT & DEVAUX (1997b): Variation de la morphologie de la carapace et des colorations chez la tortue d'Hermann. – La Tortue, Gonfaron, **38**: 22-25.

GUYOT & LESCURE (1994): Etude préliminaire du comportament alimentaire en enclos semi-naturel chez la tortue d'Hermann (*Testudo hermanni hermanni* GMELIN, 1789). – Bulletin de la Société Herpétologique de France, Paris: 69-70.

GUYOT & PRITCHARD (1999): First record of introduced eastern Mediterranean tortoises, *Testudo hermanni boettgeri*, in southern France. – Chelonian Conservation and Biology, Lunenburg, **3** (3): 518-520.

GUYOT, PIEAU & RENOUS (1994): Développement embryonnaire d'une tortue terrestre, la tortue d'Hermann, *Testudo hermanni* GMELIN, 1789. – Annales des Sciences Naturelles, Zoologie, Paris, 13e Serie, **15**: 115-137.

GUYOT JACKSON (2003): Chers lectrices et lecteurs. – Manouria, Mezzavia, **20**: 1.

GUYOT JACKSON (2004): Manouria 22. Numéro Spécial Testudo. – CD-ROM, Mezzavia (SARL MANOURIA editions).

HAACKER (1960): Zoologische Beobachtungen in der Camargue und an der Cte d'Azur, Varoise. – DATZ, Stuttgart, **13** (4): 221-223.

HAAG (1996): Tortoise news from Romania. – British Chelonia Group Newsletter, **114**: 6-7.

HAAS (1968): Freude an Schildkröten. – Bremen (Heimtier-Bücherei): 14, 31.

HABSBURG-LOTHRINGEN (1894): Die Liparischen Inseln – Allgemeiner Teil. – Prague (H. Merey), X, 159 pp.

HACKETHAL (1993): Haltungsrichtlinien für Schildkröten in menschlicher Obhut. – Journal der AG Schildkröten & Panzerechsen der DGHT, Bennstedt, **2** (3): 23-27.

HACKETHAL (1994): Ergänzungen der Haltungsrichtlinien für Schildkröten. – Journal der AG Schildkröten & Panzerechsen der DGHT, Bennstedt, **3** (3): 13.

HACKETHAL (1995a): Zusammenfassung des AG S & P Workshops in Dresden vom 25. bis 27.11.1994. – Journal der AG Schildkröten & Panzerechsen der DGHT, Bennstedt, **4** (1): 11-12.

HACKETHAL (1995b): Diskussion zur temperaturabhängigen Geschlechtsausbildung bei Schildkröten wird gewünscht! – Journal der AG Schildkröten & Panzerechsen der DGHT, Bürstadt, **4** (1): 13.

HADZI (1935): Kurze zoogeographische Übersicht Jugoslaviens. – Verhandlungen der Internationalen Vereinigung für theoretische und angewandte Limnologie, Kiel, **7**: 36-45.

HÄFELI & RYTZ (1991): Therapiemöglichkeiten der Unterkieferfraktur bei Landschildkröten. – Proceedings of the 4th International Colloquium for Pathology and Medicine of Reptiles and Amphibians, Bad Nauheim: 251-254.

HÄFELI & ZWART (2000): Panzerweiche bei jungen Landschildkröten und deren mögliche Ursachen. – Der praktische Tierarzt, Hannover, **81** (2): 129-132. – SIGS-Info, Siblingen, **7** (1): 29.

HAFFNER (1994): Les Reptiles. – In: MAURIN (Ed.): Inventaire de la faune menacée en France. – Paris (Editions Nathan/MNHN/WWF): 88-99.

HAGIST (1963): Salat als Todesursache bei Schildkröten. – DATZ, Stuttgart, **16** (9): 349.

HAHN (1996): Schildkröten-Kauf. – Ein Herz für Tiere, Ismaning, **9**: 73.

HAILEY (1988a): Population ecology and conservation of tortoises: the estimation of density and dynamics of a small population. – The Herpetological Journal, London, **1**: 263-271.

HAILEY (1988b): Tortoise Conservation in Greece. – Testudo, **2** (6): 57-68.

HAILEY (1989): How far do animals move? Routine movements in a tortoise. – Canadian Journal of Zoology, Ottawa, **67**: 208-215.

HAILEY (1990): Adult survival and recruitment and the explanation of an uneven sex ratio in a tortoise population. – Canadian Journal of Zoology, Ottawa, **68**: 547-555.

HAILEY (1991): Regulation of a Greek tortoise population. – British Ecological Society Bulletin, London, **22**: 119-123.

HAILEY (1999): Variation of adult body size of the tortoise *Testudo hermanni* in Greece: proximate and ultimate causes. – Journal of Zoology, London, **248**: 379-396.

HAILEY (2000a): Assessing body mass conditions in the tortoise *Testudo hermanni*. – The Herpetological Journal, London, **10** (2): 57-61.

HAILEY (2000b): Implications of high intrinsic growth rate of a tortoise population for conservation. – Animal Conservation, London, **3**: 185-189.

HAILEY (2000c): The effects of fire and mechanical habitat destruction on survival of the tortoise *Testudo hermanni* in northern Greece. – Biological Conservation, **92**: 321-333.

HAILEY (2001): Home range area in the tortoise *Testudo hermanni* in relation to habitat complexity: implications for conservation and biodiversity. – Biodiversity and Conservation, **10**: 1131-1140.

HAILEY & COULSON (1999): The growth pattern of the African tortoise *Geochelone pardalis* and other chelonians. – Canadian Journal of Zoology, Ottawa, **77**: 181-193.

HAILEY & GOUTNER (1991): Villas, villagers and tortoises in Greece – a sequel. – Oryx, Cambridge & Washington, 25 (3): 169-171.

HAILEY & GOUTNER (1991): Changes in the Alyki Kitrous wetland in northern Greece: 1990-1999, and future prospects. – Biodiversity and Conservation, 11: 357-377.

HAILEY & LOUMBOURDIS (1988): Egg size and shape, clutch dynamics, and reproductive effort in European tortoises. – Canadian Journal of Zoology, Ottawa, 66: 1527-1536.

HAILEY & LOUMBOURDIS (1990): Population ecology and conservation of tortoises: demographic aspects of reproduction in Testudo hermanni. – The Herpetological Journal, London, 1: 425-434.

HAILEY & THEOPHILIDIS (1987): Cardiac responses to stress and activity in the armored legless lizard Ophisaurus apodus in comparison with snake and tortoise. – Comparative Biochemistry and Physiology, A, Comparative Physiology, Vancouver, 88 (2): 201-206.

HAILEY & WILLEMSEN (1988): Status and conservation of tortoises in Greece. – The Herpetological Journal, London, 1, 315-330.

HAILEY & WILLEMSEN (2000): Population density and adult sex ratio of the tortoise Testudo hermanni in Greece: evidence for intrinsic population regulation. – Journal of Zoology, London, 251 (3): 325-338.

HAILEY & WILLEMSEN (2003): Changes in the status of tortoise populations in Greece 1984-2001. – Biodiversity and Conservation, 12: 991-1011.

HAILEY, PULFORD & STUBBS (1984): Summer activity patterns of Testudo hermanni GMELIN in Greece and France. – Amphibia-Reptilia, Leiden, 5 (1): 69-78.

HAILEY, WRIGHT & STEER (1988): Population ecology and conservation of tortoises: the effects of disturbance. – The Herpetological Journal, London, 1: 294-301.

HALLMEN (2004): Reptilienhaltung in der Schule. – DATZ, Stuttgart, 57 (11): 6-11.

HANGER (1984): Some reptiles of Corfu. – British Herpetological Society Bulletin, London, 10: 39-42.

HANSBACH (1995a): Der Tierarztbesuch. – Schildkröten, Linden, 2 (3): 6-9.

HANSBACH (1995b): Regenzeit statt Legezeit. – Schildkröten, Linden, 2 (4): 24-26.

HANSBACH (2001): Eigrube ist nicht gleich Eigrube. – Schildkröten, Linden, 8 (3): 25.

HANSEN (1990): So lebt die Schildkröte. – Luzern (Kinderbuchverlag Luzern), 40 pp.

HARCOURT-BROWN (1997): The Effects of Captivity on Tortoise Behaviour. – Testudo, 4 (4): 19-25.

HARLESS & MORLOCK (Eds.) (1979): Turtles – Perspectives and Research. – New York (John Wiley & Sons): 16, 140, 193, 210, 334-335, 361, 366, 369, 372, 385, 409, 425, 490, 511, 543, 557, 559.

HARPER (1983): European tortoises – what now? – British Chelonia Group Newsletter, 40: 4-5.

HARPER (1986): Hibernating tortoise. – The Veterinary Record, London, 118: 408.

HARRISON (1989): Regeneration of the Tail Spur in Testudo hermanni. – Testudo, 3 (1): 81-83.

HARTL (1999): Ernährung europäischer Landschildkröten. – Ein Herz für Tiere, Ismaning, 1: 28.

HARTMANN (1977): Zeitigung von Landschildkröteneiern. – Aquarien Terrarien, Leipzig, Jena & Berlin, 24 (5): 152-153.

HAWES (1998): Sale of juvenile tortoises in UK. – Tortoise Trust Newsletter, London, 13 (2): 10.

HAXHIU (1979): Përcaktues i reptileve te Shqipërise. – Shtepia botuese e Universitetit Tiranë, Tirana, 144 pp.

HAXHIU (1981): Emërtime popullore të zvaranikeve. – Studime Filologjike, Tirana, 4: 209-217.

HAXHIU (1982): Mbi gjarprinjtë giysëm helmues dhe helmues të vendit tonë. – Buletin Shkencave Mjeksore, Tirana, 1: 57-65.

HAXHIU (1985): Rezultate të studimit të breshkavetë ne vendit tonë (Rendi Testudines). – Buletin Shkencave Natyres, Tirana, 39 (2): 99-104.

HAXHIU (1986): Studim për bretkosat e gjelbra të vendit tonë. – Buletin Shkencave Natyres, Tirana, 40 (3): 47-55, (4): 79-84.

HAXHIU (1987): Studim për bretkosat e gjelbra të vendit tonë. – Buletin Shkencave Natyres, Tirana, 41 (1): 106-114.

HAXHIU (1995a): Results of studies on the chelonians of Albania. – Chelonian Conservation and Biology, Lunenburg, 1 (4): 324-326.

HAXHIU (1995b): Current data on the chelonians of Albania. – Chelonian Conservation and Biology, Lunenburg, 1 (4): 326-327.

HAXHIU (1998): The Reptilia of Albania: species composition, distribution, habitats. – Bonner Zoologische Beiträge, Bonn: 48: 35-57.

HAXHIU & ORUÇI (2002): Current status of Testudo genus in Albania. – Chelonii, Gonfaron, 3: 190-192.

HAYNES (1996): Story from the stock officer. – British Chelonia Group Newsletter, 114: 20.

HAYWOOD (2001): A veterinary treatment experience. – Tortoise Trust Newsletter, London, 15 (4)/16 (1): 8.

HEATHCOTE (1994): Some Notes to Aid Successful Hibernation for the Mediterranean Tortoise. – Reptilian Magazine, 10: 33-35.

HEDIGER (1958): Zum Überwinterungs-Verhalten der Griechischen Landschildkröte. – Natur und Volk, Frankfurt am Main, **88** (4): 121-123.

VON HEGEL (1997): Möglichkeiten der Kennzeichnung von im Anhang A der EU-Verordnung genannten Reptilienarten. – BNA-aktuell, Hambrücken, 4: 69-70.

HEIMANN (1986): Zur Aufzucht junger Landschildkröten. – elaphe, Berlin, **8** (2): 30-31.

HEIMANN (1987-1988): Vorschläge zur zweckmäßigen Haltung und effektiven Zucht europäischer Landschildkröten. – Aquarien Terrarien, Leipzig, **34** (11): 386-391, **34** (12): 414-416, **35** (1): 23-27.

HEIMANN (1989): Betr. »Aktivität von Landschildkröten-Weibchen bei der Paarung« (DATZ 9/88). – DATZ, Stuttgart, **42** (2): 125.

HEIMANN (1990): Testudo hermanni GMELIN. – Sauria Supplement, Amphibien-Reptilien-Kartei, Berlin, **12** (3): 175-178.

HEIMANN (1991): Europäische Landschildkröten – Haltung, Zucht. – Vortragszusammenfassung der DGHT-Jahrestagung, Bonn: 20-21.

HEIMANN (1992): Eine F2-Generation bei Testudo hermanni boettgeri MOJSISOVICS 1889 in Gefangenschaft. – Sauria, Berlin, **14** (2): 19-22.

HEIMANN (2000): Eine F3-Generation bei Testudo hermanni boettgeri MOJSISOVICS 1889 in menschlicher Obhut. – Sauria, Berlin, **22** (3): 41-44.

HEISSENBÜTTEL (1993): Diebstahl von Landschildkröten aus Freilandanlage in Bremen. – Journal der AG Schildkröten & Panzerechsen der DGHT, Bürstadt, **2** (3): 7-8.

HELDREICH (1878): La faune de Grèce – 1er part – Animaux vertébrés. – Philocalie, Athens, 113 pp.

HELDSTAB & BESTETTI (1982): Spontaneous viral hepatitis in a spur-tailed Mediterranean land tortoise (Testudo hermanni); Journal of Zoo Animal Medicine, 13: 113-120.

HELDSTAB & BESTETTI (1984): Herpesviridae causing glossitis and meningoencephalities in land tortoises (Testudo hermanni). – Proc. Int. Coll. Pathol. Rept. Amphib., Nottingham.

HELDSTAB & BESTETTI (1989): Herpesviridae causing glossitis and meningoencephalities in land tortoises (Testudo hermanni). – Herpetopathologia, Angers, **1** (2): 5-9.

HELLWING (1990): Testudo hermanni – Wer hat die größte im ganzen Land? – DATZ, **43** (5): 313.

HELMER, STRIJBOSCH & SCHOLTE (1988): Two addenda to the Greek herpetofauna and some new distributional data on mainland Greece. – Amphibia-Reptilia, Leiden, **9**: 421-422.

HELMER & SCHOLTE (1985): Herpetological research in Evros, Greece – proposal for a biogenetic reserve.

– Societas Europaea Herpetologica, Conservation Committee, Bonn, 142 pp.

HELLMICH (1956): Die Lurche und Kriechtiere Europas. – Winters naturwissenschaftliche Taschenbücher, Heidelberg (Carl Winter, Universitätsverlag), 26: 84.

HENIN, BIANCHI & LIPPE (1969): Active transport of Cl-across the isolated intestinal mucosa of Testudo hermanni. – Experientia, Bangor, **25**: 701-702.

HENKEL & SCHÖNE (Eds.) (1967): Emblemata – Handbuch zur Sinnbildkunst des XVI. und XVII. Jahrhunderts. – Stuttgart (Metzler), 1045 pp.

HENLE (1980): Herpetologische Beobachtungen in der Umgebung Rovinjs (Jugoslawien). – herpetofauna, Weinstadt, **2** (6): 6-10.

HENLE (1999): Die Kennzeichnung von Reptilien. – In: BUNDESMINISTERIUM FÜR UMWELT, NATURSCHUTZ UND REAKTORSICHERHEIT (Eds.): Methoden der Kennzeichnung lebender Wirbeltierarten nach der künftigen Bundesartenschutzverordnung und der EG-Durchführungsverordnung Nr. 939/97 vom 26.05.1997. – Bonn (Bundesministerium für Umwelt, Naturschutz und Reaktorsicherheit): 44-46.

HENNEN (2000): Optimierung von Freilandanlagen für europäische Landschildkröten. – Radiata, Bennstedt, **9** (1): 9-16.

HENNIG (1966): Phylogenetische Systematik. – Berlin & Hamburg (Parey-Verlag), 246 pp.

HENRY, NOUGARÈDE, PRADEL & CHEYLAN (1998): Survival rates and demography of the tortoise Testudo hermanni in Corsica. – In: MIAUD & GUYÉTANT (Eds.): Current Studies in Herpetology. – Proceedings of the 9th Ordinary Meeting of the Societas Europaea Herpetologica, Le Bourget du Lac: 189-196.

HERBEL (2003): Schildkrötenbeobachtung auf der Peloponnes. – Radiata, Lingenfeld, **12** (2): 31-34.

HERMANN (1804): Observationes zoologicae. – Strasbourg & Paris.

HERON (1968): Tortoises in a French Garden. – International Turtle and Tortoise Society Journal, Los Angeles, **2** (1): 18-19, 30-33, 39-40.

HERSCHE (1991): Merkblatt zur Haltung von europäischen Landschildkröten. – SIGS, 2 pp.

HERSCHE (1992): Merkblatt zur Aufzucht Europäischer Landschildkröten. – SIGS, 2 pp.

HERSCHE (1995): Haltung von europäischen und aus dem Mittelmeerraum stammenden Landschildkröten; SIGS-Informationsblatt, 1, 2 pp.

HERSCHE (1996): Buchbesprechung: BRIAN PURSALL: Ratgeber Europäische Landschildkröten. – SIGS-Info, Siblingen, **5** (3): 23-24.

HERSCHE (1998a): Problem Winterschlaf. – Fachmagazin Schildkröte, Rothenfluh, **1** (1): 43.

HERSCHE (1998b): Schutzhaus für mediterrane Landschildkröten. – Fachmagazin Schildkröte, Rothenfluh, 1 (3): 48-53.

HERSCHE (1998c): Wer ist die größte Griechin? – Fachmagazin Schildkröte, Rothenfluh, 1 (3): 58.

HERSCHE (1998d): Schildkröten auf Sardinien. – Fachmagazin Schildkröte, Rothenfluh, 1 (4); 16-23.

HERSCHE (1999/2000a): Temperaturbedürfnisse von Schildkröten. – Fachmagazin Schildkröte, Rothenfluh, 2 (1): 18-21.

HERSCHE (1999/2000b): Aufzuchtbehälter für Schildkröten. – Fachmagazin Schildkröte, Rothenfluh, 2 (1): 30-31.

HERSCHE (1999/2000c): Sie fragen, wir antworten. – Fachmagazin Schildkröte, Rothenfluh, 2 (2): 23.

HERSCHE (1999/2000d): Testudo hermanni, Griechische Landschildkröte. – Fachmagazin Schildkröte, Rothenfluh, 2 (3): 56-57.

HERSCHE (1999/2000e): Schildkrötenausstellung – Die Vielfalt der Schildkröten. – Fachmagazin Schildkröte, Rothenfluh, 2 (4): 12-23

HERSCHE & BAUR (1998): Herpes – tatsächlich noch nie was davon gehört? – Fachmagazin Schildkröte, Rothenfluh, 1 (4): 50-52.

HERSCHE & HOHL (1999/2000): Die Aufzucht mediterraner Landschildkröten. – Fachmagazin Schildkröte, Rothenfluh, 2 (1): 52-61.

HERVET (2000): Tortues du Quaternaire de France. Critères de détermination, répartitions chronologique et géographique. – Marseille (Mésogée), 58: 3-47.

HERVET (2001): Etude du peuplement chélonien de la Corse à partir de la répartition des tortues fossiles de la Méditerranée occidentale. – Bul. Soc. Sciences Hist. et Nat. de la Corse, Ajaccio, 696-669:147-163.

HERZ (1994): Beobachtungen an Breitrandschildkröten Testudo marginata SCHOEPFF, 1792 in freier Natur. – Sauria, Berlin, 16 (1): 27-30.

HERZ (2002): Testudo hermanni boettgeri MOJSISOVICS, 1889 in Norddalmatien. – Sauria, Berlin, 24 (4): 19-22.

HERZ (2005): Unerwartete Nachzucht von Testudo hercegovinensis WERNER, 1899. – Radiata, Lingenfeld, 14 (4): 13-19.

HERZOG (2000): Und noch eine Schildkrötengeschichte ... – SIGS-Info, Siblingen, 9 (4): 26-27.

HEWITT (1999): Post-glacial re-colonization of European biota. – Biological Journal of the Linnean Society, London, 68: 87-112.

HIBBERD (1980): Hibernation difficulties in a Hermann's tortoise. – Testudo, 1 (3): 22-23.

HIEDELS (2001a): Schildkröten in Griechenland. – Schildkrötenfreunde intern, Gelsenkirchen, 4 (1): 12-13, (2): 32-33.

HIEDELS (2001b): Der Vergleich zwischen Griechenland und hier!!! – Schildkrötenfreunde intern, Gelsenkirchen, 4 (1): 13-15.

HIGHFIELD (1985): Incubation of eggs and care of hatchlings. – Journal of Chelonian Herpetology, London: 1-24.

HIGHFIELD (1986): Safer Hibernation and Your Tortoise. – Tortoise Trust, Norwich.

HIGHFIELD (1987a): Recommended diet for captive tortoises. – Tortoise Trust, Norwich.

HIGHFIELD (1987b): Causal Factors of Mortality in Captive Collections. – Testudo, 2 (5): 15-17.

HIGHFIELD (1988a): Practical dietary recommendations for hatchling tortoises. – Tortoise Trust technical bulletin, London, 18.

HIGHFIELD (1988b): A new size record for T. hermanni GMELIN 1789? – The Rephibiary, Burford, 132: 5-6.

HIGHFIELD (1989a): Diagnostic characters of tortoises (1) – Division of the supracaudal scute in Testudo and its relevance as a taxonomic diagnostic character. – British Herpetological Society Bulletin, London, 30: 14-18.

HIGHFIELD (1989b): Revision of Taxonomic Status and Nomenclature, Genus Testudo – A brief chronology. – The Rephibiary, Banbury: 141.

HIGHFIELD (1989c): Feeding Your Tortoise. – Tortoise Trust, Norwich.

HIGHFIELD (1989d): General Care of Tortoises. – Tortoise Trust, Norwich.

HIGHFIELD (1989e): Notes on dietary constituents for herbivorous terrestrial chelonia and their effects on growth and development. – ASRA Journal, Burford, 3 (3): 7-20.

HIGHFIELD (1990a): Keeping and Breeding Tortoises in Captivity. – Portishead (R & A Publishing): 2, 4-5, 9, 26, 36-37, 58, 97-101.

HIGHFIELD (1990b): Artificial incubation techniques in relation to Testudo graeca and Testudo hermanni with notes on embryonic anoxia as a possible factor in hatchling mortality. – Testudo, 3 (3): 2-4.

HIGHFIELD (1990c): Observations on the incidence and taxonomic significance of divided supracaudal scutes in Mediterranean tortoises genus Testudo. – Tortoise Trust Newsletter, London, 5 (1): 8-9.

HIGHFIELD (1992): New disease problems in Hermann's tortoises? – Tortoise Trust Newsletter, London, 7 (1): 6-7.

HIGHFIELD (1994): Tortoise Trust Guide to Tortoises & Turtles. – London (Carapace Press): 6-8, 10, 16-17, 25-28, 50.

HIGHFIELD (1996a): Practical Encyclopedia of Keeping and Breeding Tortoises and Freshwater Turtles. – London (Carapace Press): 5, 9, 29, 33-34, 36-38, 51, 237-241, plates X-XV, XXIV.

HIGHFIELD (1996b): Tortoises – do they need to drink? – Tortoise Trust Newsletter, London, 11 (1): 10-11.

HIGHFIELD (1996c): Shell disease (»shell-rot«) in tortoises. – Tortoise Trust Newsletter, London, 11 (4): 15.

HIGHFIELD (1996d): Observations on the incidence and taxonomic significance of divided supracaudal scutes in Mediterranean tortoises genus Testudo. – Tortoise Trust Newsletter, London, 11 (2): 8-9.+

HIGHFIELD (1997a): An effective method of artificial incubation for Mediterranean tortoise eggs. – Tortoise Trust Newsletter, London, 12 (1): 6-7.

HIGHFIELD (1997b): Bebrüten von eiern von mediterranen Landschildkröten. – SIGS-Info, Siblingen

HIGHFIELD (1998): When tortoises won't feed. – Tortoise Trust Newsletter, London, 13 (4): 6-7.

HIGHFIELD (1999): Shell rot revisited. – Tortoise Trust Newsletter, London, 14 (1): 15.

HIGHFIELD (2000): The Tortoise and Turtle Feeding Manual. London (Carapace Press): 3-5, 7, 9, 29, 37-38, 51, 237-240, plate XXIV.

HIGHFIELD (2001a): Critical care – when hatchlings arrive! – Tortoise Trust Newsletter, London, 16 (2): 17.

HIGHFIELD (2001b): Tortoises – do they need to drink? – the Tortuga Gazette, Van Nuys, 37 (6): 7.

HIGHFIELD (2002): Natural and artificial nest sites for terrestrial tortoises. – Tortoise Trust Newsletter, London, 17 (3/4): 19-20.

HIGHFIELD (2003): Caring for juvenile tortoises: basic guidelines. – Tortoise Trust Newsletter, London, 18 (2): 8, 12.

HIGHFIELD (2005): Tortoises: do they need to drink? – the Tortuga Gazette, Van Nuys, 41 (3): 8-10.

HIGHFIELD & MARTIN (1989): A revision of the Testudines of North Africa, Asia and Europe. – Journal of Chelonian Herpetology, London, 1 (1): 1-12.

HILL (1981): Success at last – hatching of T. hermanni and T. graeca. – British Chelonia Group Newsletter, 24: 3-5.

HILL (1984): Breeding success in Southampton. – British Chelonia Group Newsletter, 41: 4-5.

HILL (2003): Bemerkungen zur Herpetofauna von Korfu (Griechenland). – ÖGH-Aktuell, Vienna, 12: 10-13.

HILLER (2002): Schildkröten in der Literatur des 19. Jahrhunderts. – Radiata, Haan, 11 (4): 45-47.

HILLER (2005): Schildkröten im Zweiten Weltkrieg. – Minor, Lingenfeld, 4 (3): 28-29.

HOARE (2002): Homeopathy. – Testudo, 5 (4): 17-24.

HOCHLEITNER (1990): Papillom im Bereich der Kloake bei einer Griechischen Landschildkröte (Testudo hermanni). – Wiener Tierärztliche Monatsschrift, Vienna, 77 (7): 234-235.

HOFER (1967): Beiträge zur Herpetologie Korfus. – Unveröffentlichtes Manuskript, Universität Innsbruck, 9 pp.

HOFER (2004): Freilandbeobachtungen an der Griechischen Landschildkröte Testudo hermanni boettgeri. – Sacalia, Stiefern, 2 (4): 37-40.

HOFF (1937): Méditation in solitude. – Journal of the Warburg Institute, London, 1 (4): 292-294.

HOFFMANN & BAUR (1999/2000a): Die Verdauung bei Landschildkröten unter Berücksichtigung der anatomischen Strukturen. – Fachmagazin Schildkröte, Rothenfluh, 2 (2): 17-21.

HOFFMANN & BAUR (1999/2000b): AGROBS – Biofutter für Landschildkröten. – Fachmagazin Schildkröte, Rothenfluh, 2 (2): 24-25.

HOHL & HERSCHE (1999/2000): Briefkasten. – Fachmagazin Schildkröte, Rothenfluh, 2 (2): 48-49.

HOLFERT & HOLFERT (1999): Europäische Landschildkröten im Freilandterrarium. Langjährige Erfahrungen im Haltung und Vermehrung. – Reptilia (D), Münster, 17: 24-31.

HOLMAN (1998): Pleistocene Amphibians and Reptiles in Britain and Europe. – Oxford Monographs in Geology and Geophysics, Oxford (Oxford University Press), X, 254 pp.

HOLT (1978): Radiological studies of the alimentary tract in two Greek tortoises. – The Veterinary Record, London, 103: 198-200.

HOLT (1980): Worm infestations in tortoises – Part 1 – Diagnosis. – Testudo, 1 (3): 10-14.

HOLT & COOPER (1976): Stomatitis in the Greek tortoise. – The Veterinary Record, London, 98: 156.

HOLT, COOPER & NEEDHAM (1979): Diseases of tortoises: a review of seventy cases. – Journal of Small Animal Practice, 20: 269-286.

HONEGGER (1974): The reptile trade. – International Zoo Yearbook, London, 14: 47-52.

HONEGGER (1975a): Breeding and maintaining reptiles in captivity. – In: MARTIN (Ed.): Breeding endangered species in captivity. – London (Academy Press).

HONEGGER (1975b): The public aquarium and terrarium as a consumer of wildlife. – International Zoo Yearbook, London, 15: 269-271

HONEGGER (1978): Threatened amphibians and reptiles in Europe. – Strasbourg (European Council), 123 pp.

HONEGGER (1980a): Testudo hermanni (GMELIN, 1789) – Code A-301.011.010.002. – In: DOLLINGER (Ed.): Convention on International Trade in Endangered Species of Wild Fauna and Flora Identification Manual, Band 3, Reptilia, Amphibia, Pisces. – Lausanne & Paris (Secretariat for the Convention): 1-2.

HONEGGER (1980b): Breeding endangered species of amphibians and reptiles – some critical remarks and suggestions. – British Journal of Herpetology, London, 16 (6): 113-118.

HONEGGER (1981): Threatened Amphibians and Reptiles in Europe – Handbuch der Reptilien und Amphibien Europas, Ergänzungsband. – Wiesbaden (Akademische Verlagsgesellschaft): 5, 14, 24-26, 29-30, 40-42, 44, 51, 99-102.

HONEGGER (1982): Schildkröten – verehrt und begehrt. – Natur und Museum, Frankfurt am Main, 112 (9): 294-302.

HORSTHUIS (1965): Waarnemingen bij Testudo graeca en T. hermanni. – Lacerta, Zoetermeer, 23 (7): 50, (10-11): 87..

HRABE, OLIVA & OPATRNY (1973): Klic Nasich Ryb, Obojzivelniku a Plazu. – Statni Pedagogicke Nakladatelstvi, Prague, 347 pp.

HRISTOVIC (1892): Matériaux pour l'étude de la faune bulgare. – Sbornik za narodni umotvorenija, Sofia, VII: 413-428.

HUBER (1999): Würmchen inbegriffen. – Ein Herz für Tiere, Ismaning, 7: 58-59.

HUMMEL (2004a): Das Carapax Center in Massa Marittima. – Reptilia (D), Münster, 47: 14-15.

HUMMEL (2004b): Naturkundliche Einrichtungen in Berlin und Potsdam. – Sacalia, Stiefern, 2 (3): 24-31.

HUMMEL (2004c): Urlaubsgrüße aus Griechenland. – Sacalia, Stiefern, 2 (3): 41-44.

HUMMEL (2006): Zu den Unterschieden der Europäischen Landschildkröten. – Sacalia, Stiefern, 4 (10): 46-48.

HUOT-DAUBREMENT (1996): Contribution à l'étude écophysiologique de differents aspects du cycle annuel de la tortue d'Hermann (Testudo hermanni hermanni) dans le Massif des Maures (Var). – Dissertation, Univ. du Tours, Tours, 180 pp.

HUOT-DAUBREMENT (1997): Contribution à l'étude écophysiologique de differents aspects du cycle annuel de la tortue d'Hermann dans le Massif des Maures. – La Tortue, Gonfaron, 38: 18-21

HUOT-DAUBREMENT (2002): Étude de la thermorégulation de la Tortue d'Hermann (Testudo hermanni hermanni) au cours de son cycle annuel, à l'aide d'une sonde intracorporelle – rythme nycthéméral et échelle thermobiologique. – Chelonii, Gonfaron, 3: 145-154.

HUOT-DAUBREMONT & GRENOT (1996a): Thermoregulation study of the Hermann tortoise (Testudo hermanni hermanni) by radio-telemetry – first results. – In: SOPTOM (Eds.): International Congress of Chelonian Conservation – Proceedings. – Gonfaron (Editions SOPTOM): 324.

HUOT-DAUBREMENT & GRENOT (1996b): Suivi de la thermorégulation de la Tortue d'Hermann (Testudo

hermanni hermanni), à l'aide d'une sonde intracorporelle – étude préliminaire. – Bulletin de la Société Herpétologique de France, Paris, 78: 35-41.

HUOT-DAUBREMENT & GRENOT (1997): Rythme d'activité de la tortue d'Hermann (Testudo hermanni hermanni) en semi-liberté dans le massif des Maures (Var). – Terre Vie, Rabat-Agdal, 52: 331-344.

HUOT-DAUBREMENT, GRENOT & BRADSHAW (1996): Temperature regulation in Hermann's tortoise, Testudo hermanni, studied with indwelling probes. – Amphibia-Reptilia, Leiden, 17: 91-102.

HUOT-DAUBREMENT, BRADSHAW, BRADSHAW & KUCHLING (2002): Testosterone and progesterone levels during the activity period of Hermann's tortoise (Testudo hermanni hermanni) in captivity and in the wild. – Chelonii, Gonfaron, 3: 331.

HUOT-DAUBREMONT, BRADSHAW, BRADSHAW, KUCHLING & GRENOT (2003): Variation of plasma sex steroid concentrations in wild and captive populations of Hermann's tortoise (Testudo hermanni hermanni) in southern France. – General and Comparative Endocrinology, 130 (3): 299-307.

HUSBAND (1980): Tortoises and veterinary surgeons. – Testudo, 1 (3): 73-75.

IFTIME (2002): Testudo hermanni GMELIN, 1789 in Dobroudja (SE Romania), with comments on conservation. – Herpetozoa, Vienna, 15 (3/4): 183-186.

IGALFFY, MLADINOV & PAVLETIC (1965): Contribution à l'étude de la faune de l'île de Pag. – Rapp. P.-v. Réun. Comm. Int. Explor. Scient. Mer. Méditerr., XVIII (2): 531-535.

INNES (1988): The protection of reptiles in Bulgaria. – British Chelonia Group Newsletter, 62: 12.

INNIS (1994): Considerations in formulating captive tortoise diets. – Bulletin of Association of Reptilian and Amphibian Veterinarians, Chester Heights, 4 (1): 8-11.

INNIS (1995): Per cloacal worming of tortoises. – Journal of Herpetological Medicine and Surgery, Chester Heights, 5 (2): 4.

INNIS (1997): Observations on urinalyses of clinically normal captive tortoises. – Proceedings of the Association of Reptilian and Amphibian Veterinarians: 109-112.

INSTITUTO NACIONAL PARA LA CONSERVACIÓN DE LA NATURALEZA (1992): Libro rojo de los vertebrados Españoles. – Publicaciones del Ministerio de Agricultura, Pesca y Alimentación, Madrid.

IONEV (1999): Temps difficiles en Bulgarie! – La Tortue, Gonfaron, 46/47: 16.

IPPEN (1962): Die spontane Tuberkulose bei Kaltblütern. – Verhandlungsbericht über Erkrankungen der Zootiere, 4: 183-192.

IPPEN (1972): Ein Beitrag zu Spontantumoren bei Reptilien. – Verhandlungsbericht über Erkrankungen der Zootiere, **14**: 409-418.

IPPEN (1978): Ein Beitrag zu den Thyreopathien bei Reptilien. – Verhandlungsbericht über Erkrankungen der Zootiere, **20**: 357-371.

IPPEN (1992): General review of parasites in turtles and tortoises. – Congrès international sur la pathologie des chéloniens, Gonfaron.

IRCHEK (1899): Principality of Bulgaria – II – Journey to Bulgaria. – 942 pp.

ISENBÜGEL (1981): Hautveränderungen bei Landschildkröten unbekannter Ursache. – Tagungsbericht der 1. Arbeitstagung der Zootierärzte im deutschsprachigen Raum: 20-21.

ISHII & ISHII (1986): Glossopharyngeal innervation of chemo- and baroreceptors in the dorsal carotid artery of the tortoise Testudo hermanni. – Respiratory Physiology, **65** (3): 295-302.

ISHII, ISHII & DEJOURS (1986): Activity of vagal afferent fibers innervating carbon dioxide sensitive receptors in the tortoise Testudo hermanni. – The Japanese Journal of Physiology, Tokyo, **36** (5): 1015-1026.

ISHII, ISHII & KUSAKABE (1987): Baroreceptor and chemoreceptor areas in tortoise. – 64th Annual Meeting of the Physiological Society of Japan, Tokyo, 01.-03.04.1987.

IUCN (Eds.) (1991): Tortoises and Freshwater Turtles – An Action Plan for their Conservation. – Gland (IUCN): 6, 12, 15-16, 40.

IUCN (Eds.) (1996): 1996 IUCN Red List of Threatened Animals. – Gland & Cambridge (IUCN): 166.

IUCN (1998): Guidelines for Re-introduction. – Gland & Cambridge (IUCN SSC Reintroduction Specialist Group).

IUCN (2001): IUCN Red List Categories and Criteria – Version 3.1. – Gland & Cambridge (IUCN Species Survival Commission), 30 pp.

IUCN (2003): Guidelines for Application of IUCN Red List Criteria at Regional Levels – Version 3.0. – Gland & Cambridge (IUCN Species Survival Commission), 26 pp.

IVANOV (1936): Nos tortues. – Priroda i Nauka, Sofia, **VI** (8/9): 131-133.

IVERSON (1982): Biomass in turtles (order Testudines) – a neglected subject. – Oecologia, **55**: 69-76.

IVERSON (1985): Checklist of the Turtles of the World with English Common Names. – Society for the Study of Amphibians and Reptiles, Athens, Herpetological Circular No. 14: 10.

IVERSON (1990): Patterns of survivorship in turtles (order Testudines). – Canadian Journal of Zoology, Ottawa, **69**: 385-391.

IVERSON (1992): A Revised Checklist with Distribution Maps of the Turtles of the World. – Richmond (privately printed): 288.

JACKSON (1978a): A method of assessing the health of European and North African tortoises. – British Veterinary Zoological Society, London: 25-26.

JACKSON (1978b): A method of assessing the health of European and North African tortoises. – Testudo, **1** (1): 6-7.

JACKSON (1980a): The results of weights and measurements on healthy and sick tortoises, both Testudo graeca and T. hermanni. – Testudo, **1** (3): 15-19.

JACKSON (1980b): Weight and measurement data on tortoises (Testudo graeca and Testudo hermanni) and their relationship to health. – Journal of Small Animal Practice, **21**: 409-416.

JACKSON (1981): The sick chelonian. – In: COBORN (Ed.): Proceedings of the 1980 European Herpetological Symposium, Oxford, Cotswold Wild Life Park, Burford: 1-4.

JACKSON (1982): Chelonian diets. – Testudo, **2** (1): 17-21.

JACKSON (1985): The clinical examination of reptiles. – In: TOWNSON & LAWRENCE (Eds.): Reptiles: breeding, behaviour and veterinary aspects. – London (British Herpetological Society): 91-97.

JACKSON (1987): Carapace & Other Bone Injuries in Chelonians. – Testudo, **2** (5): 18-21.

JACKSON (1990a): Diagnosis and Treatment of Diseases in Captive Chelonians. – Testudo, **3** (2): 9-17.

JACKSON (1990b): Tortoises and hibernation. – The Veterinary Record, London, **119**: 244.

JACKSON (1991a): The Jackson Ratio. – British Chelonia Group Newsletter, 84: 15.

JACKSON (1991b): Chelonians. – In: BEYNON & COOPER (Eds.): Manual of exotic pets. – Cheltenham (BSAVA Publications): 221-243.

JACKSON & LAWTON (1997): Untersuchung des Patienten und Diagnosestellung. – In: BEYNON, LAWTON & COOPER (Eds.): Kompendium der Reptilienkrankheiten: Haltung – Diagnostik – Therapie. – Hannover (Schlütersche Verlagsanstalt): 39-46.

JACKSON & NEEDHAM (1983): Rhinitis and virus antibody titres in chelonians. – Journal of Small Animal Practice, **24**: 31-36.

JACOBSON (1994): Causes of mortality and diseases in tortoises – a review. – Journal of Zoo and Wildlife Medicine, Media, **25** (1): 2-17.

JACOBSON, WEINSTEIN, BERRY, HARDENBROOK, TOMLINSON & FREITAS (1993): Problems with using weight versus carapace length relationships to assess tortoise health. – The Veterinary Record, London, **132**: 222-223.

JAHANDIEZ (1914): Les îles d'Hyères. – Carqueiranne (privately printed), 447 pp.

JAHN (1963): Kleine Terrarienkunde. – Minden (Albrecht Philler Verlag): 106.

JAHN (1981): Schildkröten. – Minden (Albrecht Philler Verlag): 57-59, Fotos 1, 4.

JAHN (1995): Schildkröten. – Hannover (Landbuch-Verlag): 82-92.

JAKOB (2002): Neue Rubrik »Gestohlen/Gefunden«. – Minor, Haan, 1 (1): 5.

JAKUBOWICZ (2002): Le commerce des tortues du genre Testudo en Belgique. – Chelonii, Gonfaron, 3: 288-292.

JAROFKE & LANGE (1993): Reptilien – Krankheiten und Haltung. – Berlin und Hamburg (Verlag Paul Parey): 50-51, 55, 59-60, 71.

JAROSCH (2002): Eine artgerechte Schildkrötenanlage. – Schildkröten, Linden, 9 (2): 40-41.

JENNEMANN (2003): Panzergangrän bei Europäischen Landschildkröten – Ein Fallbeispiel zur Diagnose, Ursachenanalyse und Behandlung. – Radiata, Lingenfeld, 12 (2): 23-30.

JEPSON (2006): Mediterranean Tortoises. – Havant (Kingdom Books): 6-7, 11, 23-24, 33, 43, 51-52, 54, 59, 62-64, 76-77, 79, 90.

JEROEN (2004): Herpetological trip in northern Greece 30 April – 14 May 2004. – http://users.skynet.be/stefanie.delarue/greece2004.htm.

JESU (1994): Testuggine comune, Testudo hermanni GMELIN, 1789. – In: DORIA & SALVIDIO (Eds.): Atlante degli anfibi e rettili della Liguria. – Genua (Museo Civico di Storia Naturale), 74-75.

JIMÉNEZ & GUILLEM (1997): Diseño y resultados previos del proyecto de (re-)introducción de la tortuga mediterránea (Testudo hermanni) en el Paraje Natural del Desert de les Palmes (Castellón). – Proceedings Jornadas de Conservación de la Tortuga Mediterránea, Benicassim: 80-88.

JIMÉNEZ-FUENTES & MARTÍN (1989): Quelonios fósiles de la cuenca de Guadix-Baza (Granada). – In: ALBERDI & BONADONNA (Eds.): Geología y paleontología de la cuenca de Guadix-Baza. – Trabajos sobre Neógeno/Cuaternario, Museo Nacional de Ciencias Naturales, Madrid, 11: 167-171.

JIMÉNEZ-FUENTES & MARTÍN (1991): Ejemplares-tipo de Quelonios fósiles españoles. – Revista Española de Paleontología, Madrid, 6: 98-106.

JIMÉNEZ-FUENTES, CARDOSO & CRESPO (1998): Presencia de Agrionemys (= Testudo) hermanni (GMELIN, 1789) en el Paleolítico medio de la Gruta Nova da Columbeira (Bombarral, provincia de Estremadura, Portugal). – Studia Geologica Salmanticensia, Salamanca, 34: 123-139.

JIMÉNEZ-FUENTES, GIL & POLLOS (1995): Quelonios del Pleistoceno medio de Las Grajas (Archidona: Málaga). – Studia Geologica Salmanticensia, Salamanca, 31: 55-62.

JOCHER (1967): Schildkröten. – Stuttgart (Franckh'sche Verlagshandlung): 10, 12, 24-25, 34-35, 57-60.

JOHNSON (1973a): Remarks on the nematode species Atractis dactyluris from tortoises from Afghanistan and Albania. – Vestn. Cesk. Spo. Zool., Prague, 37 (4): 265-272.

JOHNSON (1973b): Some oxyurid nematodes of the genera Mehdiella and Thaparia from the tortoise Testudo hermanni. – Folia Parasitologica, Prague, 20 (2): 141-148.

JOHNSON (1983): Cheers! – British Chelonia Group Newsletter, 37: 5.

JOHNSON (1989): Excerpts of members' letters. – British Chelonia Group Newsletter, 71: 12.

DE JONG (1987): Waarnemingen in het Massif des Maures in Zuid-Frankrijk. – Lacerta, Zoetermeer, 45 (7): 108-110.

DE JONG (1998): In search of historical biogeographic patterns in the western Mediterranean terrestrial fauna. – Biological Journal of the Linnean Society, London, 65: 99-164.

JOST (1994): Referatezusammenfassung des 4. Nationalen Schildkrötentages vom 22. Oktober 1994 in Emmenbrücke. – SIGS-Info, Siblingen, 3 (4): 11-17.

JOST (1995): Bau von Freilandanlagen zur Haltung von europäischen Landschildkröten. – SIGS-Informationsblatt 6, 4 pp.

JOST (1996): Wer denkt denn jetzt ans Überwintern. – SIGS-Info, Siblingen, 5 (1): 24-26.

JOST (1998a): Die Schildkrötenfauna Südost-Korsikas und Bemerkungen zur weiteren Herpetofauna der Insel. – Emys, Sitzenberg-Reidling, 5 (2): 5-23.

JOST (1998b): Die Schildkrötenfauna Südostkorsikas. – SIGS-Info, Siblingen, 7 (2): 4-19.

JOST (1999): Die Freilandanlage für Europäische Landschildkröten. – Merkblatt 10, SIGS, 4 pp.

JOST (2004): A Cupulatta – das Schildkrötenzentrum auf Korsika. – Testudo (SIGS), Wimmis, 13 (4): 18-27.

JOUBERT & CHEYLAN (1989): La tortue d'Hermann de Corse – résultats des recherches menées en 1985 et 1986. – Travaux Scinetifiques du Parc Naturel Régional du Corse, Ajaccio, 22: 1-54.

JUNG (1990): Ein Blumentopf als Gartenhaus. – Das Tier, Leinfelden-Echterdingen, 31 (8): 60.

JUNGE (1995): Unsere Kröten halten Winterschlaf. – Schildkröten, Linden, 2 (3): 14-16.

JUNGE (1996): Holzhütte oder Luxusvilla. – Schildkröten, Linden, 3 (1): 19-23.

JUNGNICKEL (1983a): Etwas über das Verhalten von Landschildkröten. – elaphe, Berlin, 5 (3): 36.

JUNGNICKEL (1983b): Aufzucht von jungen Testudo h. hermanni. – elaphe, Berlin, 5 (4): 56-57.

JUNGNICKEL (1984a): Behandlung einer Zwischengewebserkrankung bei Testudo h. hermanni. – elaphe, Berlin, 6 (2): 36.

JUNGNICKEL (1984b): Zur Überwinterung von Landschildkröten. – elaphe, Berlin, 6 (4): 66.

JUNGNICKEL (1985a): Aufzucht von jungen Testudo h. hermanni. – elaphe, Berlin, 7 (1): 13-14.

JUNGNICKEL (1985b): Beobachtungen bei der Futteraufnahme von Landschildkröten. – elaphe, Berlin, 7 (2): 24-25.

JUNGNICKEL (1986): Bemerkungen zur Problematik der Höckerbildung bei der Aufzucht von Schildkröten. – Sauria, Berlin, 8 (1): 19-22.

JUON & DOVAT (1977): Observations sur les Tortues terrestres, Grèce 1977. – Unveröffentlicher Bericht, Geneva, 10 pp.

KAADEN (2001): Viruskrankheiten der Tiere. – In: ROLLE & MAYR (Hrsg.): Medizinische Mikrobiologie, Infektions- und Seuchenlehre. – 7. Auflage, Stuttgart (Enke): 147.

KABISCH (1990): Wörterbuch der Herpetologie. – Jena (VEB Gustav Fischer Verlag): 423.

KABISCH & FROST (1994): Isolation of herpesvirus from Testudo hermanni and Agrionemys horsfieldii. – Verhandlungsbericht über Erkrankungen der Zootiere, 36: 241-245.

KAHL, GAUPP & SCHMIDT (1980): Das Terrarium. – Niedernhausen (Falken-Verlag): 99, 104, 106.

KAHN (1968): Herpetology in Kindergarten. – International Turtle and Tortoise Society Journal, Los Angeles, 2 (6): 6-8.

KALMES (2001): Dickie und Kapitän Hook. – Schildkröten, Linden, 8 (3): 26-29.

KALMES (2003): Testudos Weihnachtsgedanken. – Schildkröten, Linden, 10 (4): 53-55.

KAMMERER (1908a): Schildkrötenzucht. – Blätter für Aquarien- und Terrarienkunde, Stuttgart, 19: 757-763.

KAMMERER (1908b): Über gefangene Landschildkröten. – Blätter für Aquarien- und Terrarienkunde, Stuttgart, 19: 737-742.

KANELLIS & LEGAKIS (1979): Bibliographia faunae Graecae 1967-1978 et supplementum. – Thessaloníki, 70 pp.

KANTZ (1983): Zufallstreffer? Nachzucht von Testudo hermanni hermanni. – Sauria, Berlin, 5 (4): 5-6.

KANTZ (1984): Ergänzung zum Nachzuchtbericht Testudo h. hermanni. – Sauria, Berlin, 6 (4): 23.

KANTZ (1986): Wurmbefall an Testudo hermanni hermanni. – Sauria, Berlin, 8 (1): 11-12.

KAPLAN (1996): Bürgermeister im Schildkrötendorf. – Das Tier, Leinfelden-Echterdingen, 37 (1): 64.

KARAMAN (1921): Beiträge zur Herpetologie von Jugoslavien. – Glasnik Hrvatskog Prirodoslovnog druëtva, Zagreb, 33: 194-209.

KARAMAN (1922): Beiträge zur Herpetologie von Mazedonien. – Glasnik Skopsk. Naucn. Drust., Skopje, 4: 129-143.

KARAMAN (1928): III. Prilog cherpetologiji Jugoslavije. – Glasnik skopsk. naucn. drust., Skopje, 4: 129-143.

KARAMAN (1939): Über die Verbreitung der Reptilien in Jugoslavien. – Ann. Mus. Serb. Merid., Skopje, 1 (1): 1-20.

KARBE, KARBE & NIEHAUS-OSTERLOH (1991): Bunte Terrarienwelt. – Melle (Tetra-Verlag): 83, 92-93.

KASPAREK (1997): Rückführungsaktion für geschmuggelte Schildkröten in Südosteuropa. – elaphe (N. F.), Rheinbach, 5 (4): 28.

KÄSTLE (1969): Ein Beitrag zur Haltung von Babyschildkröten. – DATZ, Stuttgart, 22 (7): 219-221.

KATALAN-GATEVA & DIMITROV (1961): Recherches sur les Nemathelminthes infestant des tortues de la région de Petric. – Bull. Lab. Helm. Centr., Sofia, VI: 109-118.

KATHARINER & ESCHERICH (1895): Beitrag zur Biologie der Landschildkröten. – Biologische Centralblätter, 15: 815-816.

KATTINGER (1972): Beiträge zur Reptilienkunde der südwestlichen Balkanhalbinsel. – Berichte der Naturforschenden Gesellschaft Bamberg, 47: 42-75.

KELLER (1897): Die Schildkröte im Altertum. – Prague.

KELLER (1913): Die antike Tierwelt. Band 2. – Leipzig (W. Engelmann).

KEYMAR (1984): Vorläufige Ergebnisse herpetologischer Aufsammlungen auf den Ionischen Inseln – I – Korfu und Paros. – Annalen des Naturhistorischen Museums, Vienna, 86 (B): 285-286.

KEYMAR (1986a): Liste der Amphibien und Reptilien der Peloponnes-Halbinsel, GR. – ÖGH-Nachrichten, Vienna, 6/7: 3-26.

KEYMAR (1986b): Die Amphibien und Reptilien der ionischen Region (Griechenland). Analyse ihrer rezenten Ausbreitungsmuster und Überlegungen zu ihrer Ausbreitungsgeschichte. – ÖGH-Nachrichten, Vienna, 8/9: 8-44.

KEYMAR (1988): Vorläufige Ergebnisse herpetologischer Aufsammlungen auf den Ionischen Inseln. II. Zakynthos und Marathonisi. – Annalen des Naturhistorischen Museums, Vienna, 90 (B): 17-25.

KEYMER (1978): Diseases of chelonians: (1) Necropsy survey of tortoises. – The Veterinary Record, London, **103**: 548-552.

KIESEWALTER, RUDAT & SEIDEL (1960): Salmonellen aus Reptilien. – Zbl. Bakt., I. Abt. Orig., **180**: 503-509.

KILIAN & WERNER (1986): Fallbericht – Ein ungewöhnlich großer Fremdkörper bei einer Griechischen Landschildkröte (T. hermanni). – Kleintierpraxis, Alfeld, **31**: 401-405.

KING & BURKE (1989): Crocodilian, Tuatara, and Turtle Species of the World. – Washington (Association of Systematics Collections): 100.

KIRSCH & VIVIEN-ROELS (1984): Oxygen consumption in the tortoise Testudo hermanni subjected to sudden temperature changes in summer and autumn. – Comparative Biochemistry and Physiology, A, Comparative Physiology, Vancouver, **79** (4): 513-518.

KIRSCHE (1967): Zur Haltung, Zucht und Ethologie der griechischen Landschildkröte (Testudo hermanni hermanni). – Salamandra, Frankfurt am Main, **3** (3): 36-66.

KIRSCHE (1969): Frühzeitigung bei Testudo hermanni hermanni GMELIN. – Der Zoologische Garten (N. F.), Jena, **37** (1/3): 1-11.

KIRSCHE (1971): Metrische Untersuchungen über das Wachstum der Griechischen Landschildkröte (Testudo hermanni hermanni) in Beziehung zum jahreszeitlichen Rhythmus. – Der Zoologische Garten (N. F.), Jena, **40** (1/2): 47-71.

KIRSCHE (1972): Über Panzeranomalien bei Landschildkröten. – Aquarien Terrarien, Leipzig, Jena & Berlin, **19** (8): 259-261.

KIRSCHE (1979): The housing and regular breeding of Mediterranean tortoises in captivity. – International Zoo Yearbook, London, **19**: 42-49.

KIRSCHE (1980a): Conservation of Tortoises by breeding. – Proceedings of the European Herpetological Symposium, Oxford: 125.

KIRSCHE (1980b): Conservation of Tortoises by breeding. – ASRA Journal, Burford, **1** (3): 27-44.

KIRSCHE (1983): Über einen besonderen Typus von Carapax-Missbildungen aus 3 Gelegen (1979-1981) einer Testudo hermanni hermanni. – In: VAGO & MATZ (Eds.): Proceedings of the First International Colloquium on Pathology of Reptiles and Amphibians, Angers: 239-244.

KIRSCHE (1984a): An F2-generation of Testudo hermanni hermanni GMELIN bred in captivity with remarks on the breeding of Mediterranean tortoises 1976-1981. – Amphibia-Reptilia, Leiden, **5** (1): 31-35.

KIRSCHE (1984b): Bastardierung von Testudo horsfieldii (GRAY) und Testudo h. hermanni GMELIN. – Amphibia-Reptilia, Leiden, **5** (3/4): 311-322.

KIRSCHE (1986): Zucht von Landschildkröten und Artenschutz. – Der Zoologische Garten (N. F.), Jena, **56** (6): 389-402.

KIRSCHE (1993): Haltung und Nachzucht von Landschildkröten im Zusammenhang mit dem Natur- und Artenschutz. – DATZ, Stuttgart, **46** (3): 172-178.

KIRSCHE (1997): Die Landschildkröten Europas. – Melle (Mergus Verlag): 5-6, 14, 17-22, 37-42, 44-55, 57-58, 60-75, 78, 80, 82-84, 88-93, 95.

KIRSCHE (1999): Zur Biologie europäischer Landschildkröten. – Radiata, Bennstedt, **8** (3): 20-25.

KIRSCHEY (1995): Betr.: »Landschildkröten – Die Pflege nach der Winterruhe«. – DATZ, Stuttgart, **48** (12): 813.

KIRSCHNER, SEUFER & KIRCHHAUSER (1991): Vorläufige Empfehlungen zur Haltung von Reptilien und Amphibien bei Händlern und Privatpersonen. – Tierärztliche Umschau, Konstanz, **46**: 213-222.

KIRSCHEY (1996): Winterkatastrophe für Landschildkröten. – DATZ, Stuttgart, **49** (7): 412.

KLAPTOCZ (1910): Beiträge zur Herpetologie der europäischen Türkei. – Zoologische Jahrbücher für Systematik, Jena, **29** (3/4): 415-421.

KLEE (1969): Ungeschlachte Ungetüme? Die Griechischen Landschildkröten – und ihre Pflege. – aquarien magazin, **3**: 396-401.

KLEE (1979): Nachzucht von Testudo hermanni. – DATZ, Stuttgart, **32** (1): 34.

KLEINSCHMIDT (1956): Lautäußerungen bei einer griechischen Landschildkröte. – DATZ, Stuttgart, **9** (6): 166-167.

KLEMENS (Ed.) (2000): Turtle Conservation. – Washington & London (Smithsonian Institution Press): 9, 16, 22, 34, 54, 187, 191-192, 195-196, 201, 237-238.

KLENK (2006): Leserbriefe. – Marginata, Münster, **3** (1): 3.

KLERKS (2006): De Dalmatische landschildpad, een »oude« bekende. – Trionyx, Eindhoven, **4** (1): 2-10.

KLINGELHÖFFER & SCHERPNER (1955): Terrarienkunde – Band I – Allgemeines und Technik. – 2., vollständig neubearbeitete Auflage, Stuttgart (Alfred Kernen Verlag): 145, 156.

KLINGELHÖFFER & SCHERPNER (1959): Terrarienkunde – Band IV – Schlangen, Schildkröten, Panzerechsen, Reptilienzucht. – 2., vollständig neubearbeitete Auflage, Stuttgart (Alfred Kernen Verlag): 193, 197-202, 208, 213-214.

KLINGENBERG (1993): Understanding Reptiles Parasites. – Lakeside (Advanced Vivarium Systems), 54 pp.

KNOEPFFLER (1961): Contribution à l'étude des Amphibiens et des Reptiles de Provence. I + II. Généralités. – Vie et Milieu, Banyuls-sur-Mer, **12** (1/3): 67-76, 517-528.

KNOEPFFLER (1979): *Testudo hermanni* robertmertensi WERMUTH, 1952 (Chéloniens, Testudinoidea, Testudinidé), la tortue de MERTENS. – Doc. Atlas Zoogéogr. Languedoc-Roussillon, Montpellier, **15**, 4 pp.

KNOEPFFLER & SOCHUREK (1956): Amphibien und Reptilien zwischen Banyuls und Mentone. – Aquarien Terrarien, Leipzig & Jena, **3** (5/6): 147-151, 181-183.

KNON (2004): Von allen Schildkrötenhaltern gefürchtet: Herpes. – Minor, Lingenfeld, **3** (1): 27-33.

KNORR (1766-1768): Deliciae naturae selectae; oder auserlesenes Natüralien-Cabinet welches aus den drey Reichen der Natur zeiget: was von curiösen Liebhabern aufbehalten und gesammlet zu werden verdienet / Ehemals herausgegeben von G. W. KNORR ... fortgesetzt von dessen Erben, beschrieben von P. L. S. MÜLLER... und in das Französische übersetzet von M. VERDIER DE LA BLAQUIÈRE [Délices physiques choisies, etc.]. II. – Nuremberg (G. W. Knorr).

KNOTEK, FISCHER, JEKL & KNOTKOVA (2005): Fatal myiasis caused by *Calliphora vicina* in Hermann's tortoise (*Testudo hermanni*). – Acta Veterinaria Brno, Brno, **74** (1): 123-128.

KOCH (1932): Sammeltage auf der Insel Korfu, Oktober/November 1929. – Blätter für Aquarien- und Terrarienkunde, Stuttgart, **43**: 200-203, 230-232.

KOEN & MATEVA (1962): Rare *Salmonella* species and wildlife from the region of Petrich – B – Natural source of infections in Petrichko and Gotsedelchevsko. – Bulgarian Academy of Science, Sofia: 60-64.

KÖHLER (1996): Krankheiten der Amphibien und Reptilien. – Stuttgart (Verlag Eugen Ulmer): 20, 25-26, 103, 105-106, 108, 135, 138.

KÖHLER (2004): Inkubation von Reptilieneiern. – 2. erweiterte überarbeitete Neuauflage, Offenbach (Herpeton, Verlag Elke Köhler): 26, 31, 36, 67, 109, 115, 163, 176.

KÖHLER (2005): Incubation of Reptile Eggs. – Malabar (Krieger Publishing), 214 pp.

KÖHLER (2006): *Testudo graeca* – The Mediterranean Spur-Thighed Tortoise on the Turkish Riviera. – Reptilia (GB), Castelldefels, **44**: 52-58.

KOKOSCHA (2002): Geschützte Schildkröten. – DATZ-Sonderheft Schildkröten, Stuttgart (Verlag Eugen Ulmer): 67-69.

KÖLLE (1994): Blutparameter als Hilfe in der Diagnostik von Reptilienkrankheiten. – Tagungsunterlagen (Berlin Juni 1994) der AG Reptilienkrankheiten der DGHT, Rheinbach.

KÖLLE (2002): Reptilienkrankheiten. – Stuttgart (Franckh-Kosmos Verlag): 16, 23, 25, 27, 34, 44-45, 60, 62-63, 65-66, 70, 75-76, 80, 90-91, 101, 105-106.

KÖLLE, BAUR & HOFFMANN (1996): Ernährung von Schildkröten. – DATZ, **49** (5): 292-294, (6): 380-382.

KÖLLE, BAUR & HOFFMANN (1997): Ernährung von Schildkröten. – Journal der AG Schildkröten & Panzerechsen der DGHT, Bürstadt, **6** (1): 21-33.

KÖLLE, BAUR & HOFFMANN (1998/1999): Elf Kardinalfehler bei der Landschildkrötenpflege. – DATZ, **51** (12): 796-799, **52** (1): 38-41.

KÖLLE, HOFFMANN & BAUR (1995): Betr.: »Landschildkröten – Die Pflege nach der Winterruhe«. – DATZ, **48** (12): 812-813.

KÖLLE, BAUR, OIDTMANN & HOFFMANN (1997): Kritische Stellungnahme zu: Haltungsrichtlinien, Mindestansprüche für Schildkröten (E. BRABENETZ, H. SCHWAMMER & F. LUTTENBERGER), *Literas-Verlag*, Wien. – Emys, Sitzenberg-Reidling, **4** (1): 24-29.

KÖLLE, DONHAUSER, KRAUSE & HOFFMANN (2001): Blutwerte bei europäischen Landschildkröten (*Testudo hermanni*, *Testudo graeca*, *Testudo marginata*, *Agrionemys horsfieldii*). – Die Tierärztliche Praxis, Stuttgart, **29**: 386-391.

KOLOMBATOVIC (1882): Mammiferi anfibi e rettili della Dalmazia. – Spalato.

VAN KOOLWIJK (1987): Collection, trade and protection of European herpetofauna. – Traffic report, **4**, 101 pp.

KOPSTEIN & VON WETTSTEIN (1921): Reptilien und Amphibien aus Albanien. – Verhandlungen der zoologisch-botanischen Gesellschaft Wien, **70**: 387-409.

KORSÓS & CORBETT (1998): IUCN Action Plan of European Reptiles and Amphibians. – In: Drafting and implementing action plans for threatened species. – Environmental encounters, Strasbourg, **39**: 87-93.

KOTSAKIS (1978): I resti di anfibi e rettili pleistocenici della grotta di Spinagallo (Siracusa, Sicília). – Geol. Rom., Rome, **16**: 211-229.

KOTSAKIS (1980a): Anfibi e rettili del Plio-Pleistocene. – In: I vertebrati fossili italiani. – Verona (Catalogo della Mostra): 205-208.

KOTSAKIS (1980b): I resti di anfibi e rettili Pleistocenici della grotta di Dragonera (Capo Caccia, Sardegna). – Geol. Rom., Rome, **19**: 85-90.

KOTSAKIS (1980c): Révision des tortues (Emydidae, Testudinidae, Trionychidae) du Plio-Pléistocène de Valdarno supérieur (Toscane, Italie); Quaternaria, **22**: 11-37.

KOTSAKIS (1980d): Osservazioni sui vertebrati quaternari della Sardegna. – Bolletino della Società Geologica Italiana, Rome, **99**: 151-165.

KOTSAKIS (1981a): Resti di anfibi e rettili pleistocenici a Loreto di Venosa (Potenza, Italia meridionale). – Rome (Accademia Nazionale Lincei), **8** (69): 61-70.

KOTSAKIS (1981b): Gli anfibi e i rettili del Pleistocene del Lazio (Italia centrale). – Geol. Rom., Rome, **20**: 57-67.

KOUZMANOV, STOYANOV & TODOROV (1996): Sur la biologie et la protection de l'Aigle royal *Aquila chrysaetos* en Bulgarie. – In: MEYBURG & CHANCELLOR (Eds.): Eagle Studies, WWGBP, Berlin, Paris & London: 505-516.

KOVACEV (1905): Contribution à l'étude des Amphibiens et des Reptiles en Bulgarie. – Sbor. Nat. umotvor. Sofia, **21**: 1-13.

KOVACEV (1912): Cherpetologicnata fauna na Bulgarija. – Pecatniza Chr. G. Danov, Plovdiv, 90 pp.

KRADOLFER (1995): Paarungsverhalten der Schildkröten in Gefangenschaft. – SIGS-Info, Siblingen, **4** (4): 9-12.

KRADOLFER (1996): Das Paarungsverhalten von Landschildkröten in Gefangenschaft. – Emys, Sankt Pölten, **3** (2): 23-26.

KRADOLFER (1997a): Schildkröten sind nicht langweilig! – SIGS-Info, Siblingen, **6** (1): 37-39.

KRADOLFER (1997b): Begegnungen mit Wildschildkröten. – SIGS-Info, Siblingen, **6** (4): 24-27.

KRADOLFER (2001): Leben mit Schildkröten. – SIGS-Info, Siblingen, **10** (2): 21-24.

KRAGH (1981): Report on the destruction of the Alyki heath in Macedonia. – British Chelonia Group Newsletter, 28: 4-5.

KRAGH (1981): Alyki heath fires. – British Chelonia Group Newsletter, 29: 1-2.

KRAGL (1988): Zuchterfolg bei Landschildkröten. – Das Tier, Leinfelden-Echterdingen, **29** (6): 55.

KRAMER (1995): Tortoises and Terrapins on Mallorca. – In: BALLASINA (Ed.): Red Data Book on Mediterranean Chelonians. – Bologna (Edagricole): 35-40.

KRAMER & VICKERS (1983): *Testudo hermanni robertmertensi* WERMUTH on Mallorca (Balearic Is.). – Testudo, **2** (2): 7-11.

KRAUT (1995): Endoskopie bei Schildkröten unter Praxisbedingungen. – Dissertation, Univ. München, Munich.

KREBS (1960): Schildkröten. – Perlen-Reihe, Band 117, Vienna, Munich & Zürich (Verlag A. Pechan): 15-18, 66, 75.

KREFFT (1949): Die Schildkröten. – Braunschweig (Verlag Gustav Wenzel & Sohn): 68, 81.

KREINDL (1995): Bericht über ein unangenehmes Schlupferlebnis. – Emys, Sankt Pölten, **2** (6): 20-21.

KREINDL & ARTNER (1996): Hilfe bei einem Fall von Legenot bei *Testudo hermanni*. – Emys, Sankt Pölten, **3** (5): 20-21.

KRIEGER & KRIEGER (1995): Observations sur la croissance des jeunes tortues terrestres. – CITS bulletin, Bramois, 4: 19-21.

KRÜGER & PIER (1994): Fallbericht – Futterverweigerung durch einen intestinalen Fremdkörper (Stein) bei einer Griechischen Landschildkröte (*Testudo hermanni*). – Kleintierpraxis, Alfeld, **39**: 117-119.

KÜBBER-HEISS (1999): Herpesvirusinfektion bei Landschildkröten in Österreich. – Wiener Tierärztliche Monatsschrift, Vienna, **86**: 78-82.

KÜCHLER (1979): Herpetologische Ferien auf Korfu. – DATZ, Stuttgart, **32** (3): 211-215.

KUCHLING (1979): Zur Steuerung der Gonadenaktivität und der Winterruhe der männlichen Griechischen Landschildkröte (*Testudo hermanni hermanni* GMELIN). – Dissertation, Univ. Wien, Vienna.

KUCHLING (1981a): Le cycle sexuel mâle de la tortue *Testudo hermanni hermanni* GMELIN dans une population naturelle et en captivité. – Bulletin de la Société Herpétologique de France, Paris, **19**: 29-35.

KUCHLING (1981b): Seasonal variations of the oxygen consumption and the blood glucose concentration under low temperature conditions in the male tortoise (*Testudo hermanni*). – Amphibia-Reptilia, Leiden, **2** (3): 235-242.

KUCHLING (1982a): Effect of temperature and photoperiod on spermatogenesis in the tortoise *Testudo hermanni* GMELIN. – Amphibia-Reptilia, Leiden, **2** (4): 329-341.

KUCHLING (1982b): Environmental temperature spermatogenesis and plasma testosterone concentration in the tortoise *Testudo hermanni hermanni*. – Acta Endocrinologica, **99** (Supplementum 246): 29-30.

KUCHLING (1986): Diurnal fluctuations of the plasma testosterone concentration in the male tortoise, *Testudo hermanni hermanni* GMELIN – the role of temperature and season. – In: ASSENMACHER & BOISSIN (Eds.): Endocrine regulations as adaptive mechanisms to the environment. – Paris (Centre National de la Recherche Scientifique): 103-108.

KUCHLING (1997): Restoration of epidermal scute patterns during regeneration of the chelonian carapace. – Chelonian Conservation and Biology, Lunenburg, **2** (4): 500-506.

KUCHLING (1999): The Reproductive Biology of the Chelonia. – Berlin, Heidelberg & New York (Springer-Verlag): 29, 52-65, 775, 109-110, 115-116, 125-129, 135-136, 138, 146, 165-166, 169, 191.

KUCHLING, SKOLEK-WINNISCH & BAMBERG (1981): Histochemical and biochemical investigation on the annual cycle of testis, epididymis, and plasma testosterone of the tortoise, *Testudo hermanni hermanni* GMELIN. – General and Comparative Endocrinology, **44** (2): 194-201.

KÜHNE (1996): Betr.: »Winterkatastrophe für Landschildkröten«. – DATZ, Stuttgart, **49** (11): 743.

KÜHNEMANN (1981): Fachexkursion in die VR Bulgarien. – elaphe, Berlin, **3** (2): 23-26.

KUIPERS (2004): Winterslaap bij *Testudo*'s. – Trionyx, Eindhoven, **2** (4): 108-112.

KUNDERT (2002): Schildkröten im Internet: Schildkröten-Schutzprogramme. – *Testudo* (SIGS), Wimmis, **11** (4): 6-8.

KUNDERT (2003a): Schildkröten im Internet: Gehegebau für Schildkröten. – *Testudo* (SIGS), Wimmis, **12** (1): 16-18.

KUNDERT (2003b): Naturbruten im Jahrhundert-Sommer. – *Testudo* (SIGS), Wimmis, **12** (4): 41-43.

KUNDERT (2005): Buchbesprechung: Sardinien, die Insel der europäischen Schildkröten. – *Testudo* (SIGS), Wimmis, **14** (1): 29-33.

KUNZ (1995): Odysseus – ein griechischer Held. – Schildkröten, Linden, **2** (3): 9-11.

KUSAKABE, ISHII & ISHII (1988): Dense granule-containing cells in arterial chemoreceptor areas of the tortoise *Testudo hermanni*. – Journal of Morphology, **197** (2): 183-192.

VAN DER KUYL, BALLASINA, DEKKER, MAAS, WILLEMSEN & GOUDSMIT (2002): Phylogenetic relationships among the species of the genus *Testudo* (Testudines: Testudinidae) inferred from mitochondrial 12S rRNA gene sequences. – Molecular Phylogenetics and Evolution, **22**: 174-183.

LABENDA (2003): Climate & Outdoor Enclosures. – Tortoise Trust Newsletter, London, **18** (3/4): 7-9.

LABORDE (2001): Zuflucht für bedrohte Schildkröten. – auf einen Blick, November: 20-21.

LABORDE (2003): Eine Klinik für gepanzerte Patienten. – auf einen Blick, August: 17.

LAFRANCO (1955): Reptiles, amphibians of the Maltese islands. – Malta Year Book, Valletta: 198-203.

LAFRANCO (1957): Reptiles of Malta – 1 – The tortoise and turtle. –Sunday Times of Malta, Valletta, **314**.

LAMBERT (1967): Some observations on the herpetofauna of Corsica. – British Journal of Herpetology, London, **3** (42): 303-306

LABENDA (2000): Housing Your Turtles and Tortoises Outdoors. – Homestead (Green Nature Books): 21, 31, 55, 57, 88-89.

LABENDA (2001): Separation of Tortoise Species in Outdoor Habitats. – Reptile & Amphibian Hobbyist, Neptune, **3**: 38-42.

LAMBERT (1977): Mediterranean tortoises and captive breeding as a tool for their conservation in the wild – Mediterranean tortoise information, successfull management and captive breeding in Britain. – British Herpetological Society Newsletter, London, **16**: 21-25.

LAMBERT (1978): Captive breeding of Mediterranean tortoises – Letter to Editor. – British Journal of Herpetology, London, **5**: 749.

LAMBERT (1979): Trade and the Mediterranean tortoises. – Oryx, Cambridge & Washington, **15**: 81-82.

LAMBERT (1984): Threats to Mediterranean (West Palearctic) tortoises and their effects on wild populations – an overview. – Amphibia-Reptilia, Leiden, **5** (1): 5-15.

LAMBERT (1986a): On growth of captive-bred Mediterranean *Testudo* in Europe. – In: ROCEK (Ed.): Studies in Herpetology, Karls-Universität, Prague: 309-314.

LAMBERT (1986b): Natural Bioclimatic Range and the Growth of Some Home-Bred Mediterranean Tortoises in Northern Europe – Implications for Conservation Farming. – *Testudo*, **2** (4): 41-43.

LAMBERT (1988): Natural Bioclimatic range and the growth of captive-bred Mediterranean *Testudo* L. in Northern Europe – Implications für conservation farming. – British Herpetological Society Bulletin, London, **24**: 6-7.

LAMBERT & COGALNICEANU (1999): Preliminary observations addressing herpetofaunal diversity in southern Romania (August 1997). – British Herpetological Society Bulletin, London, **69**: 31-35.

LAMBERT, COLLINS & EVANS (1988): Report on Growth and Survivorship of Home-Bred Mediterranean Tortoises (*Testudo*) in Southern England. – *Testudo*, **2** (6): 31-56.

LANCASTER (1997): Safety comes first. – Tortoise Trust Newsletter, London, **12** (2): 7.

LANDWEER (1992): Otto – die Geschichte eines Schildkrötenlebens. – SIGS-Info, Siblingen, **1** (3): 7-8.

LANDWEER (1993): Fragebogen zur Überwinterung unserer Landschildkröten. – SIGS-Info, Siblingen, **2** (3): 9-10.

LANDWEER (1999): SIGS Schildkröten-Schlupfstatistik 1998, 1993-1998. – SIGS-Info, Siblingen, **8** (2): 25-31.

LANG (2001): Das Schildkrötendorf »A Cupulatta« (Centre d'Élevage et de protection de la tortue). – Radiata, Haan, **10** (1): 23-28.

LANGE (1984): Endocrinology of Reproduction in Male Reptiles. – Symposium of the Zoological Society of London, **52**: 357-383.

LANGE, HERBST, WIECHERT & SCHLIESSER (1989): Elektronenmikroskopischer Nachweis von Herpesviren bei einem Massensterben von Griechischen Landschildkröten (*Testudo hermanni*) und Vierzehenschildkröten (*Agrionemys horsfieldii*) . – Die Tierärztliche Praxis, Stuttgart, **17**: 319-321.

LANGTON (1989a): Conservation Corner. – British Chelonia Group Newsletter, 68: 9-11.

LANGTON (1989b): Conservation Corner. – British Chelonia Group Newsletter, 69: 3-4.

LANGTON (1989c): Conservation Corner. – British Chelonia Group Newsletter, 71: 10-12.

LANGTON (1990): Conservation Corner. – British Chelonia Group Newsletter, 75: 6.

LANGTON (1991): Conservation Corner. – British Chelonia Group Newsletter, 79: 7.

LANGTON (1993): Conservation Corner. – British Chelonia Group Newsletter, 91: 2-4.

LANGTON (1994a): Conservation Corner. – British Chelonia Group Newsletter, 97: 4.

LANGTON (1994b): Conservation Corner. – British Chelonia Group Newsletter, 99: 2.

LANGTON (1994c): The British Chelonia Group and the Conservation of Chelonia Worldwide. – Testudo, 4 (1): 4-9.

LANGTON (2002): Interview with BERNARD DEVAUX, founder of the tortoise village, Gonfaron, France. – British Chelonia Group Newsletter, 150: 9-11.

LANGTON (2004): Member's letters. – British Chelonia Group Newsletter, 157: 15-16.

LANKA & VÍT (1984): Lurche und Kriechtiere. – Prague (Artia): 86-87.

LANKA & ZAVADIL (1985): Amphibians and reptiles. – Prague (Artia), 224 pp.

LANKES (1932): Herpetologisches aus Bulgarien. – Blätter für Aquarien- und Terrarienkunde, Stuttgart, 18: 129-131.

LANZA (1955): Notizie su alcuni Anfibi e Rettili dell'Italia centrale e della Sardegna. – Monitore Zoologico Italiano, Florence, 63: 300-308.

LANZA (1968): Rettili. – In: TORTONESE & LANZA (Eds.): Piccola fauna italiana – Pesci, Anfibi e Rettili. – Milan (Martello Editore): 135-174.

LANZA (1972): The natural history of the Cerbicales islands (southeastern Corsica) with particular reference to their herpetofauna. – Milan (Natura), 63:345-407.

LANZA (1973): Gli Anfibi e i Rettili delle isole circumsiciliane. – Lavori della Società italiana di Biogeografia (N. S.), 3: 755-804.

LANZA (1983a): Ipotesi sulle origini del popolamento erpetologico della Sardegna. – Lavori della Società italiana di Biogeografia (N. S.), 8: 723-744.

LANZA (1983b): Guide per il riconoscimento delle specie animali dell'acque interne italiane.27. Anfibi, Rettili (Amphibia, Reptilia). – AQ/1/205, Verona (Consiglio Nazionale delle Ricerche), 196 pp.

LANZA (1986): I Rettili e gli Anfibi. – In: CAMARDA, FALCHI & NUDDA (Eds.): L'ambiente naturale in Sardegna (Elementi di base per la conoscenza e la gestione del territorio). – Sassari (Ed. Delfino): 289-321, 549-550.

LANZA (1988): Hypothèses sur les origines de la faune herpétologique corse. – Bull. Ecol., 19: 163-170.

LANZA & BRUZZONE (1960): Reptilia. – In: ZAVATTARI (Ed.): Biogeografia delle isole Pelagie. – Rendiconti della Accademia Nazionale delle Scienze detta dei XL, Memorie di Scienze Fisiche e Naturali, Serie V, Parte II, Rome, 11 (4): 288-328.

LANZA & CORTI (1993): Erpetofauna italiana: »Acquisizioni« ed estinzioni nel corso del novecento. – Supplemento Ricerche Biologia Selvaggina, 21: 5-49.

LANZA & CORTI (1996): Evolution of knowledge on the Italian herpetofauna during the 20th century. – Bollettino del Museo Civico di Storia Naturale di Verona, Verona, 20: 373-436.

LANZA & POGGESI (1986): Storia naturale delle isole satelliti della Corsica. – Florence (L'Universo), 66 (1): 1-198.

LAPINI (1983): Anfibi e Rettili. – Udine (Carlo Lorenzini Ed., Tricesimo), 142 pp.

LAPINI, DALL'ASTA, BRESSI & DOLCE (1996): Atlante preliminare dell'erpetofauna della Regione Friúli-Venezia Giulia (Italia nord-orientale). – Studi Trentini di Scienze Naturali, Acta Biologica, Trient, 71: 43-51.

LAPINI, DALL'ASTA, BRESSI, DOLCE & PELLARINI (1999): Atlante Corologico: Degli anfibi e dei rettili del Friuli-Venezia Giulia. – Udine (Comune di Udine, Edizioni del Museo Friulano di Storia Naturale, Pubblicazione), 43 pp.

DE LAPPARENT DE BROIN (2000): Les chéloniens de Sansan. – In: GINSBURG (Ed.): La faune miocène de Sansan et son evironnement. – Mémoires du Muséum d'Histoire Naturelle, Paris, 183: 219-261.

DE LAPPARENT DE BROIN (2001): The European turtle fauna from the Triassic to the Present. – Dumerilia, Paris, 4 (3): 155-217.

LATASTE (1881): Diagnose d'une nouvelle Tortue Testudo graeca Bettai, n. sbsp. – Le Naturaliste, Paris, 50 (3): 396.

LAUTNER (1955): Griechische Landschildkröte überwintert in der freien Natur: – DATZ, 8 (1): 56.

LAWRENCE (1987a): The tortoise trade – mortality in transport:an analysis of 21 years of importations into the United Kingdom. – British Veterinary Journal, London, 143 (5): 432-438.

LAWRENCE (1987b): Mortality of Mediterranean tortoises (Testudo graeca and Testudo hermanni) in pet shops prior to sale. – British Veterinary Journal, London, 143 (6): 567-573.

LAWRENCE (1987c): Post-hibernation anorexia in captive Mediterranean tortoises (Testudo graeca and Testudo hermanni). – The Veterinary Record, London, 120 (4): 87-90.

LAWRENCE (1987d): Seasonal variation in blood biochemistry of long-term captive Mediterranean tortoises (Testudo graeca and Testudo hermanni). – Research in Veterinary Science, 43 (3): 379-383.

LAWRENCE (1988a): Mortality in imported tortoises (*Testudo graeca* and *Testudo hermanni*) in the United Kingdom. – British Veterinary Journal, **144** (2): 187-195.

LAWRENCE (1988b): Some aspects of the biology of captive Mediterranean tortoises. – Thesis, University of Kent, Canterbury.

LAWRENCE & HAWKEY (1986): Seasonal variations in haematological data from Mediterranean tortoises (*Testudo graeca* and *Testudo hermanni*) in captivity. – Research in Veterinary Science, **40** (2): 225-230.

LAWRENCE & JACKSON (1982): Passage of ingesta in tortoises. – The Veterinary Record, London, 20.11.1982: 492-493.

LAWRENCE & JACKSON (1983): Inappetent tortoises. – The Veterinary Record, London, 14.5.1983: 487-488.

LAWRENCE & NEEDHAM (1985): Rhinitis in longterm captive Mediterranean tortoises (*Testudo graeca* and *Testudo hermanni*). – The Veterinary Record, London, **117** (25/26): 662-664.

LAWRENCE, PALMER & NEEDHAM (1986): Use of carbenicillin in two species of tortoise (*Testudo graeca* and *Testudo hermanni*). – Research in Veterinary Science, **40** (3): 413-415.

LAWTON (1989): Post Hibernation Health Check for Your Tortoises. – British Chelonia Group Newsletter, 68: 11.

LAWTON & STOAKES (1989): Post hibernation blindness in tortoises. – Proceedings of the Third International Colloquium of Pathology of Reptiles and Amphibians: 97-98.

LEBECKA (1963): Hydrolytic enzymes of the Greek tortoises's Kinde. – Folia Biologica, Warsaw, **11**: 145-155.

LE GARFF (1991): Les Amphibiens et les Reptiles dans leur milieu. – Paris (Éditions Bordas), 250 pp.

LE GARFF (1998): Dictionnaire étymologique de Zoologie. – Lausanne & Paris (Delachaux et Niestlé), 205 pp.

LE GARFF (1999): Etymologie des noms d'Amphibiens et de Reptiles d'Europe. – Bulletin de la Société Herpétologique de France, Paris, **90**: 23-40.

LE HOUEROU (1980): L'impact de l'homme et de ses animaux sur la forêt méditerranéenne – I. – Forêt méditerranéenne, Marseille, **2** (1): 31-44.

LEHRER (1994): Die geheimnisvolle Welt der Schildkröten. – Erlangen (Karl Müller Verlag): 82.

LEIHS (1998): Ein gepanzerter Mini aus dem Ei. – Öffentlicher Anzeiger Bad Kreuznach, 25./26.7.1998.

LEMMER (1999): Schildkröte leidet. – Das Tier, Leinfelden-Echterdingen, **40** (12): 52.

LEPSI (1925): Din viata broastelor testoase. – Rev. stiint. »V. Adamachi«, Bukarest, **11**: 1-8.

LEPSI (1927): Beiträge zur Reptilienfauna der südöstlichen Dobrudscha. – Verhandlungen und Mitteilungen des Siebenbürgischen Vereins für Naturwissenschaften zu Hermannstadt, Hermannstadt, **78**: 27-50.

LESCURE, BOUR & INEICH (1990): Les noms scientifiques français des Reptiles d'Europe. – Bulletin de la Société Herpétologique de France, Paris, **49**: 1-12.

LESHEM (1981): Golden eagles in our backyard. – The Hawk Trust, Annual Report, Taunton, **11**: 35-40.

LEUTSCHER (1961): Notes on the common tortoise – 2 – Biology of the common pet tortoise kept in Britain. – The Veterinary Record, London, **73**: 314-316.

LEVER (2003): Naturalized Reptiles and Amphibians of the World. – New York (Oxford University Press): 24, 233-234.

LEWIS (1982): Importation of Mediterranean tortoises, species *T. graeca* and *T. hermanni*. – British Chelonia Group Newsletter, 32: 2.

LIEBSCHER (2003): Naturreiseführer Griechenland. – Natur und tier-Verlag, Münster, 463 pp.

LIMACHER (2004): SIGS Sektion Zentralschweiz: Gast an der LUGA in Luzern. – *Testudo* (SIGS), Wimmis, **13** (3): 25-28.

LINDFORS (1976): Herpetologiska notiser fran ett omrade runt Korinthos, Peloponnesos, i Grekland. – Snoken, Stockholm, **6**: 188-192.

LINDHOLM (1929): Revidiertes Verzeichnis der Gattungen der rezenten Schildkröten nebst Notizen zur Nomenklatur einiger Arten. – Zoologischer Anzeiger, Leipzig, **81** (11/12): 275-295.

LINGEN (Ed.) (197?): Großes Lexikon der Tierwelt. – Lingen-Verlag, Köln: 85-87.

LINGEN (1996): Betr. »Ernährung von Schildkröten«. – DATZ, Stuttgart, **49** (8): 541.

LINNAEUS (1758): Systema Naturae per Regna tria Naturae secundum Classes, Ordines, Genera, Species, cum Characteribus, Differentiis, Synonymis, Locis. – 10. Auflage, Band 1, Stockholm (Salvii): 197.

LIPPE & GIORDANA (1967a): Alcune differenze di permeabilitá tra intestino tenie e colon. – Boll. Soc. ital. Biol. sper., **43**: 962-964.

LIPPE & GIORDANA (1967b): Effects of Amphotericin B on the permeability of the small and large intestines of *Testudo hermanni*. – Biochimica et Biophysica Acta, **135**: 966-972.

LIPPE & GIORDANA (1967c): Effetts dell' anfotericina B sulla permeabilità alla tiourea attraverso l'intestino tenue e del colon di tartaruga greca. – Boll. Soc. ital. Biol. sper., **43**: 435-437.

LIPPE & GIORDANA (1967d): Interpretazione dell' effets dell' anfotericina B sulla permeabilità dell' intestino tenue e del colon di tartaruga greca. – Boll. Soc. ital. Biol. sper., **43**: 437-439.

LIPPE & GIORDANA (1968): Permeability differences between some epithelial tissues – Testudo hermanni intestine, Bufo bufo bladder, Amphotericin B. – In: PETERS (Ed.): Protides of the biological fluids, Proceedings of the 15th Colloquium. – Amsterdam (Elsevier), 1: 209-211.

LIPPE, CREMOSCHI & CAPRARO (1966): Solvent drag on urea and thiourea across intestins of Testudo hermanni and Bufo bufo urinary bladder. – Comparative Biochemistry and Physiology, Vancouver, 19: 179-186.

LIPPE, GIORDANA & CAPRARO (1968): Polyene antibiotics and membrane composition of epithelia Testudo hermanni, Bufo bufo viscera sterol structure. – In: BOLIS & PETHICA (Eds.): Membrane models and the formation of biological membranes, Proceedings of the 1967 Meeting of the International Conference on Biological Membranes. – New York (John Wiley and Sons): 160-165.

LIPPE, BIANCHI, CREMASCHI & CAPRARO (1965): Different types of asymmetric distribution of hydrosoluble and lipospluble substances at the two sides of a mucosal intestinal preparation. – Archives Internationales de Physiologie et de Biochimie, 73: 43-54.

LIVOREIL (1998): Projet de réintroduction de tortues d'Hermann dans le Massif de l'Estérel – Etude de faisabilité. – Unpublished report, Gonfaron (SOPTOM), 6 pp.

LIVOREIL (1999): Réflexions et suggestions après une année au Village des Tortues de Gonfaron – Bilan annuel 98-99. – Unpublished report, Gonfaron (SOPTOM), 32 pp.

LIVOREIL (2003): Conservation programmes for Hermann's tortoises in France – the SOTOM experience. – Testudo, 5 (4): 5-13.

LIVOREIL & REBUFFEL (2002): Le projet Esterel – étude de faisabilité avant la réintroduction de Testudo hermanni hermanni, selection de sites de lâcher et étude phytosociologique. – Chelonii, Gonfaron, 3: 342-345.

LIVOREIL, BOURLET & DENECKER (2002): Soft versus hard release/an experimental approach with Hermann's tortoises. – Chelonii, Gonfaron, 3: 233-239.

LIVOREIL, PICARD & HIGNARD (2002): Effect of domestication on withdrawal behaviour of Hermann's tortoises Testudo hermanni hermanni. – Chelonii, Gonfaron, 3: 337-341.

LIZANA & BARBADILLO (1997): Legislación, protección y estado de conservación de los anfíbios y reptiles espanoles. – PLEGUEZUELOS (Ed.): Distribución y biogeografia de los anfibios y réptiles en España y Portugal. – Monografias de Herpetología, Volumen 3, Asociación Herpetológica Española y Universidad de Granada/Asociación Herpetológica Española, Granada: 477-516.

LLORENTE, MONTORI, CARRETERO & SANTOS (1997): Testudo hermanni (GMELIN, 1789). – In: PLEGUEZUELOS (Ed.): Distribución y biogeografia de los anfibios y réptiles en España y Portugal. – Monografias de Herpetología, Volumen 3, Asociación Herpetológica Es-

pañola y Universidad de Granada/Asociación Herpetológica Española, Granada: 181-183.

LLORENTE, MONTORI, SANTOS & CARRETERO (1995): Atlas dels Amfibis i Rèptils de Catalunya i Andorra. – Figueres (Ed. El Brau), 191 pp.

LLORENTE, FONTANET, MONTORI, SANTOS & CARRETERO (1991): Herpetofauna del delte de l'Ebre – Distribució i Conservació de les espècies. – Butlleti del Parc Natural Delta de l'Ebre, Deltebre, 6: 14-21.

LLOYD (1992): Second generation. – British Chelonia Group Newsletter, 88: 13, 89: 10-11.

LLOYD (1994): Members' letters. – British Chelonia Group Newsletter, 97: 9.

LLOYD (1999a): Members' letters. – British Chelonia Group Newsletter, 127: 8.

LLOYD (1999b): Members' letters. – British Chelonia Group Newsletter, 131: 18.

LLOYD (2001): Members' letters. – British Chelonia Group Newsletter, 142: 14.

LOEHR (1997): A model for an incubator with electronically regulated daily temperature cycle. – Tortoise Trust Newsletter, London, 12 (2): 3-4.

LOEHR (2002): Visits to CRT and SOPTOM. – Emys, Sitzenberg-Reidling, 9 (4): XIX-XX, 9 (5): X-XI.

LONGEPIERRE (2001): Ecophysiologie de Testudo hermanni hermanni GMELIN, 1789: évaluation des contraintes environnementales et alimentaires en milieu naturel dans le sud de la France. – Dissertation, Univ. Claude Bernard Lyon I, Ecole Normale Supérieure de Paris.

LONGEPIERRE & GRENOT (1997): Distribution de la tortue d'Hermann (Testudo hermanni hermanni). – Compte-Rendu de l'étude écologique de 10 secteurs dans la Plaine des Maures, Le Luc, SIVOM du Centre Var.

LONGEPIERRE & GRENOT (1999): Some effects of intestinal nematodes on the plant foraging behaviour of Testudo hermanni hermanni in the south of France. – In: MIAUD & GUYÉTANT (Eds.): Current Studies in Herpetology, Societas Europaea Herpetologica/Société Herpétologique de France, Le Bourget du Lac: 277-284.

LONGEPIERRE, GRENOT & HAILEY (2003): Individual, local and subspecific variation in female Hermann's tortoise (Testudo hermanni) reproductive characters. – Contributions to Zoology, Bangor, 72: 221-226.

LONGEPIERRE, HAILEY & GRENOT (2001): Home range area of the tortoise Testudo hermanni in relation to habitat complexity: implications for conservation of biodiversity. – Biodiversity and Conservation, 10: 1131-1140.

LÓPEZ-JURADO, TALAVERA TORRALBA, IBÁÑEZ GONZÁLEZ, MacIVOR & GARCÍA ALCÁZAR (1979): Las tortugas terrestres Testudo graeca y Testudo hermanni en España. – Naturalia Hispánica, Icona, Madrid, 17: 1-63.

LORTET (1883): Études zoologiques sur la faune du Lac de Tiberiade. – Archives du Muséum d'Histoire Naturelle, Lyon, **3**: 99-189.

LORTET (1887): Observations sur les tortues terrestres et paludines du Bassin de la Méditerranée. – Archives du Muséum d'Histoire Naturelle, Lyon, **4**: 26 + VIII pp.

LOSTAKOVÁ, KNOZ und HANÁK (1979): Notes on food habits in testudinid turtles (Chelonia: *Testudo*). – Folia Facultatis Scientiarum Naturalium Universitatis Purkynianae Brunensis, Biologia, **9** (2): 79-84.

LOUCHART (2002): Législation: sommes-nous tous plus ou moins hors la loi? – Info Tortues, Ucciani, **38**: 2.

LO VALVO & LONGO (2002): Anfibi e rettili in Sicilia. – Palermo (WWF Italia, ed. DoraMarkus & Societá Siciliana di Scienze Naturali), 88 pp.

LOVERIDGE & WILLIAMS (1957): Revision of the African tortoises and turtles of the suborder Cryptodira. – Bulletin of the Museum of Comparative Zoology, Cambridge, **115** (6): 163-557.

LOZANO & TARIN (1994): Projecte de reintroducció de la tortuga mediterrània al Massif del Garraf. – II Trobada d'Estudiosos del Garraf, Gavà, Diputació de Barcelona, **2**: 37-41.

LÜBBERT (2003): ... über Sinn und Unsinn der Preisdifferenzen bei Reptilien. – elaphe (N. F.), Rheinbach, **11** (4): 20-21.

LUGARO (1957): Elenco sistematico die Rettili italiani conservati nella collezione esistente presso il Museo di Storia Naturale di Milano con brevi note critiche ed esplicative. – Atti Soc. italiana Sci. Nat. Mus. Civ. Stor. Nat., Milan, **96** (1-2): 20-36.

LÜTHI & PAGAN (1992): Grassierendes Schildkrötensterben. – SIGS-Info Extra, 2 pp.

LUTZ & COLLIN (1967): Sur la régression des cellules photoréceptrices épiphysaires chez la tortue terrestre – *Testudo hermanni* (GMELIN) et la phylogénie des photorécepteurs épiphysaires chez les vertébrés. – Bulletin de la Société Zoologique de France, Paris, **92**: 797-808.

LYKAKIS (1974): A phylogenetic study on turtle hemoglobins. – Comparative Biochemistry and Physiology, B, **48**: 231-240.

LYKAKIS & HARITOS (1973): Electrophoretic and antigenic properties of turtle myoglobins. – Comparative Biochemistry and Physiology, B, **46**: 117-122.

MADEC (1996): La prédation dans le processus de conservation de la tortue d'Hermann *Testudo hermanni hermanni*. – In: SOPTOM (Eds.): International Congress of Chelonian Conservation – Proceedings, Editions SOPTOM, Gonfaron: 181-183.

MADEC (1997a): Importance de la prédation dans le processus de raréfaction de la tortue d'Hermann dans le Massif des Maures. – La Tortue, Gonfaron, **38**: 26-29.

MADEC (1997b): Bestandsrückgang der Griechischen Landschildkröte (*Testudo hermanni hermanni*). – SIGS-Info, Siblingen, **4**: 2-6.

MADEC (1999): La prédation des Ponies dans le processus de raréfaction de la tortue d'Hermann *Testudo hermanni hermanni* dans le massif des Maures (Var). – Dissertation, École Pratique des Hautes Études, Montpellier, 99 pp.

MADER (2005): Reptile Medicine and Surgery. – Philadelphia (W. B. Saunders Company), 1264 pp.

MADGE (1991): From other sources. – British Chelonia Group Newsletter, 80: 6.

MAGNAN (2000): Tortues siamoises. – Manouria, Mezzavia, 7: 4.

MAGNAN & MARAN (1999): L'encyclopédie terrariophile, les tortues passionnément. – JEH Editions, 86 pp.

MÄHN (2000): Inkubation von Schildkröteneiern. – Reptilia (D), Münster, 24: 55-61.

MÄHN & WILMS (2001): Tropische Landschildkröten. – Draco, Münster, 8: 4-25.

MAHNERT (1973): Recherches zoologiques dans les îles Ioniennes. – Rev. Mens. Mus., Geneva, **131**: 2-6.

MALKMUS (1972/1973): Herpetologische Beobachtungen auf Sizilien. – Aqua-Terra, Solothurn, **9** (6): 64-67, **10** (2): 22-23.

MALUQUER (1917): De re herpetológica. – Bull. Inst. Catalan. Hist. Nat., Barcelona, **17**: 108-111.

MALUQUER (1918): Notas herpetológicas – III – La *Testudo graeca* LINNÉ, en Formentera?. – Bol. Real. Soc. Espa. Hist. Natur., Madrid, **18**: 402-406.

MALUQUER (1919): Presencia de la *Testudo iberia* PALLAS en Formentera. – Bol. Real. Soc. Espa. Hist. Nat., Madrid, **19** (7): 384-385.

MALUQUER & MALUQUER (1919): Les tortugues de Catalunya. – Treb. Mus. Cien. Nat., Barcelona: 93-159.

MARA (1996): Wasser- und Landschildkröten. – Ruhmannsfelden (bede-Verlag): 37, 40, 92-94.

MARAN (1999): L'Élevage des Tortues Terrestres. – Paris (Philippe Gérard Editions): 7, 27, 35-36, 38-40, 43, 51, 56-57, 59-60, 81.

MARAN (2004): Sardaigne l'île oubliée. – La Tortue, Gonfaron, 66: 60-65.

MARCUS (1983): Amphibien und Reptilien in Heim, Labor und Zoo. – Stuttgart (Ferdinand Enke Verlag), Stuttgart: 100.

MAROLT (1996): Literaturangaben im Vergleich mit eigenen Erfahrungen – Die Griechische Landschildkröte *Testudo hermanni boettgeri*. – Emys, Sankt Pölten, **3** (5): 22-24, (6): 16.

MARQUARDT (1987a): Merkwürdiges Verhalten bei *Testudo h. hermanni* vor die Eiablage. – Die Schildkröte (N. F.), Heinsberg, **2** (3): 21-25.

MARQUARDT (1987b): Auf der Suche nach der Westrasse der Griechischen Landschildkröte (*Testudo* h. *robertmertensi*) an der Cte d'Azur. – Die Schildkröte (N. F.), Heinsberg, **2** (3): 25-27.

MARSCHANG, BECHER & POSTHAUS (1999): Isolation and characterization of an iridovirus from Hermann's tortoises (*Testudo hermanni*). – Archives of Virology, Vienna, **144** (10): 1909-1922.

MARSCHANG, GRAVENDYCK & KALETA (1997a): Herpesviruses in tortoises – Investigations into virus isolation and the treatment of viral stomatitis in *Testudo hermanni* and *T. graeca*. – Journal of Veterinary Medicine, B, **44**: 385-394.

MARSCHANG, GRAVENDYCK & KALETA (1997b): New investigations on herpesviruses in tortoises. – 38. Internationales Symposium über Erkrankungen der Zoo- und Wildtiere, 7.-11. Mai 1997, Zürich: 29-34.

MARSCHANG, MILDE & BELLAVISTA (2001): Virus isolation and vaccination of Mediterranean tortoises against a chelonid herpesvirus in a chronically infected population in Italy. – Deutsche Tierärztliche Wochenschrift, Hannover, **108** (9): 361-400; the Tortuga Gazette, Van Nuys **38** (3): 3.

MARSCHANG, POSTHAUS & GRAVENDYCK (1998): Isolation of viruses from land tortoises in Switzerland. – Proceedings of the American Association of Zoo Veterinarians and AAWV Joint Conference, Omaha, Nebraska, 17.-22. Oktober 1998: 281-284.

MARSCHANG, POSTHAUS & WILD (1998): Isolation of an irido-like virus from Hermann's tortoises (*Testudo hermanni*). – European Association of Zoo and Wildlife Veterinarians Second Scientific Meeting, Chester, 21.-24. Mai 1998: 287-294.

MARSCHANG, FROST, GRAVENDYCK & KALETA (2001): Comparison of 16 Chelonid Herpesviruses by Virus Neutralization Tests and Restriction Endonuclease Digestion of viral DNA. – Journal of Veterinary Medicine, B, **48**: 393-399.

MARSHALL & DU PRÉ (1967): Turtles in Art and Legend. – International Turtle and Tortoise Society Journal, Los Angeles, **1** (3): 24-30.1

MARTIN (2003): Waking up from hibernation. Basic steps to ensure a good start to the new season. – Tortoise Trust Newsletter, London, **18** (3/4): 9.

MARTIN, LAWTON & COOPER (1992): Manual of Reptiles. – London (British Small Animal Veterinary Association).

MARTÍNEZ (1996): Auswilderung von Schildkröten im Garraf-Massiv (Katalonien/Spanien). – Reptilia (D), Münster, **1**: 7.

MARTÍNEZ I GINER (1993): Contribución al conocimiento de la distribución de anfibios y reptiles en el país Valencià. – Boletín de la Asociación Herpetológica Española, Leganés, **4**: 2-4.

MARTÍNEZ RICA (1967): Las comunidades naturales del Sur de Menorca. – Revista de Menorca, Maó, **4**: 233-301.

MARTÍNEZ RICA (1983): Atlas herpetológica del Pirineo. – Munibe, **35** (1/2): 51-80.

MARTÍNEZ RICA (1989): El Atlas provisional de los anfibios y reptiles de España y Portugal (Aparep). Presentación y situación actual. – Monografías de herpetología, Madrid, **1**: 1-74.

MARTÍNEZ RICA & PLEGUEZUELOS (Eds.) (2005): Distribución y Biogeografía de los anfibios y reptiles en España y Portugal. – Granada (Asociación Herpetológica Española & Universidad de Granada).

MARTÍNEZ RICA & REINÉ (1988): Altitudinal distribution of Amphibians and Reptiles in the Spanish Pyrenees. – Pirineos, **131**: 57-82.

MARTÍNEZ (1998): Aspectos fundamentales en la reproducción de reptiles en cautividad. – In: GERPAC (Ed.): Proceedings of I Evssar Congress, Clinic and Reproduction. – Barcelona (AVEPA): 255-258.

MARTÍNEZ (1999): Libération de tortues en Espagne par la Comam. – La Tortue, Gonfaron, **48**: 34-35.

MARTÍNEZ & SOLER (1997): Aspectos biomédicos en el mantenimiento y reintroducción de quelonios ibéricos. – Jornadas de Conservación de la tortuga mediterránea, Conselleria de Medi Ambient, Generalitat Valenciana: 9-19.

MARTÍNEZ & SOLER (1998): Criteris de selecció de la tortuga mediterrània (*Testudo hermanni hermanni*) reintroduïda al Parc Natural del Garraf. – II Trobada d'Estudiosus del Garraf, Gavá, Diputació de Barcelona, **3**: 29.

MARTÍNEZ & SOLER (1999): Aspectes bàsics en la nutrició de rèptils mediterranis en captivitat. – Butlletí de la Societat Catalana d'Herpetologia, Leganés, **14**: 44-47.

MARTÍNEZ & SOLER (2000a): Comportamiento depredatorio de la Urraca (*Pica pica*) sobre puestas y neonatos de *Testudo hermanni*. – Boletín de la Asociación Herpetológica Española, Leganés, **11** (2): 69-71.

MARTÍNEZ & SOLER (2000b): Regeneración del caparazón en *Testudo hermanni hermanni* después de un incendio forestal. – Boletín de la Asociación Herpetológica Española, Leganés, **11** (2): 90-92.

MARTÍNEZ & SOLER (2000c): Criteris de selecció de la tortuga mediterrània (*Testudo hermanni hermanni*) reintroduïda al Parc Natural del Garraf. – In: HERNANDEZ & MELERO (Eds.): Monografies 30: III Trobada d'Estudiosos del Garraf. – Diputació de Barcelona, Servei de Parcs Naturals: 109-113.

MARTÍNEZ & SOLER (2001): An amelanistic Hermann's tortoise (*Testudo hermanni hermanni*) from the Balearic islands (Spain). – Testudo, **5** (3): 35-36.

MARTÍNEZ, SOLER & SOLÉ (2000): La tortuga mediterranea regresa al macizo del Garraf. – Animalia, **119**: 52-59.

MARTÍNEZ, SOLER, SAMPERE & SOLÉ (1998): Polidactilia en Testudo hermanni (GMELIN 1788) y causas teratogénicas en reptiles. – Boletín de la Asociación Herpetológica Española, Leganés, 9 (1): 35-38.

MARTÍNEZ, SOLER, SOLÉ & MEDINA (2001): Reproducción de quelonios aloctonos en Cataluña en condiciones naturales. Boletín de la Asociación Herpetológica Española, Leganés, 12 (1): 41-43.

MASCORT (1997a): Aspectos ecológicos de una población de tortuga mediterránea (Testudo hermanni) en la Sierra de l'Albera. – Jornadas de conservación de la tortuga mediterránea, Consellería de Medio Ambiente, Generalitat Valenciana, 6 pp.

MASCORT (1997b): Land Tortoises in Spain – Their Status and Conservation. – In: VAN ABBEMA (Ed.): Proceedings – Conservation, Restoration, and Management of Tortoises and Turtles – An International Conference, New York Turtle and Tortoise Society, New York: 307-312.

MASCORT (1998): La última población autóctona de tortuga mediterránea en la península Ibérica. – Quercus, 144: 31-34.

MASSA & DI PALMA (1988): Rettili, anfibi e uccelli terrestri dell isole circum-siciliane. – Bulletin d'Ecologie, Paris, 19 (2/3): 225-234.

MATEEV, KUOMDZHIEV & STOYANOV (1961): Natural reservoirs of Leptospirosis in Petrichko and Gotsedelchevsko – B – Natural source of infection in Petrichko and Gotsedelchevsko. – Bulgarian Academy of Science, Sofia: 33-49.

MATEEV, KUOMDZHIEV & STOYANOV (1962): Leptospirosis in Burgaske region among their natural reservoirs – B – Natural source of infection in Strandzha mountains. – Bulgarian Academy of Science, Sofia: 21-39.

MATHES (1997): Pathologie et épidémiologie de Testudo hermanni et Testudo graeca en captivité et dans la nature. – La Tortue, Gonfaron, 38: 31.

MATHES (1999): Erkrankungen der oberen Atemwege bei Schildkröten. – SIGS-Info, Siblingen, 8 (2): 14.

MATHES (2000): Einblicke in die natürliche Lebensweise von Testudo hermanni hermanni. – Draco, Münster, 2: 18-24.

MATHES (2004): Mycoplasma and Herpesvirus detection in mediterranean terrestrial tortoises in France and Morocco. – 7. Symposium of Pathology and Medicine of Reptiles and Amphibians, Berlin.

MATHES, BLAHAK, JACOBSON, BRAUN, SCHUMACHER & FERTARD (2002): Investigations for mycoplasma and herpesvirus in European terrestrial tortoises in France. – Chelonii, Gonfaron, 3: 155-156.

MATOFF (1943): Über die Möglichkeit der Entwicklung von Trichinella spiralis bei Kaltblütern. – Ann. Univ. Sofia, Fac. Méd.-Vet., Sofia, XIX: 307-336.

MATOFF (1944a): Über die Möglichkeit der Entwicklung von Trichinella spiralis bei Kaltblütern. – Zeitschrift für Parasitenkunde, Stuttgart, XIII (2/3): 156-176.

MATOFF (1944b): Zur Frage der Muskeltrichinose der Kaltblüter. – Ann. Univ. Sofia, Fac. Méd.-Vet., Sofia, XX: 347-353.

MATVEJEV (1961): Biogeografija Jugoslavije. Osnovni principi. – Bioloski Institut N. R. Srbije, Belgrade, 9, 232 pp., 1 map.

MATZ & VANDERHAEGE (1980): BLV Terrarienführer. – Munich, Vienna & Zürich (BLV Verlagsgesellschaft): 62, 335

MATZ & WEBER (1983): BLV Bestimmungsbuch Amphibien und Reptilien. – Munich, Vienna, Zürich (BLV Verlagsgesellschaft): 219, 223-224.

MATZANKE (1998): Freilandbeobachtungen und Unterschiede der Nominatform (Westrasse) der Griechischen Landschildkröte Testudo hermanni hermanni in ihren Verbreitungsgebieten. – Fachmagazin Schildkröte, Rothenfluh, 1 (5): 59-60.

MATZANKE (2000): Die Schildkrötenfauna Sardiniens. – In: ARTNER & MEIER (Eds.): Schildkröten. – Natur und Tier-Verlag, Münster: 39-44.

MAX (2001): Fritz! – Schildkröten, Linden, 8 (2): 28-29.

MAX (2002a): Die spannende Zeit der Eiablagen. – Schildkröten, Linden, 9 (3): 36-39.

MAX (2002b): Findling. – Schildkröten, Linden, 9 (4): 31-33.

MAYER (1987): Schildkrötenexkursion im Maurengebirge. – Die Schildkröte (N. F.), Heinsberg, 2 (2): 28-31.

MAYER (1992a): Zwillinge bei Testudo hermanni hermanni GMELIN 1789 w Testudo hermanni boettgeri MOJSISOVICS 1889. – Sauria, Berlin, 14 (3): 37-38.

MAYER (1992b): Bastarde zwischen den Rassen der Griechischen Landschildkröte – Testudo hermanni hermanni w T. h. boettgeri. – DATZ, Stuttgart, 45 (6): 369-371.

MAYER (1992c): Zwillinge bei einer Griechischen Landschildkröte. – DATZ, Stuttgart, 45 (9): 568.

MAYER (1994a): Die Schildkröten Sardiniens. – DATZ, Stuttgart, 47 (4): 438-440.

MAYER (1994b): Eiablage der Griechischen Landschildkröte. – Schildkröten, Linden, 1 (3): 30-32.

MAYER (1995a): Das Freilandterrarium für europäische Landschildkröten. – Schildkröten, Linden, 2 (1): 43-47.

MAYER (1995b): Aufzucht von Babyschildkröten. – Schildkröten, Linden, 2 (2): 4-7.

MAYER (1995c): Überwinterung bei europäischen Landschildkröten. – Schildkröten, Linden, 2 (4): 3-6.

MAYER (1996a): Krankheiten bei Landschildkröten. – Schildkröten, Linden, 3 (2): 11-15.

MAYER (1996b): Europäische Landschildkröten. – Kempten (Agrar Verlag Allgäu): 7-8, 11-16, 27, 29, 31-36, 38-39, 41, 43, 45, 47-48, 50, 54-55, 60-71, 81, 91-92, 99, 104, 108-109, 113-115, 117-118, 125, 127.

MAYER (1997a): Schildkrötenhaltung in der Poebene. – Schildkröten, Linden, 4 (1): 19-24.

MAYER (1997b): Haltung von Landschildkröten in einem Gartenhaus. – Schildkröten, Linden, 4 (2): 31-33.

MAYER (2001): Eiablage im Jahre 2000. – Schildkröten, Linden, 8 (2): 3-5.

MAYER (2002): Das Schildkrötendorf Massa Marittima. – Schildkröten, Linden, 9 (2): 35-37.

MAYER, RICHTER & KAMMEL (1990): Kartierung der Herpetofauna des Beckens von Feneos (Griechenland: Nord-Peloponnes). – Herpetozoa, Vienna, 2 (3/4): 87-106.

MAYOL (1985): Manuals d'Introducció a la Naturalesa. 6. Rèptils i Amfibis de les Balears. – Palma de Mallorca (Editorial Moll): 132-135, 149-151.

MAYOL SERRA (2003): Manuals d'Introducció a la Naturalesa. 6. Rèptils i Amfibis de les Balears. – Palma de Mallorca (Editorial Moll): 31, 90, 184-198.

MAYR (1967): Artbegriff und Evolution. – Hamburg & Berlin (Parey-Verlag), 617 pp.

MAZZOTTI (1992): Indagini eco-zoogeografiche sull' erpetofauna dell' Emilia-Romagna. – Boll. Mus. reg. Sci. nat. Torino, Turin, 10 (1): 73-87.

MAZZOTTI (2004): Hermann's Tortoises (Testudo hermanni): current distribution in Italy and ecological data on a population from the north Adriatic coast (Reptilia, Testudinidae). – Italian Journal of Zoology, Modena, 71 (Suppl. 1): 97-102.

MAZZOTTI (2006): Testudo hermanni GMELIN, 1789. Testuggine di Hermann/Hermann's tortoise. – In: SINDACO, DORIA, RAZZETTI & BERNINI (Eds.): Atlante degli Anfibi e die Rettili d'Italia/Atlas of Italian Amphibians and Reptiles. – Florence (Edizioni Polistampa): 390-395.

MAZZOTTI & STAGNI (1993): Gli anfibi e i rettili dell' Emilia-Romagna (Amphibia, Reptilia). – Quad. Staz. Ecol. Museo Civico di Storia Naturale di Ferrara, Ferrara, 5, 148 pp.

MAZZOTTI & VALLINI (1994): Struttura di popolazione di Testudo hermanni GMELIN nel Bosco della Mesola (Delta del Po) (Testudines, Testudinae). – Studi Trentini di Scienze Naturali, Acta Biológica, 71: 205-207.

MAZZOTTI & VALLINI (1996): Struttura di popolazione di Testudo hermanni GMELIN nel Bosco della Mesola (Delta del Po) (Testudines, Testudinidae). – In: AMATO, CALDONAZZI, RIVABEN & ZANGHELLINI (Eds.): Atti del 1° Convegno italiano di Erpetologia montana. – Studi trent. Sci. Nat., Acta biol., Trento, 71: 205-207.

MAZZOTTI & VALLINI (1999): Seasonal activity and thermal relations of Testudo hermanni GMELIN in bare patches of the Bosco della Mesola (Po Delta, Northern Italy). – In: GIACOMA (Ed.): Atti I Congresso Societas Herpetologica Italica. – Turin (Museo Regionale Scienze Naturali): 133-141.

MAZZOTTI & VALLINI (2000): Seasonal activity and thermal relations of Testudo hermanni GMELIN in bare patches of the Bosco della Mesola (Po Delta, Northern Italy). – In: GIACOMA (Ed.): Atti I Congresso Nazionale Societas Herpetologica Italica, Torino. – Mus. Reg. Sci. Nat., Torino: 133-137.

MAZZOTTI, BERTORELLE & FASOLA (2004): Le popolazioni italiane della Testuggine di Hermann (Testudo hermanni) – puzzle ecologico e tassonomico per una strategia di conservazione. – In: ZUFFI (Ed.): V° Congresso Nazionale della Societas Herpetologica Italica, 29 settembre - 3 ottobre 2004, Calci (Pisa). – Societas Herpetologica Italica, Pavia: 13-14.

MAZZOTTI, CARAMORI & BARBIERI (1999): Atlante degli Anfibi e dei Rettili dell'Emilia-Romagna (Aggiornamento 1993/1997). – Museo Civico di Storia Naturale di Ferrara, Ferrara, 121 pp.

MAZZOTTI, PISAPIA & FASOLA (2002): Activity and home range of Testudo hermanni in northern Italy. – Amphibia-Reptilia, Leiden, 23 (3): 305-312.

McARTHUR (1996): Veterinary Management of Tortoises and Turtles. – Oxford, London, Edinburgh, Cambridge & Carlton (Blackwell Science): 2, 18-29, 34-35, 50, 78, 119, 126, 134.

McARTHUR (1997): Herpes Virus infection associated with Lymphoma in Testudo hermanni. – Tortoise Trust Newsletter, London, 12 (1): 3-4.

McARTHUR (1998): Lymphoproliferative disease in Testudo hermanni and Geochelone pardalis tortoises associated with herpesvirus-like infection. – Testudo, 4 (5): 33-40.

McARTHUR (1999): A health survey of captive chelonia and a serological survey of plasma herpesvirus neutralising antibody status. – Tortoise Trust Newsletter, London, 14 (1): 8-9.

McARTHUR (2001): Emerging viral-associated diseases of chelonians in the United Kingdom. – Proceedings ARAV, Orlando: 103-116.

McARTHUR (2004): Post-hibernation anorexia (PHA) (Testudo species). – Testudo, 6 (1): 1-9.

McARTHUR, WILKINSON & MEYER (2004): Medicine and Surgery of Tortoises and Turtles. – Oxford, Ames & Carlton (Blackwell Publishing): 18-19, 29-30, 38, 40, 46-48, 50, 52-55, 57, 59-62, 64-65, 75-76, 78, 82, 85, 87, 90-91, 99, 102, 105, 115, 125-126, 133-134, 139-140, 142-143, 148, 155-158, 160, 162-166, 168-170, 177, 179-183, 203, 219, 221, 223, 226, 235-236, 249, 270-271, 277, 282, 284-286, 289, 291-292, 296-297, 300, 315-316, 321, 339-340, 349, 351, 371-

372, 395, 443, 456-457, 471, 481, 492-493, 502, 514-516, 521, 525, 527-529, 531, 533, 535-538.

MCARTHUR, BLAHAK, KÖLLE, JACOBSON, MARSCHANG & ORIGGI (2002): Chelonian Herpesvirus (Roundtable). – Journal of Herpetological Medicine and Surgery, 12 (2): 14-31.

MCGRATTAN (1982a): Importation of Mediterranean tortoises. – British Chelonia Group Newsletter, 31: 2.

MCGRATTAN (1982b): Egg retention in Testudo hermanni. – British Chelonia Group Newsletter, 34: 3.

MEBAN (1980): Physical properties of surfactant from the lungs of the tortoise Testudo hermanni. – Comparative Biochemistry and Physiology, A, Comparative Physiology, Vancouver, 67 (2): 253-258.

MEBAN (1981): Evaporative resistance of pulmonary surfactant films. – Experientia, Bangor, 37 (8): 867-868.

MEBS (1964): Eine seltene Schildkrötenkrankheit. – DATZ, Stuttgart, 17 (1): 39.

MEEK (1982): Allometry in chelonians. – British Journal of Herpetology, London, 6: 198-199.

MEEK (1984a): Amphibians and reptiles in Montenegro, Yugoslavia. – British Herpetological Society Bulletin, London, 9: 43-49.

MEEK (1984b): Thermoregulatory behaviour in a population of Hermann's tortoise (Testudo hermanni) in southern Yugoslavia. – British Journal of Herpetology, London, 6: 387-391.

MEEK (1985): Aspects of the ecology of Testudo hermanni in southern Yugoslavia. – British Journal of Herpetology, London, 6: 437-445.

MEEK (1988a): The thermal ecology of Hermann's tortoise (Testudo hermanni) in summer and autumn in Yugoslavia. – Journal of Zoology, London, 215: 99-111.

MEEK (1988b): Thermal loads experienced by a nesting Testudo hermanni. – Amphibia-Reptilia, Leiden, 9: 311-312.

MEEK (1989): The comparative population ecology of Hermann's tortoise, Testudo hermanni in Croatia and Montenegro, Yugoslavia. – The Herpetological Journal, London, 1 (9): 404-414.

MEEK (1995): Reptiles, Thermoregulation and the Environment. – Testudo, 4 (2): 56-78.

MEEK & AVERY (1988): Mini Review: Thermoregulation in Chelonians. – The Herpetological Journal, London, 1: 253-259.

MEEK & INSKEEP (1979): Observations on the herpetofauna of a costal region of southern Yugoslavia. – Herptile, London, 4 (1): 18-28.

MEEK & INSKEEP (1981): Aspects of the field biology of a population of Hermann's Tortoise (Testudo hermanni) in southern Yugoslavia. – British Journal of Herpetology, London, 6: 159-164.

MEHRING (1972): Light microscopic and electron microscopic investigation of the pineal organ of Testudo hermanni. – Anatomischer Anzeiger, Jena, 131 (3/4): 184-203.

MEIER (2000): Aus Fehlern lernt man, oder? – SIGS-Info, Siblingen, 9 (4): 17-18.

MEIJIDE (1985): Localidades nuevas o poco conocidas de Anfibios y Reptiles de la España continental. – Doñana Acta Vertebrata, Sevilla, 12 (2): 318-323.

MEJÍAS GARCÍA & AMENGUAL RAMIS (2000): Llibre Vermell dels Vertebrats de les Balears. – Documents Tècnics de Conservació, II època, núm. 8, Govern de les Illes Balears, Conselleria de Medi Ambient.

MELLADO, VALAKOS, GIL, GUERRERO, LULCH, NAVARRO & MARAGOU (1999): Herpetological notes from mainland and insular Greece. – British Herpetological Society Bulletin, London, 67: 33-38.

MÉNARD (1999): Détermination et étude des sites potentiels à la réintroduction de la tortue d'Hermann dans le Massif de l'Estérel. – Unveröffentlichter Bericht, BTS GPN Legta Arras/CRCC Soptom, 41 pp.

MENDT (1995): Das »Schildkrötendorf«. – elaphe (N. F.), Rheinbach, 3 (3): 70-73.

MENDT & BENDER (2001): Änderung der Bundesartenschutz-Verordnung in Aussicht gestellt. – elaphe (N. F.), Rheinbach, 9 (1): 21-23.

MENZEL-TETTENBORN (Ed.) (1973): Das neue Tierreich nach Brehm. – Gütersloh, Berlin, Munich & Vienna (Verlagsgruppe Bertelsmann GmbH/Bertelsmann Lexikonverlag): 227-228.

MENZEL-TETTENBORN (1967): Das bunte Terrarien-Buch. – Gütersloh (C. Bertelsmann Verlag): 104, 125.

MERCHÁN & MARTÍNEZ (1999): Tortugas de España Biología, patología y conservación de las especies ibéricas, baleares y canarias. – Madrid (Ediciones Antiqvaria): 8, 15-16, 18, 71-73, 92-111, 130-131, 134-135, 138-139, 142, 221-225, 236-237, 240-241, 244-245, 255, 259-264, 267, 275-278, 280-282, 284-288, 291, 294, 296-300, 303-308, 310, 312-313, 315, 317, 325, 329, 332-334, 337, 342, 350-351.

MERREM (1820): Versuch eines Systems der Amphibien. Tentamen Systematis Amphibiorum. – Marburg (Kreiger): 29.

MERTENS (1921a): Die Amphibien und Reptilien der Walachei und der Dobrudscha. II. Die Reptilien. – Senckenbergiana Biologica, Frankfurt am Main, 3: 21-23.

MERTENS (1921b): Zoologische Streifzüge in Rumänien. – Blätter für Aquarien- und Terrarienkunde, Stuttgart, 32: 247-252, 311-314, 323-327.

MERTENS (1923): Beiträge zur Herpetologie Rumäniens. – Senckenbergiana Biologica, Frankfurt am Main, 5 (5/6): 207-227.

MERTENS (1925): Amphibien und Reptilien aus dem nördlichen und östlichen Spanien, gesammelt von Dr. F.

HAAS. – Abhandlungen der Senckenbergischen Naturforschenden Gesellschaft, Frankfurt am Main, **39** (1): 27-129.

MERTENS (1926a): Herpetologische Mitteilungen. XV. Nachträge zu:»Amphibien und Reptilien aus dem nördlichen und östlichen Spanien«. – Senckenbergiana Biologica, Frankfurt am Main, **8**: 137-155.

MERTENS (1926b): Zoologische Ergebnisse einer Reise nach den Pelagischen Inseln und Sizilien. – Senckenbergiana Biolica, Frankfurt am Main, **8** (5/6): 225-271.

MERTENS (1927): Eine zoologische Sammelreise nach den Pelagischen Inseln. – Blätter für Aquarien- und Terrarienkunde, Stuttgart, **38**: 385-396.

MERTENS (1946a): Die Warn- und Drohreaktionen der Reptilien. – Abhandlungen der Senckenbergischen Naturforschenden Gesellschaft, Frankfurt am Main, 471: 1-103.

MERTENS (1946b): Über einige mediterrane Schildkröten-Rassen. – Senckenbergiana, Frankfurt am Main, **27** (4/6): 111-118.

MERTENS (1947): Die Lurche und Kriechtiere des Rhein-Main-Gebietes. – Frankfurt am Main (Verlag Dr. Waldemar Kramer): 22, 101.

MERTENS (1949): *Medaestia* WUSSOW, 1916, a synonym of *Testudo* LINNAEUS, 1758. – Copeia, Lawrence, 3: 232.

MERTENS (1952a): Amphibien und Reptilien aus der Türkei. – Istanbul Üniv. Fen Fac. Mecm., Ser. B, **17** (1) 41-75.

MERTENS (1952b): Nachtrag zu »Amphibien und Reptilien aus der Türkei«. – Istanbul Üniv. Fen Fac. Mecm., Ser. B, **17** (4): 353-355.

MERTENS (1955): Unterlagen zu einer »Herpetologia tyrrhenica«. III. Die Amphibien und Reptilien der Insel Elba. – Senckenbergiana Biologica, Frankfurt am Main, **36**: 287-296.

MERTENS (1957a): Die Amphibien und Reptilien Korsikas. – Senckenbergiana Biologica, Frankfurt am Main, **38** (3/4): 175-192.

MERTENS (1957b): Tierleben im Donaudelta. 1. Lurche und Kriechtiere. – Natur und Volk, Frankfurt am Main, **87** (5): 160-168.

MERTENS (1957c): Unterlagen zu einer »Herpetologia tyrrhenica« – V – Die Amphibien und Reptilien Korsikas. – Senckenbergiana Biologica, Frankfurt am Main, **38** (3/4): 175-192.

MERTENS (1958): Wie orientieren sich Schildkröten? – Natur und Volk, Frankfurt am Main, **88** (4): 116-121.

MERTENS (1960): Zoologische Wandertage auf Korfu, der Insel der Phäaken. – Natur und Volk, Frankfurt am Main, **90**: 321-333, 356-366.

MERTENS (1961): Die Amphibien und Reptilien der Insel Korfu. – Senckenbergiana Biologica, Frankfurt am Main, **42** (1/2): 1-29.

MERTENS (1964): Über Reptilienbastarde III. – Senckenbergiana Biologica, Frankfurt am Main, **45** (1): 33-49.

MERTENS (1968a): Über Reptilienbastarde IV. – Senckenbergiana Biologica, Frankfurt am Main, **49** (1): 1-12.

MERTENS (1968b): Nachträge zur Reptilienfauna der Insel Korfu. – Senckenbergiana Biologica, Frankfurt am Main, **49** (3/4): 173-180.

MERTENS (1970): Über die Lebensdauer einiger Amphibien und Reptilien in Gefangenschaft. – Der Zoologische Garten (N. F.), Jena, **39** (1/6): 193-209.

MERTENS (1972): Über Reptilienbastarde V. – Senckenbergiana Biologica, Frankfurt am Main, 53 (1/2): 1-19.

MERTENS & MÜLLER (1928): Liste der Amphibien und Reptilien Europas. – Abhandlungen der Senckenbergischen Naturforschenden Gesellschaft, Frankfurt am Main, **41** (1): 1-62.

MERTENS & MÜLLER (1940): Die Amphibien und Reptilien Europas – Zweite Liste, nach dem Stand vom 1. Januar 1940. – Abhandlungen der Senckenbergischen Naturforschenden Gesellschaft, Frankfurt am Main, 451: 1-56.

MERTENS & WERMUTH (1955): Die rezenten Schildkröten, Krokodile und Brückenechsen. – Zoologische Jahrbücher für Systematik, Jena, **83**: 379.

MERTENS & WERMUTH (1960): Die Amphibien und Reptilien Europas (Dritte Liste, nach dem Stand vom 1. Januar 1960). – Frankfurt am Main (Verlag Waldemar Kramer): 66.

MERWALD (1977): Tiere der Welt. – Linz (Rudolf Trauner Verlag): 21-22, plate 7.

MERTZANIS (1992): Aspects biogéographiques et écologiques des populations helléniques d'ours brun (*Ursus arctos* L.). Cas d'une sous-population du Pinde – application à la conservation de l'espèce et de son habitat. – Dissertation, Univ. de Montpellier, Montpellier, 247 pp.

MÉTRAILLER (1994): *Graeca ou hermanni?* – CITS bulletin, Bramois, 2: 8.

MÉTRAILLER (1997): Distinguer les deux sous-espèces de *Testudo hermanni*. – CITS bulletin, Bramois, 9: 23-25.

METTLER, PALMER, RÜBEL & ISENBÜGEL (1982): Gehäuft auftretende Fälle von Parakeratose mit Epithelablösung der Haut bei Landschildkröten. – Verhandlungsbericht über Erkrankungen der Zootiere, **24**: 245-248.

MEYER (1748): Angenehmer und nützlicher Zeitvertreib mit Betrachtung curioser Vorstellungen allerhand kriechender, fliegender und schwimmender, auf dem Land und im Wasser sich befindender und nährender Thiere, sowohl nach ihrer Gestalt und äusserlichen Beschaffenheit als auch nach der Accuratest davon verfertigten Structur ihrer Scelete oder Beincörper, nebst einer Beschreibung derselben nach der Natur gezeichnet, gemahlet, in Kupfer gestochen und verlegt von Johann Daniel Meyer... I. – Nuremberg (Mahler), IV + 56 pp., 100 plates.

MEYER (1985): Die Reptilienfauna des südlichen Peloponnes. – Sauria, Berlin, 7 (1): 13-16.

MEYER (1996): Röntgenologische, computertomographische und kernspintomographische Untersuchungen zum Verdauungstrakt der Griechischen Landschildkröte (Testudo hermanni). – Dissertation, Univ. Wien, Vienna, 196 pp.

MEYER (1998): Erfahrungen bei der Haltung und Nachzucht der Griechischen Landschildkröte Testudo hermanni hermanni. – Journal der AG Schildkröten der DGHT, Bennstedt, 7 (1): 11-15.

MEYER (2001): Schildkrötenernährung. – Frankfurt am Main (Edition Chimaira): 9-11, 19-22, 40, 42, 49, 57, 75, 77-78, 88, 91-93, 102, 104-105, 108, 115.

MEYER (2003): Artgerechte Ernährung von Landschildkröten. – DATZ, Stuttgart, 56 (6): 60-64.

MICHELOT (1980): Quelques notes sur la faune herpétologique de la Corse. – Bulletin de la Société Herpétologique de France, Paris, 15 (3): 27-44.

MICHELOT (1984): Le peuplement herpétologique de la Corse. – Bulletin de la Société Herpétologique de France, Paris, 29: 18-23.

MICHELUCCI (1962): Ricerche autoradiografiche sul corpo ultimobranchiale du cheloni (Testudo hermanni) (Nota preliminare). – Atti della Società Toscana di Scienze Naturali, Ser. B, Pisa, 68: 195-196.

MICHELUCCI (1969): Il corpo ultimobranchiale nei cheloni (Testudo hermanni). – Archo Ital. Anat. Embriol., 74: 161-176.

VAN MIDDELKOOP (1999): Centraal kweekarchief. Een overzicht van gekweekte dieren in 1995/1996/1997/1998. – De Schildpad, Ijsselstein, 25 (1): 79-80.

MILTSCHEV & GEORGIEVA (1992): Eine Studie zum Bestand, zur Brutbiologie und Ernährung des Steinadlers, Aquila chrysaetos (L.), im Strandsha-Gebirge. – Beiträge zur Vogelkunde, Leipzig, 38: 334-357.

MINCH (2005a): Futterpflanzen im Überblick: Wilde Malve (Malva sylvestris). – Radiata, Lingenfeld, 14 (3): 33-34.

MINCH (2005b): Futterpflanzen im Überblick: Wegwarte (Cichorium intybus). – Radiata, Lingenfeld, 14 (4): 33-34.

MINCH (2006a): Futterpflanzen im Überblick: Knoblauchsrauke (Alliaria petiolata). – Radiata, Lingenfeld, 15 (1): 33-34.

MINCH (2006b): PraxisRatgeber Freilandanlagen für Schildkröten. – Frankfurt am Main (Edition Chimaira), 158 pp.

MIRIMIN, VERNESI, BERTOLUCCI, MAZZOTTI & BERTORELLE (2004): Mitochondrial DNA variation and divergence in three Hermann's tortoise (Testudo hermanni) populations. – Italian Journal of Zoology, Modena, 71 (Suppl. 2): 199-201.

MIRLACH (2002a): Zusammenfassung der wichtigsten Unterscheidungsmerkmale der Europäischen Landschildkröten. – Schildkröten, Linden, 9 (3): 20-26.

MIRLACH (2002b): Über die Haltung europäischer Landschildkröten. – Schildkröten, Linden, 9 (4): 3-11.

MIRLACH (2003): Bau eines Frühbeetes für Europäische Landschildkröten. – Schildkröten, Linden, 10 (1): 8-11.

MITCHELL (2004): An eggs-traordinary summer! – Tortoise Trust Newsletter, London, 19 (1): 4-5.

MITTENZWEI (2004): Der Tierrarzt hilft. Die Seite für die Gesundheit der Schildkröten. – turtles press international, Rodenbach, 2 (2): 22-23.

MLYNARSKI (1955): Zolwie z pliocenu Polski. – Acta Geologica Polonica, Warsaw, 5 (2): 161-214, Consp.: 46-62.

MLYNARSKI (1956): Studies on the morphology of the shell of recent and fossil tortoises – I-II. – Acta Zoologica Cracoviensia, Krakow, 1 (1): 1-14.

MLYNARSKI (1962): Notes on the amphibians and reptilian fauna of the Polish Pliocene and early Pleistocene. – Acta Zoologica Cracoviensia, Krakow, 15: 177-192.

MLYNARSKI (1969): Tortoises in the Zoological Gardens. – Przegl. zool., Warsaw, 13: 122-133.

MLYNARSKI (1976): Handbuch der Paläoherpetologie – Teil 7 – Testudines. – Stuttgart & New York (Gustav Fischer Verlag): 97.

MLYNARSKI (1980): The Pleistocene turtles of central and eastern Europe – determination key. – Folia Quartern., Krakow, 52: 1-44.

MLYNARSKI & WERMUTH (1980): Die Schildkröten. – In: GRZIMEK (Ed.): Grzimeks Tierleben, Band 6, Kriechtiere. – Munich (Deutscher Taschenbuch Verlag): 20, 82, 102-104, 115, 123-124, 127, 500, 546.

MOCCI DEMARTIS (1987): Isole sarde: vi abita anche il corso. – Airone, Milan, 7 (76): 120-127.

MODLMAYR (2001): Johnny ist weg! – Schildkröten, Linden, 8 (4): 30-31.

MOJSISOVICS (1889): Zoogeographische Notizen über Süd-Ungarn aus den Jahren 1886-1888. Zugleich ein III. Nachtrag zur »Fauna von Béllye und Darda«. – Mitteilungen des Naturwissenschaftlichen Vereins der Steiermark, Graz, 25: 233-269.

MONDINI (1990): Les tortues de France – images et utilisations d'hier et d'aujourd'hui. – Bulletin de la Société Herpétologique Française, 56: 39-47.

MONDOR (2001): Mariage de tortues! – La Tortue, Gonfaron, 55: 64.

MONTORI (1996): Amfibis i rèptils del massís de Garraf. – La Sentiu, Quaderns de Divulgació, 22, Gavà (Museu de Gavà), 65 pp.

MONTORI & LLORENTE (Hrsg.) (2005): Lista patrón actualizada de la herpetofauna española: Conclusiones de nomenclatura y taxonomía para las especies de anfibios y reptiles de España. – Leganés (Asociación Herpetológica Española),

MONTORI, LLORENTE & FÉLIX (1993): Estado y gestión de la poblaciones de Testudo hermanni hermanni del nordeste de la peninsula Iberica. – In: EUROPEAN COUNCIL (Eds.): Seminar on Recovery Plans for Species of Amphibians and Reptiles. – El Hierro, T-PVS (93), 34: 72-83.

MÖRCK (1998): Untersuchungen über die bakterielle Zusammensetzung der Rachen- und Darmflora von gesunden in Süddeutschland gehaltenen Landschildkröten. – Dissertation, Univ. München, Munich.

MÖSEL (1997): Urlaubsüberraschung. – Schildkröten, Linden, 4 (2): 6-8.

MÖSEL (1999): Eine phantasievolle Terrarienvergrößerung. – Schildkröten, Linden, 6 (3): 28-30.

MOXLEY (1987): Breeding Mediterranean tortoises at Whipsnade. – Zoo Reptile News, 2: 25.

MRSIC (1978): A contribution to the knowledge of the taxonomy, zoogeography and ecology of the reptiles of the Velebit mountain-chain. – Dissertation, Academia Scientiarum et Artium Slovinica, Classis IV, 21, Ljubljana, 43 pp.

MRSIC (1997): Plazilci Slovenije. – Zavod Republika Slovenije za ëolstvo, Ljubljana, 167 pp.

MRSIC, NEMESCHKAI, POTOCNIK, SCHWAMMER & SCHWAMMER (1989): Ein Beitrag zur Herpetofauna der Quarner-Inseln (Jugoslawien – Croatien). – Biol. Vestn., Ljubljana, 37: 57-74.

MÜHLSTEIN (1994): Überraschende Nachzucht. – Schildkröten, Linden, 1 (4): 22-25.

MÜLLER (1932/1934): Beiträge zur Herpetologie der südosteuropäischen Halbinsel. Herpetologisch Neues aus Bulgarien. – Zoologischer Anzeiger I 100: 299-309, II 104: 1-14, III 107: 273-284.

MÜLLER (1940): Über die von den Herren Dr. V. JORDANS und Dr. WOLF im Jahre 1938 in Bulgarien gesammelten Amphibien und Reptilien. – Bull. Inst. Roy. Hist. Natur. Sofia, 13: 1-17.

MÜLLER (1975): Schildkröten sind kein Kinderspielzeug. – Das Tier, Leinfelden-Echterdingen, 16 (7): 48-50.

MÜLLER (1995a): Eine Urlaubsüberraschung: Testudo hermanni am Wegrand. – DATZ, Stuttgart, 48 (7): 452-453.

MÜLLER (1995b): Schildkröten. – Stuttgart (Verlag Eugen Ulmer): 15, 34, 148-150.

MÜLLER (1995c): Verlust von juvenilen Landschildkröten durch Steinmarder. – Emys, Sankt Pölten, 2 (6): 18-19.

MÜLLER (1996): Nachtrag zum Merkblatt (Beilage zur EMYS 3/2) über die Haltung und Nachzucht von Testudo hermanni. – Emys, Sankt Pölten, 3 (3): 34.

MÜLLER (1998): Turtles in the Terrarium. – Neptune City (T. F. H. Publications): 37, 52-53, 137, 140.

MÜLLER (1999): Spaß mit Schildkröten. – Schildkröten, Linden, 6 (3): 5-9.

MÜLLER & NIEDERHUBER (1996): Eindrücke vom Winter-Quartalstreffen in Salzburg am 3.12.1995. – Emys, Sankt Pölten, 3 (1): 10-11.

MÜLLER & SCHMIDT (1995): Landschildkröten. – Münster (Natur und Tier-Verlag): 12, 36-37, 41-42, 45, 48, 53, 56, 58, 67, 71-72, 81, 84, 170-174.

MÜLLER & SCHWEIGER (1998): Winterruhe europäischer Schildkröten. – Emys, Sitzenberg-Reidling, 5 (6): III-IV.

MÜLLER & SCHWEIGER (1999a): Auswinterung von Land- und Wasserschildkröten. – Emys, Sitzenberg-Reidling, 6 (2): III-V.

MÜLLER & SCHWEIGER (1999b): Inkubation (Ausbrüten) von Eiern der europäischen und mediterranen Land- und Wasserschildkröten. – Emys, Sitzenberg-Reidling, 6 (3): I-IV.

MÜLLER & SCHWEIGER (1999c): Die Ernährung Europäischer Landschildkröten. – Emys, Sitzenberg-Reidling, 6 (4): I-III.

MÜLLER & SCHWEIGER (1999d): Vorbereitung zur Winterruhe europäischer Land- und Wasserschildkröten. – Emys, Sitzenberg-Reidling, 6 (5): I-III.

MÜLLER & SCHWEIGER (1999/2000): Bau einer Freilandanlage (nicht nur) für Europäische Landschildkröten. – Emys, Sitzenberg-Reidling, 6 (6): I-V, 7 (1): I-IV.

MÜLLER & SCHWEIGER (2000): Auswinterung europäischer (mediterraner) Landschildkröten. – Emys, Sitzenberg-Reidling, 7 (2): I-II.

MÜLLER & SCHWEIGER (2002): Die Jackson-Kurve – Eine kritische Verifikation. – Radiata, Haan, 11 (1): 23-30.

MÜLLER, SACHSSE & ZANGGER (1990): Herpesvirus-Epidemie bei den Griechischen (Testudo hermanni) und der Maurischen Landschildkröte (Testudo graeca) in der Schweiz. – Schweizerisches Archiv für Tierheilkunde, Bern, 132 (1): 199-203.

MÜLLER, ZANGGER & DENZER (1988): Iridovirus-Epidemie bei der Griechischen Landschildkröte (Testudo hermanni hermanni). – Verhandlungsbericht des 30. Internationalen Symposiums über die Erkrankung der Zoo- und Wildtiere, Sofia, 30: 271-274.

MURAKAMI, MATSUBA, UNE, NOMURA & FUJITANI (2001): Deevelopment of species-specific PCR techniques for the detection of tortoise herpesvirus. – J. Vet. Diagn. Invest., 13: 513-516.

MURPHY & COLLINS (1983): A Review of the Diseases and Treatments of Captive Turtles. – Lawrence (AMS Publishing): 28-29, 31.

MURRAY (1987): The cure worse than the disease. – British Chelonia Group Newsletter, 56: 6.

MUSQUERA, MASSEGÚ & PLANAS (1976): Blood proteins in turtles (*Testudo hermanni*, *Emys orbicularis* and *Caretta caretta*). – Comparative Biochemistry and Physiology, A, Comparative Physiology, Vancouver, 55 (3): 225-230.

MUTZ (1995): Die Herpetofauna von Korsika. – elaphe (N. F.), Rheinbach, 3 (1): 35-36.

NARVESTAD (1991): First tortoises bred in Norway by Tortoise Trust member. – Tortoise Trust Newsletter, London, 6 (5/6): 11.

NARVESTAD (1995): Breeding tortoises in Norway. – Tortoise Trust Newsletter, London, 9 (1): 8.

NEDERLOF (2002): Toon en Joepie. – De Schildpad, Eindhoven, 28 (2): 101-103.

NEMURAS (1970): Creatures on Land. – International Turtle and Tortoise Society Journal, Los Angeles, 4 (4): 18-19, 30-31.

NEUBERT (1997): Das kleine Wunder. – Schildkröten, Linden, 4 (2): 29-31.

NEUMANN (2004): *Testudo hermanni* – Schlupf in freier Natur in Deutschland. – elaphe (N. F.), Rheinbach, 12 (3): 43-44.

NICKEL-HIEDELS (2002a): Ein Naturschutzgebiet in Griechenland. – Turtle-News, 2: 9-13.

NICKEL-HIEDELS (2002b): Unsere Patenschildkröten in Griechenland; Turtle-News, 2: 34-38.

NIESSEN (1996): »Höckerbildung« bei Landschildkröten. – Journal der AG Schildkröten & Panzerechsen der DGHT, Bürstadt, 5 (3): 16-18.

NIETZKE (1980): Die Terrarientiere 1. – 3., überarbeitete und verbesserte Auflage, Stuttgart (Verlag Eugen Ulmer): 225, 302-303, 336.

NIETZKE (1984): Fortpflanzung und Zucht der Terrarientiere. – Hannover (Landbuch-Verlag): 42, 57, 104, 165, 181-183, 187-189.

NIETZKE (1988): Die Terrarientiere 1. – 4., neubearbeitete und neugestaltete Auflage, Stuttgart (Verlag Eugen Ulmer): 260-261.

NIETZKE (1998): Die Terrarientiere 2. – 4., neubearbeitete und neugestaltete Auflage, Stuttgart (Verlag Eugen Ulmer): 49-50, 68, 73, 78, 80-81, 161-166.

NIETZKE (2002): Die Terrarientiere 3. – 4., neubearbeitete und neugestaltete Auflage, Stuttgart (Verlag Eugen Ulmer): 330.

NIJS (1984): Pseudomannelijk gedrag bij twee vrouwelijke landschildpadden (*Testudo graeca* en *T. hermanni*). – Lacerta, Zoetermeer, 42 (12): 240-243.

NILSSON (1906): Griechische Feste von religiöser Bedeutung mit Ausschluss der attischen. – Leipzig, 98 pp.

VAN NISPEN (2005): De pen van ... ANKIE VAN NISPEN. – Trionyx, Eindhoven, 3 (2): 59-61.

NOACK (1956): Lautäußerungen bei Griechischen Landschildkröten. – DATZ, Stuttgart, 9 (9): 250.

NOËL-HUME & NOËL-HUME (1954): Tortoises, Terrapins & Turtles. – London (W. & G. Foyle): 8-11, 20-21, 24-26, 111.

NÖLLERT (1972): Über einige Panzeranomalien bei Schildkröten (Reptilia, Testudines). – Der Zoologische Garten (N. F.), Jena, 50: 271-276.

NÖLLERT (1984): Einige Bemerkungen zur Kälteresistenz bei Schildkröten. – elaphe, Berlin, 6 (3): 42-43.

NÖLLERT (1992): Schildkröten. – Hannover (Landbuch-Verlag): 18, 29, 31, 42-43, 49-50, 53-54, 57, 72, 81, 84, 155-158, 180.

NÖLLERT & NÖLLERT (1981): Einige Bemerkungen zu den Landschildkröten Bulgariens. – Die Schildkröte, Haar, 4 (1): 5-15.

NÖLLERT, NÖLLERT & RITTER (1986): Einige Beobachtungen zur Herpetofauna der bulgarischen Schwarzmeerküste und Südwestbulgariens (Teil 2 – Die Reptilien). – herpetofauna, Weinstadt, 8 (44): 30-34.

NOUGARÈDE (1998): Principaux traits d'histoire naturelle d'une population de tortue d'Hermann (*Testudo hermanni*) dans le sud de la Corse. – Dissertation, École Pratique des Hautes Études, Montpellier, 344 pp.

VAN NUNEN (2003): Goois pardijsje voor Griekse gasten. – Trionyx, Eindhoven, 1 (6): 171-173.

NUSSEAR, SIMANDLE & TRACY (2000): Misconceptions about colour, infrared radiation, and energy exchange between animals and their environments. – The Herpetological Journal, London, 10: 119-122.

OBST (1980): Schildkröten. – Leipzig, Jena & Berlin (Urania-Verlag): 22, 59.

OBST (1985): Die Welt der Schildkröten. – Rüschlikon-Zürich, Stuttgart & Vienna (Albert Müller Verlag): 23, 52, 94, 192, 212, 215, 219.

OBST (1992): Wasser- und Landschildkröten. – In: COGGER & ZWEIFEL (Eds.): Reptilien & Amphibien. – Gütersloh (Bertelsmann Club): 121.

OBST & AMBROSIUS (1971): Taxonomische Studien an europäischen Landschildkröten (Reptilia: Testudinidae) mit serologisch-immunologischen Methoden. – Zoologische Abhandlungen des Staatlichen Museums für Tierkunde, Dresden, 30 (22): 297-331.

OBST & MEUSEL (1963): Die Landschildkröten Europas und der Mittelmeerländer. – Die Neue Brehm-Bücherei, Band 319, Wittenberg Lutherstadt (A. Ziemsen Verlag): 3-6, 12-13, 16, 19, 21, 24-26, 28-33, 35, 39-40, 43, 45, 48-50, 53, 65, 67.

OBST, RICHTER & JACOB (1984): Lexikon der Terraristik und Herpetologie. – Hannover (Landbuch-Verlag): 420.

ODDY (1985): Breeding tortoises. – Ratel, Edinburgh, 12 (6): 184-190.

OETTLE, STETYTLER & WILLIAM (1990): High mortality in a tortoise colony. – South African Journal of Wildlife Research, Bloubergstrand, 20 (1): 21-25.

O'MEARA (2002): BCG trip to CARAPAX 12th-17th September 2002. – British Chelonia Group Newsletter, 150: 5-8.

O'MEARA (2004a): Tortoises together? That is the question. – British Chelonia Group Newsletter, 158: 18-19.

O'MEARA (2004b): Tortoises on towels – that is the question. – British Chelonia Group Newsletter, 159: 7-10.

ONDRIAS (1968): Liste des Amphibiens et des Reptiles de la Grèce. – Biologia Gallo-Hellenica, Toulouse, 1 (2): 111-135.

OOSTERBROEK & ARNTZEN (1992): Area-cladograms of Circum-Mediterranean taxa in relation to Mediterranean palaeogeography. – Journal of Biogeography, 19: 3-20.

ORENSTEIN (2001): Turtles, Tortoises & Terrapins – Survivors in Armor. – Buffalo (Firefly Books): 9, 102, 115, 117-118, 195.

ORIGGI (2001): Enzyme-Linked Immunosorbent Assay for detecting Herpesvirus exposure in mediterranean tortoises (spur-thighed tortoise [Testudo graeca] and hermann's tortoise [Testudo hermanni]. – Journal of Clinical Microbiology, Washington, 39: 3156-3163.

ORIGGI & JACOBSON (1999): Development of an ELISA and an immunoperoxidase based test for herpesvirus exposure detection in tortoises. – Proceedings of the A.R.A.V., 6: 65-67.

ORIGII & JACOBSON (2000): Disease of the respiratory tract of chelonians. – Vet. Clin. North Am. Exot. Anim. Pract., 3 (2): 537-549.

ORIGGI, JACOBSON, ROMERO & KLEIN (2000): Diagnostic tools for herpesvirus detection in chelonians. – Proceedings of the A.R.A.V., 7: 127-129.

ORLANDELLA (1967): Ricerche sui serbatoi‘ di Salmonella indagini sulla tartaruga (Testudo hermanni Gm.) sulla lacertola (Lacerta sicula sicula RAF.) e sul ricco (Erinaceus europaeus L.). – Atti della Societa Peloritana di Scienze Fisiche Matematiche e Naturali, Messina, 13 (3/4): 193-199.

ORLANDELLA & ALOSI (1968): Prime ricerche zul ruolo epidemio-epizootologico della tartaruga (Testudo hermanni GM.) nella diffusione di Salmonella e Arizona. – Zooprofilassi, 23: 119-146.

ORÓS, RODRÍGUEZ & DÉNIZ (1998): Cutaneous poxvirus-like infection in a captive Hermann's tortoise (Testudo hermanni). – The Veterinary Record, London, 143: 508-509.

OSTADAL & SCHIEBLER (1971): The terminal blood bed in the heart of the turtle Testudo hermanni. – Zeitschrift für Anatomie und Entwicklungsgeschichte, Berlin, 134 (1): 111-116.

OTTIS (2001a): Besprechung ausgewählter Krankheitsbilder anhand von Bildern aus der Röntgendiagnostik – Verstopfung (Koprostase). – Schildkröten, Linden, 8 (3): 12-16.

OTTIS (2001b): Interessante Beispiele aus der tierärztlichen Praxis – Röntgenologische Darstellung von Fremdkörpern. – Schildkröten, Linden, 8 (4): 10-12.

OTTIS (2002): Angeborene Missbildungen bei Landschildkröten. – Schildkröten, Linden, 9 (2): 5, 7.

OTTIS & GERBIG (1982a): Legenot bei Landschildkröten – Diagnose, Therapie und Prophylaxe. – Die Tierärztliche Praxis, Stuttgart, 10: 257-260.

OTTIS & GERBIG (1982b): Legenot bei Landschildkröten – Diagnose, Therapie und Prophylaxe. – Die Schildkröte, Haar, 4 (1/2): 36-41.

OTTO (1956): Theophania. Der Geist der altgriechischen Religion. – rowohlts deutsche enzyklopädie 15, Hamburg (Rowohlt Taschenbuch Verlag), 134 pp.

OVTSCHAROFF (1972): Histochemistry and electron microscopy of the red nucleus of the turtle Testudo hermanni. – Histochemie, 29 (3): 240-247.

PACHL (1990a): Keine Muschelschalen für Schildkröten. – Das Tier, Leinfelden-Echterdingen, 31 (10): 60.

PACHL (1990b): Der richtige Terrarienboden. – Das Tier, Leinfelden-Echterdingen, 31 (12): 60.

PACHL (1991): Am besten mit Augenwatte. – Das Tier, Leinfelden-Echterdingen, 32 (3): 57.

PAGE & MAUTINO (1990): Clinical management of tortoises. – Cont. Educ., 12 (2): 221-228.

PAGLIONE (1988): Comportamento termico e ritmi stagionali in una popolazione di Testudo hermanni del Parco Naturale della Maremma. – Università di Genova, Genua, 68 pp.

PAGLIONE & CARBONE (1990): Biologia di popolazione di Testudo hermanni nel Parco della Maremma (GR). – In: Atti VI Convegno Naz. Ass. »Alessandro Ghigi«. – Turin (Museo Regionale Scienze Naturali): 197-199.

PALIKA (2001): Turtles & Tortoises for Dummies. – New York, Cleveland und Indianapolis (Hungry Minds): 40, 115-116, 204, 259.

PALLAS (1814): Zoographia Rosso-Asiatica. Tom III. Animalia monocardia seu frigidi sanguinis imperii Rosso-Asiatici. – Saint Petersburg, VII, 428, 125 pp.

PALMER (1984): Experimentell erzeugte Hautveränderungen bei Landschildkröten durch hohe parenterale Gaben von Vitamin A. – Zentralblatt für Veterinär-Medizin, Berlin & Hamburg, A (31): 625-633.

PALMER (1998): The hibernation of a late 1997 hatchling T. hermanni boettgeri. – Tortoise Trust Newsletter, London, 13 (3): 6.

PALMER, RÜBEL, METTLER & VOLKER (1984): Experimentell erzeugte Hautveränderungen bei Landschildkröten durch hohe parenterale Gaben von Vitamin A; Zentralblatt für Veterinärmedizin, 31: 625-633

PALOMEQUE, SESÉ & PLANAS (1977): Respiratory properties of the blood of turtles. – Comparative Biochemistry and Physiology, A, Vancouver, 57: 479-483.

PANAGIOTA & VALAKOS (1992): Contribution to the thermal ecology of Testudo marginata and Testudo hermanni (Chelonia: Testudinidae) in semi-captivity. – The Herpetological Journal, London, 2: 48-50.

PARELLADA (1997): Proyecto de reintroducción de la tortuga mediterránea (Testudo hermanni) en el macizo de Garraf. – Jornadas de Conservación de la tortuga mediterránea, Conselleria de Medi Ambient, Generalitat Valenciana: 28-32.

PARENT (1976): Remarques à propos d'une récente faune herpétologique française. – Naturalistes Belges, Rhode-Sainte-Genèse, 57: 64-68.

PARENT (1981): Matériaux pour une herpétofaune de l'Europe occidentale. Contribution à la révision chorologique de l'herpétofaune de la France et du Benelux. – Bulletin Mensuel de la Société Linneenne de Lyon, 50 (3): 86-111.

PARENT (1982): Bibliographie de l'Herpétofaune française. – Inv. Faune Flore, 17/18, 431 pp.

PARENZAN (1932): Revisione delle specie delle Gen. Testudo della Balcania. – Atti del Reale Istituto Veneto di Scienze, Lettere ed Arti, Venedig, 91 (2): 1149-1169, plates XXX-XXXIII.

PARENZAN (1933): Relazione su due spedizioni scientifiche in Albania (1929-1930). – Riv. Fis. Mat. Sci. Nat., Naples, 7 (8-10), 43 pp.

PARHAM, MACEY, PAPENFUSS, FELDMAN, TÜRKOZAN, POLYMENI & BOORE (2006): The phylogeny of Mediterranean tortoises and their close relatives based on complete mitochondrial genome sequences from museum specimens. – Molecular Phylogenetics and Evolution, 38 (1): 50-64.

PARKER (1995): Members' letters. – British Chelonia Group Newsletter, 108: 14.

PARKER & BELLAIRS (1972): Die Amphibien und Reptilien. – Lausanne (Editions Rencontre): 312.

PARLANTI, LANZA, POGGESI & SBORDONI (1988): Anfibi e rettili delle isole del Mediterraneo: un test dell'ipotesi dell'equilibrio insulare. – Bulletin d'Ecologie, Paris, 19 (2/3): 335-348.

PAULER (2000): Kranke Schildkröten ausgesetzt. – elaphe (N. F.), Rheinbach, 8 (3): 25.

PAULER (2001a): Liebe Mitglieder. – elaphe (N. F.), Rheinbach, 9 (3): 25.

PAULER (2001b): Liebe Mitglieder. – elaphe (N. F.), Rheinbach, 9 (4): 25.

PALAUS (1974): Nuevos datos sobre la distribución geográfica de los anfibios y reptiles ibéricos. – Doñana Acta Vertebrata, Sevilla, 1 (1): 19-27.

PARRY (1986): Tortoise recovery after submersion. – British Chelonia Group Newsletter, 49: 4.

PAULL (1997): The Small and Medium-Sized Tortoises. – Homestead (Green Nature Books): 154-157, 198.

PAUNOVIC (1983): Kopnene kornjace roda Testudo LINNÉ, 1758 iz pleistocenskih naslaga crvene stijene kod Petrovi°a u Crnoj Gori. – Rad. Jugoslavenska Akademija Znanosti i Umjetnosti, Zagreb, 404: 109-123.

PAUNOVIC (1984): Fische, Amphibien und Reptilien aus oberpleistozänen Ablagerungen von Sandalja bei Pula (Istrien, Kroatien). – Palaeontologia Jugoslavica, Zagreb, 31: 5-44.

PAUNOVIC (1990): Grundzüge der Herkunft und das Alter der Herpetofauna Jugoslawiens. – Rad JAZU 449, Razred za prirodne znanosti, 24: 309-317.

PAVLETIC (1962): Prilog istrazivanju herpetofaune otoka Paga. – VI. Plenum Prirodoslovne Sekcije Saveza Muzejskih Drustava Jugoslavije, Zagreb: 26-29.

PAWLOWSKI & KRÄMER (2006): Schildkrötenhaltung in Zoogeschäften und Fachmärkten im Großraum Rhein-Neckar. – elaphe (N. F.), 14 (1): 58-66.

PAWLOWSKI, JAKOB, PATZEWITZ, ANNOSOVA & SAUER (2004): Ein herpetologischer Eindruck von der italienischen Insel Elba im Frühjahr 2003. – Sauria, Berlin, 26 (2): 23-30.

PELAZ (1988): Aspectos históricos para la actual corología de Testudo hermanni en el Mediterráneo Occidental. – Vida Silvestre, 64: 28-35.

PENEDER & PENEDER (1998): Zur Verbreitung von Testudo marginata, Testudo weissingeri und Testudo hermanni boettgeri in Griechenland. – Informationsblatt der Fachgruppe Schildkröten der ÖGH, Vienna, 4 (3): 3-13.

PARHAM, MACEY, PAPENFUSS, FELDMAN, TÜRKOZAN, POLYMENI & BOORE (2006): The phylogeny of Mediterranean tortoises and their close relatives based on complete mitochondrial genome sequences from museum specimens. – Molecular Phylogenetics and Evolution, 38 (1): 50-64.

PERÄLÄ (2001): A new species of Testudo (Testudines: Testudinidae) from the Middle East, with implications for conservation. – Journal of Herpetology, New Haven, 35: 567-582.

PERÄLÄ (2002a): The genus Testudo (Testudines: Testudinidae) – phylogenetic inferences. – Chelonii, Gonfaron, 3: 32-39.

PERÄLÄ (2002b): Biodiversity in relatively neglected taxa of Testudo L., 1758 s. l.. – Chelonii, Gonfaron, 3: 40-53.

PERÄLÄ (2002c): The genus Testudo LINNAEUS, 1758 sensu lato (Testudines: Testudinidae): Phylogeny, taxonomy, conservation. – Dissertation, School of Biological Sciences, Bristol, 328 pp.

PERÄLÄ (2004a): Testudo hercegovinensis WERNER, 1899. – Manouria, Mezzavia, 22: 19-20.

PERÄLÄ (2004b): Tortoise systematics: a critique of a recent paper by VAN DER KUYL et al. (2002). – The Herpetological Journal, London, 14: 51-53.

PERRIER (1954): La faune de la France illustrée. Band X: Vertébrées. – Delagrave, Paris, 214 pp.

PERRY (1980): A home for tortoises. – British Chelonia Group Newsletter, 21: 9-10.

PERSCHMANN (1956): Über die Bedeutung der Nierenpfortader insbesondere für die Ausscheidung von Harnstoff und Harnsäure bei Testudo hermanni GML. und Lacerta viridis LAUR. sowie über die Funktion der Harnblase bei Lacerta viridis LAUR. – Zoologische Beiträge, Berlin, 2: 447-480.

PESCHKES-KESSEBOHM (2003): Fundtiere und der Artenschutz. – Minor, Haan, 2 (1): 31-32.

PESHEV & BOEV (1962): Fauna de Bulgarie – clé succincte des Vertébrés. – Sofia (Narodna Prosveta): 71-105.

PETERS (1967): Klasse Reptilia – Kriechtiere. In: Urania Tierreich – Fische, Lurche, Kriechtiere. – Leipzig, Jena & Berlin (Urania-Verlag).

PETIT & KNOEPFFLER (1959): Sur la disparition des amphibiens et reptiles méditerranéens. – Revue d'Ecologie (Terre et Vie), Supplément Colloque U.I.C.N., Animaux et végétaux rares de la région méditerranée, Athens: 50-53.

PETROV (2002): Review of the reptiles (Reptilia) in the Eastern Rhodopes. – In: Project report, Assessment of existing information on biodiversity in the Eastern Rhodopes. – Sofia (Bulgarian Society for the Protection of Birds), UN Development Program: 12.

PETROV (2004): The herpetofauna (Amphibia and Reptilia) of the Eastern Rhodopes (Bulgaria and Greece). – In: BERON & POPOV (Eds.): Biodiversity of Bulgaria. 2. Biodiversity of Eastern Rhodopes (Bulgaria and Greece). – Sofia (Pensoft & Nat. Mus. Natur. Hist.): 863-879.

PETROV, STOEV & BESHKOV (2001): Review of the species composition and distribution of Amphibians (Am-phibia) and Reptiles (Reptilia) in the Eastern Rhodopes Mt. – Hist. Nat. bulg., Sofia, 13: 127-153.

PETROV, BESHKOV, POPGEORGIEV & PLA-CHIISKI (2004): Action plan for conservation of tortoises in Bulgaria. – Sofia (Bulgarian Society for the Protection of Birds), Bulgarian Biodiversity Foundation, National Museum of Natural History, 58 pp.

PETTER (1966): Equilibre des espèces dans les populations de nématodes parasites du colon des tortues terrestres. – Mémoires du Muséum National d'Histoire Naturelle Paris, N. S., 39 (A), 252 pp.

PETZOLD (19??): Kurze Anleitung zur Pflege europäischer Land- und Wasserschildkröten. – Tierpark-Merkblatt Nr. 1, Tierpark Berlin, 12 pp.

PETZOLD (1966): Kleine herpetologische Notizen von der montenegrinischen Adriaküste. – Aquarien Terrarien, Leipzig, Jena & Berlin, 13 (7): 236-239.

PETZOLD (1981): AT Terrarientierlexikon Testudo hermanni GMELIN 1789 – Griechische Landschildkröte. – Aquarien Terrarien, Leipzig, Jena & Berlin, 28 (2): 72.

PETZOLD (1982): Aufgaben und Probleme der Tiergärtnerei bei der Erforschung der Lebensäußerungen der Niederen Amnioten (Reptilien). – Milu, Berlin, 5 (4/5): 528, 612, 620, 623, 635, 724-725.

PFEIFFER (1996): Gebrauchsanweisung für Schildkröten. – Journal der AG Schildkröten & Panzerechsen, Bürstadt, 5 (2): 7-10.

PHILIPPE (1953): Zum Vorkommen von Testudo hermanni robertmertensi WERMUTH. – DATZ, Stuttgart, 6 (9): 238-239.

PHILIPPEN (1986a): Protokoll eines Schildkröten-Schicksals. – Die Schildkröte (N. F.), Heinsberg, 1 (1/2): 17-23.

PHILIPPEN (1986b): Hinweise zum Aufspüren mediterraner Landschildkröten. – Die Schildkröte (N. F.), Heinsberg, 1 (3): 3-4.

PHILIPPEN (1997): Rezension: BRABENETZ, E., H. SCHWAMMER & F. LUTTENBERGER (Eds.): Haltungsrichtlinien – Mindestansprüche für Schildkröten. – Emys, Sitzenberg-Reidling, 4 (3): 20-28.

PHILIPPEN (2003): Aktuelle Checkliste der bis heute bekannt gewordenen Schildkrötenhybriden – Eine Literaturstudie, inklusive unveröffentlichter Hinweise – Teil 2. – Schildkröten, Linden, 10 (1): 13-23, 25.

PHILIPPEN (2005): ShellShock-Naturschutzkampagne. Umsetzung der Schildkrötenschutzkampagen in den Zoologischen Gärten und Aquarien. – Marginata, Münster, 2 (3): 55-59.

PIANKA (1970): On r- and K-selection. – The American Naturalist, Chicago, 104: 592-597.

PICARIELLO, SCILLITANI, FRITZ, GÜNTHER & MUTSCHMANN (1993): Zur Herpetofauna Süditaliens. Teil 2. Die Amphibien und Reptilien des Picentini-Gebirges (Appennin, Kampanien). I. Allgemeines und Amphibien. – herpetofauna, Weinstadt, **15** (85): 19-26.

PICCOLI, GERDOL & FERRARI (1983): Carta della vegetazione del Bosco della Mesola (Ferrara). – Atti Istituto Botanico Laboratorio Crittogamico Ferrara, **2**: 3-23.

PIEAU (1971): Sur la proportion sexuelle chez les embryons deux Chéloniens (*Testudo graeca* L. et *Emys orbicularis*) issus d'Oeufs incubés artificiellement. – Comptes Rendus de l'Académie des Sciences, Série D, Sciences Naturelles, Paris, **277**: 3071-3074.

PIEAU (2001): Affaire S.O.P.T.O.M. .... suite et fin. – Bulletin de la Société Herpétologique de France, Supplément, **90**: 14-17.

PIEAU (2002): Temperature-dependent sex determination in *Testudo graeca* and *Testudo hermanni*. – Chelonii, Gonfaron, **3**: 144.

PIEAU & DORIZZI (2004): Temperaturabhängige Geschlechtsfixierung bei Sumpf-, Wasser- und Landschildkröten. Teil 2. – Marginata, Münster, **2** (1): 36-40.

PIEH (2000): Arten und Unterarten der Landschildkröten des Mittelmeergebietes. – Draco, Münster, **2**: 4-17.

PIEH & SÄTTELE (2002): Die Herpetofauna Mallorcas. – DATZ, Stuttgart, **55** (2): 68-72.

PIEPER (1970): Neue Beiträge zur Kenntnis der Herpetofauna der südägäischen Inseln. – Senckenbergiana Biologica, Frankfurt am Main, **51**: 55-65.

PIROTTA (1999): Tartarughe Terrestri. – Bologna (Edagricole): 2, 4-5, 9, 12-14, 16-17, 19-27, 34-36, 38, 44-45, 52, 54, 56-57, 58-66, 74-75, 79, 87.

PISAPIA (1998): Ritmi di attività di *Testudo hermanni* nel Bosco della Mesola (FE). – Master's Thesis, Università degli Studi di Milano, Milan.

PITZER (2000): O AETOS – Der Adler – Unser 1996 gegründeter Verein für Tier- und Umweltschutz in Griechenland steht vor einem schwierigen Problem! – Radiata, Haan, **9** (2): 22-24.

PITZER & TRAPP (2003): Das Schildkröten-Projekt. – M & S Reptilien Katalog 4/2003, Villingen-Schwenningen: 66-67.

PLATEL, BECKERS & NIEUWENHUYS (1973): The cortical areas of *Testudo hermanni* (Reptilia, Chelonia) and *Caiman crocodilus* (Reptilia, Crocodylia). – Acta Morphologica Neerlando-Scandinavica, **11** (2): 121-150.

PLEGUEZUELOS, MÁRQUEZ & LIZANA (Eds.) (2004): Atlas y libro rojo de los anfibios y reptiles de España. Dirección General de Conservación de la Naturaleza. – Leganés (Asociación Herpetológica Española), 587 pp.

PLETSCHER (1997): Der Brief des Präsidenten. – SIGS-Info, Siblingen, **6** (2): 2-3.

PLETSCHER (1998): Gehegebau für Europäische Landschildkröten. – Fachmagazin Schildkröte, Rothenfluh, **1** (5): 61.

PLIENINGER (1847): Verzeichnis der Reptilien Württembergs. – Jahrbuch des Vereins für vaterländische Naturkunde, Stuttgart, **3**: 194-208.

PLOUVIER (2002): Schildpaddenpoëzie. – De Schildpad, Eindhoven, **28** (4): 172-173.

PODLOUCKY (1987): Frankreich – Spendenaktion für ein Schutzprogramm für die Griechische Landschildkröte. – DGHT-Rundbrief, Bonn, **95**: 3132.

PODLOUCKY (1988): S.O.P.T.O.M. – Spendenaktion erfolgreich, Schutzprojekt macht Fortschritte. – DGHT-Rundbrief, Bonn, **97**: 3.

PODLOUCKY (1989): S.O.P.T.O.M. – DGHT finanziert Quarantäne-Gehege für Schildkröten. – DGHT-Rundbrief, Bonn, **100**: 7-8.

PODLOUCKY (2002): International efforts for the conservation of European tortoises (genus *Testudo*) – legislation and conservation strategies. – Chelonii, Gonfarob, **3**: 302-311.

POINTET (1998): Courrier des lecteurs. – Manouria, Mezzavia, **1**: 7.

POLASCHEK & POLASCHEK (1997): Die Griechische Landschildkröte (*Testudo hermanni*) – Artbeschreibung sowie Tips zur Pflege, Haltung und Zucht. – Eichgraben (G. & K. Verlag), 124 pp.

POLLS (1985): The herpetofauna of the Alto Ampurdan, Spain – Faunistic. – Misc. Zool., **9**: 295-314.

PONS, FELIX & BUDÓ (1996): Caracterización morfológica de la tortuga mediterránea (*Testudo hermanni hermanni* GMELIN) – Método PIT de aplicación de técnicas de procesado de imagen. – IV Congreso Luso-Espaol de Herpetologia, Porto.

PORLIER (1989a): La tortue d'Hermann. – Bibliothèque de Travail 1008, Publications de l'Ecole moderne française, Cannes (La Bocca).

PORLIER (1989b): Das Dorf der Schildkröten. – Das Tier, Leinfelden-Echterdingen, **30** (8): 32-34.

PORTIS (1890): I Rettili pliocenici del Valdarno superiore ed alcune altre località plioceniche di Toscana. – Florence (Le Monnier): 1-32.

POSTHAUS (1996a): Herpesvirusinfektion bei Landschildkröten. – SIGS-Info, Siblingen, **5** (2): 13-15.

POSTHAUS (1996b): Neues über Herpes. – SIGS-Info, Siblingen, **5** (3): 9-11.

POSTHAUS (1997): Herpesvirusinfektion bei Landschildkröten. – Emys, Sitzenberg-Reidling, **4** (2): 25-28.

POZIO & FRISENDA (1980): Gli Anfibi e i Rettili della Regione Puglia. – In: SCALERI LIACI (Ed.): Atti del

VII Simposio Nazionale sulla Conservazione della Natura, Cacucci, Bari: 233-257.

POZZI (1966): Geonemia e catalogo ragionato degli Anfibi e dei Rettili della Jugoslavia. – Natura, Milan, **57** (1): 1-55.

PRASCHAG (1995): Schildkröten – die handlichen Heimtiere – DATZ, Stuttgart, **48** (8): 531-535.

PRASCHAG (2002): Landschildkröten. – Stuttgart (Verlag Eugen Ulmer): 1, 4-5, 7, 10, 18, 32-33, 36-42, 45-49, 52, 58-61, 65-66, 70-71, 80-81, 83, 88-89.

PREISER (1990a): S.O.P.T.O.M. – Schutzprojekt macht weiter gute Fortschritte. – DGHT-Rundbrief, Bonn, 104: 19.

PREISER (1990b): S.O.P.T.O.M. – Projekt expandiert, deutscher Tochterverein geplant. – DGHT-Rundbrief, Bonn, 105: 17.

PREISER (1991): Das Schildkrötendorf. – Ökowerkmagazin, Berlin, **5**: 32-33.

PREISER (1993): Das Schildkröten-Schutzprojekt S.O.P.T.O.M. – Journal der AG Schildkröten & Panzerechsen der DGHT, Bürstadt, **2** (3): 14-16.

PRENZEL (1997): Kiki, die Ausreißerin. – Schildkröten, Linden, **4** (2): 23-26.

PRENZEL (1998): Freud und Leid mit Schildkröten – Erinnerungen einer alten Dame. – Schildkröten, Linden, **5** (3): 19-23.

PRESTREAU (2001): Alimentation naturelle et équilibrée pour les tortues terrestres méditerranéennes.– Manouria, Mezzavia, 13: 10-15.

PRIETO (1996): Metodologia bàsica per la deteccio de Paràsits helmints a partir de femtes de reptils. – L'Entorn natural, COMAM. 10.

PRITCHARD (1979): Encyclopedia of Turtles. – Neptune City (T. F. H. Publications): 348, 402-403, 406-407, 566.

PRITCHARD (1988): A survey of neural bone variation among recent chelonian species, with functional interpretations. – Acta Zoologica Cracoviensia, Krakow, **31** (26): 625-686.

PRITCHARD (2002): Overview of the genus Testudo. – Chelonii, Gonfaron, 3: 10-11.

PRUKSARAJ (1967): Unteruchungen über das Vorkommen von Salmonellen bei Landschildkröten der Arten Testudo graeca und Testudo hermanni. – Dissertation, Univ. Hannover, Hannover.

PUCHADES LLORIS (1996): Notas sobre la reproducción de una población semicautiva de tortuga mediterránea Testudo h. hermanni en Valencia (E. España). – Doñana Acta Vertebrata, Sevilla, **23**: 99-103.

PUDDU, VIARENGO & ERMINIO (1988): Animali di Sardegna. Gli anfibi e i rettili. – Cagliari.

PULFORD, HAILEY & STUBBS (1984): Thermal relations of Testudo hermanni **robertmertensi** WERMUTH in S. France. – Amphibia-Reptilia, Leiden, **5** (1): 37-41.

PURSALL (1995): Europäische Landschildkröten. – Ruhmannsfelden (bede-Verlag): 5, 10-11, 13-15, 18, 22, 29, 32, 35, 41, 44-45, 51-52, 55-56, 58-59, 73, 75, 81, 88, 94.

PURSALL & PURSALL (1987): Case History of a Sick Testudo hermanni. – Testudo, **2** (5): 22-24.

RADOVANOVIC (1941): Zur Kenntnis der Herpetofauna des Balkans. – Zoologischer Anzeiger, Leipzig, **136** (7/8): 145-159.

RADOVANOVIC (1951): Vodozemci i gmizavci nase zemlje. – Belgrade (Srpsko Biolosko Drustvo), 250 pp.

RADOVANOVIC (1961): Résultats des recherches faites dans les îles Adriatiques sous le jour de l'evolutionnisme. – Bull. T. XXVI, Acad. Serbe Sc., **8**.

RADOVANOVIC (1964): Die Verbreitung der Amphibien und Reptilien in Jugoslawien. – Senckenbergiana Biologica, Frankfurt am Main, **45** (3-5): 553-561.

RAGNI, DI MURO, SPILINGA & MANDRICI (2004): L'Atlante degli Anfibi e dei Rettili dell'Umbria. – In: ZUFFI (Ed.): V° Congresso Nazionale della Societas Herpetologica Italica, 29 settembre - 3 ottobre 2004, Calci (Pisa). – Turin (Societas Herpetologica Italica): 21-22.

RAMIREZ, VARGAS & GUERRERO (1992): Distribution patterns and diversity in European reptiles. – In: KORSOS & KISS (Eds.): Proceedings of the 6th Ordinary General Meeting of the Societas Europaea Herpetologica. – Budapest: 371-376.

R.A.N.A. INTERNATIONAL FOUNDATION (1994): R.A.N.A. News, 1.

RANZI (1971): Ricerche zoologichenelle isole di Tavolara e Molara. – In: PASQUINI (Ed.): Relazione preliminare delle ricerche sulle popolazioni insulari compiute nel triennio 1965-1968. – Quaderni de »La Ricerca Scientifica«, Rome, **73**: 25-28.

RATHBAUER (2002): Feldherpetologische Exkursion nach Cres (2002). – ÖGH-Aktuell, Vienna, **10**: 6-10.

RAU (1966): Schildkröten-Verluste durch Ratten beim Überwintern. – DATZ, Stuttgart, **19** (1): 23-25.

RAU (1981): Erstaunliche Genesung einer Griechischen Landschildkröte (Testudo hermanni hermanni). – DATZ, **34** (7): 245-246.

RAUH (2000): Grundlagen der Reptilienhaltung. – Münster (Natur und Tier-Verlag): 30, 95, 115, 129, 132, 142, 191-193.

RAXWORTHY (1984): Hermann's Tortoise (Testudo hermanni **robertmertensi** WERMUTH) on Menorca, Balearic Islands. – British Journal of Herpetology, London, **6**: 385-386

RAZNOSANU (1900): On the Romanian species (T. graeca, **ibera**, **marginata**). – Bull. Soc. Bucuresti, **9**: 278.

RAZZETTI, BADER, BILEK, DELFINO, DI CERBO, DUDA, HILL, RATHBAUER, RIEGLER & SACCHI (2004): A contribution to the knowledge of the herpetofauna of the Greek island of Corfu. – In: ZUFFI (Ed.): V° Congresso Nazionale della Societas Herpetologica Italica, 29 settembre - 3 ottobre 2004, Calci (Pisa). – Turin (Societas Herpetologica Italica): 22.

REBUFFEL (1999): Projet de réintroduction de la tortue d'Hermann dans la forêt domaniale de l'Estérel – Etude Botanique (systématique et couvert végétal). – Unveröffentlichter Bericht, Gonfaron (SOPTOM), 17 pp.

RECHINGER-MOSER, WETTSTEIN & BEIR (1959): Was finde ich in Italien, an den Mittelmeerküsten Frankreichs, Spaniens und des Balkans? – Stuttgart (Franckh'sche Verlagshandlung), 220 pp.

RECKLIES (1989): Krankheiten der Schildkröten – Eine Literaturstudie. – Dissertation, Freie Univ. Berlin, Berlin: 5, 28-29, 39, 52-53, 58-60, 80, 83, 90, 110, 123, 139, 149-150, 158, 160, 168, 174, 180-181, 184, 196, 208, 211, 213-214, 216-217, 288.

REDROBE (1996): Shell Diseases in Chelonia. – Reptilian Magazine, 12: 51-56.

REDROBE (1997): An Introduction to Chelonian Radiography and Ultrasonography. – Testudo, 4 (4): 41.

REESE (1985): Appendix VIII(E): The Kition Tortoise Carapace. – In: KARAGEORGHIS (Ed.): Excavations at Kition. – Nicosia (Department of Antiquities), 5 (2): 411.

REGENSBURGER (1982): Untersuchungen über die Entwurmung von Landschildkröten mit Flubenol®, Panacur® und Rintal®. – Dissertation, Univ. München, Munich.

REICHENBACH-KLINKE & ELKAN (1963): Krankheiten der Reptilien. – Stuttgart (Gustav Fischer Verlag): 119, 124, 126.

REISS (2004): Doppelköpfiger Schlüpfling einer Testudo hermanni boettgeri MOJSISOVICS, 1889. – elaphe (N. F.), Rheinbach, 12 (2): 46-49.

RENGIFO (1991): Activité et déplacements de la tortue d'Hermann (Testudo hermanni h.) après lâcher dans la région des Maures. Programme radiotracking SOPTOM Mars-Juillet 91. – Gonfaron (SOPTOM).

RENGIFO (1994): Activité et déplacements de la tortue d'Hermann après lâcher dans la région des Maures. – Editions SOPTOM, Gonfaron.

RIABININ (1915): Sur les tortues des dépts méotiens de Bessarabie. –Trudy Geol. Min. Muz. Petra Velikago Imper. Akad. Nauk, Saint Petersburg, 1: 1-16.

RICHARDS & RICHARDS (1990): A Field Study of Testudo hermanni hermanni Tortoises on Corfu, June 1989. – Testudo, 3 (2): 33-41.

RIEMERSMA & VAN DER STAAY (2002): Op locatie in...'s Gravendeel. – De Schildpad, Eindhoven, 28 (2): 80-85.

RIERA (1999): Rien ne sert de courir ... – La Tortue, Gonfaron, 48: 40-43.

RISCH (1979): Les tortues terrestres paléarctiques (Testudo spp.) en France. Présence à l'état sauvage, maintien et réproduction en captivité, protection (Reptilia, Testudines, Testudinidae). – Bulletin de la Société Zoologique de France, Paris, 103 (4): 524-527.

RIVAL (2000): Rhinite des tortues terrestres. – Maisons-Alfort (Editions du Point Vétérinaire), 208: 57-58.

RIVERA & ARRIBAS (1993): Anfibios y reptiles introducidos de la fauna espaola. – Quercus, 84: 12-16.

ROCHESTER (2002): The visit. – British Chelonia Group Newsletter, 145: 14.

RODAMER (1998): Mit ein wenig Liebe geht alles. – Schildkröten, Linden, 5 (4): 18-20.

RÖDEL (1994): Beiträge zur Kenntnis der Verbreitung, Habitatwahl und Biologie griechischer Amphibien und Reptilien. Daten aus 7 Exkursionen von 1987 bis 1991. – Faunistische Abhandlungen des Staatlichen Museums für Tierkunde Dresden, 19 (29): 227-246.

ROGNER (1987): Die Reptilien auf Korsika – Schildkröten und Schlangen. – DATZ, Essen, 40 (10): 564-566.

ROGNER (1989a): Probleme beim Zeitigen von Schildkröten-Eiern. – DATZ, Stuttgart, 42 (2): 148-150.

ROGNER (1989b): Herpetologisches aus der Umgebung von Ulcinj. – DATZ, Stuttgart, 42 (12): 748-749.

ROGNER (1995): Zur Herpetofauna der Insel Korfu. – Das Aquarium, Wuppertal, 315: 39-42.

ROGNER (1996): Schildkröten 2. – Hürtgenwald (Heidi-Rogner-Verlag): 109-110, 116-117.

ROGNER (2001): Landschildkröten. – Stuttgart (Franckh-Kosmos): 8, 18-19, 32, 36, 44-45, 48, 72, 82-83, 88-90, 94, 97, 100, 102-103, 106, 108, 112.

ROGNER (2005): Griechische Landschildkröten (Testudo hermanni hermanni, T. h. boettgeri, T. h. hercegovinensis). Verbreitung, Lebensräume, Haltung und Vermehrung. – Münster (Natur und Tier-Verlag), 167 pp.

ROHR (1970): Die Bedeutung des Wärmefaktors für die Fortpflanzungsperiodik und Eiablageverhalten südeuropäischer Landschildkröten im Terrarium. – Salamandra, Frankfurt am Main, 6 (3/4): 99-103.

ROOCK (1952): Die westliche Rasse von Testudo h. hermanni GMELIN. – DATZ, Stuttgart, 5 (12): 326-327.

ROSCHER (1884): Ausführliches Lexikon der Griechischen und Römischen Mythologie. – Leipzig.

ROSENBERG (1970): Excitation and inhibition of motoneurons in the tortoise. – The Journal of Physiology, London, 221: 715-730.

ROSENBERG (1986): Carapace and plastron sensitivity to touch and vibration in the tortoise Testudo hermanni and Testudo graeca. – Journal of Zoology, London, **208** (3): 443-456.

RÖSSEL (2001a): Die neue Bundesartenschutzverordnung mit der Kennzeichnungsregelung. – BNA-aktuell, Hambrücken, 2: 11-15.

RÖSSEL (2001b): Die neue Bundesartenschutzverordnung mit der Kennzeichnungsregelung. – Reptilia (D), Münster, 30: 14, 16.

RÖSSLER (1903): Verzeichnis der Reptilien und Amphibien der kroatischen Fauna, welche an das zoologische Nationalmuseum in Zagreb bis zum Schluß des Jahres 1900 eingesendet wurden. – Glasnik hrvatskoga Naravoslovnoga drustva, Zagreb, **15**: 221-224.

ROTTNER & NEUBERT (2003): Überwinterung von Schlüpflingen der Griechischen Landschildkröte. – Schildkröten, Linden, **10** (1): 3-8.

ROZHAJA, RIZANOLLI & BERISHA (1977): Nitrogen gas exchange in turtles in hypoxia and hypercapnia under confinement conditions. – Acta Biol. Med. Esp., **21** (1): 33-36.

ROZHAJA, DERMAKU, HALILI & BERISHA (1980): Some biochemical characteristics of the blood sera of the turtle Testudo hermanni from the immediate surrounding of lead and zinc foundry in Zvecan, Yugoslavia. – Acta Biol. Med. Esp., **5** (1): 43-46.

ROZYLOWICZ, TETELEA & POPESCU (2003): Assessing the distribution of Hermann's tortoise (Testudo hermanni boettgeri MOJSISOVICS, 1888) in the Iron Gates Natural Park, Romania. – Proceedings of the First International Conference on Environmental Research and Assessment, Bukarest.

RÜCK (1965): Nachzucht bei der griechischen Landschildkröte. – DATZ, Stuttgart, **18** (4): 117-119.

RUDLOFF (1990): Schildkröten. – Leipzig, Jena & Berlin (Urania-Verlag): 46, 70, 114, 121-122, 150.

RUGIERO (2004): Composition of the reptile communities in five urban protected areas of different isolation degrees. – Herpetozoa, Vienna, **16** (3/4): 151-155.

RUMPF (1892): Aus dem Leben der griechischen Landschildkröten. – Der Zoologische Garten, Berlin, **33**: 260-264.

RUST (1941): Gestaltung von Freilandanlagen für Schildkröten und Panzerechsen in Zoologischen Gärten. – Das Aquarium, Wuppertal, 15: 11-12, 22-23.

RUTSCHKE, KOEPE & DEICHSEL (2004): Beobachtungen zu anthropogenen Einflüssen auf die Reptilienfauna des Peloponnes (Griechenland). – herpetofauna, Weinstadt, 143: 17-28.

RYSAVY & JOHNSON (1979): On some oxyurid nematodes of the genus Tachygonetria parasitizing tortoises in Afghanistan and Albania. – Vestn. Ceskoslov. Spolec. Zool., Prague, 2: 148-160.

SACCHI, GALEOTTI & FASOLA (2004): Meccanismi di produzione e diffusione delle vocalizzazioni nei Cheloni. – In: ZUFFI (Ed.): V° Congresso Nazionale della Societas Herpetologica Italica, 29 settembre - 3 ottobre 2004, Calci (Pisa). – Turin (Societas Herpetologica Italica): 36.

SAHRHAGE (1976): Erlebnisse mit Griechischen Landschildkröten. – DATZ, Stuttgart, **29** (5): 174-175.

SAILER, PYCZAK & HARTMANN (1997): Siamesische Zwillinge bei Testudo hermanni boettgeri. – herpetofauna, Weinstadt, 106: 12-13.

SAINT-GIRONS (1971): Catalogue des reptiles. – In: La grande encyclopédie de la nature, Volume 10, Reptiles. – Paris & Montréal (Bordas): 639-761.

SAINT-GIRONS (1975): Sperm survival and transport in the female genital tract of reptiles. – In: HEFEZ & THIBAULT (Eds.): The Biology of Spermatozoa. – Basel (S. Karger A.G.): 105-113.

SAINT-GIRONS (1982a): Influence des climats de type méditerranéen sur l'écophysiologie et la répartition des Reptiles. – Eco. Mediter., Marseille, **8** (1/2): 245-252.

SAINT-GIRONS (1982b): Remarques générales sur la biogéographie des reptiles méditerranéens. – P. Cent. Pir. Biol. exp., **13**: 111-115.

SAINT-GIRONS & DUGUY (1963): Notes de cytologie sanguine comparée sur les reptiles de France. – Bulletin de la Société Zoologique de France, Paris, **88**: 613-624.

SAJOVIC (1911): Zelve v lubljanski okolici – Testudines, quae prope Labacum inventae sunt. – Carniola (N. F.), Ljubljana, **2**: 178-180.

SAJOVIC (1914): Beiträge zur Reptilienkunde Krains. – Verhandlungen der zoologisch-botanischen Gesellschaft Wien, **64**: 150-175.

SALOTTI, BAILON, BONIFAY, COURTOIS, DUBOIS, FERRANDINI, LA MILZA, MOURER-CHAUVIRÉ, POPELARD, QUINIF, RÉAL-TESTUD, MINICONI, PEREIRA & PERSIANI (1997): Castiglione 3, un nouveau remplissage fossilifère d'âge Pléistocène moyen dans le karst de la région d'Oletta (Haute-Corse). – Comptes Rendus de l'Académie des Sciences, Série II a, Paris, **324**: 67-74.

SALVADOR (1974): Guía de los anfibios y reptiles españoles. – Madrid (Icona), 282 pp.

SALVADOR (1985): Guía de Campo de los Anfibios y Reptiles de la Península Ibérica, Islas Baleares y Canarias. – León (Santiago García), 212 pp., 128 plates, 78 maps.

SALVADOR & PÉREZ MELLADO (1984): The amphibians and reptiles of the Pityusic Islands. – In: KUBBIER (Ed.): Biogeography and Ecology of the Pityusic Islands. – Alcover (Guerau d'Arellano Tur): 429-439.

SALVADOR & PLEGUEZUELOS (2002): Reptiles Españoles. Identificación, historia natural y distribución. – Talavara de la Reina (Canseco Editores), 490 pp.

SALZBERG (1996): Report on import / export turtle trade in the United States. – In: SOPTOM (Eds.): International Congress of Chelonian Conservation – Proceedings. – Gonfaron (Editions SOPTOM): 314-322.

SÄNGER (1934): Eigenartiges Benehmen zweier Testudo graeca im Freien. – Blätter für Aquarien- und Terrarienkunde, Stuttgart, 45: 134-135.

SARA (1996): Uomo e Fauna Nelle Isole Mediterranee. – Palermo (Medical Books).

SART (1966): Resultados de una expedición zoológica a las islas Pitiusas – I – Vertebrados. – Boln. R. Soc. Esp. Hist. Nat. (Sec. Biol.), 64: 15-46.

SATORHELYI & SRETER (1993): Studies on internal parasites of tortoises. – Parasit. Hung., Budapest, 26: 51-55.

SASSENBURG (1983): Beiträge zur Physiologie und Pathologie der Fortpflanzung in Gefangenschaft gehaltener Reptilien aus der Sicht des praktischen Tierarztes. – Dissertation, Humboldt Univ., Berlin.

SASSENBURG (2000): Schildkrötenkrankheiten. – Ruhmannsfelden (bede-Verlag): 6, 12, 16, 21-23, 25-27, 30, 32-33, 36, 46, 52-56, 69, 72-73, 75-79, 81, 84-87, 91, 93.

SASSENBURG (2005): Handbuch Schildkrötenkrankheiten. – Ruhmannsfelden (bede-Verlag): 7, 14, 20, 27-28, 31-34, 38, 40, 46, 58-59, 68-70, 72-73, 83, 91, 96, 98, 100, 104-105, 109-111, 119-121, 123.

SAVELLI & BRIFFAUT (2004): Réhydratation d'une Testudo hermanni repêchée en mer, soins apportés pour le rétablissement de l'animal. – Manouria, Mezzavia, 25: 14-16.

SCALERA (2003): Anfibi e Rettili italiani, Elementi di tutela e conservazione. Collana Verde, 104. – Rome (Corpo Forestale dello Stato & Ministero per le politiche agricole e forestali), 232 pp.

SCHADEWALDT (1956): Die Sternsagen der Griechen. – Frankfurt am Main (Fischer), 192 pp.

SCHAFFER (2006): Futterpflanzen von der Wiese. – Sacalia, Stiefern, 4 (10): 40-45.

SCHAMBONY (1994): Fuchs, du hast die ... gestohlen – Ein unerwartetes Problem bei der Freilandhaltung von Landschildkröten. – Schildkröten, Linden, 1 (4): 33-35.

SCHÄR (1995): Betr.: »Landschildkröten – Die Pflege nach der Winterruhe«. – DATZ, Stuttgart, 48 (12): 812.

SCHEFFER (1995): De griekse landschildpad (Testudo hermanni boettgeri en Testudo hermanni hermanni). – In: VAN BAKEL, BRUEKERS, DE BRUIN, KELDERMANN & WIEBERDINK (Eds.): Special ter gelegenheid van het 20-jarig bestaan van de Nederlandse Schildpadden Vereniging 1975-1995: 54-58.

SCHEFFER (1996a): SOPTOM has a tenth anniversary. – British Chelonia Group Newsletter, 113: 23-24.

SCHEFFER (1996b): The biotope of Testudo hermanni hermanni. – British Chelonia Group Newsletter, 114: 20-21.

SCHELER (1986): Unsere »Salatschildkröten«. – Die Schildkröte (N. F.), Heinsberg, 1 (1/2): 32-34.

SCHENKELDIJK & SCHENKELDIJK (2002): Op locatie in...Apeldoorn. – De Schildpad, Eindhoven, 28 (5): 215-218.

SCHILDE (2001): Nachzuchtstatistik 2000. – Radiata, Haan, 10 (4): 33-34.

SCHILDE (2003): Nachzuchtstatistik 2001. – Minor, Lingenfeld, 2 (2): 8-9.

SCHILDE (2004a): Nachzuchtstatistik 2002. – Minor, Lingenfeld, 3 (2): 17.

SCHILDE (2004b): Nachzuchtstatistik 2003. – Minor, Lingenfeld, 3 (4): 12-13.

SCHILDE (2005): Nachzuchtstatistik 2004. – Minor, Lingenfeld, 4 (4): 27-29.+

SCHILDGER & HÄFELI (1989): Chirurgische Therapie der Legenot bei Reptilien. – Die Tierärztliche Praxis, Stuttgart, 17: 420-425.

SCHILDGER & HERZBERGER (1993): Einige blutchemische Parameter von Echsen und Schildkröten. – Reflotron Vet-Info 17, Mannheim (Prämix Wirkstoff GmbH).

SCHILDGER & TAYLOR (1998): Endoscopy in birds, reptiles, amphibians and fish. – Tuttlingen (Endo-Press).

SCHILLIGER (1990): Les affections parasitaires chez les reptiles – étude bibliographique et expérimentale. Applications prophylactiques et thérapeutiques en terrariophilie. – Master's thesis, École vétérinaire de Nantes, Nantes.

SCHILLIGER (2001): Fiche vétérinaire 3 – Les maladies respiratoires (partie 2). – Manouria, Mezzavia, 13: 6-9.

SCHILLIGER (2003): Hibernation. – Manouria, Mezzavia, 21: 6-9.

SCHILLIGER (2004a): Les affections hépatiques des chéloniens. – Manouria, Mezzavia, 25: 18-25.

SCHILLIGER (2004b): Guide Pratique des Maladies des reptiles en captivité. – Paris (éditions Med'Com), 224 pp.

SCHIPPAN (2004): Das Verhältnis von Größe zu Alter und Gewicht bei der Griechischen Landschildkröte (Testudo hermanni boettgeri). – Minor, Lingenfeld, 3 (2): 30-31.

SCHIPPERIJN (2000): Kwekers aan het woord over – de Griekse landschildpad (Testudo hermanni). – De Schildpad, Eindhoven, 26 (5): 188-192.

SCHLAGER (Ed.) (2003): GRZIMEK'S Animal Life Encyclopedia – Volume 7 – Reptiles. – Farmington Hills (Gale): 145, 148-149.

SCHLEFF (1996): Der Einfluß der Inkubationstemperatur auf das Geschlechterverhältnis bei europäischen

Landschildkröten. – Bremer Schildkröten-Interessen-Gemeinschaft Info, Bremen, 4: 5-9.

SCHLEFF (1998): Die Schildkrötenfreunde der Balearen A.D.L.T. – Amigos de las tortugas. – Journal der AG Schildkröten der DGHT, Bennstedt, 7 (1): 23-25.

SCHLEICH (1981): Jungtertiäre Schildkröten Süddeutschlands unter besonderer Berücksichtigung der Fundstelle Sandelzhausen. – Courier Forschungsinstitut Senckenberg, Frankfurt am Main, 48, 378 pp., 19 plates.

SCHLEICH (1998): Die ewig Verdammten – Wissenswertes aus der Welt der Amphibien und Reptilien. – Wuppertal (Fuhlrott-Museum): 13.

SCHLÜTER (2005): Die Herpetofauna der bulgarischen Schwarzmeerküste – Teil 1: Naturraum und Schildkröten. – elaphe (N. F.), Rheinbach, 13 (3): 48–56.

SCHMIDT (1981): Geschützte Amphibien und Reptilien in Freundesland 3. VR Bulgarien. – Aquarien Terrarien, Leipzig, Jena & Berlin, 28: 104-105.

SCHMIDT (1989): Wehenspritze für Schildkröte. – Das Tier, Leinfelden-Echterdingen, 30 (1): 57.

SCHMIDT (1995a): Herpes – Ein Virus wirft Fragen über Fragen auf! – SIGS-Info, Siblingen, 4 (1): 14-17.

SCHMIDT (1995b): Eine männliche Schildkröte legt befruchtete Eier. – Schildkröten, Lingen, 2 (2): 11-13.

SCHMIDT (1995c): Die Eiablage bei unseren griechischen Landschildkröten. – Schildkröten, Lingen, 2 (3): 3-6.

SCHMIDT (1995d): Überwinterung von Landschildkröten. – Schildkröten, Lingen, 2 (4): 16-18.

SCHMIDT (1999): Testudos auf Menorca. – Schildkröten, Lingen, 6 (4): 30-32.

SCHMIDT (2000a): Testudo hermanni hermanni auf Menorca. – Radiata, Haan, 9 (3): 16-18.

SCHMIDT (2000b): Schildkröten auf Menorca – 2. Teil. – Radiata, Haan, 9 (4): 13-16.

SCHMIDT (2004a): Testudo hermanni hermanni auf Menorca – Teil 3. – Radiata, Lingenfeld, 13 (1): 31-33.

SCHMIDT (2004b): Testudo hermanni hermanni auf Menorca – Teil 4. – Radiata, Lingenfeld, 13 (2): 25-30.

SCHMIDT (2006): 30 Jahre Reptilienzoo HAPP. – Reptilia (D), Münster: 81-83.

SCHMIDT & HENKEL (1998): Terrarientiere. – Stuttgart (Verlag Eugen Ulmer): 58, 98, 140.

SCHMIDT & INGER (1957): Knaurs Tierreich in Farben – Band II – Reptilien. – Munich & Zürich (Droemersche Verlagsanstalt Th. Knaur Nachf.): 27-28, 38.

SCHMIDTGEN (1907): Die Cloake und ihre Organe bei den Schildkröten. – Zoologische Jahrbücher, Abteilung für Anatomie, Jena, 24: 357-414.

SCHMIDT-RÖGER (1999): Urvieh für Einsteiger. – Das Tier, Leinfelden-Echterdingen, 40 (8): 44-47.

SCHMITT (1948): Beobachtungen über das Verhalten gezähmter Schildkröten. – Zeitschrift für Tierpsychologie, Berlin & Hamburg, 6: 274-283.

SCHMITZ (1995): O Schreck, o Schreck – die Kröt ist weg. – Schildkröten, 2 (1): 38-39.

SCHMITZ (1997): Terrarientiere. – Munich (BLV Verlagsgesellschaft): 77-81.

SCHNEIDER (1783): Allgemeine Naturgeschichte der Schildkröten nebst einem systematischen Verzeichnisse der einzelnen Arten und zwey Kupfern. – Leipzig (J. G. Müller): 348.

SCHNEIDER (1971): Das Tyrrhenisproblem. Interpretation auf zoogeographischer Grundlage. Dargestellt an Amphibien und Reptilien. – Dissertation, Univ. des Saarlandes, Saarbrücken, VI + 362 pp.

SCHNEIDER (2005): Überlegungen zur Gehegebepflanzung für Landschildkröten. – Schildkröten im Fokus, Bergheim, 2 (3): 13-20.

SCHOEPFF (1793): Historia Testudinum Iconibus Illustrata. – Erlangen (J. J. Palm): 38, plates VIII, IX.

SCHOMBURG & STEFFENS (1988): Rhythmic motor activity and phase dependent reflex transmission in the spinal tortoise (Testudo graeca, Testudo hermanni). – Journal of Comparative Physiology, A, Sensory, Neural, and Behavioral Physiology, 163 (4): 537-548.

SCHONEBOOM (2002): Schildpadden wel en wee. – De Schildpad, Eindhoven, 28 (4): 173.

SCHOOLDERMAN & SCHOOLDERMAN (1986): Griekse landschildpadden (Testudo hermanni) in de tuin. – Lacerta, Zoetermeer, 47 (3): 67-71.

SCHRAMM (1993): Über die allgemeine Anatomie und das Repirationssystem der Landschildkröten (Testudinidae). – Thesis, Universität Basel, Basel.

SCHREIBER (1875): Herpetologia Europaea. – Braunschweig (F. Viehweg und Sohn), XVII + 639 pp.

SCHREIBER (1912): Herpetologia Europaea. – 2. Auflage, Jena (Fischer Verlag), X + 960 pp.

SCHRÖDER (1973): Lurche und Kriechtiere in Farben. – Ravensburg (Otto Maier Verlag): 116, plate 40.

SCHÜRGERS (2004): Zo kweek ik mijn Testudo's op. – Trionyx, Eindhoven, 2 (2): 40-43.

SCHWARDMANN (1986): Unbekanntes Krankheitsbild bei Testudo h. hermanni. – Die Schildkröte (N. F.), Heinsberg, 1 (1/2): 30-31.

SCHWEIGER (1989): Über die Auswirkungen der Hitzewelle 1988 auf einige Schildkrötenpopulationen in Griechenland. – herpetofauna, Weinstadt, 58: 24-26.

SCHWEIGER (1992a): Das Stachelschwein Hystrix cristata LINNAEUS, 1758 als populationslimitierender

Faktor von *Testudo hermanni hermanni* GMELIN, 1789. – Salamandra, Bonn, **28** (1): 86-88.

SCHWEIGER (1992b): *Testudo hermanni hermanni* in der Toscana (Festland) – Verbreitung, Lebensraum und Status. – Vortragszusammenfassungen der DGHT-Jahrestagung, Bonn: 7.

SCHWEIGER (2005): Ile Of Walls – Herpetologische Beobachtungen auf der Kroatischen Insel Pag – 2. Teil: Amphibien und Schildkröten. – ÖGH-aktuell, Vienna, **15**: 4-6.

SCHWEIZER (1955): Wie werden europäische Landschildkröten überwintert? – DATZ, Stuttgart, **8** (12): 331.

SEBA (1734): Locupletissimi rerum naturalium thesauri accurata descriptio, et iconibus artificiosissimus expressio, per universam physices historiam. Opus, cui, in hoc rerum genere, nullum par existit. Ex toto terrarum orbe collegit, digessit, descripsit, et depingendum curavit. Tomus I. – Amsterdam (Janssonio-Waesbergios, J. Wetstenium & Gul. Smith), XXXII + 178 pp., 111 plates.

SÉCRETARIAT DE LA FAUNE ET DE LA FLORE (1983): Livre rouge des espèces menacées en France. Tome I: Vertébrés. – In: BEAUFOURT (Ed.): Inventaires de faune et de flore. – Paris (Sécretariat de la Faune et de la Flore): 19-23.

SEDLAG (1995): Urania Tierreich – Tiergeographie. – Leipzig, Jena & Berlin (Urania-Verlag): 326.

SEEGER (1998): Landschildkröten. – Augsburg (Naturbuch Verlag): 1, 6-7, 9, 11-12, 18, 20, 22, 30-32, 36-39, 45-46, 48-57.

SEHNAL & SCHUSTER (1999): Herpetologische Beobachtungen auf der Kvarnerinsel Cres, Kroatien – Ergebnisse von fünf Exkursionen. – Herpetozoa, Vienna, **12** (3/4): 163-178.

SEMENZATO (1985): Osservazioni sull' erpetofauna dell' entroterra veneziano. – Natura, Milan, **76**: 53-62.

SENN (1992): Eine Naturgeschichte der Schildkröten. – »Fortkommen« Schriften im R + R Verlag Nr. 14, Bottmingen: 50.

SHERRARD (1996): Don't get into a mix. – Tortoise Trust Newsletter, London, **11** (4): 11.

SHKORPIL (1897): Sur la flore de Plovdiv (avec des remarques géologiques et faunistiques). – Otchetna Plovdivsketa Gimnaziya »Alexander I« za 1896-1897 Uchebna Godina, Plovdiv: 3-23.

SICKENBERG (1971): Revision der Wirbeltierfauna der Höhle Petralona (Griech. Mazedonien). – Ann. Géol. Pays Hellén., Athens, **23**: 230-264, plates 39-40.

SIEBENROCK (1903): Über zwei seltene und eine neue Schildkröte des Berliner Museums. – Sitzungsberichte der Akademie der Wissenschaften Wien, Mathematisch-naturwissenschaftliche Klasse, Vienna, **112** (1): 439-445.

SIEBENROCK (1906): Zur Kenntnis der mediterranen *Testudo*-Arten und über ihre Verbreitung in Europa. – Zoologischer Anzeiger, Leipzig, **30** (25): 847-854.

SIEBENROCK (1909): Synopsis der rezenten Schildkröten, mit Berücksichtigung der in historischer Zeit ausgestorbenen Arten. – Zoologische Jahrbücher, Jena, Supplement **10**: 542.

SIEBENROCK (1910): Schildkröten aus Süd- und Südwestafrika. – Sitzungsberichte der Akademie der Wissenschaften Wien, Vienna, **119** (1): 693-720.

SIEBENROCK (1913): Schildkröten aus Syrien und Mesopotamien. – Annalen des Naturhistorischen Museums Wien, Vienna, **27**: 171-225, plates 10-12.

SIEBENROCK (1916): Die Schildkröten Niederösterreichs vor der Eiszeit. – Blätter für Naturkunde und Naturschutz in Niederösterreich, Vienna, **3**: 1-7.

SIERING (1979): Über die Ökologie der mediterranen Landschildkröten. – Die Schildkröte, Haar, **2** (1): 30-35.

SIMON (2000): Planung und Bau einer Freilandanlage für europäische Landschildkröten. – Draco, Münster, **2**: 42-47.

SIMONETTA (1960): Distribuzione e significata dell'organo paratimpanico del Vitali. – Atti della Società Toscana di Scienze Naturali, Ser. B, Pisa, **66**: 39-55.

SINGER (1991): Griechische Landschildkröten naturgemäß gepflegt. – DATZ, Stuttgart, **44** (2): 97-99.

SJØSTRAND (1969): Noradrenaline containing cells in the epididymis and vas deferens of the tortoise *Testudo hermanni*. – Acta Zoologica, **50** (3): 271-275.

SLAVENS (1980): Inventory of live reptiles and amphibians in North American collections. – Seattle (privately printed), 156 pp.

SLAVENS (1985): Inventory of live reptiles and amphibians in captivity. – Seattle (privately printed), 341 pp.

SLAVENS (1989): Reptiles and amphibians in captivity – breeding-longevity and inventory. – Seattle (privately printed), 474 pp.

SLAVENS & SLAVENS (1994): Reptiles and amphibians in captivity – breeding-longevity and inventory current January 1, 1994. – Seattle (Slaveware), 536 pp.

SLAVENS & SLAVENS (1998): Reptiles and amphibians in captivity – breeding-longevity and inventory current January 1, 1998. – Seattle (Slaveware), 423 pp.

VAN DER SLOOT (1968): Termination of dorsal root fibres in the spinal cord of the turtle *Testudo hermanni*. – Acta Morphologica Neerlando-Scandinavica, **7** (2): 200-201.

VAN SLOUN (2004): De bouw van een buitenverblijf. – Trionyx, Eindhoven, **2** (6): 186-189.

SMART & BRIDE (1993): The UK Trade in Live Reptiles and Amphibians – A Report to the RSPCA on the Nature and Status of the Reptile and Amphibian Pet Trade between

1980 and 1992. – Canterbury (Durrell Institute of Conservation and Ecology, University of Kent).

SMITH (1986): Anatomy of Male and Female Genitalia of Tortoises (specifically *Testudo graeca* and *Testudo hermanni*). – *Testudo*, **2** (4): 1-7.

SMOLIK (1968): rororo Tierlexikon – Band 4 – Kriechtiere, Lurche, Fische. – Reinbek (Rowohlt Taschenbuch Verlag): 15.

SMOLIK (1982): Weltreich der Tiere. – Munich & Mönchengladbach (Naturalis): 395.

SOARES, CHALKER, ERLES, HOLTBY, WATERS & MCARTHUR (2004): Prevalence of *Mycoplasma agassizii* and Chelonian herpesvirus in captive tortoises (*Testudo* sp.) in the United Kingsom. – Journal of Zoo and Wildlife Medicine, Media, **35** (1): 25-33.

SOCHUREK (1954): Amphibien- und Reptilienleben auf Elba. – Aquarien Terrarien, Leipzig & Jena, **1** (7): 213-214.

SOCHUREK (1955): Herpetologische waarnemingen in Noord-Sardinien. – Lacerta, Zoetermeer, **14** (1): 13.

SOCHUREK (1985): Krk – ein herpetologischer Überblick. – elaphe, Berlin, 7 (1): 13.

SOCIETAS EUROPAEA HERPETOLOGICA (Eds.) (1990): Threatened reptiles in Europe requiring special conservation measures. – Strasbourg (European Council), T-PVS (90), **57**, 51 pp.

SOCIETAS EUROPAEA HERPETOLOGICA (Eds.) (1994): Threatened amphibians and reptiles of eastern Europe requiring special conservation measures. – Strasbourg (European Council), T-PVS (94), **3**, 87 pp.

SOFIANIDOU (1996): Tetrapoda of Greece. – In: Systematics of Tetrapoda, with appendix of the Greek species. – Thessaloníki (Giachudis Giapulis), 384 pp.

SOFSKY (1982): Freilandbeobachtungen an der Griechischen Landschildkröte. – DATZ, Stuttgart, **35** (2): 119.

SOKOLOV (Ed.) (1988): Dictionary of animal names in five languages – Amphibians and Reptiles. – Moscow (Russy Yazik Publishers), 557 pp.

SOLER (1995): Distribución geográfica de la *Testudo hermanni hermanni* en la Peninsula Ibérica. – In: BALLASINA (Ed.): Red Data Book on Mediterranean Chelonians. – Bologna (Edagricole-Edizioni Agricole Calderini): 50-58.

SOLER (2002): Estat actual de la població reintroduida de tortuga mediterrània (*Testudo hermanni hermanni*) al Parc Natural del Garraf. – Trobades d'Estudiosos del Garraf, VI: 25.

SOLER & MARTÍNEZ (1999): Europäische Landschildkröten. – Reptilia (D), Münster, 17: 18-23.

SOLER & MARTÍNEZ (1999a): European tortoises. – Reptilia (GB), Barcelona, 8: 43-48.

SOLER & MARTÍNEZ (1999b): Las tortugas terrestres europeas. – Reptilia (E), Barcelona, 21: 43-47.

SOLER & MARTÍNEZ (2001): Des de fa 26 milions d'anys: el cicle vital de la tortuga mediterrània. – Descobrir Catalunya, 47: 15.

SOLER & MARTÍNEZ (2005): La tortuga mediterrània a Catalunya. – Tarragona (Edicions l'Agulla de Cultura Popular), 196 pp.

SOLER, MARTÍNEZ, & SOLÉ (2000): Estatus y conservación de la tortuga mediterranea en Mallorca. – Animalia, 116: 52-55.

SOLER, MARTÍNEZ, PARELLADA & BALLUS (2005): Participacio ciutadana en la conservació de *Testudo hermanni hermanni* a Catalunya. – Jornades de formació i divulgació de resultats sobre fauna, Flora i Animals de Companyia, II: 12.

SOLER, MARTÍNEZ, TARÍN & PARELLADA (2002): Premiers résultats de la réintroduction de la Tortue d'Hermann (*Testudo hermanni hermanni*) dans le Massif du Garraf (Catalogne, Espagne). – Chelonii, Gonfaron, 3: 230-232.

SOLER, MARTÍNEZ, TARÍN & PARELLADA (2003): Evolució de la població reintroduïda de tortuga mediterrània (*Testudo hermanni hermanni*) al Parc del Garraf. – Jornades d'Estudiosos del Garraf, IV: 93-97.

SOLER, SAMPERE, MARTÍNEZ & MEDINA (2002): Nuevos datos sobre la distribucion de *Testudo hermanni hermanni* en la comarca de l'Anoia (Barcelona). – Boletín de la Asociación Herpetológica Española, Leganés, **13** (1-2): 7-11.

SOLER, VALLESPIR, MARTÍNEZ, MEDINA, & SOLÉ, R. (2001): Patrón melánico en una población de *Testudo hermanni hermanni* del sudoeste de Mallorca. – Boletín de la Asociación Herpetológica Española, Leganés, **12** (1): 19-21.

SOPTOM (Eds.) (1985): Plan de sauvegarde de la Tortue d'Hermann. – Gonfaron (Editions Soptom), 41 pp.

SOPTOM (Eds.) (2002): Programme de conservation de la tortue d'Hermann *Testudo hermanni hermanni* en France continentale. – Gonfaron (Editions Soptom), 44 pp.

SPANGENBERG (1996): Exoten gehören nicht in die Wohnung. – Mainzer Allgemeine Zeitung, 03./04.10.1996.

SPEAKE, SURAI & GORE (2001): Lipid composition, fatty acid profiles, and lipid-soluble antioxidants of eggs of the Hermann's tortoise (*Testudo hermanni boettgeri*). – Zoo Biology, **20**: 75-87.

SPÖRLE (1992): Untersuchungen zu den Blutspiegelverläufen der Antiinfektiva *Ampicillin, Doxycyclin* und *Enrofloxacin* bei der Griechischen Landschildkröte (*Testudo hermanni*). – Dissertation, Univ. Gießen, Gießen.

SPÖRLE, GÖBEL & SCHILDGER (1991): Blood-levels of some anti-infectives in the Hermann's Tortoise (*Testudo hermanni hermanni*). – Proceedings of the 4th International Colloquium for Pathology and Medicine of Reptiles and Amphibians, Bad Nauheim: 120-128.

SPÖRRI (1999): Auffangstation der Sektion Zentralschweiz erweitert. – SIGS-Info, Siblingen, **8** (3): 31-32.

SPÖRRI (2000a): Sind unsere Pfleglinge Überlebenskünstler? – SIGS-Info, Siblingen, **9** (3): 22.

SPÖRRI (2000b): Aufzucht von Landschildkröten aus dem Mittelmeerraum. – Merkblatt 13, SIGS, 4 pp.

SQUALLI-HOUSSAINI & BLANC (1990): Genetic variability of four species of the genus *Testudo* (LINNAEUS, 1758). – Journal of the Herpetological Association of Africa, Johannesburg, **37** (5): 1-12.

STAESCHE (1961): Beobachtungen am Panzer von *Testudo graeca* und *Testudo hermanni*. – Stuttgarter Beiträge zur Naturkunde, Stuttgart, **74**: 1-16.

STANZEL (1991): Die Tierreste aus dem Artemis-/Apollon-Heiligtum bei Kalapodi in Böotien. – Dissertation, Ludwig-Maximilians-Univ., Munich: 15, 131, 162.

STAROSTA (2004): La tortue – Etonnante centenaire. – Toulouse (Éditions Milan-Jeunesse), 32 pp.

STAUFFER (1983): Landschildkröten im Garten – ja oder nein? – Das Tier, Leinfelden-Echterdingen, **24** (4): 52.

STEEHOUDER (1987): Over bultvorming in het schild bij de opkweek van landschildpadden. – Lacerta, Zoetermeer, **48** (3): 89-95.

STEFANI (1971): Ricerche zoologiche e botaniche nelle isole sarde di S.E. e S.O. – In: PASQUINI (Ed.): Relazione preliminare delle ricerche sulle popolazioni insulari compiute nel triennio 1965-1968. – Quaderni de »La Ricerca Scientifica«, Rome, **73**: 30-36.

STEFFEN (2001): Schildkrötenurlaub auf Menorca. – Schildkrötenfreunde intern, Gelsenkirchen, **4** (2): 23-28.

STEFFENS, SCHOMBURG & BEHRENDS (1978): Segmental reflex pathways from cutaneous afferents to alpha motor neurons in the tortoise *Testudo graeca* and *Testudo hermanni*. – Neuroscience Letters, Supplement 1: 104.

STEFFENS, SCHOMBURG & KOEHLER (1979): Spinal locomotion in the tortoise *Testudo hermanni*. – Third European Neuroscience Association Meeting, Rome, 11.-14.9.1979.

STEFFENS, SCHOMBURG & KOEHLER (1985): Spinal reflex pattern in the tortoise (*Testudo graeca*, *Testudo hermanni*). – Journal of Comparative Physiology, A, Sensory, Neural, and Behavioral Physiology, **156** (2): 153-164.

STEINLE (1977): Ein rätselhaftes Gelege – Eier von *Testudo horsfieldii* durch *T. hermanni* befruchtet? – DATZ, Stuttgart, **30** (1): 33-34.

STEMMLER (1957): Schildkröten in Griechenland. – Zeitschrift für Vivaristik, Mannheim, **3** (11): 159-164.

STEMMLER (1959): Sardische Schildkröten. – Zeitschrift für Vivaristik, Mannheim, **5** (1): 42-50.

STEMMLER (1968a): Zur Kenntnis von *Testudo hermanni* im tyrrhenischen Gebiet. – Aqua-Terra, Solothurn, **5** (6): 41-47, (7): 49-52.

STEMMLER (1968b): Herpetologische Beobachtungen auf den Inseln Elba, Topi, Ortano, Palmajola, Cerboli und dem Monte Massoncello (Italien). – Revue Suisse Zoologique, Geneva, **75** (4): 883-926.

STEMMLER & MATZ (1967): Les tortues terrestres. – Aquarama, **1** (3): 21-24.

STEMMLER-MORATH (1953): Ein weiterer Fundort von *Testudo hermanni robertmertensi*. – DATZ, Stuttgart, **6** (3): 71-72.

STEMMLER-GYGER (1963): Ein Beitrag zur Brutbiologie der mediterranen Landschildkröten. – DATZ, Stuttgart, **16** (3): 181-183.

STEMMLER-GYGER (1964a): Zur Brutbiologie der mediterranen Landschildkröten – II. – Aqua Terra, Solothurn, **1** (9): 65-68.

STEMMLER-GYGER (1964b): Zur Brutbiologie der mediterranen Landschildkröten – III. – Aquaria, Sankt Gallen, **11** (3): 164-169.

STEPÁNEK (1944): Zur Herpetologie Griechenlands. – Vestnik Ceskoslov. Spolecnosti Zool., Prague, **9**: 123-147.

STEVENS (1994): Notes on the herpetofauna of two geographically separate Greek islands. – Reptilian Magazine, **3** (3): 26-32.

STOCK (1972): Karyological relationships in turtles (Reptilia: Chelonia). – Canadian Journal of Genetics and Cytology, Ottawa, **14**: 859-868.

STOEV (2000): On the distribution, biology and ecology of amphibians and reptiles in the Derventski Heights and the Sakar Mountain, South-East Bulgaria. – Historia naturalis bulgarica, Sofia, **12**: 59-69.

STOEV (2003): Diversity and Conservation Significance of the Amphibians and Reptiles in Rila Monastery Nature Park. – In: PEEV (Ed.): Rapid Ecological Assessment of Rila Monastery Nature Park. – Burlington (United States Agency for International Development): 139-142.

STOYCHEV & PETROVA (2003): Protectes areas in Eastern Rhodopes and Sakar mountains. – Sofia (Bulgarian Society for the Protection of Birds), Conservation Series, Band 7, 49 pp.

STRATHEMANN (1986): Herpetologische Beobachtungen westlich des Prespasees in Südjugoslawien. – Sauria, Berlin, **8** (2): 19-21.

STREET (1979): The Reptiles of Northern and Central Europe. – London (B. T. Batsford), 268 pp.

STREET (1980): Pet tortoises (*Testudo graeca* and hermanni). – British Chelonia Group Newsletter, 20: 5-7.

STREJCKOVA & SERVIT (1973): Isolated head of the turtle – a useful experimental model in the physiology and patho-physiology of the brain. – Physiologica Bohemoslovenica, Bratislava, **22** (1): 37-41.

STRIEGL (1996): Erworbener Augenfehler bei einer Schildkröte. – Schildkröten, Linden, **3** (4): 34.

STRIEGL (1997a): Nachzuchtbericht 1996. – Schildkröten, Linden, **4** (1): 19.

STRIEGL (1997b): Ich Johanna – oder das Ei der Johanna. – Schildkröten, Linden, **4** (2): 20.

STRIEGL (1997c): Der Sache auf den Knochen gehen!! – Schildkröten, Linden, **4** (2): 21.

STRIEGL (1998): Das Terrarium. – Schildkröten, Linden, **5** (1): 17-18.

STRIEGL (2001): Überwinterung. – Schildkröten, Linden, **8** (3): 11-12.

STRIEGL (2003): Mallorca – einmal ganz anders! – Schildkröten, **10** (4): 49-53.

STRIJBOSCH (1985): Determinatielabel van de amfibieÁn en reptielen op Corsica. – Lacerta, Zoetermeer, **44** (3): 44-51.

STROMMER (1996): Betreff –»Beipacktext« für Nachzuchten unserer griechischen Landschildkröten. – Informationsblatt der Fachgruppe Schildkröten der ÖGH, Vienna, **2** (2): 3.

STUBBS (1981a): University of London Union Natural History Society Expedition to Greece 1980. – Bulletin of the Hellenic Society for the Protection of Nature, Athens, **9** (119): 49-50.

STUBBS (1981b): Villas, villagers and tortoises in Greece. – Oryx, Cambridge & Washington, **16** (2): 176-178.

STUBBS (1981c): Wildlife of the Alyki heaths – I – Destruction by fire and plough. – Animals, **8**: 10-11.

STUBBS (1981d): Wildlife of the Alyki heaths – II – Before and after the fire. – Animals, **9**: 14-16.

STUBBS (1984): Alyki revisited – Wildlife of the Alyki heaths Part 3 – Recovery. – RSPCA Today, London, **1**: 16-17.

STUBBS (1986a): Tortoise trade post-mortem. – BBC Wildlife, London, **2**: 78.

STUBBS (1986b): Action program for protecting Testudo hermanni in southern France. – Environment Conservation, **13** (2): 167.

STUBBS (1987a): La plaine au nord des Maures – la dernière plaine basse sauvage et naturelle en Provence – Notes sur la flore et faune.

STUBBS (1987b): French tortoise village appeal. – British Chelonia Group Newsletter, **58**: 4-5

STUBBS (1988): Action programme for protecting Testudo hermanni in southern France. – British Herpetological Society Bulletin, London, **24**: 5-6.

STUBBS (1989): Testudo hermanni – Hermann's Tortoise. – In: SWINGLAND & KLEMENS (Eds.): The Conserva-

tion Biology of Tortoises. – Occasional Papers of the IUCN Species Survival Commission, No. 5, Gland (IUCN): 34-36.

STUBBS (1990): Care of Chelonia in Their Natural Environment – The French Tortoise Village. – Testudo, **3** (2): 21-24.

STUBBS (1995): Testudo hermanni in France. – In: BALLASINA (Ed.): Red Data Book on Mediterranean Chelonians. – Bologna (Edagricole: 94-102.

STUBBS & SWINGLAND (1985): The ecology of a Mediterranean tortoise (Testudo hermanni): a declining population. – Canadian Journal of Zoology, Ottawa, **63** (1): 169-180.

STUBBS & SWINGLAND (1986a): Recent developments in the conservation of Testudo hermanni in France. – In: ROCEK (Ed.): Studies in Herpetoloy. – Proceedings of the European Herpetological Meeting (3rd Ordinary General Meeting of Societas Europaea Herpetologica), Prague: 739-742.

STUBBS & SWINGLAND (1986b): Recent developments in the conservation of Testudo hermanni in France. – Testudo, **2** (4): 31-36.

STUBBS, DEVAUX & BOUR (1991): Recensement tortue d'Hermann continentale (plaine et massif des Maures). Campagne 87-88-89-90. – Gonfaron (Editions SOPTOM).

STUBBS, ESPIN & MATHER (1979): Report on an expedition to Greece 1979. – London (University of London Union Natural History Society), 130 pp.

STUBBS, HAILEY, PULFORD & TYLER (1984): Population ecology of European tortoises: review of field techniques. – Amphibia-Reptilia, Leiden, **5** (1): 57-68.

STUBBS, HAILEY, TYLER & PULFORD (1981): University of London Natural History Society Expedition to Greece 1980 – A report. – London (University of London Union Natural History Society), 136 pp.

STUBBS, SWINGLAND, HAILEY & PULFORD (1985): The ecology of the Mediterranean tortoise Testudo hermanni in northern Greece (The effects of a catastrophe on population structure and density). – Biological Conservation, **31** (2): 125-152.

STUGREN & KAVVADIAS (1989): Infraspezifische Systematik der Griechischen Landschildkröte (Testudo hermanni GMELIN) aus Korfu. – Stud. Univ. Babes-Bolyai, Biologia, Cluj-Napoca, **34** (2): 78-83.

STUMPEL, PODLOUCKY, CORBETT, ANDRÉN, BEA, NILSON & OLIVEIRA (1992): Threatened reptiles in Europe requiring special conservation measures. – In: KORSÓS & KISS (Eds.): Proceedings of the Sixth Ordinary General Meeting of the Societas Europaea Herpetologica, Budapest 1991: 25-34.

STUMPEL-RIENKS (1992): Handbuch der Reptilien und Amphibien Europas – Ergänzungsband – Nomina Herpetofaunae Europaeae. – Wiesbaden (AULA-Verlag): 111,

121, 123-124, 127, 131, 135, 137, 141, 144, 149, 152, 157, 162-164, 169, 172, 175, 180, 182, 184, 187, 190, 193, 195, 248.

STURGREN (1958): Noi contributii la problema originii faunei herpetologice din Republica Populare Romina in Lumina glaciatiunilor. – Bul. Stintific, Biol. Stiinte Agric. Zool., Bukarest, 9 (1): 35-47.

VAN SUCHTELEN & VAN SUCHTELEN (2002): Eerst denken dan doen – schildpadden thuis. – De Schildpad, Eindhoven, 28 (2): 98-101.

SUNDERLAND & VEAL (2001): An investigation into the faecal flora of clinically healthy tortoises. – Testudo, 5 (3): 23-34.

SURA (1981): Notes on the reptiles of Bulgaria. – British Herpetological Society Bulletin, London, 3: 25-28.

SUSEBACH (1956): Lautäußerungen bei griechischen Landschildkröten. – DATZ, Stuttgart, 9 (11): 308.

SÜSS & MALTER (1991): Vom Mythos der Schildkröte – Das Urtier als Glücksbringer. – Dortmund (Harenberg Edition); 35, 51, 58, 73-74, 77-80, 82, 89-91, 105-108, 117, 122-123, 129-140, 167-170.

SUTTNER (2005): Günter – unsere Griechische Landschildkröte. – Aquarien-Praxis, Stuttgart, 5: 2-5.

SWINGLAND (1984a): Dietary preferences of free-living chelonians. – British Chelonia Group Newsletter, 42: 2-3.

SWINGLAND (1984b): The ecology of the Mediterranean tortoise – a long term study. – British Veterinary Zoological Society, London, 17: 12-14.

SWINGLAND (1986): Movement patterns in Testudo hermanni and implications for management. – In: ROCEK (Ed.): Studies in Herpetoloy. – Proceedings of the European Herpetological Meeting (3rd Ordinary General Meeting of Societas Europaea Herpetologica), Prague: 573-578.

SWINGLAND & STUBBS (1985): The ecology of a Mediterranean tortoise Testudo hermanni: reproduction. – Journal of Zoology, London (A), 205 (4): 595-610.

SWINGLAND, STUBBS, NEWDICK & WORTON (1986): Movement patterns in Testudo hermanni and implications for management. – In: ROCEK (Ed.): Studies in Herpetoloy. – Proceedings of the European Herpetological Meeting (3rd Ordinary General Meeting of Societas Europaea Herpetologica), Prague: 573-578.

SWINGLAND, STUBBS, NEWDICK & WORTON (2001): Bewegungsmuster von Testudo hermanni und Folgerungen für die Haltung. – Schildkrötenfreunde intern, Gelsenkirchen, 4 (1): 23-33.

SZERBAK & SHARPILO (1966): Data on the systematics, ecology, and parasitofauna of the Black Sea coast of Bulgaria. – In: Ecology and history of the vertebrate fauna of the Ukraine, Kiev: 160-168.

TAKÁCS (1987): Exploitation of tortoises in Eastern Europe. – British Herpetological Society Bulletin, London, 19: 27-28.

TEIFKE, LOHR, MARSCHANG, OSTERREIDER & POSTHAUS (2000): Detection of chelonid herpesvirus DNA by nonradioactive in situ hybridization in tissue from tortoises suffering from stomatistis-rhinitis complex in europe and North America. – Veterinary Pathology, 37: 377-385.

TELECKY (2001): United States Import and Export of Live Turtles and Tortoises. – Turtle and Tortoise Newsletter, Lunenburg, 4: 8-13.

TEMBROCK (1961): Diskussionsbemerkungen zu: Können Schildkröten und Schlangen hören? – Aquarien Terrarien, Leipzig, Jena & Berlin, 8: 383.

TERRILL (1994): Harrington »Houdini« Tortoise. – British Chelonia Group Newsletter, 101: 16.

TEYNIÉ (1987): Observations herpétologiques en Turquie. 1ère partie. – Bulletin de la Société Herpétologique de France, Paris, 43: 9-18.

TEYNIÉ (1991): Observations herpétologiques en Turquie. 2ème partie. – Bulletin de la Société Herpétologique de France, Paris, 58: 21-30.

THALMANN (2005): Schildkrötenanlagen in Südfrankreich. – Testudo (SIGS), Wimmis, 14 (4): 24-27.

THEIL (1958): Licht- und elektronenmikroskopische Studie über das Nierenkörperchen der Griechischen Landschildkröte (Testudo hermanni). – Zeitschrift für Zellforschung und mikroskopische Anatomie, Berlin, 47: 288-319.

THEILE (2002): International trade in live Testudinidae – review of trade levels and trends over two decades. – Chelonii, Gonfaron, 3: 268-276.

THIBAULT, DELAUGERRE, CHEYLAN, GUYOT & MINICONI (1987): Les Vertébrés terrestres non domestiques des îles Lavezzi (sud de la Corse). – Bulletin Mensuel de la Société Linneenne de Lyon, 56: 117-152.

THIEL, GEISS & BRAUN (1988): A new herpes-virus induced in tortoise. – Proceedings of the European Society of Veterinary Pathology, San Remo.

THIEME (1986): Die Amphibien- und Reptilienfauna der südostbulgarischen Küste – III – Reptilien III. – Sauria, Berlin, 8 (1): 7-9.

THIERFELDT (2004): Der 3. Rheinische Workshop der DGHT-AG Schildkröten am 15. Mai im Aquazoo Düsseldorf. – Minor, Lingenfeld, 3 (2): 8-13.

THIERFELDT & HÖFLER-THIERFELDT (2002): Überwinterung von Schildkröten im Kühlschrank. – Radiata, Haan, 11 (4): 42-44.

THINÈS (1968): Activity regulation in the tortoise Testudo hermanni GMELIN. – Psychologica Belge, Brussels, 8 (2): 131-138.

THOMAS (1969): Fortpflanzungsverhalten bei jungen Griechischen Landschildkröten (Testudo h. hermanni). – Salamandra, Frankfurt am Main, 5 (3/4): 147-148.

THOMSON (1932): The anatomy of the tortoise. – Science Proceedings of the Royal Dublin Society, Dublin, 20: 359-461.

THOMPSON (2001): A walk on the wild side with Testudo hermanni. – Tortoise Trust Newsletter, London, 15 (4)/16 (1): 21.

THOMPSON (2004): A first time breeding experience with Testudo hermanni. – Tortoise Trust Newsletter, London, 19 (1): 3-4.

TIEDEMANN (1978): Herpetologische Aufsammlungen in Nordsardinien. – Annalen des Naturhistorischen Museums Wien (Ser. B), 81: 447-463.

TILLEY (1999): Virology in Chelonia. – British Chelonia Group Newsletter, 132: 11-12.

TILLEY (2006): Know your tortoise – Part 3: The skin. – British Chelonia Group Newsletter, 169: 8.

TIPPMANN (1998a): Zusammenfassung der Jahrestagung der Schildkrötenfreunde Österreich in Wien. – Journal der AG Schildkröten der DGHT, Bennstedt, 7 (1): 4-9.

TIPPMANN (1998b): Datenerhebung zur Größe und dem Gewicht von in Menschenhand gepflegten Landschildkröten der Gattung Testudo. – Journal der AG Schildkröten der DGHT, Bennstedt, 7 (2): 4.

TIPPMANN (1998c): Jahrestagung der DGHT-AG Schildkröten 1998 in Gera – Zusammenfassung einiger Vorträge. – Journal der AG Schildkröten der DGHT, Bennstedt, 7 (2): 5-9.

TIPPMANN (2000): Die europäischen und mediterranen Landschildkröten der Gattung Testudo und ihre Nachzucht. – In: ARTNER & MEIER (Eds.): Schildkröten. – Münster (Natur und Tier-Verlag): 9-20.

TOMASETTI (1997): Indagini morfometriche ed ecologiche su una popolazione di Testudo hermanni hermanni GMELIN die Monti Nebrodi (Sicilia). – Dissertation, Univ. Studi, Catania.

TOMASINI (1894): Skizzen aus dem Reptilienleben Bosniens und der Hercegovina. – Wissenschaftliche Mitteilungen des Bosnisch-Herzegovinischen Landesmuseums Sarajevo, Vienna, 2: 560-661.

TOME (1996): Pregled razsirjenosti plazilcev v Sloveniji. – Ann. istr. mediter. stud., Koper, 9: 217-228.

TORTONESE (1941/1942): Gli anfibi e i rettili italiani del R. Museo Zoologico di Torino. – Boll. Musei Zool. Anat. comp. R. Univ. Torino, Turin, 49 (127): 203-222.

TORTONESE & LANZA (1968): Piccola fauna italiana. Pesci, Anfibi e Rettili. – Milan (Martello), 185 pp.

TÓTH, KRECSÁK, MADSEN & ÚJVÁRI (2002): Herpetofaunal locality records on the Greek island of Corfu. – Herpetozoa, Vienna, 15 (3/4): 149-169.

TRABUCCO (1899): L'isola di Linosa – Studio geofisico. – Atti III Congr. Geogr. Ital., 2: 148-162.

TRAPP (2002): Über Naturschutz und Drachenfliegen: Das Schildkrötenprojekt am Olymp. – Reptilia (D), Münster, 38: 7-9.

TRAPP (2004a): Schildkröten und Olympia 2004. – Reptilia (D), Münster, 46: 6.

TRAPP & VALVERDE (2004a): Testudo hermanni boettgeri MOJSISOVICS, 1889 – Griechische Landschildkröte. – Reptilia (D), Münster, 46: 51-54.

TRAPP & VALVERDE (2004b): Testudo hermanni boettgeri MOJSISOVICS, 1889 – Eastern Hermann's Tortoise. – Reptilia (GB), 35: 39-42.

TRAPP & VALVERDE (2004c): Fichas de especies y póster – Testudo hermanni boettgeri. Reptilia (E), 48: 43- 46.

TRAUTWEIN & PRUKSARAJ (1967): Über Amyloidose bei Schildkröten. – Deutsche Tierärztliche Wochenschrift, Hannover, 74: 184-186.

TREPTE (1993): Lebensräume der Griechischen Landschildkröte Testudo h. hermanni in der Toskana. – Journal der AG Schildkröten und Panzerechsen der DGHT, Bürstadt, 2 (2): 11-16.

TRIPEPI, ROSSI & TRECROCI (1993): Situazione dell'erpetofauna in Calabria con particolare riguardo alle specie minacciate. – Suppl. Ric. Biol. Selvaggina, Ozzano dell'Emilia, 21: 407-413.

TRONCO (1992): Importance des conditions d'entretien dans la pathologie des chéloniens en captivité. – Proceedings of the 1st International Congress on Chelonian Pathology, Gonfaron (SOPTOM): 8-18.

TRUTNAU (1975): Europäische Amphibien und Reptilien. – Stuttgart (Belser Verlag): 137-138, 42-43.

TRUTNAU (1994): Terraristik. – Stuttgart (Verlag Eugen Ulmer): 65, 239.

TULESHKOV (1955): Les tortues – monument naturel. – Priroda Znanie, Sofia, VIII (8): 14-17.

TUR (1981): Paralysis in the back legs of a tortoise. – British Chelonia Group Newsletter, 25: 3.

TUR & TUR (1982): Observations of the behaviour of European tortoises. – Testudo, 2 (1): 33-36.

TURRISI & VACCARO (1998): Anfibi e Rettili del Monte Etna (Sicilia orientale). – Boll. Accad. Gioenia Sci. Nat., Catania, 36 (363): 5-103.

TURTLE CONSERVATION FUND (2002): A Global Action Plan for Conservation of Tortoises and Freshwater Turtles – Strategy and Funding Prospectus 2002-2007. – Washington (Conservation International & Chelonian Research Foundation): 14, 24.

ULLRICH (1999): Landschildkröten. – Niedernhausen (Falken Verlag): 9, 15-17, 28, 32-33, 39, 48-49, 75-76, 96-97, 118.

UNE, MURAKAMI, UEMURA, FUJITANI, ISHIBASHI & NOMURA (2000): Polymerase chain Reaction (PCR) for the Detection of herpesvirus in Tortoises. – Journal of Veterinary Medicine Science, 62 (8): 905-907.

URBANSKI (1962): The new legislation relating to the protection of animals in the Bulgarian People's Republic. – Chronmy Przyr. Ojezsta (N. S.), Sofia,, 18 (6): 31-39.

URECH (2001): Schlupferfolg einer Jungzüchterin aus dem Tessin. – SIGS-Info, Siblingen, 10 (4): 15.

UVA & VALLARINO (1982): Renin angiotensin system and osmoregulation in the terrestrial Chelonian Testudo hermanni. – Comparative Biochemistry and Physiology, A, Comparative Physiology, Vancouver, 71 (3): 449-452.

UVA, VALLARINO, MANDICH & ISOLA (1982): Plasma aldo sterone levels in the female tortoise Testudo hermanni in different experimental conditions. – General and Comparative Endocrinology, 46 (1): 116-123.

VALAKOS & MYLONAS (1992): Distribution and ecological aspects of the herpetofauna of Strofadhes Islands (Ionian Archipelago, Greece). – Herpetozoa, Vienna, 5 (1): 33-39.

VALLARINO (1984): Seasonal kidney and plasma renin concentration in Testudo hermanni; Comparative Biochemistry and Physiology, A, Comparative Physiology, Vancouver, 79 (4): 529-532.

VALLARINO, UVA & ISOLA (1985): Effect of hypophysectomy on plasmaelectrolytes and adrenal mineralocorticoid secretion in the terrestrial Chelonian Testudo hermanni. – Comparative Biochemistry and Physiology, A, Comparative Physiology, Vancouver, 81 (2): 283-286.

VARGA (1995): Geographical patterns of biological diversity in the Palearctic region and the Carpathian basin. – Acta Zoologica Academiae Scientiarum Hungaricae, 41: 71-92.

VASILIU & SOVA (1968): Fauna Vertebratica Romaniae (Index) II. Amphibia. III. Reptilia. – Studii si comunicari, Muzeul Judetean Bacau, Sectia Stiintele Naturii, Bacau.

VEIDT & FRITZ (2001): Bastarde der Griechischen Landschildkröte. – DATZ, 54 (2): 57-59.

VEITH (1991): Die Reptilien Bosniens und der Herzegowina – Teil I. – Herpetozoa, Vienna, 4 (3); 107-194

VENTO, ROCA, PRADES, QUERALT & SÁNCHEZ (1992): Atlas provisional de los Anfibios y Reptiles de la Comunidad Valenciana: mitad septentrional. – Revista Española de Herpetología, Leganés, 6: 119-128.

VENTURA (1985): The fossil herpetofauna of the Maltese Islands – a review. – Naturalista Siciliana, Palermo, 8 (3/4): 93-106.

VERHOEKS (2006): Identificatie bij landschildpadden op lijst A. – Trionyx, Eindhoven, 4 (2): 44-47.

VETTER (1986): Verstopfung bei Schildkröten. – Das Tier, Essen, 39 (1): 53.

VETTER (2002a): Schildkröten der Welt – Band 1 – Afrika, Europa und Westasien. – Frankfurt am Main & Rodgau (Edition Chimaira & Verlag ACS): 6-7, 13, 64-65, 69-70.

VETTER (2002b): Schildkröten auf Briefmarken und ihr Vorkommen in den jeweiligen Ländern. – Schildkröten, Linden, 9 (1): 4-43.

VEYSSET (1999): Minorque et ses tortues. – La Tortue, Gonfaron, 48: 20-21.

VIGNE (1989): Les Mammifères post-glaciaires de Corse et leurs rapports avec l'Homme. – 26ème supplément à Gallia-Préhistorique, CNRS, Paris, 334 pp.

VIGNE & ALCOVER (1985): Incidence des relations historiques entre l'Homme et l'Animal dans la composition actuelle du peuplement amphibien, reptilien et mammalien des îles de Méditerranée occidentale. – 11ème Congrès Sociétés Savantes, Montpellier, 2: 79-91.

VILELLA (1979): Herpetofauna of Catalonia: Preliminary note on the Herpetofauna of Vidra (Gerona). – Miscellànea Zoológica, Barcelona, 5: 180-183.

VILLENEUVE (1821): Statistique du département des Bouches-du-Rhne. – Marseile (Ricar), 944 pp.

VINKE & VINKE (1997): Schildkröten lieben es warm. – Journal der AG Schildkröten der DGHT, Bennstedt, 6 (3): 4-8.

VINKE & VINKE (2001a): Projekt »Fotodokumentation von Jungtieren« angelaufen. – Radiata, Haan, 10 (4): 23.

VINKE & VINKE (2001b): Kleine Pflegeanleitung für Europäische Landschildkröten. – Haan (DGHT-AG Schildkröten), 4 pp.

VINKE & VINKE (2001c): Aktueller Stand bei der Umsetzung der Kennzeichnungspflicht in der BartSchVO. – Radiata, Haan, 10 (2): 15-17.

VINKE & VINKE (2002a): Europäische Landschildkröten. – M & S Reptilien, Villingen-Schwenningen, 3: 74-75 57-58.

VINKE & VINKE (2002b): Vom Niedergang eines Schildkrötenbiotops. – Radiata, Haan, 11 (3): 44-49.

VINKE & VINKE (2003): Betrifft: Ernährung von Schildkröten. – DATZ, Stuttgart, 56 (8): 560.

VINKE & VINKE (2004a): Vermehrung von Landschildkröten. – Offenbach (Herpeton, Verlag Elke Köhler): 6, 11-13, 15, 20, 26-29, 32-33, 36-38, 45, 59-60, 63-64, 72, 79-80, 85-86, 89-90, 98, 104, 108, 111, 115, 122-124, 133-134, 163, 166, 176-177, 179, 181.

VINKE & VINKE (2004b): Testudo hercegovinensis WERNER, 1899 – die Dalmatinische Landschildkröte. – Schildkröten im Fokus, Bergheim, 1 (1): 22-34.

VINKE & VINKE (2004c): Die Rolle ungesättigter Fettsäuren in der Landschildkrötenernährung – eine Annäherung an einen vernachlässigten Aspekt. – Schildkröten im Fokus, Bergheim, **1** (2): 11-15.

VINKE & VINKE (2006): Ist die Abschaffung der EU-Bescheinigung und/oder der Meldepflicht bei Europäischen Landschildkröten wirklich sinnvoll? – Reptilia (D), Münster, 57: 6-8.

VINTER & GREEN (1961): Notes on the common tortoise – 1 – The trade in tortoises. – The Veterinary Record, London, **73**: 313-314.

VISINESCU (1968): Inflenta temperaturii scazute asupra metabolismului energetic al unor specii de animale heteroterme si poikiloterme. – Studii si cercetari de Biologie, Seria Zoologie, Bukarest, **20**: 501-506.

VISSENAEKENS (2005): De pen van … HILDE VISSENAEKENS. – Trionyx, Eindhoven, **3** (6): 191–194.

VISSER (2002): Schildpadden op enkele Griekse eilanden. – De Schildpad, Eindhoven, **28** (6): 243-246.

VISSER (2005): Heucops. – Trionyx, Eindhoven, **3** (2): 62.

VIVES-BALMAÑA (1982): Contribución al conocimiento de la fauna herpetológico del NE de la Península Ibérica. – Master's thesis, Universitat de Barcelona, Barcelona.

VIVES-BALMAÑA (1984a): Els Amfibis i els Rèptils de Catalunya. – Barcelona (Ketres Editora), 229 pp.

VIVES-BALMAÑA (1984b): Herpetofaune de Catalogne: Aspects biogéographique et écologique. – Bulletin de la Société Herpétologique de France, Paris, **29**: 33-34.

VIVES-BALMAÑA (1990): Contribució al coneixement de la fauna herpetológica de Catalunya. – Barcelona (Institut d'Estudis Catalans).

VIVES-BALMAÑA & GOSALBEZ (1987): Història Natural dels Països Catalans – Vol. 13 – Amfibis, Reptils i Mamifers. – Enciclopèdia Catalana, Barcelona, 498 pp.

VIVIEN-ROELS (1976): Differentiation of secretory photoreceptors in the embryonic epiphysis of *Testudo hermanni* (Reptilia, Chelonia). – J. Microscopy, **26** (2/3): 30 A.

VIVIEN-ROELS & ARENDT (1979): Circadian and circannual fluctuations of pineal melatonin content in *Testudo hermanni* (Reptilia, Chelonia) under natural conditions of photoperiod and temperature. – Annals of Endocrinology, Paris, **40** (1): 93-94.

VIVIEN-ROELS & ARENDT (1981a): Relative roles of environmental factors, photoperiod and temperature in the control of serotonin and melatonin circadian variations in the pineal organ and plasma of the tortoise *Testudo hermanni*. – In: BIRAU & SCHLOOT (Eds.): Melatonin – current status and perspectives, International Symposium, Bremen, 28.-30.9.1980. – Pergamon Press: 401-406

VIVIEN-ROELS & ARENDT (1981b): Environmental control of pineal and gonadal function in reptiles – preliminary results on the relative role of photoperiod and

temperature. – In: Photoperiodism and Reproduction, Colloque I.N.R.A., 6: 273-288.

VIVIEN-ROELS & ARENDT (1983): How does the indoleamine production of the pineal gland respond to variations of the environment in a nonmammalian vertebrate *Testudo hermanni*. – Psychoneuroendocrinology, **8** (3): 327-332.

VIVIEN-ROELS & HUMBERT (1977): The lipo pigments of the pineal gland of *Testudo hermanni* reptile Chelonian microprobe analysis and physiological significance. – Journal of Ultrastructural Research, **61** (1): 134-139.

VIVIEN-ROELS & PETIT (1975): Spectro fluorometric measurement of serotonin 5 Hydroxy tryptamine in the pineal gland of reptiles – seasonal variations of pineal 5 Hydroxy tryptamine rate in the turtle *Testudo hermanni*. – Comptes Rendus de l'Académie des Sciences, Série D, Sciences Naturelles, Paris, **280** (4): 467-470.

VIVIEN-ROELS & PEVET (1983): The pineal gland and the synchronisation of reproductive cycles with variations of the environmental climatic conditions, with special reference to temperature. – Pineal Research Review, **1**: 91-143.

VIVIEN-ROELS, ARENDT & BRADTKE (1979); Circadian and circannual fluctuations of pineal indolamines (serotonin and melatonin) in *Testudo hermanni* GMELIN (Reptilia, Chelonia) – I. Under natural conditions of photoperiod and temperature. – General and Comparative Endocrinology, **37** (2): 197-210.

VIVIEN-ROELS, FÈVRE-MONTANGE & ARENDT (1984a): Long-term effect of environmental factors on indolic synthesis in the pineal gland and on the functioning of male gonads in *Testudo hermanni*. – In: Fourteenth Colloquium of the Société de Neuroendocrinologie Experimentale, Besan‚on, 27.28.9.1984.

VIVIEN-ROELS, FÈVRE-MONTANGE & ARENDT (1984b): Long-term effect of environmental factors on pineal and gonadal function in the male tortoise *Testudo hermanni*. – In: Satellite Symposia of the Seventh International Congress of Endocrinology, Québec, 1.-7.7.1984.

VLACHOS & PAPAGEORGIOU (1996): Breeding biology and feeding of the lesser spotted eagle *Aquila pomarina* in Dadia Forest, north-eastern Greece. – In: MEYBURG & CHANCELLOR (Eds.): Eagle Studies, WWGBP, Berlin, Paris & London: 337-347.

VLACHOS, PAPAGEORGIOU & BAKALOUDIS (1996): Effects of the feeding station establishment on the Egyptian Vulture *Neophron percnopterus* in Dadia forest, north-eastern Greece. – In: MEYBURG & CHANCELLOR (Eds.): Eagle Studies, WWGBP, Berlin, Paris & London: 197-207.

VODDEN (1983): The R.S.P.C.A. and the Tortoise Trade. – Testudo, **2** (2): 23-26.

VOGEL (1963): Wunderwelt Terrarium. – Leipzig, Jena & Berlin (Urania-Verlag): 122-123, 198, Abb. 228-229.

VOGEL (1966): Apollinisch und Dionysisch: Geschichte ines genialen Irrtums. – Regensburg (Gustav Bosse).

VOGEL (1994a): Die Schildkröte in der griechischen Mythologie. – Schildkröten, Linden, 1 (2): 10-12.

VOGEL (1994b): Ein wildes Tier. – Schildkröten, Linden, 1 (2): 24.

VOGEL (1994c): Hans. – Schildkröten, Linden, 1 (2): 25-26.

VOGEL (1994d): Erstaunliche Verhaltensweise bei einer Griechischen Landschildkröte. – Schildkröten, Linden, 1 (4): 36-37.

VOGEL (1995): Bau eines Freilandgeheges. – Schildkröten, 2 (1): 39-42.

VOGEL (1998): Die Futterpflanzen für Landschildkröten. – Schildkröten, 5 (2): 26-32.

VOGEL (1999): Möglichkeit der Überwinterung von Schlüpflingen der Griechischen Landschildkröte Testudo hermanni. – Radiata, Bennstedt, 8 (2): 3-6.

VOGEL (2000a): Ein Besuch auf dem Rauscherhof in Degerndorf. – Schildkröten, Linden, 7 (1): 46-48.

VOGEL (2000b): Überwinterung einer zweijährigen Testudo hermanni im Freiland. – SIGS-Info, Siblingen, 9 (4): 41.

VOGEL (2001a): Einiges zur Farbsehfähigkeit der Schildkröten. – Schildkröten, Linden, 8 (1): 29-36, 2: 15-23.

VOGEL (2001b): Auf Schildkrötensuche im Urlaub. – SIGS-Info, Siblingen, 10 (3): 18-19.

VOGEL (2005a): Futterpflanzen für Landschildkröten. Teil 1. – Marginata, Münster, 2 (2): 35-41.

VOGEL (2005b): Futterpflanzen für Landschildkröten. Teil 2. – Marginata, Münster, 2 (3): 45-50.

VOGEL (2005c): Futterpflanzen für Landschildkröten. Teil 3. – Marginata, Münster, 2 (4): 46-51.

VOGEL (2006): Futterpflanzen für Landschildkröten. Teil 4. – Marginata, Münster, 3 (1): 35-40.

VOGRIN (1997a): An overview of the herpetofauna of Slovenia. – British Herpetological Society Bulletin, London, 58: 26-35.

VOGRIN (1997b): On the herpetofauna of Lake Vrana and its vicinity (Dalmacia, Croatia). – Herpetozoa, Vienna, 10 (1/2): 85-88.

VOGT (1998): Wie man junge Landschildkröten richtig hält. – Schildkröten, Lingen, 5 (2): 12-21.

VOGT (2002): Kennzeichnungspflicht. – M & S Reptilien, Villingen-Schwenningen, 3: 77-79.

VOGT & WERMUTH (1980): Knaurs Aquarien- und Terrarienbuch. – Munich & Zürich (Droemersche Verlagsanstalt Th. Knaur Nachf.): 222-223, 232.

DE VOSJOLI (1996): General Care and Maintenance of Popular Tortoises. – Santee (Advanced Vivarium Systems): 4-5, 34.

VROOM (1979a): Schildpadden in Montenegro. – Verenigingsblad Nederlandse Schildpadden Vereniging, Eindhoven, 3 (5): 1-8.

VROOM (1979b): Schildpadden in Ampurias. – De Schildpad, Eindhoven, 5 (1): 16-19.

VROOM (1979c): Herfstreis naar Mallorca. – De Schildpad, Eindhoven, 5 (6): 1-12.

VROOM (1981): Herpetologische Waarnemingen in het gebied van de Rio Orlina. – De Schildpad, Eindhoven, 7 (1): 21-26.

VROOM (1983): Testudo hermanni robertmertensi WERMUTH and Mauremys caspica leprosa (SCHWEIGGER) in the Monts Alberes habitat, El Ampurdan, NE Spain. – Testudo, 2 (2): 12-17.

VROOM (1984): Herbstreise nach Mallorca. – Die Schildkröte, Haar, 6 (4): 19-30.

WERNER (1899): Beiträge zur Kenntnis der Reptilien- und Batrachierfauna der Balkanhalbinsel. – Wissenschaftliche Mittheilungen aus Bosnien und der Herzegovina, 6: 817-841.

WAGLER (1830): Natürliches System der Amphibien, mit Vorangehender Classification der Säugethiere un Vögel. – Munich, Stuttgart & Tübingen (Cotta'schen): 138.

WAGNER (2005): Zuchtziele und Zuchtmethoden. – Schildkröten im Fokus, Bergheim, 2 (2): 3-20.

WALLACE (1979): Comparisons between the Hermann's and Spur-thighed tortoise. – Testudo, 1 (2): 15.

WALLACE (1995): More tortoises in the wild. – British Chelonia Group Newsletter, 107: 9.

WALLACE & WALLACE (1985a): Observations of a Population of Hermann's Tortoise (Testudo hermanni) in Southern Yugoslavia. – Testudo, 2 (3): 15-25.

WALLACE & WALLACE (1985b): Observations on a Population of Hermann's Tortoise (Testudo hermanni) on Corfu. – Testudo, 2 (3): 56-61.

WALLACE & WALLACE (1986): Observations of Hermann's Tortoise (Testudo hermanni robertmertensi) and Other Reptiles on Menorca, Balearic Islands. – Testudo, 2 (4): 44-53.

WALLACE & WALLACE (2000): Potamos (Corfu) revisited. – British Chelonia Group Newsletter, 136: 4-5.

WALLACE & WALLACE (2005): Unlikely Hatching. – British Chelonia Group Newsletter, 165: 12-13.

WALLER (1995a): Jacki und Jenni. – Schildkröten, Linden, 2 (3): 18-19.

WALLER (1995b): Ein langer Tag auf kurzen Beinchen. – Schildkröten, Linden, 2 (4): 34-35.

WALLS (1997): Landschildkröten. – Ruhmannsfelden (bede-Verlag): 11, 17-22.

WALSER (2000): Rettungsaktion. – Ein Herz für Tiere, Ismaning, 7: 74.

WALSH (1980): The tortoise trade! – British Chelonia Group Newsletter, 21: 6.

WANDOLLECK (1904): Eine bucklige Testudo graeca L. – Zoologische Jahrbücher für Systematik, Jena, 20: 151-166.

WARMUTH (2002): Schicksalhafte Verbindung. – Testudo (SIGS), Wimmis, 11 (3): 27-28.

WATSON (1962): Notes on copulation and distribution of Aegean land tortoises. – Copeia, Lawrence, 3: 317-321.

WEBB (1980): Notes on some reptiles and amphibians of N. E. Greece. – British Herpetological Society Bulletin, London.

WEBER & GÖBEL (1994): Fallbericht – Bericht über ein Adenokarzinom der Lunge bei einer Griechischen Landschildkröte (Testudo hermanni robertmertensi). – Kleintierpraxis, Alfeld, 39: 117-119.

WEBER & PIETZSCH (1974): Ein Beitrag zum Vorkommen von Salmonellen bei Landschildkröten aus Zoohandlungen und Privathaushalten. – Berliner und Münchener Tierärztliche Wochenschrift, Berlin & Munich, 87: 257-260.

WEGEHAUPT (2003): Die natürliche Haltung und Zucht der Griechischen Landschildkröten. – Kressbronn (Wegehaupt Verlag), 224 pp.

WEGEHAUPT (2004a): Sardinien, die Insel der europäischen Schildkröten. – Sacalia, Stiefern, 2 (2): 5-16.

WEGEHAUPT (2004b): Sardinien, die Insel der europäischen Schildkröten. – Kressbronn (Wegehaupt Verlag): 4-6, 8, 15-16, 31, 38, 40, 42, 50, 53, 55, 57, 60-63, 66, 68-71, 73, 75-79, 84-117, 125-127, 147, 153, 173-185, 192.

WEGEHAUPT (2005): Kroatien-Exkursion – Die Dalmatinische Landschildkröte Testudo (hermanni) hercegovinensis WERNER, 1899. – www.Testudo-farm.de

WEGER (1977): Schildkröten-Zucht im Freiland von Bozen – ein Versuch. – DATZ, Stuttgart, 30 (10): 355-358.

WEGER (1983): Überwinterung von Schildkröten-Gelegen in Südtirol. – DATZ, Stuttgart, 36 (4): 159.

WEHNER (1966): Kleine Terrarienkunde. – Leipzig, Jena & Berlin (Urania-Verlag): 85, 108, 118, Abbildung 28.

WEICHMANN (1989): Extreme Höcker auf dem Panzer einer Landschildkröte. – DATZ, Stuttgart, 42 (10): 585.

WEINDL & KUCHLING (1982): Immunohistochemistry of somatostatin in the central nervous system of the tortoise Testudo hermanni GMELIN. – Verhandlungen der Deutschen Zoologischen Gesellschaft, Munich: 209.

WEINDL, KUCHLING & WETZSTEIN (1983): The distribution of neuro-hypophyseal peptides in the central nervous system of the tortoise Testudo hermanni hermanni. – Acta Endocrinologica, 102 (Supplement 253): 67-68.

WEINDL, TRIEPEL & KUCHLING (1984): Somatostatin in the brain of the turtle Testudo hermanni – an immuno-histochemical mapping study. – Peptides, 5 (Supplement 1): 91-100.

WEINDL, KUCHLING, TRIEPEL & REINECKE (1983): Immunohistochemical localization of substance P in the brain and spinal cord of the tortoise Testudo hermanni GMELIN. – In: SKRABANEK & POWELL (Eds.): Substance P. – Dublin (Boole Press): 265-266.

WEISGRAM & SPLECHTNA (1990): Intervertebral movability movability in the neck of two turtle species (Testudo hermanni hermanni, Pelomedusa subrufa). – Zoologisches Jahrbuch für Anatomie, 120: 425-431.

WELCH (1994): Turtles, Tortoises and Terrapins – A Checklist. – R & A Research and Information, Taunton: 69, 71.

WELLING (1994): Herr auf dem Haus. – Ein Herz für Tiere, Ismaning, 6: 47.

WELSCH (2000): Europäische Landschildkröten – Sensible Urviecher. – Ein Herz für Tiere, Ismaning, 9: 28-30.

WENNING (2004): Testudo hermanni – Schlupf in freier Natur in Deutschland. – elaphe (N. F.), Rheinbach, 12 (3): 41-42.

WERMUTH (1952): Testudo hermanni robertmertensi n. subsp. und ihr Vorkommen in Spanien. – Senckenbergiana, Frankfurt am Main, 33 (1/2): 157-164.

WERMUTH (1953): Überwinterung Griechischer Landschildkröten. – Fischen und Angeln, Berlin, 5: 23.

WERMUTH (1954a): Wie die westliche Rasse der Griechischen Landschildkröte, Testudo hermanni robertmertensi, »entdeckt« wurde. – Aquarien Terrarien, Leipzig, Jena & Berlin, 1 (2): 83-85.

WERMUTH (1954b): Kann ich Terrarientieren ihren natürlichen Lebensraum ersetzen? – Aquarien Terrarien, Leipzig, Jena & Berlin, 1 (7): 206-209.

WERMUTH (1956): Versuch der Deutung einiger bisher übersehener Schildkröten-Namen. – Zoologische Beiträge (N. F.), Berlin, 2: 399-423.

WERMUTH (1961): Anomalien bei einer Griechischen Landschildkröte (Testudo hermanni hermanni GMELIN). – Sitzungsberichte der Gesellschaft der Naturforschenden Freunde Berlin (N. F.), Berlin, 1 (1/5): 139-142.

WERMUTH (1971a): Eine totalalbinotische Landschildkröte (Testudo hermanni). – DATZ, Stuttgart, 24 (8): 276.

WERMUTH (1971b): Schildkrötenarten. – In: ZOLL (Ed.): Das neue Heimtierlexikon. – Bergisch Gladbach (Gustav Lübbe Verlag): 294.

WERMUTH (1977): Wie überwintern wir unsere Landschildkröten? – Aquarien-Magazin, Stuttgart, 11 (9): 268-273.

WERMUTH (1985): Neuer Nachweis von *Testudo hermanni robertmertensi* für das spanische Festland. – DATZ, Stuttgart, **38** (1): 39-41.

WERMUTH & MERTENS (1961): Schildkröten – Krokodile – Brückenechsen. – Jena (VEB Gustav Fischer Verlag): 210-212.

WERMUTH & MERTENS (1977): Liste der rezenten Amphibien und Reptilien: Testudines, Crocodylia, Rhynchocephalia. – Das Tierreich, Lieferung 100, Berlin & New York (Walter de Gruyter): 86-87.

WERNER (1891): Beiträge zur Kenntnis der Reptilien und Amphibien von Istrien und Dalmatien. – – Sitzungsberichte der Zoologisch-Botanischen Gesellschaft, Mathematisch-naturwissenschaftliche Klasse, Wien, **41**.

WERNER (1894): Die Reptilien- und Batrachierfauna der Ionischen Inseln. – Sitzungsberichte der Zoologisch-Botanischen Gesellschaft, Mathematisch-naturwissenschaftliche Klasse, Vienna, **44**: 225-237.

WERNER (1897): Die Reptilien und Amphibien Österreich-Ungarns und der Occupationsländer. – Vienna (A. Pichler's Witwe & Sohn), 162 pp.

WERNER (1898): Prilozi poznavanju faune reptilija i batrachija Balkanskog poluostrva. – Glasnik Zem. Mus. U Bosni i Herz, Sarajevo, X: 131-156.

WERNER (1899): Beiträge zur Kenntniss der Reptilien- und der Balkanhalbinsel. – Wissenschaftliche Mitteilungen aus Bosnien und der Hercegowina, Vienna, **6**: 817-841.

WERNER (1902a): Zoologische Reiseabenteuer in Griechenland. – Der Zoologische Garten, Berlin, **43** (1): 1-18.

WERNER (1902b): Reptilien. – In: GALVAGNI (Ed.): Beiträge zur Kenntniss der Fauna einiger dalmatischer Inseln. – Verhandlungen der königlich kaiserlichen zoologisch-botanischen Gesellschaft, Vienna, **52**: 381-388.

WERNER (1912a): Brehms Tierleben. Lurche und Kriechtiere. Erster Band. – Leipzig & Vienna (Bibliographisches Institut), XVI + 572 pp.

WERNER (1912b): Beiträge zur Kenntnis der Reptilien und Amphibien Griechenlands. – Archiv für Naturgeschichte, Berlin, **78** A (5): 169-180.

WERNER (1918a): Zur Kenntnis der Reptilienfauna von Südalbanien. – Blätter für Aquarien- und Terrarienkunde, Stuttgart, **29** (21): 250-251.

WERNER (1918b): Über Reptilien und Amphibien aus Albanien gesammelt von Prof. R. EBNER und Dr. H. KARNY im Sommer 1918. – Archiv für Naturgeschichte, Berlin, **84** (10): 140-150.

WERNER (1920): Zur Kenntnis der Reptilien- und Amphibienfauna Albaniens. – Zoologischer Anzeiger, Leipzig, **51** (1/2): 20-23.

WERNER (1927): Beiträge zur Kenntnis der Fauna Griechenlands (Reptilia – Amphibia – Scorpiones – Orthoptera – Isoptera – Apterygota). – Zoologischer Anzeiger, Jena, **70**: 135-151.

WERNER (1929): Zoologische Forschungsreise nach den Ionischen Inseln und dem Peloponnes – V. Teil – Reptilia, Amphibia, Orthoptera, Embidaria und Scorpiones. – Sitzungsberichte der Akademie der Wissenschaften, mathematisch-naturwissenschaftliche Klasse, Abteilung I, Vienna, **138**: 471-485.

WERNER (1930): Contribution to the Knowledge of the Reptiles and Amphibians of Greece, especially the Aegean Islands. – Occasional Papers of the Museum of Zoology, University of Michigan, Ann Arbor, **211**, 34 + VI pp.

WERNER (1933): Ergebnisse einer zoologischen Studien- und Sammelreise nach den Inseln des Ägäischen Meeres. I. Reptilien und Amphibien. – Sitzungsberichte der Österreichischen Akademie der Wissenschaften, mathematisch-naturwissenschaftliche Klasse, Abteilung I, Vienna, **142** (3/4): 103-133.

WERNER (1935): Reptilien der Ägäischen Inseln. – Sitzungsberichte der Östereichischen Akademie der Wissenschaften, mathematisch-naturwissenschaftliche Klasse, Abteilung I, Vienna, **144** (3/4): 81-117.

WERNER (1938): Die Amphibien und Reptilien Griechenlands. – Zoologica, Stuttgart, **35** (94): 1-117.

WERNING (2000): Artenschutzgesetze und Kennzeichnung mediterraner Landschildkröten – aktueller Stand. – Draco, Münster, 2: 89-92.

WERNING (2005): Novellierung der Bundesartenschutzverordnung. – Reptilia (D), Münster, 51: 15.

WESER (1988): Zur Höckerbildung bei der Aufzucht von Landschildkröten. – Sauria, Berlin, **10** (3): 23-25.

The following are just some of the most important and interesting links to websites relevant to the species discussed here. A search of the name "*Testudo hermanni*" on the search engine *Google* in April of 2006 revealed that not less than 81,500 websites contained this name. Other search engines may find other and/or additional sites.

ANONYMUS: Griekse landschildpad. – http://home.hccnet. nl/euro.emys/hermanni.html

ANONYMUS: Griekse landschildpad Testudo hermanni. – www.schildpad.nl/r_allesover_004.html

ANONYMUS: Haltungstipps. – www.dght.de/ag/schild-kroeten/haltungstipps.htm

ANONYMUS: La Tortue d'Hermann (*Testudo hermanni hermanni*). – www.espaces-naturels-provence.com/tortue.html

ANONYMUS: Recherche de sites par espèce: Amphibiens et reptiles: Tortue d'Hermann (*Testudo hermanni*) – 1217. – http://natura2000.environnement.gouv.fr/especes/1217.html#FR83

ANONYMUS: Slowcoach Homepage. – www.slowcoach.org.uk

ANONYMUS: Tartarughe.org. – www.tartarughe.org

ANONYMUS: *Testudo hermanni*. – http://testudohermanni.interfree.it

ANONYMUS: *Testudo hermanni boettgeri* – Eastern Hermann's Tortoise. – www.empireoftheturtle.com/testudo_hermanni_boettgeri.htm

ANONYMUS: *Testudo hermanni* GMELIN, 1789. – http://membres.lycos.fr/testudo/testudohermanni.html

ANONYMUS: *Testudo hermanni* GMELIN, 1789 – Hermann's Tortoise. – www.herp.it/indexjs.htm?SpeciesPages/TestuHerma.htm

ANONYMUS: *Testudo hermanni* GMELIN, 1789 – Testuggine di Hermann – Hermann's Tortoise. – www.tartaclubitalia.it/specieterrestri/hermanni/stancher/stancher001.htm

ANONYMUS: *Testudo hermanni hermanni* und *Testudo hermanni boettgeri*. – www.beepworld.de/members36/landschildkroetenseite/index.htm

ANONYMUS: *Testudo hermanni* site. – www.geocities.com/Petsburgh/6356

BECK: schroete.de. – http://home.arcor.de/schroete/arten/index.html

BLANCK: *Testudo hermanni*. – www.geocities.com/landschildkroete/testudo_hermanni.htm

BUDISCHEK: *Testudo hermanni boettgeri*, MOJSISOVICS, 1889. – www.isv.cc/THB/thb.htm

CONNOR: Hermann's Tortoise, *Testudo hermanni*. – www.tortoise.org/archives/herman.html

CONNOR: *Testudo hermanni hermanni*. – http://tortuga.iespana.es/hermanni.htm

DIETHELM: Meine Schildkröten. Haltung und Aufzucht. – www.udena.ch/wilf/schildkroeten.htm

EGER: Villa-Testudo. Die Landschildkröten Europas. – www.villa-testudo.de

EGGENSCHWILER & JOST: Die Griechische Landschildkröte (*Testudo hermanni*, GMELIN 1789). – www.sigs.ch/blatt1.aspx

JENNINGS: The Beginners Guide To Keeping Hermanns Tortoises. – http://greenfield.fortunecity.com/wilderness/446/

KNON: Die Griechische Landschildkröte, andere Landschildkröten und Echsen. – www.t-hermanni.de

LOSSAU: *Testudo hermanni* – Beschreibung. – www.lossau-at-home.de/AndereTiere/Testudo/Beschreibung.htm

MINCH: Schildfutter. – www.schildifutter.de

MÜLLER: Die Schildkröten-Farm – Mediterrane Landschildkröten. – www.schildkroeten-farm.de

MÜLLER: Griechische Landschildkröte – Testudo hermanni. – www.ug-mueller.de/landschildkroeten.htm

POPOVIC: Die Griechische Landschildkröte (*Testudo hermanni*). – www.kaspar-p.privat.t-online.de/26868.html?*session*id*key*=*session*id*val*

RENTSCHLER: Elke's Schildkrötenseite. – www.fam-rentschler.de/Intro.htm

SENNEKE: Hermann's Tortoises – Testudo hermanni. – www.chelonia.org/Articles/hermannstortoisecare.htm

SONNENDECKER: Die Panzerpiraten. – www.panzerpiraten.de

VAUCHER: La tortue léopard, *Geochelone pardalis*, et la tortue d'Hermann, *Testudo hermanni*. – www.batraciens-reptiles.com/geochelone_pardalis.htm#hermann

VOGT: REHA-Station für Landschildkröten. – www.schildkroete.de

WEGEHAUPT: Testudo-Farm. – www.testudo-farm.de

WÜTHRICH: *Testudo hermanni boettgeri*, Griechische Landschildkröte Ostrasse. – http://home.datacomm.ch/fritz.wuethrich/bilder/testudo_hermanni_boettgeri.html

WÜTHRICH: *Testudo hermanni hermanni*, Griechische Landschildkröte Westrasse. – http://home.datacomm.ch/fritz.wuethrich/bilder/testudo_hermanni_hermanni.html

Photographs on front cover:
Large photograph: *Testudo hermanni* (G. JAKUBOWICZ)
Small photograph: Juvenile *Testudo boettgeri* (H.-U. SCHMIDT)

Photographs on rear cover:
Large photograph: Male *Testudo hermanni* from the Albera Mountains in Catalonia, Spain
(J. MARAN)
Small photograph: Female Boettger's tortoise from the Peloponnesus, Greece (J. MARAN)

Photograph, page 3: Male *Testudo hermanni* on Sardinia (Italy) (W. WEGEHAUPT)

Chapter headers
Systematics (p. 10): Plate 30 (depicting *Testudo boettgeri*) from MEHELY'S Herpetologia
Hungarica
Description (p. 19): Boettger's tortoise in Bulgaria (G. POPGEORGIEV)
Fossil Records (p. 58): Fossil shell remains of *Testudo antiqua* BRONN, 1831, from the Miocene
of Germany (H.-H. SCHLEICH)
Natural Habitat (p. 60): *Testudo hercegovinensis* in Croatia (W. WEGEHAUPT)
Diet (p. 84): Very old female *Testudo boettgeri* feeding on greens (F. WÜTHRICH))
Reproduction (p. 92): A baby *Testudo boettgeri* hatching on the Peloponnesus (Greece)
(J.MARAN)
Growth & Life Expectancy (p. 108): Hatchling Boettger's tortoise (B. SEEGER)
Diseases & Parasites (p. 112): Herpes infection in a tortoise (S. BLAHAK)
Husbandry (p. 116): Outdoor enclosure for Boettger's tortoises (B. SEEGER)
Tortoises & Man (p. 168): Antique string instrument (chelyes) manufactured from a tortoise
shell (B. DEVAUX)
Threats (p. 176): A *Testudo hermanni* that burnt to death in a fire in southern France
(B. DEVAUX)
Conservation (p. 201): Reintroduction of *Testudo hermanni* in the Maure Plains of southern
France (B. DEVAUX)

HOLGER VETTER

Leopard- and African Spurred Tortoise

220 pages, 194 pictures

ISBN 3 – 89973 – 601 – x

HOLGER VETTER:

Red-footed tortoise and Yellow-footed tortoise

2008, 355 pages,
285 pictures

ISBN 3 – 89973 – 503 – x

MANFRED BOGNER:

European Pond Turtles

2009, 255 pages,
150 pictures

ISBN 3 – 89973 – 604–4

Chelonian Library

For further information please contact:
Chimaira Buchhandelsgesellschaft mbH
Heddernheimer Landstraße 20 | 60439 Frankfurt am Main | Germany
Phone: +49 (0) 69 – 49 72 23 | Telefax: +49 (0) 69 – 49 78 26 | E-Mail: frogbook@aol.de
www.chimaira.de